**PHILIP'S**

T0301084

**Royal Geographical Society**

with IBG

Advancing geography and geographical learning

## ATLAS FOR ADVENTURE

# OUTDOOR BRITAIN

- Ultimate outdoor companion • National parks • Walking trails
- Scenic journeys • Nature reserves • Ancient monuments

www.philips-maps.co.uk

First published in 2024 by Philip's
a division of Octopus Publishing Group Ltd
www.octopusbooks.co.uk
Carmelite House, 50 Victoria Embankment
London EC4Y 0DZ
An Hachette UK Company
www.hachette.co.uk

First edition 2024
First impression 2024

ISBN 978-1-84907-677-7

Cartography by Philip's
Copyright © 2024 Philip's

**Ordnance Survey**
**Licensed Data**

This product includes mapping data licensed from Ordnance Survey®, with the permission of the Controller of His Majesty's Stationery Office. © Crown copyright 2024. All rights reserved. Licence number AC0000851689.

Information for National Parks, National Landscapes, National Trails and Country Parks in Wales supplied by the Countryside Council for Wales.

Information for National Parks, National Landscapes, National Trails and Country Parks in England supplied by Natural England. Data for Regional Parks, Long Distance Footpaths and Country Parks in Scotland provided by Scottish Natural Heritage.

Gaelic name forms used in the Western Isles provided by Comhairle nan Eilean.

Data for the National Nature Reserves in England provided by Natural England. Data for the National Nature Reserves in Wales provided by Countryside Council for Wales. Darparwyd data'n ymwneud â Gwarchodfeydd Natur Cenedlaethol Cymru gan Gyngor Cefn Gwlad Cymru.

Information on the location of National Nature Reserves in Scotland was provided by Scottish Natural Heritage.

Data for National Scenic Areas in Scotland provided by the Scottish Government. Crown copyright material is reproduced with the permission of the Controller of HMSO and the King's Printer for Scotland. Licence number C02W0003960.

Front cover photograph: Summit of Ben A'an overlooking Loch Katrine, Loch Lomond and the Trossachs National Park, Scotland. Kay Roxby / Alamy Stock Photo

Printed in China

# CONTENTS

**II   Key to map symbols**

**III   The Best of Outdoor Britain**
IV   National parks
VI   Map of Britain: protected areas
VII   National Trails
VIII   Forest parks and
        National Nature Reserves
XI   Dark skies
XII   Other natural features
XIV   Ancient and historic sites
XVI   Pilgrimage routes
XVII   Parks and gardens
XX   Outdoor museums
XXIII   Festivals
XXVI   Transport
XXIX   Cycle routes
XXX   Scenic journeys
XXXI   Animal attractions
XXXIV   Outdoor activities
XXXVII   Eccentric Britain

**XXXVIII   Route planner**

**XL   Distances and journey times**

**1   Key to road map pages**

**2   Road maps of Britain**

**161   Index to road maps of Britain**

Inside back cover:
**County and unitary authority boundaries**
**Inclusive activity networks**

## Road map symbols

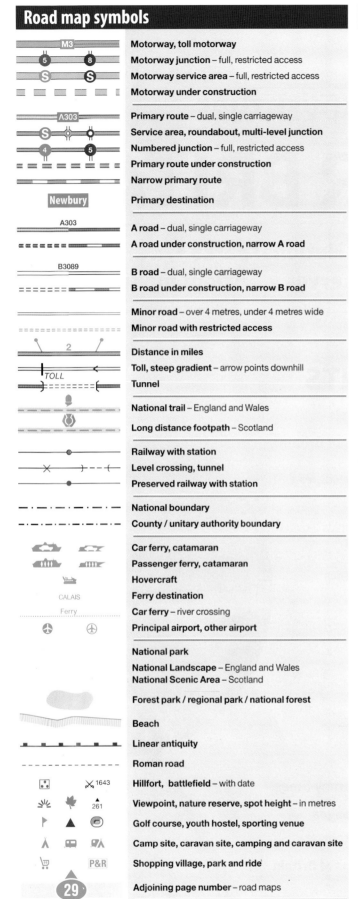

Motorway, toll motorway

Motorway junction – full, restricted access

Motorway service area – full, restricted access

Motorway under construction

Primary route – dual, single carriageway

Service area, roundabout, multi-level junction

Numbered junction – full, restricted access

Primary route under construction

Narrow primary route

Primary destination

**Newbury**

A303

A road – dual, single carriageway

A road under construction, narrow A road

B3089

B road – dual, single carriageway

B road under construction, narrow B road

Minor road – over 4 metres, under 4 metres wide

Minor road with restricted access

Distance in miles

Toll, steep gradient – arrow points downhill

Tunnel

National trail – England and Wales

Long distance footpath – Scotland

Railway with station

Level crossing, tunnel

Preserved railway with station

National boundary

County / unitary authority boundary

Car ferry, catamaran

Passenger ferry, catamaran

Hovercraft

Ferry destination

Car ferry – river crossing

Principal airport, other airport

National park

National Landscape – England and Wales
National Scenic Area – Scotland

Forest park / regional park / national forest

Beach

Linear antiquity

Roman road

Hillfort, battlefield – with date

Viewpoint, nature reserve, spot height – in metres

Golf course, youth hostel, sporting venue

Camp site, caravan site, camping and caravan site

Shopping village, park and ride

Adjoining page number – road maps

## Tourist information

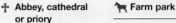

✝ Abbey, cathedral or priory

🏛 Ancient monument

🦭 Aquarium

🏛 Art gallery

🦅 Bird collection or aviary

🏰 Castle

⛪ Church

Country park
🎖 England and Wales
🎖 Scotland

🐎 Farm park

❄ Garden

⛵ Historic ship

🏠 House

🏡 House and garden

▦ Motor racing circuit

🏛 Museum

Ⓐ Picnic area

🚂 Preserved railway

🏇 Race course

Roman antiquity

Safari park

🎡 Theme park

ℹ Tourist information

🐘 Zoo

✦ Other place of interest

### Road map scales

1 : 200 000 • 1cm = 2km • 1 inch = 3·15 miles

### Parts of Scotland

1 : 265 000 • 1 cm = 2.65 km • 1 inch = 4.18 miles

### Scottish Highlands and Islands

1 : 332 000 • 1 cm = 3.32km • 1 inch = 5.24 miles

Orkney and Shetland Islands 1 : 400 000 • 1cm = 4 km • 1 inch = 6.31 miles

**Royal Geographical Society**
with IBG

Advancing geography and geographical learning

**Philip's Atlases** are published in association with The Royal Geographical Society (with The Institute of British Geographers).

The Society was founded in 1830 and given a Royal Charter in 1859 for 'the advancement of geographical science'. Today it is a leading world centre for geographical learning – supporting education, teaching, research and expeditions, and promoting public understanding of the subject.

Further information about the Society and how to join may be found on its website at: www.rgs.org

# The Best of Outdoor Britain

## Introduction

The maps in this atlas will guide you to the best places for outdoor adventures whether it be exploring Britain's finest national parks or finding quiet places to gaze at the mesmerizing depths of dark skies.

The following pages present a selection of some of the best places to enjoy the outdoors across the whole of Great Britain. To make it easier to find places in your area, the entries have been grouped by the regions shown on the map on this page. For extra detail, there is a comprehensive county map on the inside back cover of the atlas.

At the end of each entry there is a page and grid reference to enable you to locate the attraction on the maps. Larger attractions will be named on the map – for events and smaller places use the reference to the nearest town or village given at the start of each entry to locate them.

Find your adventure!

▼ A hillwalking trail in the Cairngorms Iwom22 / Dreamstime

Scotland

North East

North West

Yorkshire & the Humber

East Midlands

West Midlands

Wales

East of England

South East

South West

# National parks

**Brecon Beacons (Bannau Brycheiniog)** *Libanus, Powys*
Occupying 520 square miles, the Brecon Beacons National Park is named after its rugged mountains, known as the Beacons, the highest of which is Pen y Fan, at 886m/2,900ft. The scenery is diverse, with moorlands and forests dotted with lakes and waterfalls, as well as man-made history, such as stone circles, castles and industrial heritage. With 1,200 miles of rights of way, the park is a magnet for walkers, cyclists and horse riders, and the rocky landscape is popular with climbers and cavers. In addition, it is known for its dark skies, good for stargazers. There is a visitor centre at Libanus.
🖥 www.breconbeacons.org
**34 B3**

**The Broads** *Hoveton, Norfolk*
More than 125 miles of navigable lakes (or Broads) and rivers fringed by marshes and meadows. Activities include all types of boating, with many visitors hiring pleasure boats in order to enjoy the lock-free waterways, as well as canoeing, kayaking and paddleboarding. Rare birds and plant species flourish in the wetland habitats, particularly in the many nature reserves, which include Hickling Broad, How Hill and Ranworth Broad. It is also a popular area for walking and cycling, with many miles of footpaths and nature trails. There are visitor centres are at Hoveton, Ranworth and Toad Hole Cottage at How Hill Nature Reserve.
🖥 www.visitthebroads.co.uk
**69 D7**

**Cairngorms** *Braemar, Aberdeenshire*
The UK's largest national park, an area of approximately 1,750 square miles. It encompasses the Cairngorm plateau, location of most of the UK's highest mountains, including its second-highest peak, Ben Macdui, at 1,309m/4,296ft, and 55 'Munros' (mountains above 914m/3,000ft). The varied landscape includes steep valleys (glens), rivers, lochs, forests and moorland, which offer a wide range of activities, including walking, cycling, horse riding, golf, water sports and fishing. There are three ski resorts. The park boasts a large number of national nature reserves, with endangered animal and plant species flourishing throughout the area. There are visitor centres throughout the park.
🖥 www.cairngorms.co.uk **139 E7**

**Dartmoor** *Postbridge, Devon* National park, about 370 square miles in area, known for its dramatic scenery of high open moorland, steep valleys and hilltop tors (granite outcrops). Among its diverse and rare habitats are blanket bogs and upland heath, important for many threatened animal and plant species. There are walking routes of varying lengths and difficulty, cycle trails and bridlepaths, and it is a popular area for horse riding. The tors offer climbing and bouldering opportunities, with two of the most popular being Haytor and Bonehill Rocks. Water sports are available on the park's lakes and reservoirs. There are visitor centres in Postbridge, Princetown and Haytor.
🖥 www.dartmoor.gov.uk **6 B4**

▲ The 17th-century stone bridge at Malmsmead on Exmoor Rhatton / Dreamstime

**Exmoor** *Lynmouth, Devon* Area of moorland, woodland and rolling hills, with a dramatic rugged coastline overlooking the Bristol Channel. The park is home to red deer and endangered Exmoor ponies, as well as other rare species, including butterflies and bats. Over 600 miles of footpaths and bridleways make this a popular park for walkers, and it is on the route of several long-distance paths. Cycling is well catered for with quiet roads, steep climbs and mountain biking opportunities. Its dark skies are popular with stargazers. All the traditional seaside activities are available on the coast. There are visitor centres in Dulverton, Dunster and Lynmouth.
🖥 www.exmoor-nationalpark.gov.uk
**21 E6**

**Lake District** *Bowness-on-Windermere, Westmorland & Furness* UNESCO World Heritage Site, a dramatic landscape of mountains (fells), lakes and valleys. There are boat trips and sailing available on most of the lakes, including Windermere, Ullswater, Coniston Water and Derwentwater, but some, including the Northern Lakes of Buttermere, Crummock, Loweswater and Bassenthwaite, do not allow motor boats, and are popular for canoeing, kayaking and paddleboarding. Rydal Water is known for wild swimming. The national park is criss-crossed with footpaths and cycling routes of varying lengths and difficulties, many with spectacular views, and its dark skies are popular with stargazers. There

◄ **Hillwalking in the Cairngorm Mountains** Iwom22 / Dreamstime

▼ **Derwent Water in the Lake District** Matthew Dixon / Dreamstime

are visitor centres in Bowness-on-Windermere, Keswick and Ullswater.
🖥 www.lakedistrict.gov.uk **99 E5**

**Loch Lomond and the Trossachs** *Aberfoyle, Stirling* National park straddling the geological fault line dividing the Scottish Highlands from the Lowlands. It contains 22 lochs, including Loch Lomond, Scotland's largest, and 21 'Munros' (mountains above 914m/3,000ft), as well as hills, woodlands and valleys. There are walking trails in all terrains, including gentler lochside walks, and cycle paths for both on-road riders and mountain bikers. Other activities include climbing, fishing and water sports, such as sailing and paddleboarding. Rare wildlife can sometimes be spotted, notably golden eagles, red squirrels and adders, or – on the coast – porpoises and seals. There are visitor centres at Balmaha, Aberfoyle, Duke's Pass, Balloch and Glen Finglas. 🖥 www.lochlomond-trossachs.org **126 D4**

**New Forest** *Lyndhurst, Hampshire* Area of ancient woodland and open heathland created by William the Conqueror in 1079 as his 'new hunting forest'. It is known for the New Forest ponies that roam freely. The park is home to five species of deer and many rare plant and animal species, which flourish in the lowland heath and bog habitat. It is popular with walkers, but also has much to offer on- and off-road cyclists and horse riders. Water sports such as sailing, paddleboarding and kayaking are available on its coastline and inland waterways. There is a heritage centre at Lyndhurst and visitor information points throughout the park. 🖥 www.thenewforest.co.uk
**14 D4**

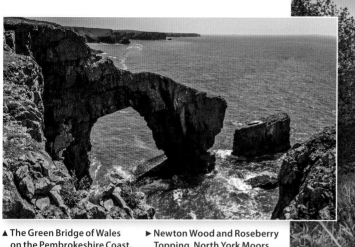

▲ The Green Bridge of Wales
on the Pembrokeshire Coast,
Nicola Pulham / Dreamstime.com

► Newton Wood and Roseberry
Topping, North York Moors
David Head / Dreamstime

**North York Moors** *Danby, North
Yorkshire* Large area of moorland and
woods with a 26-mile coastline on the
North Sea. Wildlife flourishes, with
whales, dolphins and seals frequently
sighted, and large seabird colonies
near Flamborough and Filey. Birds of
prey are spotted inland, with bird hides
around the park. Walkers and horse
riders can enjoy quiet trails, bridleways
and disused railway lines, and cyclists
benefit from the 150-mile cycle route
that makes up the Moor to Sea Cycle
Network. The park's dark skies make
it an excellent location for stargazing,
and water sports are available on the
coast. There are national park centres at
Danby Lodge and Sutton Bank.
🖳 www.northyorkmoors.org.uk
**103 D5**

**Northumberland** *Hexham,
Northumberland* Large national park
just south of the Scottish border,
characterised by open moorland and

peaceful hills, notably the Cheviot and
Simonside ranges. The area is popular
with walkers for its quiet and plentiful
rights of way, bird-watching, and the
chance to get up close to Hadrian's
Wall, which snakes through the park. A
UNESCO World Heritage Site, Hadrian's
Wall can be visited on foot or by car,
with popular viewpoints at Steel Rigg
and Cawfields. The park is popular
with stargazers and is designated an
International Dark Sky Park. There is a
visitor centre, The Sill, at Once Brewed.
🖳 www.northumberlandnationalpark.
org.uk **109 C7**

**Peak District** *Castleton, Derbyshire*
National park covering 555 square miles,
comprising the 'Dark Peak' area in the
north and east, which is characterised
by dramatic gritstone cliffs, moorland
and steep-sided valleys, and the
'White Peak', an area of limestone
plateau with steep dales. The park
is popular with walkers and cyclists,

with trails to suit all abilities, and is the
start of the long-distance route the
Pennine Way. It is well known for its
excellent bouldering and rock climbing
opportunities, notably at Stanage Edge.
Other activities include horse riding
and caving. There are visitor centres
in Bakewell, Castleton, Derwent and
Edale. 🖳 www.peakdistrict.gov.uk
**88 F2**

**Pembrokeshire Coast**
*St David's, Pembrokeshire* National
park encompassing most of the
Pembrokeshire coast, all its offshore
islands and varied inland habitats.
Walkers can enjoy more than 600
miles of footpaths and bridleways,
including the 186-mile coastal path,
which showcases the diverse geology
of the coast, from craggy outcrops to
sandy beaches. Seals, dolphins and
porpoises can be spotted, and the
rare heathland and estuarine habitats
are havens for rare birds. The offshore
islands, particularly Skomer, are famous
for seabirds, especially guillemots,
razorbills and puffins, and can be visited
by boat. Other activities include water
sports, horse riding and cycling. There
is a visitor centre at St Davids. 🖳 www.
pembrokeshirecoast.wales **44 C2**

**Snowdonia (Eryri))** *Betws-y-Coed,
Conwy* Large national park covering
823 square miles of dramatic mountain
scenery, lakes, rivers, woodlands and
coast. It contains nine mountain ranges,
with 15 peaks over 914 m / 3000 ft ,
and many nature reserves. There
are walking trails to suit all abilities,
from gentle walks through ancient
woodlands to strenuous routes up
Yr Wyddfa (Snowdon), the highest
mountain in England and Wales,
and Cader Idris. Cycling is popular,
with both road and mountain biking
routes; other activities include water

sports, wild swimming and climbing.
The park is popular with stargazers
for its dark skies. There are information
centres in Betws-y-Coed, Beddgelert
and Aberdyfi.
🖳 https://snowdonia.gov.wales **83 F7**

**South Downs** *Midhurst, West Sussex*
Area of rolling hills, ancient woodland,
pastures and forests and the famous
Seven Sisters chalk cliffs. It has vitally
important areas of threatened habitat:
chalk grassland, which supports a huge
variety of wildflowers and butterflies;
and lowland heath, particularly
Woolmer Forest, home to threatened
reptile and amphibian species. There
are footpaths, bridleways and cycle
trails throughout, the most famous
being the 100-mile long distance
path the South Downs Way, which is
popular not only with walkers but also
with cyclists and horse riders. The park
is good for stargazing thanks to its
dark skies. There is a visitor centre in
Midhurst. 🖳 www.southdowns.gov.uk
**16 B2**

**Yorkshire Dales** *Hawes, North Yorkshire*
An upland landscape of rolling valleys
(dales), exposed hills and moorland.
It is known for its limestone scenery
– the sheer cliff face at Malham Cove,
steep gorges such as Gordale Scar, and
dramatic waterfalls, including Aysgarth
and Hardraw Force. The dales are criss-
crossed by ancient dry-stone walls.
There are walking routes for all abilities,
including the famous Three Peaks
Challenge, and routes for road cyclists
and mountain bikers, as well as fell
running trails, horse riding and some
of the UK's best climbing and caving.
Its dark skies make it popular with
stargazers. There are visitor centres at
Aysgarth Falls, Grassington, Hawes,
Malham and Reeth.
🖳 www.yorkshiredales.org.uk **100 E3**

▲ Brentor Church in Dartmoor
National Park Helen Hotson / Dreamstime

▼ Crag Lough and Hadrian's Wall in
Northumberland National Park
David Head / Dreamstime

# Map of Britain: protected areas

- National Park
- National Landscape
- National Scenic Area
- Built-up area
- Long-distance footpath

*Shetland Islands*

Lerwick

SHETLAND

*Orkney Islands*

HOY & WEST MAINLAND
Kirkwall
Stromness

Thurso

*Outer Hebrides*

N.W. SUTHERLAND

KYLE OF TONGUE

ASSYNT-COIGACH

Stornoway

SOUTH LEWIS, HARRIS & NORTH UIST

Ullapool

DORNOCH FIRTH

WESTER ROSS

Invergordon

Formartine & Buchan Way

LOCH TORRIDON

*Skye*

Inverness

Nairn

Speyside Way

CUILLINS

GLEN AFFRIC

Great Glen Way

Aviemore

CAIRNGORMS

Aberdeen

**Scotland**

Fort William

BEN NEVIS AND GLENCOE

Rob Roy Way

West Highland Way

Dundee

Arbroath

Perth

Oban

LOCH LOMOND & THE TROSSACHS

St Andrews

Fife Coastal Path

Stirling

Dunbar

Dunoon

KYLES OF BUTE

John Muir Way

Edinburgh

St Cuthbert's Way

Glasgow

*Kintyre Way*

UPPER TWEEDDALE

NORTHUMBERLAND COAST

*Arran*

Ayr

**UNITED KINGDOM**

Ayrshire Coastal Path

Southern Upland Way

NITH ESTUARY

NORTHUMBERLAND

Hadrian's Wall Path

Newcastle-upon-Tyne

Stranraer

Carlisle

NORTH PENNINES

King Charles III England Coast Path

Cleveland Way

*Isle of Man*

King Charles III England Coast Path

LAKE DISTRICT

Middlesbrough

NORTH YORK MOORS

Scarborough

Windermere

YORKSHIRE DALES

Bridlington

Douglas

Morecambe

Pennine Way

York

Yorkshire Wolds Way

FOREST OF BOWLAND

Leeds

Hull

Blackpool

Southport

King Charles III England Coast Path

Manchester

PEAK DISTRICT

Sheffield

LINCOLNSHIRE WOLDS

King Charles III England Coast Path

ANGLESEY

Liverpool

Lincoln

Skegness

Holyhead

Llandudno

CLWYDIAN RANGE

Chester

**England**

Peddars Way & Norfolk Coast Path

Wales Coast Path

SNOWDONIA (ERYRI)

Stoke-on-Trent

Derby

Nottingham

THE BROADS

King Charles III England Coast Path

Glyndwr's Way

Shrewsbury

CANNOCK CHASE

Leicester

Kings Lynn

Norwich

Great Yarmouth

SHROPSHIRE HILLS

Wolverhampton

Bury St Edmunds

Aberystwyth

**Wales**

Birmingham

SUFFOLK & ESSEX COAST & HEATHS

Offa's Dyke Path

Stratford-upon-Avon

Cambridge

Felixstowe

Cotswold Way

The Ridgeway

Harwich

PEMBROKESHIRE COAST

Fishguard

Cheltenham

COTSWOLDS

Oxford

CHILTERN HILLS

Clacton

King Charles III England Coast Path

Pembrokeshire Coast Path

BRECON BEACONS (BANNAU BRYCHEINIOG)

Thames Path

LONDON

Southend

Tenby

Swansea

Bristol

Greenwich

Margate

Wales Coast Path

GOWER

Cardiff

Bath

KENT DOWNS

Dover

King Charles III England Coast Path

Weston-super-Mare

North Downs Way

Folkestone

Ilfracombe

Minehead

Winchester

HIGH WEALD

EXMOOR

Salisbury

SOUTH DOWNS

Hastings

South West Coast Path

NORTH DEVON

Exeter

DORSET

Poole

NEW FOREST

Southampton

Brighton

Eastbourne

Newhaven

King Charles III England Coast Path

Newquay

DARTMOOR

South West Coast Path

Weymouth

Bournemouth

Portsmouth

ISLE OF WIGHT

Worthing

South Downs Way

St. Ives

Torbay

CORNWALL

Plymouth

SOUTH DEVON

King Charles III England Coast Path

Penzance

*Isles of Scilly*

*Channel Islands*

Cherbourg

**FRANCE**

Calais

Boulogne

Dieppe

Le Havre

*Guernsey*

*Jersey*

COPYRIGHT PHILIP'S

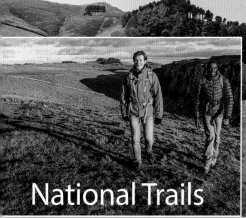

# National Trails

## England

National Trails are long distance footpaths and bridleways in England and Wales. They are managed by Natural England and Natural Resources Wales. See www.nationaltrail.co.uk

**Cleveland Way** *109 miles / 175 km Helmsley to Filey, North Yorkshire* This trail covers two contrasting landscapes: the inland section runs across the heather moorland of the North York Moors National Park, then, after it reaches the coast at Saltburn-by-the-Sea, it passes fishing villages and coastal towns. **102 F4 / 97 A7**

**Cotswold Way** *102 miles / 164 km Chipping Campden, Gloucestershire to Bath, Somerset* Running along the edge of the Cotswold escarpment, this path offers meadows, woodlands, quaint villages and historic sites along with wide-ranging views to the north and west. **51 F6 / 24 C2**

**Hadrian's Wall Path** *84 miles / 135 km Wallsend, Tyne and Wear to Bowness-on-Solway, Cumberland* For most of its length, the path stays close to the line of the Hadrian's Wall UNESCO World Heritage Site. Stretching from coast to coast across northern England, it includes rolling fields and rough moorland. **111 C5 / 108 C2**

**King Charles III England Coast Path** *2,700 miles / 4,300 km* The trail is planned to follow the entire coastline of England. Once all sections are completed, and linked up, it will be around 2,700 miles (4,300 km) long. It will allow access, in most places, to the coastal margin – where land meets the sea.

**North Downs Way** *153 miles / 246 km Farnham, Surrey to Dover, Kent* Offering an escape close to London, this trail offers a mix of picturesque villages and glorious countryside. It passes many sites of historic interest including Stone Age burial sites, cathedrals and pilgrim churches. **27 E6 / 31 E7**

**Peddar's Way & Norfolk Coast Path** *92 miles / 148 km Knettishall Heath Country Park, Suffolk to Cromer, Norfolk* Although nominally in two parts, this forms one continuous route from the inland Breckland to the Norfolk coast. The coastal stretch passes seaside towns and villages, tidal marshes teeming with birdlife, wide sandy beaches, pine woodlands and big skies. **68 A2 / 81 C8**

▲ The Pennine Way near Edale in the Peak District
Davidmartyn / Dreamstime

**Pennine Way** *268 miles / 431 km Edale, Derbyshire to Kirk Yetholm, Scottish Borders* This is Britain's oldest trail and one of the most popular – and the toughest to walk. It follows the 'backbone of England' and just crosses the border into Scotland. Inspired by the Appalachian Trail in the US, it uses mainly public footpaths, rather than bridleways, and is not accessible to horse riders or cyclists. **88 F2 / 116 B4**

**Pennine Bridleway** *205 miles / 330 km Middleton Top, Derbyshire to Ravenstonedale, Westmorland & Furness* Running roughly parallel to the main Pennine Way, this trail has been designed to accommodate horse riders and cyclists. It uses both ancient packhorse routes and the trackbed of the former Cromford and High Peak Railway. **76 D2 / 100 D2**

**South Downs Way** *100 miles / 160 km Winchester, Hampshire to Eastbourne, East Sussex* An ancient route affording wide views of the best of the English countryside from the chalk escarpment and ridges of the South Downs. Most of the route is on bridleways, allowing access for walkers, cyclists and horse riders. **15 B5 / 18 F3**

**South West Coast Path** *630 miles / 1,014 km Minehead, Somerset to Poole Harbour, Dorset* This is England's longest waymarked National Trail and is quite challenging due to its many ups and downs. The rewards are rugged cliff tops, sheltered estuaries, beaches, hidden coves and picturesque villages. **21 E8 / 13 E8**

**Thames Path** *185 miles / 298 km Near Coates, Gloucestershire to Woolwich, London* From the source to the sea, the path follows England's most iconic river. The path was first proposed in 1948 but not opened until 1996. Winding through meadows, and passing unspoilt villages and historic towns, it navigates walkers through London to meet the King Charles III England Coast Path. **37 D6 / 28 B5**

**The Ridgeway** *87 miles / 140 km Avebury, Wiltshire to Ivinghoe Beacon, Buckinghamshire* This ancient trackway is known as 'Britain's oldest road' and has been in use since prehistoric times. The high dry ground gave a reliable and safe trading route from Dorset to The Wash. The official guide to the trail divides it into six, easy to tackle, sections. **25 C6 / 40 C2**

**Yorkshire Wolds Way** *79 miles / 127 km Hessle, East Riding of Yorkshire to Filey, North Yorkshire* This is a relatively undemanding meander, without steep climbs, through gentle countryside. One of least well-known trails, it introduces visitors to the Yorkshire Wolds via dry chalk valleys and rolling hills, giving expansive views. **90 B4 / 97 A7**

◀ Disused Tamdhu station on The Speyside Way
David Massie / Dreamstime

▲ Strumble Head on the Pembrokeshire Coast Path
steved_np3 / iStock

## Wales

**Glyndwr's Way** *135 miles / 217 km Knighton to Welshpool, Powys* Named after the Welsh prince, Owain Glyndwr, this trail offers open moorland, rolling farmland and forests. Birds seen may include red kites, peregrine falcons and ospreys. It meanders in an extended loop. **48 B4 / 60 D2**

**Offa's Dyke Path** *177 miles / 285 km Sedbury Cliffs, Gloucestershire to Prestatyn, Denbighshire* The route loosely follows the England/Wales border from the cliffs of Sedbury in the south to Prestatyn in the north. Offa's Dyke is an earthwork constructed in the late 8th century although its original purpose is subject to conjecture. **36 E2 / 72 A4**

**Pembrokeshire Coast Path** *186 miles / 299 km St Dogmaels to Amroth, Pembrokeshire* The best of the Welsh coastline can be experienced on this trail from rugged cliff tops to hidden coves and wide open sandy beaches. Although not very strenuous, there are constant undulations and many stiles and footbridges. **45 E3 / 32 D2**

## Scotland

**The Great Trails:** 29 trails managed by NatureScot/NàrAlba. See www.scotlandsgreattrails.com. Some of the most popular are listed below.

**Great Glen Way** *79 miles / 125 km Fort William to Inverness, Highland* A variety of modes of transport can be used on this route: walking, cycling and boating. Although mainly low level – and following canal towpaths, forest tracks and roads – there are some challenging sections. Experienced walkers can make detours to tackle nearby Munros or Corbetts. **131 B5 / 151 G9**

**Southern Upland Way** *214 miles / 344 km Portpatrick, Dumfries & Galloway to Cockburnspath, Scottish Borders* Tackling the whole route is quite a challenge and can take 12 to 16 days to complete the full length, though some sections are more suitable for families. This, the longest of the Great Trails, is mainly designed for walkers but some sections are accessible to cyclists and horse riders. **104 D4 / 122 B3**

**Speyside Way** *85 miles / 137 km Buckie, Moray to Newtonmore, Highland* Much of the route follows the river with some parts crossing open moorland. Short diversions allow visits to whisky distilleries. Wildlife on view includes deer, red squirrels, capercaillie and maybe the elusive Scottish wildcat. **152 B4 / 138 E3**

**West Highland Way** *96 miles / 154 km Milngavie, Glasgow to Fort William, Highland* Traditionally walked from south to north to take advantage of prevailing winds, the whole trail takes 5-8 days to complete. This is a busy route despite travelling through some remote areas including the very exposed Rannoch Moor. **119 B5 / 131 B5**

▼ The South Downs Way in Sussex
Dmitry Naumov / Dreamstime

▲ A boardwalk across wetlands at Thursley Common Ac Manley / Dreamstime

◀ Kynance Cove on the Lizard Peninsula Andrew Michael / iStock

# Forest parks and National Nature Reserves

## Forest parks

### Wales

**Gwydyr Forest Park** *Betws-y-Coed, Conwy* A forest park ranging across eastern Snowdonia's hills, with more than 20 miles (32 km) of trails through mountain forest, plus riding, canoeing and mountain biking. 🖥 www.visitconwy.org.uk **83 E7**

### Yorkshire & the Humber

**Duncombe Park** *Helmsley, North Yorkshire* This parkland is home to many ancient trees, which provide a home for rare invertebrates and fungi. Birds include woodpecker, nuthatch and the elusive hawfinch. In spring the woodland floor is covered in sheets of bluebells, primroses and wild garlic. 🖥 www.woodlandtrust.org.uk **102 F4**

### Forge Valley Woodlands

*West Ayton, North Yorkshire* This, the largest community managed woodland in England, provides a home to nationally rare flora and fauna. It also contains over 200 historic environment and built heritage features including ancient charcoal pits and holloways. 🖥 www.woodlandtrust.org.uk **103 F7**

### North East

**Kielder Water & Forest Park** *Northumberland* Northern Europe's largest man-made lake, and England's largest forest, also home to around half of England's red squirrel population. The forest contains a number of art and architectural installations including a 'Skyspace' to frame stargazing. 🖥 www.visitkielder.com **116 E2**

### Scotland

**Galloway Forest Park** *New Galloway, Dumfries and Galloway* Britain's largest forest park with habitats ranging from forest, moorland and loch to mountains and beaches. There are extensive walking and cycle trails, horse riding, fishing, and stunning views. 🖥 https://forestryandland.gov.scot **112 F3**

## National Nature Reserves

### South West

**East Dartmoor Woods and Heaths** *Bovey Tracey, Devon* Internationally important western oakwood. Pied flycatchers, woodpeckers and wood warblers in the woods. Dartford warblers, ponies and fritillary butterflies around the moorland, and dippers along the River Bovey. 🖥 www.exploredevon.info **7 B5**

**Golitha Falls** *St Cleer, Cornwall* A steeply sided wooded valley where the river Fowey drops in a series of spectacular cascades. This ancient woodland is carpeted with bluebells and wood anemones in spring. 🖥 www.woodlandtrust.org.uk **5 C7**

**Purbeck Heath** *Studland, Dorset* Designated as the UK's first 'super' nature reserve. It spans lowland wet and dry heath, valley mires, acid grassland and woodland, coastal sand dunes, lakes and saltmarsh which makes it one of the most biodiverse places in the UK. 🖥 https://purbeckheaths.org.uk **13 F8**

◀ Swallow Falls in Gwydyr Forest, Snowdonia Eddie Cloud / Dreamstime

▶ Sunset at Kielder Water Forest Park Nurmala Taberham / Dreamstime

▼ Loch Trool in the Galloway Forest Park Mark Dean / Dreamstime

**Shapwick Heath** *Meare, Somerset* Situated at the heart of the Avalon Marshes in the Somerset Levels, there is a chance to spot the elusive bittern or even otters in the reed beds. Today's landscape owes much to the extraction of peat for horticultural use. 🖥 https://avalonmarshes.org **23 F6**

**Slapton Ley** *Torcross, Devon* This large freshwater lake is separated from the open sea by the shingle beach of Slapton Sands. There are trails and hides for bird watching. Guided walks and events are held throughout the year. 🖥 www.exploredevon.info **7 E6**

**The Lizard** *Helston, Cornwall* This is the most southerly tip of Britain and offers stunning beaches, cliff top walks, and heathland landscapes. Spring and summer bring carpets of wild flowers. The local serpentine rock is especially distinctive. 🖥 www.nationaltrust.org.uk **3 E6**

▲ A rare British Raft Spider at Lopham Fen Dubsy21 / Dreamstime

## South East

**Aston Rowant** *near Stokenchurch, Oxfordshire* Located on the north-western scarp of the Chiltern Hills with wide views, the main habitats are flower and butterfly-rich chalk grassland, beech woodland and juniper scrub. Bird life includes winter visitors such as fieldfare and redwing.
🖥 www.chilternsaonb.org **39 E7**

**Kingley Vale** *West Stoke, West Sussex* There are large areas of grass downland with pockets of forest with yew trees that are up to 2,000 years old. Views stretch over Sussex to the south coast. There are a number of walks featuring Iron and Bronze Age remains.
🖥 www.woodlandtrust.org.uk **16 C2**

**Old Winchester Hill** *Warnford, Hampshire* Topped by an Iron Age hill fort, the summit gives all round views of the South Downs National Park. The chalk downs support a wide variety of butterflies and orchids.
🖥 www.visit-hampshire.co.uk **15 B7**

**Stodmarsh** *Canterbury, Kent* Extensive network of footpaths through the reedbeds allow sightings of migrating birds and rare plants. There are 'sensory' trails with wheelchair access.
🖥 www.visitkent.co.uk **31 C6**

**Thursley** *Godalming, Surrey* Lying between the villages of Thursley and Elstead, there are trails through the heathland with boardwalks in the boggy areas. Dragonflies and damselflies flit around the open ponds.
🖥 https://surreyhills.org **27 E7**

**Wye** *Ashford, Kent* The Wye Downs are popular with walkers giving wide-ranging views from the North Downs Way. The chalk escarpment is interrupted by combes (steep narrow valleys) with the most spectacular being the Devil's Kneading Trough.
🖥 https://explorekent.org **30 E4**

## East of England

**Barnack Hills & Holes** *Stamford, Cambridgeshire* Once the site of a medieval quarry, this is one of Britain's most important wildlife sites. Covering an area of 50 acres, it is rich in wild flowers which support a wide variety of wildlife, especially insects.
🖥 www.woodlandtrust.org **65 D7**

**Holkham** *Wells-next-the-Sea, Norfolk* Pine trees given way to vast swathes of salt-marsh and sand on the North Norfolk coast. This, England's largest National Nature Reserve, is important for its wintering wildfowl especially pink-footed geese.
🖥 www.holkham.co.uk **80 C5**

**Orford Ness** *Suffolk*
Apart from its important vegetated shingle habitat, there are buildings left from its time as a base for the Atomic Weapons Research Establishment. Access is by boat from Orford Quay and must be booked in advance.
🖥 www.nationaltrust.org.uk **57 E8**

**Redgrave and Lopham Fen**
*South Lopham, Norfolk* The fen is the source of both the Waveney and Little Ouse rivers. Sheep, cattle and wild Konik ponies are used to manage the vegetation. 🖥 www.suffolkwildlifetrust.org **68 F3**

**Suffolk Coast** *Walberswick, Suffolk* Lying south of the town of Southwold the reserve can be accessed from a

▲ Ancient oaks in Sherwood Forest
Steven Bramall / Dreamstime

▶ **The Stiperstones** Paul Brewster / Dreamstime

number of car parks leading to walking routes. There are two other reserves along this coast at Benacre and Westleton Heath.
🖥 www.thesuffolkcoast.co.uk **57 B8**

**Wicken Fen** *Ely, Cambridgeshire* One of Britain's oldest nature reserves with fenland, marsh and reedbeds. To keep the land clear of scrub, wild Konik ponies and Highland cattle have been introduced. There is a National Trust visitor centre.
🖥 www.nationaltrust.org.uk **55 B6**

## East Midlands

**Cribbs Meadow** *Sewstern, Leicestershire* The embankment of a disused railway runs through this landscape providing access. The wealth of flora includes adder's tongue fern, hayrattle and green-winged orchid.
🖥 www.lrwt.org.uk **65 C5**

**Derbyshire Dales** *near Bakewell, Derbyshire* Consisting of a group of five dales within the White Peak area of the Peak District National Park: Lathkill Dale; Cressbrook Dale; Monk's Dale; Long Dale and Hay Dale. Lathkill Dale is the most popular and easily accessible with a good path. 🖥 www.naturalengland.co.uk **75 B8**

**Gibraltar Point** *near Skegness, Lincolnshire* The great variety of wildfowl, waders and gulls can be seen from the bird observatory and visitor centre close to Gibraltar Point. The sand dunes, which make up the reserve, stretch from the southern end of Skegness for 3 miles. 🖥 www.lincstrust.org.uk **79 D8**

**Saltfleetby-Theddlethorpe Dunes**
*Saltfleet, Lincolnshire* Mainly sand dunes, salt marsh and tidal mudflats. A large part of the reserve near the car

▲ **Reed beds at Wicken Fen**
Andremichel / Dreamstime

◀ **A barn owl hunting at Holkham Marsh** Lee Amery / Dreamstime

park is wheelchair accessible. To the south, just to the north of Mablethorpe, is a seal sanctuary and wildlife centre.
🖥 www.lincstrust.org.uk **91 E8**

**Sherwood Forest** *Edwinstowe, Nottinghamshire* Sherwood is the remnants of an ancient royal forest and is full of ancient oaks that are over 500 years old. Home to a wide variety of wildlife, visitors can go on a guided bat or glow-worm walk.
🖥 www.rspb.org.uk **77 C6**

## West Midlands

**Aqualate Mere** *Coton, Staffordshire* This is a good place to see overwintering wildfowl from the public observation hide. Mammals include otter, polecat, stoat, water vole, harvest mouse, and bats such as pipistrelle.
🖥 www.woodlandtrust.org.uk **61 B7**

**Chaddesley Woods** *Bromsgrove, Worcestershire* Mentioned in the Domesday Book, this ancient woodland has indicator species such as yellow archangel, herb paris and dog's mercury as well as wild service trees.
🖥 www.worcswildlifetrust.co.uk **50 B4**

**Stiperstones** *The Bog, Shropshire* The long summit ridge consists of several distinctive jagged outcrops of rock. A five mile walk, suitable for families, makes the most of the views. Facilities available at the Bog Centre. The Shropshire Way passes through the reserve. 🖥 http://www.shropshiresgreatoutdoors.co.uk **60 E3**

**Wybunbury Moss** *Nantwich, Cheshire East* This is a rare raised lowland bog. Access is limited, but a permitted wildlife walk leaves a public footpath north of Wybunbury Tower, running west over boardwalks towards the centre of the reserve.
🖥 www.woodlandtrust.org.uk **74 D3**

## Wales

**Cors Caron** *Tregaron, Ceredigion* A fully accessible boardwalk allows access over the south-east bog and to the large hide where visitors can view the landscape and wildlife. The multi-user trail can be used by walkers, cyclists and horse riders, and follows on an old railway track along the edge of the reserve. 🖥 https://naturalresources.wales **47 C5**

**Cors Goch** *Pentraeth, Isle of Anglesey* Complex geology and a wealth of habitats make this one of Wales's most diverse and colourful nature reserves. Dragonflies and damselflies can be seen from the boardwalk. 🖥 www. northwaleswildlifetrust.org.uk **82 C4**

**Dyfi** *Near Aberystwyth, Ceredigion* A nature reserve, with a sandy beach and spectacular dunes, at the mouth of the River Dyfi. Mudflats and saltmarshes provide feeding and roosting areas for wetland birds. There is a visitor centre and a network of footpaths. 🖥 https://naturalresources.wales **58 E3**

**Kenfig** *Pyle, Bridgend* This beautiful sand dune nature reserve, with spectacular views across Swansea Bay to the Gower, is one of the largest active sand dune systems in Europe. There is an Information Centre. 🖥 www.visitwales.com **34 F1**

**Oxwich** *Swansea* Close to Swansea, this reserve is made up of a mix of beach, sand dunes, lakes, woodlands, cliffs and salt and freshwater marshes. In summer, many kinds of chalk-loving wildflowers bloom. 🖥 https://naturalresources. wales **33 F6**

## North West

**Drumburgh Moss** *Near Carlisle, Cumberland* This lowland raised mire is one of Western Europe's most threatened habitats. Sphagnum moss and other bog-loving plants thrive in these wetlands. Curlew and red grouse breed and adders and roe deer can be seen. 🖥 www.cumbriawildlifetrust.org.uk **108 D2**

**Duddon Mosses** *Broughton in Furness, Westmorland & Furness* Wildlife includes deer, adders, lizards, frogs and barn owls. Typical of the vegetation are bog plants such as sphagnum mosses, cotton grasses and the carnivorous sundew. 🖥 www.woodlandtrust.org.uk **98 F4**

**Finglandrigg Woods** *Near Carlisle, Cumberland* One of the largest areas of semi-natural woodland on the Solway Plain. Wildlife ranges from red squirrel and roe deer to badgers and otters. 🖥 www.woodlandtrust.org.uk **108 D2**

**Gait Barrows** *Silverdale, Lancashire* The reserve covers both limestone pavements and peat habitats giving home to often rare wildlife. Meadows are grazed by native breeds of cattle and ponies. **92 B4**

**Ribble Estuary** *Lancashire* An important site for wintering wildfowl, the reserve occupies land on both sides of the Estuary. A footpath runs along the flood embankment on the southern edge of the reserve from Crossens pumping station to Hundred End near Hesketh Bank village. 🖥 www.rspb.org.uk **85 B4**

## Yorkshire & the Humber

**Ingleborough** *Ingleton, North Yorkshire* Ingleborough is one of the famous Three Peaks of the Yorkshire Dales National Park and there are several routes to the summit. Along the edge of the plateau there are the remains of an Iron Age hill fort. Nearby is the Ingleborough showcave and the pothole of Gaping Gill. **93 B7**

**Malham Tarn** *Settle, North Yorkshire* The tarn is the highest limestone lake in Britain and is rich in wildlife. The adjacent raised bog includes plants such as wild cranberry, bog rosemary and crowberry. There is a boardwalk around the fen. 🖥 www.yorkshiredales. org.uk **93 C8**

**Skipwith Common** *Barlby, North Yorkshire* Skipwith Common is one of the last remaining areas of northern lowland heath in England. The open heath, ponds, woodland and scrub are an ancient landscape showing the land as it was before intensive agriculture. 🖥 https://freshwaterhabitats.org.uk **96 F2**

**Spurn** *East Riding of Yorkshire* Spurn Point is a constantly moving peninsula which curves between the North Sea and the Humber Estuary. It is over 3 miles /5 km long but as little as 50 yds / 45 m wide. Footpaths are open at all times (unless bad weather closes the nature reserve). 🖥 www.ywt.org.uk **91 C8**

## North East

**Castle Eden Dene** *Peterlee, Durham* A rare survivor of the 'wildwood' that once covered much of Britain. A tangle of trees, rocky outcrops and steep limestone cliffs. The Dene is 3.5 miles / 5.6 km long and runs down to the coast between Sunderland and Hartlepool. 🖥 www.woodlandtrust.org.uk **111 F7**

**Durham Coast** *Hartlepool to South Shields, Durham* A Site of Special Scientific Interest stretching from north of the Tees estuary to the Tyne at South Shields. The rugged cliffs and beaches provide bracing walks along the coastline of the North Sea. **111 F7**

**Farne Islands** *Seahouses, Northumberland* An archipelago of some 20 islands. The islands are an internationally important wildlife habitat with puffins in the summer and a breeding colony of grey seals in the autumn. The waters round the islands are popular with scuba divers. Boat trips are available from Seahouses. 🖥 www.nationaltrust.org.uk **123 F8**

**Lindisfarne** *Northumberland* This tidal island lies less than a mile from the coast and is surrounded by the nature reserve that protects the sand dunes and intertidal habitats. A causeway (with pedestrian refuges) provides access at low tide. Tide tables are posted at both ends of the causeway. 🖥 www.lindisfarne.org.uk **123 E7**

**Moor House-Upper Teesdale** *Forest-in-Teesdale, Durham/ Westmorland & Furness* Designated a UNESCO biosphere reserve, it sits high on the Pennines close to the Pennine Way and is one of England's largest National Nature Reserves. It covers a wide range of landscapes from hay meadows to bleak high fells with blanket bog and juniper woods. 🖥 https://explorenorthpennines.org. uk **109 F7**

## Scotland

**Ben Lawers** *Milton Morenish, Perth & Kinross* This reserve has a unique range of arctic-alpine plants that flower in early to mid- summer. There is a nature trail, and ranger-led walks are available. 🖥 www.nts.org.uk **132 E3**

**Forvie** *Collieston, Aberdeenshire* The Ythan estuary, riverside, sand dunes, coastal heath and seacliffs make this a rich area for a variety of plants and wildlife, including seals. It is renowned for its birdlife with breeding eider duck. 🖥 www.nature.scot **153 F10**

**Glen Affric** *Cannich, Highland* Glen Affric is among the most beautiful glens and has one of the largest remaining ancient pinewoods in Scotland. Wildlife present includes some of Scotland's most elusive species – black grouse, capercaillies and pine martens. 🖥 www.visitscotland.com **136 B4**

**Rùm** *Highland* The spectacular Isle of Rùm home to otters, red deer, sea eagles and a mountain top colony of Manx shearwaters. Access is via ferry from Mallaig. 🖥 www.nature.scot **146 B6**

**St Abb's Head** *St Abbs, Scottish Borders* The stunning cliffs support large breeding colonies of fulmars, guillemots, kittiwakes, puffins, razorbills and shags. In spring and summer the grasslands are full of flowers. In autumn and spring large numbers of migrant birds pass close to the cliffs. 🖥 www.nts.org.uk **122 C5**

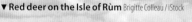

# Dark skies

The International Dark-Sky Association recognises four categories of dark-sky sites in the UK. A Dark Sky Sanctuary is noted for exceptionally dark nights and a nocturnal environment protected for its scientific and cultural heritage, often in a remote location. Dark Sky Reserves are generally large, and consist of a very dark core region surrounded by a peripheral area where lighting is minimal. Smaller regions with exceptionally low light pollution are designated Dark Sky Parks. A town, village or complete island that's actively fighting light pollution can be designated a Dark Sky Community.

## Dark Sky Sanctuary

**Bardsey Island** *Gwynedd* Europe's first designated Dark Sky Sanctuary is home to a major bird observatory, with an emphasis on nocturnal species. It lies 2 miles / 3 km off the Welsh coast, and is accessible only by small boat during good weather.
www.bardsey.org/darkskysanctuary **70 E2**

## Dark Sky Reserves

**Brecon Beacons National Park** *Powys* Situated in the mountains of South Wales, where sheep outnumber humans 30 to 1, this Reserve is home to 33,000 people – yet lighting is controlled so that the core zone has some of the darkest skies in Wales.
www.breconbeaconsparksociety.org **34 B4**

**Cranborne Chase** *Wiltshire* Not far from Stonehenge, Cranborne Chase is a chalk plateau rising to 901 ft / 277 m at Win Green. This area has commanding views to the west and to some extent to the north.
https://cranbornechase.org.uk **13 B7**

**Exmoor National Park** *Somerset* The first Dark Sky Reserve site to be designated in Britain, Exmoor is a moorland area with much preserved history and many monuments within its core zone. www.exmoor-nationalpark.gov.uk/enjoying/stargazing **21 E7**

**Moore's Reserve (South Downs)** *Brighton* Named after the British astronomy populariser Sir Patrick Moore (1923–2012) who lived nearby, this reserve is sandwiched between London and the busy seaside resorts of Brighton and Worthing – yet it retains remarkably dark skies. www.southdowns.gov.uk **17 D7**

**North York Moors National Park** *North Yorkshire* Despite its proximity to the busy tourist destinations of Whitby and Scarborough, the North York Moors is a largely deserted expanse of heather and bog moorland, with wide views of the night sky.
www.northyorkmoors.org.uk **103 E5**

**Snowdonia National Park** *Gwynedd* The national park encompasses around 10 per cent of the total land area of Wales, and the darkest skies are to be seen from the rugged central area around Mount Snowdon.
www.snowdonia.gov.wales **83 F6**

**Yorkshire Dales National Park** *North Yorkshire* The largest dark-sky site in Britain, the Yorkshire Dales National Park boasts impressive waterfalls and caves, and brilliant night skies within reach of major cities like Leeds and Manchester. www.yorkshiredales.org.uk **100 E3**

▲ **The Milky Way over Horsey Windpump, Norfolk** Ollie Taylor / Dreamstime

▶ **The Milky Way at Kielder Forest Dark Skies, Northumberland** Anita Nicholson / iStock

## Dark Sky Parks

**Bodmin Moor Dark Sky Landscape** *Cornwall* This remote, rugged area of granite moorland in north-east Cornwall is a working agricultural landscape, protecting it from large-scale development that would threaten dark skies. www.cornwall-aonb.gov.uk/bodminmoor **5 B6**

**Elan Valley Estate** *Powys* The city of Birmingham purchased this Welsh valley in 1892 to construct reservoirs that would provide a regular supply of pure water. Views of the starry night over the reservoirs are particularly impressive. www.elanvalley.org.uk **47 C8**

**Galloway Forest Park** *Dumfries & Galloway* Galloway Forest Park is the largest forest park in the UK, and 20 per cent has been set aside as a core area with no illumination allowed. It's a mecca not just for astronomers but for nocturnal wildlife whose lives are often disrupted elsewhere by light pollution.
www.forestryandland.gov.scot **112 F3**

**Northumberland National Park and Kielder Water & Forest Park** *Rothbury, Northumberland* Near Hadrian's Wall, built to keep the Picts from Roman Britain, this Dark Sky Park was designated as a bulwark against light pollution invading the darkness of northern England. It contains the largest reservoir and most extensive forest in northern Europe.
www.northumberlandnationalpark.org.uk **116 C4**

**Tomintoul and Glenlivet, Cairngorms** *Highland* Containing the dramatic landscape of the Cairngorm Mountains, this Dark Sky Park is home to Britain's only herd of wild reindeer. And, if the weather is cloudy, the Park also contains the Glenlivet whisky distillery! www.cairngormsdarkskypark.org **139 C7**

**West Penwith** *Cornwall* The very western tip of Cornwall, stretching down to Land's End, West Penwith is a wild landscape, with stunning sea views and ancient archaeological remains – some thought to be astronomically aligned.
www.cornwall-aonb.gov.uk **2 C3**

▶ **The Milky Way over Great Staple Tor, Dartmoor National Park** MattStansfield / iStock

## Dark Sky Communities

**Coll** *Argyll & Bute* The Scottish island of Coll is home to just 200 permanent residents, plus myriad birds in its extensive nature reserve. The island has adopted a light-management plan to ensure its skies remain dark. https://visitcoll.co.uk/dark_sky **146 F5**

**Moffat** *Dumfries & Galloway* This former spa town is a tourist base for southern Scotland. It has strict outdoor lighting policies to reduce light pollution in its hinterland. https://visitmoffat.co.uk **114 D3**

**North Ronaldsay** *Orkney* The northernmost island in Orkney. Many visitors come to its bird observatory, and the island's appeal extends to astronomers with its Dark Sky Community designation. www.northronaldsay.co.uk **159 C8**

# Other natural features

## South West

**Chesil Beach** *Weymouth, Dorset*
Long shingle barrier beach, stretching 18 miles/29 km between West Bay and Portland on the Jurassic Coast. For much of its length, it is separated from the mainland by the brackish Fleet Lagoon. **13 F4**

**Durdle Door** *West Lulworth, Dorset*
Natural limestone arch jutting out to sea. A famous geological landmark, it was formed by the erosion of softer rocks by wave power; with continued erosion, the arch will collapse leaving just a sea stack. **13 F6**

**Valley of Rocks** *Lynton, Devon*
Dry valley running parallel to the coast and known for its unusual rock formations and caves, as well as for the feral goats that graze on its precipitous cliffs. **21 E6**

**Wistman's Wood** *Two Bridges, Devon*
High-altitude oak woodland within the Dartmoor National Park. It is an unusual and rare habitat, where fragile mosses and lichen flourish. **6 B4**

## South East

**Cuckmere Haven & Seven Sisters**
*Seaford, East Sussex* Chalk cliffs in the form of seven peaks, created when ancient rivers cut valleys through the chalk. They run between Beachy Head

▲ Ancient forest Wistman's Wood on Dartmoor, Devon. Savo Ilic / Dreamstime

and Cuckmere Haven, a country park where the meandering River Cuckmere reaches the sea.
🖥 www.sevensisters.org.uk **18 F2**

**Devil's Punch Bowl** *Hindhead, Surrey* Large basin forming a natural amphitheatre. Its open heathland and ancient woodland are full of wildlife, and its surrounding slopes have fine views over the area. It is popular with walkers. 🖥 www.nationaltrust.org.uk **27 F6**

**Dunstable Downs** *Dunstable, Central Bedfordshire* Chalk escarpment within the Chiltern Hills, known for its chalk grasslands and associated flora and fauna, fine views and ancient monuments, including the Bronze Age barrow cemetery Five Knolls and a medieval rabbit warren.
🖥 www.nationaltrust.org.uk **40 C3**

**The Needles** *Alum Bay, Isle of Wight* Three distinctive chalk stacks protruding from the sea, with a lighthouse perched on the outermost. They are next to the multi-coloured cliffs of Alum Bay. A chairlift provides dramatic views of both.
🖥 www.theneedles.co.uk **14 F3**

## East of England

**Blakeney Point** *Blakeney, Norfolk*
Shingle spit and sand dunes, backed by salt marshes and mudflats. It is known for its large grey seal colony, and as an important site for breeding and migrating birds.
🖥 www.nationaltrust.org.uk **81 C5**

**Epping Forest** *Epping, Essex* Large area of ancient woodland and grassland, dotted with streams, ponds and bogs. It is an important site for rare mosses and fungi, many of which flourish on its 55,000 veteran pollarded trees.
🖥 www.visiteppingforest.org **41 E7**

**Hickling Broad** *Potter Heigham, Norfolk* The largest of the Norfolk Broads, a haven for birds, in particular waders and birds of prey, as well as deer, otters and butterflies. **69 B7**

**Orford Ness** *Orford, Suffolk* Spit of land separating the River Alde from the North Sea. Unusual wildlife and plant species thrive in its rare habitats, which include vegetated shingle, saltmarsh and brackish lagoons. **57 E8**

## East Midlands

**Castleton Caverns** *Derbyshire* Show caves in the Peak District – Blue John, Treak Cliff, Peak and Speedwell. Only Peak Cavern is entirely natural, the others being part natural and part mine-workings. Speedwell has an underground canal and boat trips.
🖥 https://visitcastleton.co.uk **88 F2**

**Rutland Water** *Oakham, Rutland* Reservoir created in the 1970s and covering over 3,000 acres, one-third of which is nature reserve. Waterfowl and birds of prey flourish in its network of lagoons and wetlands. **65 D6**

**Sherwood Forest** *Edwinstowe, Nottinghamshire* Large area of ancient woodland, closely associated with the legend of Robin Hood. It is known for its ancient oaks, oak-birch woodland and wide variety of animal life, especially birds and insects.
🖥 www.nationaltrust.org.uk **77 C6**

**The Wash** *Boston, Lincolnshire* Tidal estuary and shallow bay opening into the North Sea. It is rich in wildlife, in particular wading birds, waterfowl and seals, which flourish on its sandbanks, mudflats and saltmarshes. **79 E7**

## West Midlands

**Bredon Hill** *Evesham, Worcestershire* Outlier of the Cotswold Hills; on its summit are the remains of an Iron Age hillfort and a tower known as Parsons Folly. **50 F4**

**Golden Valley** *Bromyard, Herefordshire* Rolling countryside between the valleys of the rivers Dore and Monnow and the Black Mountains. The Neolithic burial chamber Arthur's Stone and the ruined Norman Snodhill Castle overlook the valley. **49 D8**

**Thor's Cave** *Wetton, Staffordshire* Natural cavern in a steep limestone crag, with fine views over the Manifold Valley. Evidence for human occupation has been found dating from the Stone Age up until Roman times. **75 D8**

**The Wrekin** *Telford, Shropshire* Prominent hill overlooking the Shropshire Plain, with wooded slopes and a rocky summit, where the remains of an Iron Age hillfort can be found. **61 D6**

## Wales

**Newborough Warren** *Anglesey* Extensive sand dune system and conifer forest, known for its red squirrels, behind Llanddwyn Beach. There are excellent views from Llanddwyn Island, a narrow promontory at the west end of the beach. **82 E3**

**Pistyll Rhaeadr** *Tan-y-pistyll, Powys* Highest waterfall in Wales, where the River Disgynfa drops 80 m/240 ft down a steep rock face into the River Rhaeadr below. It is situated within the Berwyn Mountains. **59 B7**

**Snowdon summit** *Llanberis, Gwynedd* Yr Wyddfa, or Snowdon, in the Eryri National Park, is the highest mountain in Wales (and England), at an altitude of 1085 m/2560 ft. It is a popular but challenging peak to climb. A mountain railway travels to the summit in summer. **83 F6**

**Worms Head and Rhossili Bay** *Rhossili, Swansea* Worms Head is an island at the westernmost point of the Gower Peninsula. It can be reached by a rocky causeway exposed for a few hours either side of low tide. North of the promontory is the beautiful long sandy beach, Rhossili Bay. **32 F4**

▼ Durdle Door in Dorset allou / iStock

▲ Rhossili Beach and Worm's Head, D4cus_cymru / iStock

◄ The Druid's Writing Desk at Brimham Rocks Jeremy Campbell / Dreamstime

► High Force Waterfall on the River Tees David Head / Dreamstime

## North West

**Alderley Edge** *Cheshire* Red sandstone escarpment overlooking the Cheshire plain, with dramatic views over the surrounding countryside. There is evidence of copper mining from the Bronze Age onwards. **74 B5**

**Buttermere** *Cumberland* Lake in a dramatic setting, surrounded by steep mountains, or fells. Unlike many of the other Cumbrian lakes, it has an easy footpath running all the way round. 💻www.nationaltrust.org.uk **98 C3**

**Morecambe Bay** *Arnside, Westmorland & Furness* Large estuary whose mudflats, shifting sands and salt marshes are important habitats for birds and shellfish. The Bay has an official 'King's Guide' appointed to lead walkers across the treacherous quicksand and unpredictable water channels. 💻https://guideoversands.co.uk **92 B4**

**Trough of Bowland** *Slaidburn, Lancashire* High valley and pass in the Forest of Bowland, a sparsely populated area of gritstone fells, steep valleys and peat moorland. **93 D6**

## Yorkshire & the Humber

**Brimham Rocks** *Pateley Bridge, North Yorkshire* Cluster of unusual rock formations, created over millions of years by the movement of the earth's plates combined with the action of ice, wind and rain. Huge and strangely shaped, they tower over the surrounding moorland. 💻www.nationaltrust.org.uk **94 C5**

**Buttertubs Pass** *Hawes, North Yorkshire* Scenic mountain pass in the Yorkshire Dales, crossing the high moorland between Hawes and Thwaite, and named after the deep limestone potholes in the area. It is a famously challenging cycle climb. **100 E3**

**Gaping Gill** *Ingleton, North Yorkshire* Natural cave known for its extremely large underground chamber complete with dramatic waterfall. Visitors can be winched into the chamber during occasional events run by local potholing clubs. **93 B7**

**Spurn Head** *Easington, East Riding of Yorkshire* Narrow sand peninsula, over 3 miles/5 km long, jutting into the North Sea at the mouth of the Humber Estuary. Many rare birds visit its varied habitats, which include sand dunes, chalk grassland and mudflats. **91 C8**

## North East

**Farne Islands** *Seahouses, Northumberland* Cluster of rocky islands off the Northumberland Coast, known for seabird colonies and seals. Puffins in particular flourish here, as do razorbills, guillemots and many others. Boat trips run to the islands from Seahouses. 💻www.nationaltrust.org.uk **123 F8**

**High Force** *Middleton-in-Teesdale, Durham* Picturesque waterfalls on the River Tees, where the river drops 70 m/21 ft over a sheer cliff face. There are woodland walks near the falls, and they are also on the route of the long-distance Pennine Way. **100 B3**

**Kielder Water** *Northumberland* Large man-made lake in the heart of the Kielder Forest. Wildlife flourishes in the varied habitats, which include marsh and bogs as well as woodland, and it is home to a large population of red squirrels. **116 F2**

**Yeavering Bell** *Wooler, Northumberland* Distinctive dome-shaped hill on the edge of the Cheviot Hills. On its summit are the remains of the largest Iron Age hillfort in Northumberland, with its encircling stone wall still visible. **117 B5**

## Scotland

**Dunnet Head** *Dunnet, Highland* Most northerly point of mainland Britain, a rugged landscape of steep cliffs home to large numbers of seabirds, including puffins, razorbills and fulmars. **158 C3**

**Falls of Clyde** *New Lanark, Lanarkshire* Series of waterfalls on the River Clyde, within a wooded gorge, part of the Clyde Valley Woodlands Nature Reserve. It is popular with walkers keen to spot badgers and otters. **119 E8**

**Fingal's Cave** *Staffa, Argyll & Bute* Sea cave on the uninhabited island of Staffa; it is formed from striking hexagonal basalt columns, which are of volcanic origin. The cave's unique natural acoustics inspired Felix Mendelssohn to compose his famous Hebrides Overture. **146 H6**

**Glen Coe** *Highland* U-shaped valley surrounded by a dramatic backdrop of mountains, including the famous Three Sisters of Glen Coe. Waterfalls tumble down the slopes into the glen, and the whole area is popular with walkers and mountaineers. **131 D5**

▼ Glencoe in the Scottish Highlands Helen Hotson / Dreamstime

# Ancient and historic sites

## South West

**Avebury Henge and Stone Circle**
*Avebury, Wiltshire* Neolithic circular earth bank and ditch enclosing the world's large prehistoric stone circle, within which are the remains of two smaller circles. The Avebury World Heritage Site is an internationally significant collection of Neolithic and Bronze Age monuments.
🖥 www.nationaltrust.org.uk **25 C6**

**Barbury Castle** *Broad Hinton, Wroughton, Wiltshire* Iron Age hillfort with impressive double ditch and far-reaching views over the surrounding countryside. The large area of chalk grassland is an important habitat for wildflowers and insects.
🖥 www.swindon.gov.uk **25 B6**

**Belas Knap Long Barrow**
*Winchcombe, Gloucestershire* Restored Neolithic burial mound, probably dating from 3000 BC. The barrow is surrounded by a drystone wall and has an imposing false entrance, with the actual burial chambers accessed via separate entrances.
🖥 www.english-heritage.org.uk **37 B7**

**Blackbury Camp** *Southleigh, Devon* Iron Age hillfort dating from the 4th century BC, comprising a bank and ditch surrounding an oval area, with an unusual triangular earthwork near its entrance. The area is known for bluebells in spring.
🖥 www.english-heritage.org.uk **11 E6**

**Bratton Camp** *Bratton, Westbury, Wiltshire* Earth banks and ditches that are the remains of an Iron Age hillfort. The double banks protected round houses, workshops and stores. Nearby is a Neolithic long barrow and the Westbury White Horse.
🖥 www.english-heritage.org.uk **24 D4**

**Carn Euny Ancient Village** *Brane or Sancreed, Cornwall* Remains of an ancient settlement occupied from Iron Age to Roman times. Some walls and foundations of the stone houses are visible, as well as a well-preserved underground passage ('fogou').
🖥 www.english-heritage.org.uk **2 D3**

**Chysauster Ancient Village**
*New Mill, Penzance, Cornwall* Remains of between 18 and 20 stone houses and an underground passage or 'fogou', dating from about 2,000 years ago, lining what was once a village street.
🖥 www.english-heritage.org.uk **2 C3**

**Halliggye Fogou** *Mawgan, Cornwall* Complex of underground tunnels within the Trelowarren Estate. Thought to date from the 5th to 4th century BC, they are typical of Iron Age settlements in this part of Cornwall.
🖥 www.english-heritage.org.uk **3 D6**

**Maiden Castle** *Winterborne Monkton, Dorchester, Dorset* Iron Age hillfort, one of the largest in Europe. It has multiple earth ramparts and ditches, mostly dating from the 1st century BC, best appreciated by walking around the perimeter bank.
🖥 www.english-heritage.org.uk **12 F4**

**Old Sarum** *Salisbury, Wiltshire* Well-preserved earthworks marking the site of an Iron Age hillfort, within which are the ruins of a 12th-century castle and cathedral, including a gatehouse and keep. There are impressive views over the Wiltshire plains.
🖥 www.english-heritage.org.uk **25 F6**

**Stonehenge** *Amesbury, Wiltshire* Circle of huge standing stones, with some horizontal lintel stones connecting them, believed to be about 4,500 years old. Its purpose is unclear, but its alignment with the sun on solstices is thought to be significant.
🖥 www.english-heritage.org.uk **25 E6**

**Tarr Steps** *Knaplock, Ashwick, Liscombe, Somerset* Britain's longest 'clapper' bridge – piles of stones placed at intervals across a river to support flat stone slabs – known to have existed in Tudor times and possibly much older.
🖥 www.exmoor-nationalpark.gov.uk **21 F7**

▲ Tarr Steps, a medieval clapper bridge on Exmoor Julian Gazzard / Dreamstime

**The Hurlers Stone Circle** *Minions, Cornwall* Three stone circles, dating from late Neolithic or early Bronze Age, arranged in a line. The southernmost is incomplete. Nearby are two standing stones, 'the Pipers', and the Bronze Age burial chamber Rillaton Barrow.
🖥 www.english-heritage.org.uk **5 B7**

**Trethevy Quoit** *Tremar or Darite, Cornwall* Well-preserved burial chamber or 'dolmen' consisting of five standing stones supporting an impressive capstone. It is thought to date from between 3500 and 2500 BC, during the Neolithic period.
🖥 www.english-heritage.org.uk **5 C7**

**West Kennet Long Barrow and Silbury Hill** *Beckhampton, Wiltshire* Neolithic burial mound and impressive standing stones dating from about 3650 BC, with five burial chambers. There is a good view towards Silbury Hill, an ancient artificial mound whose purpose is not known.
🖥 www.english-heritage.org.uk **25 C6**

**Woodhenge** *Durrington, Amesbury, Wiltshire* Neolithic monument made up of a series of concentric ovals of timber posts, now marked with concrete pillars, surrounded by an earth bank and ditch. The posts are aligned with midsummer sunrise.
🖥 www.english-heritage.org.uk **25 E6**

## South East

**Kit's Coty House** *Aylesford, Kent* Megalithic long barrow (burial chamber), dating from between 4000 and 3000 BC and comprising three huge standing stones surmounted by a large capstone. Little Kit's Coty nearby is also a chambered long barrow, but its sarsen stones are no longer standing.
🖥 www.english-heritage.org.uk **29 C8**

**Rollright Stones** *Little Rollright, Oxfordshire* Three groups of ancient stone monuments built from local limestone. The Whispering Knights burial chamber and King's Men stone circle date from the early and late Neolithic respectively; the King Stone from the Bronze Age.
🖥 www.rollrightstones.co.uk **38 B2**

**The Long Man of Wilmington**
*Wilmington, East Sussex* Large hill figure (235 ft / 72 m tall), now marked out with concrete blocks, on Windover Hill. Its origins are unclear, with some claiming it to be prehistoric and others dating it to the 17th century.
🖥 www.sussexpast.co.uk **18 E2**

**Uffington Castle** *Uffington, Wantage, Oxfordshire* Remains of a large Iron Age hillfort, atop Whitehorse Hill. Two earth ramparts separated by a deep ditch surround the site. It lies near the ancient route known as the Ridgeway.
🖥 www.english-heritage.org.uk **38 F3**

◄ Belas Knap Neolithic long barrow in Gloucestershire Davidmartyn / Dreamstim

▼ Castlerigg stone circle, located near Keswick in Cumbria MNStudio / Dreamstime e

▲ Callanais stone circle on the Isle of Lewis in the Outer Hebrides
*Helen Hotson / Dreamstime*

▶ Cairn and standing stones at Clava near Inverness *Travelling-light / Dreamstime*

## East of England

**Grimes Graves** *Lynford, Thetford, Norfolk* Neolithic flint mining complex, comprising roughly 400 pits (some up to 42 ft / 13 m deep) dug between 2650 and 2100 BC. There is an exhibition area and one of the shafts can be climbed down. 🖥 www.english-heritage.org.uk **67 F8**

## East Midlands

**Arbor Low Henge** *Monyash, Derbyshire* Neolithic stone circle made up of 50 limestone slabs (none standing) surrounded by earthworks and a ditch. Its central stone 'cove' indicates that it was a very important sacred site in pre-historic times. 🖥 www.english-heritage.org.uk **75 C8**

**Nine Ladies Stone Circle** *Stanton in Peak, Derbyshire* Early Bronze Age stone circle, made up of large sandstone blocks of varying shapes and sizes. In the late 20th century a tenth stone was uncovered but it may have been a later addition. 🖥 www.english-heritage.org.uk **76 C2**

## West Midlands

**Old Oswestry Hill Fort** *Oswestry, Shropshire* Large Iron Age hillfort with impressive multiple ramparts, visible as banks and ditches surrounding the site. It is thought to have been the base of one of the many Iron Age tribes active in Britain at that time. 🖥 www.english-heritage.org.uk **73 F6**

## Wales

**Offa's Dyke** *Wye Valley National Landscape* Linear defensive earthwork constructed in the 8th century, comprising an earth bank and ditch (or dyke), which roughly traces the border between Wales and England. The long-distance Offa's Dyke Path is a 177 mile / 285 km trail which follows the route. 🖥 www.english-heritage.org.uk **36 D2**

**Penrhos Standing Stones** *Holyhead, Isle of Anglesey* Pair of standing stones about 10 ft / 3 m high, dating from the Bronze Age. Their purpose is unknown. 🖥 www.cadw.gov.wales **82 C2**

## North West

**Castlerigg Stone Circle** *Keswick, Cumberland* One of the UK's oldest stone circles, dating from about 3000 BC, in a dramatic location with views towards the surrounding fells. It is unusual in containing a small rectangle of stones within it. 🖥 www.english-heritage.org.uk **99 B5**

**Manx Crosses** *Isle of Man* Over 200 carved stone crosses, mostly early medieval, found throughout the island, used as grave markers, altar fronts and memorials. The carved decorations range from simple crosses to complicated designs combining Christian and Viking subjects, sometimes with runic inscriptions. 🖥 www.manxnationalheritage.im **84 C4**

## Scotland

**Aberlemno Sculptured Stones** *Aberlemno, Angus* Four stones dating from 500 to 800 AD. One is probably a reused prehistoric standing stone, one is unshaped, and two are cross-slabs. They are decorated with Pictish carvings, some combining Pictish symbols with Christian imagery. 🖥 www.historicenvironment.scot **135 D5**

**Calanais Standing Stones** *Calanais, Isle of Lewis* 5,000-year old stone circle and rows of standing stones that together form a cruciform pattern. At the centre is a 17.7 ft / 4.8 m-tall monolith and a small, chambered tomb. Nearby are other smaller stone circles. 🖥 www.historicenvironment.scot **154 D7**

**Clava Cairns** *Leanach, Inverness* Bronze Age cemetery, dating from 4,000 years ago. At Balnuaran are three well-preserved burial cairns of different types, each surrounded by standing stones. Traces of a smaller cemetery can be seen at nearby Milton of Clava. 🖥 www.historicenvironment.scot **151 G10**

**Kilmartin** *Kilmartin, Argyll* Area known for its abundance of historic monuments, many of them from the Neolithic and Bronze Age. There are standing stones, burial cairns and a stone circle, as well as an Iron Age hillfort at Dunadd. 🖥 www.visitscotland.co.uk **124 F4**

**Kirkmadrine Stones** *Sandhead, Dumfries and Galloway* Eight carved stones dating from 6th to 12th centuries AD. The three earliest stones, some of the oldest Christian memorials in Scotland, date from the 500s and are carved with Latin inscriptions and Greek crosses. 🖥 www.historicenvironment.scot **104 E4**

**Mousa Broch** *Sandwick (accessible by boat from here), Island of Mousa, Shetland* Well-preserved Iron Age round tower or 'broch', 42 ft / 13 m tall, dating from about 300 BC. A staircase winds between its two unusually thick, concentric drystone walls to the top of the tower, overlooking Mousa Sound. 🖥 www.historicenvironment.scot **160 L6**

**Ring of Brodgar** *Stennes, Mainland, Orkney* Large circle of standing stones, dating from 2600 to 2000 BC, originally comprising 60 megaliths of which about half remain. The circle is surrounded by a rock-cut ditch or 'henge', and there are burial mounds nearby. 🖥 www.historicenvironment.scot **159 G3**

**Ruthwell Cross** *Ruthwell, Dumfries and Galloway* Anglo Saxon stone cross dating from the early 700s, carved with New Testament scenes, Latin inscriptions, Northumbrian designs and Anglo Saxon runes. It stands at an impressive 17 ft / 5.2 m tall, and is in Ruthwell Parish Church. 🖥 www.historicenvironment.scot **107 C8**

**Skara Brae** *Skaill, Orkney* Unusually well-preserved Neolithic settlement, a UNESCO World Heritage Site. The houses were built of flat stone slabs, with walls supported by earth mounds, and had stone hearths and built-in box-beds that can still be seen. 🖥 www.historicenvironment.scot **159 G3**

▼ Skara Brae Neolithic settlement in the Orkney Islands
*Juan Vilata Simón / Dreamstime*

# Pilgrimage routes

## South West

**Avebury** *11 or 7 miles / 18 or 11 km, Avebury, Wiltshire* A circular day route to connect with the world's largest prehistoric stone circle and West Kennet's 5700 year old Long Barrow. This is a pilgrimage to connect with prehistory and celebrate connections both pagan and Christian. **25 C6**

**Cornish Celtic Way** *125 miles / 200 km, St Germans Priory to St Michael's Mount, Cornwall* Designed to highlight Cornwall's spiritual inheritance including St German's Priory, St Issey Church and St Michael's Mount. The 'Cornish Celtic Way Passport' can be stamped along the way and allows access to budget accommodation in churches. **5 D8 / 2 D4**

## South East

**Canterbury** *4 miles / 6 km, Kent* The place where St Augustine first settled to convert England to Christianity. Canterbury is the focal point for several pilgrim routes. Once in the city, a 4-mile circular route visits its most significant holy places. **30 D5**

**Pilgrims' Way** *120 miles / 192 km, Winchester, Hampshire to Canterbury, Kent* Traditionally held to be the route taken by Pilgrims from Winchester to the shrine of Thomas à Becket in Canterbury. It follows a trackway in use since prehistoric times along the slopes of the North Downs. **15 B8 / 30 D5**

## East of England

**London to Walsingham Camino** *180 miles / 290 km, London to Little Walsingham, Norfolk* A newly-established route from the capital to England's greatest holy shrine. The journey can be broken into 13 stages averaging 14 miles / 23 km per day and follows footpaths and quiet country lanes that have been in use since medieval times. **41 F6 / 80 D5**

**St Edmund Way** *79 miles / 127 km, Manningtree, Essex to Brandon, Suffolk* Starting by following the River Stour valley path, the route reaches Bury St Edmunds to visit the shrine of St Edmund, England's original patron saint, at the Abbey. Moving north, the route goes through the vast area of the King's Forest before reaching Brandon. **56 F4 / 67 F7**

▲ Holy Island (Lindisfarne) on the Northumberland coast Andrew Martin / Dreamstime

## East Midlands

**Peak District Old Stones Way** *38 miles / 61 km, Carl Wark Hill Fort to Minninglow Hill, Derbyshire* This route celebrates ancient history by linking the Iron Age fort of Carl Wark and the chambered tomb and barrows of Minninglow Hill. The route passes the old stones of the Nine Ladies and Arbor Low. **88 F3 / 76 D2**

**St Thomas Way** *Swansea to Hereford* This is not a linear route but a collection of 13 locations in the Welsh Marches each with its own circular route. There are many historic medieval sites to visit including castles and cathedrals. **33 E7 / 49 E7**

## West Midlands

**Abbesses' Way** *20 miles / 32 km, Wenlock Priory to Shrewsbury Abbey, Shropshire* The abbesses in question here are St Milburga and St Winefride. The route climbs Wenlock Edge which affords views of the rolling Shropshire countryside. Churches to visit along the way include those at Kenley and Atcham. **61 D6 / 60 C4**

**Golden Valley Pilgrim Way** *59 miles / 95 km, Hereford* This starts and ends at Hereford Cathedral and travels via the Wye Valley, the Golden Valley and the foothills of the Black Mountains. It is possible to sleep in the Night Sanctuaries of participating churches. **49 E7**

## Wales

**Lleyn Pilgrims Trail** *72 miles / 116 km, Aberdesach to Porthmadog, Gwynedd* Journey around the coast of the peninsula with the opportunity to visit Bardsey Island at the western tip. Many 6th-century churches dot the way. **82 F4 / 71 D6**

**Welsh Cistercian Way** *672 miles / 1081 km, Caerphilly* This is a long-distance circular route that gives the opportunity to experience Wales in depth – from valley bottom to mountain top. **35 F5**

**For more information** on these Pilgrimage routes and others see:
🖥 https://britishpilgrimage.org/routes and 🖥 www.english-heritage.org.uk/pilgrimage

## North West

**Cumbrian Cistercian Way** *25 miles / 40 km, Piel Island to Cartmel Priory, Westmorland & Furness* Starting with a short ferry trip to Piel Island, this trail follows in the footprints of the Cistercian monks. Then visit the ruins of Furness Abbey, once the most powerful Cistercian monastery in England. End at the 12th-century Cartmel Priory. **92 C2 / 92 B3**

**Two Saints Way** *92 miles / 148 km, Chester, Cheshire to Lichfield, Staffordshire* Named after St Werburgh and St Chad, this was a popular pilgrim route in the late Middle Ages. St Chad's shrine at Lichfield attracted so many visitors that a cathedral had to be built. **73 C8 / 62 D5**

## Yorkshire & the Humber

**St Hilda's Way** *22 miles / 35 km, Hinderwell to Whitby, North Yorkshire* The remarkable St Hild was an Anglo-Saxon princess, and this trail visits many places associated with her. The route meanders over the, often bleak, North York Moor and finishes at Whitby Abbey. **103 C5 / 103 C6**

**Whitby Way** *70 miles / 113 km, York to Whitby, North Yorkshire* Linking two iconic buildings – York Minster and Whitby Abbey. The flat Vale of York gives way to rolling hills before crossing the North York Moors. Following the valley of the river Esk, the path ends at Whitby Abbey. **95 D8 / 103 C6**

## North East

**Finchale Camino Inglé** *22 miles / 35 km, Finchale Priory to Escomb, Durham* Starting at the ruins of Finchale Priory, the route visits the magnificent Durham Cathedral with the shrines of the Venerable Bede and St Cuthbert. The Weardale Way is then followed to Bishop Auckland and the nearby Saxon church of Escomb. **111 E5 / 101 B6**

**Pilgrim's Way to Holy Island** *3 miles / 5 km, Holy Island (Lindisfarne), Northumberland* Many trails bring pilgrims to the crossing from the mainland to Holy Island. The ancient route (bypassing the modern causeway) lies across the sands at low tide. The way is marked by wooden poles but is safer to be accompanied by an experienced guide. **123 E7**

## Scotland

**St Columba's Way** *260 miles / 418 km, Iona, Argyll & Bute to St Andrews, Fife* From the west coast island of Iona, St Columba set out to convert the Picts to Christianity. Following his lead, this trail traverses the Isle of Mull to cross to Oban on the mainland where the steeper climbs begin. Eventually, the river Tay is followed downhill to St Andrews. **146 J5 / 129 C7**

**St Magnus' Way** *58 miles / 93 km, Egilsay to Kirkwall, Orkney* This traces the procession of St Magnus' body following his martyrdom on Egilsay, via Birsay, to end at St Magnus' Cathedral in Kirkwall. 'Mansie' or Magnus Stones once marked the places where Magnus's coffin was rested along the way. **159 F5 / 159 G5**

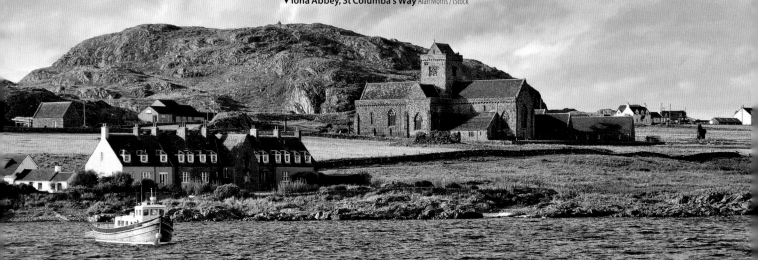

▼ Iona Abbey, St Columba's Way Alan Morris / iStock

# Parks and gardens

## Arboretums

### South West

**Westonbirt Arboretum** *Tetbury, Gloucestershire* This, the National Arboretum, is home to a spectacular collection of trees featuring a notable collection of Japanese maples. Numerous 'grass rides' divide the trees into glades for special plantings. There is a treetop walkway.
🖥 www.forestryengland.uk **37 F5**

### South East

**Winkworth Arboretum**
*Godalming, Surrey* With glorious views from the hillside, and vibrant spring and autumn colour, this is a stunning setting for over 1000 species of trees and shrubs, many of them rare.
🖥 www.nationaltrust.org.uk **27 E7**

### East Midlands

**Derby Arboretum**
*Arboretum Square, Derby*
The country's first urban arboretum has over 40 species of trees including an Indian bean tree and a silver pendant lime. There is a tree trail and trees are numbered to aid identification.
🖥 www.inderby.org.uk **76 F3**

### West Midlands

**National Memorial Arboretum**
*Alrewas, Staffordshire* Established as a national focus for Remembrance, the arboretum was opened in 2001. 400 memorials have been placed among over 25,000 trees. Daily activities include guided walks, buggy tours, Land Train rides and free talks.
🖥 www.thenma.org.uk
**63 C5**

▲ Armed Forces Memorial, National Memorial Arboretum, Arenaphotouk / Dreamstime

### Wales

**Bute Park Arboretum** *Cardiff*
A significant arboretum with over 3000 individually catalogued trees, some of which are rare and there are 41 champion trees. The avenue of Ginkgo biloba trees are striking all year round. 🖥 https://bute-park.com/arboretum **22 B3**

### Yorkshire & the Humber

**Thorp Perrow** *Bedale, North Yorkshire* With over 2000 species this is one of the finest collections of trees in England with many champion specimens. There is a tree trail to guide visitors. A bog garden can be viewed from a raised walkway.
🖥 www.thorpperrow.com **101 F7**

### Scotland

**Dawyck Botanic Garden**
*Peebles, Scottish Borders* Set in a picturesque glen, the arboretum boasts a fine collection of rare and exotic species planted over a period of 300 years. Visit in February for snowdrops and autumn for glorious colour. 🖥 www.rbge.org.uk **120 F4**

◄ Bluebell woods in Winkworth Arboretum Grahamprentice / Dreamstime

▼ The Palladian Bridge and Pantheon at Stourhead Gardens Steve Luck / Dreamstime

► Crocuses in the Conifer Lawn at RHS Wisley Leklek73 / Dreamstime

## Gardens

### South West

**Antony** *Torpoint, Cornwall*
Landscaped by Humphrey Repton in the 18th century, the garden is set in grounds sweeping down to the river. The formal gardens are in contrast to the woodland area with magnolias and scented rhododendrons.
🖥 www.nationaltrust.org.uk **6 D2**

**Prior Park Landscape Garden** *Bath, Somerset* A prime example of a garden in the style of the romantic landscape movement. A lake and Rococo bridge create a theatrical effect along with a cascade and grotto. The 'Priory Path' gives a panoramic view over Bath.
🖥 www.nationaltrust.org.uk **24 C2**

**Stourhead** *Mere, Wiltshire* One of the world's finest landscape gardens with something of interest in every season. Follow the path round the lake to take in glimpses of classical temples. Exotic tree species were introduced such as tulip trees and Indian bean trees.
🖥 www.nationaltrust.org.uk **24 F2**

### South East

**Exbury Gardens**
*Southampton, Hampshire* Famed for its collection of colourful azaleas, rhododendrons and camellias on a hilly woodland site. Each season has its highlights here. A steam railway has opened up the southeast corner of the site. 🖥 www.exbury.co.uk **14 D5**

**Penshurst Place** *Tonbridge, Kent* The formal walled gardens retain their Elizabethan splendour after 600 years. Yew-hedged 'garden rooms' have individual planting schemes.

There is a cycle route from Tonbridge into the estate parkland.
🖥 www.penshurstplace.com **29 E6**

**RHS Garden Wisley**
*Woking, Surrey* The flagship garden of the RHS is a maze of planting, open spaces and specialist areas spread across 200 acres. Highlights include the lily canal and the deep herbaceous borders running up Battleston Hill.
🖥 www.rhs.org.uk **27 D8**

**Rousham House** *Steeple Aston, Oxfordshire* The gardens surrounding the house are the main attraction here – this is William Kent's masterpiece of landscaping. Essentially preserving the original 1738 design, walled gardens, a parterre and rose gardens can be visited. 🖥 https://rousham.org **38 B4**

**Sheffield Park Garden** *Uckfield, East Sussex* Renowned for its fabulous autumn colours, the park has four lakes in a valley linked by cascades. The extensive grounds are punctuated by towering mature specimen trees.
🖥 www.nationaltrust.org.uk **17 B8**

**Stowe Landscape Gardens**
*Buckingham* The grounds surrounding the school buildings have been hugely influential in garden design. Thoughtfully restored, visitors can wander for miles enjoying views dotted with the many listed garden buildings.
🖥 www.nationaltrust.org.uk **52 F4**

▲ The Carolean Garden at Packwood
House Stuart Andrews / Dreamstime

◀ Japanese Maple Tree at Bodnant
Garden David Murray / Dreamstime

▲ A fallow deer near the stables and
carriage hall at Dunham Massey
Steve Allen / Dreamstime

## East of England

**Anglesey Abbey** *Lode, Cambridgeshire*
This tranquil garden is noted for its
collection of statuary. It has a popular
mile-long winter walk with white-
stemmed birches and snowdrops.
There is a wildlife discovery area and
working watermill.
🖳 www.nationaltrust.org.uk **55 C6**

**Helmingham Hall Gardens**
*Stowmarket, Suffolk* Elegant gardens, set
in an ancient deer park, surround the
double-moated Tudor mansion house.
There is a classic parterre, Elizabethan
kitchen garden and a knot garden.
🖳 www.helmingham.com **57 D5**

**Pensthorpe** *Fakenham, Norfolk*
Part of the gardens at this nature
reserve were designed by Piet Oudolf
in the naturalistic prairie style using
perennials and grasses. There are
250 acres of lakes and riverside walks
to explore.
🖳 https://pensthorpe.com **81 E5**

**RHS Garden Hyde Hall**
*Chelmsford, Essex* This is a challenging
site for a garden, an exposed hill with
low rainfall, but it shows what can
be done with the right plants in the
right places. Styles range from formal
schemes to more naturalistic planting.
🖳 www.rhs.org.uk **42 E3**

**Wrest Park** *Clophill, Central Bedfordshire*
A Baroque formal garden with a canal
as its formal axis and an elegant pavilion
at its head. The great landscaper
'Capability' Brown created a naturalistic
river to surround the grounds.
🖳 www.english-heritage.org.uk **53 F8**

## East Midlands

**Belvoir Castle** *Grantham, Leicestershire*
The gardens are laid out in Italian-
style terraces divided into smaller
compartments using topiary and
hedging. Sited on a hill top, the gardens
give wide views of the Vale of Belvoir.
🖳 www.belvoircastle.com **77 F8**

**Clumber Park** *Worksop,
Nottinghamshire* The design was laid
out in the 18th century as a pleasure
garden with serpentine walks and
shrubberies. The Atlantic cedars and
sweet chestnuts are of breathtaking
size. There is a large glasshouse.
🖳 www.nationaltrust.org.uk **77 B6**

**Coton Manor** *Guilsborough, West
Northamptonshire* Benefitting from its
position on a south-facing slope, with
an abundance of springs, this is one of
the finest gardens in the East Midlands.
The more formal area near the house
gives way to a fine woodland walk.
🖳 www.cotonmanor.co.uk **52 B4**

**Normanby Hall** *Scunthorpe, North
Lincolnshire* There is much to explore
in the 300 acres of historic parkland.
There is a Victorian kitchen garden
and fern house, as well as a vinery with
sub-tropical plants. The range of trees
includes unusual species like the Tulip
Tree, Judas Tree and Handkerchief Tree.
🖳 www.normanbyhall.co.uk **90 C2**

## West Midlands

**Hergest Croft Gardens**
*Kington, Herefordshire* Reminiscent of
a Himalayan hillside, this garden is set
in a steep sided valley. There is a
collection of rare trees, including
around 20 champions. Park Wood has
a stunning collection of camellias,
magnolias and rhododendrons.
🖳 www.hergest.co.uk **48 D4**

**Packwood House** *Lapworth,
Warwickshire* The most striking feature
of this garden is the topiary with a
collection of yews said to represent
the Sermon on the Mount. There is
an attractive lakeside walk and wild-
flower meadows.
🖳 www.nationaltrust.org.uk **51 B6**

**Trentham Gardens**
*Stoke-on-Trent, Staffordshire* The
restoration of the Italian Gardens
was led by Tom Stuart-Smith with Piet
Oudolf being responsible for the
Rivers of Grass and the Floral Labyrinth.
The results are stunning.
🖳 https://trentham.co.uk **75 E5**

**Witley Court**
*Great Witley, Worcestershire*
Witley Court is now a spectacular ruin
but the gardens have been restored
to their former glory with an Italianate
fountain at the centre of elaborate
parterres, pools and pavilions.
🖳 www.english-heritage.org.uk **50 C2**

**Wollerton Old Hall** *Hodnet, Shropshire*
In the classic English style, this garden
has contrasting areas of hot planting
and a scented white garden. The
summer months are filled with the
scent of English roses, spires of blue
delphiniums and fragrant phlox.
🖳 www.wollertonoldhallgarden.com
**61 B6**

## Wales

**Bodnant** *Tal-y-Cafn, Conwy*
Ablaze with colour in spring and
autumn, the garden is comprised of a
series of terraces above a woodland
area with views over the river Conwy
towards Snowdonia.
🖳 www.nationaltrust.org.uk **83 D8**

**Dyffryn Gardens** *St Nicholas, Cardiff*
Designed in the Arts and Crafts
style, more than 30 themed garden

rooms are enclosed by yew hedges,
including Italian, rose and lavender
gardens. There are open pleasure
grounds and an arboretum.
🖳 www.nationaltrust.org.uk **22 B2**

**National Botanic Garden of Wales**
*Llanarthne, Carmarthenshire*
Here, the largest single-span
glasshouse in the world houses rare
and endangered species that thrive
in a Mediterranean climate. There is
a walled garden and a 'Woods of the
World' in the extensive parkland.
🖳 https://botanicgarden.wales **33 C6**

**Plas Newydd** *Llanfairpwll, Isle of
Anglesey* The grounds slope down to
the Menai Strait with superb views
of Snowdonia. The gardens are a mix
of formal terraces and informal areas
loosely planted with shrubs.
🖳 www.nationaltrust.org.uk **82 E5**

**Powis Castle** *Welshpool, Powys*
The most striking feature here are
the enormous yews looming over the
terraces. These terraces form hanging
gardens of extravagant and colourful
plantings. An orangery houses
conservatory plants.
🖳 www.nationaltrust.org.uk **60 D2**

## North West

**Dunham Massey** *Altrincham, Cheshire*
The grounds include one of the
country's largest winter gardens with a
camellia walk and swathes of bulbs. The
Garden Wood has colourful azaleas and
hydrangeas. Fallow deer roam freely.
🖳 www.nationaltrust.org.uk **86 F5**

**Holker Hall** *Grange-over-Sands,
Westmorland & Furness* The woodland
gardens are at their best in spring and
summer. There are formal gardens near
the house with an Italian influence.
The woods contain many rare trees
which are labelled for identification.
🖳 www.holker.co.uk **92 B3**

**Levens Hall** *Kendal, Westmorland &
Furness* Looking like giant chess pieces,
the topiary specimens are some of the
oldest in the world. Delightful at any
time of the year, the spring sees an
explosion of tulips followed by glorious
summer colour.
🖳 www.levenshall.co.uk **99 F6**

◀ Lavender Court, Dyffryn Gardens
Tazzymoto / Dreamstime

**RHS Garden Bridgewater** *Salford, Greater Manchester* The latest RHS garden to open, this has been a mammoth restoration project. Award-winning designers have brought the gardens to life with a walled garden, colourful borders, meadows and lakes.
💻 www.rhs.org.uk **86 D5**

**Tatton Park** *Knutsford, Cheshire East* With grounds landscaped by Humphrey Repton, the gardens are among the finest in Britain. There is an elegant Italian garden, orangery and masses of azaleas and rhododendrons.
💻 www.tattonpark.org.uk **86 F5**

## Yorkshire & the Humber

**Harewood House** *Leeds* Designed by 'Capability' Brown and Charles Barry, the grounds include an Italianate terrace and a lakeside garden. At the top of the lake is a sunken Himalayan garden with a Buddhist stupa.
💻 https://harewood.org **95 E6**

**RHS Garden Harlow Carr** *Harrogate, North Yorkshire* The beautifully planted streamside garden is criss-crossed by numerous packhorse bridges. From the lake, a magnificent avenue sweeps through woodland to an arboretum.
💻 www.rhs.org.uk **95 D5**

**Scampston Hall** *Malton, North Yorkshire* Piet Oudolf, a leader designer of 'New Wave Planting', was commissioned to design a scheme for the walled garden. His contemporary design of grasses and meadow planting is inspirational.
💻 www.scampston.co.uk **96 B4**

**Sheffield Botanical Gardens** *Sheffield* Winding paths take visitors through over 18 garden areas based on geographical or botanical themes. A major attraction are some of the country's oldest glasshouses.
💻 www.sbg.org.uk **88 F4**

## North East

**Alnwick Garden** *Northumberland* The centrepiece of this garden is a grand cascade sending water tumbling down 27 weirs. Other highlights include a poison garden, a bamboo labyrinth and an enormous treehouse.
💻 www.alnwickgarden.com **117 C7**

▲ Dunrobin Castle and gardens
Wirestock / Dreamstime

**Belsay Hall** *Northumberland* The quarry garden, with lichen covered rocks, lends a romantic air to walks. Of particular note are the snowdrop and lily collections. There is a winter garden.
💻 www.english-heritage.org.uk **110 B3**

**Cragside House** *Rothbury, Northumberland* Europe's largest sandstone rock garden is planted with heathers and alpines. Carpet bedding gives a colourful display. The grounds, on a steep hillside, contain rare coniferous trees.
💻 www.nationaltrust.org.uk **117 D6**

**Gibside** *Rowlands Gill, Tyne & Wear* Once one of the finest 18th-century designed landscapes in England, restored buildings have been sited at key points. They include a decorative banqueting house, a Palladian chapel and stables.
💻 www.nationaltrust.org.uk **110 D4**

**Wallington** *Cambo, Northumberland* An attractive woodland walk leads to a walled garden with a restored peach house. Walks step down from a classical fountain to beds with heathers and herbaceous perennials.
💻 www.nationaltrust.org.uk **117 F6**

▼ An aerial view of the landform sculptures *Cells of Life* by Charles Jencks at Jupiter Artland Iain Masterton/Alamy

## Scotland

**Dunrobin Castle Gardens** *Golspie, Highland* Inspired by Versailles, the gardens were designed in grand French style by Sir Charles Barry. Two parterres are laid out around circular ponds each with its own fountain.
💻 www.dunrobincastle.co.uk **157 J11**

**Glamis Castle** *Forfar, Angus* The extensive grounds include an Italian Garden, surrounded by yew hedges, which was created in 1910 by King Charles III's great-grandmother. There is a nature trail which winds through the pinetum.
💻 www.glamis-castle.co.uk **134 E3**

**Logan Botanic Garden** *Port Logan, Dumfries & Galloway* Although remote, this exotic garden is worth the trip. The balmy Gulf Stream allows tender tree ferns and eucalyptus to flourish. The highest point gives fine views over the Rhins to the Galloway Hills.
💻 www.rbge.org.uk **104 E4**

**Manderston** *Duns, Scottish Borders* Set around a grand classical house, Edwardian formal terraces give way to a picturesque landscape with a lake and Chinese-style bridge. The woodland garden is at its best in May.
💻 www.manderston.com **122 D4**

# Sculpture parks

## South West

**Barbara Hepworth Sculpture Garden** *St Ives, Cornwall* Once the home of Barbara Hepworth and her husband, the artist Ben Nicholson, the bronzes are placed in the garden in the locations chosen by Hepworth.
💻 www.tate.org.uk **2 B4**

**Forest of Dean Sculpture Trail** *Coleford, Gloucestershire* The trail is part of Forestry England's Beechenhurst site and features artworks inspired by their setting in the Forest of Dean. There are routes to follow – terrain can be steep with uneven surfaces. 💻 www.forestofdean-sculpture.org.uk **36 C3**

## East of England

**Henry Moore Studios & Gardens** *Perry Green, Hertfordshire* Once the home of Henry Moore, his studios and gardens in the small village of Perry Green are now the perfect setting for some of his monumental sculptures that are best appreciated in an outdoor setting.
💻 https://henry-moore.org **41 C7**

**Sainsbury Centre** *Norwich, Norfolk* Sculptures sit in extensive parkland around the Norman-Foster designed Sainsbury Centre. Includes works by Antony Gormley, Henry Moore and Elisabeth Frink.
💻 www.sainsburycentre.ac.uk **68 D4**

## North West

**Grizedale Forest Sculpture Trail** *Hawkshead, Westmorland & Furness* Scattered throughout the forest are over 50 sculptures fashioned out of natural materials. Over time they will decay and return to the forest. There are several footpaths plus cycle trails.
💻 www.forestryengland.uk **99 E5**

## Yorkshire & the Humber

**Yorkshire Sculpture Park** *West Bretton, Wakefield, West Yorkshire* With a changing exhibition programme, sculptures are set in 500 acres of parkland. Artists include Barbara Hepworth, Henry Moore and Eduardo Paolozzi. 💻 https://ysp.org.uk **88 C3**

## Scotland

**Jupiter Artland** *Wilkieston, Edinburgh* Contemporary sculpture garden just to the west of Edinburgh. Over 30 permanent sculptures by artists such as Anish Kapoor and Charles Jencks. Seasonal events and temporary exhibitions. 💻 www.jupiterartland.org **120 C4**

# Outdoor museums

## Historic sites

### South West

**Cerne Abbas Giant** *Dorchester, Dorset*
A chalk hill figure, with distinctive features, sits high above the village. His exact origin is subject to dispute, but one of the best guesses is that he resembles the Roman god Hercules.
💻 www.nationaltrust.org.uk **12 D4**

**Corfe Castle** *Swanage, Dorset*
The gaunt castle ruins can be seen from miles away. Once one of the mightiest castles in the country, its unhappy history lends it an atmospheric melancholy air.
💻 www.nationaltrust.org.uk **13 F7**

**Glastonbury Tor** *Somerset*
Believed, by some, to be the location of the Holy Grail as brought to England by Joseph of Arimathea. The 14th-century tower of the chapel of St Michael at the summit is a later addition.
💻 www.nationaltrust.org.uk **23 F7**

**Tintagel Castle** *Cornwall*
Long associated with the legend of King Arthur, this rocky and romantic ruin is reached by crossing an award-winning footbridge.
💻 www.english-heritage.org.uk **8 F2**

▲ Sculpture of King Arthur at **Tintagel Castle** Chris Dorney / Dreamstime

▼ **Glastonbuy Tor** Ashley Stewart / iStock

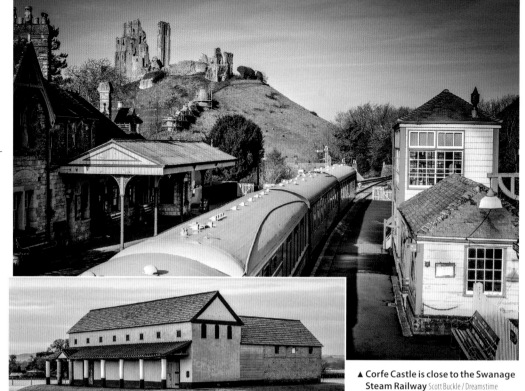

▲ Corfe Castle is close to the Swanage Steam Railway Scott Buckle / Dreamstime

◀ A reconstructed Roman town house at Wroxeter Roman City
Nicola Pulham / Dreamstime

### South East

**Portchester Castle** *Fareham, Hampshire* The well-preserved 3rd-century Roman sea walls protect a Norman stronghold and church. The whole fortress can be viewed from the top of the 12th-century keep.
💻 www.english-heritage.org.uk **15 D7**

**Silchester Roman town** *Basingstoke, Hampshire* Once a large and important town known as Calleva Atrebatum, the defensive walls and amphitheatre at Silchester are unusually well-preserved.
💻 www.english-heritage.org.uk **26 C4**

**Verulamium Roman Theatre**
*St Albans, Hertfordshire* Lying on the Roman route of Watling Street, this theatre is unique in Britain as it has a stage rather than an amphitheatre. At its height, it could seat 2000 spectators. St Albans Verulamium Museum is nearby.
💻 www.gorhamburyestate.co.uk **16 D2**

### East of England

**Dunwich** *Suffolk* The compelling story of a village lost to the sea brings visitors to this stretch of coast. Little remains of the once important Saxon port, except maybe the echoes of bells from the nine churches under the waves.
💻 www.thesuffolkcoast.co.uk **57 B8**

**Tilbury Fort** *Essex* A 17th-century fort with arrowhead shaped bastions on the shore of the river Thames. Built to protect London from invasion by the French and Dutch, it never saw military service.
💻 www.english-heritage.org.uk **29 B7**

### East Midlands

**Bolingbroke Castle** *Spilsby, Lincolnshire* The birthplace of King Henry IV, this site was first fortified by the Saxons in the 6th or 7thcentury. What remains now is the imprint of the 13th-century hexagonal castle. In summer, outdoor events are held.
💻 www.english-heritage.org.uk **79 C6**

**Bosworth Battlefield** *Leicestershire* Marking the alleged site of the battle of 1485 where Henry VII, the first of the Tudors, was proclaimed king after the defeat and death of Richard III. A heritage centre explains the story.
💻 www.bosworthbattlefield.org.uk **63 D8**

**Eleanor Cross** *Geddington, North Northamptonshire* The cross marks one of the resting places of Eleanor of Castile's funeral cortege on its way to London. This is the best preserved of the three surviving crosses erected in 1294. 💻 www.english-heritage.org.uk **65 F5**

**Eyam** *Derbyshire* When the Great Plague struck the village in 1666, the inhabitants quarantined themselves to stop the spread of the disease. Touching memorials and plaques on several houses commemorate the event.
💻 www.eyamvillage.org.uk **76 B2**

**Laxton** *Ollerton, Nottinghamshire* A visitor centre explains how this is the only remaining working 'open field' farming village in Europe still operating this ancient system. Three walks start from the Dovecote Inn.
💻 www.laxtonvisitorcentre.org.uk **77 C7**

### West Midlands

**Kinver Edge rock houses** *Stourbridge, Staffordshire* Occupied until the 1960s, these houses were carved out of soft red sandstone. The community peaked in the 1860s with 11 families living here.
💻 www.nationaltrust.org.uk **61 F8**

**Lunt Roman Fort** *Coventry* A wooden gateway has been reconstructed to mark the entrance to the fort. Open for public, school visits and organised tours. 💻 www.luntromanfort.org **51 B8**

▲ A Roman legionnaire's helmet at Segedunum Roman Fort
Barry32 / Dreamstime

▶ Tintern Abbey WhitcombeRD / iStock

**Wroxeter Roman City** *Shrewsbury, Shropshire* One of the largest examples of Roman masonry still standing in England. Located on the banks of the river Severn, the city had a population of 5000 in the 2nd century.
🖥 www.english-heritage.org.uk **61 D5**

## Wales

**Beaumaris Castle** *Isle of Anglesey* Built by Edward I to contain the Welsh, this was the last in a line of strongholds. It is a fortress of immense size and near-perfect symmetry.
🖥 https://cadw.gov.wales **83 D6**

**Caerleon Roman Fortress and Baths** *Newport* Spread across the town of Caerleon, near the city of Newport, are the remains of the Legionary Fortress of Isca Augusta. It has the most complete Roman amphitheatre in Britain.
🖥 https://cadw.gov.wales **35 E7**

**Llanthony Priory** *Abergavenny, Monmouthshire* Substantial parts of this grand church still remain including eight bays of an arcade, two sides of the tower and the west end.
🖥 https://cadw.gov.wales **35 B6**

**Tintern Abbey** *Chepstow, Monmouthshire* These soaring romantic ruins inspired the painter J.M.W. Turner and the poet William Wordsworth. The remains that stand today date from the 13th century.
🖥 https://cadw.gov.wales **36 D2**

## North West

**Beeston Castle** *Tarporley, Cheshire* Its ruined state belies how powerful this stronghold once was. Built in 1225, it had defensive features inspired by those of fortresses in the Holy Land from the time of the Crusades.
🖥 www.english-heritage.org.uk **74 D2**

**Birdoswald** *Gilsland, Cumberland* A fort built by the Romans to protect the crossing of the nearby river Irthing. A walk, half a mile to the east, arrives at the remains of Roman bridges at Willowford. 🖥 www.english-heritage.org.uk **109 C6**

**Lowther Castle** *Penrith, Westmorland and Furness* From a distance this majestic building looks almost complete, but up close it can be seen that only the façade and outer walls of the castle remain. Once abandoned, the gardens have undergone an amazing transformation.
🖥 https://lowthercastle.org **99 B7**

**Wycoller** *Colne, Lancashire* Wycoller Hall, now a ruin, is said to have been the inspiration for Ferndean Manor in Charlotte Bronte's 'Jane Eyre'. The leafy dene has many bridges including a 13th century packhorse bridge.
🖥 www.historic-uk.com **94 F2**

## Yorkshire & the Humber

**Aldborough Roman Town** *Boroughbridge, North Yorkshire* This was once the main town of the Romanised Brigantes, the largest tribe in Britain. Two mosaic pavements can be seen and there is a museum.
🖥 www.english-heritage.org.uk **95 C7**

**Fountains Abbey** *Ripon, North Yorkshire* This 14th-century abbey was among the largest in Europe. To the east are the 18th-century water gardens of Studley Royal.
🖥 www.nationaltrust.org.uk **95 C5**

**Wharram Percy Medieval Village** *Malton, North Yorkshire* A roofless church, cottages and a gaunt tower are all that is left of this former prosperous village. Abandoned soon after 1500, it affords evidence of how life was lived in medieval times.
🖥 www.english-heritage.org.uk **96 C4**

**Wheeldale Moor Roman Road** *Goathland, North Yorkshire* High on the bleak moorland is a mile-long stretch of an ancient road. Most likely it is Roman, but it may be earlier or later. A hard-core surface and drainage ditches survive.
🖥 www.english-heritage.org.uk **103 E6**

▼ St Mary's Lighthouse, Whitley Bay
Helen Hotson / Dreamstime

## North East

**Dunstanburgh Castle** *Craster, Northumberland* Standing on a remote headland, this was a grand castle as can be seen by its impressive outline against the sky. It is reached by a short walk from the village of Craster.
🖥 www.english-heritage.org.uk **117 B8**

**Housesteads Fort** *Bardon Mill, Northumberland* Built high on the crest of the Whin Sill, this is one of the best preserved of Hadrian's Wall's forts and gives spectacular views. Foundations remain of the barracks and baths.
🖥 www.english-heritage.org.uk **109 C7**

**Segedunum Roman Fort** *Wallsend, North Tyneside* At the eastern end of Hadrian's Wall, Segedunum is right in the middle of the urban area. A high tower gives a bird's-eye view of the site which has a reconstructed bath-house.
🖥 https://segedunumromanfort.org.uk **111 C6**

**St Mary's Lighthouse** *Whitley Bay, North Tyneside* Opened in 1898, the lighthouse is a popular end-point of a stroll from Whitley Bay. It is perched on a small island with a causeway that is covered at high tide. It has a small visitor centre. 🖥 www.visitnorthtyneside.com **111 B6**

**Vindolanda** *Bardon Mill, Northumberland* This Roman fort pre-dates Hadrian's Wall and grew large as a civilian settlement. The museum houses a fascinating collection of everyday items including shoes, pots, jewels and household bric-a-brac.
🖥 www.vindolanda.com **109 C7**

▲ Fountains Abbey and Studley Royal Water Garden Anyutagillespie / Dreamstime

▲ Street scene at Beamish Museum
Roger Harrison / Dreamstime

▲ An historic 15th-century tŷ hir or long house at St Fagans National Museum Dudlajzov / Dreamstime

◄ Inside the 1930s ironmonger's shop at the Black Country Living Museum
Stuart Andrews / Dreamstime

## Scotland

**Culloden** *Inverness, Highland* The romantic dreams of 'Bonnie Prince Charlie' came to an end in 1746 on this battlefield when confronted by the overwhelming forces of the Duke of Cumberland. The visitor centre tells the story of the end of the Jacobite cause. 🖥 www.nts.org.uk **151 G10**

**Dunnottar Castle** *Stonehaven, Aberdeenshire* Battlements and towers appear to rise straight from the sea on this headland. Practically impregnable, its walls have housed a lion, and its dungeon almost 200 Covenanters! 🖥 www.dunnottarcastle.co.uk **141 F7**

**Jedburgh Abbey** *Scottish Borders* Founded by David I in 1138 the ruins of this large abbey has both Romanesque and Gothic arches. A small museum has a model of the church in its heyday, along with excavated artefacts. 🖥 www.historicenvironment.scot **116 B2**

**Tantallon Castle** *North Berwick, East Lothian* Protected on three sides by North Sea cliffs, this has always been a formidable castle. It has repelled many sieges, and bears the scars of cannon fire on its ruined ramparts. 🖥 www.historicenvironment.scot **129 F7**

# Open-air museums

## South East

**Chiltern Open Air Museum** *Chalfont St Giles, Buckinghamshire* A collection of vernacular historic buildings at risk of demolition that have been dismantled and reconstructed in the museum grounds. There are costumed inhabitants on selected days. 🖥 https://coam.org.uk **40 E3**

**Weald and Downland Living Museum** *Singleton, West Sussex* Over 50 historic buildings dating from 950 AD to the 19th century, assembled to create the illusion of a real village. Also gardens, livestock, walks and a mill pond. 🖥 www.wealddown.co.uk **16 C2**

## East of England

**Flag Fen** *Peterborough, Cambridgeshire* The Archaeology Park allows exploration of a reconstructed prehistoric landscape, including a typical Iron Age roundhouse dwelling. There is a visitor centre. 🖥 https://flagfen.org.uk **66 E2**

◄ Replica Iron Age roundhouse at Chiltern Open Air Museum
Peter Fleming Dreamstime

**Food Museum** *Stowmarket, Suffolk* Formerly the Museum of East Anglian Life, this museum presents agricultural history through a mixture of exhibits and living history demonstrations. It also hosts the East Anglian Living History Fair. 🖥 https://foodmuseum.org.uk **56 D4**

**West Stow Anglo-Saxon Village** *Bury St Edmunds, Suffolk* A recreation of an early Anglo-Saxon village, occupied from 420–650 AD, surrounded by 125 acres of countryside. The site now has eight buildings and rare breed pigs and chickens. 🖥 www.weststow.org **56 B2**

## West Midlands

**Avoncroft Museum of Historic Buildings** *Bromsgrove, Worcestershire* An open-air museum of over 30 historic buildings which have been relocated and re-built in rural Worcestershire. The collection represents over 700 years of Midlands history. 🖥 https://avoncroft.org.uk **50 C4**

**Black Country Living Museum** *Dudley* This shows what a typical village in this area would look like in the late 18th century. There are many buildings to explore and you can take a narrowboat trip along one of the canals into the mine workings. 🖥 https://bclm.com **62 E3**

**Blists Hill Victorian Town** *Telford, Shropshire* Lying to the eastern edge of Ironbridge and its many attractions, Blists Hill demonstrates every aspect of life and work during its industrial heyday. 🖥 www.ironbridge.org.uk **61 D6**

## Wales

**Castell Henllys Iron Age Village** *Newport, Pembrokeshire* Four roundhouses and a granary have been reconstructed on their original Iron Age foundations, the only place where this has been done in Britain. Guides, in costume, explain what life would have been like. 🖥 www.visitwales.com **45 F3**

**St Fagans National Museum of History** *Cardiff, Vale of Glamorgan* One of Europe's biggest open-air museums, it celebrates the lifestyle, culture and architecture of the Welsh people. After a major refurbishment, it was named UK's Museum of the Year 2019. 🖥 https://museum.wales **22 B3**

## Yorkshire & the Humber

**Ryedale Folk Museum** *Hutton le Hole, North Yorkshire* Set in the North York Moors, this museum offers more than twenty heritage buildings and 40,000 objects to explore. Buildings range from an Iron Age roundhouse to a medieval Manor House. 🖥 www.ryedalefolkmuseum.co.uk **103 E5**

## North East

**Beamish Museum** *Stanley, Durham* Beamish pioneered the concept of a living museum, allowing visitors to interact with their surroundings. Mainly featuring life in the late Victorian and Edwardian eras, it also highlights the effects of the industrial revolution on the countryside. 🖥 www.beamish.org.uk **110 D5**

## Scotland

**Highland Folk Museum** *Newtonmore, Highland* With heather-thatched roofs and open peat fires, this award-winning museum recreates a township of the 1700s. Actors in costume bring day-to-day living to life and there are opportunities to try traditional crafts. 🖥 www.visitscotland.com **138 E3**

▼ Weald and Downland Open Air Museum at Singleton Aiselin82 / iStock

# Festivals

## Arts & Culture

### South East

**Brighton Festival** *Stanmer Park, Brighton* A large, annual, curated multi-arts festival in England. It includes music, theatre, dance, circus, art, film, literature, debate, outdoor and family events, and takes place in venues across Brighton and Hove each May.
🖥️https://brightonfestival.org **17 D7**

**Notting Hill Carnival** *Notting Hill, London* An annual Caribbean Carnival event that has taken place in London since 1966 on the streets of the Notting Hill area of Kensington, over the August Bank Holiday weekend.
🖥️https://nhcarnival.org/ **41 F5**

### East of England

**Cambridge Literary Festival** *Newnham College, Cambridge* Two festivals and events throughout the year, hosting literary greats, debut writers, scientists, artists, politicians, comedians and children's authors.
🖥️www.cambridgeliteraryfestival.com **55 D5**

### East Midlands

**Wirksworth Festival** *Wirksworth, Derbyshire* A 10 day Festival of Arts set within the historic market town of Wirksworth, with an indoor and outdoor art trail that hosts over 150 artists and thousands of visitors annually.
🖥️https://wirksworthfestival.co.uk **76 D2**

### Wales

**Caerleon Arts Festival** *Caerleon, Newport* A yearly arts, literature and entertainment event in the town of Caerleon, Wales.
🖥️https://caerleon-arts.org **35 E7**

### Scotland

**Edinburgh Fringe** *Edinburgh* The world's largest performance arts festival, with indoor and outdoor performances. 🖥️www.edfringe.com **121 B5**

▼ An Australian troupe dressed as kangaroos on Calton Hill during the Edinburgh Festival Fringe *Arch White / Alamy*

▲ Notting Hill Carnival *Anizza / Dreamstime Vittorio Caramazza / Dreamstime*  ▶ Edinburgh Food Festival *Sally Anderson / Alamy*

## Food & Drink

### South East

**Foodies** *Syon Park, London* A celebration of food, with festivals in each region of England encouraging artisan producers, street food traders and local food and drink producers to take part.
🖥️https://foodiesfestival.com **28 B2**

**Sausage and Cider Fest** *Stoke Park, Guildford, Surrey* Multiple locations across the UK, featuring local acts, tribute acts, an array of food and drinks, and a disco for children. This one in Guildford is held in June.
🖥️www.sausageandciderfest.co.uk/guildford **27 E8**

### East Midlands

**Wingfest** *Bustler Market, Derby* The world's largest chicken wings festival. It is spread across two days and features a tasting contest and live music, attracting thousands of attendees each year to the centre of Derby.
🖥️www.wingfest.co.uk **76 F3**

**Taste of London Festival** *Regent's Park, London* Part of a food company that runs a series of food festivals across the world, with 36 restaurants, 50 chefs and 150 artisan producers. 🖥️https://london.tastefestivals.com **41 F5**

**The Big Feastival** *Kingham, Stow-on-the-Wold, Gloucestershire* A festival of first-class food and live music for all the family, set within a secluded Cotswolds farm. Held over three days in August. Camping available. 🖥️https://thebigfeastival.com **38 B2**

### Wales

**Abergavenny Food Festival** *Abergavenny* Held in September, seven venues offer the best produce from Wales. There is a programme of talks and demonstrations from suppliers and chefs. 🖥️www.abergavennyfoodfestival.com **35 C7**

**The Great British Food Festival** *Port Talbot* Combines excellent food and drink with some of the most treasured locations across Britain including this one at Margam Country Park, held in early September.
🖥️https://greatbritishfoodfestival.com/margam-park **34 F2**

## Yorkshire & The Humber

**Harrogate Food Festival** *Ripley, Harrogate, Yorkshire* Showcases the region's best talent in food, drink, performing arts and music at Ripley Castle. 🖥 https://harrogatefoodfestival.com **95 C5**

## Scotland

**Edinburgh Food Festival** *George Square Gardens, Edinburgh* Edinburgh's only free-to-enter food festival with food and drink for visitors to enjoy throughout the day, produce to take home and a programme of interesting and informative live events in the Treehouse Kitchen. 🖥 https://www.edfoodfest.com **121 B5**

**Stranraer Oyster Festival** *Stranraer, Dumfries & Galloway* One of Scotland's top food festivals that celebrates Scotland's last remaining native oyster. There are celebrity chef demos, live music, oyster shucking championships, watersports, and a renowned oyster bar. 🖥 https://stranraeroysterfestival.com **104 C4**

# Great Outdoors

## East Midlands

**Alpkit Big Shakeout** *Great Longstone, Bakewell, Derbyshire* Held in the Peak District, this popular festival organises outdoor adventures for the whole family. Held in September at the Thornbridge Outdoors Centre. 🖥 https://alpkit.com **76 B2**

**The Bushcraft Show** *Swinford, Lutterworth, Leicestershire* A family-friendly festival showcasing bushcraft and outdoor skills, with a kids zone and activities including archery, axe throwing and basketry. Held at Stanford Hall. 🖥 https://thebushcraftshow.co.uk **64 F2**

## North West

**Keswick Mountain Festival** *Keswick, Cumberland* Held in May, Mountain Festival hosts outdoor sports, speakers, live music on two stages and a range of other activities in Crow Park and in Theatre by the Lake. 🖥 https://keswickmountainfestival.co.uk **98 B4**

**OMM Festival** *Grasmere, Westmorland & Furness* A family friendly trail running weekend based in the heart of the Lake District, with orienteering and workshops. Held in September. 🖥 https://theomm.com **99 D5**

# Music

## South West

**Camp Bestival** *Lulworth Castle, Dorset* Held at Lulworth Castle, one of two locations in England – the other being Shropshire – in July. It is aimed at families with young children and offers a huge range of activities to enjoy. 🖥 www.campbestival.net **13 F6**

**Glastonbury Festival** *Pilton, Somerset* A five-day festival of contemporary performing arts which has become one of the most high-profile outdoor arts festivals in Britain with an attendance of over 200,000 people. In addition to contemporary music, the festival

◄ An inflatable ball that makes it possible to walk on water, during the Keswick Mountain Festival.
PA Images / Alamy Stock Photo

hosts dance, comedy, theatre, circus and cabaret. There is a wide range of camping facilities available. 🖥 https://glastonburyfestivals.co.uk **23 E7**

**World of Music, Arts and Dance** *Charlton, Malmesbury, Wiltshire* Set in Charlton Park, this is an international arts festival, dedicated to celebrating the world's many forms of music, arts and dance. 🖥 www.womad.co.uk **37 F6**

**Wychwood Festival** *Cheltenham, Gloucestershire* An annual music festival held at Cheltenham racecourse in Gloucestershire. As well as music, the family-friendly three-day festival includes workshops, comedy, the Children's Literature Festival and a Headphone Disco. 🖥 www.wychwoodfestival.com **37 B6**

## South East

**Boomtown Fair (Winchester)** *Ovington, Winchester, Hampshire* Held annually on the Matterley Estate in the South Downs National Park, Boomtown embraces environmentalism and social equality. Diverse range of themed music events. Camping available. 🖥 www.boomtownfair.co.uk **26 F3**

**Fairport's Cropredy Convention** *Cropredy, Oxfordshire* Fairport's Cropredy Convention is an annual festival of folk and rock music, headed by British folk-rock band Fairport Convention. Staged in August on the edge of the village of Cropredy. 🖥 https://fairportconvention.com **52 E2**

**Isle of Wight Festival** *Newport, Isle of Wight* Held annually in June in Seaclose Park, this was one of the earliest festivals to be established and has attracted major international headline acts. 🖥 https://isleofwightfestival.com **15 F6**

◄ The famous Pyramid Stage at Glastonbury Festival *Amylaughinghouse / Dreamstime.com*

▼ Glastonbury Festival with Glastonbury Tor in the distance
Raggedstone / Shutterstock

**Reading Festival** *Little Johns Farm, Reading* The longest running music festival in the UK. Twinned with the Leeds Festival, they share the performers over the same weekend. Camping available. 🖥 www.readingfestival.com **26 B5**

**Sidmouth Folk Festival** *Sidmouth, Devon* A week-long seaside celebration of music, dance and song. It has been running since 1955 and features over 700 diverse events. 🖥 https://sidmouthfolkfestival.co.uk **11 F6**

**Truck Festival** *Steventon, Oxfordshire* Known as 'the Godfather of the small festival scene' and held in the idyllic Oxfordshire countryside at Hill Farm, this annual independent music festival started in 1988 and has since become more mainstream. 🖥 https://truckfestival.com **38 E4**

**Victorious Festival** *The Common and Castle Field, Southsea, Portsmouth* Known by some as the most 'beautifully located festival in the UK' it is based in the seaside town of Portsmouth. This three-day music festival hosts some of the world's leading artists. 🖥 www.victoriousfestival.co.uk **15 E7**

**Wireless Festival** *Finsbury Park, London* One of the UK's leading music festivals, based in London. It started primarily as a rock and pop festival, but since the early 2010s, it has focused more on hip-hop and rap. 🖥 https://wirelessfestival.co.uk **41 F6**

## North West

**Africa Oyé** *Sefton Park, Liverpool* The country's largest annual celebration of African music and culture held in the city's Sefton Park. Held over two days in June. No admission charge and no tickets required. No camping. 🖥 https://africaoye.com **85 F4**

**Kendal Calling** *Hackthorpe, Westmorland & Furness* A major four-day music festival held at Lowther Deer Park, south of Penrith, in the Lake District during August. 🖥 www.kendalcalling.co.uk **99 B7**

**Parklife** *Heaton Park, Manchester* An annual two-day music festival that takes place in June each year. The festival predominantly features dance and electronic music, as well as pop and hip-hop artists. 🖥 https://parklife.uk.com **87 D6**

## East of England

**Cambridge Folk Festival** *Cherry Hinton, Cambridge* One of the world's longest running folk festivals held over four days in July. An eclectic mix of traditional and contemporary acts, it is held in Cherry Hinton Hall Park, a short distance south of Cambridge's city centre. Camping available. 💻www. cambridgefolkfestival.co.uk **55 D5**

**FolkEast** *Little Glenham, Suffolk* Held over three days in August and set in the ancient parkland at Glemham Hall. It includes a mix of music, dance and crafts. 💻https://folkeast.co.uk **57 D7**

**Latitude Festival** *Blythburgh, Southwold, Suffolk* Held within the grounds of Henham Park, near Southwold, in July, this is one of the larger festivals. It hosts a wide range of events including music, dance, comedy, poetry, theatre, literature, family activities and wellness. 💻www.latitudefestival.com **57 B8**

**Strawberry Fair** *Midsummer Common, Cambridge* A free, volunteer-run music and arts festival in Cambridge, with performances, workshops, benefit gigs and the Cambridge Band Competition for under 18s. 💻https://strawberry-fair.org.uk **55 D5**

## East Midlands

**Download Festival** *Donington Park, Leicestershire* Download Festival is a three-day rock festival held in June at the Donington Park motorsport circuit. Camping available. 💻https://downloadfestival.co.uk **63 B8**

**Greenbelt Festival** *Kettering, North Northamptonshire* Greenbelt has grown from being an evangelical Christian music festival to one which now celebrates arts, faith and justice. Held annually at Boughton House over the August Bank Holiday. 💻www.greenbelt.org.uk **65 F6**

**Splendour in Nottingham** *Wollaton Hall, Nottingham* Nottinghamshire's biggest festival, where attendees can enjoy music that spans all genres. There is also a funfair, a silent disco, an array of food and drink and activities for children. 💻www.splendourfestival.com **76 F5**

**Y Not** *Pikehall, Matlock, Derbyshire* A weekend music festival based in the Peak District, with comedy shows, paint fights and carnivals. Camping available. 💻https://ynotfestival.com **75 D8**

## West Midlands

**Camp Bestival** *Weston Park, Shropshire* Held at Weston Park, one of two locations in England – the other being Lulworth Castle – in August. It is aimed at families with young children and offers a huge range of activities to enjoy. 💻www.campbestival.net **61 C8**

## Wales

**Cardiff Mela** *Roald Dahl Plass, Cardiff* This free event showcases a wide diversity of cultures, music, dance, arts, fashion and food – mainly from Asia. Normally held in June, this is a free event. The Mela is part of Cardiff Festivals – a series of events that includes live music, street theatre, open-air theatre, children's entertainment and funfairs. 💻www.cardiffmela.com **22 B3**

**Green Man Festival** *Crickhowell, Powys* Set in the Brecon Beacons, this festival offers music, science and arts based entertainment over a week in mid-August. Camping available. 💻www.greenman.net **35 C6**

**Llangollen International Musical Eisteddfod** *Llangollen, Denbighshire* Takes place every year during the second week of July in North Wales. Based in and around the Royal International Pavilion, an area rich with medieval and industrial history. 💻https://international-eisteddfod.co.uk **73 E6**

**Monmouth Festival** *Monmouth, Monmouthshire* Situated in a historic Welsh border town, this nine day free festival showcases an eclectic mix of talent across a huge range of genres. It is widely considered to be one of the longest running, largest and best free volunteer organised festivals in Europe. 💻www.monmouthfestival.co.uk **36 C2**

**Tafwyl** *Bute Park, Cardiff* An annual Welsh language festival, that is split into two events: Tafwyl Fair, the main event at the weekend, and Tafwyl Week, a seven day fringe that showcases Welsh culture. 💻https://tafwyl.org **22 B3**

## Yorkshire & Humber

**Leeds Festival** *Bramham Park, Leeds* Takes place over the August Bank Holiday in Bramham Park, near Wetherby. Twinned with the Reading Festival, they share performers over the same weekend. Camping available. 💻www.leedsfestival.com **95 E7**

## Scotland

**Tartan Heart Festival** *Kiltarlity, Beauly, Highland* A music and arts festival, held on the Belladrum Estate in Kiltarlity near Beauly, known for its eclectic line-ups, off-beat non-musical entertainments and its all-ages approach. 💻www.tartanheartfestival.co.uk **151 G8**

**TRNSMT** *Glasgow Green, Glasgow* Awarded 'best new festival' in 2017, TRNSMT (pronounced as 'Transmit') is a music festival staged over three days at Glasgow Green in the heart of the city. 💻https://trnsmtfest.com **119 C5**

**West End Festival** *Glasgow* Also known as WestFest, this annual culture and music festival delivers a wide array of high-quality, vibrant and inclusive events to various locations in the West End of Glasgow. 💻https://westfest.uk **119 C5**

# Religion

## South West

**Buddhafield** *Culmhead, Taunton, Somerset* A family-friendly celebration of song, dance, arts and crafts and yoga that is open to everyone, with Buddhist workshops and rituals throughout. Held over five days in July. 💻https://festivalcalendar.uk/buddhafield **11 C7**

**Creation Fest** *Wadebridge, Cornwall* A faith-based skate and music festival in Cornwall, featuring Bible lessons, worship, seminars, sports activities, a kids and youth programme, an arts stream, bonfires, barn dances, silent discos, and late night film screenings. 💻https://creationfest.org.uk **4 B5**

## South East

**Big Church Festival** *Wiston House, Steyning, West Sussex* Formally known as Big Church Day Out, or BCDO, this Christian non-profit music festival is best known for its contemporary Christian music. 💻www.bigchurchfestival.com **17 C5**

**Diwali on the Square** *Westminster, London* A line up of music, dance and performances from London's Hindu, Sikh and Jain communities, with puppet shows, cooking theatres and comedy. 💻www.diwaliinlondon.com **41 F5**

**Eid In The Square** *Westminster, London* An annual Muslim festival held on the first Saturday after the Islamic religious holiday of Eid al-Fitr at Trafalgar Square in London. The event has grown to become one of the key cultural highlights of London's events calendar and sees attendances of over 25,000 people. 💻www.london.gov.uk/events **41 F5**

**Sri Krishna Janmashtami** *Letchmore Heath, Watford, Hertfordshire* An annual Hindu festival that celebrates the birth of Krishna. This is the largest festival held at Bhaktivedanta Manor. 💻www.krishnatemple.com **40 E4**

## East Midlands

**Holi** *Leeds* The Hindu festival of colour with live acts, Bollywood artists performing live, a bouncy castle and rides for children. Held at the Beaverworks in the centre of Leeds. 💻https://leedsholifestival.com **95 F5**

## North West

**Limmud Festival** *Pendigo Lake, Birmingham* A celebration of Jewish life, learning and culture. It showcases a roster of speakers, thought leaders, and artists hailing from all corners of the Jewish world. Held at Pendigo Lake, beside the National Exhibition Centre. 💻https://limmud.org/festival/ **63 F5**

# Transport

## Boats

### South West

**Brunel's SS Great Britain** *Bristol* One of Bristol's top attractions, this museum ship and former passenger steamship offers interactive tours, talks and activities for the whole family. www.ssgreatbritain.org **23 B7**

### South East

**Portsmouth Historic Dockyard** *Portsmouth* An area of HM Naval Base Portsmouth which is open to the public, containing several historic buildings and world famous ships. https://historicdockyard.co.uk **15 D7**

### Wales

**West Wales Maritime Heritage Museum** *Pembroke Dock, Pembrokeshire* An outdoor boatyard and museum, with interactive displays, maritime artifacts and a comprehensive library. www.wwmhs.org.uk **44 E4**

### North West

**Windermere Jetty Museum** *Bowness-on-Windermere, Westmorland & Furness* A lakeside museum, with family activities, displays of heritage boats and steam-launch tours. https://lakelandarts.org.uk/windermere-jetty-museum/ **99 E6**

▼ **SS Great Britain** Dudlajzov / Dreamstime

### North East

**National Museum of the Royal Navy Hartlepool** *Hartlepool* A quayside attraction of the oldest floating British warship, with a museum and costumed guides. www.nmrn.org.uk/visit-us/hartlepool **111 F8**

### Scotland

**Glenlee Tall Ship** *Glasgow* A restored Victorian sailing ship, with an outdoor deck for visitors to explore, plus maritime-themed exhibitions, tours and a mini cinema. https://thetallship.com **119 C5**

## Cable cars

### South East

**IFS Cloud Cable Car** *London* The UK's first and only urban cable car. Aerial views across London's skyline. www.visitlondon.com **41 F6**

▼ **HMS Warrior, the Royal Navy's first ironclad warship at Portsmouth**
Julian Gazzard / Dreamstime

▲ **The Falkirk Wheel, rotating boat lift**
Creativehearts / Dreamstime

◄ **The IFS Cloud Cable Car over the River Thames at Greenwich**
Ben Gingell / Dreamstime

► **A barge entering Caen Hill Locks in Wiltshire**
Njarvis5 / Dreamstime

### East Midlands

**Heights of Abraham** *Matlock, Derbyshire* A hilltop park with cavern tours, reached by Britain's first alpine style cable car. www.heightsofabraham.com **76 D2**

### Wales

**Llandudno Cable Car** *Llandudno, Conwy* The longest passenger cable car system in Britain, taking passengers to the top of the Great Orme summit. www.llandudno.com **83 C7**

## Canals

### South West

**Caen Hill Locks** *Devizes, Wiltshire* A flight of 29 locks on the Kennet and Avon Canal, originally built in the 1800s. https://canalrivertrust.org.uk **24 C5**

### East Midlands

**Foxton Locks** *Market Harborough, Leicestershire* The largest flight of such staircase locks on the English canal system. The Foxton Canal Museum nearby tells the story of the lifts, locks and lives associated with this landmark. https://canalrivertrust.org.uk **64 F4**

### West Midlands

**Delph Locks** *Brierley Hill, Dudley* A flight of eight (originally nine) canal locks of conservation status, that link the Dudley and Stourbridge canals in Brierley Hill. https://industrialtour.co.uk/delph-locks **62 F3**

### Wales

**Fourteen Locks** *Rogerstone, Newport* A flight of 14 locks, built during the Industrial Revolution, with a visitor's centre and computer based information points, taking visitors on a virtual journey along the canal. www.newport.gov.uk **35 F6**

### Scotland

**Falkirk Wheel** *Falkirk* The world's only rotating boat lift, connecting the Forth and Clyde Canal with the Union Canal in a half-turn that takes only five minutes. www.scottishcanals.co.uk **127 F7**

# Preserved railways

## South West

**Avon Valley Railway** *Bitton, Bristol* A heritage and educational railway based at Bitton station, with a station buffet and events year-round.
🖥 www.avonvalleyrailway.org **23 C8**

**Devon Railway Centre** *Bickleigh, Devon* A tourist attraction with various railway experiences, including model, miniature and narrow gauge, plus indoor play areas, a model funfair and a model village. 🖥 https://devonrailwaycentre.co.uk **10 D4**

**Perrygrove Railway** *Coleford, Gloucestershire* A heritage railway of 15 inch gauge, located on Perrygrove farm, with unlimited train rides, as well as play areas, woodland walks and events for children.
🖥 www.perrygrove.co.uk **36 C2**

## South East

**Bluebell Railway** *Uckfield, Sussex* A heritage steam railway running 11 miles / 18 km through the Sussex Weald between Sheffield Park and East Grinstead. The stations along the line have been restored to different periods from the 1880s to the 1950s and are sometimes used as film and TV locations. There is a museum and gift shop at Sheffield Park station.
🖥 www.bluebell-railway.com **17 B8**

▼ The Bluebell Railway at Sheffield Park *Philip Bird / Dreamstime*

▲ The Severn Valley Railway near Upper Arley *Nigel Cliff / Dreamstime*

**Didcot Railway Centre** *Didcot, Oxfordshire* A heritage railway museum and preservation engineering site, set within 21 acres alongside Didcot Parkway Station.
🖥 www.didcotrailwaycentre.org.uk **39 E5**

**Hampton & Kempton Waterworks Railway** *Feltham, London* The only operational 1915 heritage narrow-gauge railway 'loop' in London, offering rides to visitors on a restored steam locomotive. 🖥 https://hamptonkemptonrailway.org.uk **27 B8**

**Isle of Wight Steam Railway** *Ryde, Isle of Wight* A multi-award winning heritage railway and museum, offering train rides, VIP experiences, woodland walks and a children's play area.
🖥 https://iwsteamrailway.co.uk **15 F6**

**Ruislip Lido Railway** *Ruislip, London* A 12 inch gauge miniature railway around Ruislip Lido in Ruislip, operated by volunteers.
🖥 www.ruisliplidorailway.org **40 F3**

**Watercress Line** *New Alresford, Hampshire* A 19th-century heritage line with steam trains travelling through vintage stations, and year-round events. 🖥 https://watercressline.co.uk **26 F3**

## East of England

**Colne Valley Railway** *Castle Hedingham, Essex* A heritage railway based at the Castle Hedingham Station, plus a model railway, Brewster Museum, woodland walk and miniature railway.
🖥 www.colnevalleyrailway.co.uk **55 F8**

▶ Bridgnorth Cliff Railway
*roberthyrons / iStock*

**Epping Ongar Railway** *Chipping Ongar, Essex* Essex's longest heritage railway, running through countryside, forest and historic towns.
🖥 www.eorailway.co.uk **41 D7**

**Leighton Buzzard Railway** *Leighton Buzzard, Central Bedfordshire* One of the UK's longest and oldest narrow-gauge lines, with a worldwide collection of locomotives and one of the largest collections of narrow-gauge stock in England.
🖥 https://www.buzzrail.uk **40 B2**

**North Norfolk Railway** *Sheringham, Norfolk* Also known as the 'Poppy Line', this heritage steam railway runs between the towns of Sheringham and Holt. 🖥 www.nnrailway.co.uk **81 C7**

**Wells & Walsingham Light Railway** *Wells-next-the-Sea, Norfolk* The longest 10¼ inch narrow gauge steam railway in the world. It runs between the coastal town of Wells-next-the-Sea and the inland village of Walsingham.
🖥 www.wlr.co.uk **80 C5**

**Whitwell & Reepham Railway Station** *Reepham, Norwich* A heritage railway with working steam and diesel engines, as well as a licensed bar, restaurant and café.
🖥 https://whitwellstation.com **81 E6**

## East Midlands

**Battlefield Line Railway** *Shackerstone, Leicestershire* The last remaining part of the former Ashby and Nuneaton joint railway, this heritage railway runs from Shackerstone to Shenton for a total of five miles.
🖥 www.battlefieldline.co.uk **63 D7**

**Nottingham Heritage Railway** *Ruddington, Nottingham* A 10 mile heritage railway, passing through some of Nottinghamshire's most picturesque scenery. 🖥 www.gcrn.co.uk **77 F5**

**Peak Rail** *Matlock, Derbyshire* Heritage railway and steam train rides, based in the Peak District, with seasonal events, fine dining and activities year-round.
🖥 www.peakrail.co.uk **76 C2**

**Sherwood Forest Railway** *Edwinstowe, Nottingham* Nottinghamshire's only narrow gauge steam railway, with trains running regularly everyday, plus refreshments and an outdoor play area.
🖥 www.sherwoodforestrailway.com **77 C6**

## West Midlands

**Bridgnorth Cliff Railway** *Bridgnorth, Shropshire* A funicular railway that has been transporting the people of Bridgnorth up and down the 111 ft sandstone cliffs that separate High Town from Low Town for over a century.
🖥 www.bridgnorthcliffrailway.co.uk **61 E7**

**Midland Railway** *Ripley, Derbyshire* A museum complex with heritage train rides, a Victorian railwayman's church, a children's playground and country park for visitors. 🖥 www.midlandrailway-butterley.co.uk **76 D4**

**Severn Valley Railway** *Kidderminster, Worcestershire* An award-winning heritage railway and museum, displaying a fleet of engines. There are on-train dining and train driving experiences that visitors can book in advance. 🖥 https://svr.co.uk **50 B2**

▲ A train on the Welsh Highland Railway hauled by a rare Garratt articulated steam locomotive Denis Kabanov / iStock

## Wales

**Brecon Mountain Railway** *Merthyr Tydfil, Mid Glamorgan* A heritage railway, offering visitors vintage train rides through the Brecon Beacons. 🖥️www.bmr.wales **34 C4**

**Rhyl Miniature Railway** *Rhyl, Denbighshire* Britain's oldest miniature railway, providing train rides around the Marine Lake since 1911. 🖥️https://rhylminiaturerailway.co.uk **72 A4**

**Welsh Highland Railway** *Porthmadog, Gwynedd* The UK's longest heritage railway, stretching for 25 miles / 40 km through Snowdonia National Park. 🖥️www.visitwales.com **71 C6**

## North West

**Ravenglass and Eskdale Railway** *Ravenglass, Cumberland* The Lake District's oldest, longest and most scenic railway, home to the world's oldest narrow gauge engine built in 1894. 🖥️https://ravenglass-railway.co.uk **98 E2**

**Ribble Steam Railway** *Preston, Lancashire* A standard gauge preserved railway, plus industrial heritage museum, outdoor playground and educational centre. 🖥️https://ribblesteam.org.uk **86 B3**

**South Tynedale Railway** *Alston, Westmorland & Furness* A preserved, 2 ft narrow gauge heritage railway, with nearby cycle trails, special events and a café. 🖥️www.south-tynedale-railway.org.uk **109 E7**

## Yorkshire & the Humber

**Embsay & Bolton Abbey Steam Railway** *Skipton, North Yorkshire* A heritage railway that runs regular steam services throughout the year, and special events. 🖥️www.embsayboltonabbeyrailway.org.uk **94 D3**

**Keighley & Worth Valley Railway** *Haworth, West Yorkshire* A 5-mile branch line railway, running heritage steam and diesel trains from Keighley to Oxenhope. 🖥️https://kwvr.co.uk **94 F3**

**North Yorkshire Moors Railway** *Pickering, North Yorkshire* A heritage railway running through the North York Moors National Park, hosting photography workshops, dining experiences and events. 🖥️https://www.nymr.co.uk **103 F6**

**Scarborough North Bay Railway** *Scarborough, North Yorkshire* Running services for over 90 years, this miniature railway offers rides as well as other lakeside activities. 🖥️http://www.snbr.org.uk **103 F8**

## North East

**Tanfield Railway** *Stanley, Durham* The oldest railway in Britain, with sections dating back to 1725. It runs preserved steam and diesel rolling stock. 🖥️www.tanfield-railway.co.uk **110 D4**

**Weardale Railway** *Stanhope, Durham* An 18 mile heritage line, offering rides, photography experiences and dining for visitors. 🖥️www.weardale-railway.org.uk **110 F3**

## Scotland

**Bo'ness and Kinneil Railway** *Bo'ness, Falkirk* A heritage railway with steam and diesel locomotives, running through through woodlands, past waterfalls and over the Avon Viaduct. 🖥️www.bkrailway.co.uk **127 F8**

**Fife Heritage Railway** *Leven, Fife* A heritage railway run by the The Kingdom of Fife Railway Preservation Society, which aims to preserve and restore rolling stock in Fife. 🖥️www.fifeheritagerailway.co.uk **129 D5**

**Keith and Dufftown Railway** *Keith, Moray* The most northerly heritage railway in Scotland, with cycling routes, mountain biking, rafting, sailing and hiking nearby. 🖥️https://morayspeyside.com **152 D4**

**Royal Deeside Railway** *Banchory, Aberdeenshire* A standard gauge steam and diesel hauled heritage railway, running alongside the River Dee. 🖥️www.deeside-railway.co.uk **141 E6**

**West Highland Line** *Glasgow* Tours along this railway line have been described as some of the most scenic in the world. The route is known to millions as one that took Harry Potter from Platform 9¾ all the way to Hogwarts. 🖥️www.visitscotland.com **119 C5**

# Tramways

## South West

**Seaton Tramway** *Seaton, Devon* A narrow gauge, heritage tramway running three miles from Seaton to Colyton through the scenic Axe Valley. 🖥️www.tram.co.uk **11 E7**

## East Midlands

**Crich Tramway Village** *Crich, Matlock, Derbyshire* A period village with indoor exhibitions and an outdoor fleet of trams for visitors to ride. 🖥️www.tramway.co.uk **76 D3**

## North East

**Saltburn Cliff Tramway** *Saltburn-by-the-Sea, Redcar & Cleveland* A landmark tramway, opened in 1884, with stained glass windows, offering rides with views of the sea. 🖥️https://redcarcleveland.co.uk **102 B4**

▼ A World War II themed event at Crich Tramway Village Ian Good / Dreamstime

▼ The Jacobite steam train crossing Glenfinnan Viaduct on the West Highland Line Pmstock / Dreamstime

# Cycle routes

**The National Cycle Network (NCN)** is a UK-wide network of signed paths and routes for cycling and walking. Many of the routes below use parts of the Network. For more details see www.sustrans.org.uk

## South West

**Camel Trail** *Padstow to Wenfordbridge* Following a disused railway line, this 18 mile / 29 km route is largely traffic free, fairly flat, and therefore suitable for families. Shared with walkers and horse-riders, this trail is a good one to spot wildlife, birds and wild flowers. 🖳 www.cornwall.gov.uk/environment **4 B4 / 5 B5**

**West Kernow Way** *Penzance* Circular route through the western half of the Cornish peninsula taking in Land's End, St Michael's Mount and Lizard Point. With the official starting point in Penzance, it is a challenging route, with some stiff climbs. 🖳 www.cyclinguk.org/west-kernow-way **2 C3**

## South East

**Crab & Winkle Way** *Canterbury to Whitstable* With a climb out of Canterbury and an undulating middle section, this route requires a bit of effort. The reward is a fine view of Whitstable from the hill top. The trail follows the route of a disused railway line and is mainly traffic-free. 🖳 www.sustrans.org.uk **31 D5 / 30 C5**

**Viking Coastal Trail** *Margate/Broadstairs/Ramsgate* A 32 mile circular route on the Isle of Thanet in Kent. The inland section follows quiet country lanes but the main attraction hugs the coastline using large stretches of traffic-free paths, sharing the promenades with walkers. 🖳 https://explorekent.org/activities/viking-coastal-trail **31 C7**

## East of England

**Peterborough Green Wheel** *Peterborough* Spokes radiate out from the city centre using urban cycle lanes and quiet roads to link with the route around the outside of the city. The section running through Ferry Meadows Country Park is particularly suitable for beginners and young children. 🖳 www.sustrans.org.uk **65 E8**

**Rebellion Way** *Norwich* Norfolk is famed for 'big skies' and this long distance route is a good way to appreciate the rolling landscape. Numerous noteworthy churches can be visited along with chances to spot seals and migrating birds along the coastline. Towns along the route include King's Lynn, Cromer and Norwich. 🖳 www.cyclinguk.org/rebellion-way **68 D5**

## East Midlands

**Tissington Trail** *Parsley Hay to Ashbourne* Set in the Peak District National Park. Will suit most skill levels, mainly paved surfaces on the track of the former Buxton to Ashbourne railway. The one-way trip of 13 miles / 21 km is mostly flat and traffic free. 🖳 www.peakdistrict.gov.uk **75 C8 / 75 E8**

**Water Rail Way** *Lincoln to Boston* Following the route of a disused railway line, this is flat and almost traffic-free. Viewing platforms allow inspiring views over the river Witham and the vast fenland landscapes. Dotted along the way are specially commissioned sculptures. 🖳 www.sustrans.org.uk **78 B2 / 79 E6**

## West Midlands

**Lias Line** *Rugby to Royal Leamington Spa* This route is part of the National Cycle Network in Warwickshire. The trail leaves Rugby by following a disused railway line to arrive at Draycote Water. Pretty lanes and the Grand Union Canal towpath take riders into the centre of Royal Leamington Spa. 🖳 www.sustrans.org.uk **52 B3 / 51 C8**

**Shropshire Cycleway** *Shrewsbury* An unsigned 185 miles / 298 km route that follows the Shropshire boundary. Can be ridden as a long cycle touring holiday or broken into five shorter day rides. There is also the Shrewsbury Circular – a ride through the countryside around the county town. 🖳 www.shropshiresgreatoutdoors.co.uk **60 C5**

## Wales

**Cardiff to Castell Coch** *Cardiff* Part of the 55 mile / 88 km Taff Trail from Cardiff to Brecon, this short section is a perfect ride for families to explore the green heart of the capital. 🖳 www.visitwales.com **22 B3**

**North Wales Coaster** *Holyhead to Connah's Quay* Using National Cycle Network Route 5, this trail follows much of the North Wales coastline from Anglesey to the Welsh/English border. It crosses the Menai Bridge and passes Conwy Castle. A few climbs along the way. 🖳 www.visitwales.com **82 C2 / 73 C7**

## North West & North East

**Coast to Coast (C2C)** *Whitehaven to Sunderland/Tynemouth* This popular trail runs across northern England from the Irish Sea to the North Sea. It is traditional to dip your wheel in the sea at the beginning and end of the ride. It involves some challenging climbs across the North Pennines. 🖳 www.sustrans.org.uk **98 C1 / 111 D7 & C6**

**Hadrian's Wall Cycleway** *Bowness-on-Solway to Tynemouth* A good introduction to long-distance cycling that would be suitable for families. With plenty of places of interest, including the Roman sites of Birdoswald and Vindolanda. The market town of Hexham is a good place to take a break. 🖳 www.sustrans.org.uk **108 C2 / 111 C6**

## North West

**Lancashire Cycleway** Constructed in two loops of roughly 130 miles / 210 km each: the northern loop takes in the Forest of Bowland and Lancaster and the southern one includes Pendle and Blackburn. 🖳 www.visitlancashire.com

## North East

**Coasts & Castles** *Newcastle upon Tyne to Edinburgh* This route follows the beautiful coast of North East England as far as Berwick-upon-Tweed then continues inland into the Scottish Borders. There are sandy beaches to enjoy and views of iconic castles at Bamburgh and Dunstanburgh. A short detour can take in the tidal island of Lindisfarne. 🖳 www.sustrans.org.uk **111 C5 / 121 B5**

## Yorkshire & the Humber

**Way of the Roses** *Morecambe to Bridlington* A relatively challenging coast-to-coast route with some hills. Most people ride this route from west to east hoping for a tailwind. It weaves through some of the county's best countryside, including the Forest of Bowland, Yorkshire Dales National Park and the Vale of York. 🖳 www.sustrans.org.uk **92 C4 / 97 C7**

**Yorkshire Wolds** *Beverley* This is a 170 mile / 274 km circular ride starting and ending in Beverley in the East Riding of Yorkshire. The rolling countryside gives a relatively easy ride – good for beginners. The route heads west to Market Weighton before heading north toward Bridlington. 🖳 www.sustrans.org.uk **97 F6**

## Scotland

**Ayrshire Coast Cycle Way** *Irvine to Ayr* Mainly off-road, this linear route follow the coast with views of the Isle of Arran. An easy section of the longer National Cycle Network. 🖳 www.visitscotland.com **118 / 112 B3**

**Caledonia Way** *Campbeltown to Inverness* Featuring the best of Scotland's scenery, this 235 mile / 378 km route uses quiet rural roads, traffic free cycle ways and some gravel sections. Highlights include riding through Glen Coe then climbing high above Loch Ness to finish in Inverness. 🖳 https://caledoniaway.com **143 F8 / 151 G9**

## National

**Land's End to John o'Groats** 1,042 miles / 1676 km This is Britain's ultimate cycle challenge – LEJOG. Best ridden from south to north to take advantage of the prevailing winds. There are variations on the route but it mainly utilises sections of the National Cycle Network. Tackling it all in one ride requires a certain level of fitness but it can be broken down into smaller sections. 🖳 www.sustrans.org.uk

**Cycle routes listed here** are not shown on the maps in this atlas, but details can be found by following links to the websites where full route descriptions and maps can be found.

## Further information

**National Cycle Network**
A country-wide network of signed paths for cycling and walking 🖳 www.sustrans.org.uk

**Cycling UK** Lists many long-distance cycle routes 🖳 www.cyclinguk.org/routes

**Wheels for All** With centres across Britain to help disabled people to cycle 🖳 https://wheelsforall.org.uk

# Scenic journeys

## South West

**The Atlantic Highway** *70 miles / 112 km* Travelling south from Barnstaple on the A39, this route has rugged inland landscapes to one side and stunning views of the Atlantic to the other. There are numerous places to stop off at along the way, such as the pretty coastal village of Clovelly, King Arthur's Tintagel Castle and Port Isaac – 'Portwenn' in the TV series, Doc Martin. The trip ends in the popular seaside resort of Newquay. **20 F4 / 4 C3**

## South East

**Military Road, Isle of Wight** *13 miles / 20 km* Hugging the south-west coast of the island, the A3055, known as the Military Road, links St Catherine's Point in the south with Freshwater Bay near The Needles. There are several official parking places to stop to enjoy sea views but care needs to be taken travelling to the east of Niton as part of the main road has been lost to erosion and an inland detour is in place. **15 G5 / 14 F4**

## East of England

**Norfolk Coastal Drive Trail** *56 miles / 90 km* Starting in the pilgrimage centre of Little Walsingham, this route has plenty of places to visit along the way: Holkham Hall, Blakeney, Cley and the Georgian town of Holt. Leave the car in Holt to take a steam train on the 'Poppy Line' to Sheringham. The last point on this trail is the impressive National Trust's Blickling Hall. ⌨ www.thetouristtrail.org/trails/england/norfolk/coastal-drive/ **80 D5 / 81 E7**

## East Midlands & North West

**Cat and Fiddle Road, Peak District** *11 miles / 18 km* Leave Buxton on the A54, then fork right on the A537 towards Macclesfield. This high-level route with many sharp bends, and expansive views over Greater Manchester, the Cheshire Plain and the Peak District National Park, is a favourite with motorcyclists. The former pub, which gave its name to this stretch of road, is now a whisky distillery. **75 B7 / 75 B6**

## West Midlands

**The Watkins Way, Herefordshire** *106 miles / 170 km* Explore the ancient landscapes of Herefordshire by car or bike to celebrate Alfred Watkin's discovery of hillside ley lines. Drive through the Wye Valley, the Golden Valley and the picturesque black and white villages in the north of the county. Start in the village of Woolhope in the Wye Valley and circle round to complete the tour in Hereford. ⌨ www.visitherefordshire.co.uk/see-do/scenic-trails/ley-lines-landscape/watkins-way **49 F8 / 49 F7**

## Wales

**The Coastal Way, Wales** *180 miles / 290 km* This route runs the whole length of Cardigan Bay from Aberdaron on the Llyn Peninsula to Wales' smallest city, St David's. It is possible to utilise a variety of transport options to explore the many diversions along the way: drive; walk; cycle; take train (steam or standard) or even sail. This is one of three routes that make up the Wales Way. ⌨ www.visitwales.com/inspire-me/wales-way/coastal-way **70 E2 / 44 C2**

## North West

**Kendal to Keswick, Lake District** *30 miles / 48 km* The A591 links two of the most popular towns in the Lake District. A short drive, but it takes in some of the best scenery in the area passing Windermere, Grasmere and Thirlmere. An adventurous detour on

◀ **The River Glaven in Cley, Norfolk**
Nicola Pulham / Dreamstime

▲ **The fishing village of Port Isaac on the North Cornwall coast** Ian Woolcock / Dreamstime

minor roads west from Ambleside goes up and over the notorious Wrynose and Hard Knott Pass. **99 E7 / 98 B4**

## Yorkshire & the Humber

**Buttertubs Pass, Yorkshire Dales** *28 miles / 45 km* Buttertubs Pass is a very popular scenic road winding north from Hawes in Wensleydale over the top of the remote fells to sweep down into Swaledale in the Yorkshire Dales. Stop to look deep into the fissures known as the Buttertubs – so called due to their resemblance to those used to store butter. Continue through the hay meadows of Swaledale to Richmond. **100 F3 / 101 D6**

## North East

**Alnmouth to Lindisfarne** *36 miles / 57 km* This coastal route, from the wide sands of Alnmouth to Holy Island along the B1339, gives views of castles at Dunstanburgh, Bamburgh and Lindisfarne. The causeway to Holy Island is covered by the sea at high tide twice a day. Tide tables are posted at both ends of the causeway and should be checked to avoid needing to use the emergency refuges. ⌨ https://holyislandcrossingtimes.northumberland.gov.uk **117 C8 / 123 E7**

## Scotland

**North Coast 500** *516 miles / 830 km* Launched in 2015 to attract more visitors to this remote area, it has become very popular with drivers, motorcyclists and cyclists. The circular route starts in Inverness before heading west to Applecross. Running across the north coast it takes in Cape Wrath and John o'Groats along with stunning beaches and fairy tale castles such as Dunrobin. There are several short-cuts for heavier vehicles to avoid the narrowest roads. ⌨ www.northcoast500.com **151 G9**

▼ **Kylesku Bridge across Loch a' Chàirn Bhàin on the North Coast 500 route** Helen Hotson / Dreamstime

# Animal attractions

## Bird collections

### South West

**Birdland Park & Gardens** *Bourton-on-the-Water, Gloucestershire* Home to over 500 species of birds and 50 aviaries, this centre offers shows, experiences and an interactive discovery zone for children. 🖥 www.birdland.co.uk **38 B1**

### South East

**Eagle Heights Wildlife Foundation** *Eynsford, Kent* A wildlife sanctuary, home to the largest bird of prey centre in the UK, with over 50 avian species. 🖥 www.eagleheights.co.uk **29 C6**

**Hawk Conservancy Trust** *Andover, Hampshire* An award-winning birds of prey centre, with some of the best flying displays in the country. 🖥 www.hawk-conservancy.org **25 E8**

**London Falconry** *Fulham Palace, Bishop's Avenue, London* Gardens and woodland, where vistors can learn of origins of falconry, as well as meeting a variety of hawks, falcons and owls. 🖥 https://londonfalconry.com/fulham-palace **28 B3**

### East Midlands

**Baytree Owl & Wildlife Centre** *Spalding, Lincolnshire* Suitable for families, there is a collection of over 60 owls and birds of prey. The centre supports a successful conservation breeding programme. 🖥 www.bowc.co.uk **66 B2**

**Rutland Falconry & Owl Centre** *Exton, Oakham, Rutland* The sanctuary, in a woodland setting, is home to a superb collection of birds of prey including hawks, buzzards, eagles and vultures. Some birds can be held while others can be admired at a safe distance. 🖥 www.rutlandwildlifesanctuary.co.uk **65 D6**

**Tropical Birdland** *Desford, Leicester* A visitor attraction which is home to over 250 birds including macaws and exotic parrots, providing hands-on experiences. 🖥 https://tropicalbirdland.com/ **63 D8**

### Wales

**The British Bird of Prey Centre** *Llanarthne, Carmarthenshire* The only bird of prey centre in the UK that focuses solely on British native species with daily flying displays, housed in the National Botanic Gardens of Wales. 🖥 www.britishbirdofpreycentre.co.uk **33 C6**

**Gigrin Farm Red Kite Feeding Centre** *Rhayader, Powys* Provides a breathtaking spectacle when hundreds of red kites come here to feed once a day. Watch from a general hide or one of the specialist photographic hides. 🖥 https://gigrin.co.uk **47 C8**

### North West

**Cumberland Bird of Prey Centre** *Thurstonfield, Cumberland* Situated west of Carlisle, the centre offers a wide variety of training courses and activities – from one-hour Hawk Walks to Family Experiences. Visits should be booked in advance. 🖥 www.birdofpreycentre.co.uk **108 D3**

### North East

**Kielder Water Birds of Prey Centre** *Kielder, Northumberland* The centre is located within the lakeside surroundings of Kielder Water at Leaplish Waterside Park. Home to over 60 birds including eagles, owls, falcons, hawks and vultures, as well as a family of wallabies. 🖥 www.kielderbopc.com **116 F2**

**North East Falconry** *Ryton, Tyne & Wear* With almost 16 years of experience, this birds of prey centre hosts hawk, owl and falcon experiences daily. Located west of Newcastle upon Tyne city centre. 🖥 www.northeastfalconry.com **110 C4**

### Scotland

**Scottish Seabird Centre** *North Berwick, East Lothian* With an interactive Discovery Experience and seasonal boat trips around the local islands that are teeming with wildlife, including the spectacular Bass Rock gannet. 🖥 www.seabird.org **129 F7**

▲ **Gannets on the Bass Rock**
Colin Hugill / Alamy

▼ **West Midland Safari Park**
Chon Kit Leong / Dreamstime

**World of Wings** *Luggiebank, Glasgow* Scotland's largest bird of prey centre, with flying demos, handling experiences, as well as conservation projects. 🖥 https://worldofwings.co.uk **119 B7**

## Farm parks

### South West

**Cotswold Farm Park** *Guiting Power, Cheltenham, Gloucestershire* Popular farm attraction run by Adam Henson, the park has been involved in conserving rare breeds for over 50 years. Visitors can interact with over 50 breeds across 7 different species of British farm animals. 🖥 https://cotswoldfarmpark.co.uk **37 B8**

### South East

**South of England Rare Breeds Centre** *Ashford, Kent* Approved by the Rare Breeds Survival Trust (RBST), offering indoor and outdoor encounters with rare and native farm animals and bird species. 🖥 www.rarebreeds.org.uk **19 B6**

### East Midlands

**Northcote Heavy Horse Centre** *Spilsby, Lincolnshire* Activities include animal handling – from small Shetland ponies to big Shire horses. There are opportunities to walk with goats and llamas. 🖥 www.northcotehorses.com **79 C7**

### Wales

**Dyfed Shire Horse Farm** *Eglwyswrw, Crymch, Pembrokeshire* Meet these gentle yet giant horses on a traditional Welsh working farm. 🖥 https://dyfed-shires.co.uk **45 F3**

### North East

**Wild Cattle of Chillingham** *Wooler, Northumberland* The wild cattle have been bred in isolation for hundreds of years. A warden leads small groups on foot to find where the cattle are grazing – they are sometimes easily accesssible, but at other times, it can involve a long walk. 🖥 https://chillinghamwildcattle.com **117 B6**

▼ A red kite over Gigrin Farm Feeding Centre
Xpalleja87/Dreamstime

## Safari parks

### East of England

**Woburn Safari Park** *Woburn, Central Bedfordshire* Part of the estates of the Duke of Bedford, where visitors can drive through the animal enclosures. Included are species such as elephants, tigers, rhinos and North American bison. The Great Woburn Railway transports visitors to the Alpaca Outpost. 🖥 www.woburnsafari.co.uk **53 F7**

### West Midlands

**West Midland Safari Park** *Bewdley, Worcestershire* A safari and leisure park with over 165 species of exotic animals, and other attractions such as a small theme park. 🖥 www.wmsp.co.uk **50 B3**

### North West

**Knowsley Safari Park** *Prescot, Merseyside* A safari park that has welcomed visitors for over 50 years, with animal talks, displays and rides. 🖥 www.knowsleysafariexperience.co.uk **86 E2**

**Lake District Wildlife Park** *Bassenthwaite Lake, Keswick, Cumberland* Sitting in the shadow of Skiddaw, and close to Bassenthwaite Lake, the park is home to over 100 species of wild and domestic animals. Daily activites allow visitors to engage with the animals. 🖥 www.lakedistrictwildlifepark.co.uk **108 F2**

▲ A blue and gold macaw at South Lakes Safari Zoo
Sueburtonphotography / Dreamstime

## Scotland

**Blairdrummond Safari Park** *Stirling* One of the country's earliest safari parks, this is a family friendly attraction near Stirling. Animals roam free or in large enclosures. It has four main reserves dedicated to Africa, Asia, Lions and Barbary macaques.
🖳 www.blairdrummond.com **127 E6**

# Sea life sanctuaries
## South West

**Cornish Seal Sanctuary** *Gweek, Cornwall* A sanctuary for injured seal pups, owned by The Sea Life Trust.
🖳 www.sealsanctuary.co.uk **3 D6**

## East Midlands

**Natureland Seal Sanctuary** *Skegness, Lincolnshire* Primarily a seal rescue centre dedicated to rescuing, rehabilitating and eventually releasing them back into the wild. Watch the seals at feeding time in the Resident Seal pool. Other animals include penguins, meerkats and alpacas. 🖳 https:// skegnessnatureland.co.uk **79 C8**

**The Seal Sanctuary Wildlife Centre** *Mablethorpe, Lincolnshire* A wildlife centre and tourist attraction, working to rehabilitate sick and injured seals along with reptiles, meerkats and primates.
🖳 www.thesealsanctuary.co.uk **91 F9**

## Scotland

**Scottish Dolphin Centre** *Spey Bay, Moray* Based at the mouth of the River Spey, this centre is a haven for wildlife including bottlenose dolphins, ospreys, grey and common seals and the occasional otter. 🖳 https:// dolphincentre.whales.org **152 B3**

# Wildlife parks
## South East

**Crocodiles of the World** *Carterton, Oxfordshire* A conservation and education centre specialising in crocodilia with under-water viewing, talks and animal encounters. 🖳 www. crocodilesoftheworld.co.uk **38 D2**

**New Forest Wildlife Park** *Southampton* An animal and safari park, located on the edge of The New Forest, specialising in native and past-native wildlife of Britain. 🖳 https:// newforestwildlifepark.co.uk **14 D4**

## East of England

**Shepreth Wildlife Park** Join daily keeper talks to appreciate the collection of lemurs, meerkats, red pandas and a Sumatran tiger. 🖳 https:// sheprethwildlifepark.co.uk **54 E4**

**Thrigby Hall Wildlife Gardens** *Great Yarmouth. Norfolk* Animals inlcude a pair of critically endangered Sumatran tigers along with red pandas. Snow leopards have been sucessfully bred at the gardens.
🖳 www.thrigbyhall.com **69 C7**

## East Midlands

**Catanger Llama Trekking** *Weston, Towcester, West Northants* A llama breeding farm with a trekking centre, open for visitors year-round.
🖳 www.llamatrekking.co.uk **52 E3**

**Lincolnshire Wildlife Park** *Friskney, Boston, Lincolnshire* A zoo with the largest collection of Bengal tigers in Europe and one of the largest parrot rescue centres in the world. Also home to the National Parrot Sanctuary.
🖳 www.lincswildlife.com **79 D7**

**Woodside Wildlife Park** *Langworth, Lincolnshire* Conservation activities include supporting both local and international programmes. Animals include a tiger, rescued from a circus, and a colony of Humboldt penguins.
🖳 https://woodsidewildlife.com **78 B3**

## West Midlands

**All Things Wild** *Evesham, Worcestershire,* Scenic retreat with farm animals, lemurs, camels and more – suitable for families. A train ride runs past dinosaur statues. There is a year round programme of events and animal experiences.
🖳 www.allthingswild.co.uk **51 E6**

**Peak Wildlife Park** *Leek, Staffordshire* 'Walkthroughs' allow guests to come face to face with red squirrels, penguins, wallabies and lemurs.
🖳 www.peakwildlifepark. co.uk **75 D7**

▲ Reindeer roaming free in the Cairngorms Andi Probert / Dreamstime

## Wales

**Manor Wildlife Park** *Tenby, Pembrokeshire* A 52-acre zoo, home to some of the world's most endangered animals.
🖳 www.manorwildlifepark.co.uk **32 D1**

## North West

**Lakeland Wildlife Oasis** *Milnthorpe, Westmorland & Furness* Established for over 25 years, the zoo hosts a collection of insects, fish, amphibians, reptiles, birds and mammals.
🖳 https://wildlifeoasis.co.uk **92 B5**

## Yorkshire & the Humber

**Bridlington Animal park** *Bridlington, East Riding of Yorkshire* Collection of both animals and birds with flying displays every day. Species include parrots, owls, flamingos, zebra, meerkats, lemur, camels and raccoons.
🖳 https://bridlingtonanimalpark.co.uk **97 C7**

**Yorkshire Wildlife Park** *Doncaster, South Yorkshire* A wildlife conservation and rehabilitation centre. Recent additions include the Atlantic Forest habitat which is themed around the Amazon lowlands and houses several animals from the South American continent, including bush dogs, maned wolves and lowland tapirs. 🖳 www. yorkshirewildlifepark.com **89 D7**

## Scotland

**Auchingarrich Wildlife Park** *Comrie, Perth & Kinross* Keeper Days and Animal Experiences allow visitors to appreciate time with a wide variety of animals and birds. 🖳 www. auchingarrichwildlifepark.co.uk **127 C6**

**Cairngorm Reindeer Centre** *Glenmore Lodge, Cairngorm, Highland* Established in 1952 in the Cairngorm mountains, this is Britain's only free-ranging herd of reindeer. Guided hill trips and paddock visits allow visitors to interact with the reindeer. 🖳 www. cairngormreindeer.co.uk **139 C5**

**Highland Wildlife Park** *Kincraig, Kingussie, Highland* Owned by the Royal Zoological Society of Scotland, this 105-hectare safari park and zoo hosts animal attractions, events and educational programmes. 🖳 www. highlandwildlifepark.org.uk **138 D4**

# Zoos
## South West

**Bristol Zoo Project** *Easter Compton, Bristol* Formerly known as the Wild Place Project, this was the sister site of Bristol Zoo until that site closed in 2022. It has been designed to link specific ecosystems and conservation programmes around the world. A wide variety of species includes gorilla, zebra and cheetah.
🖳 https://bristolzoo.org.uk **36 F2**

**Dartmoor Zoo** *Sparkwell, Plymouth, Devon* A family-owned zoo located in 33 acres of parkland, with endangered animals and a conservation centre.
🖳 www.dartmoorzoo.org.uk **6 D3**

**Exmoor Zoo** *Bratton Fleming, Barnstaple, Devon* The former Exmoor Bird Gardens, now a zoo and education centre dedicated to the conservation of smaller animals.
🖳 www.exmoorzoo.co.uk **21 E5**

**Newquay Zoo** *Newquay, Cornwall* Nestled within 13 acres of sub-tropical farms, with children's play areas, events and easy access for wheelchair and pushchair users.
🖳 www.newquayzoo.org.uk **4 C3**

▼ Bottlenose dolphins breaching in the Moray Firth
Thomas A Langlands / Dreamstime

▲ A glasswing butterfly in London Zoo
Matthew Omojola / Dreamstime

### Noah's Ark Zoo Farm
*Wraxall, Clevedon, North Somerset*
A zoo with lions, tigers and rhinos, set in 110 acres of countryside, plus a children's playground.
🖥 www.noahsarkzoofarm.co.uk **23 B6**

### Tropiquaria Zoo *Watchet, Somerset*
A small tropical house and zoo, housed in a former Art Deco radio transmitter station.
🖥 www.tropiquaria.co.uk **22 E2**

## South East

### Drusillas Park *Berwick, Polegate, East Sussex* One of the best small zoos in Europe, with exhibits targeted for children between 2 and 10 years old.
🖥 www.drusillas.co.uk **18 E2**

### London Zoo *Regent's Park, London*
Dating from 1828, this is the world's oldest scientific zoo and is situated in the heart of London. It has several architect-designed landmark features including the Snowdon Aviary, Tiger Territory and the Mappin Terraces, an early move to recreate natural environments for the animals without cages and bars.
🖥 www.londonzoo.org **41 F5**

### Marwell Zoo *Owslebury, Winchester, Hampshire* A zoo and tropical house, home to hundreds of exotic and endangered animals within a landscaped 140-acre park.
🖥 www.marwell.org.uk **15 B6**

## East of England

### Africa Alive! *Kessingland, Suffolk*
A conservation based zoo located south of Lowestoft. Offers the chance to learn about conservation through a variety of activities and displays.
🖥 www.zsea.org/reserve **69 F8**

### Amazonia Zoo *Cromer, Norfolk*
Features over 200 South American animals including jaguar, monkeys, pumas, peccaries, macaws, parrots, capuchins and snakes.
🖥 https://amazonazoo.co.uk **81 C8**

### Banham Zoo
*Banham, Norfolk* Hundreds of animals – with giraffes, tigers, leopards, meerkats, penguins and more. Birds of the World displays. 🖥 www.zsea.org/banham **68 F3**

### Colchester Zoo *Colchester, Essex*
Established over 60 years ago and now home to many rare and endangered species, including big cats, primates and birds plus many invertebrates and fish species.
🖥 www.colchester-zoo.com **43 B5**

### Linton Zoo *Linton, Cambridgeshire*
Animals range from 'big cats' to kangaroos and wallabies, many of them endangered species. Also a collection of exotic birds in this family run zoo.
🖥 www.lintonzoo.com **55 E6**

### Paradise Wildlife Park *Broxbourne, Hertfordshire* A family-run wildlife park with a wide range of experiences and animals, including the largest green anaconda on-show in the UK. Houses a superb collection of 'big cats', including white lions, tigers and snow leopards.
🖥 www.pwpark.com **41 D6**

### Whipsnade Zoo *Dunstable, Central Bedfordshire* The UK's largest zoo and one of Europe's largest wildlife conservation parks, home to over 3,000 animals, many of which are endangered. Set in extensive grounds, visitors can walk, use the zoo's bus service or drive their own cars through many of the habitats. A narrow gauge railway, 'the Jumbo Express', also takes visitors round the park.
🖥 www.whipsnadezoo.org **40 C3**

## East Midlands

### Twycross Zoo *Little Orton, Leicestershire,* Zoo and conservation charity with hundreds of animals within a nature reserve. Talks and a range of activities are on offer.
🖥 https://twycrosszoo.org **63 D7**

## West Midlands

### Dudley Zoo & Castle *Dudley, West Midlands* The zoo is located within the grounds of Dudley Castle. Consisting of 12 modernist animal enclosures, the collection of large animals includes giraffes, tigers, lions, reindeer and snow leopards.
🖥 www.dudleyzoo.org.uk **62 E3**

### Hoo Zoo & Dinosaur World *Telford, Shropshire* Animal zoo and model dinosaur park. Visitors can walk through a lemur forest and help feed some of the range of exotic cat species.
🖥 www.hoo-zoo.com **61 C6**

## Wales

### Welsh Mountain Zoo *Colwyn Bay, Conwy* A zoological garden, education and conservation centre, with sea lion and penguin feeding displays. 🖥 www.welshmountainzoo.org **83 D8**

▼ Giraffes at the South Lakes Safari Zoo *Wellsie82 / Dreamstime*

▲ Sleepy seals in Edinburgh Zoo
John Keenan / Dreamstime

◄ A snow leopard in Northumberland Zoo John Blaise / Dreamstime

## North West

### Blackpool Zoo *Blackpool* An award-winning zoo, and one of the UK's best animal parks, with over 1,000 different species from around the world. 🖥 www.blackpoolzoo.org.uk **92 F3**

### Chester Zoo *Chester* One of the UK's largest zoos, providing seasonal events and animal encounter experiences.
🖥 www.chesterzoo.org **73 B8**

### South Lakes Safari Zoo *Lindal in Furness, Ulverston, Westmorland and Furness* A safari zoo near the Lake District, with interactive and educational experiences for visitors of all ages. 🖥 www.southlakessafarizoo.com **92 B2**

## North East

### Northumberland Zoo *Felton, Morpeth, Northumberland* A family-run, not-for-profit zoo with over 100 different species of mammals, birds, reptiles and invertebrates to see. Animal talks, including Birds of Prey flying displays, are hosted daily. 🖥 www.northumberlandzoo.co.uk **117 D7**

## Scotland

### Edinburgh Zoo *Corstorphine, Edinburgh* A 82-acre non-profit zoological park in Edinburgh, hosting keeper experiences, team-building activities and events. One of the first zoos to keep animals in spacious conditions rather than cages. 🖥 www.edinburghzoo.org.uk **120 B5**

# Outdoor activities

## Activity Centres

### South West

**Calvert Exmoor** *Wistlandpound, Kentisbury, Devon* An accessible residential activity centre and charity for people with physical, learning, behavioural, sensory and complex disabilities, alongside their families, friends and carers.
🖥 https://calvertexmoor.org.uk **20 E5**

### South East

**Walton Firs Activity Centre** *Cobham, Surrey* Adventure, activity and learning combine here, nestled within 36 acres of forest in Surrey.
🖥 https://waltonfirs.co.uk **27 C8**

### East of England

**Hilltop Outdoor Centre** *Sheringham, Norfolk* An award-winning outdoor adventure centre in Norfolk, offering adventure days for schools, families and groups.
🖥 www.hilltopoutdoorcentre.co.uk **81 C7**

### Wales

**Llangorse Multi Activity Centre** *Llangors, Powys* A multi-award-winning indoor and outdoor activity centre, set in the Breacon Beacons.
🖥 www.activityuk.com **35 B5**

## Cricket

### South East

**Lord's Cricket Ground** *St John's Wood, Westminster* Named after its founder, this is the largest cricket venue in the UK, home to the Middlesex Cricket Club. 🖥 www.lords.org **41 F5**

**The Oval** *Kennington, Lambeth* One of the most popular cricket grounds in the UK, home to the Surrey County Cricket Club. The final Test match of the season is traditionally played here.
🖥 www.kiaoval.com **28 B4**

**The Rose Bowl** *West End, Southampton* Also known as The Ageas Bowl, this is a hotel complex and cricket ground in West Hampshire.
🖥 www.ageasbowl.com **15 C5**

### North West

**Edgbaston Cricket Ground** *Edgbaston Rd, Birmingham* The only English Cricket ground, apart from Lord's, to host an ICC ODI final, this lively cricket ground is home to the Warwickshire County Cricket Club.
🖥 https://edgbaston.com **62 F4**

**Old Trafford** *Talbot Rd, Old Trafford, Manchester* Current home of Lancashire County Cricket Club, with the quickest cricket pitch in the UK.
🖥 https://emiratesoldtrafford. lancashirecricket.co.uk **87 E6**

## Cycling

### South West

**Forest of Dean Cycle Centre** *Cannop, Coleford, Gloucestershire* A cycle centre with activities for all ages and abilities, including the Family Cycle Trail, skills areas, singletrack trails and demanding downhill runs. Nearby, Beechenhurst Lodge has a family activity trail, sculpture trail and refreshments.
🖥 www.forestryengland.uk/forest-dean-cycle-centre **36 C3**

### South East

**Lee Valley VeloPark** *Queen Elizabeth Olympic Park, Stratford* Track cycling in the velodrome, road-circuit racing, mountain bike trails and the re-modelled Olympic BMX track.
🖥 www.visitleevalley.org.uk/lee-valley-velopark **41 F6**

### Wales

**The Geraint Thomas National Velodrome of Wales** *Velodrome Way, Newport* An indoor cycling arena, previously known as the Wales National Velodrome, home to Olympic, Paralympic and Commonwealth Games athletes. 🖥 www.newportlive.co.uk/en/venues/geraint-thomas-national-velodrome-wales **35 F7**

### North West

**The National Cycling Centre** *Stuart St, Manchester* Britain's first indoor cycling track, now the headquarters of British Cycling, Team Sky and part of the National Cycling Centre. Outdoor MTB Trails at Clayton Vale. 🖥 www.nationalcyclingcentre.com **87 E6**

▲ Mountain biking in Wales
Tosca Weijers / Dreamstime

### Yorkshire and the Humber

**Dales Bike** *Fremington, North Yorkshire* The centre of cycling and mountain biking in the Yorkshire Dales National Park, offering e-bike, hybrid bike, mountain bike and road bike hire.
🖥 www.dalesbikecentre.co.uk **101 E5**

## Football

### South East

**Wembley Stadium** *Wembley, Brent* The largest football stadium in the UK. It hosts major football matches, including home matches of the England national football team, and the FA Cup Final. 🖥 www.wembleystadium.com **40 F4**

## Golf

### South East

**Royal St George's Golf Club** *Sandwich, Kent* Site of many Open Championships, with fine dining at its clubhouse.
🖥 www.royalstgeorges.com **31 D7**

### North West

**Royal Birkdale** *Southport, Sefton* A renowned golf course, founded in 1889 and a regular venue of The Open, with green fees for non-members.
🖥 https://royalbirkdale.com **85 C4**

**Royal Lytham and St Annes** *Lytham St Annes, Lancashire* A premier links courses, host to eleven Open Championships, two Ryder Cups and several other major tournaments.
🖥 www.royallytham.org **85 B4**

### Scotland

**Carnoustie** *Carnoustie, Angus* One of the toughest golf links in the world, and host of The Senior Open in 2024.
🖥 www.carnoustiegolflinks.com **135 F5**

**Muirfield** *Gullane, East Lothian* A privately owned golf links, and one of the golf courses used in rotation for The Open Championship.
🖥 www.muirfield.org.uk **129 F6**

**St Andrews** Golf had been played in this town on the coast of Fife for over 600 years. With seven golf courses, it is the largest golf complex in Europe.
🖥 https://standrews.com **129 C7**

## Hang-gliding and Paragliding

### South East

**Airsports Sussex** *Mile Oak Rd, Brighton and Hove* An airsports centre, offering hang gliding lessons and experiences.
🖥 www.airsportssussex.co.uk **17 D6**

### East Midlands

**Parapente Paragliding** *New Mills, Derbyshire* One of the oldest established paragliding schools, and has been teaching students to paraglide since 1987. 🖥 www.fly-paragliders.co.uk **87 F7**

**Peak Airsports** *New Whittington, Chesterfield, Derbyshire* A fully accredited paragliding school located in the Peak District, providing a range of taster days, courses and tandem flights.
🖥 https://peakairsports.com **76 B4**

▼ St Andrews Golf Course Fintastique / Dreamstime

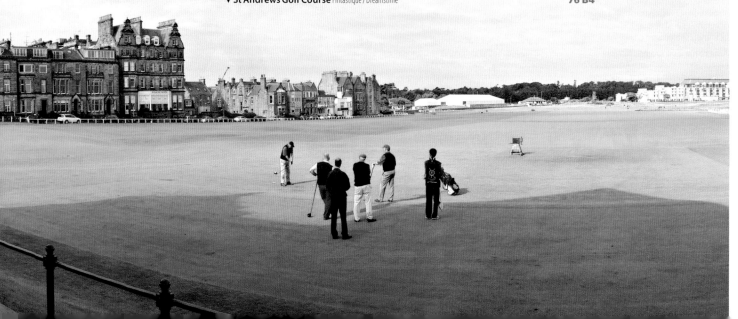

## Wales

**Axis Paragliding and Paramotoring**
*Abergavenny, Monmouthshire*
A paragliding and paramotoring school located in scenic South East Wales. https://paraglide.co.uk **35 C6**

# Horseracing
## South West

**Cheltenham Racecourse** *Cheltenham, Gloucestershire* The home of Jump Racing and host to National Hunt horse racing. The biggest event of the year is the Cheltenham Festival held in March. www.thejockeyclub.co.uk/cheltenham **37 B6**

## South East

**Ascot Racecourse** *Ascot, Windsor and Maidenhead* A dual-purpose British racecourse, running 13 of Britain's 36 annual flat Group 1 horse races and three Grade 1 Jumps races. www.ascot.com **27 C7**

## North West

**Aintree Racecourse** *Aintree, Liverpool* This racecourse has hosted the Grand National steeplechase annually since 1839. www.thejockeyclub.co.uk **85 E4**

## Yorkshire and the Humber

**Doncaster Racecourse** *Bawtry Rd, Doncaster* One of Britain's oldest horse racecourses. There are typically 37 race fixtures here annually. www.doncaster-racecourse.co.uk **89 D7**

## Scotland

**Musselburgh Racecourse**
*Musselburgh, East Lothian* Flat racing in summer, National Hunt racing during winter. www.musselburgh-racecourse.co.uk **121 B6**

# Horseriding
## South East

**Brockenhurst Riding Stables**
*Brockenhurst, Hampshire* A stables that takes visitors on horse rides directly into the New Forest. Pony rides can also be organized for special occasions. www.brockenhurstridingstables.co.uk **14 D4**

**Wimbledon Village Stables**
*Wimbledon, Merton* An award-winning stables with 25 well-schooled horses and fully qualified instructors offering lessons and courses for members and non-members. www.wvstables.com **28 B3**

## East of England

**Magpie Centre** *Runcton Holme, King's Lynn, Norfolk* Run by the West Norfolk Riding for the Disabled Association, this centre provides activities such as riding and carriage driving to people of all ages, with any disability. https://rda-westnorfolk.org.uk **67 D6**

▼ Horses crossing the river in Lower Slaughter, Cotswolds
Chun Ju Wu / Dreamstime

## Scotland

**Gleneagles Equestrian School**
*Auchterarder, Perth & Kinross* A riding school in Scotland, with lessons dedicated to fine tuning advanced techniques for showjumping, cross-country, dressage and more. https://gleneagles.com/pursuits/riding **127 C8**

# Motorsports
## South East

**Brands Hatch** *West Kingsdown, Kent* A motor racing circuit with bike racing, car racing and MSV driving experiences. www.brandshatch.co.uk **29 C6**

**Thruxton Circuit** *Andover, Hampshire* The fastest racetrack in the country, with a karting centre and driving experiences. https://thruxtonracing.co.uk **25 E7**

## East Midlands

**Donington Park Circuit** *Castle Donington, Derby* The oldest motorsport circuit in the UK that is still in operation; racing first began here in 1931. www.donington-park.co.uk **63 B8**

**Silverstone** *Towcester, West Northamptonshire* Home to the British Grand Prix and FIA Formula One World Championship since 1950, as well as numerous automobile events. There is also the Silverstone museum on-site. www.silverstone.co.uk **52 E4**

## Wales

**Trac Mônglesey Circuit** *Llangwyfan-isaf, Anglesey* A motor racing circuit set dramatically on the coast for all skill levels. It hosts events including car racing, motorcycle racing, car sprints, stage rallies. Both Porsche and Lotus have a dedicated track day here. www.angleseycircuit.co.uk **82 E3**

## North West

**Aintree Motor Racing Circuit** *Aintree, Liverpool* The UK's only purpose-built 3-mile Grand Prix motor racing circuit, offering 'track days' open to the public to try out this historic track. www.liverpoolmotorclub.com **85 E4**

▼ A paraglider over Luskentyre Bay on the Isle of Harris in the Outer Hebrides
Alan5766 / Dreamstime

# Orienteering
## Scotland

**Glenmore Lodge, National Outdoor Training Centre** *Glenmore Lodge, Aviemore, Highland* The Scottish centre for orienteering, offering information, news and events about the sport across the country is based at the Lodge. Other organisations representing outdoor activities are also based here. A number of training courses are available. www.scottish-orienteering.org **139 C5**

# Rugby
## South East

**Twickenham Stadium** *Twickenham, Richmond* The official home of rugby in the UK, with a World Rugby Museum, stadium tours and store. www.englandrugby.com/twickenham **28 B2**

## Wales

**Principality Stadium** *Westgate St, Cardiff* The national rugby stadium of Wales and the third largest stadium in Britain. www.principalitystadium.wales **22 B3**

## Scotland

**Murrayfield Stadium** *Roseburn St, Edinburgh* The largest stadium in Scotland, home to the Scottish Rugby Union. https://scottishrugby.org **120 B5**

# Shooting
## South West

**Barbury Shooting School** *Wroughton, Swindon* A clay pigeon shooting school, with other activities including archery, air rifles and simulated game days. Located high on the Marlborough Downs at Barbury Castle Country Park. www.barburyshootingschool.com **25 B6**

**The Tunnel** *Axminster Road, Charmouth, Dorset* The UK's premier shooting centre and miniature rifle club, providing a range of shooting experiences. www.thetunnel.co.uk **11 E8**

▲ Paddle boarders at Walsham Lock on the River Wey, Surrey Ian Shaw / Alamy

## South East

**National Shooting Centre**
*Bisley, Woking, Surrey* The UK's largest shooting complex with several ranges covering different disciplines. The site has some relocated historic buildings, dating from the Victorian era.
🖳 www.bisleyshooting.co.uk **27 D7**

## East of England

**Barrow Sporting Clays** *Risby, Bury St Edmunds, Suffolk* A premier clay pigeon ground, recognised by the Clay Pigeon Shooting Association.
🖳 www.cpsa.co.uk **55 C8**

## Yorkshire and the Humber

**Coniston Shooting Ground** *Coniston Cold, Skipton, North Yorkshire* Situated on a 1,400-acre Coniston Estate near Skipton, this clag-pigeon shooting ground is CPSA Premier Plus meaning it is one of the best in the UK. 🖳 www. conistonshootingground.co.uk **93 D8**

# Skiing
## North West

**Lake District Ski Club** *Glenridding, Westmorland & Furness* Founded in 1936, this ski club offers up to 60 days of skiing a year, depending on conditions, across nine slopes in the Lake District National Park. Day tickets are available. There are ski lift and basic facilites for experienced skiers. Located an hour's walk from Genridding.
🖳 www.ldscsnowski.co.uk **99 C5**

## North East

**Weardale Ski Club** *Daddry Shield, Weardale, Durham* A club for experienced skiers promoting natural snow sports in the North Pennines and, an area with the longest ski tow in England. 🖳 www.skiweardale.com **110 F2**

## Scotland

**Glenshee** *Old Military Rd, Braemar, Aberdeenshire* Scotland's largest ski area with 22 lifts allowing access to 25 miles / 40 km of pistes on four mountains on either side of the road linking Blairgowrie and Braemar.
🖳 www.ski-glenshee.co.uk **133 B8**

**The Lecht** *Tomintoul, Moray* A skiing area more suitable for beginners than some others, located high on the road between Cock Bridge and Tomintoul, one of the highest main roads in Britain. The Lecht Ski Centre now offers activities all year round.
🖳 www.lecht.co.uk **139 C8**

# Surfing
## North East

**Tynemouth surfing** *Tynemouth, North Tyneside* Long Sands at the foot of the cliffs at Tynemouth is one of the best places for surfing in the North East. Surf schools offer tuition and equipment hire.
🖳 https://tynemouthsurf.co.uk/surf-school/ and www.longsandsurf.com **111 B6**

# Watersports
## South West

**Lizard Adventure** *Lizard, Cornwall* An outdoor adventure provider, with six watersports activities for visitors to choose from.
🖳 https://lizardadventure.co.uk **3 E6**

**Newquay Activity Centre**
*Newquay, Cornwall* An award-winning activity centre for watersports, offering kayaking, stand-up paddle boarding, body-boarding, coastal adventures and more. 🖳 https:// newquayactivitycentre.co.uk **4 C3**

**Rock Solid Coasteering**
*Maidencombe, Torquay, Devon* Coasteering specialists in South Devon, offering extreme experiences such as cliff jumping, bouldering, caving and extreme boating.
🖳 https://rocksolidcoasteering.uk **7 C7**

## South East

**Docksailing and Watersports Centre** *Isle of Dogs, Tower Hamlets* An award-winning, purpose-built water sports facility and training centre, providing adult activities, youth activities and open-water swimming.
🖳 www.dswc.org **28 B4**

**Duck-2-Water** *Ocean Village Marina, Southampton* A premier powerboat training centre offering boat tuition, RYA training and theory. 🖳 https:// www.duck-2-water.co.uk/ **14 C5**

## East of England

**Curve Water Sports** *St Osyth, Essex* An aqua park, wakeboarding, kayaking and paddle boarding centre in Essex
🖳 https://curvewatersports.co.uk **43 C7**

**Hunstanton Watersports** *Hunstanton, Norfolk* A professional kitesurfing and paddle boarding provider, with over 20 years of experience. 🖳 www. hunstantonwatersports.com **80 C2**

**Lee Valley White Water Centre**
*Waltham Cross, Hertfordshire* Offers white water rafting on the 2012 Olympic slalom course to family paddling on the lake. 🖳 www.better.org.uk/leisure-centre/lee-valley/white-water-centre **41 D6**

## East Midlands

**Carsington Sports and Leisure Activity Centre** *Carsington, Ashbourne* Multiple water-based activities at Carsington Water, one of Britain's largest reservoirs. Try out stand paddle boarding, kayaking and windsurfing. There is also cycle hire and fly-fishing from boats.
🖳 www.visitpeakdistrict.com **76 D2**

## West Midlands

**Shropshire Raft Tours** *Coalport Rd, Ironbridge, Telford* A canoe, kayak, mini-raft and stand up paddle board hire, located along the River Severn. 🖳 www. shropshirerafttours.co.uk **61 D6**

# Wild Swimming
## South East

**Freshwater Bay** *Freshwater, Isle of Wight* One of the most picturesque beaches for wild swimming on the Isle of Wight. 🖳 www.visitisleofwight.co.uk **14 F4**

## South East

**Hampstead Heath** *Hampstead Heath, Camden* Swimming ponds including three natural bathing ponds and one 60m Lido. Set within 790 acres of ancient heath. 🖳 www.cityoflondon. gov.uk/things-to-do/green-spaces/hampstead-heath **41 F5**

## Wales

**Pen-ffordd-goch Pond** *Blaenavon, Torfaen* A man-made pond, built in the early 19th century, has become a beauty spot for swimmers and walkers alike. Near Pwll Du, on the hill above Blaenavon. 🖳 www. visitmonmouthshire.com **35 D6**

**Sgwd Gwladys** *Pontneddfechan, Powys* A swimming area surrounded by woodland with a 7 ft / 2m high waterfall, in the Brecon Beacons National Park.
🖳 www.wildswimming.co.uk **34 D2**

## Scotland

**Stroan Loch** *Mossdale, New Galloway, Dumfries and Galloway* A freshwater lake within one of the largest forests in the UK. Swimming is also popular in the nearby larger Loch Ken. **106 B3**

▼ Surfing at North Fistral, Newquay, Cornwall David Pick / Alamy

# Eccentric Britain

## South West

**Cheese-Rolling** *Cooper's Hill, Great Witcombe, Gloucester* Traditional race, dating back at least to the early 1800s, in which participants run down Cooper's Hill in an attempt to catch a large wheel of Double Gloucester cheese. **37 C5**

**Stonehenge Solstice** *Amesbury, Wiltshire* Celebrations on the summer and winter solstices, when the huge standing stones at this prehistoric monument align with the sun at sunrise and sunset respectively. It is a gathering point for Druids and other pagans. **25 E6**

## South East

**Bonfire Night** *Lewes, East Sussex* Town-wide event, where members of 'bonfire societies' parade through the streets in costumes, bearing burning crosses and effigies, often of contemporary figures, which are burned on the bonfires, or blown up with fireworks. 🖥 www.lewesbonfirecelebrations.com **17 C8**

**Pancake Race** *Olney, Milton Keynes* Shrove Tuesday event when local Olney women race through the streets with a frying pan and pancake which must be tossed at the beginning and end. The race is said to date from 1445. **53 D6**

## East of England

**House in the Clouds** *Thorpeness, Suffolk* Water tower, 70ft/21m tall, built in the 1920s and disguised as a house. It appears to float above the surrounding trees. The water tank was removed in 1979 and the tower is now purely residential. **57 D8**

**Mud Race** *Maldon, Essex* Annual race in which competitors wade across and back through the mud and shallow water of the River Blackwater at low tide. 🖥 https://maldonmudrace.com **42 D4**

## East Midlands

**Royal Shrovetide Football** *Ashbourne, Derbyshire* Match played on Shrove Tuesday and Ash Wednesday through the whole of Ashbourne, with thousands of players, goals three miles apart, and a duration of up to eight hours each day. **75 E8**

**World Conker Championships** *Southwick, North Northamptonshire* Annual tournament in which competitors of all ages and from all over the world compete to smash each other's conker. 🖥 www.worldconkerchampionships.com **65 E7**

## West Midlands

**Hawkstone Park & Follies** *Weston-under-Redcastle, Shrewsbury, Shropshire* Landscaped parkland surrounding a ruined castle; it is dotted with follies that can be explored, including a tower, arches, a bridge, a 100ft/30m-tall monument and cave grottos. 🖥 www.hawkstoneparkfollies.co.uk **61 B5**

**Well Dressing** *Endon, Leek, Staffordshire* Tradition of decorating wells with artworks that are created mosaic-like by hand on large wooden frames, made from natural materials such as petals, leaves and moss. A festival follows the installation of the artwork. 🖥 www.enjoystaffordshire.com **75 D6**

## Wales

**Bog Snorkelling** *Llanwrtyd Wells, Powys* Annual event in which competitors of all ages, some in fancy dress, take part in a swimming race through a peat bog. Spectators can enjoy the carnival-like atmosphere. 🖥 www.visitwales.com **47 E7**

▲ The Up Helly Aa festival on Shetland
konstantin belovtov / Shutterstock

◀ The annual cheese rolling contest on Coopers Hill, Gloucestershire Guy Corbishley/Alamy

▲ Maldon Mud Race, Essex SOPA Images Limited/Alamy
▶ World Gravy Wrestling Championships PA Images / Alamy

**Portmeirion** *Gwynedd* Unusual Italianate-style village built between 1925 and 1973 on a steep cliff overlooking the Dwyryd estuary. It is known for its colourful and fanciful folly-type buildings and lush gardens. 🖥 https://portmeirion.wales **71 D6**

## North West

**Crab Fair & Gurning Competition** *Egremont, Cumberland* Annual festival originally celebrating harvest. Events include an outdoor concert, an apple cart parade and unusual competitions, including the world-famous 'gurning' championships, in which participants compete to pull the most grotesque face. 🖥 www.egremontcrabfair.com **98 C2**

**World Gravy Wrestling Championships** *Rossendale, Rawtenstall, Lancashire* Competition in which contestants, some in fancy dress, wrestle in a pool of gravy. The short bouts are scored on entertainment value as well as skill. **87 B6**

## Yorkshire & the Humber

**Jorvik Viking Festival** *York* A week-long, city-wide event celebrating the region's Norse heritage. There are hands-on activities in the Viking Encampment, a Viking Banquet, competitions, and a march of warriors through the streets. 🖥 https://jorvikvikingfestival.co.uk **95 D8**

**Scarecrow Festival** *Kettlewell, Skipton, North Yorkshire* A display of hundreds of scarecrows, often created to a particular theme and some extremely elaborate are scattered around the village. A trail guides visitors to the scarecrows, and there are stalls and other activities. 🖥 www.kettlewellscarecrowfestival.co.uk **94 B2**

## North East

**Hedley Barrel Race** *Hedley on the Hill, Northumberland* Easter Monday competition in which teams of three race up a steep hill carrying an empty beer barrel. 🖥 https://calendarcustoms.com/articles/hedley-barrel-race/ **110 D3**

**North East Skinny Dip** *Amble, Northumberland* Annual event, around the autumn equinox, in which usually more than a thousand people take a brief, naked dip in the North Sea at Druridge Bay. **117 E8**

## Scotland

**Stonehaven Fireballs** *Stonehaven, Aberdeenshire* New Year's Eve ceremony in which local people swing balls of fire around their heads at midnight to burn off the old year's bad spirits. It is preceded by a street parade and followed by fireworks. 🖥 www.stunningstonehaven.com **141 F7**

**Up Helly Aa** *Lerwick, Shetland* Fire festival held every January in which squads of 'guizers' disguised in costumes take part in a torchlit procession that culminates in the burning of a specially built Viking-style galley. 🖥 www.uphellyaa.org **160 J6**

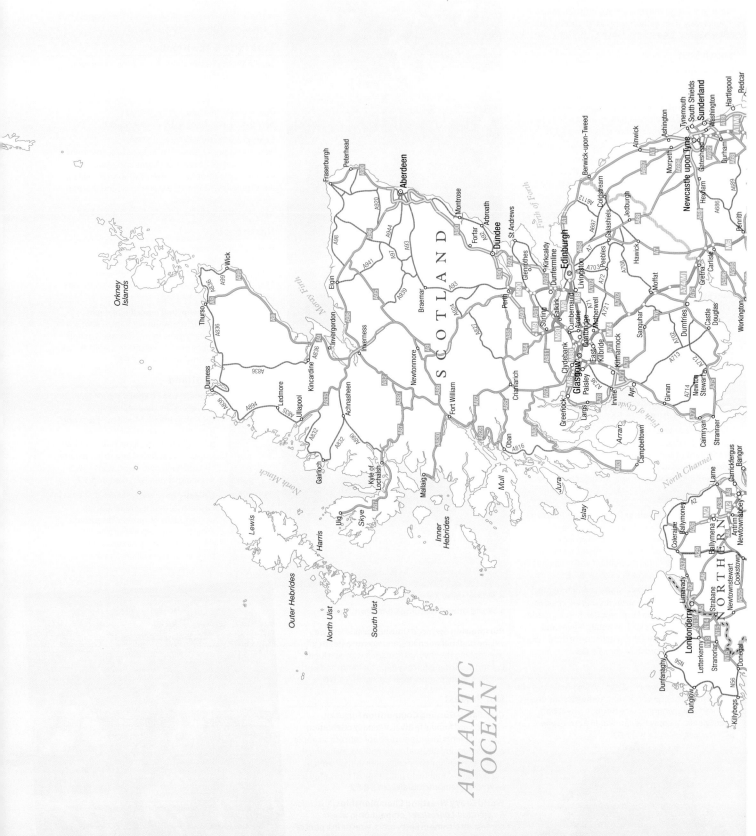

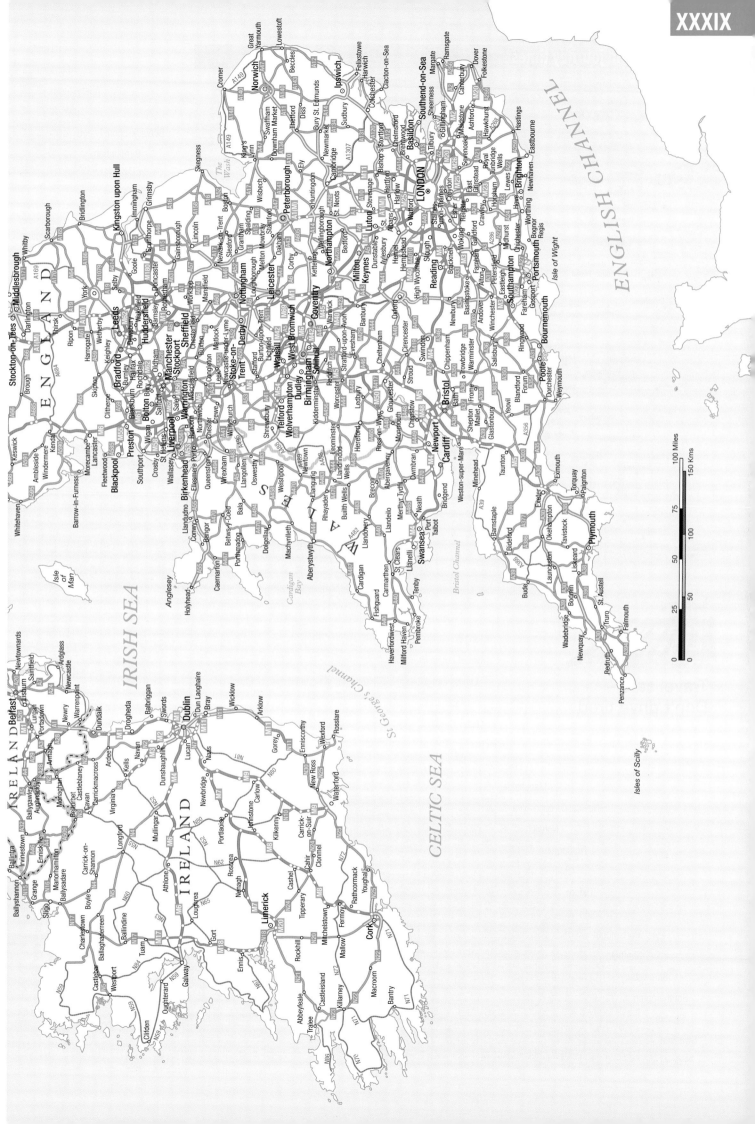

# Distances and journey times

## How to use this table

Distances are shown in miles and kilometres with estimated journey times in hours and minutes.

For example: the distance between Dover and Fishguard is 331 miles or 533 kilometres with an estimated journey time of 6 hours, 20 minutes.

Estimated driving times are based on an average speed of 60mph on Motorways and 40mph on other roads. Drivers should allow extra time when driving at peak periods or through areas likely to be congested.

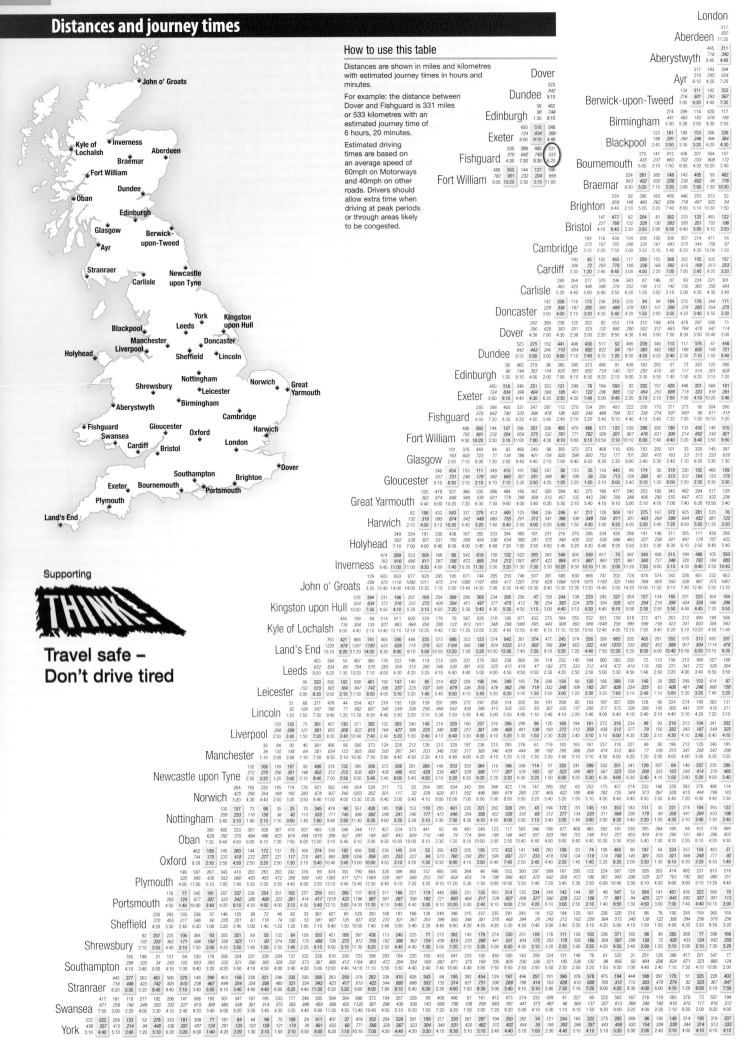

Supporting

THINK!

Travel safe –
Don't drive tired

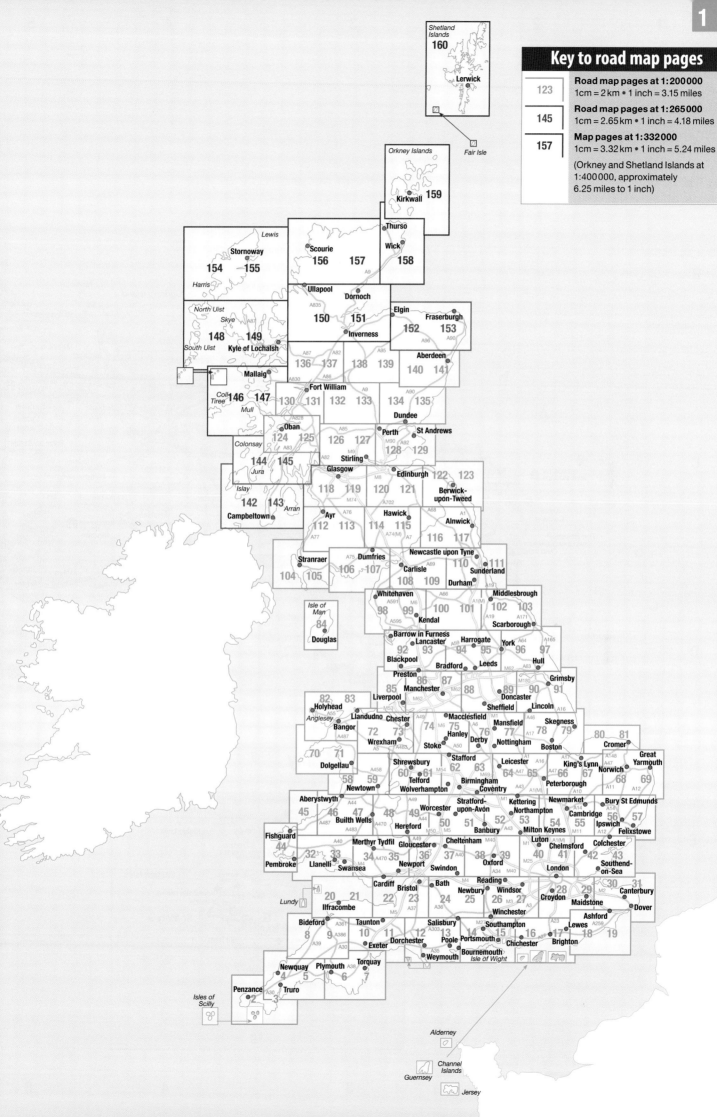

Shetland
Islands
**160**
Lerwick

## Key to road map pages

| | |
|---|---|
| 123 | **Road map pages at 1:200000**<br>1cm = 2 km • 1 inch = 3.15 miles |
| 145 | **Road map pages at 1:265000**<br>1cm = 2.65 km • 1 inch = 4.18 miles |
| 157 | **Map pages at 1:332000**<br>1cm = 3.32 km • 1 inch = 5.24 miles<br>(Orkney and Shetland Islands at<br>1:400000, approximately<br>6.25 miles to 1 inch) |

Fair Isle

Orkney Islands
Kirkwall **159**

Lewis
Stornoway
Thurso
**154 155**
Scourie
Wick
**156 157 158**
Harris
Ullapool
Dornoch
North Uist
**150 151**
Skye
Elgin
Fraserburgh
**148 149**
Inverness
**152 153**
South Uist
Kyle of Lochalsh
Aberdeen
Mallaig
**136 137 138 139**
**140 141**
Coll
Tiree
**146 147**
Fort William
**130 131 132 133 134 135**
Mull
Dundee
Oban
**124 125 126 127**
Perth St Andrews
Colonsay
**128 129**
**144 145**
Stirling
Jura
Glasgow
Islay
**118 119 120 121 122 123**
Edinburgh
**142 143**
Berwick-
upon-Tweed
Campbeltown
Arran
Ayr
Hawick
**112 113 114 115**
Alnwick
**116 117**
Stranraer
Dumfries
Newcastle upon Tyne
**104 105 106 107**
Carlisle
**110 111**
Sunderland
**108 109**
Durham
Whitehaven
Middlesbrough
Isle of
Man
**98 99 100 101 102 103**
**84**
Kendal
Scarborough
Douglas
Barrow in Furness
Harrogate
**92 93 94 95 96 97**
Blackpool
York
Lancaster
Bradford
Leeds
Hull
Preston
**85 86 87 88**
Grimsby
Manchester
**89 90 91**
Liverpool
Doncaster
**82 83**
Sheffield
Lincoln
Holyhead
Macclesfield
Anglesey
Llandudno
Chester
Skegness
Bangor
**72 73 74 75 76 77 78 79**
Mansfield
**80 81**
Hanley
Derby
Wrexham
Stoke
Nottingham
Boston
Cromer
**70 71**
Great
Yarmouth
Dolgellau
Stafford
Leicester
King's Lynn
**60 61 62 63 64 65 66 67 68 69**
Telford
Shrewsbury
Norwich
**58 59**
Birmingham
Peterborough
Newtown
Wolverhampton
Coventry
Aberystwyth
Kettering
Newmarket
Bury St Edmunds
**45 46 47 48 49**
Worcester
Stratford-
upon-Avon
Northampton
Cambridge
Ipswich
Builth Wells
**50 51 52 53 54 55 56 57**
Hereford
Banbury
Milton Keynes
Felixstowe
Fishguard
Luton
Colchester
**44**
Merthyr Tydfil
Gloucester
Cheltenham
Oxford
**40 41 42 43**
Pembroke
**32 33 34 35 36 37 38 39**
Chelmsford
Llanelli
Newport
London
Southend-
Swansea
Swindon
on-Sea
Cardiff
Bristol
Bath
Reading
**20 21 22 23 24 25 26 27 28 29 30 31**
Newbury
Windsor
Croydon
Lundy
Ilfracombe
Maidstone
Canterbury
Winchester
Ashford
Dover
Bideford
Taunton
Salisbury
Southampton
Lewes
**8 9 10 11 12 13 14 15 16 17 18 19**
Exeter
Dorchester
Poole
Portsmouth
Chichester
Brighton
Weymouth
Bournemouth
Newquay
Plymouth
Torquay
Isle of Wight
**4 5 6 7**
Penzance
Truro
**2 3**
Isles of
Scilly

Alderney

Channel
Islands
Guernsey
Jersey

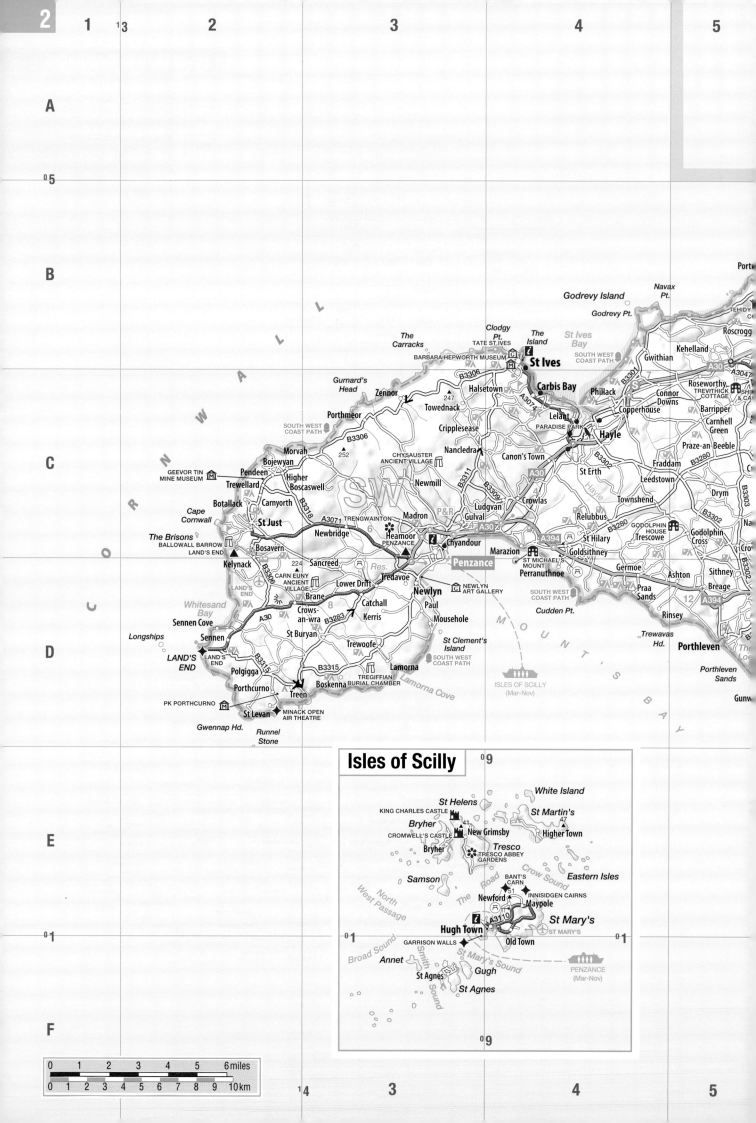

A

B

C

D

E

F

Godrevy Island
Navax Pt.
Godrevy Pt.
Port
Roscrogg
TEHIDY C
Kehelland
The
Clodgy
Pt.
St Ives Bay
SOUTH WEST COAST PATH
Gwithian
The Carracks
TATE ST IVES
The Island
BARBARA HEPWORTH MUSEUM
**St Ives**
Roseworthy
TREVITHICK COTTAGE
SH
& CA
A30
A3047
Gurnard's Head
B3306
Halsetown
Carbis Bay
Phillack
Connor Downs
Barripper
Zennor
A3074
Lelant
Copperhouse
Carnhell Green
Porthmeor
247
Towednack
PARADISE PARK
**Hayle**
Praze-an-Beeble
SOUTH WEST COAST PATH
B3306
Cripplesease
St Erth
Fraddam
B3280
Morvah
252
Nancledra
Canon's Town
B3302
Leedstown
Drym
Bojewyan
CHYSAUSTER ANCIENT VILLAGE
Newmill
B3311
A30
Townshend
B3302
GEEVOR TIN MINE MUSEUM
Pendeen
Higher Boscaswell
SW
B3309
Crowlas
Relubbus
Townshend
Trewellard
Ludgvan
P&R
St Hilary
GODOLPHIN HOUSE
Trescowe
Godolphin Cross
Carnyorth
B3318
TRENGWAINTON
Madron
Gulval
A30
A394
Goldsithney
Sithney
Botallack
A3071
Heamoor
PENZANCE
Chyandour
Marazion
ST MICHAEL'S MOUNT
Germoe
Ashton
Breage
Cape Cornwall
**St Just**
Newbridge
**Penzance**
Perranuthnoe
A394
The Brisons
BALLOWALL BARROW
LAND'S END
Bosavern
224
Sancreed
Res.
Tredavoe
**Newlyn**
NEWLYN ART GALLERY
SOUTH WEST COAST PATH
Praa Sands
Rinsey
Kelynack
B3306
CARN EUNY ANCIENT VILLAGE
Lower Drift
Paul
Cudden Pt.
LAND'S END
Brane
Catchall
Mousehole
Trewavas Hd.
**Porthleven**
Whitesand Bay
A30
8
Crows-an-wra
B3283
Kerris
St Clement's Island
Porthleven Sands
The Lo
Sennen Cove
St Buryan
Trewoofe
SOUTH WEST COAST PATH
Longships
Sennen
ISLES OF SCILLY (Mar-Nov)
Gunw
**LAND'S END**
LAND'S END
B3315
Lamorna
Polgigga
B3315
Boskenna
TREGIFFIAN BURIAL CHAMBER
Lamorna Cove
Porthcurno
Treen
PK PORTHCURNO
St Levan
MINACK OPEN AIR THEATRE
Gwennap Hd.
Runnel Stone

# Isles of Scilly

9

St Helens
White Island
KING CHARLES CASTLE
St Martin's
**Bryher**
41
Higher Town
CROMWELL'S CASTLE
New Grimsby
47
Bryher
**Tresco**
TRESCO ABBEY GARDENS
Samson
Eastern Isles
North West Passage
The Road
BANT'S CARN
Crow Sound
Newford
51
INNISIDGEN CAIRNS
Maypole
**St Mary's**
1
Hugh Town
ST MARY'S
1
Broad Sound
GARRISON WALLS
Old Town
PENZANCE (Mar-Nov)
Annet
St Mary's Sound
Smith Sound
Gugh
St Agnes
St Agnes

9

0  1  2  3  4  5  6 miles
0  1  2  3  4  5  6  7  8  9  10km

4  3  4  5

## Jersey

3½ miles to 1 inch

*JERSEY*

**A**

**B**

**C**

**D**

**E**

**F**

**G**

5  6  7  8  9

TR

ENGLISH CHANNEL

Maltman's Hill
Smarden
Haffenden Quarter
Wissenden
Standen
Tanden
High Halden
Biddenden Vineyards
St Michael's
Henghurst
Shirkoak
Woodchurch
Shadoxhurst
Stubbs Cross
Kingsnorth
Cheeseman's Green
Bromley Green
Aldington Frith
Bonnington
Clap Hill
Aldington
Court-at-Street
Sellindge
Sellindge Lees
Smeeth
Mersham
Sevington
Willesborough
Ashford
Great Chart
Hinxhill
Willesborough Lees
Brabourne
Stowting
Brabourne Lees
Lyminge
Postling
Etchinghill
Paddlesworth
Stanford
Beachborough
Newingreen
Pedlinge
Lympne
West Hythe
Saltwood
Brockhill
Palmarsh
Burmarsh
Hythe
Sandgate
Folkestone
Cheriton
Newington
Hawkinge
Capel le Ferne
West Hougham
Densole
Drellingore
Swingfield Minnis
Ottinge
Rhodes Minnis
Lymbridge Green
Elham
Snave
Snargate
Ivychurch
Brenzett
Brookland
Old Romney
New Romney
Lydd
Littlestone on Sea
Romney Sands
Greatstone on Sea
Lydd on Sea
St Mary's Bay
St Mary in the Marsh
Dymchurch
Newchurch
ROMNEY MARSH
Romney Warren
Denge Marsh
DUNGENESS
Denge Beach
THE OLD LIGHTHOUSE
Tenterden
Small Hythe
Leigh Green
Reading Street
Appledore Heath
Appledore
Stone
Peening Quarter
Wittersham
Ham Green
The Stocks
ISLE OF OXNEY
Four Oaks
Iden
Houghton Green
Playden
Rye Foreign
Peasmarsh
Rye
Rye Harbour
Camber
Winchelsea
Winchelsea Beach
Icklesham
Pett
Cliff End
Fairlight
Fairlight Cove
Udimore
Brede
East Guldeford
Walland Marsh
Rye Bay
KENT & EAST SUSSEX RAILWAY
COLONEL STEPHENS RAILWAY MUSEUM
SOUTH OF ENGLAND RARE BREEDS CEN
HAM STREET WOODS
HORNE'S PLACE CHAPEL
SMALLHYTHE PLACE
AERONAUTICAL MUSEUM
ROMNEY MARSH VISITOR CENTRE
ROMNEY, HYTHE AND DYMCHURCH RAILWAY
PORT LYMPNE WILD ANIMAL PARK AND GARDENS
KENT BATTLE OF BRITAIN MUSEUM
ELHAM VALLEY RLY MUS
LYDD (LONDON ASHFORD)
LYDD INTERNATIONAL RACEWAY
RYE HERITAGE CENTRE
CAMBER CASTLE
WINCHELSEA COURT HALL MUSEUM
CONNINGBROOK LAKE
GODINTON HOUSE
CHANNEL TUNNEL
CLIFF LIFT
MARTELLO TOWER
NORTH DOWNS WAY
Royal Military Canal
E. Stour
Tillingham
HASTINGS CAVES & MUSEUMS
AQUARIUM

**1**   **2**   **3**   **4**   **5**

A

<sub>1</sub>8

B

**5**
²2

North West
Point    North East
Point

LUNDY MARINE
NATURE RESERVE    *LUNDY*

C    142▲

⛴
ILFRACOMBE
BIDEFORD
(April-Oct)

South West
Point    Surf
Point

²1
¹4

SS

D

*NORTH DEVON*

⛴
LUNDY
(April-Oct)    HELE CORN MILL

Rillage Pt.    Combe Martin
Bay    Trentisho

**Ilfracombe**    ILFRACOMBE
MUSEUM    WATERMOUTH CASTLE    Girt Down    349▲    Heale

Bull Pt.    Hele
Lee    206    Berrynarbor    **Combe
Martin**    10    WILDLIFE & DINOSAUR PARK

*Rockham Bay*    Whitestone    Slade    A361    Sterridge    269    A3123    Kentisbury

Morte Point    Trimstone    *Berry
Down*    Berry Down
Cross    Patchole    Kentisbury
Ford

E    Woolacombe    B3343    Cheglinch    Bittadon    East Down    EXMO

*MORTE
BAY*    210    Dean    West
Down    Churchill    Arlington
ARLINGTON
COURT

Woolacombe Sand    North
Buckland    B3230    Loxhore    Knightac
SOUTH WEST
COAST PATH    Pickwell    Nethercott    Milltown    198    Shirwell

Baggy Pt.    Putsborough    Halsinger    Muddiford    Shirwell
Cross    Stoke
Rivers    B
F

*Croyde Bay*    Georgeham    Knowle    Marwood    Guineaford    Yeo

Croyde    Darracott    MARWOOD
HILL GARDENS    Kingsheanton    Prixford

B3231    158    Lobb    Pippacott
Saunton    14    **Braunton**    Heanton
Puncharoon    Ashford    Burridge    Goodleigh    Gunn

ELLIOT GALLERY    Wrafton    Chivenor    A361    **Barnstaple**

*Saunton
Sands*    TOLL    Pilton    MUSEUM OF BARNSTAPLE
& NORTH DEVON

F    *Braunton
Burrows*    Fremington    P&R    Newport    Westacott

⛴
LUNDY
(April-Oct)    Yelland    B3233    Bickington    Landkey
Instow    A39    Bishops
Tawton    Swimbridge
Newland    Bu

NORTH DEVON
MARITIME MUSEUM    TAPELEY    Swimbridge

*BIDEFORD BAY*    NORTHAM BURROWS    TAPELEY
PARK GDNS

**9**    **9**

**Appledore**    Westward Ho!

¹3    Northam    A386    Westleigh

0 1 2 3 4 5 6 miles    THE BIG SHEEP    Orchard
Hill    Horwood    Newton
Tracey    Herner    Co
0 1 2 3 4 5 6 7 8 9 10km

Titchb    ²4    Abbotsham    BUNTON ART
GALL & MUS    **Bideford**    ³3    Eastleigh    Woodtown    Hiscott    Chapelton    ⁴4    COBBATON    East S    ⁵5

ABBEY    CLOVELLY VILLAGE    East-the-W    Handy

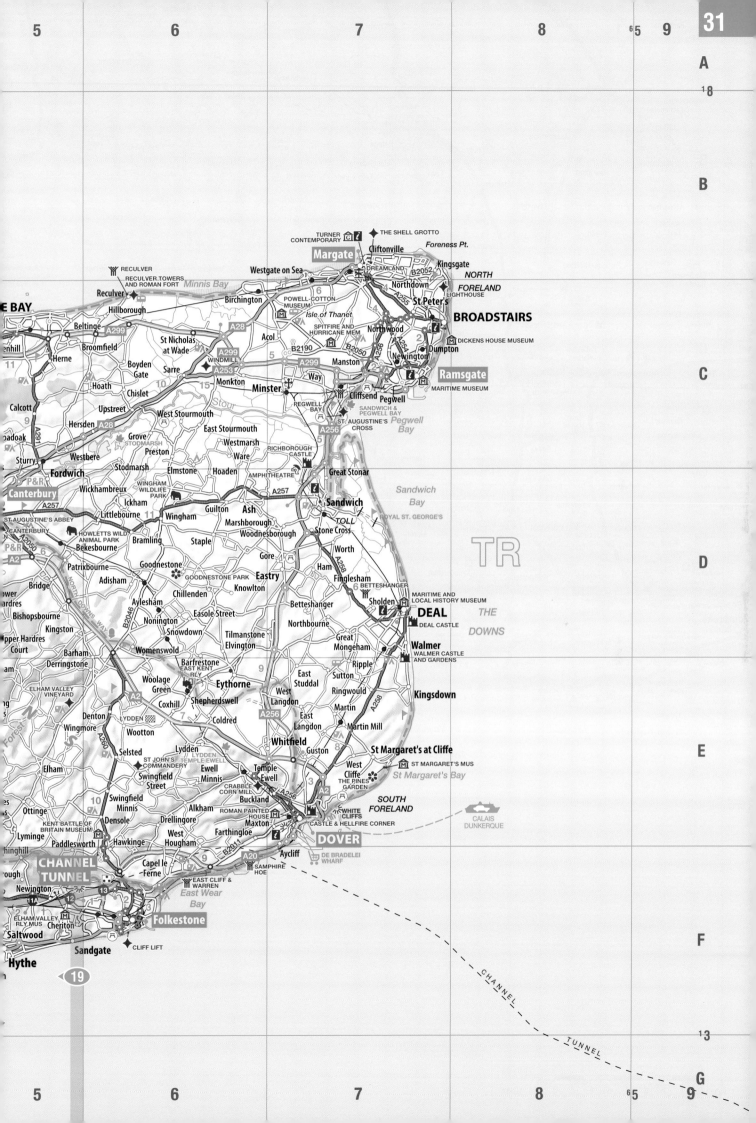

1    1    2    3    4    5

A

B

C

D

E

F

**C A E R N A R F O N**

**B A Y**

**B A E**

**C A E R N A R F O N**

82

Clynnog-fawr

Gyrn-goch

Bryn-yr-eryr

Capel Ucha

Trefor

509
BWLCH
MAWR

522
GYRN DDU

564
YR EIFL    6

Llanaelhaearn

Pen-sarn

Llithfaen

Pencaenewydd

Pistyll

Llwyndyrys

7

Llangybi

*Carreg Ddu*    *Porth Dinllaen*

WALES COAST PATH

B4417

Llanarmon

**Morfa Nefyn**

**Nefyn**

LLYN MARITIME MUSEUM

Fron

Rhos-fawr

B4354

Chwilc

Edern

Tan-y-graig

Y Ffôr

PENARTH FAWR MEDIEVAL HOUSE

*Porth Ysgadan*

B4417

Glanrhyd

Boduan

Llannor

A497

Rhos-y-llan

CORS GEIRCH

Efailnewydd

Abererch

Tudweiliog

Dinas

Rhyd-y-clafdy

Denio

**Pwllheli**

*Carreg yr Imbill*

*Porth Golmon*

14

Garnfadryn

Llaniestyn

B4415

Penrhos

South Beach

Bryn-mawr

7

Pen-y-graig

Rhedyn

Llangwnnadl

Sarn Meyllteyrn

Llanbedrog

*Trwyn Llanbedrog*

Penrhyn Mawr

Pen-y-groeslon

Botwnnog

Nanhoron

Mynytho

*St Tudwal's Road*

*Angorfa St Tudwal*

Ty-hen

Bryncroes

B4413

Methlem

Llandegwning

Rhydlios

304
MYNYDD
RHIW

PLAS-YN-RHIW

Llawrdref
Bellaf

Llangian

**Abersoch**

Rhoshirwaun

Rhiw

*St Tudwal's Island East*
*Ynys St Tudwal Dwyrain*

Capel Carmel

B4413

Llanengan

Sarn Bach

Marchroes

*St Tudwal's Island West*
*Ynys St Tudwal Gorllewin*

191

Bwlchtocyn

Uwchmynydd

Aberdaron

Llanfaelrhys

*Porth Neigwl or Hell's Mouth*

Cilan Uchaf

Bodermid

*Bardsey Sound
Swnt Enlli*

Pen-y-cil

*Trwyn Cilan*

167

YNYS ENLLI

**Bardsey
Island**

**Ynys Enlli**

**L L E Y N**

**Ý Ý**

**L L E Y N**

SH

**L L Y N**

**P E N R H Y N**

*Malltraeth Bay*
*Bae Malltraeth*

*Newborough Forest*

ANGLESEY MODEL VILLAGE

*Llanddwyn I.*

**Ynys Llanddwyn**

*The Bar*

CA
REGIMENT

*Abermenai
Pt.*
**Trwyn
Abermenai**

AIRWORLD
AVIATION MUSEUM

**Morfa Dinlle**

**Dinas Dinlle**

Ff

Llandwro

GLYNLL

14

Pontllyfni

Aberdesach

Ta

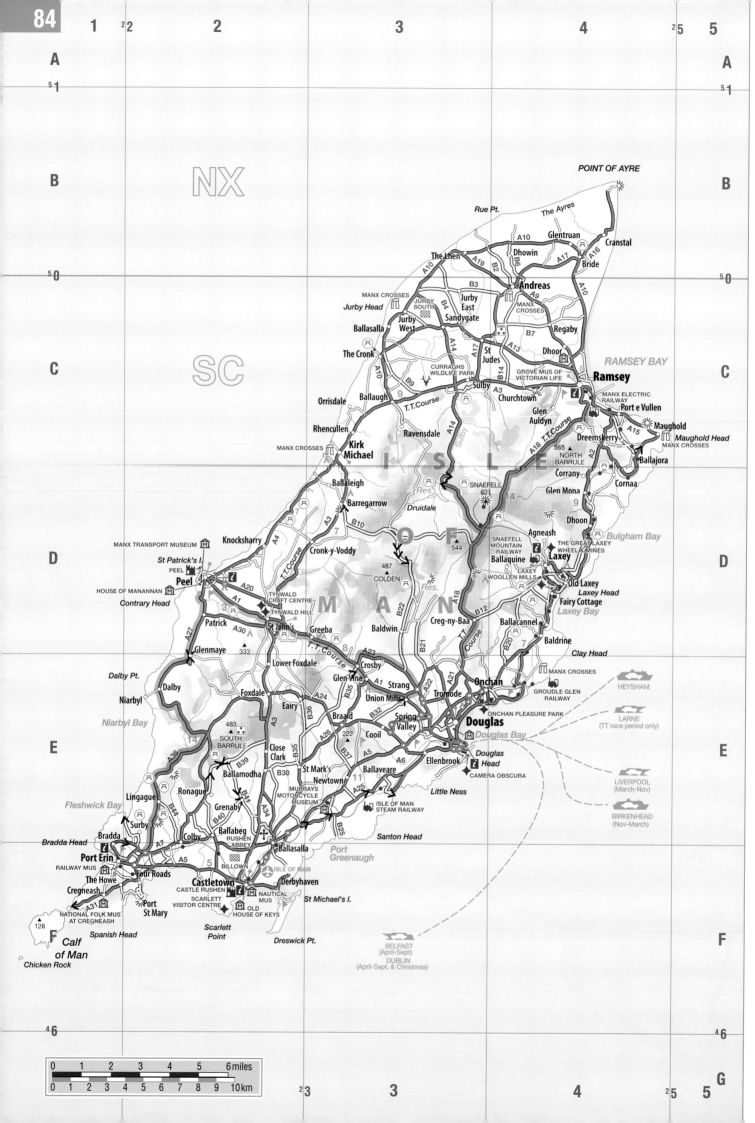

A

B

C

D

E

F

G

5 6 7 8 9

**Map labels (place names):**

Thirtleby  Sproatley  Humbleton  Fitling  Hilston
Instead  Lelley  Elstronwick  Owstwick  Tunstall
Bilton  B1238  B1240  Burton  North End
Preston  B1239  Roos  B1242
West End  Salt End  Waxholme  Owthorne
Hedon  Rimswell  Withernsea
Haven Side  Burstwick  B1362  East End  Hollym
A1033  Camerton  Halsham  Winestead  B1033
Thorngumbald  18  Keyingham  Holmpton
Paull  Ryehill  Ottringham  Out Newton
Little Humber  Patrington  B1445  Welwick  Weeton
Thorney Crofts  Cherry Cob Sands  Skeffling  Easington
TA  Sunk Island  Kilnsea
SPURN DISCOVERY CENTRE
SPURN
ROTTERDAM EUROPOORT  SPURN HEAD
MOUTH OF THE HUMBER

A160  Immingham  Pyewipe  Grimsby
Stallingborough  A180  West Marsh
Healing  Old Clee  CLEETHORPES
Keelby  Great Coates  FISHING HERITAGE CENTRE  CLEETHORPES COAST LIGHT RAILWAY
Riby Cross Roads  Aylesby  A46  Scartho  A1098  CLEETHORPES
Riby  Laceby  Nunsthorpe  A16  Humberston
NORTH EAST  Bradley  Waltham  B1219  New Waltham
LINCOLNSHIRE  Irby upon Humber  A18  Barnoldby le Beck  WALTHAM WINDMILL  Holton le Clay
Swallow  Beelsby  brigsley  A1031  Tetney Lock
Cuxwold  Hatcliffe  Ashby cum Fenby  Waithe  North Cotes
East Ravendale  B1209  Grainsby  Tetney  Marshchapel
Thorganby  Wold Newton  B1201  Eskham  Donna Nook
Swinhope  Ludborough  North Thoresby  Fulstow  Wragholme
Brookenby  LINCOLNSHIRE WOLDS RLY  Grainthorpe
Stainton le Vale  Covenham St Bartholomew  Conisholme  North Somercotes
Binbrook  TF  Covenham St Mary  South Somercotes  Skidbrooke North End
Kirmond le Mire  Utterby  Yarburgh  DONNA NOOK  Saltfleet
B1203  North Ormsby  Alvingham  Skidbrooke  A1031
Tealby  Great Tows  Fotherby  North Cockerington  Saltfleetby St Clements
Kelstern  Little Grimsby  RUSHMOOR  SALTFLEETBY THEDDLETHORPE
North Elkington  Saltfleetby All Saints
15  Ludford  A631  South Elkington  South Cockerington  B1200  Saltfleetby St Peter  Theddlethorpe St Helen
Willingham  Welton le Wold  Louth  Keddington  Grimoldby  Saltfleetby All Saints  Theddlethorpe All Saints
Burgh on Bain  ST JAMES  Stewton  Manby  SEAL SANCTUARY & WILDLIFE CENTRE
Sixhills  Grimblethorpe  Legbourne  Little Carlton  Meers Bridge
Hainton  Gayton le Wold  Hallington  Great Carlton  Mablethorpe
South Willingham  Biscathorpe  Raithby  A157  South Reston  Gayton le Marsh  Trusthorpe
Donington on Bain  Withcall  Little Cawthorpe  North Reston  Strubby  A1104  Sutton on Sea
Benniworth  Tathwell  Muckton  Withern  A157  Thorpe  Sandilands
East Barkwith  Haugham  13  Tothill  Maltby le Marsh  Beesby
West Barkwith  B1225  Stenigot  CADWELL PARK  Authorpe  B1373  Woodthorpe
Sotby  Market Stainton  Cawkwell  Maidenwell  A16  Burwell  78  79  CLAYTHORPE WATER AND WILDFOWL GARDENS  Saleby  Hannah
Panton  Dalby  Scamblesby  Farforth  White Pit  Belleau  Markby  KING CHA ENGLAND
Hatton  Ranby  Oxcombe  Ruckland  Swaby  Aby  Asserby
Great Sturton  Belchford  Ketsby  South Thoresby  ALFORD MANOR HOUSE  Bilsby  Huttoft
Rigsby  Alford  B1449  A52

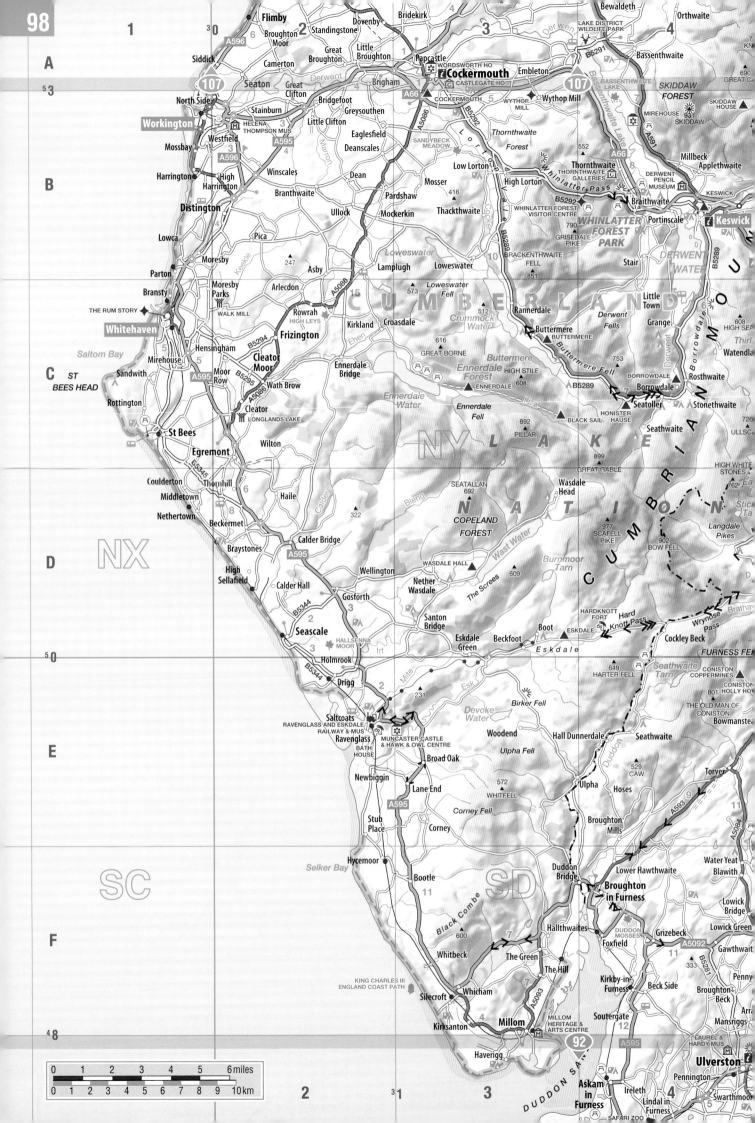

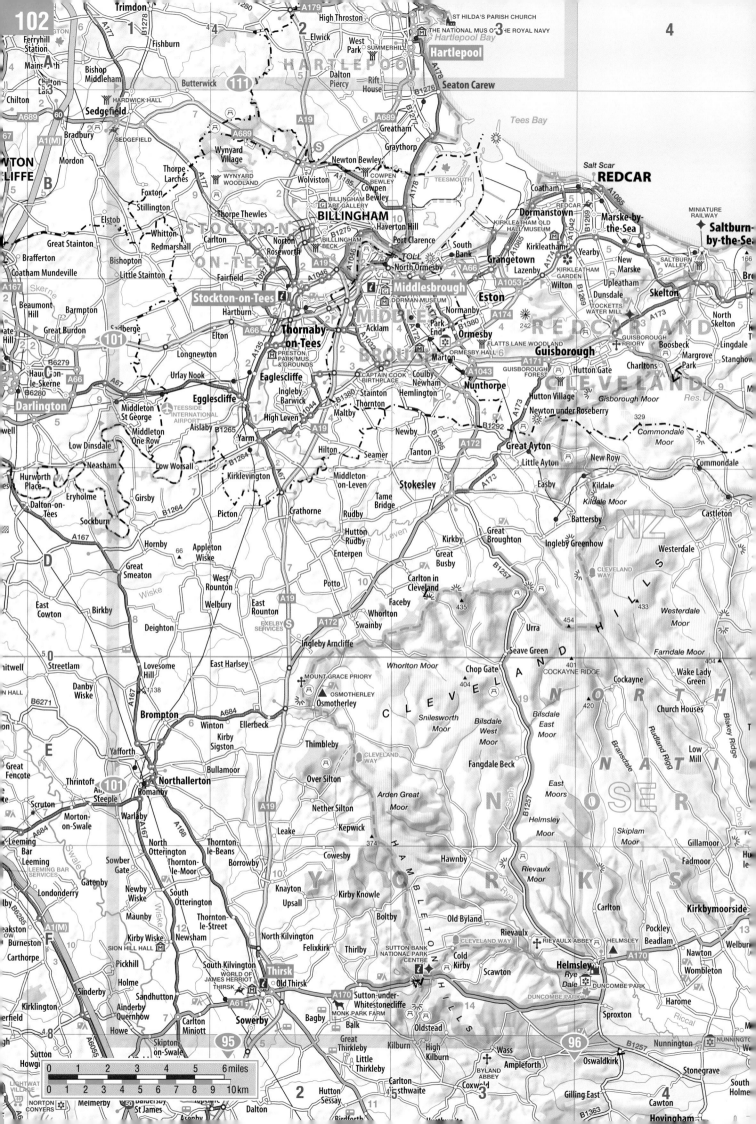

CARLETON CASTLE
Bennane Hd.
112
Colmone
B734 265
Knockdoliar
Heronsford
Ballantrae Bay
Glen Tig
Ballantrae
Balk
Downan Pt.
Auchencrosh
439
BENERAIF
A77
Mark
257
Glen App
17

BELFAST

LARNE

Milleur Pt.
Corsewall Pt.
Portencalzie
Barnhills
North Cairn
South Cairn
Corsewall
Cairnryan
B738
Loch Connell
Kirkcolm
Dounan Bay
Penwhirn Res.
Mains of Airies
Ervie
Low Salchrie
The Wig
Braid Fell
B798
LOCH RYAN
Slouchnawen Bay
Knocknain
B738
Leswalt
A77
B7043
Craigencross
Innermessan
Auchma
A718
Black Loch
CASTLE KENNEDY
Glenstockadale
GARDENS
Stranraer
Aird
White Loch
Broadsea Bay
CASTLE OF ST. JOHN VISITOR CENTRE
Castle Kennedy
T  H  E        E        R        H
Mark
Knockglass
STRANRAER MUSEUM
Soulseat Loch
A75
Black Hd.
B738
Lochans
182
Dunskey Ho.
A17
5
A716
5
Mark
B7077
6
Torrs W
5
Awhirk
B7084
6
Portpatrick
8
Stoneykirk
Luce S
Port of Spittal Bay
B7042
Cairngarroch
Sandhead
KIRKMADRINE STONES
Sandhead Bay
Cairngarroch Bay
Money Hd.
Clachanmore
Ardwell
Ardwell Mains
Chapel Rossa
Hole Stone Bay
10
Ardwell Pt.
Logan Mains
Balgowan
LOGAN BOTANIC GARDEN
Mull of Logan
Port Nessock or Port Logan Bay
Port Logan
Cairnywellan Hd.
B7065
A716
Clanyard Bay
Low Clanyard
Laggantalluch Hd.
Kirkmaiden
Drum
164
Damnaglaur
B7041
Crammag Hd.
Cairngaan
Port Kemin

NW

0  1  2  3  4  5  6miles
0 1 2 3 4 5 6 7 8 9 10km

NX

NY

SOLWAY

SOLWAY FIRTH COAST

NITH ESTUARY

**Dumfries**

Maxwelltown

Lincluden

**Annan**

Eastrigg

**Lockerbie**

**Silloth**
Greenrow

**Kirkbride**

**Newton Arlosh**

**Maryport**

**Cockermouth**

**Workington**

**Aspatria**

**Allonby**

Lochmaben

Marjoriebanks

Applegarthtown

Bankshill

Burnswark

Waterbeck

Middlebie

Eaglesfield

Creca

Kirtlebridge

Ecclefechan

Hoddomcross

Hoddom Mains

Brydekirk

Charlesfield

Welldale

Dornock

Shawhill

Powfoot

Cummertrees

Ruthwell

Clarencefield

Bowness-on-Solway

Port Carlisle

Glasson

Drumburgh

Cardurnock

Anthorn

Whitrigg

Bowness Common

Calvo

Seaville

Causewayhead

Blitterlees

Highlaws

Abbey Town

Kingside Hill

Beckfoot

Pelutho

Newtown

Mawbray

Holme St Cuthbert

Edderside

New Cowper

Westnewton

Watchhill

Blencogo

Bromfield

Langrigg

Kelsick

Dundraw

Waverbridge

Waterton

Waterside

Oulton

Lessonhall

Bolton Low Houses

Mealsgate

Boltongate

Blennerhasset

Oughterside

Prospect

Hayton

Allerby

Crosscanonby

Crosby

Crosby Villa

Parsonby

Bullgill

Gilcrux

Plumbland

Bothel

Threapland

Torpenhow

Whitrigg

Ireby

Uldale

Sandale

High Ireby

Sunderland

Bewaldeth

Binsey

Crossby

Dearham

Tallentire

Blindcrake

Flimby

Dovenby

Bridekirk

Broughton Moor

Standingstone

Little Broughton

Great Broughton

Papcastle

Embleton

Bassenthwaite

Siddick

Camerton

Brigham

Bridgefoot

Seaton

Great Clifton

North Side

Little Clifton

Greysouthen

Eaglesfield

Deanscales

Dean

Brigham

Wythop Mill

Low Lorton

Thornthwaite

Thornthwaite Forest

Mirehouse

SKIDDAW FOREST

Westfield

Mossbay

Harrington

High

Winscales

Stainburn

A  B  C  D  E  F

Crossroads
DUNDONALD CASTLE
Barassie
North Bay
Muirhead
Loans
Symington
Craigie
Bogend
Troon
South Bay
ROYAL TROON
Hansel Village
Monkton
GLASGOW PRESTWICK
Tarbolton
BACHELOR'S CLUB
BURN'S HOUSE MUSEUM
Mossgiel
Mauchline
Prestwick
Woodfield
St Quivox
Mossblown
Failford
AYR GORGE WOODLANDS
Haugh
Newton on Ayr
Wallacetown
Whitletts
Stair
Crosshill
Annbank
Ayr
AYR
Belston
Trabboch
Ochiltree
Seafield
Masonhill
Coylton
Côalhall
Belmont
ROBERT BURNS BIRTHPLACE MUS.
MACLAURIN GALLERY & ROZELLE HOUSE
Joppa
Hillhead
Drongan
Doonfoot
Laigh Glengall
Sinclairston
Heads of Ayr
HEADS OF AYR FARM PARK
Alloway
Martnaham Loch
Barbieston
Hayhill
Littlemill
Fisherton
BURNS NATIONAL HERITAGE PARK
Rankinston
Dunure
Culroy
Minishant
Hollybush
ELECTRIC BRAE
Dalrymple
Polnessan
KII MFIN HILL
429
NS
Culzean Bay
Patna
Burnfoot
CULZEAN CASTLE
Whitefaulds
Maybole
Kirkmichael
Waterside
DOON VALLEY RAILWAY
DENDCOOL
464
CULZEAN
Maidonhead Bay
COLLEGIATE CHURCH
Aitkenhead
Loch Spallander Reservoir
Burnton
Maidens
Kirkoswald
CROSSRAGUEL ABBEY
Crosshill
Dalmellington
TURNBERRY
SOUTER JOHNNIE'S COTTAGE
Bellsbank
Turnberry Bay
Turnberry
Ruglen
Straiton
Brest Rocks
Townhead
BIG HILL OF GLENMOUNT
Wallacetown
SOUTH
AYRSHIRE
Dipple
Burnhead
Dailly
Old Dailly
BARGANY GARDENS
Loch Finlas
Girvan
Penkill
Tairlaw Forest
LOCH DOON
Glendoune
Houdston
Linfern Loch
Loch Bradan
Laml
Penwhapple Res.
LOCH DOON CASTLE
Woodland Bay
Dalwyne
Craigmalloch
Kennedy's Pass
Pinminnoch
Tormitchell
MULL OF MILJOAN
Loch Riecawr
GREY HILL
Auchensoul
Barr
South Balloch
CARRICK FOREST
Loch Macaterick
Curraie
Pinmore
CHANGUE FOREST
MEAUL
Straid
Merkland
CORSERINE
Lendalfoot
Pinmore Mains
CRAIGENREOCH
NX
CARLETON CASTLE
Pinwherry
PINDONNAN
MULLWHARCHAR
RHINNS OF KELLS
Poundland
Bellamore
GALLOWAY
MERRICK
Loch Enoch
Colmonell
Ballochmorrie
Black Clauchrie
Loch Moan
Palgowan
Loch Neldricken
SILVER FLOWE
Knockdolian
Heronsford
Barrhill
Laggan
Eldrick
FOREST
Glentrool
BRUCE'S STONE
Loch Valley
Balkissock
Glen Trool Lodge
Troon
LAMACHAN HILL
Glen Trool
PARK
Arecleoch Forest
Glentrool Village
GLENTROOL VISITOR CENTRE
Loch Trool
Loch Dee
Drumlamford Loch
Dornal
Bargrennan

0  1  2  3  4  5  6 miles
0  1  2  3  4  5  6  7  8  9  10km

5    40    6    7    8    43    9

A

68

B

C

EYEMOUTH MUSEUM
mouth

D

NU

NORTHUMBERLAND COAST

Lamberton
Beach

1333

Highfields

**Berwick-upon-Tweed**

BERWICK-UPON-TWEED
BARRACKS & MAIN GUARD

BERWICK

East
Ord

Tweedmouth

Spittal

B6461

B698

Prior
Park

A167

Redshin Cove

108

DEVIL'S CAUSEWAY

Scremerston

West Allerdean

Shoresdean

Cheswick

Ancroft

Goswick

B6525

Haggerston

North Low

Berrington

South Low

Bowsden

A1

Beal

Causeway
Holy
Island
Sands

82

12

B6353

Barmoor
Castle

Barmoor
Lane End

West
Kyloe

Fenwick

Fenham

Lowick

Kyloe
Hills

East
Kyloe

WATERFORD HALL

157

Buckton

Holburn

Detchant

SLAW

B6353

Kimmerston

Nesbit

Fenton
Town

Doddington

200

South
Hazelrigg

West
Horton

Newtown

East Horton

Weetwood Hall

B6625

1402

B6348

166

Humbleton

**Wooler**

WOOLER

Earle

40

Haugh Head

Middleton Hall

Middleton

North Hazelrigg

211

Belford

B1342

Elwick

Ross

Budle
Bay

Easington

Waren
Mill

Spindlestone

Mousen

Bellshill

B6349

Warenton

10

Chatton

6

B6348

Greendikes

CHILLINGHAM
CASTLE

Chillingham

WILD CATTLE OF
CHILLINGHAM

ADDERSTONE
SERVICES

NEWHAM BOG

Warenford

Newham
Hall

A1

Newstead

Rosebrough

7

Newham

Ellingham

B134

Fleetham

Swinhoe

Chathill

8

LINDISFARNE

Holy Island
(Lindisfarne)

Emmanuel Hd.

LINDISFARNE CASTLE

Holy
Island

Castle Pt.

HERITAGE
CENTRE

LINDISFARNE
PRIORY

Guile
Pt.

E

Farne
Islands

Staple Sound

FARNE ISLANDS

Inner Sound

BAMBURGH
CASTLE

**Bamburgh**

Budle

F

63

Burton

Glororum

Bradford

B1341

B1340

Adderstone

Lucker

Elford

North
Sunderland

**Seahouses**

Bead

117

Benthall

KING CHARLES III
ENGLAND COAST PATH

Bead ll Bay

High Newton-

G

5    40    6    7    8    43    9

117

Thornyhive B

A

B

C

D

E

F

G

5   6   7   8

Glen Dye

778 MOUNT BA 5 CK

Burn of Ten

Drumtochty Forest

464

525 MELUNCART

140

Cairn o' Mount

Tannachie
Carmont
New ?ll 8

7

Mains of Dellavaird

BURNS FAMILY MEMORIALS

Glenfarquhar Lodge

Drumlithie

Glenbervie

141

Fiddes

Barras

Mill of Uras

10

Crawton

Crawton Bay

across
THE RETREAT GLEN ESK FOLK MUS

Milden Lodge

Clatterin Bridge

Glensaugh

Strath Finella

Drumtochty Castle

Auchenblae

Monboddo House

14

Mondynes

Pitforthie

Roadside of Catterline

Catterline

Braidon Bay

Todhead Point

Auchmull

Mains of Balnakettle

Thainston

FETTERCAIRN DISTILLERY VISITOR CENTRE

Fettercairn

B974

East Cairnbeg

Howe of the Mearns

Brownmuir

Scotston

Fordoun

B967

Parkneuk

Arbuthnott

GRASSIC GIBBON CENTRE

ARBUTHNOTT CHURCH

Roadside of Kinneff

Kinneff

678 HILL OF WIRREN

Dalbog

B966

Inch of Arnhall

Meikle Strath

Mains of Thornton

Bent

B9120

A90

Laurencekirk

ARBUTHNOTT HOUSE GARDENS

Mains of Allardice

Inverbervie

Little John's Haven

440

Witton

Gannochy

Edzell

B966

Sauchieburn

Luthermuir

Dykelands

Garvock

Garvock Hill

Redford

Benholm

Gourdon

Bervie Bay

Bridgend
Balfield

EDZELL CASTLE AND GARDENS

Dunlappie

North Water Bridge

B974

North Esk

Marykirk

Ecclesgreig

Johnshaven

13

B9120

llyarblet

BROWN CATERTHUN
WHITE CATERTHUN

Inchbare
Newtonmill

Pert

Craigo

Logie

Lochside
Morphie

St Cyrus

ST CYRUS

Milton Ness

Kirkton of Menmuir

Tigerton

Little Brechin

Keithock

STRACATHRO SERVICES

Logie Pert

Muirton of Ballochy

A937

Pathhead

Mains of Balhall

Lochty
Belliehill

West Muir

Trinity

Hillside

Kirkhill

Careston Castle

BRECHIN CASTLE CENTRE

A935

Brechin

CATHEDRAL & ROUND TOWER

Dun

HOUSE OF DUN

A935

CALEDONIAN RAILWAY

Montrose Basin

Montrose

MUSEUM AND ART GALLERY

South Esk

14

Netherton Mains of Melgund

Aldbar Castle

Middle Drums

Kinnaird Castle

A933

Farnell

Bridge of Dun

Barnhead

MONTROSE BASIN VISITOR CENTRE

Inchbraoch

Ferryden

Scurdie Ness

WILLIAM LAMB MEMORIAL STUDIO

NO

ABERLEMNO SCULPTURED STONES

Aberlemno

Pitkennedy

Montreathmont Forest

A934

Bonnyton
Carcary

Maryton

Dunninald

Kirkton of Craig

Long Craig
Fishtown of Usan

252

Turin

B9113

Montreathmont Moor

Dubton

11

Rossie Moor

Westerton

Boddin Pt.

Rescobie

eswallie

Burnside A932

9

Balgavies

Milldens

Glasterlaw

Guthrie

Kinnell

Bolshan

A92

13

Braehead of Lunan

Lunan

Redcastle

LUNAN BAY

Letham

Pitmuies

PITMUIES GARDEN

Friockheim

Boysack

Lunan Water

Inverkeilor

Lang Craig

nichen

Idvies

Chapelton

B965

Ethie Mains

Red Head

Tulloes

Leysmill

Cauldcots

Ethie Castle

12

B961

Mosston

Colliston

Drunkendub

B978
B912R

Greystone

Redford

7

Letham Grange

Auchmithie

Meg's Craig

B9127

B9127

Carmyllie

Denhead of Arbilot

St Vigeans

Marywell

ST VIGEANS STONES & MUSEUM

Hayhillock

Cliffburn

The Deil's Heid

CROMBIE

B9128

Arbirlot

6

Arbroath

ARBROATH ABBEY

Hayshead

Kirkton of Monikie

Balmirmer

A92

Elliot

SIGNAL TOWER MUSEUM

Craigton

A930

Salmond's Muir

CARLUNGIE SOUTERRAIN

wbigging

Muirdrum

East Haven

BARRY MILL

Barry

Panbride

Mains of Ardestie

Carnoustie

nifieth

Barry Links

Buddon Ness

129

3

73

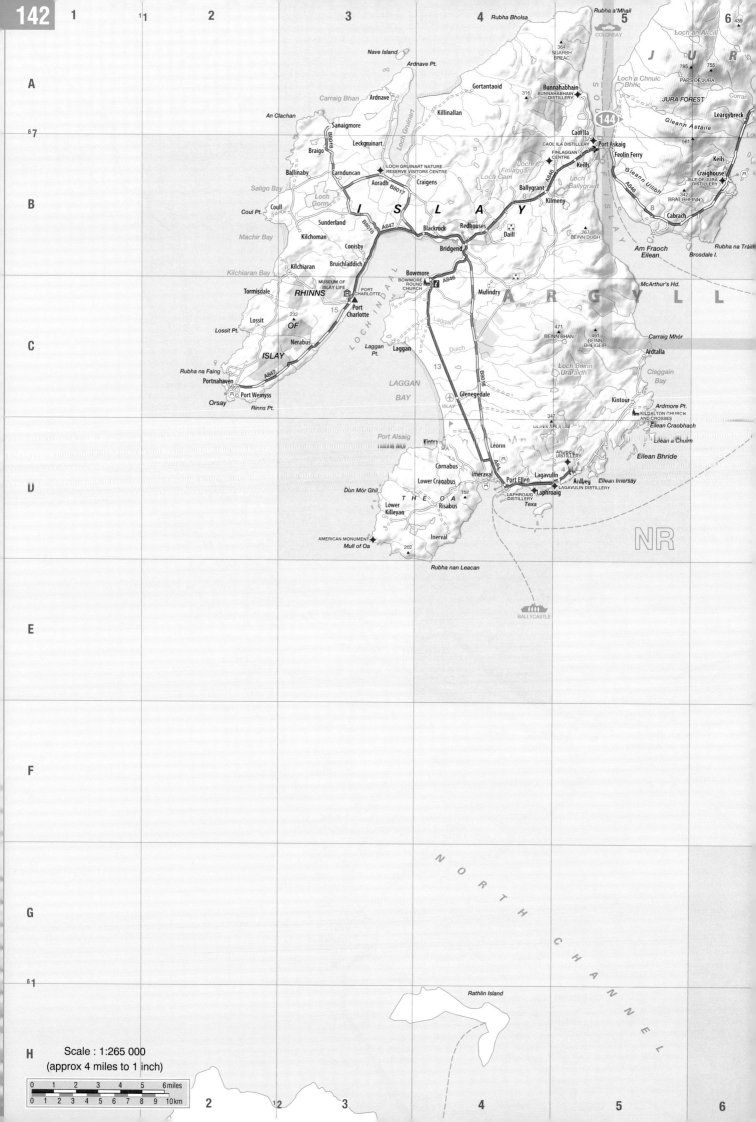

1    1    2    3    4    5    6

Rubha Bholsa
Rubha a'Mhail
439

Nave Island
COLONSAY
Loch an Aircll

Ardnave Pt.
SGARBH BREAC 364

**A**

Carraig Bhan
Gortantaoid
Bunnahabhain
BUNNAHABHAIN DISTILLERY
316

Ardnave
Killinallan
785
755
PAPS OF JURA

An Clachan
JURA FOREST

Sanaigmore
Caol Ila
CAOL ILA DISTILLERY
Corran

**7**
Leckgruinart
144
Gleann Astaile

Braigo
Port Askaig
561
Leargybreck

B8018
Carnduncan
Craigens
FINLAGGAN CENTRE
Feolin Ferry
Gleann Uillich

Ballinaby
Aoradh
B8017
LOCH GRUINART NATURE RESERVE VISITORS CENTRE
Ballygrant
Keills
A846
A846
Craighouse
ISLE OF JURA DISTILLERY

**B**
Saligo Bay
Kilmeny
342
Loch Ballygrant
BRAT BHEINN

Loch Gorm
Coull
**I S L A Y**
Loch Finlaggan
Cabrach

Coul Pt.
Sunderland
Blackrock
Redhouses
Loch Cam
8

Machir Bay
B8016
A847
Daill
267
BEINN DUBH
Am Fraoch Eilean
Rubha na Tràill

Kilchoman
Bridgend
Brosdale I.

Conisby

Kilchiaran Bay
Kilchiaran
Bruichladdich
Bowmore
BOWMORE ROUND CHURCH
A846
Mulindry
McArthur's Hd.

**C**
Tormisdale
**RHINNS**
MUSEUM OF ISLAY LIFE
Port Charlotte
**A R G Y L L**
Carraig Mhór

Lossit
**OF**
232
Port Charlotte
15
Laggan
Ardtalla

Lossit Pt.
Nerabus
Laggan Pt.
Laggan
Duich
471
BEINN BHAN
491
BEINN BHEIGEIR
Loch Beinn Uraraidh
Claggain Bay

**ISLAY**
13

Rubha na Faing
A847
**LAGGAN BAY**
347
Kintour
Ardmore Pt.

Portnahaven
Port Wemyss
ISLAY
B8016
Glenegedale
BEINN SHOLUM
KILDALTON CHURCH AND CROSSES

Orsay
Rinns Pt.
Kintra
Léorin
Eilean Craobhach

**D**
Dùn Mòr Ghil
Cornabus
Lilean a'Chuirn

Lower Cragabus
Imeraval
Lagavulin
ARDBEG DISTILLERY
Eilean Bhride

Lower Killeyan
Risabus
152
Port Ellen
Ardbeg
Eilean Imersay

**T H E O A**
LAPHROAIG DISTILLERY
Laphroaig
LAGAVULIN DISTILLERY

AMERICAN MONUMENT
Inerval
Texa

Mull of Oa
202
8

Rubha nan Leacan
**NR**

BALLYCASTLE

**E**

**F**

**N O R T H**

**C H A N N E L**

**G**

**1**

Rathlin Island

**H**

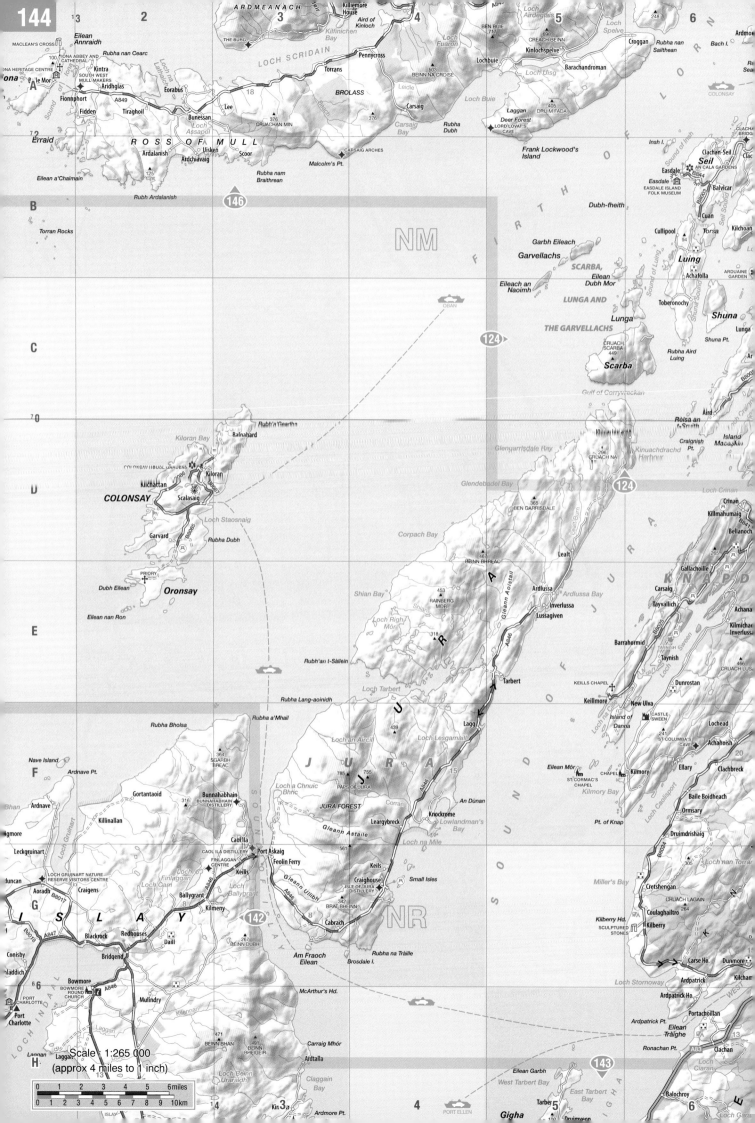

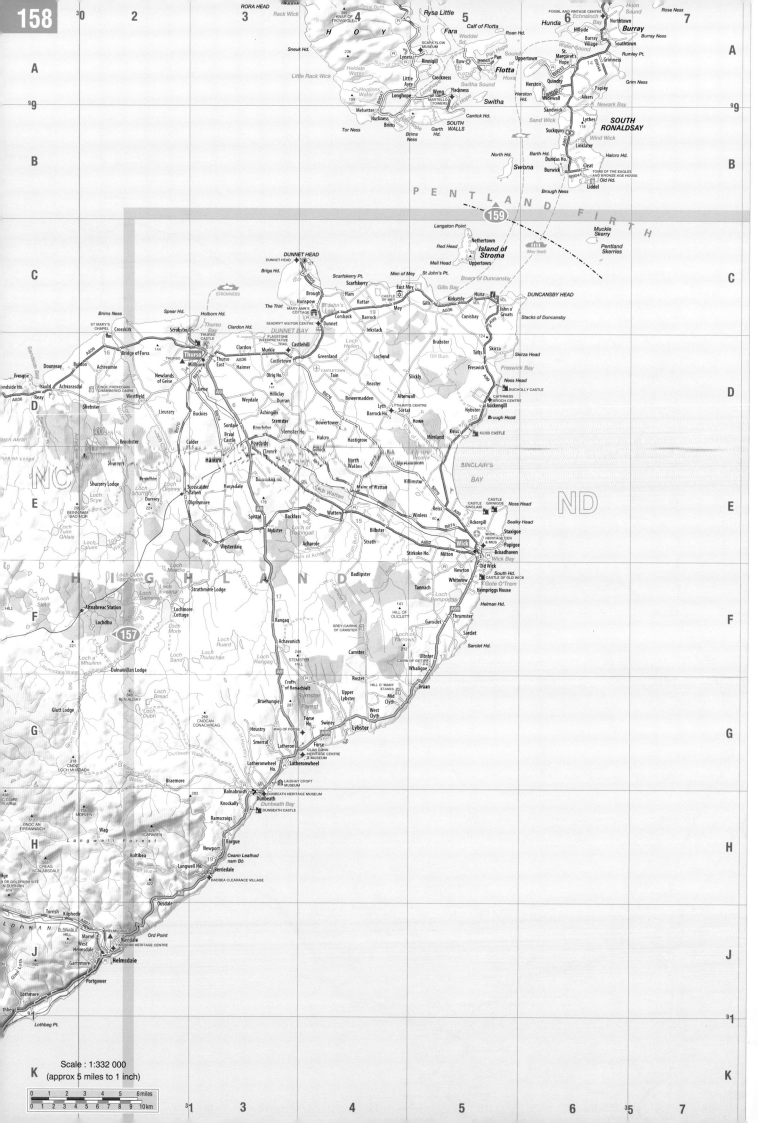

**1** **2** **3** **4** **5** **6** **7** **8**

³1
107
³8

B

**North Ronaldsay**
NORTH RONALDSAY
Hollandstoun
BROCH OF BURRIAN

C

Papa Westray
Holm of Papa
Aikerness
PAPA WESTRAY
Holland
PAPA WESTRAY
NORTH RONALDSAY FIRTH
Backaskaill
Gayfield
NOUP HEAD
PIEROWALL CHURCH
Rackwick
Pierowall
NOLTLAND CASTLE
Broughton
Braehead
THE NORTH SOUND
Scar
Burness
Lettan
B9068
Sellibister
KIRKWALL
Newark
START PT.
WESTRAY
FITTY HILL
159
Midbea
Skelwick
Broughtown
Lady
SANDAY
Langskaill
WESTSIDE CHURCH
Rapness
Overbister
Sulland
SANDAY
SOUND

D
107
³8

WESTRAY FIRTH
HY
Calf of Eday
Carrick Ho.
CARRICK HOUSE
Calfsound
Kettletoft
QUOYNESS CHAMBERED CAIRN
Faray
Laminess
Odie
Papa Stronsay
Guith
Braeswick
Whitehall Village
Millbounds
Stove
Linga Holm
Wardhill
Everbay STRONSAY
WASBISTER
Loth
Grobister
Kirbister
ROUSAY
Sourin
Dishes
MIDHOWE BROCH
Skaill
ST MAGNUS CHURCH
Rothiesholm
Holland
EYNHALLOW CHURCH
Westness
Egilsay
SANDAY SOUND
Eynhallow
KNOWE OF YARSO CAIRN
Brinian
Muckle Green Holm
Backaland
EDAY
101
Veness

E

BROUGH OF BIRSAY
BROUGH HEAD
Costa
GUBBIE ROO'S CASTLE AND ST MARY'S CHAPEL
EARL'S PALACE
The Barony
Abune-the-Hill
Burgar
Frotoft
STRONSAY
MARWICK HEAD NATURE RESERVE
Marwick
Stara
Kirbuster
Stenso
Wyre
FIRTH
Twatt
B9057
Redland
Gairsay
ORKNEY
Isbister
Beaquoy
CLICK MILL
Tingwall
Click Mill
Edmonstone
Scarwell
Quoyloo
Skeabrae
Dounby
Hackland
Northdyke
Mirbister
CORRIGALL FARM MUSEUM
Gorseness
Shapinsay
Kierfield Ho.
Brough
Isbister
SKARA BRAE
Settiscarth
Breck of Cruan
Balfour
Aith
SKAILL HOUSE
Skaill
Hestwall
Tenston
Netherbrough
Bimbister
Newlot
AUSKERRY
Auskerry

F

Yesnaby
Voy
Arion
Finstown
Work
ABERDEEN LERWICK
Quholm
RING OF BROGGAR
Grimbister
ORTAK JEWELLERY CENTRE
Craigiefield
158
STENNESS STANDING STONES
TORMISTON MILL
Heddle
ORKNEY WIRELESS MUS.
ORKNEY MUSEUM
KIRKWALL
Bridge of Waith
MAES HOWE
Nisthouse
ST MAGNUS CATHEDRAL
Berstane
Outertown
Clouston
BISHOP'S & EARL'S PALACE
Scapa
Ireland
HIGHLAND PARK DISTILLERY
Hall of Tankerness
PIER ARTS CENTRE STROMNESS
Stromness
Kirbister
WARD HILL
Tradespark
Whitecleat
North Halley
STROMNESS MUSEUM
Clestrain
Hobbister
Greenigoe
Deerness
Skaill
Grindigar
HOY AND WEST MAINLAND
Breckan
Cairnton
Smoogro
WAULKMILL LODGE
Toab
Gritley
Murra
Graemsay
Crya
Gyre
Swanbister
Foubister
Upper Sanday
NORTH HOY NATURE RESERVE
Linksness
Petertown
Houton
North Dawn
SCRABSTER
Hoy
Quoyness
ST NICHOLAS CHURCH
Copinsay

G
³8
8

OLD MAN OF HOY
Murra
SCAPA FLOW
St Mary's
ITALIAN CHAPEL
Braehead
RORA HEAD
RACKWICK
Rackwick
Cava
Cornquoy
KNAP OF TROWIEGLEN
Rysa Little
FOSSIL AND VINTAGE CENTRE
Northtown
HOY
Fara
Hunda
Hillside
Burray
LYNESS
SCAPA FLOW MUSEUM
Rinnigill
Bow
Uppertown
Southtown
Lyness
Pan
St Margaret's Hope
Grimness
Little Ayre
Crockness
Flotta
Herston
Quindry
Longhope
Wyng
Hackness
Widewall
Papley
Aikers
Melsetter
MARTELLO TOWERS
Swartha
Sandwick
Lythes
SOUTH RONALDSAY
Hurliness
Brims
SOUTH WALLS
Suckquoy
Linklater
Dundas Ho.
Swona
Burwick
Cleat
LIMB OF THE EAGLES AND BRONZE AGE HOUSE
Liddel

J

K

PENTLAND FIRTH

158
DUNNET HEAD
DUNNET HEAD
Island of Stroma
Nethertown
Uppertown
(May-Sept)
DUNCANSBY HEAD

L

Scarfskerry
East Mey
STROMNESS
Brough
CASTLE OF MEY
Hunspow
Ham
Rattar
Mey
Kirkstyle
Huna
MARY ANN'S COTTAGE
Corsback
Barrock
Gills
John o'Groats
SEADRIFT VISITOR CENTRE
Dunnet
Canisbay
FLAGSTONE INTERPRETATIVE TRAIL
Scrabster
THURSO CASTLE
DUNNET BAY
Inkstack
Brabster
Skirza
Thurso
Clardon
Murkle
Castlehill
Tofts
Freswick
Thurso East
Haimer
Castletown
Tain
Reaster
Slickly
BUCHOLLY CASTLE
Millbank
Olrig Ho.
Scale : 1:400 000
Geise
Alterwall
Nybster
CAITHNESS BROCH CENTRE
Weydale
Hilliclay
Durran
Bowermadden
Lyth
(approx 6¼ miles to 1 inch)
LYTH ARTS CENTRE
Auckengill
Achingills
Stemster
Sortat
ND
Buckies
Sordale
Braal
Roadside
Bowertower
Halcro
Howe
Keiss
Calder Mains
Castle
Stemster Ho.
Hastigrow
Mireland
KEISS CASTLE
Olgrindmore
Knockdee
Gillock
Kirk
Halkirk
Clayock
North Watten
Myrelandhorn
Harpsdale
Banniskirk Ho.
Killimster
Scotscalder Station
Mains of Watten
SINCLAIR'S BAY

M
³6
9

N

**2** **3** **4** **5** **6** **7** **8**

Scale bar: 0 1 2 3 4 5 6 miles / 0 1 2 3 4 5 6 7 8 9 10km

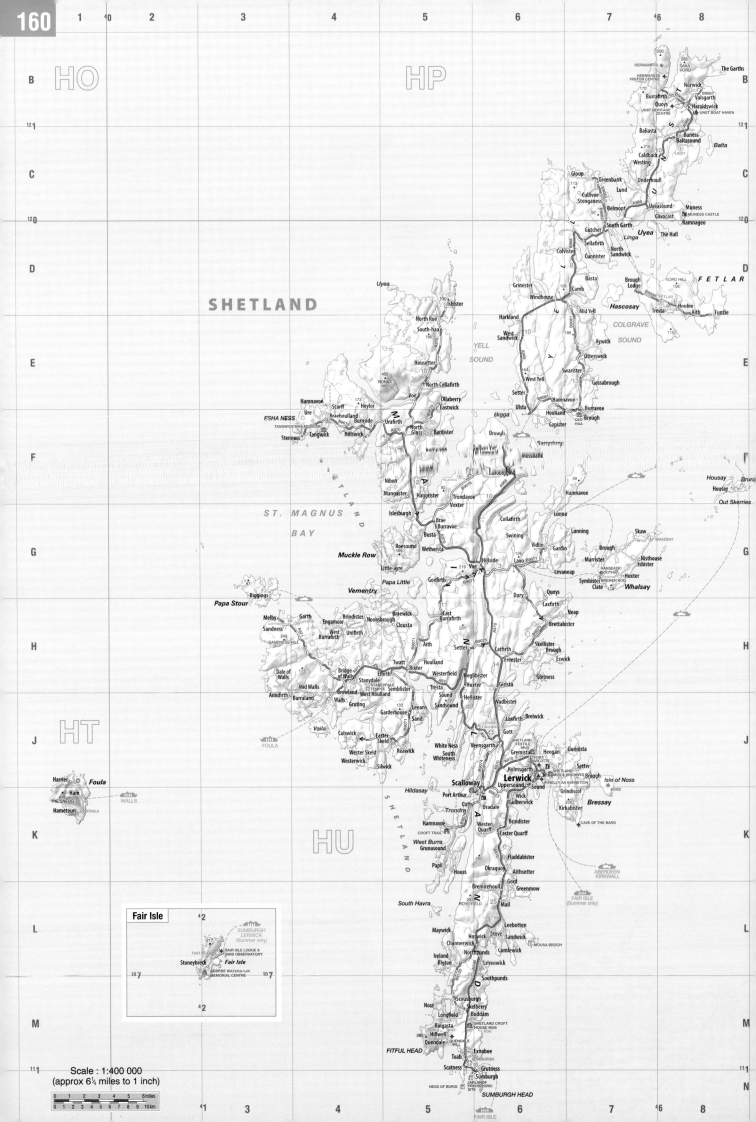

# Index

## Abbreviations used in the index

| | | | |
|---|---|---|---|
| Aberdeen | Aberdeen City | Bucks | Buckinghamshire |
| Aberds | Aberdeenshire | Caerph | Caerphilly |
| Ald | Alderney | Cambs | Cambridgeshire |
| Anglesey | Isle of Anglesey | Cardiff | Cardiff |
| Angus | Angus | Carms | Carmarthenshire |
| Argyll | Argyll and Bute | C Beds | Central Bedfordshire |
| Bath | Bath and North East Somerset | Ceredig | Ceredigion |
| BCP | Bournemouth, Christchurch and Poole | Ches E | Cheshire East |
| | | Ches W | Cheshire West and Chester |
| Bedford | Bedford | Clack | Clackmannanshire |
| Blackburn | Blackburn with Darwen | Conwy | Conwy |
| | | Corn | Cornwall |
| Blackpool | Blackpool | Cumb | Cumberland |
| Bl Gwent | Blaenau Gwent | Darl | Darlington |
| Borders | Scottish Borders | Denb | Denbighshire |
| Brack | Bracknell | Derby | City of Derby |
| Bridgend | Bridgend | Derbys | Derbyshire |
| Brighton | City of Brighton and Hove | Devon | Devon |
| | | Dorset | Dorset |
| Bristol | City and County of Bristol | Dumfries | Dumfries and Galloway |
| | | Dundee | Dundee City |
| | | Durham | Durham |
| | | E Ayrs | East Ayrshire |
| | | Edin | City of Edinburgh |
| | | E Dunb | East Dunbartonshire |
| | | E Loth | East Lothian |
| | | E Renf | East Renfrewshire |
| | | Essex | Essex |
| | | E Sus | East Sussex |
| | | E Yorks | East Riding of Yorkshire |
| | | Falk | Falkirk |
| | | Fife | Fife |
| | | Flint | Flintshire |
| | | Glasgow | City of Glasgow |
| | | Glos | Gloucestershire |
| | | Gtr Man | Greater Manchester |
| | | Guern | Guernsey |
| | | Gwyn | Gwynedd |
| | | Halton | Halton |
| | | Hants | Hampshire |
| | | Hereford | Herefordshire |
| | | Herts | Hertfordshire |
| | | Highld | Highland |
| | | Hrtlpl | Hartlepool |
| | | Hull | Hull |
| | | Invclyd | Inverclyde |
| | | IoM | Isle of Man |
| | | IoW | Isle of Wight |
| | | Jersey | Jersey |
| | | Kent | Kent |

| | | | |
|---|---|---|---|
| Lancs | Lancashire | S Glos | South Gloucestershire |
| Leicester | City of Leicester | Shetland | Shetland |
| Leics | Leicestershire | Shrops | Shropshire |
| Lincs | Lincolnshire | S Lanark | South Lanarkshire |
| London | Greater London | Slough | Slough |
| Luton | Luton | Som | Somerset |
| Mbro | Middlesbrough | Soton | Southampton |
| Medway | Medway | Southend | Southend-on-Sea |
| Mers | Merseyside | Staffs | Staffordshire |
| Midloth | Midlothian | Stirling | Stirling |
| M Keynes | Milton Keynes | Stockton | Stockton-on-Tees |
| Mon | Monmouthshire | Stoke | Stoke-on-Trent |
| Moray | Moray | Suff | Suffolk |
| M Tydf | Merthyr Tydfil | Sur | Surrey |
| N Ayrs | North Ayrshire | Swansea | Swansea |
| Neath | Neath Port Talbot | Swindon | Swindon |
| NE Lincs | North East Lincolnshire | S Yorks | South Yorkshire |
| Newport | City and County of Newport | T&W | Tyne and Wear |
| | | Telford | Telford and Wrekin |
| N Lanark | North Lanarkshire | Thurrock | Thurrock |
| N Lincs | North Lincolnshire | Torbay | Torbay |
| N Nhants | North Northamptonshire | Torf | Torfaen |
| | | V Glam | The Vale of Glamorgan |
| Norf | Norfolk | W&F | Westmorland and Furness |
| Northumb | Northumberland | | |
| Nottingham | City of Nottingham | Warks | Warwickshire |
| Notts | Nottinghamshire | Warr | Warrington |
| N Som | North Somerset | W Berks | West Berkshire |
| N Yorks | North Yorkshire | W Dunb | West Dunbartonshire |
| Orkney | Orkney | | |
| Oxon | Oxfordshire | Wilts | Wiltshire |
| Pboro | Peterborough | Windsor | Windsor and Maidenhead |
| Pembs | Pembrokeshire | | |
| Perth | Perth and Kinross | W Isles | Western Isles |
| Plym | Plymouth | W Loth | West Lothian |
| Powys | Powys | W Mid | West Midlands |
| Ptsmth | Portsmouth | W Nhants | West Northamptonshire |
| Reading | Reading | | |
| Redcar | Redcar and Cleveland | Wokingham | Wokingham |
| Renfs | Renfrewshire | Worcs | Worcestershire |
| Rhondda | Rhondda Cynon Taff | Wrex | Wrexham |
| Rutland | Rutland | W Sus | West Sussex |
| S Ayrs | South Ayrshire | W Yorks | West Yorkshire |
| Scilly | Scilly | York | City of York |

## How to use the index

Example

**Trudoxhill** Som **24 E2**

- grid square
- page number
- county or unitary authority

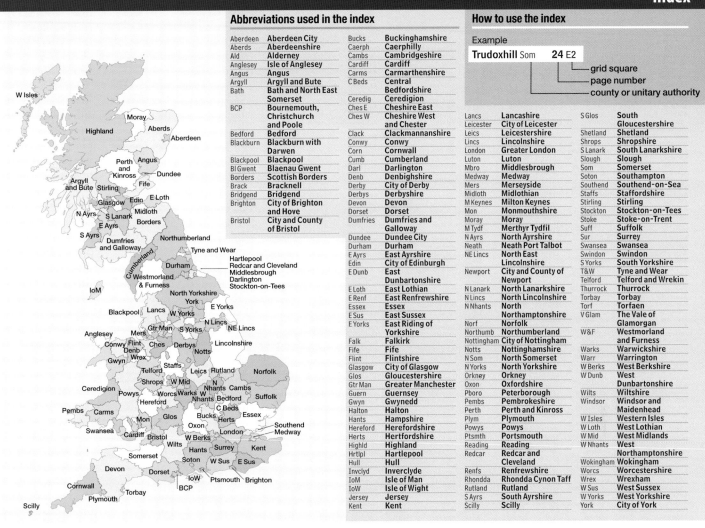

### A

Abbas Combe . . . . . 12 B5
Abberley . . . . . . . . . 50 C2
Abberton Essex . . . 43 C6
Worcs . . . . . . . . . . 50 D4
Abberwick . . . . . . . 117 C7
Abbess Roding . . . . 42 C1
Abbey . . . . . . . . . . . 11 C6
Abbey-cwm-hir . . . 48 B2
Abbeydale . . . . . . . . 88 F4
Abbey Dore . . . . . . 49 F5
Abbey Field . . . . . . 43 B5
Abbey Hulton . . . . . 75 E6
Abbey St Bathans. 122 C3
Abbeystead . . . . . . 93 D5
Abbey Town . . . . . 107 D8
Abbey Village . . . . . 86 B4
Abbey Wood . . . . . . 29 B5
Abbots Bickington. . 9 C5
Abbots Bromley . . . 62 B4
Abbotsbury . . . . . . 12 F3
Abbotsham . . . . . . . 9 B6
Abbotskerswell . . . . 7 C6
Abbots Langley . . . 40 D3
Abbots Leigh . . . . . 23 B7
Abbotsley . . . . . . . . 54 D3
Abbots Morton . . . . 50 D5
Abbots Ripton . . . . 54 B3
Abbots Salford . . . . 51 D5
Abbotswood . . . . . . 14 B4
Abbotts Ann . . . . . . 25 E8
Abcott . . . . . . . . . . . 49 B5
Abdon . . . . . . . . . . . 61 F5
Aber . . . . . . . . . . . . . 46 E3
Aberaeron . . . . . . . 46 C3
Aberaman . . . . . . . . 34 D4
Aberangell . . . . . . . 58 C5
Aber-Arad . . . . . . . . 46 F2
Aberarder . . . . . . . 137 F7
Aberarder House . 138 B2
Aberarder Lodge . 137 F8
Aberargie . . . . . . . 128 C3
Aberarth . . . . . . . . . 46 C3
Aberavon . . . . . . . . 33 E8
Aber-banc . . . . . . . . 46 E2
Aberbeeg . . . . . . . . 35 D6
Abercanaid . . . . . . . 34 D4
Abercarn . . . . . . . . . 35 E6
Abercastle . . . . . . . 44 B3
Abercegir . . . . . . . . 58 D5
Aberchirder . . . . . 152 C6
Aber Cowarch . . . . 59 C5
Abercraf . . . . . . . . . 34 C2
Abercrombie . . . . . 129 D7
Abercych . . . . . . . . . 45 E4
Abercynafon . . . . . 34 C4
Abercynon . . . . . . . 34 E4
Aberdalgie . . . . . . 128 B2
Aberdâr
= Aberdare . . . . 34 D3
Aberdare
= Aberdâr . . . . . 34 D3
Aberdaron . . . . . . . 70 E2

Aberdaugleddau
= Milford Haven . . 44 E4
Aberdeen . . . . . . . 141 D8
Aberdesach . . . . . . . 82 F4
Aberdour . . . . . . . . 128 F3
Aberdovey
= Aberdyfi . . . . . 58 E3
Aberdulais . . . . . . . 34 D1
Aberdyfi
= Aberdovey . . . . 58 E3
Aberedw . . . . . . . . . 48 E2
Abereiddy . . . . . . . . 44 B2
Abererch . . . . . . . . . 70 D4
Aberfan . . . . . . . . . . 34 D4
Aberfeldy . . . . . . . 133 E5
Aberffraw . . . . . . . . 82 E3
Aberffrwd . . . . . . . . 47 B5
Aberford . . . . . . . . . 95 F7
Aberfoyle . . . . . . . 126 D4
Abergavenny
= Y Fenni . . . . . . 35 C6
Abergele . . . . . . . . . 72 B3
Aber-Giâr . . . . . . . . 46 E4
Abergorlech . . . . . . 46 F4
Abergwaun
= Fishguard. . . . 44 B4
Abergwesyn . . . . . . 47 D7
Abergwili . . . . . . . . 33 B5
Abergwynant . . . . . 58 C3
Aber-gwynfi . . . . . . 34 E2
Abergwyngregyn . . 83 D6
Abergynolwyn . . . . 58 D3
Aber-Hirnant . . . . . 72 F3
Aberhonddu
= Brecon . . . . . . 34 B4
Aberhosan . . . . . . . 58 E5
Aberkenfig . . . . . . . 34 F2
Aberlady . . . . . . . . 129 F6
Aberlemno . . . . . . 135 D5
Aberllefenni . . . . . . 58 D4
Abermagwr . . . . . . 47 B5
Abermaw
= Barmouth . . . . 58 C3
Abermeurig . . . . . . 46 D4
Abermule . . . . . . . . 59 E8
Abernaint . . . . . . . . 59 B8
Abernant . . . . . . . . . 32 B4
Aber-nant . . . . . . . . 34 D4
Abernethy . . . . . . . 128 C3
Abernyte . . . . . . . . 134 F2
Aberpennar
= Mountain Ash . . 34 E4
Aberporth . . . . . . . . 45 D4
Aber-Rhiwlech . . . . 59 B6
Abersoch . . . . . . . . . 70 E4
Abersychan . . . . . . 35 D6
Abertawe
= Swansea . . . . . 33 E7
Aberteifi
= Cardigan . . . . . 45 E3
Aberthin . . . . . . . . . 22 B2
Abertillery
= Abertyleri . . . . 35 D6
Abertridwr Caerph. 35 F5
Powys . . . . . . . . . 59 C7

Abertyleri
= Abertillery . . . . 35 D6
Abertysswg . . . . . . 35 D5
Aberuthven . . . . . . 127 C8
Aber-Village . . . . . . 35 B5
Aberyscir . . . . . . . . 34 B3
Aberystwyth . . . . . . 58 F2
Abhainn Suidhe . 154 G5
Abingdon-on-
Thames . . . . . . . 38 E4
Abinger Common . . 28 E2
Abinger Hammer . . 27 E8
Abington . . . . . . . . 114 B2
Abington Pigotts . . 54 E4
Ab Kettleby . . . . . . 64 B4
Ab Lench . . . . . . . . . 50 D5
Ablington Glos . . . . 37 D8
Wilts . . . . . . . . . . 25 E6
Abney . . . . . . . . . . . 75 B8
Aboyne . . . . . . . . . 140 E4
Abram . . . . . . . . . . . 86 D4
Abriachan . . . . . . . 151 H8
Abridge . . . . . . . . . . 41 E7
Abronhill . . . . . . . . 119 B7
Abson . . . . . . . . . . . 24 B2
Abthorpe . . . . . . . . 52 E4
Abune-the-Hill . . . 159 F3
Aby . . . . . . . . . . . . . . 79 B7
Acaster Malbis . . . . 95 E4
Acaster Selby . . . . . 95 E8
Accrington . . . . . . . 87 B5
Acha . . . . . . . . . . . 146 F4
Achabraid . . . . . . . 145 E7
Achachork . . . . . . . 149 D9
Achafolla . . . . . . . 124 D3
Achagary . . . . . . . 157 D10
Achahoish . . . . . . . 144 F6
Achalader . . . . . . . 133 E8
Achallader . . . . . . . 131 E7
Acha Mor . . . . . . . 155 E8
Achanalt . . . . . . . . 150 E5
Achanamara . . . . . 144 E6
Achandunie . . . . . . 151 D9
Achany . . . . . . . . . 157 J8
Achaphubuil . . . . . 130 B4
Acharacle . . . . . . . 147 E9
Acharn Highld . . . 147 F10
Perth . . . . . . . . . 132 E4
Acharole . . . . . . . . 158 E4
Achath . . . . . . . . . . 141 C6
Achavanich . . . . . . 158 F3
Achavraat . . . . . . . 151 G12
Achddu . . . . . . . . . . 33 D5
Achduart . . . . . . . . 156 J3
Achentoul . . . . . . . 157 F11
Achfary . . . . . . . . . 156 F5
Achgarve . . . . . . . 155 H13
Achiemore Highld 156 C6
Highld . . . . . . . . . 157 D11
A'Chill . . . . . . . . . . 148 H7
Achiltibuie . . . . . . 156 J3
Achina . . . . . . . . . 157 C10
Achinduich . . . . . . 157 J8
Achinduin . . . . . . . 124 B4

Achingills . . . . . . . 158 D3
Achintee Highld . . 131 B5
Highld . . . . . . . . . 150 G2
Achintraid . . . . . . 149 E13
Achlean . . . . . . . . 138 E4
Achleck . . . . . . . . . 146 G2
Achluachrach . . . . 137 F5
Achlyness . . . . . . . 156 D5
Achmelvich . . . . . 156 G3
Achmore Highld . . 149 E13
Stirling . . . . . . . 132 F2
Achnaba Argyll . . 124 B5
Argyll . . . . . . . . . 145 E8
Achnabat . . . . . . . 151 H8
Achnacarnin . . . . . 156 F3
Achnacarry . . . . . . 136 F4
Achnacloich Argyll 125 B5
Highld . . . . . . . . . 149 H10
Achnaconeran . . . 137 C7
Achnacraig . . . . . . 146 G7
Achnacroish . . . . . 130 E2
Achnadrish . . . . . . 146 F7
Achnafalnich . . . . 125 C8
Achnagarron . . . . 151 E9
Achnaha . . . . . . . . 146 E7
Achnahanat . . . . . 151 B8
Achnahannet . . . . 139 B5
Achnairn . . . . . . . 157 H8
Achnaluachrach. . 157 J9
Achnasaul . . . . . . 136 F4
Achnasheen . . . . . 150 F4
Achosnich . . . . . . . 146 E7
Achranich . . . . . . 147 G10
Achreamie . . . . . . 157 C13
Achriabhach . . . . 131 C5
Achriesgill . . . . . . 156 D5
Achrimsdale . . . . 157 J12
Achtoty . . . . . . . . 157 C9
Achurch . . . . . . . . . 65 F7
Achuvoldrach . . . . 157 D8
Achvaich . . . . . . . 151 B10
Achvarasdal . . . . . 157 C12
Ackergill . . . . . . . 158 E5
Acklam Mbro . . . . 102 C2
N Yorks . . . . . . . 96 C3
Ackleton . . . . . . . . 61 E7
Acklington . . . . . . 117 D8
Ackton . . . . . . . . . . 88 B5
Ackworth Moor
Top. . . . . . . . . . . 88 C5
Acle . . . . . . . . . . . . 69 C7
Acock's Green. . . . 62 F5
Acol . . . . . . . . . . . . 31 C7
Acomb Northumb . 110 C2
York . . . . . . . . . . 95 D8
Aconbury . . . . . . . 49 F7
Acre . . . . . . . . . . . . 87 B5
Acrefair . . . . . . . . . 73 E6
Acre Street . . . . . . 15 E8
Acton Ches E . . . . 74 D3
Dorset . . . . . . . . 13 G7
London . . . . . . . . 41 F5
Shrops . . . . . . . . 60 F3
Suff . . . . . . . . . . 56 E2
Wrex . . . . . . . . . 73 D7

Acton Beauchamp . 49 D8
Acton Bridge . . . . . 74 B2
Acton Burnell . . . . 60 D5
Acton Green . . . . . 49 D8
Acton Pigott . . . . . 60 D5
Acton Round . . . . . 61 E6
Acton Scott . . . . . . 60 F4
Acton Trussell . . . . 62 C3
Acton Turville . . . . 37 F5
Adbaston . . . . . . . . 61 B7
Adber . . . . . . . . . . . 12 B3
Adderley . . . . . . . . 74 E3
Adderstone . . . . . 123 F7
Addiewell . . . . . . . 120 C2
Addingham . . . . . . 94 E3
Addington Bucks . . 39 B7
Kent . . . . . . . . . . 29 D7
London . . . . . . . . 28 C4
Addinston . . . . . . 121 D8
Addiscombe . . . . . 28 C4
Addlestone . . . . . . 27 C8
Addlethorpe . . . . . 79 C8
Adel . . . . . . . . . . . . 95 F5
Adeney . . . . . . . . . 61 C7
Adfa . . . . . . . . . . . . 59 D7
Adforton . . . . . . . . 49 B6
Adisham . . . . . . . . 31 D6
Adlestrop . . . . . . . 38 B2
Adlingfleet . . . . . . 90 B2
Adlington . . . . . . . 86 C4
Admaston Staffs . . 62 B4
Telford . . . . . . . . 61 C6
Admington . . . . . . 51 E7
Adstock . . . . . . . . . 52 F5
Adstone . . . . . . . . . 52 D3
Adversane . . . . . . . 16 B4
Advie . . . . . . . . . . 152 E1
Adwalton . . . . . . . 88 B3
Adwell . . . . . . . . . . 39 E6
Adwick le Street. . 89 D6
Adwick upon
Dearne . . . . . . . 89 D5
Adziel . . . . . . . . . 153 C9
Ae Village . . . . . . 114 F2
Affleck . . . . . . . . . 141 B7
Affpuddle . . . . . . . 13 E6
Affric Lodge . . . . 136 B4
Afon-wen . . . . . . . 72 B5
Afton . . . . . . . . . . . 14 F4
Agglethorpe . . . . 101 F5
Agneash . . . . . . . . 84 D4
Aigburth . . . . . . . . 85 F4
Aiginis . . . . . . . . . 155 D9
Aike . . . . . . . . . . . 97 E6
Aikerness . . . . . . 159 C5
Aikers . . . . . . . . . 159 J5
Aiketgate . . . . . . 108 E4
Aikton . . . . . . . . . 108 D2
Ailey . . . . . . . . . . . 48 E5
Ailstone . . . . . . . . 51 D7
Ailsworth . . . . . . . 65 E8
Ainderby
Quernhow . . . . 102 F1
Ainderby Steeple. 101 E8
Aingers Green. . . . 43 B7

Ainsdale . . . . . . . . 85 C4
Ainsdale-on-Sea . . 85 C4
Ainstable . . . . . . . 108 E5
Ainsworth . . . . . . . 87 C5
Ainthorpe . . . . . . . 103 D5
Aintree . . . . . . . . . . 85 E4
Aird Argyll . . . . . . 124 E3
Dumfries . . . . . . 104 C4
Highld . . . . . . . . 149 A12
W Isles . . . . . . . 155 D10
Aird a Mhachair . . 148 D2
Aird a' Mhulaidh . 154 F6
Aird Asaig . . . . . . 154 G6
Aird Dhail . . . . . . 155 A9
Airdens . . . . . . . . 151 B9
Aird Mhidhinis . . 148 H2
Aird Mhighe
W Isles . . . . . . . 154 H6
W Isles . . . . . . . 154 J5
Aird Mhor . . . . . . 148 H2
Aird of Sleat . . . . 149 H10
Airdrie . . . . . . . . . 119 C7
Aird Thunga . . . . 155 D9
Airdtorrisdale . . . 157 C9
Aird Uig . . . . . . . . 154 D5
Airidh a Bhruaich . 154 F7
Airieland . . . . . . . 106 D4
Airmyn . . . . . . . . . 89 B8
Airntully . . . . . . . 133 F7
Airor . . . . . . . . . 149 H12
Airth . . . . . . . . . . 127 F7
Airton . . . . . . . . . . 94 D2
Airyhassen . . . . . 105 E7
Aisby Lincs . . . . . . 78 F3
Lincs . . . . . . . . . 90 E2
Aisgernis . . . . . . . 148 F2
Aiskew . . . . . . . . 101 F7
Aislaby N Yorks . . 103 D6
N Yorks . . . . . . . 103 F5
Stockton. . . . . . 102 C2
Aisthorpe . . . . . . . 78 A2
Aith Orkney . . . . 159 G3
Shetland . . . . . . 160 D8
Shetland . . . . . . 160 H5
Aithsetter . . . . . . 160 K6
Aitkenhead . . . . . 112 D3
Aitnoch . . . . . . . 151 H12
Akeld . . . . . . . . . . 117 B5
Akeley . . . . . . . . . . 52 F5
Akenham . . . . . . . 56 E5
Albaston . . . . . . . . . 6 B2
Alberbury . . . . . . . 60 C3
Albourne . . . . . . . . 17 C6
Albrighton Shrops . 60 C4
Shrops . . . . . . . . 62 D2
Albury Herts . . . . . 41 B7
Sur . . . . . . . . . . . 27 E8
Albury End . . . . . . 41 B7
Alby Hill . . . . . . . . 81 D7
Alcaig . . . . . . . . . 151 F8
Alcaston . . . . . . . . 60 F4
Alcester . . . . . . . . 51 D5
Alciston . . . . . . . . 18 E2
Alcombe Som . . . . 21 E8

Alcombe continued
Wilts . . . . . . . . . 24 C3
Alconbury . . . . . . 54 B2
Som . . . . . . . . . . 23 F8
Alconbury Weald
Cambs. . . . . . . . 54 B3
Alconbury Weston. 54 B2
Aldborough Norf . . 81 D7
N Yorks . . . . . . . 95 C7
Aldbourne . . . . . . 25 B7
Aldbrough . . . . . . . 97 F8
Aldbrough St
John . . . . . . . . 101 C7
Aldbury . . . . . . . . 40 C2
Aldcliffe . . . . . . . . 92 C4
Aldclune . . . . . . . 133 C6
Aldeburgh . . . . . . 57 D8
Aldeby . . . . . . . . . 69 E7
Aldenham . . . . . . . 40 E4
Alderbury . . . . . . . 14 B2
Aldercar . . . . . . . . 76 E4
Alderford . . . . . . . 68 C4
Alderholt . . . . . . . 14 C2
Alderley . . . . . . . . 36 E4
Alderley Edge . . . . 74 B5
Aldermaston . . . . . 26 C3
Aldermaston
Wharf . . . . . . . . 26 C4
Alderminster . . . . 51 E7
Alder's End . . . . . . 49 E8
Aldersey Green . . . 73 D8
Aldershot . . . . . . . 27 D6
Alderton Glos . . . . 50 F5
Shrops . . . . . . . . 60 B4
Suff . . . . . . . . . . 57 E7
Wilts . . . . . . . . . 37 F5
W Nhants. . . . . . 52 E5
Alderwasley . . . . . 76 D3
Aldfield . . . . . . . . 95 C5
Aldford . . . . . . . . . 73 D8
Aldham Essex . . . . 43 B5
Suff . . . . . . . . . . 56 E4
Aldie . . . . . . . . . 151 C10
Aldingbourne . . . . 16 D3
Aldingham . . . . . . 92 B2
Aldington Kent . . . 19 B7
Worcs . . . . . . . . . 51 E5
Aldington Frith . . . 19 B7
Aldochlay . . . . . . 126 E2
Aldreth . . . . . . . . . 54 B5
Aldridge . . . . . . . . 62 D4
Aldringham . . . . . . 57 C8
Aldsworth . . . . . . . 38 C1
Aldunie . . . . . . . . 140 B2
Aldwark Derbys . . 76 D2
N Yorks . . . . . . . 95 C7
Aldwick . . . . . . . . 16 E3
Aldwincle . . . . . . . 65 F7
Aldworth . . . . . . . 26 B3
Alexandria . . . . . 118 B3
Alfardisworthy . . . . 8 C4
Alfington . . . . . . . 11 E6
Alfold . . . . . . . . . . 27 F8
Alfold Bars . . . . . . 27 F8
Alfold Crossways . 27 F8

Alford Aberds . . . 140 C4
Lincs . . . . . . . . . 79 B7
Som . . . . . . . . . . 23 F8
Alfreton . . . . . . . . 76 D4
Alfrick . . . . . . . . . 50 D2
Alfrick Pound . . . . 50 D2
Algaltraig . . . . . . 145 F9
Algarkirk . . . . . . . 79 F5
Alhampton . . . . . . 23 F8
Aline Lodge . . . . 154 F6
Alisary . . . . . . . . 147 D10
Alkborough . . . . . 90 B2
Alkerton . . . . . . . . 51 E8
Alkham . . . . . . . . . 31 E6
Alkington . . . . . . . 74 F2
Alkmonton . . . . . . 75 F8
Alladale Lodge . . 150 C7
Allaleigh . . . . . . . . . 7 D5
Allanaquoich . . . 139 E7
Allangrange
Mains . . . . . . . 151 F9
Allanton Borders . 122 D4
N Lanark . . . . . . 119 D8
Allathasdal. . . . . . 148 H1
Allendale Town . . 109 D8
Allenheads . . . . . 109 E8
Allensford . . . . . . 110 D3
Allens Green . . . . . 41 C7
Allensmore . . . . . . 49 F6
Allenton . . . . . . . . 76 F3
Aller . . . . . . . . . . . 12 B2
Allerby . . . . . . . . 107 F7
Allerford . . . . . . . . 21 E8
Allerston . . . . . . . 103 F6
Allerthorpe . . . . . . 96 E3
Allerton Mers . . . . 86 F2
W Yorks . . . . . . . 94 F4
Allerton Bywater . 88 B5
Allerton
Mauleverer . . . 95 D7
Allesley . . . . . . . . 63 F7
Allestree . . . . . . . 76 F3
Allet . . . . . . . . . . . . 3 B6
Allexton . . . . . . . . 64 D5
Allgreave . . . . . . . 75 C6
Allhallows . . . . . . 30 B2
Allhallows-on-Sea 30 B2
Alligin Shuas . . . 149 C13
Allimore Green . . . 62 C2
Allington Lincs . . . 77 E8
Wilts . . . . . . . . . 25 C5
Wilts . . . . . . . . . 25 F7
Allithwaite . . . . . . 92 B3
Alloa . . . . . . . . . . 127 E7
Allonby . . . . . . . . 107 E7
Alloway . . . . . . . . 112 C3
All Saints South
Elmham . . . . . . 69 F6
All Stretton . . . . . . 60 E4
Allt . . . . . . . . . . . . 33 D6
Alltbeithe . . . . . . 136 C4
Alltcaillich . . . . . 156 E7
Allt na h-Airbhe . 150 B4
Allt-nan-sùgh . . . 136 B2
Alltsigh . . . . . . . . 137 C7
Alltwalis . . . . . . . . 46 F3
Alltwen . . . . . . . . . 33 D8
Alltyblaca . . . . . . . 46 E4
Allwood Green . . . 56 B4
Almeley . . . . . . . . 48 D5
Almer . . . . . . . . . . 13 E7
Almholme . . . . . . . 89 D6
Almington . . . . . . . 74 F4
Alminstone Cross . . 8 B5
Almondbank . . . . 128 B2
Almondbury . . . . . 88 C2
Almondsbury . . . . 36 F3
Alne . . . . . . . . . . . 95 C7
Alness . . . . . . . . . 151 E9
Alnham . . . . . . . . 117 C5
Alnmouth . . . . . . 117 C8
Alnwick . . . . . . . . 117 C7
Alperton . . . . . . . . 40 F4
Alphamstone . . . . 56 F2
Alpheton . . . . . . . 56 D2
Alphington . . . . . . 10 E4
Alport . . . . . . . . . . 76 C2
Alpraham . . . . . . . 74 D2
Alresford . . . . . . . 43 B6
Alrewas . . . . . . . . 63 C5
Alsager . . . . . . . . . 74 D4
Alsagers Bank . . . 74 E5
Alsop en le Dale . . 75 D8
Alston Devon . . . . 11 D8
Cumb . . . . . . . . 109 E7
W&F. . . . . . . . . 109 E7
Alstone . . . . . . . . . 50 F4
Alstonefield. . . . . . 75 D8
Alswear . . . . . . . . 10 B2
Altandhu. . . . . . . 156 H2
Altanduin . . . . . . 157 G11
Altarnun . . . . . . . . . 8 F4
Altass . . . . . . . . . 156 J7
Alterwall . . . . . . 158 D4
Altham . . . . . . . . . 93 F7
Althorne . . . . . . . . 43 E5
Althorpe . . . . . . . . 90 D2
Alticry . . . . . . . . . 105 D6
Altnabreac
Station . . . . . . 157 E13
Altnacealgach
Hotel. . . . . . . . 156 H5
Altnacraig . . . . . . 124 C4
Altnafeadh . . . . . 131 D6
Altnaharra . . . . . 157 F8
Altofts . . . . . . . . . . 88 B4
Alton Derbys . . . . . 76 C3
Hants . . . . . . . . . 26 F5
Staffs . . . . . . . . . 75 E7
Alton Pancras . . . . 12 D5
Alton Priors . . . . . 25 C6
Altrincham . . . . . . 87 F5
Altrua . . . . . . . . . 136 F5
Altskeith . . . . . . . 126 D3

Altyre House 151 F13
Alva 127 E7
Alvanley 73 B8
Alvaston 76 F3
Alvechurch 50 B5
Alvecote 63 D6
Alvediston 13 B7
Alveley 61 F7
Alverdiscott 9 B7
Alverstoke 15 E7
Alverstone 15 F6
Alverton 77 E7
Alves 152 B1
Alvescot 38 D2
Alveston
S Glos 36 F3
Warks 51 D7
Alvie 138 D4
Alvingham 91 E7
Alvington 36 D3
Alwalton 65 E8
Alweston 12 C4
Alwinton 116 D5
Alwoodley 95 E5
Alyth 134 E2
Amatnatua 150 B7
Am Baile 148 G2
Ambergate 76 D3
Amber Hill 78 E5
Amberley Glos 37 D5
W Sus 16 C4
Amble 117 D8
Amblecote 62 F2
Ambler Thorn 87 B8
Ambleside 99 D5
Ambleston 44 C5
Ambrosden 39 C6
Am Buth 124 C4
Amcotts 90 C2
Amersham 40 E2
Amesbury 25 E6
Amington 63 D6
Amisfield 114 F2
Amlwch 82 B4
Amlwch Port 82 B4
Ammanford
=Rhydaman 33 C7
Amod 143 E8
Amotherby 96 B3
Ampfield 14 B5
Ampleforth 95 B8
Ampney Crucis 37 D7
Ampney St Mary 37 D7
Ampney St Peter 37 D7
Amport 25 E7
Ampthill 53 F8
Ampton 56 B2
Amroth 32 D2
Amulree 133 F5
Anagach 139 B6
Anaheilt 130 C2
Anancaun 150 E3
An Caol 149 C11
Ancaster 78 E2
Anchor 59 F8
Anchorsholme 92 E3
An Cnoc 155 D9
Ancroft 123 E5
Ancrum 116 B2
Anderby 79 B8
Anderson 13 E6
Anderton 74 B3
Andover 25 E8
Andover Down 25 E8
Andoversford 37 C7
Andreas 84 C4
Anfield 85 E4
Angersleigh 11 C6
Angle 44 E3
An Gleann Ur 155 D9
Angmering 16 D4
Angram N Yorks 95 F8
N Yorks 100 E3
Anie 126 C4
Ankerville 151 D11
Anlaby 90 B4
Anmer 80 E3
Annan 107 C8
Annat Argyll 125 C6
Highld 149 C13
Anna Valley 25 E8
Annbank 112 B4
Annesley 76 D5
Annesley
Woodhouse 76 D4
Annfield Plain 110 D4
Annifirth 160 J3
Annitsford 111 B5
Annscroft 60 D4
Ansdell 85 B4
Ansford 23 F8
Ansley 63 E6
Anslow 63 B6
Anslow Gate 63 B5
Anstey Herts 54 F5
Leics 64 D2
Anstruther
Easter 129 D7
Anstruther
Wester 129 D7
Ansty Hants 26 E5
Warks 63 F7
Wilts 13 B7
W Sus 17 B6
Anthill Common 15 C7
Anthorn 107 D8
Antingham 81 D8
An t-Ob
=Leverburgh 154 J5
Anton's Gowt 79 E5
Antonshill 127 F7
Antony 5 D8
Anwick 78 D4
Anwoth 106 D2
Aoradh 142 B3
Apes Hall 67 E5
Apethorpe 65 E7
Apeton 62 C2
Apley 78 B4
Apperknowle 76 B3
Apperley 37 B5
Apperley Bridge 94 F4
Appersett 100 E3
Appin 130 E3
Appin House 130 E3
Appleby 90 C3
Appleby-in-
Westmorland 100 B1
Appleby Magna 63 D7
Appleby Parva 63 D7
Applecross 149 D12
Applecross
House 149 D12
Appledore Devon 11 C5
Devon 20 F3
Kent 19 C6
Appledore Heath 19 B6
Appleford 39 E5
Applegarthtown 114 F4
Appleshaw 25 E8
Applethwaite 98 B4
Appleton Halton 86 F3
Oxon 38 D4
Appleton-le-
Moors 103 F5
Appleton-le-
Street 96 B3
Appleton Roebuck 95 E8
Appleton Thorn 86 F4
Appleton Wiske 102 D1
Appletreehall 115 C8
Appletreewick 94 C3
Appley 11 B5
Appley Bridge 86 D3
Apse Heath 15 F6
Apsley End 54 F2
Apuldram 16 D2
Aquhythie 141 C6
Arabella 151 D11
Arbeadie 141 E5
Arberth
=Narberth 32 C2
Arbirlot 135 E6
Arboll 151 C11
Arborfield 27 C5
Arborfield Cross 27 C5
Arborfield
Garrison 27 C5
Arbourthorne 88 F4
Arbroath 135 E6
Arbuthnott 135 B7
Archiestown 152 D2
Arclid 74 C4
Ardachu 157 J9
Ardalanish 146 K6
Ardanaiseig 125 C6
Ardaneaskan 149 E13
Ardanstur 124 D4
Ardargie House
Hotel 128 C2
Ardarroch 149 E13
Ardbeg Argyll 142 D5
Argyll 145 E10
Ardcharnich 150 C4
Ardchiavaig 146 K6
Ardchullarie
More 126 C4
Ardchyle 126 B4
Ard-dhubh 149 D12
Arddleen 60 C2
Ardechvie 136 E4
Ardeley 41 B6
Ardelve 149 F13
Arden 126 F2
Ardens Grafton 51 D6
Ardentinny 145 E10
Ardentraive 145 F9
Ardeonaig 132 F3
Ardersier 151 F10
Ardessie 150 C3
Ardfern 124 E4
Ardgartan 125 E8
Ardgay 151 B8
Ardgour 130 C4
Ardheslaig 149 C12
Ardiecow 152 B5
Ardindrean 150 C4
Ardingly 17 B7
Ardington 38 F4
Ardlair 140 B4
Ardlamont House 145 G8
Ardleigh 43 B6
Ardler 134 E2
Ardley 39 B5
Ardlui 126 C2
Ardlussa 144 E5
Ardmair 150 B4
Ardmay 125 E8
Ardminish 143 D7
Ardmolich 147 D10
Ardmore Argyll 124 C3
Highld 151 C10
Highld 156 D5
Ardnacross 147 G8
Ardnadam 145 F10
Ardnagrask 151 G8
Ardnarff 149 E13
Ardnastang 130 C2
Ardnave 142 A3
Ardno 125 E7
Ardo 153 E8
Ardoch 133 F7
Ardochy House 136 D5
Ardo House 141 B8
Ardoyne 141 B5
Ardpatrick 144 G6
Ardpatrick House 144 H6
Ardpeaton 145 E11
Ardrishaig 145 E7
Ardross Fife 129 D7
Highld 151 D9
Ardrossan 118 E2
Ardross Castle 151 D9
Ardshealach 147 E9
Ardsley 88 D4
Ardslignish 147 E8
Ardtalla 142 C5
Ardtalnaig 132 F4
Ardtoe 147 D9
Ardtrostan 127 B5
Arduaine 124 D3
Ardullie 151 E8
Ardvasar 149 H11
Ardvorlich 126 B5
Ardwell 104 E5
Ardwell Mains 104 E5
Ardwick 87 E6
Areley Kings 50 B3
Arford 27 F6
Argoed Caerph 35 E5
Powys 47 C8
Arichamish 124 E5
Arichastlich 125 B8
Aridhglas 146 J6
Arileod 146 F4
Arinacrinachd 149 C12
Arinagour 146 F5
Arion 159 G3
Arisaig 147 C9
Ariundle 130 C2
Arkendale 95 C6
Arkesden 55 F5
Arkholme 93 B5
Arkleton 115 E6
Arkle Town 101 D5
Arkley 41 E5
Arksey 89 D6
Arkwright Town 76 B4
Arle 37 B6
Arlecdon 98 C2
Arlesey 54 F2
Arleston 61 C6
Arley 86 F4
Arlingham 36 C4
Arlington Devon 20 E5
E Sus 18 E2
Glos 37 D8
Armadale Highld 157 C10
W Loth 120 C2
Armadale
Castle 149 H11
Armathwaite 108 E5
Arminghall 69 D5
Armitage 62 C4
Armley 95 F5
Armscote 51 E7
Armthorpe 89 D7
Arnabost 146 F5
Arncliffe 94 B2
Arncroach 129 D7
Arne 13 F7
Arnesby 64 E3
Arngask 128 C3
Arnisdale 149 G13
Arnish 149 D10
Arniston Engine 121 C6
Arnol 155 C8
Arnold E Yorks 97 E7
Notts 77 E5
Arnprior 126 E5
Arnside 92 B4
Aros Mains 147 G8
Arowry 73 F8
Arpafeelie 151 F9
Arrad Foot 99 F5
Arram 97 E6
Arrathorne 101 E7
Arreton 15 F6
Arrington 54 D4
Arrivain 125 B8
Arrochar [illegible]
[illegible]
Arthington 95 E5
Arthingworth 64 F4
Arthog 58 C3
Arthrath 153 E9
Arthurstone 134 E2
Artrochie 153 E10
Arundel 16 D4
Aryhoulan 130 C4
Asby 98 B2
Ascog 145 G10
Ascot 27 C7
Ascott 51 F8
Ascott-under-
Wychwood 38 C3
Asenby 95 B6
Asfordby 64 C4
Asfordby Hill 64 C4
Asgarby Lincs 78 E4
Lincs 79 C6
Ash Kent 29 C6
Kent 31 D6
Som 12 B2
Sur 27 D6
Ashampstead 26 B3
Ashbocking 57 D5
Ashbourne 75 E8
Ashbrittle 11 B5
Ash Bullayne 10 D2
Ashburton 7 C5
Ashbury Devon 9 E7
Oxon 38 F2
Ashby 90 D3
Ashby by Partney 79 C7
Ashby cum Fenby 91 D6
Ashby de la
Launde 78 D3
Ashby-de-la-
Zouch 63 C7
Ashby Folville 64 C4
Ashby Magna 64 E2
Ashby Parva 64 F2
Ashby Puerorum 79 B6
Ashby St Ledgers 52 C3
Ashby St Mary 69 D6
Ashchurch 50 F4
Ashcombe 7 B7
Ashcott 23 F6
Ashdon 55 E6
Ashe 26 E3
Asheldham 43 D5
Ashen 55 E8
Ashendon 39 C7
Ashfield Carms 33 B7
Stirling 127 D6
Suff 57 C6
Ashfield Green 57 B6
Ashfold Crossways 17 B6
Ashford Devon 20 F4
Hants 14 C2
Kent 30 E4
Sur 27 B8
Ashford Bowdler 49 B7
Ashford Carbonell 49 B7
Ashford Hill 26 C3
Ashford in the
Water 75 C8
Ashgill 119 E7
Ash Green 63 F7
Ashill Devon 11 C5
Norf 67 D8
Som 11 C8
Ashingdon 42 E4
Ashington
Northumb 117 F8
Som 12 B3
W Sus 16 C5
Ashintully Castle 133 C8
Ashkirk 115 B7
Ashlett 15 D5
Ashleworth 37 B5
Ashley Cambs 55 C7
Ches E 87 F5
Ashley *continued*
Devon 9 C8
Dorset 14 D2
Glos 37 E6
Hants 14 E3
Hants 25 F8
N Nhants 64 E4
Staffs 74 F4
Ashley Green 40 D2
Ashley Heath
Dorset 14 D2
Staffs 74 F4
Ash Magna 74 F2
Ashmanhaugh 69 B6
Ashmansworth 26 D2
Ashmansworthy 8 C5
Ash Mill 10 B2
Ashmore 13 C7
Ashorne 51 D8
Ashover 76 C3
Ashow 51 B8
Ashprington 7 D6
Ash Priors 11 B6
Ashreigney 9 C8
Ash Street 56 E4
Ashtead 28 D2
Ash Thomas 10 C5
Ashton Ches W 74 C2
Corn 2 D5
Hants 15 C6
Hereford 49 C7
Invclyd 118 B2
N Nhants 65 F7
W Nhants 53 E5
Ashton Common 24 D3
Ashton-in-
Makerfield 86 E3
Ashton Keynes 37 E7
Ashton under Hill 50 F4
Ashton-under-
Lyne 87 E7
Ashton upon
Mersey 87 E5
Ashurst Hants 14 C4
Kent 18 B2
W Sus 17 C5
Ashurstwood 28 F5
Ash Vale 27 D6
Ashwater 9 E5
Ashwell Herts 54 F3
Rutland 65 C5
Som 11 C8
Ashwellthorpe 68 E4
Ashwick [illegible]
Ashwicken 67 C7
Ashybank 113 C8
[illegible]
Askern 89 C6
Askerswell 12 E3
Askett 39 D8
Askham Notts 77 B7
W&F 99 B7
Askham Bryan 95 E8
Askham Richard 95 E8
Asknish 145 D8
Askrigg 100 E4
Askwith 94 E4
Aslackby 78 F3
Aslacton 68 E4
Aslockton 77 F7
Asloun 140 C4
Aspatria 107 E8
Aspenden 41 B6
Asperton 79 F5
Aspley Guise 53 F7
Aspley Heath 53 F7
Aspull 86 D4
Asselby 89 B8
Asserby 79 B7
Assington 56 F3
Assynt House 151 E8
Astbury 74 C5
Astcote 52 D4
Asterley 60 D3
Asterton 60 E3
Asthall 38 C2
Asthall Leigh 38 C3
Astley Shrops 60 C5
Warks 63 F7
Worcs 50 C2
Astley Abbotts 61 E7
Astley Bridge 86 C5
Astley Cross 50 C3
Astley Green 86 E5
Aston Ches E 74 E3
Ches W 74 B2
Derbys 88 F2
Hereford 49 B6
Herts 41 B5
Oxon 38 D3
Shrops 60 B5
Staffs 74 E4
S Yorks 89 F5
Telford 61 D6
W Mid 62 F4
Wokingham 39 F7
Aston Abbotts 39 B8
Aston Botterell 61 F6
Aston-by-Stone 75 F6
Aston Cantlow 51 D6
Aston Clinton 40 C1
Aston Crews 36 B3
Aston Cross 50 F4
Aston End 41 B5
Aston Eyre 61 E6
Aston Fields 50 C4
Aston Flamville 63 E8
Aston Ingham 36 B3
Aston juxta
Mondrum 74 D3
Aston le Walls 52 D2
Aston Magna 51 F6
Aston Munslow 60 F5
Aston on Clun 60 F3
Aston-on-Trent 63 B8
Aston Rogers 60 D3
Aston Rowant 39 E7
Aston Sandford 39 D7
Aston Somerville 50 F5
Aston Subedge 51 E6
Aston Tirrold 39 F5
Aston Upthorpe 39 F5
Astrop 52 F3
Astwick 54 F3
Astwood M Keynes 53 E7
Worcs 50 D3
Astwood Bank 50 C5
Aswarby 78 F3
Aswardby 79 B6
Atcham 60 D5
Atch Lench 50 D5
Athelhampton 13 E5
Athelington 57 B6
Athelney 11 B8
Athelstaneford 121 B8
Atherington 9 B7
Atherstone 63 E7
Atherstone on
Stour 51 D7
Atherton 86 D4
Atley Hill 101 D7
Atlow 76 E2
Attadale 150 H2
Attadale House 150 H2
Attenborough 76 F5
Atterby 90 E3
Attercliffe 88 F4
Attleborough Norf 68 E3
Warks 63 E7
Attlebridge 68 C4
Atwick 97 D7
Atworth 24 C3
Aubourn 78 C2
Auchagallon 143 E9
Auchallater 139 F7
Aucharnie 153 D6
Auchattie 141 E5
Auchavan 134 C1
Auchbreck 139 B8
Auchenback 118 D5
Auchenbainzie 113 E8
Auchenblae 135 B7
Auchenbrack 113 E7
Auchenbreck 145 E9
Auchencairn
Dumfries 106 D4
Dumfries 114 F2
N Ayrs 143 F11
Auchencrosh 104 B5
Auchencrow 122 C4
Auchendinny 121 C5
Auchengray 120 D2
Auchenhalrig 152 B3
Auchenheath 119 E8
Auchenlochan 145 F8
Auchenmalg 105 D6
Auchensoul 112 E2
Auchentiber 118 E3
Auchertyre 149 F13
Auchgourish 138 C5
Auchincarroch 126 F3
Auchindrain 125 E6
Auchindrean 130 C4
Auchininna 153 D6
Auchinleck 113 B5
Auchinloch 119 B6
Auchinroath 152 C2
Auchintoul 140 C4
Auchiries 153 F10
Auchlee 141 E7
Auchleven 140 B5
Auchlochan 119 F8
Auchlossan 140 D4
Auchlunies 141 E7
Auchlyne 126 B4
Auchmacoy 153 E9
Auchmair 140 B2
Auchmantle 105 C5
Auchmillan 112 B5
Auchmithie 135 E6
Auchmuirbridge 128 D4
Auchmull 135 B5
Auchnacree 134 C4
Auchnagallin 151 H13
Auchnagatt 153 D9
Auchnaha 145 E8
Auchnashelloch 127 C6
Aucholzie 140 E2
Auchrannie 134 D2
Auchroisk 139 B6
Auchronie 140 F3
Auchterarder 127 C8
Auchteraw 137 D6
Auchterderran 128 E4
Auchterhouse 134 F3
Auchtermuchty 128 C4
Auchterneed 150 F7
Auchtertool 128 E4
Auchtertyre 152 C1
Auchtubh 126 B4
Auckengill 158 D5
Auckley 89 D7
Audenshaw 87 E7
Audlem 74 E3
Audley 74 D4
Audley End 56 F2
Auds 153 B6
Aughton E Yorks 96 F3
Lancs 85 D4
Lancs 93 C5
S Yorks 89 F5
Wilts 25 D7
Aughton Park 86 D2
Auldearn 151 F12
Aulden 49 D6
Auldgirth 114 F2
Auldhame 129 F7
Auldhouse 119 D6
Ault a'chruinn 136 B2
Aultanrynie 156 F6
Aultbea 155 J13
Aultdearg 150 E5
Aultgrishan 155 J12
Aultguish Inn 150 D6
Aultibea 157 G13
Aultiphurst 157 C11
Aultmore 152 C4
Aultnagoire 137 B8
Aultnamain Inn 151 C9
Aultnaslat 136 D4
Aulton 140 B5
Aundorach 139 C5
Aunsby 78 F3
Auquhorthies 141 B7
Aust 36 F2
Austendike 66 B2
Austerfield 89 E7
Austrey 63 D6
Austwick 93 C7
Authorpe 91 F8
Authorpe Row 79 B8
Avebury 25 C6
Aveley 42 F1
Avening 37 E5
Averham 77 D7
Aveton Gifford 6 E4
Avielochan 138 C5
Aviemore 138 C4
Avington Hants 26 F3
W Berks 25 C8
Avoch 151 F10
Avon 14 E2
Avonbridge 120 B2
Avon Dassett 52 E2
Avonmouth 23 B7
Avonwick 6 D5
Awbridge 14 B4
Awhirk 104 D4
Awkley 36 F2
Awliscombe 11 D6
Awre 36 D4
Awsworth 76 E4
Axbridge 23 D6
Axford Hants 26 E4
Wilts 25 B7
Axminster 11 E7
Axmouth 11 E7
Axton 85 F2
Aycliff 31 E7
Aycliffe 101 B7
Aydon 110 C3
Aylburton 36 D3
Ayle 109 E7
Aylesbeare 10 E5
Aylesbury 39 C8
Aylesby 91 D6
Aylesford 29 D8
Aylesham 31 D6
Aylestone 64 D2
Aylmerton 81 D7
Aylsham 81 E7
Aylton 49 F8
Aymestrey 49 C6
Aynho 52 F3
Ayot St Lawrence 40 C4
Ayot St Peter 41 C5
Ayr 112 B3
Aysgarth 101 F5
Ayside 99 F5
Ayston 65 D5
Aythorpe Roding 42 C1
Ayton 122 C5
Aywick 160 E7
Azerley 95 B5


## B


Babbacombe 7 C7
Babbinswood 73 F7
Babcary 12 B3
Babel 47 F7
Babell 73 B5
Babraham 55 D6
Babworth 89 F7
Bac 155 C9
Bachau 82 C4
Backaland 159 E6
Backaskaill 159 C5
Backbarrow 99 F5
Backe 32 C3
Backfolds 153 C10
Backford 73 B8
Backford Cross 73 B7
Backhill Aberds 153 E7
Aberds 153 E10
Backhill of
Clackriach 153 D9
Backhill of
Fortree 153 D9
Backhill of
Trustach 140 E5
Backies 157 J11
Backlass 158 E4
Back of Keppoch 147 C9
Back Rogerton 113 B5
Backwell 23 C6
Backworth 111 B6
Bacon End 42 C2
Baconsthorpe 81 D7
Bacton Hereford 49 F5
Norf 81 D9
Suff 56 C4
Bacton Green 56 C4
Bacup 87 B6
Badachro 149 A12
Badanloch
Lodge 157 F10
Badavanich 150 F4
Badbury 38 F1
Badby 52 D3
Badcall 156 D5
Badcaul 150 B3
Baddeley Green 75 D6
Baddesley Clinton 51 B7
Baddesley Ensor 63 E6
Baddidarach 156 G3
Baddoch 139 F7
Baddock 151 F10
Badenscoth 153 E7
Badenyon 140 C2
Badger 61 E7
Badger's Mount 29 C5
Badgeworth 37 C6
Badgworth 23 D5
Badicaul 149 F12
Badingham 57 C7
Badlesmere 30 D4
Badlipster 158 F4
Badluarach 150 B2
Badminton 37 F5
Badnaban 156 G3
Badninish 151 B10
Badrallach 150 B3
Badsey 51 E5
Badshot Lea 27 E6
Badsworth 89 C5
Badwell Ash 56 C3
Bae Colwyn
=Colwyn Bay 83 D8
Bagby 102 F2
Bag Enderby 79 B6
Bagendon 37 D7
Bagh a Chaisteil
=Castlebay 148 J1
Baghasdal 148 G2
Bagh Mor 148 C3
Bagh
Shiarabhagh 148 H2
Bagillt 73 B6
Baginton 51 B8
Baglan 33 E8
Bagley 60 B4
Bagnall 75 D6
Bagnor 26 C2
Bagshot Sur 27 C7
Wilts 25 C8
Bagthorpe Norf 80 D3
Notts 76 D4
Bagworth 63 D8
Bagwy Llydiart 35 B8
Bail Àrd Bhuirgh 155 B9
Baildon 94 F4
Baile 154 J4
Baile Ailein 155 E7
Baile a Mhanaich 148 C2
Baile an Truiseil 155 B8
Bailebeag 137 C8
Baile Boidheach 144 F6
Baile Glas 148 C3
Baile Mhartainn 148 A2
Baile Mhic Phail 148 A3
Baile Mor Argyll 146 J5
W Isles 148 B2
Baile na Creige 148 H1
Baile nan
Cailleach 148 C2
Baile Raghaill 148 A2
Baileyhead 108 B5
Bailiesward 152 E4
Baillieston 119 C6
Bail'Iochdrach 148 C3
Bail Uachdraich 148 B3
Bail'Ur
Tholastaidh 155 C10
Bainbridge 100 E4
Bainsford 127 F7
Bainshole 152 E6
Bainton E Yorks 97 D5
Pboro 65 D7
Bairnkine 116 C2
Baker's End 41 C6
Baker Street 42 F2
Bakewell 76 C2
Bala =Y Bala 72 F3
Balachuirn 149 D10
Balavil 138 D3
Balbeg Highld 137 B7
Highld 150 H7
Balbeggie 128 B3
Balbithan 141 C6
Balbithan House 141 C7
Balblair Highld 151 B8
Highld 151 E10
Balby 89 D6
Balchladich 156 F3
Balchraggan
Highld 151 G8
Highld 151 H8
Balchrick 156 D4
Balchrystie 129 D6
[illegible]
[illegible]
Balcombe Lane 28 F4
Balcomie 129 C8
Balcurvie 128 D5
Baldersby 95 B6
Baldersby St
James 95 B6
Balderstone 93 F6
Balderton Ches W 73 C7
Notts 77 D8
Baldhu 3 B6
Baldinnie 129 C6
Baldock 54 F3
Baldovie 134 F4
Baldrine 84 D4
Baldslow 18 D4
Baldwin 84 D3
Baldwinholme 108 D3
Baldwin's Gate 74 E4
Bale 81 D6
Balearn 153 C10
Balemartine 146 G2
Balephuil 146 G2
Balerno 120 C4
Balevullin 146 G2
Balfield 135 C5
Balfour 159 G5
Balfron 126 F4
Balfron Station 126 F4
Balgaveny 153 D6
Balgavies 135 D5
Balgonar 128 E2
Balgove 153 E8
Balgowan 138 E2
Balgown 149 B8
Balgrochan 119 B6
Balgy 149 C13
Balhaldie 127 D7
Balhalgardy 141 B6
Balham 28 B3
Balhary 134 E2
Baliasta 160 C8
Baligill 157 C11
Balintore Angus 134 D2
Highld 151 D11
Balintraid 151 D10
Balk 102 F2
Balkeerie 134 E3
Balkemback 134 F3
Balkholme 89 B8
Balkissock 104 A5
Ball 60 B3
Ballabeg 84 E2
Ballacannel 84 D4
Ballachulish 130 D4
Ballajora 84 C4
Ballaleigh 84 D3
Ballamodha 84 E2
Ballantrae 104 A4
Ballaquine 84 D4
Ballards Gore 43 E5
Ballasalla IoM 84 C3
IoM 84 E2
Ballater 140 E2
Ballaugh 84 C3
Ballaveare 84 E3
Ballcorach 139 B7
Ballechin 133 D6
Balleigh 151 C10
Ballencrieff 121 B7
Ballentoul 133 C5
Ball Haye Green 75 D6
Ball Hill 26 C2
Ballidon 76 D2
Balliemore Argyll 124 C4
Argyll 145 E9
Ballikinrain 126 F4
Ballimeanoch 125 D6
Ballimore Argyll 145 E8
Stirling 126 C4
Ballinaby 142 B3
Ballindean 128 B4
Ballingdon 56 E2
Ballinger Common 40 D2
Ballingham 49 F7
Ballingry 128 E3
Ballinlick 133 E6
Ballinluig 133 D6
Ballintuim 133 D8
Balloch Angus 134 D3
Highld 151 G10
N Lanark 119 B7
W Dunb 126 F2
Ballochan 140 E4
Ballochford 152 E3
Ballochmorrie 112 F2
Balls Cross 16 B3
Balls Green 43 B6
Ballygown 146 G7
Ballygrant 142 B4
Ballyhaugh 146 F4
Balmacara 149 F13
Balmacara
Square 149 F13
Balmaclellan 106 B3
Balmacneil 133 D6
Balmacqueen 149 A9
Balmae 106 E3
Balmaha 126 E3
Balmalcolm 128 D5
Balmeanach 149 D10
Balmedie 141 C8
Balmer Heath 73 F8
Balmerino 129 B5
Balmerlawn 14 D4
Balmichael 143 E10
Balmirmer 135 F5
Balmore Highld 149 D7
Highld 150 H6
Highld 151 G11
Perth 133 D6
Balmule 128 F4
Balmullo 129 B6
Balmungie 151 F10
Balnaboth 134 C3
Balnabruaich 151 E10
Balnabruich 158 H3
Balnacoil 157 H11
Balnacra 150 G2
Balnafoich 151 H9
Balnagall 151 C11
Balnaguard 133 D6
Balnahard Argyll 144 D3
Argyll 146 H7
Balnain 150 H7
Balnakeil 156 C6
[illegible]
Balnapaling 151 E10
[illegible] 89 C6
[illegible] 143 C8
Balone 129 C6
Balornock 119 C6
Balquharn 133 F7
Balquhidder 126 B4
Balsall 51 B7
Balsall Common 51 B7
Balsall Heath 62 F4
Balscott 51 E8
Balsham 55 D6
Baltasound 160 C8
Balterley 74 D4
Baltersan 105 C8
Balthangie 153 C8
Baltonsborough 23 F7
Balvaird 151 F8
Balvicar 124 D3
Balvraid Highld 149 G13
Highld 151 H11
Bamber Bridge 86 B3
Bambers Green 42 B1
Bamburgh 123 F7
Bamff 134 D2
Bamford
Derbys 88 F3
Gtr Man 87 C6
Bampton Devon 10 B4
Oxon 38 D3
W&F 99 C7
Bampton Grange 99 C7
Banavie 131 B5
Banbury 52 E2
Bancffosfelen 33 C5
Banchory 141 E5
Banchory-
Devenick 141 D8
Bancycapel 33 C5
Bancyfelin 32 C4
Bancyffordd 46 F3
Bandirran 134 F2
Banff 153 B6
Bangor 83 D5
Bangor-is-y-coed
=Bangor-on-Dee 73 E7
Bangor-on-Dee
=Bangor-is-y-coed 73 E7
Banham 68 F3
Bank 14 D3
Bankend 107 C7
Bankfoot 133 F7
Bankglen 113 C6
Bankhead
Aberdeen 141 C7
Aberds 141 D5
Bank Newton 94 D2
Banknock 119 B7
Banks
Cumb 109 C5
Lancs 85 B4
Bankshill 114 F4
Bank Street 49 C8
Banningham 81 E8
Banniskirk House 158 E3
Bannister Green 42 B2
Bannockburn 127 E7
Banstead 28 D3
Bantham 6 E4
Banton 119 B7
Banwell 23 D5
Banyard's Green 57 B6
Bapchild 30 C3
Barabhas 155 C8
Barabhas Iarach 155 C8
Barabhas Uarach 155 B8
Barachandroman 124 C2
Barassie 118 F3
Baravullin 124 E4
Barbaraville 151 D10
Barber Booth 88 F2
Barbieston 112 C4
Barbon 99 F8
Barbridge 74 D3
Barbrook 21 E6
Barby 52 B3
Barcaldine 130 E3
Barcheston 51 F7
Barcombe 17 C8
Barcombe Cross 17 C8
Barden 101 E6
Bardennoch 113 E5
Barden Scale 94 D3
Bardfield Saling 42 B2
Bardister 160 F5
Bardney 78 C4
Bardon 63 C8
Bardon Mill 109 C7
Bardowie 119 B5
Bardrainney 118 B3
Bardsea 92 B3
Bardsey 95 E6
Bardwell 56 B3
Bare 92 C4
Barfad 145 G7
Barford Norf 68 D4
Warks 51 C7
Barford St John 52 F2
Barford St Martin 25 F5
Barford St Michael 52 F2
Barfrestone 31 D6
Bargod =Bargoed 35 E5
Bargoed =Bargod 35 E5
Bargrennan 105 B7
Barham Cambs 54 B2
Kent 31 D6
Suff 56 D5
Barharrow 106 D3
Barhill 106 C5
Bar Hill 54 C4
Barholm 65 C7
Barkby 64 D3
Barkestone-le-
Vale 77 F7
Barkham 27 C5
Barking London 41 F7
Suff 56 D4
Barkingside 41 F7
Barking Tye 56 D4
Barkisland 87 C8
Barkston Lincs 78 E2
N Yorks 95 F7
Barkway 54 F4
Barlaston 75 F5
Barlavington 16 C3
Barlborough 76 B4
Barlby 96 F2
Barlestone 63 D8
Barley Herts 54 F4
Lancs 93 F8
Barley Mow 111 D5
Barleythorpe 64 D5
Barling 43 F5
Barlow Derbys 76 B3
N Yorks 89 B7
T&W 110 C4
Barmby Moor 96 E3
Barmby on the
Marsh 89 B7
Barmer 80 D4
Barmoor Castle 123 F5
Barmoor Lane
End 123 F6
Barmouth
=Abermaw 58 C3
Barmpton 101 C8
Barmston 97 D7
Barnack 65 D7
Barnacle 63 F7
Barnard Castle 101 C5
Barnard Gate 38 C4
Barnardiston 55 E8
Barnbarroch 106 D5
Barnburgh 89 D5
Barnby 69 F7
Barnby Dun 89 D7
Barnby in the
Willows 77 D8
Barnby Moor 89 F7
Barnes Street 29 E7
Barnet 41 E5
Barnetby le Wold 90 D4
Barney 81 D5
Barnham Suff 56 B2
W Sus 16 D3
Barnham Broom 68 D3
Barnhead 135 D6
Barnhill Ches W 73 D8
Dundee 134 F4
Moray 152 C1
Barnhills 104 B3
Barningham
Durham 101 C5
Suff 56 B3
Barnoldby le Beck 91 D6
Barnoldswick 93 E8
Barns Green 16 B5
Barnsley Glos 37 D7
S Yorks 88 D4
Barnstaple 20 F4
Barnston Essex 42 C2
Mers 85 F3
Barnstone 77 F7
Barnt Green 50 B5
Barnton Ches W 74 B3
Edin 120 B4
Barnwell All Saints 65 F7
Barnwell St
Andrew 65 F7
Barnwood 37 C5
Barochreal 124 C4
Barons Cross 49 D6
Barr 112 E2
Barra Castle 141 B6
Barrachan 105 E7
Barrack 153 D8
Barraglom 154 D6
Barrahormid 144 E6
Barran 124 C4
Barrapol 146 G2
Barras Aberds 141 F7
W&F 100 C3
Barrasford 110 B2
Barravullin 124 E4
Barregarrow 84 D3
Barrhead 118 D4
Barrhill 112 F2
Barrington Cambs 54 E4
Som 11 C8
Barripper 2 C5
Barrmill 118 D3
Barrock 158 C4
Barrock House 158 D4
Barrow Lancs 93 F7
Rutland 65 C5

**Barrow** continued
Suff ... 55 C8
Barroway Drove ... 67 D5
Barrowburn ... 116 C4
Barrowby ... 77 F8
Barrowcliff ... 103 F8
Barrowden ... 65 D6
Barrowford ... 93 F8
Barrow Green ... 30 C3
Barrow Gurney ... 23 C7
Barrow Haven ... 90 B4
Barrow-in-
Furness ... 92 C2
Barrow Island ... 92 C1
Barrow Nook ... 86 D2
Barrows Green
Ches E ... 74 D3
W&F ... 99 F7
Barrow's Green ... 86 F3
Barrow Street ... 24 F3
Barrow upon
Humber ... 90 B4
Barrow upon Soar ... 64 C2
Barrow upon Trent ... 63 B7
Barry ... 135 F5
Barry = Y Barri ... 22 C3
Barry Island ... 22 C3
Barsby ... 64 C3
Barsham ... 69 F6
Barston ... 51 B7
Bartestree ... 49 E7
Barthol Chapel ... 153 E8
Barthomley ... 74 D4
Bartley ... 14 C4
Bartley Green ... 62 F4
Bartlow ... 55 E6
Barton Cambs ... 54 D5
Ches W ... 73 D8
Glos ... 37 B8
Lancs ... 85 D4
Lancs ... 92 F5
N Yorks ... 101 D7
Oxon ... 39 D5
Torbay ... 7 C7
Warks ... 51 D6
Barton Bendish ... 67 D7
Barton Hartshorn ... 52 F4
Barton in Fabis ... 76 F5
Barton in the
Beans ... 63 D7
Barton-le-Clay ... 53 F8
Barton-le-Street ... 96 B3
Barton-le-Willows 96 C3
Barton Mills ... 55 B8
Barton on Sea ... 14 E3
Barton on the
Heath ... 51 F7
Barton St David ... 23 F7
Barton Seagrave ... 53 B6
Barton Stacey ... 26 E2
Barton Turf ... 69 B6
Barton-under-
Needwood ... 63 C5
Barton-upon-
Humber ... 90 B4
Barton Waterside 90 B4
Barugh ... 88 D4
Barway ... 55 B6
Barwell ... 63 E8
Barwick Herts ... 41 C6
Som ... 12 C3
Barwick in Elmet ... 95 F6
Baschurch ... 60 B4
Bascote ... 52 C2
Basford Green ... 75 D6
Bashall Eaves ... 93 E6
Bashley ... 14 E3
Basildon ... 42 F3
Basingstoke ... 26 D4
Baslow ... 76 B2
Bason Bridge ... 22 E5
Bassaleg ... 35 F6
Bassenthwaite ... 108 F2
Bassett ... 14 C5
Bassingbourn ... 54 E4
Bassingfield ... 77 F6
Bassingham ... 78 C2
Bassingthorpe ... 65 B6
Basta ... 160 D7
Baston ... 65 C8
Bastwick ... 69 C7
Baswick Steer ... 97 E6
Batchworth Heath 40 E3
Batcombe Dorset ... 12 D4
Som ... 23 F8
Bate Heath ... 74 B3
Batford ... 40 C4
Bath ... 24 C2
Bathampton ... 24 C2
Bathealton ... 11 B5
Batheaston ... 24 C2
Bathford ... 24 C2
Bathgate ... 120 C2
Bathley ... 77 D7
Bathpool Corn ... 5 B7
Som ... 11 B7
Bathville ... 120 C2
Batley ... 88 B3
Batsford ... 51 F6
Battersby ... 102 D3
Battersea ... 28 B3
Battisborough
Cross ... 6 E3
Battisford ... 56 D4
Battisford Tye ... 56 D4
Battle E Sus ... 18 D4
Powys ... 48 F2
Battledown ... 37 B6
Battlefield ... 60 C5
Battlesbridge ... 42 E3
Battlesden ... 40 B2
Battlesea Green ... 57 B6
Battleton ... 10 B4
Battram ... 63 D8
Battramsley ... 14 E4
Baughton ... 50 E3
Baughurst ... 26 D3
Baulking ... 38 E3
Baumber ... 78 B5
Baunton ... 37 D7
Baverstock ... 24 F5
Bawburgh ... 68 D4
Bawdeswell ... 81 E6
Bawdrip ... 22 F5
Bawdsey ... 57 E7
Bawtry ... 89 E7
Baxenden ... 87 B5
Baxterley ... 63 E6
Baybridge ... 15 B6

Baycliff ... 92 B2
Baydon ... 25 B7
Bayford Herts ... 41 D6
Som ... 12 B5
Bayles ... 109 E7
Baylham ... 56 D5
Baynard's Green ... 39 B5
Bayston Hill ... 60 D4
Baythorn End ... 55 E8
Bayton ... 49 B8
Beach ... 130 D1
Beachampton ... 53 F5
Beachamwell ... 67 D7
Beacharr ... 143 D7
Beachborough ... 19 B8
Beachley ... 36 E2
Beacon ... 11 D6
Beacon End ... 43 B5
Beacon Hill ... 27 F6
Beacon's Bottom ... 39 E7
Beaconsfield ... 40 F2
Beacrabhaic ... 154 H6
Beadlam ... 102 F4
Beadlow ... 54 F2
Beadnell ... 117 B8
Beaford ... 9 C7
Beal Northumb ... 123 E6
N Yorks ... 89 B6
Beamhurst ... 75 F7
Beaminster ... 12 D2
Beamish ... 110 D5
Beamsley ... 94 D3
Bean ... 29 B6
Beanacre ... 24 C4
Beanley ... 117 C6
Beaquoy ... 159 F4
Bear Cross ... 13 E8
Beardwood ... 86 B4
Beare Green ... 28 E2
Bearley ... 51 C6
Bearnus ... 146 G6
Bearpark ... 110 E5
Bearsbridge ... 109 D7
Bearsden ... 118 B5
Bearsted ... 29 D8
Bearstone ... 74 F4
Bearwood BCP ... 13 E8
Hereford ... 49 D5
W Mid ... 62 F4
Beattock ... 114 D3
Beauchamp
Roding ... 42 C1
Beauchief ... 88 F4
Beaufort ... 35 C5
Beaufort Castle ... 151 G8
Beaulieu ... 14 D4
Beauly ... 151 G8
Beaumaris
= Biwmares ... 83 D6
Beaumont Cumb ... 108 D3
Essex ... 43 B7
Beaumont Hill ... 101 C7
Beausale ... 51 B7
Beauworth ... 15 B6
Beaworthy ... 9 E6
Beazley End ... 42 B3
Bebington ... 85 F4
Bebside ... 117 F8
Beccles ... 69 E7
Becconsall ... 86 B2
Beckbury ... 61 D7
Beckenham ... 28 C4
Beckermet ... 98 D2
Beckfoot Cumb ... 98 D3
Cumb ... 107 E7
Beck Foot ... 99 E8
Beckford ... 50 F4
Beckhampton ... 25 C5
Beck Hole ... 103 D6
Beckingham Lincs ... 77 D8
Notts ... 89 F8
Beckington ... 24 D3
Beckley E Sus ... 19 C5
Hants ... 14 E3
Oxon ... 39 C5
Beck Row ... 55 B7
Beck Side ... 98 F4
Beckton ... 41 F7
Beckwithshaw ... 95 D5
Becontree ... 41 F7
Bedale ... 101 F7
Bedburn ... 110 F4
Bedchester ... 13 C6
Beddau ... 34 F4
Beddgelert ... 71 C6
Beddingham ... 17 D8
Beddington ... 28 C4
Bedfield ... 57 C6
Bedford ... 53 D8
Bedham ... 16 B4
Bedhampton ... 15 D8
Bedingfield ... 57 C5
Bedlam ... 95 C5
Bedlar's Green ... 41 B8
Bedlington
Station ... 117 F8
Bedlinog ... 34 D4
Bedminster ... 23 B7
Bedmond ... 40 D3
Bednall ... 62 C3
Bedrule ... 116 C2
Bedstone ... 49 B5
Bedwas ... 35 F5
Bedworth ... 63 F7
Bedworth Heath ... 63 F7
Bed-y-coedwr ... 71 E8
Beeby ... 64 D3
Beech Hants ... 26 F4
Staffs ... 75 F5
Beech Hill Gtr Man. 86 D3
W Berks ... 26 C4
Beechingstoke ... 25 D5
Beedon ... 26 B2
Beeford ... 97 D7
Beelsby ... 91 D6
Beenham ... 26 C3
Beeny ... 8 E3
Beer ... 11 F7
Beercrocombe ... 11 B8
Beer Hackett ... 12 C3
Beesands ... 7 E6
Beesby ... 91 F8
Beeson ... 7 E6
Ches W ... 74 D2
Norf ... 68 C2
Notts ... 76 F5

**Beeston** continued
W Yorks ... 95 F5
Beeston Regis ... 81 C7
Beeswing ... 107 C5
Beetham ... 92 B4
Beetley ... 68 C2
Begbroke ... 38 C4
Begelly ... 32 D2
Beggar's Bush ... 48 C4
Beguildy ... 48 B3
Beighton Norf ... 69 D6
S Yorks ... 88 F5
Beighton Hill ... 76 D2
Beith ... 118 D3
Bekesbourne ... 31 D5
Belaugh ... 69 C5
Belbroughton ... 50 B4
Belchamp Otten ... 56 E2
Belchamp St Paul ... 55 E8
Belchamp Walter ... 56 E2
Belchford ... 79 B5
Belford ... 123 F7
Belhaven ... 122 B2
Belhelvie ... 141 C8
Belhinnie ... 140 B3
Bellabeg ... 140 C2
Bellamore ... 112 F2
Bellanoch ... 144 D6
Bellaty ... 134 C2
Bell Bar ... 41 D5
Bell Busk ... 94 D2
Belleau ... 79 B7
Bell End ... 50 B4
Bellerby ... 101 E6
Bellever ... 6 B4
Belliehill ... 135 C5
Bellingdon ... 40 D2
Bellingham ... 116 F4
Belloch ... 143 E7
Bellochantuy ... 143 E7
Bell o'th'Hill ... 74 E2
Bellsbank ... 112 D4
Bellshill N Lanark . 119 C7
Northumb ... 123 F7
Bellspool ... 120 F4
Bellsquarry ... 120 C3
Bells Yew Green ... 18 B3
Belmaduthy ... 151 F9
Belmesthorpe ... 65 C7
Belmont Blackburn.. 86 C4
London ... 28 C3
S Ayrs ... 112 B3
Shetland ... 160 C7
Belnacraig ... 140 C2
Belowda ... 4 C4
Belper ... 76 E3
Belper Lane End ... 76 E3
Belsay ... 110 B4
Belses ... 115 B8
Belsford ... 7 D5
Belstead ... 56 E5
Belston ... 112 B3
Belstone ... 9 E8
Belthorn ... 86 B5
Beltinge ... 31 C5
Beltoft ... 90 D2
Belton Leics ... 63 B8
Lincs ... 78 F2
N Lincs ... 89 D8
Norf ... 69 D7
Belton in Rutland.. 64 D5
Beltring ... 29 E7
Belts of
Collonach ... 141 E5
Belvedere ... 29 B5
Belvoir ... 77 F8
Bembridge ... 15 F7
Bemersyde ... 121 F8
Bemerton ... 25 F6
Bempton ... 97 B7
Benacre ... 69 F8
Ben Alder Lodge . 132 B2
Ben Armine
Lodge ... 157 H10
Benbuie ... 113 E7
Ben Casgro ... 155 E9
Benderloch ... 124 B5
Bendronaig
Lodge ... 150 H3
Benenden ... 18 B5
Benfield ... 105 C7
Bengate ... 69 B6
Bengeworth ... 50 E5
Benhall Green ... 57 C7
Benhall Street ... 57 C7
Benholm ... 135 C8
Beningbrough ... 95 D8
Benington Herts ... 41 B5
Lincs ... 79 E6
Benllech ... 82 C5
Benmore Argyll ... 145 E10
Stirling ... 126 B3
Benmore Lodge ... 156 H6
Bennacott ... 8 E4
Bennan ... 143 F10
Benniworth ... 91 F6
Benover ... 29 E8
Bensham ... 110 C5
Benslie ... 118 E3
Benson ... 39 E6
Bent ... 135 B6
Bent Gate ... 87 B5
Benthall Northumb. 117 B8
Shrops ... 61 D6
Bentham ... 37 C6
Benthoul ... 141 D7
Bentlawnt ... 60 D3
Bentley E Yorks ... 97 F6
Hants ... 27 E5
Suff ... 56 F5
S Yorks ... 89 D6
Warks ... 63 E6
Worcs ... 50 C4
Bentley Heath ... 51 B6
Benton ... 21 F5
Bentpath ... 115 E6
Bents ... 120 C2
Bentworth ... 26 E4
Benwick ... 66 E3
Beoley ... 51 C5
Beoraidbeg ... 147 B9
Bepton ... 16 C2
Berden ... 41 B7
Bere Alston ... 6 C2
Bere Ferrers ... 6 C2
Berepper ... 3 D5
Bere Regis ... 13 E6

Bergh Apton ... 69 D6
Berinsfield ... 39 E5
Berkeley ... 36 E3
Berkhamsted ... 40 D2
Berkley ... 24 E3
Berkswell ... 51 B7
Bermondsey ... 28 B4
Bernera ... 149 F13
Bernice ... 145 D10
Bernisdale ... 149 C9
Berrick Salome ... 39 E6
Berriedale ... 158 H3
Berrier ... 99 B5
Berriew ... 59 D8
Berrington
Northumb ... 123 E6
Shrops ... 60 D5
Berrow ... 22 D5
Berrow Green ... 50 D2
Berry Down Cross ... 20 E4
Berryfield ... 39 C7
Berry Hill Glos ... 36 C2
Pembs ... 45 E2
Berryhillock ... 152 B5
Berrynarbor ... 20 E4
Berry Pomeroy ... 7 C6
Bersham ... 73 E7
Berstane ... 159 G5
Berwick ... 18 E2
Berwick Bassett ... 25 B5
Berwick Hill ... 110 B4
Berwick St James ... 25 F5
Berwick St John ... 13 B7
Berwick St
Leonard ... 24 F4
Berwick-upon-
Tweed ... 123 D5
Bescar ... 85 C4
Besford ... 50 E4
Bessacarr ... 89 D7
Bessels Leigh ... 38 D4
Bessingby ... 97 C7
Bessingham ... 81 D7
Bestbeech Hill ... 18 B3
Besthorpe Norf ... 68 E3
Notts ... 77 C8
Bestwood ... 77 E5
Bestwood Village ... 77 E5
Beswick ... 97 E6
Betchworth ... 28 E3
Bethania Ceredig ... 46 C4
Gwyn ... 71 C8
Gwyn ... 83 F6
Bethel Anglesey ... 82 D3
Gwyn ... 72 F3
Gwyn ... 82 E5
Bethersden ... 30 E3
Bethesda Gwyn ... 83 E6
Pembs ... 32 C1
Bethlehem ... 33 B7
Bethnal Green ... 41 F6
Betley ... 74 E4
Betsham ... 29 B7
Betteshanger ... 31 D7
Bettiscombe ... 11 E8
Bettisfield ... 73 F8
Betton Shrops ... 60 D3
Shrops ... 74 F3
Bettws Bridgend ... 34 F3
Mon ... 35 C6
Newport ... 35 E6
Bettws Cedewain ... 59 E8
Bettws Gwerfil
Goch ... 72 E4
Bettws Ifan ... 46 E2
Bettws Newydd ... 35 D7
Bettws-y-crwyn ... 60 F2
Bettyhill ... 157 C10
Betws ... 33 C7
Betws Bledrws ... 46 D4
Betws-Garmon ... 82 F5
Betws-y-Coed ... 83 F7
Betws-yn-Rhos ... 72 B3
Beulah Ceredig ... 45 E4
Powys ... 47 D8
Bevendean ... 17 D7
Bevercotes ... 77 B6
Beverley ... 97 F6
Beverston ... 37 E5
Bevington ... 36 E3
Bewaldeth ... 108 F2
Bewcastle ... 109 B5
Bewdley ... 50 B2
Bewerley ... 94 C4
Bewholme ... 97 D7
Bexhill ... 18 E4
Bexley ... 29 B5
Bexleyheath ... 29 B5
Bexwell ... 67 D6
Beyton ... 56 C3
Bhaltos ... 154 D5
Bhatarsaigh ... 148 J1
Bibury ... 37 D8
Bicester ... 39 B5
Bickenhall ... 11 C7
Bickenhill ... 63 F5
Bicker ... 78 F5
Bickershaw ... 86 D4
Bickerstaffe ... 86 D2
Bickerton Ches E .. 74 D2
N Yorks ... 95 D7
Bickington Devon ...7 B5
Devon ... 20 F4
Bickleigh Devon ...6 C3
Devon ... 10 D4
Bickleton ... 20 F4
Bickley ... 28 C5
Bickley Moss ... 74 E2
Bicknacre ... 42 D3
Bicknoller ... 22 F3
Bicknor ... 30 D2
Bickton ... 14 C2
Bicton Shrops ... 60 C4
Shrops ... 60 F2
Bidborough ... 29 E6
Biddenden ... 19 B5
Biddenham ... 53 E8
Biddestone ... 24 B3
Biddisham ... 23 D5
Biddlesden ... 52 E4
Biddlestone ... 117 D5
Biddulph ... 75 D5
Biddulph Moor ... 75 D6
Bideford ... 9 B6
Bidford-on-Avon ... 51 D6
Bidston ... 85 E3
Bielby ... 96 E3
Bieldside ... 141 D7
Bierley IoW ... 15 G6

**Bierley** continued
W Yorks ... 94 F4
Bierton ... 39 C8
Bigbury ... 6 E4
Bigbury on Sea ... 6 E4
Bigby ... 90 D4
Biggar S Lanark ... 120 F3
W&F ... 92 C1
Biggin Derbys ... 75 D8
Derbys ... 76 E2
N Yorks ... 95 F8
Biggings ... 160 G3
Biggin Hill ... 28 D5
Biggleswade ... 54 E2
Bighouse ... 157 C11
Bighton ... 26 F4
Bignor ... 16 C3
Big Sand ... 149 A12
Bigton ... 160 L5
Bilberry ... 4 C5
Bilborough ... 76 E5
Bilbrook ... 22 E2
Bilbrough ... 95 E8
Bilbster ... 158 E4
Bildershaw ... 101 B7
Bildeston ... 56 E3
Billericay ... 42 E2
Billesdon ... 64 D4
Billesley ... 51 D6
Billingborough ... 78 F4
Billinge ... 86 D3
Billingford ... 81 E6
Billingham ... 102 B2
Billinghay ... 78 D4
Billingley ... 88 D5
Billingshurst ... 16 B4
Billingsley ... 61 F7
Billington C Beds ... 40 B2
Lancs ... 93 F7
Billockby ... 69 C7
Billy Row ... 110 F4
Bilsborrow ... 92 F5
Bilsby ... 79 B7
Bilsham ... 16 D3
Bilsington ... 19 B7
Bilson Green ... 36 C3
Bilsthorpe ... 77 C6
Bilsthorpe Moor ... 77 D6
Bilston Midloth ... 121 C5
W Mid ... 62 E3
Bilstone ... 63 D7
Bilting ... 30 E4
Bilton E Yorks ... 97 F7
Northumb ... 117 C8
Warks ... 52 B2
Bilton in Ainsty ... 95 E8
Bimbister ... 159 G4
Binbrook ... 91 E6
Binchester
Blocks ... 110 F5
Bincombe ... 12 F4
Bindal ... 151 C12
Binegar ... 23 E8
Binfield ... 27 B6
Binfield Heath ... 26 B5
Bingfield ... 110 B2
Bingham ... 77 F7
Bingley ... 94 F4
Bings Heath ... 60 C5
Binham ... 81 D5
Binley Hants ... 26 D2
W Mid ... 51 B8
Binley Woods ... 51 B8
Binniehill ... 119 B8
Binsoe ... 94 B5
Binstead ... 15 E6
Binsted ... 27 E5
Binton ... 51 D6
Bintree ... 81 E6
Binweston ... 60 D3
Birch Essex ... 43 C5
Gtr Man ... 87 D6
Bircham Newton ... 80 D3
Bircham Tofts ... 80 D3
Birchanger ... 41 B8
Birchencliffe ... 88 C2
Bircher ... 49 C6
Birch Green ... 43 C5
Birchgrove Cardiff... 22 B3
Swansea ... 33 E8
Birch Heath ... 74 C2
Birch Hill ... 74 B2
Birchington ... 31 C6
Birchmoor ... 63 D6
Birchover ... 76 C2
Birch Vale ... 87 F8
Birchwood Lincs ... 78 C2
Warr ... 86 E4
Bircotes ... 89 E7
Birdbrook ... 55 E8
Birdforth ... 95 B7
Birdham ... 16 D2
Birdholme ... 76 C3
Birdingbury ... 52 C2
Birdlip ... 37 C6
Birds Edge ... 88 D3
Birdsgreen ... 61 F7
Birdsmoor Gate ... 11 D8
Birdston ... 119 B6
Birdwell ... 88 D4
Birdwood ... 36 C4
Birgham ... 122 F3
Birkby ... 101 D8
Birkdale ... 85 C4
Birkenhead ... 85 F4
Birkenhills ... 153 D7
Birkenshaw
N Lanark ... 119 C6
W Yorks ... 88 B3
Birkhall ... 140 E2
Birkhill Angus ... 134 F3
Borders ... 114 C5
Birkholme ... 65 B6
Birkin ... 89 B6
Birley ... 49 D6
Birling Kent ... 29 C7
Northumb ... 117 D8
Birling Gap ... 18 F2
Birlingham ... 50 E4
Birmingham ... 62 F4
Birnam ... 133 E7
Birse ... 140 E4
Birsemore ... 27 F5
Birstall Leics ... 64 D2
W Yorks ... 88 B3
Birstwith ... 94 D5
Birthorpe ... 78 F4
Birtley Hereford ... 49 C5

**Birtley** continued
Northumb ... 109 B8
T&W ... 111 D5
Birts Street ... 50 F2
Bisbrooke ... 65 E5
Biscathorpe ... 91 F6
Biscot ... 40 B3
Bisham ... 39 F8
Bishampton ... 50 D4
Bish Mill ... 10 B2
Bishop Auckland 101 B7
Bishopbridge ... 90 E4
Bishopbriggs ... 119 C6
Bishop Burton ... 97 F5
Bishop
Middleham ... 111 F6
Bishopmill ... 152 B2
Bishop Monkton ... 95 C6
Bishop Norton ... 90 E3
Bishopsbourne ... 31 D5
Bishops Cannings ... 24 C5
Bishop's Castle ... 60 F3
Bishop's Caundle ... 12 C4
Bishop's Cleeve ... 37 B6
Bishops Frome ... 49 E8
Bishop's Green ... 42 C2
Bishop's Hull ... 11 B7
Bishop's
Itchington ... 51 D8
Bishops Lydeard ... 11 B6
Bishops Nympton ... 10 B2
Bishop's Offley ... 61 B7
Bishop's Stortford ... 41 B7
Bishop's Sutton ... 26 F4
Bishop's
Tachbrook ... 51 C8
Bishops Tawton ... 20 F4
Bishopsteignton ... 7 B7
Bishopstoke ... 15 C5
Bishopston ... 33 F6
Bishopstone Bucks ... 39 C8
E Sus ... 17 D8
Hereford ... 49 E6
Swindon ... 38 F2
Wilts ... 13 B8
Bishopstrow ... 24 E3
Bishop Sutton ... 23 D7
Bishop's Waltham ... 15 C6
Bishopswood ... 11 C7
Bishop's Wood ... 62 D2
Bishopsworth ... 23 C7
Bishop Thornton ... 95 C5
Bishopthorpe ... 95 E8
Bishopton Darl ... 102 B1
Dumfries ... 105 E8
N Yorks ... 95 B6
Renfs ... 118 B4
Warks ... 51 D6
Bishop Wilton ... 96 D3
Bishton ... 35 F7
Bisley Glos ... 37 D6
Sur ... 27 D7
Bispham ... 92 E3
Bispham Green ... 86 C2
Bissoe ... 3 B6
Bisterne Close ... 14 D3
Bitchfield ... 65 B6
Bittadon ... 20 E4
Bittaford ... 6 D4
Bittering ... 68 C2
Bitterley ... 49 B7
Bitterne ... 15 C5
Bitteswell ... 64 F2
Bitton ... 23 C8
Bix ... 39 F7
Bixter ... 160 H5
Blaby ... 64 E2
Blackacre ... 114 E3
Blackadder West . 122 D4
Blackawton ... 7 D6
Blackborough ... 11 D5
Blackborough End. 67 C6
Black Bourton ... 38 D2
Blackboys ... 18 C2
Blackbrook Derbys . 76 E3
Mers ... 86 E3
Staffs ... 74 F4
Blackburn Aberds . 141 C7
Aberds ... 152 E5
Blackburn ... 86 B4
W Loth ... 120 C2
Black Callerton ... 110 C4
Black Clauchrie ... 112 F2
Black Corries
Lodge ... 131 D6
Blackcraig ... 113 F7
Black Crofts ... 124 B5
Blackden Heath ... 74 B4
Black Dog ... 10 D3
Blackfell ... 111 D5
Blackfield ... 14 D5
Blackford Cumb ... 108 C3
Perth ... 127 D7
Som ... 12 B4
Som ... 23 E6
Blackfordby ... 63 C7
Blackgang ... 15 G5
Blackhall Colliery 111 F7
Blackhall Mill ... 110 D4
Blackhall Rocks ... 111 F7
Blackham ... 29 F5
Blackhaugh ... 121 F7
Blackheath Essex . 43 B6
Suff ... 57 B8
Sur ... 27 E8
W Mid ... 62 F3
Black Heddon ... 110 B3
Blackhill Aberds. .153 C10
Aberds ... 153 D10
Borders ... 114 C5
Blackhills Highld .151 F12
Moray ... 152 C2
Blackhorse ... 23 B8
Blackland ... 24 C5
Black Lane ... 87 D5
Blacklaw ... 153 C6
Blackley ... 87 D6
Blacklunans ... 134 C1
Black Marsh ... 60 E3
Blackmill ... 34 F3
Blackmoor ... 27 F5
Blackmoor Gate ... 21 E5
Blackmore ... 42 D2
Blackmore End
Essex ... 55 F8
Herts ... 40 C4

Black Mount ... 131 E6
Blackness ... 120 B3
Blacknest ... 27 C5
Black Notley ... 42 B3
Blacko ... 93 E8
Black Pill ... 33 E7
Blackpool Blackpool 92 F3
Devon ... 7 E6
Pembs ... 32 C1
Blackpool Gate ... 108 B5
Blackridge ... 119 C8
Blackrock Argyll ... 142 B4
Mon ... 35 C6
Blackrod ... 86 C4
Blackshaw ... 107 C7
Blackshaw Head ... 87 B7
Blacksmith's
Green ... 56 C5
Blackstone ... 17 C6
Black Tar ... 44 E4
Blackthorn ... 39 C6
Blackthorpe ... 56 C3
Blacktoft ... 90 B2
Blacktop ... 141 D7
Black Torrington ... 9 D6
Blackwall ... 35 F6
Blackwall Tunnel ... 41 F6
Blackwater Corn ... 3 B6
Hants ... 27 D6
IoW ... 15 F6
Blackwaterfoot ... 143 F9
Blackwell Darl ... 101 C7
Derbys ... 75 B8
Derbys ... 76 D4
Warks ... 51 E7
Worcs ... 50 B4
W Sus ... 28 F4
Blackwood ... 119 E7
Blackwood
= Coed Duon ... 35 E5
Blackwood Hill ... 75 D6
Blacon ... 73 C7
Bladnoch ... 105 D8
Bladon ... 38 C4
Blaenannerch ... 45 E4
Blaenau Ffestiniog 71 C8
Blaenavon ... 35 D6
Blaencelyn ... 46 D2
Blaendyryn ... 47 F8
Blaenffos ... 45 F3
Blaengarw ... 34 E3
Blaengwrach ... 34 D2
Blaen-gwynfi ... 34 E2
Blaenpennal ... 46 C5
Blaenplwyf ... 46 B4
Blaenporth ... 45 E4
Blaenrhondda ... 34 D3
Blaen-waun ... 32 B3
Blaen-y-coed ... 32 B4
Blaenycwm ... 47 B8
Blaen-y-Cwm Denb 72 F4
Gwyn ... 71 E8
Powys ... 59 B7
Blagdon N Som ... 23 D7
Torbay ... 7 C6
Blagdon Hill ... 11 C7
Blagill ... 109 E7
Blaguegate ... 86 D2
Blaich ... 130 B4
Blain ... 147 E9
Blaina ... 35 D6
Blair Atholl ... 133 C5
Blairbeg ... 143 E11
Blairdaff ... 141 C5
Blair Drummond ... 127 E6
Blairglas ... 126 F2
Blairgowrie ... 134 E1
Blairhall ... 128 F2
Blairingone ... 127 E8
Blairland ... 118 E3
Blairlogie ... 127 E7
Blairlomond ... 125 F7
Blairmore ... 145 E10
Blairnamarrow ... 139 C8
Blairquhosh ... 126 F4
Blair's Ferry ... 145 G8
Blairskaith ... 119 B5
Blaisdon ... 36 C4
Blakebrook ... 50 B3
Blakedown ... 50 B3
Blakelaw ... 122 F3
Blakeley ... 62 E2
Blakeley Lane ... 75 E6
Blakemere ... 49 E5
Blakeney Glos ... 36 D3
Norf ... 81 C6
Blakenhall Ches E .. 74 E4
W Mid ... 62 E3
Blakeshall ... 62 F2
Blakesley ... 52 D4
Blanchland ... 110 D2
Blandford Forum . 13 D6
Blandford St Mary. 13 D6
Bland Hill ... 94 D5
Blanefield ... 119 B5
Blankney ... 78 C3
Blantyre ... 119 D6
Blar a'Chaorainn .131 C5
Blaran ... 124 D4
Blarghour ... 125 D5
Blarmachfoldach .130 C4
Blarnalearoch ... 150 B4
Blashford ... 14 D2
Blaston ... 64 E5
Blatherwycke ... 65 E6
Blawith ... 98 F4
Blaxhall ... 57 D7
Blaxton ... 89 D7
Blaydon ... 110 C4
Bleadon ... 22 D5
Bleak Hey Nook ... 87 D8
Blean ... 30 C5
Bleasby Lincs ... 90 F5
Notts ... 77 E7
Bleasdale ... 93 E5
Bleatarn ... 100 C2
Blebocraigs ... 129 C6
Bleddfa ... 48 C4
Bledington ... 38 B2
Bledlow ... 39 D7
Bledlow Ridge ... 39 E7
Blegbie ... 121 C7
Blencarn ... 109 F6
Blencogo ... 107 E8
Blendworth ... 15 C8
Blenheim Park ... 80 D5
Blennerhasset ... 107 E8
Blervie Castle ... 151 F13
Bletchingdon ... 39 C5

Bletchingley ... 28 D4
Bletchley M Keynes . 53 F6
Shrops ... 74 F3
Bletherston ... 32 B1
Bletsoe ... 53 D8
Blewbury ... 39 F5
Blickling ... 81 E7
Blidworth ... 77 D5
Blindburn ... 116 C4
Blindcrake ... 107 F8
Blindley Heath ... 28 E4
Blisland ... 5 B6
Blissford ... 14 C2
Bliss Gate ... 50 B2
Blisworth ... 52 D5
Blithbury ... 62 B4
Blitterlees ... 107 D8
Blockley ... 51 F6
Blofield ... 69 D6
Blofield Heath ... 69 C6
Blo' Norton ... 56 B4
Bloomfield ... 115 B8
Blore ... 75 E8
Blount's Green ... 75 F7
Blowick ... 85 C4
Bloxham ... 52 F2
Bloxholm ... 78 D3
Bloxwich ... 62 D3
Bloxworth ... 13 E6
Blubberhouses ... 94 D4
Blue Anchor Som ... 22 E2
Swansea ... 33 E6
Blue Row ... 43 C6
Blundeston ... 69 E8
Blunham ... 54 D2
Blunsdon St
Andrew ... 37 F8
Bluntington ... 50 B3
Bluntisham ... 54 B4
Blunts ... 5 C8
Blyborough ... 90 E3
Blyford ... 57 B8
Blymhill ... 62 C2
Blyth Northumb ... 117 F9
Notts ... 89 F7
Blyth Bridge ... 120 E4
Blythburgh ... 57 B8
Blythe ... 121 E8
Blythe Bridge ... 75 E6
Blyton ... 90 E2
Boarhills ... 129 C7
Boarhunt ... 15 D7
Boars Head ... 86 D3
Boarshead ... 18 B2
Boars Hill ... 38 D4
Boasley Cross ... 9 E6
Boat of Garten ... 138 C5
Bobbing ... 30 C2
Bobbington ... 62 E2
Bobbingworth ... 41 D8
Bocaddon ... 5 D6
Bochastle ... 126 D5
Bocking ... 42 B3
Bocking
Churchstreet ... 42 B3
Boddam Aberds .153 D11
Shetland ... 160 M5
Boddington ... 37 B5
Bodedern ... 82 C3
Bodelwyddan ... 72 B4
Bodenham
Hereford ... 49 D7
Wilts ... 14 B2
Bodenham Moor ... 49 D7
Bodermid ... 70 E2
Bodewryd ... 82 B3
Bodfari ... 72 B4
Bodffordd ... 82 D4
Bodham ... 81 C7
Bodiam ... 18 C4
Bodicote ... 52 F2
Bodieve ... 4 B4
Bodinnick ... 5 D6
Bodle Street
Green ... 18 D3
Bodmin ... 5 C5
Bodney ... 67 E8
Bodorgan ... 82 E3
Bodsham ... 30 E5
Boduan ... 70 D4
Bodymoor Heath ... 63 E5
Bogallan ... 151 F9
Bogbrae ... 153 E10
Bogend Borders . 122 E3
S Ayrs ... 118 F3
Boghall ... 120 C2
Boghead ... 119 E7
Bogmoor ... 152 B3
Bogniebrae ... 152 D5
Bognor Regis ... 16 E3
Bograxie ... 141 C6
Bogside ... 119 D8
Bogton ... 153 C6
Bogue ... 113 F6
Bohenie ... 137 F5
Bohortha ... 3 C7
Bohuntine ... 137 F5
Boirseam ... 154 J5
Bojewyan ... 2 C2
Bolam Durham ... 101 B6
Northumb ... 117 F6
Bolberry ... 6 F4
Bold Heath ... 86 F3
Boldon ... 111 C6
Boldon Colliery ... 111 C6
Boldre ... 14 E4
Boldron ... 101 C5
Bole ... 89 F8
Bolehill ... 76 D2
Boleside ... 121 F7
Bolham ... 10 C4
Bolham Water ... 11 C6
Bolingey ... 3 D6
Bollington ... 75 B6
Bollington Cross ... 75 B6
Bolney ... 17 B6
Bolnhurst ... 53 D8
Bolshan ... 135 D6
Bolsover ... 76 B4
Bolsterstone ... 88 E3
Bolstone ... 49 F7
Boltby ... 102 F2
Bolton E Loth ... 121 B8
E Yorks ... 96 D3
Gtr Man ... 86 D5
Northumb ... 117 C7

**Bolton** continued
W&F ... 99 B8
Bolton Abbey ... 94 D3
Bolton Bridge ... 94 D3
Bolton-by-
Bowland ... 93 E7
Boltonfellend ... 108 C4
Boltongate ... 108 E2
Bolton-le-Sands ... 92 C4
Bolton Low
Houses ... 108 E2
Bolton-on-Swale 101 E7
Bolton Percy ... 95 E8
Bolton Town End ... 92 C4
Bolton upon
Dearne ... 89 D5
Bolventor ... 5 B6
Bomere Heath ... 60 C4
Bonar Bridge ... 151 B9
Bonawe ... 125 B6
Bonby ... 90 C4
Boncath ... 45 F4
Bonchester
Bridge ... 115 C8
Bonchurch ... 15 G6
Bondleigh ... 9 D8
Bonehill Devon ... 6 B5
Staffs ... 63 D5
Bo'ness ... 127 F8
Bonhill ... 118 B3
Boningale ... 62 D2
Bonjedward ... 116 B2
Bonkle ... 119 D8
Bonnavoulin ... 147 F8
Bonnington Edin . 120 C4
Kent ... 19 B7
Bonnybank ... 129 D5
Bonnybridge ... 127 F7
Bonnykelly ... 153 C8
Bonnyrigg and
Lasswade ... 121 C6
Bonnyton Aberds . 153 E6
Angus ... 134 F3
Angus ... 135 D6
Bonsall ... 76 D2
Bonskeid House . 133 C5
Bont ... 35 C7
Bontddu ... 58 C3
Bont-Dolgadfan... 59 D5
Bont-goch ... 58 F3
Bonthorpe ... 79 B7
Bontnewydd
Ceredig ... 46 C5
Gwyn ... 82 F4
Bont Newydd Gwyn. 71 C8
Gwyn ... 71 E8
Bontuchel ... 72 D4
Bonvilston ... 22 B2
Bon-y-maen ... 33 E7
Booker ... 39 E8
Boon ... 121 E8
Boosbeck ... 102 C4
Boot ... 98 D3
Booth ... 87 B8
Boothby Graffoe .. 78 D2
Boothby Pagnell . 78 F2
Boothen ... 75 E5
Boothferry ... 89 B8
Boothville ... 53 C5
Booth Wood ... 87 C8
Bootle Cumb ... 98 F3
Mers ... 85 E4
Booton ... 81 E7
Boot Street ... 57 E6
Boquhan ... 126 F4
Boraston ... 49 B8
Borden Kent ... 30 C2
W Sus ... 16 B2
Bordley ... 94 C2
Bordon ... 27 F6
Bordon Camp ... 27 F5
Boreham Essex ... 42 D3
Wilts ... 24 E3
Boreham Street ... 18 D3
Borehamwood ... 40 E4
Boreland Dumfries. 114 E4
Stirling ... 132 F2
Borgh W Isles ... 148 H1
W Isles ... 154 J4
Borghastan ... 154 C7
Borgie ... 157 D9
Borgue Dumfries.. 106 E3
Highld ... 158 H3
Borley ... 56 E2
Bornais ... 148 F2
Bornesketaig ... 149 A8
Borness ... 106 E3
Boroughbridge ... 95 C6
Borough Green ... 29 D7
Borras Head ... 73 D7
Borreraig ... 148 C6
Borrobol Lodge .157 G11
Borrowash ... 76 F4
Borrowby ... 102 F2
Borrowdale ... 98 C4
Borrowfield ... 141 E7
Borth ... 58 E3
Borthwickbrae ... 115 C7
Borthwickshiels .. 115 C7
Borth-y-Gest ... 71 D6
Borve ... 149 D9
Borve Lodge ... 154 H5
Borwick ... 92 B5
Bosavern ... 2 C2
Bosbury ... 49 E8
Boscastle ... 8 E3
Boscombe BCP ... 14 E2
Wilts ... 25 F7
Boscoppa ... 4 D5
Bosham ... 16 D2
Bosherston ... 44 F4
Boskenna ... 2 D3
Bosley ... 75 C6
Bossall ... 96 C3
Bossiney ... 8 F2
Bossingham ... 31 E5
Bossington ... 21 E7
Bostock Green ... 74 C3
Boston ... 79 E6
Boston Long
Hedges ... 79 E6
Boston Spa ... 95 E7
Boston West ... 79 E5
Boswinger ... 3 B8
Botallack ... 2 C2

Burniston 103 E8
Burnlee 88 D2
Burnley 93 F8
Burnley Lane 93 F8
Burnmouth 123 C5
Burn of Cambus 127 D6
Burnopfield 110 D4
Bursall 94 C3
Burnside Angus 135 D5
E Ayrs 113 C5
Fife 128 D3
Shetland 160 F4
S Lanark 119 C6
W Loth 120 B3
Burnside of Duntrune 134 F4
Burnswark 107 B8
Burntcommon 27 D8
Burnt Heath 76 B2
Burnthouse 3 C6
Burnt Houses 101 B6
Burntisland 128 F4
Burnton 112 D4
Burntwood 62 D4
Burnt Yates 95 C5
Burnwynd 120 C4
Burpham Sur 27 D8
W Sus 16 D4
Burradon
Northumb 117 D5
T&W 111 B5
Burrafirth 160 B8
Burraland Shetland 160 F5
Shetland 160 J4
Burras 3 C5
Burravoe Shetland 160 F7
Shetland 160 G5
Burray Village 159 J5
Burrells 100 C1
Burrelton 134 F2
Burridge Devon 20 F4
Hants 15 C6
Burrill 101 F7
Burringham 90 D2
Burrington Devon 9 C8
Hereford 49 B6
N Som 23 D6
Burrough Green 55 D7
Burrough on the Hill 64 C4
Burrow-bridge 11 B8
Burrowhill 27 C7
Burry 33 E5
Burry Green 33 E5
Burry Port
= Porth Tywyn 33 D5
Burscough 86 C2
Burscough Bridge 86 C2
Bursea 96 F4
Burshill 97 E6
Bursledon 15 D5
Burslem 75 E5
Burstall 56 E4
Burstock 12 D2
Burston Norf 68 F4
Staffs 75 F6
Burstow 28 E4
Burstwick 91 B6
Burtersett 100 F3
Burtle 23 E5
Burton BCP 14 E2
Ches W 73 B7
Ches W 74 C2
Lincs 78 B2
Northumb 123 F7
Pembs 44 E4
Som 22 E3
Wilts 24 B3
Burton Agnes 97 C7
Burton Bradstock 12 F2
Burton Dassett 51 D8
Burton Fleming 97 B6
Burton Green
W Mid 51 B7
Wrex 73 D7
Burton Hastings 63 E8
Burton-in-Kendal 92 B5
Burton in Lonsdale 93 B6
Burton Joyce 77 E6
Burton Latimer 53 B7
Burton Lazars 64 C4
Burton-le-Coggles 65 B6
Burton Leonard 95 C6
Burton on the Wolds 64 B2
Burton Overy 64 E3
Burton Pedwardine 78 E4
Burton Pidsea 97 F8
Burton Salmon 89 B5
Burton Stather 90 C2
Burton upon Stather 90 C2
Burton upon Trent 63 B6
Burtonwood 86 E3
Burwardsley 74 D2
Burwarton 61 F6
Burwash 18 C3
Burwash Common 18 C3
Burwash Weald 18 C3
Burwell Cambs 55 C6
Lincs 79 B6
Burwen 82 B4
Burwick 159 K5
Bury Cambs 66 F2
Gtr Man 87 C6
Som 10 B4
W Sus 16 C4
Bury Green 41 B7
Bury St Edmunds 56 C2
Burythorpe 96 C3
Busby 119 D5
Buscot 38 E2
Bush Bank 49 D6
Bushbury 62 D3
Bushby 64 D3
Bush Crathie 139 E8
Bushey 40 E4
Bushey Heath 40 E4
Bush Green 68 F5
Bushley 50 F3
Bushton 25 B5
Buslingthorpe 90 F4
Busta 160 G5
Butcher's Cross 18 C2
Butcombe 23 C7
Butetown 22 B3
Butleigh 23 F7
Butleigh Wootton 23 F7
Butler's Cross 39 D8
Butler's End 63 F6
Butlers Marston 51 E8
Butley 57 D7
Butley High Corner 57 E7
Butterburn 109 B6
Buttercrambe 96 D3
Butterknowle 101 B6
Butterleigh 10 D4
Buttermere Cumb 98 C3
Wilts 25 C8
Buttershaw 88 B2
Butterstone 133 E7
Butterton 75 D7
Butterwick
Durham 102 B1
Lincs 79 E6
N Yorks 96 B3
N Yorks 97 B5
Butt Green 74 D3
Buttington 60 D2
Buttonoak 50 B2
Buttsash 14 D5
Butt's Green 14 B4
Buxhall 56 D4
Buxhall Fen Street 56 D4
Buxley 122 D4
Buxted 17 B8
Buxton Derbys 75 B7
Norf 81 E8
Buxworth 87 F8
Bwcle = Buckley 73 C6
Bwlch 35 B5
Bwlchgwyn 73 D6
Bwlch-Llan 46 D4
Bwlchnewydd 32 B4
Bwlchtocyn 70 E4
Bwlch-y-cibau 59 C8
Bwlchyddar 59 B8
Bwlch-y-fadfa 46 E3
Bwlch-y-ffridd 59 E7
Bwlchygroes 45 F4
Bwlch-y-sarnau 48 B2
Byermoor 110 D4
Byers Green 110 F5
Byfield 52 D3
Byfleet 27 C8
Byford 49 E5
Bygrave 54 F3
Byker 111 C5
Bylchau 72 C3
Byley 74 C4
Bynea 33 E6
Byrness 116 D3
Bythorn 53 B8
Byton 49 C5
Byworth 16 B3

## C

Cabharstadh 155 E8
Cablea 133 F6
Cabourne 90 D5
Cabrach Argyll 144 G3
Moray 140 B2
Cabrich 151 G8
Cabus 92 E4
Cackle Street 17 B8
Cadbury 10 D4
Cadbury Barton 9 C8
Cadder 119 B6
Caddington 40 C3
Caddonfoot 121 F7
Cadeby Leics 63 D8
S Yorks 89 D6
Cadeleigh 10 D4
Cade Street 18 C3
Cadgwith 3 E6
Cadham 128 D4
Cadishead 86 E5
Cadle 33 E7
Cadley Lancs 92 F5
Wilts 25 C7
Wilts 25 D7
Cadmore End 39 E7
Cadnam 14 C3
Cadney 90 D4
Cadole 73 C6
Cadoxton 22 C3
Cadoxton-Juxta-Neath 34 E1
Cadshaw 86 C5
Cadzow 119 D7
Caeathro 82 E4
Caehopkin 34 C2
Caenby 90 F4
Caenby Corner 90 F3
Caerau Bridgend 34 E2
Cardiff 22 B3
Caér-bryn 33 C6
Caerdeon 58 C3
Caerdydd = Cardiff 22 B3
Caerfarchell 44 C2
Caerffili
= Caerphilly 35 F5
Caerfyrddin
= Carmarthen 33 B5
Caergeiliog 82 D3
Caergwrle 73 D7
Caergybi
= Holyhead 82 C2
Caerleon
= Caerllion 35 E7
Caer Llan 36 D1
Caerllion
= Caerleon 35 E7
Caernarfon 82 E4
Caerphilly
= Caerffili 35 F5
Caerfyrddin
Caersws 59 E7
Caerwedros 46 D2
Caerwent 36 E1
Caerwych 71 D7
Caerwys 72 B5
Caethle 58 E3
Caim 83 C6
Caio 47 F5
Cairinis 148 B3
Cairisiadar 154 D5
Cairminis 154 J5
Cairnbaan 145 D7
Cairnbanno House 153 D8
Cairnborrow 152 D4
Cairnbrogie 141 B7
Cairnbulg Castle 153 B10
Cairncross Angus 134 B4
Cairncross continued
Borders 122 C4
Cairndow 125 D7
Cairness 153 B10
Cairneyhill 128 F2
Cairnfield House 152 B4
Cairngaan 104 F5
Cairngarroch 104 E4
Cairnhill 153 E6
Cairnie Aberds 141 D7
Aberds 152 D4
Cairnorrie 153 D8
Cairnpark 141 C7
Cairnryan 104 C4
Cairnton 159 H4
Caister-on-Sea 69 C8
Caistor 90 D5
Caistor St Edmund 68 D5
Caistron 117 D5
Caitha Bowland 121 E7
Calais Street 56 F3
Calanais 154 D7
Calbost 155 F9
Calbourne 14 F5
Calceby 79 B6
Calcot Row 26 B4
Calcott 31 C5
Caldback 160 C8
Caldbeck 108 F3
Caldbergh 101 F5
Caldecote Cambs 54 D4
Cambs 65 F8
Herts 54 F3
W Nhants 52 D4
Caldecott N Nhants 53 C7
Oxon 38 E4
Rutland 65 E5
Calderbank 119 C7
Calder Bridge 98 D2
Calderbrook 87 C7
Caldercruix 119 C8
Calder Hall 98 D2
Calder Mains 158 E2
Caldermill 119 E6
Calder Vale 92 E5
Calderwood 119 D6
Caldhame 134 E4
Caldicot 36 F1
Caldwell Derbys 63 C6
N Yorks 101 C6
Caldy 85 F3
Caledrhydiau 46 D3
Calfsound 159 E6
Calgary 146 F6
Califer 151 F13
California Falk 120 B2
Norf 69 C8
Calke 63 B7
Callakille 149 C11
Callaly 117 D6
Callander 126 D5
Callaughton 61 E6
Callestick 4 D2
Calligarry 149 H11
Callington 5 C8
Callow 49 F6
Callow End 50 E3
Callow Hill Wilts 37 F7
Worcs 50 B2
Callows Grave 49 C7
Calmore 14 C4
Calmsden 37 D7
Calne 24 B5
Calow 76 B4
Calshot 15 D5
Calstock 6 C2
Calstone Wellington 24 C5
Calthorpe 81 D7
Calthwaite 108 E4
Calton N Yorks 94 D2
Staffs 75 D8
Calveley 74 D2
Calver 76 B2
Calverhall 74 F3
Calver Hill 49 E5
Calverleigh 10 C4
Calverley 94 F5
Calvert 39 B6
Calverton M Keynes 53 F5
Notts 77 E6
Calvine 133 C5
Calvo 107 D8
Cam 36 E4
Camas-luinie 136 B2
Camasnacroise 130 D2
Camastianavaig 149 E10
Camasunary 149 G10
Camault Muir 151 G8
Camb 160 D7
Camber 19 D6
Camberley 27 C6
Camberwell 28 B4
Camblesforth 89 B7
Cambo 117 F6
Cambois 117 F9
Camborne 3 B5
Cambourne 54 D4
Cambridge Cambs 55 D5
Glos 36 D4
Cambridge Town 43 F5
Cambus 127 E7
Cambusavie Farm 151 B10
Cambusbarron 127 E6
Cambuskenneth 127 E7
Cambuslang 119 C6
Cambusmore Lodge 151 B10
Camden 41 F5
Camelford 8 F3
Camelsdale 27 F6
Camerory 151 H13
Camer's Green 50 F2
Camerton Bath 23 D8
Cumb 107 F7
E Yorks 91 B6
Camghouran 132 D2
Cammachmore 141 E8
Cammeringham 90 F3
Camore 151 B10
Campbeltown 143 F8
Camperdown 111 B5
Camp Hill 63 E7
Campmuir 134 F2
Campsall 89 C6
Campsey Ash 57 D7
Campton 54 F2
Camptown 116 C2
Camrose 44 C4
Camserney 133 E5
Camster 158 F4
Camuschoirk 130 C1
Camuscross 149 G11
Camusnagaul
Highld 130 B4
Highld 150 C3
Camusrory 147 B11
Camusteel 149 D12
Camusterrach 149 D12
Camusvrachan 132 E3
Canada 14 C3
Canadia 18 D4
Canal Side 89 C7
Candacraig House 140 C2
Candlesby 79 C7
Candy Mill 120 E3
Cane End 26 B4
Canewdon 42 E4
Canford Bottom 13 D8
Canford Cliffs 13 F8
Canford Magna 13 E8
Canham's Green 56 C4
Canholes 75 B7
Canisbay 158 C5
Cann 13 B6
Cannard's Grave 23 E8
Cann Common 13 B6
Cannich 150 H6
Cannington 22 F4
Cannock 62 D3
Cannock Wood 62 C4
Canonbie 108 B3
Canon Bridge 49 E6
Canon Frome 49 E8
Canon Pyon 49 E6
Canons Ashby 52 D3
Canonstown 2 C4
Canterbury 30 D5
Cantley Norf 69 D6
S Yorks 89 D7
Cantlop 60 D5
Canton 22 B3
Cantraybruich 151 G10
Cantraydoune 151 G10
Cantraywood 151 G10
Cantsfield 93 B6
Canvey Island 42 F3
Canwick 78 C2
Canworthy Water 8 E4
Caol 131 B5
Caolas 146 G3
Caolas Scalpaigh 154 H7
Caolas Stocinis 154 H6
Caol Ila 142 A5
Capel 28 E2
Capel Bangor 58 F3
Capel Betws Lleucu 46 D5
Capel Carmel 70 E2
Capel Coch 82 C4
Capel Curig 83 F7
Capel Cynon 46 E2
Capel Dewi Carms 33 B5
Ceredig 46 E3
Ceredig 58 F3
Capel Garmon 83 F8
Capel-gwyn 82 D3
Capel Gwyn 33 B5
Capel Gwynfe 33 B8
Capel Hendre 33 C6
Capel Hermon 71 E8
Capel Isaac 33 B6
Capel Iwan 45 F4
Capel le Ferne 31 F6
Capel Llanilltern 34 F4
Capel Mawr 82 D4
Capel St Andrew 57 E7
Capel St Mary 56 F4
Capel Seion 46 B5
Capel Tygwydd 45 E4
Capel Uchaf 70 C5
Capelulo 83 D7
Capel-y-graig 82 E5
Capenhurst 73 B7
Capernwray 92 B5
Capheaton 117 F6
Cappercleuch 115 B5
Capplegill 114 D4
Capton 7 D6
Caputh 133 F7
Carbis Bay 2 C4
Carbost Highld 149 D9
Highld 149 E8
Carbrook 88 F4
Carbrooke 68 D2
Carburton 77 B6
Carcant 121 D6
Carcary 135 D6
Carclaze 4 D5
Car Colston 77 E7
Carcroft 89 C6
Cardenden 128 E4
Cardeston 60 C3
Cardiff = Caerdydd 22 B3
Cardigan
= Aberteifi 45 E3
Cardington Bedford 53 E8
Shrops 60 E5
Cardinham 5 C6
Cardonald 118 C5
Cardow 152 D1
Cardrona 121 F6
Cardross 118 B3
Cardurnock 107 D8
Careby 65 C7
Careston Castle 135 D5
Carew 32 D1
Carew Cheriton 32 D1
Carew Newton 32 D1
Carey 49 F7
Carfrae 121 C8
Cargenbridge 107 B6
Cargill 134 F1
Cargo 108 D3
Cargreen 6 C2
Carham 122 F4
Carhampton 22 E2
Carharrack 3 B6
Carie Perth 132 D3
Perth 132 F3
Carines 4 D2
Carisbrooke 15 F5
Cark 92 B3
Carlabhagh 154 C7
Carland Cross 4 D3
Carlby 65 C7
Carlecotes 88 D2
Carlesmoor 94 B4
Carleton Cumb 108 D4
Lancs 92 F3
N Yorks 94 E2
W&F 99 B7
Carleton Forehoe 68 D3
Carleton Rode 68 E4
Carlingcott 23 D8
Carlin How 103 C5
Carlisle 108 D4
Carlops 120 D4
Carlton Bedford 53 D7
Cambs 55 D7
Leics 63 D7
Notts 77 E6
N Yorks 89 B7
N Yorks 101 C6
N Yorks 101 F5
N Yorks 102 F4
Stockton 102 B1
Suff 57 C7
S Yorks 88 C4
W Yorks 88 B4
Carlton Colville 69 F8
Carlton Curlieu 64 E3
Carlton Husthwaite 95 B7
Carlton in Cleveland 102 D3
Carlton in Lindrick 89 F6
Carlton le Moorland 78 D2
Carlton Miniott 102 F1
Carlton on Trent 77 C7
Carlton Scroop 78 E2
Carluke 119 D8
Carmarthen
= Caerfyrddin 33 B5
Carmel Anglesey 82 C3
Carms 33 C6
Flint 73 B5
Guern 16 I2
Gwyn 82 F4
Carmont 141 F7
Carmunnock 119 D6
Carmyle 119 C6
Carmyllie 135 E5
Carnaby 97 C7
Carnach Highld 136 B3
Highld 150 B3
W Isles 154 H7
Carnachy 157 D10
Càrnais 154 D5
Carnbee 129 D7
Carnbo 128 D2
Carnbrea 3 B5
Carnduff 119 E6
Carnduncan 142 B3
Carne 3 C8
Carnforth 92 B4
Carn-gorm 136 B2
Carnhedryn 44 C3
Carnhell Green 2 C5
Carnkie Corn 3 C5
Corn 3 C6
Carno 59 E6
Carnoch Highld 150 F5
Highld 150 H6
Carnock 128 F2
Carnon Downs 3 B6
Carnousie 153 C6
Carnoustie 135 F5
Carnwath 120 E2
Carnyorth 2 C2
Carperby 101 F5
Carpley Green 100 F4
Carr 89 E6
Carradale 143 E9
Carragraich 154 H6
Carrbridge 138 B5
Carrefour Selous 17 I3
Carreglefn 82 C3
Carreg-wen 45 E4
Carr Hill 111 C5
Carrick Argyll 145 E8
Fife 129 B6
Carrick Castle 145 D10
Carrick House 159 E6
Carriden 128 F2
Carrington Gtr Man 86 E5
Lincs 79 D6
Midloth 121 C6
Carrog Conwy 71 C8
Denb 72 E5
Carron Falk 127 F7
Moray 152 D2
Carronbridge 113 E8
Carron Bridge 127 F6
Carronshore 127 F7
Carrshield 109 E8
Carrutherstown 107 B8
Carrville 111 E6
Carsaig Argyll 144 E6
Argyll 147 J8
Carscreugh 105 D6
Carsegowan 105 D8
Carse Gray 134 D4
Carse House 144 G6
Carseriggan 105 C7
Carsethorn 107 D6
Carshalton 28 C3
Carsington 76 D2
Carskiey 143 H7
Carsluith 105 D8
Carsphairn 113 E5
Carstairs 120 E2
Carstairs Junction 120 E2
Carswell Marsh 38 E3
Carter's Clay 14 B4
Carterton 38 D2
Carterway Heads 110 D3
Carthew 4 D5
Carthorpe 101 F8
Cartington 117 D6
Cartland 119 E8
Cartmel 92 B3
Cartmel Fell 99 F6
Carway 33 D5
Cary Fitzpaine 12 B3
Cascob 48 C4
Cas-gwent
= Chepstow 36 E2
Cashlie 132 E1
Cashmoor 13 C7
Casnewydd
= Newport 35 F7
Cassey Compton 37 C7
Cassington 38 C4
Cassop 111 F6
Castell 72 C5
Castellau 34 F4
Castell-Howell 46 E3
Castell-Nedd
= Neath 33 E8
Castell Newydd Emlyn
= Newcastle Emlyn 46 E2
Castell-y-bwch 35 E6
Casterton 93 B6
Castle Acre 67 C8
Castle Ashby 53 D6
Castlebay
= Bagh a Chaisteil 148 J1
Castle Bolton 101 E5
Castle Bromwich 62 F5
Castle Bytham 65 C6
Castlebythe 32 B1
Castle Caereinion 59 D8
Castle Camps 55 E7
Castle Carrock 108 D5
Castlecary 119 B7
Castle Cary 23 F8
Castle Combe 24 B3
Castlecraig 151 E11
Castle Donington 63 B8
Castle Douglas 106 C4
Castle Eaton 37 E8
Castle Eden 111 F7
Castlefairn 113 F7
Castle Forbes 140 C5
Castleford 88 B5
Castle Frome 49 E8
Castle Green 27 C7
Castle Gresley 63 C6
Castle Heaton 122 E5
Castle Hedingham 55 F8
Castlehill Borders 120 F5
Highld 158 D3
W Dunb 118 B3
Castle Hill 29 E7
Castle Huntly 128 B5
Castle Kennedy 104 D5
Castlemaddy 113 F5
Castlemartin 44 F4
Castlemilk
Dumfries 107 B8
Glasgow 119 D6
Castlemorris 44 B4
Castlemorton 50 F2
Castle O'er 115 E5
Castle Pulverbatch 60 D4
Castle Rising 67 B6
Castleside 110 E3
Castle Stuart 151 G10
Castlethorpe 53 E6
Castleton Angus 134 E3
Argyll 145 E7
Derbys 88 F2
Gtr Man 87 C6
Newport 35 F6
N Yorks 102 D4
Castletown
Ches W 73 D8
Highld 151 G10
Highld 158 D3
IoM 84 F2
T&W 111 D6
Castleweary 115 D7
Castley 95 E5
Caston 68 E2
Castor 65 E8
Catacol 143 D10
Catbrain 36 F2
Catbrook 36 D2
Catchall 2 D3
Catchems Corner 51 B7
Catchgate 110 D4
Catcleugh 116 D3
Catcliffe 88 F5
Catcott 23 F5
Caterham 28 D4
Catfield 69 B6
Catfirth 160 H6
Catford 28 B4
Catforth 92 F4
Cathays 22 B3
Cathcart 119 C5
Cathedine 35 B5
Catherington 15 C7
Catherton 49 B8
Catlodge 138 E2
Catlowdy 108 B4
Catmore 38 F4
Caton 92 C5
Caton Green 92 C5
Catrine 113 B5
Cat's Ash 35 E7
Catsfield 18 D4
Catshill 50 B4
Cattal 95 D7
Cattawade 56 F5
Catterall 92 E4
Catterick 101 E7
Catterick Bridge 101 E7
Catterick Garrison 101 E6
Catterlen 108 F4
Catterline 135 B8
Catterton 95 E8
Catthorpe 52 B3
Cattistock 12 E3
Catton Northumb 109 D8
N Yorks 95 B6
Catwick 97 E7
Catworth 53 B8
Caudlesprings 68 D2
Caulcott 39 B5
Cauldcots 135 E6
Cauldhame 126 E5
Cauldmill 115 C8
Cauldon 75 E7
Caulkerbush 107 D6
Caulside 115 F7
Caunsall 62 F2
Caunton 77 D7
Causewayend 120 F3
Causeway End 105 C8
Causeway Foot 94 F3
Causewayhead
Cumb 107 D8
Stirling 127 E6
Causeyend 141 C8
Causey Park Bridge 117 E7
Cautley 100 E1
Cavendish 56 E2
Cavendish Bridge 63 B8
Cavenham 55 C8
Caversfield 39 B5
Caversham 26 B5
Caverswall 75 E6
Cavil 96 F3
Cawdor 151 F11
Cawkwell 79 B5
Cawood 95 F8
Cawsand 6 D2
Cawston 81 E7
Cawthorne 88 D3
Cawthorpe 65 B7
Cawton 96 B2
Caxton 54 D4
Caynham 49 B7
Caythorpe Lincs 78 E2
Notts 77 E6
Cayton 103 F8
Ceann a Bhaigh 148 B2
Ceannacroc Lodge 136 C5
Ceann a Deas Loch Baghasdail 148 G2
Ceann Shiphoirt 155 F7
Ceann Tarabhaigh 154 F7
Cearsiadair 155 E8
Cefn Berain 72 C3
Cefn-brith 72 D3
Cefn Canol 73 F6
Cefn-coch 83 E8
Cefn Coch 59 B8
Cefn-coed-y-cymmer 34 D4
Cefn Cribbwr 34 F2
Cefn Cross 34 F2
Cefn-ddwysarn 72 F3
Cefn Einion 60 F2
Cefneithin 33 C6
Cefn-gorwydd 47 E8
Cefn-mawr 73 E6
Cefn-y-bedd 73 D7
Cefn-y-pant 32 B2
Cei-bach 46 D3
Ceinewydd
= New Quay 46 D2
Ceint 82 D4
Cellan 46 E5
Cellarhead 75 E6
Cemaes 82 B3
Cemmaes 58 D5
Cemmaes Road 58 D5
Cenarth 45 E4
Cenin 71 C5
Central 118 B2
Ceos 155 E8
Ceres 129 C6
Cerne Abbas 12 D4
Cerney Wick 37 E7
Cerrigceinwen 82 D4
Cerrigydrudion 72 E3
Cessford 116 B3
Ceunant 82 E5
Chaceley 50 F3
Chacewater 3 B6
Chackmore 52 F4
Chacombe 52 E2
Chadderton 87 D7
Chadderton Fold 87 D6
Chaddesden 76 F3
Chaddesley Corbett 50 B3
Chaddleworth 26 B2
Chadlington 38 B3
Chadshunt 51 D8
Chad Valley 62 F4
Chadwell 64 B4
Chadwell St Mary 29 B7
Chadwick End 51 B7
Chadwick Green 86 E3
Chaffcombe 11 C8
Chagford 10 F2
Chailey 17 C7
Chainbridge 66 D4
Chain Bridge 79 E6
Chainhurst 29 E8
Chalbury 13 D8
Chalbury Common 13 D8
Chaldon 28 D4
Chaldon Herring 13 F5
Chale 15 G5
Chale Green 15 G5
Chalfont Common 40 E3
Chalfont St Giles 40 E2
Chalfont St Peter 40 E3
Chalford 37 D5
Chalgrove 39 E6
Chalk 29 B7
Challacombe 21 E5
Challoch 105 C7
Challock 30 D4
Chalton C Beds 40 B3
Hants 15 C8
Chalvington 18 E2
Chancery 46 B4
Chandler's Ford 14 B5
Channel Tunnel 19 B8
Channerwick 160 L6
Chantry Som 24 E2
Suff 56 E5
Chapel 128 E4
Chapel Allerton
Som 23 D6
W Yorks 95 F6
Chapel Amble 4 B4
Chapel Brampton 52 C5
Chapel Chorlton 74 F5
Chapel End 63 E7
Chapel-en-le-Frith 87 F8
Chapelgate 66 B4
Chapel Green
Warks 52 C2
Warks 63 F6
Chapel Haddlesey 89 B6
Chapelhall 119 C7
Chapel Head 66 F3
Chapelhill
Dumfries 114 E3
Highld 151 D11
N Ayrs 118 E2
Perth 128 B4
Perth 133 F7
Chapel Hill
Aberds 153 E10
Lincs 78 D5
Mon 36 E2
N Yorks 95 E6
Chapelknowe 108 B3
Chapel Lawn 48 B5
Chapel-le-Dale 93 B7
Chapel Milton 87 F8
Chapel of Garioch 141 B6
Chapel Row 26 C3
Chapel St Leonards 79 B8
Chapel Stile 99 D5
Chapelton Angus 135 E6
Devon 9 B7
Highld 138 C5
S Lanark 119 E6
Chapeltown
Blackburn 86 C5
Moray 139 B8
S Yorks 88 E4
Chapmanslade 24 E3
Chapmans Well 9 E5
Chapmore End 41 C6
Chappel 42 B4
Chard 11 D8
Chardstock 11 D8
Charfield 36 E4
Charford 50 C4
Charing 30 E3
Charing Cross 14 C2
Charing Heath 30 E3
Charingworth 51 F7
Charlbury 38 C3
Charlcombe 24 C2
Charlecote 51 D7
Charles 21 F5
Charlesfield 107 C8
Charleston Angus 134 E3
Renfs 118 C4
Charlestown
Aberdeen 141 D8
Corn 4 D5
Derbys 87 E8
Dorset 12 G4
Fife 128 F2
Gtr Man 87 D6
Highld 149 A13
Highld 151 G9
W Yorks 87 B7
Charlestown of Aberlour 152 D2
Charles Tye 56 D4
Charlesworth 87 E8
Charleton 7 E5
Charlton Hants 25 E8
Herts 40 B4
London 28 B5
Northumb 116 F4
Som 23 D8
Telford 61 C5
Wilts 13 B7
Wilts 25 D6
Wilts 37 F6
W Nhants 52 F3
Worcs 50 E5
W Sus 16 C2
Charlton Abbots 37 B7
Charlton Adam 12 B3
Charlton-All-Saints 14 B2
Charlton Down 12 E4
Charlton Horethorne 12 B4
Charlton Kings 37 B6
Charlton Mackerell 12 B3
Charlton Marshall 13 D6
Charlton Musgrove 12 B5
Charlton on Otmoor 39 C5
Charltons 102 C4
Charlwood 28 E3
Charlynch 22 F4
Charminster 12 E4
Charmouth 11 E8
Charndon 39 B6
Charney Bassett 38 E3
Charnock Richard 86 C3
Charsfield 57 D6
Chart Corner 29 D8
Charter Alley 26 D3
Charterhouse 23 D6
Charterville Allotments 38 C3
Chartham 30 D5
Chartham Hatch 30 D5
Chartridge 40 D2
Chart Sutton 30 E2
Charvil 27 B5
Charwelton 52 D3
Chasetown 62 D4
Chastleton 38 B2
Chasty 8 D5
Chatburn 93 E7
Chatcull 74 F4
Chatham 29 C8
Chathill 117 B7
Chattenden 29 B8
Chatteris 66 F3
Chattisham 56 E4
Chatto 116 C3
Chatton 117 B6
Chawleigh 10 C2
Chawley 38 D4
Chawston 54 D2
Chawton 26 F5
Cheadle Gtr Man 87 F6
Staffs 75 E7
Cheadle Heath 87 F6
Cheadle Hulme 87 F6
Cheam 28 C3
Cheapside 27 D8
Chearsley 39 C7
Chebsey 62 B2
Checkendon 39 F6
Checkley Ches E 74 E4
Hereford 49 F7
Staffs 75 F7
Chedburgh 55 D8
Cheddar 23 D6
Cheddington 40 C2
Cheddleton 75 D6
Cheddon Fitzpaine 11 B7
Chedglow 37 E6
Chedgrave 69 E6
Chedington 12 D2
Chediston 57 B7
Chedworth 37 C7
Chedzoy 22 F5
Cheeklaw 122 D3
Cheeseman's Green 19 B7
Cheglinch 20 E4
Cheldon 10 C2
Chelford 74 B5
Chellaston 76 F3
Chell Heath 75 D5
Chellington 53 D7
Chelmarsh 61 F7
Chelmer Village 42 D3
Chelmondiston 57 F6
Chelmorton 75 C8
Chelmsford 42 D3
Chelsea 28 B3
Chelsfield 29 C5
Chelsworth 56 E3
Cheltenham 37 B6
Chelveston 53 C7
Chelvey 23 C6
Chelwood 23 C8
Chelwood Common 17 B8
Chelwood Gate 17 B8
Chelworth 37 E6
Chelworth Green 37 E7
Chemistry 74 E2
Chenies 40 E3
Cheny Longville 60 F4
Chepstow
= Cas-gwent 36 E2
Chequerfield 89 B5
Cherhill 24 B5
Cherington Glos 37 E6
Warks 51 F7
Cheriton Devon 21 E6
Hants 15 B6
Kent 19 B8
Swansea 33 E5
Cheriton Bishop 10 E2
Cheriton Fitzpaine 10 D3
Cheriton or Stackpole Elidor 44 F4
Cherrington 61 B6
Cherrybank 128 B3
Cherry Burton 97 E5
Cherry Hinton 55 D5
Cherry Orchard 50 D3
Cherry Willingham 78 B3
Chertsey 27 C8
Cheselbourne 13 E5
Chesham 40 D2
Chesham Bois 40 E2
Cheshunt 41 D6
Cheslyn Hay 62 D3
Chessington 28 C2
Chester 73 C8
Chesterblade 23 E8
Chesterfield 76 B3
Chester-le-Street 111 D5
Chester Moor 111 E5
Chesters Borders 116 B2
Borders 116 C2
Chesterton Cambs 55 C5
Cambs 65 E8
Glos 37 D7
Oxon 39 B5
Shrops 61 E7
Staffs 74 E5
Warks 51 D8
Chesterwood 109 C8
Chestfield 30 C5
Cheston 6 D4
Cheswardine 61 B7
Cheswick 123 E6
Chetnole 12 D4
Chettiscombe 10 C4
Chettisham 66 F5
Chettle 13 C7
Chetton 61 E6
Chetwode 39 B6
Chetwynd Aston 61 C7
Cheveley 55 C7
Chevening 29 D5
Chevington 55 D8
Chevithorne 10 C4
Chew Magna 23 C7
Chew Stoke 23 C7
Chewton Keynsham 23 C8
Chewton Mendip 23 D7
Chicheley 53 E7
Chichester 16 D2
Chickerell 12 F4
Chicklade 24 F4
Chicksgrove 24 F4
Chidden 15 C7
Chiddingfold 27 F7
Chiddingly 18 D2
Chiddingstone 29 E5
Chiddingstone Causeway 29 E6
Chiddingstone Hoath 29 E5
Chideock 12 E2
Chidham 15 D8
Chidswell 88 B3
Chieveley 26 B2
Chignall St James 42 D2
Chignall Smealy 42 C2
Chigwell 41 E7
Chigwell Row 41 E7
Chilbolton 25 F8
Chilcomb 15 B6
Chilcombe 12 E3
Chilcompton 23 D8
Chilcote 63 C6
Childer Thornton 73 B7
Child Okeford 13 C6
Childrey 38 F3
Child's Ercall 61 B6
Childswickham 51 F5
Childwall 86 F2
Childwick Green 40 C4
Chilfrome 12 E3
Chilgrove 16 C2
Chilham 30 D4
Chilhampton 25 F5
Chilla 9 D6
Chillaton 9 F6
Chillenden 31 D6
Chillerton 15 F5
Chillesford 57 D7
Chillingham 117 B6
Chillington Devon 7 E5
Som 11 C8

Chilmark . . . . . . . . . . 24 F4
Chilson . . . . . . . . . . . 38 C3
Chilsworthy Corn. . . . . .6 B2
Devon. . . . . . . . . . . . . .8 D5
Chilthorne Domer . 12 C3
Chiltington . . . . . . . . 17 C7
Chilton Bucks . . . . . 39 C6
Durham . . . . . . . . 101 B7
Oxon. . . . . . . . . . . . 38 F4
Chilton Cantelo . . 12 B3
Chilton Foliat . . . . 25 B8
Chilton Lane . . . . 111 F6
Chilton Polden . . . 23 F5
Chilton Street . . . . 55 E8
Chilton Trinity . . . . 22 F4
Chilvers Coton . . . . 63 E7
Chilwell . . . . . . . . . 76 F5
Chilworth Hants. . . 14 C5
Sur . . . . . . . . . . . . . 27 E8
Chimney . . . . . . . . 38 D3
Chineham . . . . . . . 26 D4
Chingford . . . . . . . 41 E6
Chinley . . . . . . . . . 87 F8
Chinley Head . . . . 87 F8
Chinnor . . . . . . . . . 39 D7
Chipnall . . . . . . . . 74 F4
Chippenhall Green 57 B6
Chippenham Cambs 55 C7
Wilts . . . . . . . . . . . 24 B4
Chipperfield . . . . . 40 D3
Chipping Herts. . . . 54 F4
Lancs . . . . . . . . . . 93 E6
Chipping
Campden . . . . . . 51 F6
Chipping Hill . . . . . 42 C4
Chipping Norton . . 38 B3
Chipping Ongar . . 42 D1
Chipping Sodbury . 36 F4
Chipping Warden . 52 E2
Chipstable . . . . . . 10 B5
Chipstead Kent. . . 29 D5
Sur . . . . . . . . . . . . . 28 D3
Chirbury . . . . . . . . 60 E2
Chirk = Y Waun . . 73 F6
Chirk Bank . . . . . . 73 F6
Chirmorrie . . . . . 105 B6
Chirnside . . . . . . 122 D4
Chirnsidebridge . 122 D4
Chirton . . . . . . . . . 25 D5
Chisbury . . . . . . . . 25 C7
Chiselborough . . . 12 C2
Chiseldon . . . . . . . 25 B6
Chiserley . . . . . . . 87 B8
Chislehampton . . . 39 E5
Chislehurst . . . . . . 28 B5
Chislet . . . . . . . . . 31 C6
Chiswell Green . . . 40 D4
Chiswick . . . . . . . . 28 B3
Chiswick End . . . . 54 E4
Chisworth . . . . . . . 87 E7
Chithurst . . . . . . . . 16 B2
Chittering . . . . . . . 55 B5
Chitterne . . . . . . . . 24 E4
Chittlehamholt . . . .9 B8
Chittlehampton . . . .9 B8
Chittoe . . . . . . . . . 24 C4
Chivenor . . . . . . . . 20 F4
Chobham . . . . . . . 27 C7
Choicelee . . . . . . 122 D3
Cholderton . . . . . . 25 E7
Cholesbury . . . . . . 40 D2
Chollerford . . . . . 110 B2
Chollerton . . . . . 110 B2
Cholmondeston . . 74 C3
Cholsey . . . . . . . . 39 F5
Cholstrey . . . . . . . 49 D6
Chop Gate . . . . . 102 E3
Choppington . . . . 117 F8
Chopwell . . . . . . 110 D4
Chorley Ches E . . . 74 D2
Lancs . . . . . . . . . . 86 C3
Shrops. . . . . . . . . 61 F6
Staffs . . . . . . . . . 62 C4
Chorleywood . . . . 40 E3
Chorlton cum
Hardy . . . . . . . . . 87 E6
Chorlton Lane . . . . 73 E8
Choulton . . . . . . . 60 F3
Chowdene . . . . . 111 D5
Chowley . . . . . . . . 73 D8
Chrishall . . . . . . . . 54 F5
Christchurch BCP . . 14 E2
Cambs . . . . . . . . . 66 E4
Glos . . . . . . . . . . . 36 C2
Newport. . . . . . . . 35 F7
Christian Malford . 24 B4
Christleton . . . . . . 73 C8
Christmas
Common . . . . . . . 39 E7
Christon . . . . . . . . 23 D5
Christon Bank . . . 117 B8
Christow . . . . . . . . 10 F3
Chryston . . . . . . 119 B6
Chudleigh . . . . . . . .7 B6
Chudleigh Knighton 7 B6
Chulmleigh . . . . . . .9 C8
Chunal . . . . . . . . . 87 E8
Church . . . . . . . . . 86 B5
Churcham . . . . . . 36 C4
Churchbank . . . . . 48 B4
Church Brampton . 52 C5
Churchbridge . . . . 62 D3
Church Broughton 76 F2
Church Crookham 27 D6
Churchdown . . . . . 37 C5
Church Eaton . . . . 62 C2
Churchend Essex . . 43 E6
Essex . . . . . . . . . . 43 E6
S Glos . . . . . . . . . 36 E4
Church End Cambs 66 D3
Lambs . . . . . . . . . 66 F2
C Beds . . . . . . . . . 40 B2
C Beds . . . . . . . . . 53 F5
C Beds . . . . . . . . . 54 F2
Essex . . . . . . . . . . 42 B3
Essex . . . . . . . . . . 55 E6
E Yorks . . . . . . . . 97 D6
Hants . . . . . . . . . . 26 D4
Lincs. . . . . . . . . . . 78 F5
Warks . . . . . . . . . . 63 E6
Wilts . . . . . . . . . . . 24 B5
Church Enstone . . 38 B3
Church Fenton . . . 95 F8
Churchfield . . . . . . 62 E3
Churchgate Street . 41 C7

Church Green
Devon. . . . . . . . . . 11 E6
Norf . . . . . . . . . . . . 68 E3
Church Gresley . . . 63 C6
Church
Hanborough . . . 38 C4
Church Hill . . . . . . 74 C3
Church Houses . . 102 E4
Churchill Devon . . 11 D8
Devon. . . . . . . . . . 20 E4
N Som . . . . . . . . . 23 D6
Oxon. . . . . . . . . . . 38 C3
Worcs . . . . . . . . . 50 B3
Worcs . . . . . . . . . 50 D4
Churchinford. . . . . 11 C7
Church Knowle. . . . 13 F7
Church Laneham . . 77 B8
Church Langton . . 64 E4
Church Lawford . . 52 B2
Church Lawton . . . 74 D5
Church Leigh . . . . 75 F7
Church Lench . . . . 50 D5
Church Mayfield . . 75 E8
Church Minshull . . 74 C3
Church Norton . . . 16 E2
Churchover . . . . . . 64 F2
Church Preen . . . . 60 E5
Church
Pulverbatch . . . . 60 D4
Churchstanton . . . 11 C6
Church Stoke . . . . 60 E2
Churchstow . . . . . . .6 E5
Church Stowe . . . . 52 D4
Church Street . . . . 29 B8
Church Stretton . . 60 E4
Churchtown Derbys 76 C2
IoM . . . . . . . . . . . . 84 C4
Lancs . . . . . . . . . . 92 E4
Mers . . . . . . . . . . . 85 F4
Church Town
N Lincs. . . . . . . . . 89 D8
Sur . . . . . . . . . . . . 28 D4
Church Village . . . 34 F4
Church Warsop . . . 77 C5
Churnsike Lodge 109 B6
Churston Ferrers . . .7 D7
Churt . . . . . . . . . . 27 F6
Churton . . . . . . . . 73 D8
Churwell . . . . . . . . 88 B3
Chute Standen . . . 25 D8
Chwilog . . . . . . . . 70 D5
Chyandour . . . . . . .2 C3
Cilan Uchaf . . . . . 70 E3
Cilcain . . . . . . . . . 73 C5
Cilcennin . . . . . . . 46 C4
Cilfor . . . . . . . . . . 71 D7
Cilfrew . . . . . . . . . 34 D1
Cilfynydd . . . . . . . 35 E5
Cilgerran . . . . . . . 45 E2
Cilgwyn Carms . . . 33 B8
Gwyn . . . . . . . . . . 82 F4
Pembs . . . . . . . . . 45 F2
Ciliau Aeron . . . . . 46 D3
Cill Donnain . . . . 148 F2
Cille Bhrighde . . 148 G2
Cille Pheadair . . 148 G2
Cilmaengwyn . . . . 33 D8
Cilmery = Cilmeri . 48 D2
Cilmeri = Cilmeri . 48 D2
Cilsan . . . . . . . . . 33 B6
Ciltalgarth . . . . . . 72 E2
Cilwendeg . . . . . . 45 F4
Cilybebyll . . . . . . . 33 D8
Cilycwm . . . . . . . . 47 F6
Cimla . . . . . . . . . . 34 E1
Cinderford . . . . . . 36 C3
Cippyn . . . . . . . . . 45 E3
Cirbhig . . . . . . . . 157 F8
Cirencester . . . . . 37 D7
Ciribhig . . . . . . . . 154 C6
City London . . . . . 41 F6
Powys . . . . . . . . . 60 F2
City Dulas . . . . . . 82 C4
Clachaig . . . . . . 145 E10
Clachan Argyll . . . 124 D3
Argyll . . . . . . . . . 124 D3
Argyll . . . . . . . . . 130 E2
Argyll . . . . . . . . . 144 H6
Highld . . . . . . . . 149 E10
W Isles . . . . . . . . 148 D2
Clachaneasy . . . . 105 B7
Clachanmore . . . 104 E4
Clachan na Luib . 148 B3
Clachan of
Campsie. . . . . . 119 B6
Clachan of
Glendaruel . . . 145 E8
Clachan-Seil . . . . 124 D3
Clachan Strachur 125 E6
Clachbreck . . . . . 144 F6
Clachnabrain . . . 134 C3
Clachtoll . . . . . . 156 G3
Clackmannan . . . 127 E8
Clacton-on-Sea . . 43 C7
Cladach
Chireboist . . . . 148 B2
Claddach-
knockline. . . . . 148 B2
Cladich . . . . . . . 125 C6
Clanville . . . . . . . 25 E8
Claonaig . . . . . . 145 H7
Claonel . . . . . . . 157 J8
Clapgate Dorset . 13 D8
Herts . . . . . . . . . . 41 B7
Clapham Bedford . 53 D8
London . . . . . . . . 28 B3
N Yorks . . . . . . . . 93 C7
W Sus . . . . . . . . . 16 D4
Clap Hill . . . . . . . . 19 B7
Clappers . . . . . . 122 D5
Clappersgate . . . . 99 D5
Clapton . . . . . . . . 12 D2
Clapton-in-
Gordano . . . . . . 23 B6
Clapton-on-the-
Hill . . . . . . . . . . . 38 C1
Clapworthy . . . . . . .9 B8
Clarach . . . . . . . . 58 F3
Clara Vale . . . . . 110 C4
Clarbeston . . . . . . 32 B1
Clarbeston Road . 32 B1
Clarborough . . . . . 89 F8
Clardon . . . . . . . 158 D3

Clare . . . . . . . . . . 55 E8
Clarebrand. . . . . . 106 C4
Clarencefield . . . . 107 C7
Clarilaw . . . . . . . . 115 C8
Clark's Green . . . . 28 F2
Clarkston . . . . . . 119 D5
Clashandorran . . . 151 G8
Clashcoig . . . . . . 151 B9
Clashindarroch . . 152 E4
Clashmore
Highld . . . . . . . 151 C10
Highld . . . . . . . . 156 F3
Clashnessie . . . . 156 F3
Clashnoir . . . . . . 139 B8
Clate . . . . . . . . . 160 G7
Clathy . . . . . . . . 127 C8
Clatt . . . . . . . . . . 140 B4
Clatter . . . . . . . . . 59 E6
Clatterford . . . . . . 15 F5
Clatterin Bridge . 135 B6
Clatworthy . . . . . . 22 F2
Claughton Lancs . 92 E5
Lancs . . . . . . . . . . 93 C5
Mers . . . . . . . . . . 85 F4
Claverdon . . . . . . 51 C6
Claverham . . . . . . 23 C6
Clavering . . . . . . . 55 F5
Claverley . . . . . . . 61 E7
Claverton . . . . . . . 24 C2
Clawdd-newydd . . 72 D4
Clawthorpe . . . . . 92 B5
Clawton . . . . . . . . .9 E5
Claxby Lincs. . . . . 79 B7
Lincs. . . . . . . . . . . 90 E5
Claxton Norf . . . . . 69 D6
N Yorks . . . . . . . . 96 C2
Claybokie . . . . . . 139 E6
Claybrooke Magna 63 E8
Claybrooke Parva . 63 E8
Clay Common . . . 69 F7
Clay Coton . . . . . . 52 B3
Clay Cross . . . . . . 76 C3
Claydon Oxon . . . 52 D2
Suff . . . . . . . . . . . 56 D5
Claygate Dumfries 108 B3
Kent . . . . . . . . . . 29 E8
Sur . . . . . . . . . . . . 28 C2
Claygate Cross . . 29 D7
Clayhanger Devon . 10 B5
W Mid . . . . . . . . . 62 D4
Clayhidon . . . . . . 11 C6
Clayhill E Sus . . . . 18 C5
Hants . . . . . . . . . . 14 D4
Clay Hill . . . . . . . . 26 B3
Clay Lake . . . . . . . 66 B2
Clayock . . . . . . . 158 E3
Claypole . . . . . . . 77 E8
Clayton Staffs . . . . 75 E5
S Yorks . . . . . . . . 89 D3
W Sus . . . . . . . . . 17 C6
W Yorks . . . . . . . 94 F4
Clayton Green . . . 86 B3
Clayton-le-Moors 93 F7
Clayton-le-Woods 86 B3
Clayton West . . . . 88 C3
Clayworth . . . . . . 89 F8
Cleadale . . . . . . . 146 C7
Cleadon . . . . . . . 111 C6
Clearbrook . . . . . . .6 C3
Clearwell . . . . . . . 36 D2
Cleasby . . . . . . . 101 C7
Cleat . . . . . . . . . 159 K5
Cleatlam . . . . . . 101 C6
Cleator . . . . . . . . 98 C2
Cleator Moor . . . . 98 C2
Clebrig . . . . . . . . 157 F8
Cleckheaton . . . . 88 B2
Cleedownton . . . . 61 F5
Cleehill . . . . . . . . 49 B7
Clee St Margaret . 61 F5
Cleethorpes . . . . . 91 D7
Cleeton St Mary . . 49 B8
Cleeve . . . . . . . . . 23 C6
Cleeve Hill . . . . . . 37 B6
Cleeve Prior . . . . . 51 E5
Clegyrnant . . . . . . 59 D6
Clehonger . . . . . . 49 F6
Cleish . . . . . . . . . 128 E2
Cleland . . . . . . . . 119 D8
Clench Common . . 25 C6
Clenchwarton . . . . 67 B5
Clent . . . . . . . . . . 50 B4
Cleobury
Mortimer . . . . . . 49 B8
Cleobury North . . 61 F6
Cleongart . . . . . . 143 E7
Clephanton . . . . . 151 F11
Clerklands . . . . . 115 B8
Clestrain . . . . . . . 159 H4
Cleuch Head . . . . 115 C8
Cleughbrae . . . . . 107 B7
Clevancy . . . . . . . 25 B5
Clevedon . . . . . . . 23 B6
Cleveley . . . . . . . . 38 B3
Cleveleys . . . . . . . 92 E3
Cleverton . . . . . . . 37 F6
Clevis . . . . . . . . . . 21 B7
Clewer . . . . . . . . . 23 D6
Cley next the Sea . 81 C6
Cliaid . . . . . . . . . 148 H1
Cliasmol . . . . . . . 154 G5
Cliburn . . . . . . . . 99 B7
Click Mill . . . . . . 159 F4
Cliddesden . . . . . . 26 E4
Cliffburn . . . . . . . 135 E6
Cliffe Medway . . . 29 B8
N Yorks . . . . . . . . 96 F2
Cliff End . . . . . . . . 19 D5
Cliffe Woods . . . . 29 B8
Clifford Hereford . 48 E4
W Yorks . . . . . . . . 95 E7
Clifford Chambers 51 D6
Clifford's Mesne . 36 B4
Cliffsend . . . . . . . 31 C7
Clifton Bristol . . . . 23 B7
C Beds . . . . . . . . . 54 F2
Derbys . . . . . . . . . 75 E8
Lancs . . . . . . . . . . 92 F4
Northumb. . . . . . 117 F8
Nottingham . . . . . 77 F5
N Yorks . . . . . . . . 94 E4
Oxon. . . . . . . . . . . 52 F2
Stirling . . . . . . . . 131 F7
S Yorks . . . . . . . . 89 E6
W&F. . . . . . . . . . . 99 B7
Worcs . . . . . . . . . 50 E3
York . . . . . . . . . . . 95 D8
Clifton Campville . 63 C6
Cliftoncote . . . . . 116 B4

Clifton Green. . . . . 87 D5
Clifton Hampden . 39 E5
Clifton Reynes . . . 53 D7
Clifton upon
Dunsmore . . . . . 52 B3
Clifton upon Teme 50 C2
Cliftonville . . . . . . 31 B7
Climaen gwyn. . . . 33 D8
Climping. . . . . . . . 16 D4
Climpy . . . . . . . . 120 D2
Clink. . . . . . . . . . . 24 E2
Clint . . . . . . . . . . 95 D5
Clint Green. . . . . . 68 C3
Clintmains . . . . . 122 F2
Cliobh . . . . . . . . 154 D5
Clippesby . . . . . . 69 C7
Clipsham . . . . . . . 65 C6
Clipston . . . . . . . . 64 F4
Clipstone . . . . . . . 77 C5
Clitheroe . . . . . . . 93 E7
Cliuthar . . . . . . . 154 H6
Clive. . . . . . . . . . . 60 B5
Clivocast . . . . . . 160 C8
Clixby. . . . . . . . . . 90 D5
Clocaenog . . . . . . 72 D4
Clochan . . . . . . . 152 B4
Clock Face . . . . . . 86 E3
Clockmill . . . . . . 122 D3
Cloddiau . . . . . . . 60 D2
Clodock . . . . . . . . 35 B7
Clola. . . . . . . . . . 153 D10
Clophill . . . . . . . . 53 F8
Clopton N Nhants . 65 F7
Suff . . . . . . . . . . . 57 D6
Clopton Corner. . . 57 D6
Clopton Green . . . 55 D8
Closeburn . . . . . . 113 E8
Close Clark . . . . . . 84 E2
Closworth. . . . . . . 12 C3
Clothall . . . . . . . . 54 F3
Clotton . . . . . . . . 74 C2
Clough Foot . . . . . 87 B7
Cloughton . . . . . 103 E8
Cloughton
Newlands. . . . . . 103 E8
Clousta . . . . . . . 160 H5
Clouston . . . . . . . 159 G3
Clova Aberds . . . . 140 B3
Angus . . . . . . . . . 134 B3
Clovelly . . . . . . . . .8 B5
Clove Lodge . . . . 100 C4
Clovenfords. . . . . 121 F7
Clovenstone . . . . 141 C6
Clovullin . . . . . . . 130 C4
Clow Bridge . . . . . 87 B6
Clowne . . . . . . . . 76 B4
Clows Top . . . . . . 50 B2
Cloy . . . . . . . . . . . 73 E7
Cluanie Inn . . . . 136 C3
Cluanie Lodge . . 136 C3
Clun . . . . . . . . . . 60 F3
Clunbury . . . . . . . 60 F3
Clunderwen . . . . . 32 C2
Clune . . . . . . . . . 138 B3
Clunes . . . . . . . . 136 F5
Clungunford . . . . . 49 B5
Clunie Aberds . . . 153 C6
Perth . . . . . . . . . 133 E8
Clunton . . . . . . . . 60 F3
Cluny . . . . . . . . . 128 E4
Cluny Castle . . . . 138 E2
Clutton Bath . . . . . 23 D8
Ches W . . . . . . . . 73 D8
Clwt-grugoer . . . . 72 C3
Clwt-y-bont . . . . . 83 E5
Clydach Mon . . . . 35 C6
Swansea . . . . . . . 33 D7
Clydach Vale . . . . 34 E3
Clydebank . . . . . 118 B4
Clydey . . . . . . . . . 45 F4
Clyffe Pypard. . . . 25 B5
Clynder . . . . . . . 145 E11
Clyne . . . . . . . . . 34 D2
Clynelish . . . . . . 157 J11
Clynnog-fawr. . . . 82 F4
Clyro . . . . . . . . . . 48 E4
Clyst Honiton . . . 10 E4
Clyst Hydon . . . . 10 D5
Clyst St George. . 10 F4
Clyst St Lawrence . 10 D5
Clyst St Mary . . . 10 E4
Cnoc Amhlaigh. . 155 D10
Cnwch-coch . . . . 47 B5
Cnwcheaton . . . . 50 B4
Coachford . . . . . 152 D4
Coad's Green. . . . 5 B7
Coal Aston . . . . . . 76 B3
Coalbrookdale . . . 61 D6
Coalbrookvale . . . 35 D5
Coalburn . . . . . . . 119 F8
Coalburns. . . . . . 110 C4
Coalcleugh . . . . 109 E8
Coaley . . . . . . . . . 36 D4
Coalhall . . . . . . . 112 C4
Coalhill . . . . . . . . 42 E3
Coalpit Heath . . . 36 F3
Coalport . . . . . . . 61 D6
Coalsnaughton. . 127 E8
Coaltown of
Balgonie . . . . . 128 E4
Coaltown of
Wemyss . . . . . . 128 E5
Coalville . . . . . . . 63 C8
Coalway . . . . . . . 36 C2
Coat . . . . . . . . . . 12 B2
Coatbridge. . . . . 119 C7
Coatdyke . . . . . . 119 C7
Coate Swindon . . 38 F1
Wilts . . . . . . . . . . 24 C5
Coates Cambs . . . 66 E3
Glos . . . . . . . . . . . 37 D6
Lancs . . . . . . . . . . 93 E8
Notts . . . . . . . . . . 90 F2
W Sus . . . . . . . . . 16 C3
Coatham . . . . . . 102 B3
Coatham
Mundeville . . . . 101 B7
Coatsgate. . . . . . 114 D3
Cobbaton . . . . . . .9 B8
Cobbler's Green . 69 E5
Coberley . . . . . . . 37 C6
Cobham Kent . . . 29 C7
Sur . . . . . . . . . . . 28 C2
Cobholm Island . 69 D8
Cobleland . . . . . . 126 E4
Cobnash . . . . . . . 49 C6
Coburty . . . . . . . 153 B9
Cock Bank . . . . . . 73 E7

Cock Bridge . . . . 139 D8
Cockburnspath . . 122 B3
Cock Clarks . . . . . 42 D4
Cockenzie and Port
Seton . . . . . . . . 121 B7
Cockerham . . . . . 92 D4
Cockermouth . . . 107 F8
Cockernhoe Green 40 B4
Cockfield Durham . 101 B6
Suff . . . . . . . . . . . 56 D3
Cockfosters . . . . . 41 E5
Cocking . . . . . . . . 16 C2
Cockington . . . . . . .7 C6
Cocklake . . . . . . . 23 E6
Cockley Beck . . . . 98 D4
Cockley Cley . . . . 67 D7
Cockshutt . . . . . . 60 B4
Cockthorpe . . . . . 81 C5
Cockwood . . . . . . 10 F4
Cockyard . . . . . . . 49 F6
Codda . . . . . . . . . .5 B6
Coddenham . . . . . 56 D5
Coddington
Ches W . . . . . . . 73 D8
Hereford . . . . . . . 50 E2
Notts . . . . . . . . . . 77 D8
Codford St Mary . 24 F4
Codford St Peter . 24 F4
Codicote . . . . . . . 41 C5
Codmore Hill . . . . 16 B4
Codnor . . . . . . . . 76 E4
Codrington . . . . . 24 B2
Codsall . . . . . . . . 62 D2
Codsall Wood . . . 62 D2
Coed Duon
= Blackwood . . 35 E5
Coedely . . . . . . . . 34 F4
Coedkernew . . . . 35 F6
Coed Mawr . . . . . 83 D5
Coed Morgan . . . 35 C7
Coedpoeth. . . . . . 73 D6
Coed-Talon . . . . . 73 D6
Coedway . . . . . . . 60 C3
Coed-y-bryn. . . . . 46 E2
Coed-y-paen . . . . 35 E7
Coed-yr-ynys . . . . 35 B5
Coed Ystumgwern 71 E6
Coelbren . . . . . . . 34 C2
Coffinswell . . . . . . .7 C6
Cofton Hackett . . 50 B5
Cogan . . . . . . . . . 22 B3
Cogenhoe. . . . . . . 53 C6
Cogges . . . . . . . . 38 D3
Coggeshall. . . . . . 42 B4
Coggeshall Hamlet 42 B4
Coggins Mill . . . . 18 C2
Coig
Peighinnean. . . 155 A10
Coig
na f' Chinnann
Bhuirgh. . . . . . . 155 B9
Coilacriech . . . . . 140 E2
Coilantogle . . . . 126 D4
Coilleag . . . . . . . 148 G2
Coillore . . . . . . . 149 E8
Coity . . . . . . . . . . 34 F3
Col . . . . . . . . . . . 155 C9
Colaboll . . . . . . . 157 H8
Colan . . . . . . . . . . 4 C3
Colaton Raleigh . 11 F5
Colbost . . . . . . . 148 D7
Colburn . . . . . . . 101 E6
Colby IoM . . . . . . 84 E2
Norf . . . . . . . . . . . 81 D8
W&F. . . . . . . . . . 100 B1
Colchester . . . . . . 43 B6
Colcot . . . . . . . . . 22 C3
Cold Ash . . . . . . . 26 C3
Cold Ashby . . . . . 52 B4
Cold Ashton . . . . 24 B2
Cold Aston . . . . . 37 C8
Coldbackie . . . . . 157 D9
Coldblow . . . . . . . 29 B6
Cold Blow . . . . . . 32 C2
Cold Brayfield . . . 53 D7
Coldean . . . . . . . 17 D7
Coldeast . . . . . . . .7 B6
Colden . . . . . . . . 87 B7
Cold Hanworth . . 90 F4
Coldharbour Glos . 36 D2
Kent . . . . . . . . . . 29 D6
Sur . . . . . . . . . . . 28 E2
Cold Harbour . . . . 78 F2
Cold Hatton . . . . . 61 B6
Cold Hesledon . . 111 E7
Cold Higham . . . . 52 D4
Coldingham . . . . 122 C5
Cold Kirby . . . . . 102 F3
Cold Newton . . . . 64 D4
Cold Northcott . . . 8 F4
Cold Norton . . . . . 42 D4
Cold Overton . . . . 64 C5
Coldrain . . . . . . . 128 D2
Coldred . . . . . . . . 31 E6
Coldridge. . . . . . . .9 C8
Coldstream Angus. 134 F3
Borders . . . . . . . 122 F4
Coldwaltham. . . . 16 C4
Coldwells. . . . . . 153 D11
Coldwells Croft . . 140 B4
Coldyeld . . . . . . . 60 E3
Cole . . . . . . . . . . 23 F8
Colebatch . . . . . . 60 F3
Colebrook . . . . . . 10 D5
Colebrooke . . . . . 10 E2
Coleburn . . . . . . 152 C2
Coleby Lincs . . . . 78 C2
N Lincs . . . . . . . . 90 C2
Coleford Devon. . 10 D2
Glos . . . . . . . . . . . 36 C2
Som . . . . . . . . . . . 23 E8
Cole Green . . . . . 41 C5
Cole Henley . . . . . 26 D2
Colehill . . . . . . . . 13 D8
Coleman's Hatch . 29 F5
Colemere . . . . . . 73 F8
Colemore . . . . . . . 26 F5
Coleorton . . . . . . 63 C8
Colerne . . . . . . . . 24 B3
Colesbourne . . . . 37 C6
Colesden . . . . . . 54 D2
Coles Green . . . . 56 E4
Cole's Green . . . . 57 C6
Coleshill Bucks . . 40 E2
Oxon. . . . . . . . . . . 38 E2

Coleshill continued
Warks . . . . . . . . . 63 F6
Colestocks . . . . . 11 D5
Colgate . . . . . . . . 28 F3
Colgrain . . . . . . . 126 F2
Colinsburgh. . . . . 129 D6
Colinton . . . . . . . 120 C5
Colintraive . . . . . 145 F9
Colkirk . . . . . . . . 80 E5
Collace . . . . . . . 134 F2
Collafirth . . . . . . 160 G6
Collaton St Mary . 7 D6
College Milton . . 119 D6
Collessie . . . . . . 128 C4
Collier Row . . . . . 41 E8
Collier's End . . . . 41 B6
Collier's Green . . . 18 B4
Collier Street . . . . 29 E8
Colliery Row . . . . 111 E6
Collieston . . . . . . 141 B9
Collin . . . . . . . . . 107 B7
Collingbourne
Ducis . . . . . . . . . 25 D7
Collingbourne
Kingston . . . . . 25 D7
Collingham Notts . 77 C8
W Yorks . . . . . . . 95 E6
Collington . . . . . . 49 C8
Collingtree. . . . . . 53 D5
Collins Green . . . . 86 E3
Colliston . . . . . . 135 E6
Collycroft . . . . . . 63 F7
Collynie . . . . . . . 153 E8
Collyweston . . . . . 65 D6
Colmonell . . . . . 104 A5
Colmworth . . . . . . 54 D2
Coln Rogers . . . . 37 D7
Colnabaichin. . . . 139 D8
Colnbrook . . . . . . 27 B8
Colne Cambs . . . . 54 B4
Lancs . . . . . . . . . . 93 E8
Colne Edge . . . . . 93 E8
Colne Engaine . . . 56 F2
Colney . . . . . . . . . 68 D4
Colney Heath . . . . 41 D5
Colney Street . . . . 40 D4
Coln Rogers . . . . 37 D7
Coln St Aldwyn's . 37 D8
Coln St Dennis . . 37 C7
Colpy . . . . . . . . . 153 E6
Colquhar . . . . . . 121 E6
Colsterdale . . . . 101 F6
Colsterworth. . . . . 65 B6
Colston Bassett . . 77 F6
Coltfield. . . . . . . 151 E14
Colthouse . . . . . . 99 E5
Coltishall. . . . . . . 69 C5
Coltness . . . . . . . 119 D8
Colton Norf . . . . . 68 D4
N Yorks . . . . . . . . 95 E8
Staffs. . . . . . . . . . 62 B4
W Yorks . . . . . . . 95 F6
Colva . . . . . . . . . 48 D4
Colvend . . . . . . . 107 D5
Colvister . . . . . . 160 D7
Colwall Green . . . 50 E2
Colwall Stone . . . 50 E2
Colwell . . . . . . . . 110 B2
Colwich. . . . . . . . 62 B4
Colwick . . . . . . . . 77 E6
Colwinston . . . . . 21 B8
Colworth. . . . . . . 16 D3
Colwyn Bay
= Bae Colwyn . 83 D8
Colyford . . . . . . . 11 E7
Colyton . . . . . . . . 11 E7
Combe Hereford . 48 C5
Oxon. . . . . . . . . . . 38 C4
W Berks . . . . . . . 25 C8
Combe Common . 27 F7
Combe Down . . . . 24 C2
Combe Florey . . . 22 F3
Combe Hay . . . . . 24 D2
Combeinteignhead 7 B7
Combe Martin . . . 20 E4
Combe Moor . . . . 49 C5
Combe Raleigh . . 11 D6
Comberbach . . . . 74 B3
Comberton Cambs. 54 D4
Hereford . . . . . . . 49 C6
Combe St
Nicholas . . . . . . 11 C8
Combpyne . . . . . . 11 E7
Combridge. . . . . . 75 F7
Combrook . . . . . . 51 D8
Combs Derbys. . . 75 B7
Suff . . . . . . . . . . . 56 D4
Combs Ford . . . . . 56 D4
Combwich . . . . . . 22 E4
Comers . . . . . . . 141 D5
Comins Coch . . . 58 F3
Commercial End . 55 C6
Commins Coch. . . 58 D5
Commondale . . . 102 C4
Common Edge . . . 92 F3
Commonmoor . . . .5 C7
Commonside . . . . 74 B2
Common Side . . . 76 B3
Compstall. . . . . . . 87 E7
Compton Devon . . .7 C6
Hants . . . . . . . . . . 15 B5
Sur . . . . . . . . . . . 27 E6
Sur . . . . . . . . . . . 27 E7
W Berks . . . . . . . 26 B3
Wilts . . . . . . . . . . 25 D6
W Sus . . . . . . . . . 15 C8
Compton Abbas . 13 C6
Compton Abdale . 37 C7
Compton Bassett . 24 B5
Compton
Beauchamp. . . . 38 F2
Compton Bishop . 23 D5
Compton
Chamberlayne . 13 B8
Compton Dando . 23 C8
Compton Dundon 23 F6
Compton Martin . 23 D7
Compton
Pauncefoot . . . 12 B4
Compton Valence . 12 E3
Comrie Fife . . . . 128 F2
Perth . . . . . . . . . 127 B6
Conaglen House . 130 C4
Conchra . . . . . . . 145 E9
Concraigie . . . . . 133 E8
Condate . . . . . . . 74 B3

Conderton . . . . . . 50 F4
Condicote . . . . . . 38 B1
Condorrat . . . . . . 119 B7
Condover . . . . . . . 60 D4
Coneyhurst . . . . . 16 B5
Coneysthorpe . . . 96 B3
Coneythorpe . . . . 95 D6
Coney Weston. . . 56 B3
Conford. . . . . . . . 27 F6
Congash . . . . . . . 139 B6
Congdon's Shop. . 5 B7
Congerstone . . . . 63 D7
Congham . . . . . . 80 E3
Congleton . . . . . . 75 C5
Congl-y-wal . . . . . 71 C8
Congresbury . . . . 23 C6
Congreve . . . . . . . 62 C3
Conicavel . . . . . 151 F12
Coningsby . . . . . . 78 D5
Conington Cambs . 52 B5
Cambs . . . . . . . . . 65 F8
Conisbrough . . . . 89 E6
Conisby . . . . . . . 142 B3
Conisholme . . . . . 91 E8
Coniston E Yorks . . 97 F7
W&F. . . . . . . . . . . 99 E5
Coniston Cold . . . 94 D2
Conistone . . . . . . 94 C2
Connah's Quay . . 73 C6
Connel . . . . . . . . 124 B5
Connel Park . . . . 113 C6
Connor Downs . . . 2 C4
Conon Bridge . . . 151 F8
Conon House. . . . 151 F8
Cononley . . . . . . 94 E2
Conordan . . . . . 149 E10
Consall . . . . . . . . 75 E6
Consett . . . . . . . . 110 D4
Constable Burton 101 E6
Constantine . . . . . 3 D6
Constantine Bay . . 4 B3
Contin . . . . . . . . 150 F7
Contlaw . . . . . . . 141 D7
Conwy . . . . . . . . 83 D7
Conyer. . . . . . . . . 30 C3
Conyers Green . . 56 C2
Cooden . . . . . . . . 18 E4
Cooil . . . . . . . . . . 84 E3
Cookbury . . . . . . . .9 D6
Cookham . . . . . . . 40 F1
Cookham Dean . . 40 F1
Cookham Rise . . . 40 F1
Cookhill . . . . . . . . 51 D5
Cookley Suff . . . . 57 B7
Worcs . . . . . . . . . 62 F2
Cookley Green . . . 39 E6
Cookney. . . . . . . 141 E7
Cookridge. . . . . . . 95 E5
Cooksbridge . . . . 17 C8
Cooksmill Green . 42 D2
Coolham . . . . . . . 16 B4
Cooling . . . . . . . . 29 B8
Coombe Corn . . . 4 D4
Corn . . . . . . . . . . .8 C4
Hants . . . . . . . . . . 15 B7
Wilts . . . . . . . . . . 25 D6
Coombe Bissett . . 14 B2
Coombe Hill . . . . . 37 B5
Coombe Keynes . 13 F6
Coombes . . . . . . . 17 D5
Coopersale
Common . . . . . . 41 D7
Cootham . . . . . . . 16 C4
Copdock . . . . . . . 56 E5
Copford Green . . . 43 B5
Copgrove . . . . . . . 95 C6
Copister . . . . . . . 160 F6
Cople . . . . . . . . . 54 E2
Copley . . . . . . . . 101 B5
Coplow Dale . . . . 75 B8
Copmanthorpe . . 95 E8
Coppathorne . . . . .8 D4
Coppenhall . . . . . 62 C3
Coppenhall Moss . 74 D4
Copperhouse . . . . 2 C4
Coppingford . . . . 65 F8
Copplestone . . . . 10 D2
Coppull . . . . . . . . 86 C3
Coppull Moor . . . 86 C3
Copsale . . . . . . . . 17 B5
Copster Green . . . 93 F6
Copston Magna . . 63 F8
Copt Heath. . . . . . 51 B6
Copt Hewick . . . . 95 B6
Copthorne Shrops. 60 C4
Sur . . . . . . . . . . . 28 F4
Copt Oak . . . . . . . 63 C8
Copy's Green . . . . 80 D5
Copythorne . . . . . 14 C4
Corbets Tey . . . . . 42 F1
Corbridge . . . . . . 110 C2
Corby . . . . . . . . . 65 F5
Corby Glen . . . . . 65 B6
Cordon . . . . . . . 143 E11
Coreley . . . . . . . . 49 B8
Cores End . . . . . . 40 F2
Corfe . . . . . . . . . . 11 C7
Corfe Castle. . . . . 13 F7
Corfe Mullen . . . . 13 E7
Corfton . . . . . . . . 60 F4
Corgarff . . . . . . . 139 D8
Corhampton . . . . . 15 B7
Corlae . . . . . . . . 113 E6
Corley . . . . . . . . . 63 F7
Corley Ash . . . . . 63 F6
Corley Moor. . . . . 63 F6
Cornaa . . . . . . . . 84 C4
Cornabus . . . . . . 142 D4
Cornel . . . . . . . . 83 E7
Corner Row . . . . . 92 F4
Corney. . . . . . . . . 98 E3
Cornforth . . . . . . 111 F6
Cornhill . . . . . . . 152 C5
Cornhill-on-
Tweed . . . . . . . . 122 F4
Cornholme . . . . . 87 B7
Cornish Hall End . 55 F7
Cornquoy . . . . . . 159 J6
Cornsay. . . . . . . . 110 E4
Cornsay Colliery . 110 E4
Corntown Highld . 151 F8
V Glam . . . . . . . . 21 B8
Cornwell . . . . . . . 38 B2
Cornwood . . . . . . .6 D5
Cornworthy . . . . . .7 D6
Corpach . . . . . . . 130 B4
Corpusty . . . . . . . 81 D7
Corran Highld . . 130 C4
Highld . . . . . . . . 149 H13

Corranbuie . . . . . 145 G7
Corrany. . . . . . . . 84 D4
Corrie . . . . . . . . 143 D11
Corrie Common . . 114 F5
Corriecravie . . . . 143 F10
Corriemoillie. . . . 150 E6
Corriemulzie
Lodge . . . . . . . . 150 B6
Corrievarkie
Lodge . . . . . . . . 132 B2
Corrievorrie . . . . 138 B3
Corrimony . . . . . 150 H6
Corringham Lincs . 90 E2
Thurrock . . . . . . 42 F3
Corris . . . . . . . . . 58 D4
Corris Uchaf . . . . 58 D4
Corrour Shooting
Lodge . . . . . . . . 131 C8
Corrow . . . . . . . . 125 E7
Corry . . . . . . . . . 149 F11
Corrykinloch . . . 156 G6
Corrymuckloch . . 133 F5
Corrynachenchy . 147 G9
Corry of
Ardnagrask . . . 151 G8
Corsback . . . . . . 158 C4
Corscombe . . . . . 12 D3
Corse Aberds . . . 152 D6
Glos . . . . . . . . . . . 36 B4
Corse Lawn . . . . . 50 F3
Corse of Kinnoir . 152 D5
Corsewall . . . . . . 104 C4
Corsham . . . . . . . 24 B3
Corsindae . . . . . . 141 D5
Corsley . . . . . . . . 24 E3
Corsley Heath . . . 24 E3
Corsock . . . . . . . 106 B4
Corston Bath. . . . . 23 C8
Wilts . . . . . . . . . . 37 F6
Corstorphine . . . 120 B4
Cors-y-Gedol . . . . 71 E6
Cortachy . . . . . . . 134 D3
Corton Suff . . . . . 69 E8
Wilts . . . . . . . . . . 24 E4
Corton Denham . . 12 B4
Coruanan Lodge . 130 C4
Corunna . . . . . . . 148 B3
Corwen . . . . . . . . 72 E4
Coryton Devon . . . .9 F6
Thurrock . . . . . . 42 F3
Cosby . . . . . . . . . 64 E2
Coseley . . . . . . . . 62 E3
Cosgrove . . . . . . . 53 E5
Cosham . . . . . . . . 15 D7
Cosheston . . . . . . 32 D1
Cossall . . . . . . . . 76 E4
Cossington Leics . 64 C3
Som . . . . . . . . . . . 23 E5
Costa . . . . . . . . . 159 F4
Costessey . . . . . . 68 C4
Coston . . . . . . . . 64 B5
Cote . . . . . . . . . . 38 D3
Cotebrook . . . . . . 74 C2
Cotehill . . . . . . . 108 D4
Cotes Leics . . . . . 64 B2
Staffs . . . . . . . . . 74 F5
W&F. . . . . . . . . . . 99 F6
Cotesbach . . . . . . 64 F2
Cotgrave . . . . . . . 77 F6
Cothall . . . . . . . . 141 C7
Cotham . . . . . . . . 77 E7
Cothelstone . . . . . 22 F3
Cotherstone . . . . 101 C5
Cothill . . . . . . . . . 38 E4
Cotleigh . . . . . . . 11 D7
Cotmanhay . . . . . 76 E4
Cotmaton . . . . . . 11 F6
Coton Cambs . . . . 54 D5
Staffs . . . . . . . . . 62 B2
Staffs . . . . . . . . . 75 F6
N Whants. . . . . . . 52 B4
Coton Clanford . . 62 B2
Coton Hill Shrops. 60 C4
Coton in the Elms. 63 C6
Cott . . . . . . . . . . . .7 D5
Cottam E Yorks . . 97 C5
Lancs . . . . . . . . . . 92 F5
Notts . . . . . . . . . . 77 B8
Cottartown . . . . 151 H13
Cottenham . . . . . 54 C5
Cotterdale . . . . . 100 E3
Cottered . . . . . . . 41 B6
Cotteridge . . . . . . 50 B5
Cotterstock . . . . . 65 E7
Cottesbrooke . . . 52 B5
Cottesmore . . . . . 65 C6
Cotteylands . . . . 10 C4
Cottingham
E Yorks . . . . . . . . 97 F6
N Nhants . . . . . . 64 E5
Cottingley . . . . . . 94 F4
Cottisford . . . . . . 52 F3
Cotton Staffs . . . . 75 E7
Suff . . . . . . . . . . . 56 C4
Cotton End . . . . . 53 E8
Cottown Aberds . 140 B4
Aberds . . . . . . . . 141 C6
Aberds . . . . . . . . 153 D8
Cotwalton . . . . . . 75 F6
Couch's Mill . . . . .5 D6
Coughton Hereford 36 B2
Warks . . . . . . . . . 51 C5
Coulaghailtro . . . 144 G6
Coulags . . . . . . . 150 G2
Coulby Newham . 102 C3
Coulderton . . . . . 98 D1
Coulin . . . . . . . . 150 F3
Coull Aberds . . . . 140 D4
Argyll . . . . . . . . . 142 B3
Coulport . . . . . . 145 E11
Coulsdon . . . . . . 28 D3
Coulston . . . . . . . 24 D4
Coulter . . . . . . . . 120 F3
Coulton . . . . . . . . 96 B3
Cound . . . . . . . . . 61 D5
Coundon Durham. 101 B7
W Mid . . . . . . . . . 63 F7
Coundon Grange . 101 B7
Countersett . . . . 100 F4
Countess . . . . . . . 25 E6
Countess Wear . . 10 F4
Countesthorpe . . 64 E2
Countisbury . . . . 21 E6
County Oak . . . . . 28 F3
Coupar Angus . . 134 E2
Coup Green . . . . . 86 B3
Coupland . . . . . . 122 F5

Cour . . . . . . . . . . 143 D9
Courance . . . . . . 114 E3
Court-at-Street . . 19 B7
Court Henry . . . . . 33 B6
Courteenhall . . . . 53 D5
Courtsend . . . . . . 43 E6
Courtway . . . . . . . 22 F4
Cousland . . . . . . 121 C6
Cousley Wood . . . 18 B3
Cove Argyll . . . . 145 E11
Borders . . . . . . . 122 B3
Devon. . . . . . . . . 10 C4
Hants . . . . . . . . . . 27 D6
Highld . . . . . . . . 155 H13
Cove Bay . . . . . . 141 D8
Cove Bottom . . . . 57 B8
Covehithe . . . . . . 69 F8
Coven . . . . . . . . . 62 D3
Coveney . . . . . . . 66 F4
Covenham St
Bartholomew . . 91 E7
Covenham St Mary 91 E8
Coventry . . . . . . . 51 B8
Coverack . . . . . . . .3 E6
Coverham . . . . . 101 F6
Covesea . . . . . . 152 A1
Covington Cambs . 53 B8
S Lanark . . . . . . 120 F2
Cowan Bridge . . . 93 B6
Cow Ark . . . . . . . 93 E6
Cowbeech . . . . . . 18 D3
Cowbit . . . . . . . . 66 C2
Cowbridge Lincs . 79 E6
Som . . . . . . . . . . . 21 E8
Cowbridge
= Y Bont-Faen. 21 B8
Cowdale . . . . . . . 75 B7
Cowden. . . . . . . . 29 E5
Cowdenbeath . . 128 E3
Cowdenburn . . . 120 D5
Cowers Lane . . . . 76 E3
Cowes . . . . . . . . 15 E5
Cowesby . . . . . . 102 F2
Cowfold . . . . . . . 17 B6
Cowgill . . . . . . . 100 F2
Cowie Aberds . . . 141 F7
Stirling . . . . . . . . 127 F7
Cowley Devon . . . 10 E4
Glos . . . . . . . . . . . 37 C6
London . . . . . . . . 40 F3
Oxon. . . . . . . . . . . 39 D5
Cowleymoor. . . . . 10 C4
Cowling N Yorks . 101 F7
N Yorks . . . . . . . . 94 E2
Cowlinge . . . . . . . 55 D8
Cowpe . . . . . . . . 87 B6
Cowpen . . . . . . . 117 F8
Cowpen Bewley . 102 B2
Cowplain . . . . . . 15 C7
Cowshill . . . . . . 109 E8
Cowslip Green . . 23 C6
Cowstrandburn . 128 E2
Cowthorpe . . . . . 95 D7
Coxbank . . . . . . . 74 E3
Coxbench . . . . . . 76 E3
Cox Common . . . 69 F6
Coxford Norf . . . . 80 E4
Soton . . . . . . . . . 14 C4
Cox Green . . . . . 27 B6
Coxheath . . . . . . 29 D8
Coxhill . . . . . . . . 31 E6
Coxhoe . . . . . . . 111 F6
Coxley . . . . . . . . 23 E7
Cox Moor . . . . . . 76 D5
Coxwold . . . . . . . 95 B8
Coychurch . . . . . 21 B8
Coylton . . . . . . . 112 B4
Coylumbridge . . 138 D5
Coynach . . . . . . . 140 D3
Coynachie . . . . . 152 E4
Coytrahen . . . . . 34 F2
Crabadon . . . . . . .7 D5
Crabbs Cross . . . 50 C5
Crabtree . . . . . . . 17 B6
Crackenthorpe . . 100 B1
Crackington Haven .8 E3
Crackley . . . . . . . 51 B7
Crackleybank . . . 61 C7
Crackpot . . . . . . 100 E4
Cracoe . . . . . . . . 94 C2
Craddock . . . . . . 11 C5
Cradhlastadh . . . 154 D5
Cradley . . . . . . . . 50 E2
Cradley Heath . . . 62 F3
Crafthole . . . . . . . .5 D8
Craggan Highld . 139 B6
Highld . . . . . . . . 157 H11
Cragg Vale . . . . . 87 B8
Craghead . . . . . . 110 D5
Crai . . . . . . . . . . 34 B2
Craibstone . . . . . 152 C4
Craichie . . . . . . . 135 E5
Craig Dumfries . . 106 B3
Dumfries . . . . . . 106 C3
Highld . . . . . . . . 150 G3
Craiganour Lodge 132 D3
Craig Castle . . . . 140 B3
Craig-cefn-parc . . 33 D7
Craigdam . . . . . . 153 E8
Craigdarroch
Dumfries . . . . . . 113 E7
Highld . . . . . . . . 150 F7
Craigdhu . . . . . . 150 G7
Craigearn . . . . . . 141 C6
Craigellachie . . . 152 D2
Craigencross . . . 104 C4
Craigend Perth . . 128 B3
Stirling . . . . . . . . 127 F6
Craigendoran . . 126 F2
Craigends . . . . . . 118 C4
Craigens Argyll . . 142 B3
E Ayrs. . . . . . . . . 113 C5
Craighat . . . . . . . 126 F3
Craighead . . . . . 129 D8
Craighlaw Mains . 105 C7
Craighouse . . . . 144 G4
Craigie Aberds . . 141 C8
Dundee . . . . . . . 134 F4
Perth . . . . . . . . . 128 B3
Perth . . . . . . . . . 133 E8
S Ayrs. . . . . . . . . 118 F4
Craigiefield . . . . 159 G5
Craiglaw . . . . . . 121 C8
Craiglockhart . . . 120 B5
Craigmalloch . . . 112 E4
Craigmaud . . . . . 153 C8

Craigmillar ......121 B5
Craigmore .....145 G10
Craignant ......73 F6
Craigneuk
  N Lanark .....119 C7
  N Lanark .....119 D7
Craignure......124 B3
Craigo .........135 C6
Craigow ........128 D2
Craig Penllyn ... 21 B8
Craigrothie .....129 C5
Craigroy ......151 F14
Craigruie ......126 B3
Craigston Castle .153 C7
Craigton Aberdeen.141 D7
  Angus.........134 D3
  Angus.........135 F5
  Highld ........151 B9
Craigtown ....157 D11
Craig-y-don .....83 C7
Craig-y-nos .....34 C2
Craik ..........115 D6
Crail ..........129 D8
Crailing .......116 B2
Crailinghall .....116 B2
Craiselound .....89 E8
Crakehill .......95 B7
Crakemarsh .....75 F7
Crambe .........96 C3
Cramlington ....111 B5
Cramond .......120 B4
Cramond Bridge .120 B4
Cranage ........74 C4
Cranberry ......74 F5
Cranborne ......13 C8
Cranbourne .....27 B7
Cranbrook Devon..10 C5
  Kent..........18 B4
Cranbrook
  Common .......18 B4
Crane Moor .....88 D4
Crane's Corner ..68 C2
Cranfield .......53 E7
Cranford ........28 B2
Cranford St
  Andrew.........53 B7
Cranford St John ..53 B7
Cranham Glos....37 C5
  London ........42 F1
Crank ..........86 E3
Crank Wood .....86 D4
Cranleigh ......27 F8
Cranley ........57 B5
Cranmer Green ..56 B4
Cranmore .......14 F4
Cranna .......153 C6
Crannich ......147 G8
Crannoch ......152 C4
Cranoe .........64 E4
Cransford ......57 C7
Cranshaws .....122 C2
Cranstal .......84 B4
Crantock ........4 C2
Cranwell .......78 E3
Cranwich .......67 E7
Cranworth ......68 D2
Craobh Haven ..124 E3
Crapstone .......6 C3
Crarae ........125 F5
Crask Inn .....157 G8
Craskins .......140 D4
Crask of Aigas .150 G7
Craster .......117 C8
Craswall .......48 F4
Cratfield ......57 B7
Crathes .......141 E6
Crathie Aberds .139 E8
  Highld .......137 F8
Crathorne .....102 D2
Craven Arms .....60 F4
Crawcrook ....110 C4
Crawford Lancs ..86 D2
  S Lanark ......114 B2
Crawfordjohn ..113 B8
Crawick .......113 C7
Crawley Hants ...26 F2
  Oxon..........38 C3
  W Sus .........28 F3
Crawley Down ...28 F4
Crawleyside ....110 E2
Crawshawbooth ..87 B6
Crawton .......135 B8
Cray N Yorks ....94 B2
  Perth ........133 C8
Crayford .......29 B6
Crayke .........95 B8
Crays Hill ......42 E3
Cray's Pond ....39 F6
Creacombe .....10 C3
Creagan .......130 E3
Creag Ghoraidh .148 D2
Creaguaineach
  Lodge .......131 C7
Creaksea .......43 E5
Creaton ........52 B5
Creca .........108 B2
Credenhill ......49 E6
Crediton .......10 U3
Creebridge ....105 C8
Creech Heathfield .11 B7
Creech St Michael ..11 B7
Creed ...........3 B8
Creekmouth .....41 F7
Creeting Bottoms .56 D5
Creeting St Mary ..56 D4
Creeton ........65 B7
Creetown .....105 D8
Creggans ......125 E6
Cregneash ......84 F1
Creg-ny-Baa ....84 D3
Cregrina .......48 D3
Creich .........128 B5
Creigiau .......34 F4
Cremyll .........6 D2
Creslow ........39 B8
Cressage .......61 D5
Cressbrook .....75 B8
Cresselly.......32 D1
Cressing .......42 B3
Cresswell
  Northumb......117 E8
  Staffs.........75 F6
Cresswell Quay ..32 D1
Creswell .......76 B5
Cretingham .....57 C6
Cretshengan ..144 G6
Crewe Ches E....74 D4
  Ches W .......73 D8
Crewgreen ......60 C3

Crewkerne .....12 D2
Crianlarich ....126 B2
Cribyn .........46 D4
Criccieth .......71 D5
Crich ..........76 D3
Crichie .......153 D9
Crichton ......121 C6
Crick Mon .......36 E1
  W Nhants.......52 B3
Crickadarn......48 E2
Cricket Malherbie .11 C8
Cricket St Thomas .11 D8
Crickheath......60 B2
Crickhowell ....35 C6
Cricklade ......37 E8
Cricklewood.....41 F5
Cridling Stubbs ..89 B6
Crieff .........127 B7
Criggion .......60 C2
Crigglestone ....88 C4
Crimond ......153 C10
Crimonmogate .153 C10
Crimplesham ....67 D6
Crinan ........144 D6
Cringleford .....68 D4
Cringles ........94 E3
Crinow .........32 C2
Cripplesease .....2 C4
Cripplestyle ....13 C8
Cripp's Corner ..18 C4
Crockenhill .....29 C6
Crockernwell ....10 E2
Crockerton .....24 E3
Crocketford or
  Ninemile Bar ..106 B5
Crockey Hill ....96 E2
Crockham Hill ...28 D5
Crockleford Heath. 43 B6
Crockness .....159 J4
Crock Street ....11 C8
Croeserw .......34 E2
Croes-goch .....44 B3
Croes-lan ......46 E2
Croesor ........71 C7
Croesyceiliog
  Carms .........33 C5
  Torf ..........35 E7
Croes-y-mwyalch .35 E7
Croesywaun......82 F5
Croft Leics .....64 E2
  Lincs..........79 C8
  Pembs .........45 E3
  Warr ..........86 E4
Croftamie ......126 F3
Croftmalloch ...120 C2
Crofton Wilts ...25 C7
  W Yorks .......88 C4
Croft-on-Tees ..101 D7
Crofts of
  Benachielt....158 G3
Crofts of Haddo .153 E8
Crofts of
  Inverthernie ..153 D7
Crofts of Meikle
  Ardo .........153 D8
Crofty .........33 E6
Croggan .......124 C3
Croglin .......109 E5
Croich ........150 B7
Crois Dughaill ..148 F2
Cromarty ......151 E10
Cromblet ......153 E7
Cromdale ......139 B6
Cromer Herts ...41 B5
  Norf ..........81 C8
Cromford .......76 D2
Cromhall .......36 E3
Cromhall Common .36 E3
Cromor ........155 E9
Cromra ........137 E8
Cromwell .......77 C7
Cronberry .....113 B6
Crondall .......27 E5
Cronk-y-Voddy ..84 D3
Cronton ........86 F2
Crook Durham ..110 F4
  W&F...........99 E6
Crookedholm ...118 F4
Crookes ........88 F4
Crookham
  Northumb......122 F5
  W Berks........26 C3
Crookham Village .27 D5
Crookhaugh ....114 B4
Crookhouse ....116 B3
Crooklands .....99 F7
Crook of Devon .128 D2
Cropredy.......52 E2
Cropston ......64 C2
Cropthorne .....50 E4
Cropton .......103 F5
Cropwell Bishop .77 F6
Cropwell Butler ..77 F6
Cros .........155 A10
Crosbost ......155 E8
Crosby Cumb....107 F7
  IoM ..........84 E3
  N Lincs........90 C2
Crosby Garrett ..100 D2
Crosby
  Ravensworth ...99 C8
Crosby Villa ...107 F7
Croscombe .....23 E7
Cross ..........23 D6
Crossaig ......143 C9
Crossal ........149 E9
Crossapol .....146 G2
Cross Ash ......35 C8
Cross-at-Hand ..29 E8
Crossburn .....119 B8
Crossbush ......16 D4
Crosscanonby ...107 F7
Crossdale Street .81 D8
Crossens .......85 C4
Crossflatts .....94 E4
Crossford Fife ..128 F2
  S Lanark ......119 E8
Crossgate ......66 B2
Crossgatehall ..121 C6
Crossgates Fife .128 F3
  Powys .........48 C2
Crossgill .......93 C5
Cross Green Devon ..9 F5
  Suff ..........56 D2
  Suff ..........56 D3
  Warks .........51 D8
Cross-hands .....32 B2
Cross Hands Carms. 33 C6

Cross Hands continued
  Pembs .........32 C1
Crosshill E Ayrs..112 B4
  Fife ..........128 E3
  S Ayrs .........112 D3
Cross Hill ......76 E4
Crosshouse ....118 F3
Cross Houses ...60 D5
Crossings .....108 B5
Cross in Hand
  E Sus ..........18 C2
  Leics..........64 F2
Cross Inn Ceredig.. 46 C4
  Ceredig .......46 D2
  Rhondda........34 F4
Crosskeys ......35 E6
Cross Keys .....29 D6
Crosskirk .....157 B13
Cross Lane Head . 61 E7
Crosslanes .....60 B3
Cross Lanes Corn...3 D5
  N Yorks........95 C8
  Wrex ..........73 E7
Crossle ........118 C4
Crosslee ......115 C6
Crossmichael ...106 C4
Crossmoor ......92 F4
Cross Oak ......35 B5
Cross of
  Jackston .....153 E7
Cross o'th'hands .76 E2
Crossroads Aberds 141 E6
  E Ayrs.........118 F4
Cross Street ....57 B5
Crossway Hereford .49 F8
  Mon ..........35 C8
  Powys .........48 D2
Crossway Green .50 C3
Crossways ......13 F5
Crosswell ......45 F3
Crosswood ......47 B5
Crosthwaite .....99 E6
Croston ........86 C2
Crostwick ......69 C5
Crostwight .....69 B6
Crothair ......154 D6
Crouch .........29 D7
Croucheston ....13 B8
Crouch Hill .....12 C5
Crouch House
  Green .........28 E5
Croughton ......52 F3
Crovie ........153 B8
Crowan ..........2 C5
Crowborough ....18 B2
Crowcombe......22 F3
Crowdecote .....75 C8
Crowden ........87 E8
Crow Edge ......88 D2
Crowell .........39 E7
Crowfield Suff ...56 D5
  W Nhants.......52 E4
Crow Hill .......36 B3
Crowhurst E Sus...18 D4
  Sur ...........28 E4
Crowhurst Lane
  End ...........28 E4
Crowland .......66 C2
Crowlas .........2 C4
Crowle N Lincs ...89 C8
  Worcs .........50 D4
Crowmarsh
  Gifford ........39 F6
Crown Corner ...57 B6
Crownhill .......6 D2
Crownland ......56 C4
Crownthorpe ....68 D3
Crowntown ......2 C5
Crows-an-wra .....2 D2
Crowshill ......68 D2
Crowsnest ......60 D3
Crowthorne .....27 C6
Crowton .......74 B2
Croxall ........63 C5
Croxby .........90 E5
Croxdale ......111 F5
Croxden ........75 F7
Croxley Green ...40 E3
Croxton Cambs ..54 C3
  N Lincs........90 C4
  Norf ..........67 F8
  Staffs.........74 F4
Croxtonbank ....74 F4
Croxton Kerrial ..64 B5
Croy Highld .....151 G10
  N Lanark ......119 B7
Croyde ........20 F3
Croydon Cambs ..54 E4
  London ........28 C4
Crubenmore
  Lodge ........138 E2
Cruckmeole .....60 D4
Cruckton .......60 C4
Cruden Bay ....153 E10
Crudgington ....61 C6
Crudwell .......37 E6
Crug ...........48 B3
Crugmeer .......4 B4
Crugybar ........47 F5
Crulabhig .....154 D6
Crumlin =Crymlyn. 35 E6
Crumpsall ......87 D6
Crundale Kent ...30 E4
  Pembs .........44 D4
Cruwys Morchard .10 C3
Crux Easton ....26 D2
Crwbin .........33 C5
Crya ..........159 H4
Cryers Hill .....40 E1
Crymlyn ........83 D6
Crymych ........45 F3
Crynant ........34 D1
Crynfryn .......46 C4
Cuaig .........149 C12
Cuan ..........124 D3
Cubbington .....51 C8
Cubeck ........100 F4
Cubert ..........4 D2
Cubley .........88 D3
Cubley Common ..88 D3
Cublington Bucks .39 B8
  Hereford ......49 F5
Cuckfield .......17 B7
Cucklington .....13 B5
Cuckney ........77 B5
Cuckoo Hill .....89 E8
Cuddesdon ......39 D6
Cuddington Bucks. 39 C7

Cuddington continued
  Ches W ........74 B3
Cuddington Heath. 73 E8
Cuddy Hill ......92 F4
Cudham ........28 D5
Cudliptown ......6 B3
Cudworth Som ...11 C8
  S Yorks........88 D4
Cuffley .........41 D6
Cuiashader ....155 B10
Cuidhir .......148 H1
Cuidhtinis .....154 J5
Culbo ..........151 E9
Culbokie .......151 F9
Culburnie ......150 G7
Culcabock .....151 G9
Culcairn .......151 E9
Culcharry .....151 F11
Culcheth .......86 E4
Culdrain .......152 E5
Culduie .......149 D12
Culford ........56 B2
Culgaith .......99 B8
Culham .........39 E5
Culkein .......156 F3
Culkein Drumbeg 156 F4
Culkerton ......37 E6
Cullachie ......139 B5
Cullen ........152 B5
Cullercoats ....111 B6
Cullicudden ....151 E9
Cullingworth ....94 F3
Cullipool ......124 D3
Cullivoe ......160 C7
Culloch .......127 C6
Culloden ......151 G10
Cullompton .....10 D5
Culmaily ......151 B11
Culmazie ......105 D7
Culmington .....60 F4
Culmstock ......11 C6
Culnacraig .....156 J3
Culnaknock ....149 B10
Culpho .........57 E6
Culrain ........151 B8
Culross .......127 F8
Culroy ........112 C3
Culsh Aberds ...140 E2
  Aberds ........153 D8
Culshabbin ....105 D7
Culswick ......160 J4
Cultercullen ...141 B8
Cults Aberdeen ..141 D7
  Aberds ........152 E5
  Dumfries ......105 E8
Culverstone Green 29 C7
Culverthorpe ....78 E3
Culworth .......52 E3
Culzie Lodge ...151 D8
Cumberland ....119 B7
Cumbernauld
  Village .......119 B7
Cumberworth ....79 B8
Cuminestown ...153 C8
Cumlewick .....160 L6
Cummersdale ...108 D3
Cummertrees ...107 C8
Cummingston ...152 B1
Cumnock ......113 B5
Cumnor .........38 D4
Cumrew ........108 D5
Cumwhinton ...108 D4
Cumwhitton ....108 D5
Cundall ........95 B7
Cunninghamhead 118 E3
Cunnister .....160 D7
Cupar .........129 C5
Cupar Muir .....129 C5
Cupernham ......14 B4
Curbar .........76 B2
Curbridge Hants .15 C6
  Oxon..........38 D3
Curdridge ......15 C6
Curdworth ......63 E5
Curland ........11 C7
Curlew Green ...57 C7
Currarie ......112 E1
Curridge .......26 B2
Currie ........120 C4
Curry Mallet ....11 B8
Curry Rivel .....11 B8
Curtisden Green .29 E8
Curtisknowle .....6 D5
Cury ...........3 D5
Cushnie ......153 B7
Cushuish ........22 F3
Cusop ..........48 E4
Cutcloy .......105 F8
Cutcombe .......21 F8
Cutgate ........87 C6
Cutiau .........58 C3
Cutlers Green ...55 F6
Cutnall Green ...50 C3
Cutsdean .......51 F5
Cutthorpe ......76 B3
Cutts .........160 K6
Cuxham ........39 E6
Cuxton .........29 C8
Cuxwold .......91 D5
Cwm Bl Gwent ...35 D5
  Denb ..........72 B4
  Swansea .......33 E7
Cwmafan ........34 E1
Cwmaman .......34 E4
Cwmann ........46 E4
Cwmavon .......35 D6
Cwmbach Carms ..32 B3
  Carms .........33 D5
  Powys .........48 F2
  Powys .........48 F3
Cwmbelan ......59 F6
Cwmbrân
  =Cwmbrân .......35 E6
Cwmbrwyno .....58 F4
Cwm-byr ........46 F5
Cwmcarn .......35 E6
Cwmcarvan .....36 D1
Cwm-Cewydd ....59 C5
Cwm-cou .......45 E4
Cwmcych .......45 F4
Cwmdare ........34 D3
Cwmderwen .....59 D6
Cwmdu Carms ...46 F5
  Powys .........35 B5
  Swansea .......33 E7
Cwmduad .......46 F2
Cwm-Dulais .....33 D7
Cwmdwr ........47 F6

Cwmfelin Bridgend . 34 F2
  M Tydf ........34 D4
Cwmfelin Boeth ..32 C2
Cwm-felin-fach ..35 E5
Cwmfelin Mynach 32 B3
Cwmffrwd .......33 C5
Cwm Ffrwd-oer ..35 D6
Cwmgiedd .......34 C1
Cwmgors .......33 C8
Cwmgwili ......33 C6
Cwmgwrach .....34 D2
Cwm-hesgen ....71 E8
Cwmhiraeth .....46 F2
Cwm-hwnt.......34 D3
Cwmifor ........33 B7
Cwm Irfon ......47 E7
Cwmisfael ......33 C5
Cwm-Llinau .....58 D5
Cwmllynfell .....33 C8
Cwm-mawr ......33 C6
Cwmorgan ......45 F4
Cwm-parc .......34 E3
Cwmpengraig ...46 F2
Cwm Penmachno .71 C8
Cwmrhos ........35 B5
Cwmsychpant ...46 E3
Cwmtillery ......35 D6
Cwm-twrch Isaf ..34 C1
Cwm-twrch Uchaf. 34 C1
Cwmwysg .......34 B2
Cwm-y-glo Carms .82 E5
  Gwyn .........82 E5
Cwmyoy ........35 B6
Cwmystwyth .....47 B6
Cwrt ...........58 D3
Cwrt-newydd ....46 E3
Cwrt-y-cadno ...47 E5
Cwrt-y-gollen ...35 C6
Cydweli
  =Kidwelly .....33 D5
Cyffordd Llandudno
  Junction ......83 D7
Cyffylliog ......72 D4
Cyfronydd ......59 D8
Cymer .........34 E2
Cyncoed .......35 F5
Cynghordy ......47 E7
Cynheidre ......33 D5
Cynwyd .........72 E4
Cynwyl Elfed ....32 B4
Cywarch .......59 C5

### D

Dacre N Yorks .....94 C4
  W&F...........99 B6
Dacre Banks .....94 C4
Daddry Shield ...109 F8
Dadford ........52 F4
Dadlington......63 E8
Dafarn Faig .....71 C5
Dafen ..........33 D6
Daffy Green .....68 D2
Dagenham ......41 F7
Daglingworth ...37 D6
Dagnall ........40 C2
Dail Beag .....154 C7
Dail Bho Dheas .155 A9
Dail bho Thuath .155 A9
Daill .........142 B4
Dailly .........112 D2
Dail Mor ......154 C7
Dairsie or
  Osnaburgh ....129 C6
Daisy Hill ......86 D4
Dalabrog ......148 F2
Dalavich ......125 D5
Dalbeattie .....106 C5
Dalblair .......113 C6
Dalbog ........135 B5
Dalbury ........76 F3
Dalby IoM .......84 E2
  N Yorks........96 B2
Dalchalloch ....132 C4
Dalchalm ......157 J12
Dalchenna .....125 E6
Dalchirach ....152 E1
Dalchork ......157 H8
Dalchreichart ..137 C5
Dalchruin ......127 C6
Dalderby .......78 C5
Dale ...........44 E3
Dale Abbey .....76 F4
Dale Head ......99 C6
Dalelia .......147 E10
Dale of Walls ..160 H3
Daless ........151 H11
Dalfaber .......138 C5
Dalgarven ......118 E2
Dalgety Bay ....128 F3
Dalginross .....127 B6
Dalguise ......133 E6
Dalhalvaig ....157 D11
Dalham .........55 C8
Dalinlongart ..145 E10
Dalkeith ......121 C6
Dallam .........86 E3
Dallas ........151 F14
Dalleagles .....113 C5
Dallinghoo .....57 D6
Dallington E Sus .18 D3
  W Nhants.......52 C5
Dallow .........94 B4
Dalmadilly ....141 C6
Dalmally .......125 C7
Dalmarnock ....119 C6
Dalmary .......126 E4
Dalmellington ..112 D4
Dalmeny ......120 B4
Dalmigavie ....138 C3
Dalmigavie
  Lodge ........138 B3
Dalmore ......151 E9
Dalmuir .......118 B4
Dalnabreck ....147 E9
Dalnacardoch
  Lodge ........132 B4
Dalnacroich ...150 F6
Dalnaglar Castle .133 C8
Dalnahaitnach .138 B4
Dalnaspidal
  Lodge ........132 B3
Dalnavaid .....133 C7
Dalnavie ......151 D9
Dalnawillan
  Lodge .......157 E13
Dalness .......131 D5

Dalnessie .....157 H9
Dalqueich .....128 D2
Dalreavoch ....157 J10
Dalry .........118 E2
Dalrymple .....112 C3
Dalserf .......119 D8
Dalston .......108 D3
Dalswinton ....114 F2
Dalton Dumfries .107 B8
  Lancs .........86 D2
  Northum........110 B4
  Northum........110 D2
  N Yorks.........95 B7
  S Yorks.........89 E5
Dalton-in-Furness 92 B2
Dalton-le-Dale ..111 E7
Dalton-on-Tees .101 D7
Dalton Piercy ...111 F7
Dalveich ......126 B5
Dalvina Lodge ..157 E9
Dalwhinnie .....138 F2
Dalwood ........11 D7
Dalwyne .......112 E3
Damerham ......14 C2
Damgate .......69 D7
Damnaglaur ....104 F5
Damside .......120 E4
Dam Side .......92 E4
Danbury ........42 D3
Danby .........103 D5
Danby Wiske ...101 E8
Dandaleith .....152 D2
Danderhall ....121 C6
Danebridge .....75 C6
Dane End .......41 B6
Danehill ........17 B8
Danemoor Green .68 D3
Danesford ......61 E7
Daneshill .......26 D4
Dangerous Corner. 86 C3
Danskine ......121 C8
Darcy Lever ....86 D5
Darenth .........29 B6
Daresbury ......86 F3
Darfield ........88 D5
Darfoulds ......77 B5
Dargate ........30 C4
Dargavel Renfs .118 B3
Darite ...........5 C7
Darkland ......135 E5
Darlaston ......62 E3
Darley ..........94 D5
Darley Bridge ...76 C2
Darley Head ....94 D4
Darlingscott ....51 E7
Darlington ....101 C7
Darliston .......74 F2
Darlton ........77 B7
Darnall .........88 F4
Darnick .......121 F8
Darowen ........58 D5
Darra .........153 D7
Darracott ......20 F3
Darras Hall ....110 B4
Darrington .....89 B5
Darsham ........57 C8
Dartford ........29 B6
Dartford Crossing .29 B6
Dartington .......7 C5
Dartmeet ........6 B4
Dartmouth .......7 D6
Darton .........88 D4
Darvel ........119 F5
Darwell Hole ....18 D3
Darwen .........86 B4
Datchet ........27 B7
Datchworth .....41 C5
Datchworth Green .41 C5
Dauhhill ........86 D5
Daugh of
  Kinnermony ...152 D2
Dauntsey .......37 F6
Davaar ........143 H3
Davenham ......74 B3
Davenport Green .74 B5
Daventry .......52 C3
Davidson's Mains 120 B5
Davidstow .......8 F3
Davington .....115 D5
Daviot Aberds ..141 B6
  Highld ........151 H10
Davoch of
  Grange ........152 C4
Davyhulme ......87 E5
Dawley .........61 D6
Dawlish .........7 B7
Dawlish Warren ..7 B7
Dawn ..........83 D8
Daws Heath .....42 F4
Daw's House .....8 F5
Dawsmere .......79 F7
Daylesford .....38 B2
Ddôl-Cownwy ....59 C7
Ddrydwy ........82 D3
Deadwater ......116 E2
Deaf Hill ......111 F6
Deal ...........31 D7
Deal Hall .......43 E6
Dean Cumb ......98 B2
  Devon ..........6 C5
  Devon .........20 E4
  Dorset .........13 C7
  Hants .........15 B6
Deanburnhaugh .115 C6
Deane Gtr Man ...86 D4
  Hants .........26 D3
Deanich Lodge ..150 C6
Deanland ........13 C7
Deanlane End ....15 C8
Deans .........120 C3
Deanscales .....98 B2
Deanshanger ....53 F5
Deanston ......127 D6
Dearham .......107 F7
Debach .........57 D6
Debden Essex ...41 E7
  Essex .........55 F6
Debden Cross ...55 F6
Debenham ......57 C5
Dechmont .....120 B3
Deddington .....52 F2
Dedham ........56 F4
Dedham Heath ..56 F4
Deebank .......141 E5

Deene ..........65 E6
Deenethorpe ....65 E6
Deepcar ........88 E3
Deepcut ........27 D7
Deepdale ......100 F2
Deeping Gate ...65 D8
Deeping St James .65 D8
Deeping St
  Nicholas .......66 C2
Deerhill ......152 C4
Deerhurst ......37 B5
Deerness .....159 H6
Defford ........50 E4
Defynnog .......34 B3
Deganwy .......83 D7
Deighton N Yorks .102 D1
  W Yorks .......88 C2
  York ..........96 E2
Deiniolen ......83 E5
Delabole ........8 F2
Delamere .......74 C2
Delfrigs ......141 B8
Delliefure ....151 H13
Dell Lodge ....139 C6
Delnabo .......139 C6
Delnadamph ....139 D7
Delph ..........87 D7
Delves ........110 E4
Delvine .......133 E8
Dembleby .......78 F3
Denaby Main ....89 E5
Denbigh
  =Dinbych ......72 C4
Denbury .........7 C6
Denby ..........76 E3
Denby Dale .....88 D3
Denchworth .....38 E3
Dendron ........92 B2
Denel End ......53 F8
Denend ........152 E6
Denford ........53 B7
Dengie .........43 D5
Denham Bucks ...40 F3
  Suff ..........55 C8
  Suff ..........57 B5
Denham Street ..57 B5
Denhead Aberds .153 C9
  Fife ..........129 C6
Denhead of
  Arbilot .......135 E5
Denhead of Gray .134 F3
Denholm .......115 C8
Denholme ......94 F3
Denholme Clough. 94 F3
Denio ..........70 D4
Denmead .......15 C7
Dennington .....57 C6
Denny .........127 F7
Dennyloanhead .127 F7
Denny Lodge ....14 D4
Denshaw .......87 C7
Denside .......141 E7
Densole ........31 E6
Denston ........55 D8
Denstone .......75 E8
Dent ..........100 F2
Denton Cambs ...65 F8
  Darl ..........101 C7
  E Sus .........17 D8
  Gtr Man .......87 E7
  Kent ..........31 E6
  Lincs..........77 F8
  Norf ..........69 F5
  N Yorks........94 E4
  Oxon..........39 D5
  W Nhants.......53 D6
Denton's Green ..86 E2
Denver .........67 D6
Denwick .......117 C8
Deopham .......68 D3
Deopham Green .68 E3
Depden .........55 D8
Depden Green ...55 D8
Deptford London .28 B4
  Wilts .........24 F5
Derby ..........76 F3
Derbyhaven .....84 F2
Dereham ........68 C2
Deri ...........35 D5
Derril .........8 D5
Derringstone ...31 E6
Derrington .....62 B2
Derriton ........8 D5
Derry Hill ......24 B4
Derrythorpe ....90 D2
Dersingham .....80 D2
Dervaig .......146 F7
Derwen .........72 D4
Derwenlas ......58 E4
Desborough .....64 F5
Desford ........63 D8
Detchant ......123 F6
Detling ........29 D8
Deuddwr .......60 C2
Deuxhill .......61 F6
Devauden .......36 E1
Devil's Bridge ...47 B6
Devizes ........24 C5
Devol .........118 B3
Devonport .......6 D2
Devonside .....127 E8
Devoran .........3 C6
Dewar .........121 E6
Dewlish ........13 E5
Dewsbury .......88 B3
Dewsbury Moor ..88 B3
Dewshall Court ..49 F6
Dhoon .........84 D4
Dhoor .........84 C4
Dhowin .........84 B4
Dial Post .......17 C5
Dibden .........14 D5
Dibden Purlieu ..14 D5
Dickleburgh ....68 F4
Didbrook .......51 F5
Didcot .........39 F5
Diddington .....54 C2
Diddlebury ......60 F5
Didley .........49 F6
Didling ........16 C2
Didmarton ......37 F5
Didsbury .......87 E6
Didworthy .......6 C4
Digby ..........78 D3
Digg .........149 B9
Diggle .........87 D8
Digmoor ........86 D2

Digswell Park ...41 C5
Dihewyd ........46 D3
Dilham .........69 B6
Dilhorne .......75 E6
Dillarburn ....119 E8
Dillington ......54 C2
Dilston .......110 C2
Dilton Marsh ....24 E3
Dilwyn .........49 D6
Dinas Carms ....45 F4
  Gwyn .........70 D3
Dinas Cross ....45 F2
Dinas Dinlle ....82 F4
Dinas-Mawddwy ..59 C5
Dinas Powys ....22 B3
Dinbych
  =Denbigh ......72 C4
Dinbych-y-Pysgod
  =Tenby ........32 D2
Dinder .........23 E7
Dinedor ........49 F7
Dingestow ......36 C1
Dingle .........85 F4
Dingleden ......18 B5
Dingley ........64 F4
Dingwall ......151 F8
Dinlabyre .....115 E8
Dinmael ........72 E4
Dinnet ........140 E3
Dinnington Som..12 C2
  S Yorks........89 F6
  T&W ..........110 B5
Dinorwic .......83 E5
Dinton Bucks ...39 C7
  Wilts .........24 F5
Dinwoodie Mains.114 E4
Dinworthy .......8 C5
Dippen ........143 F11
Dippenhall ......27 E6
Dipple Moray ...152 C3
  S Ayrs .........112 D2
Diptford ........6 D5
Dipton ........110 D4
Dirdhu ........139 B6
Dirleton ......129 F7
Dirt Pot ......109 E8
Discoed ........48 C4
Diseworth ......63 B8
Dishes ........159 F7
Dishforth ......95 B6
Disley .........87 F7
Diss ...........56 B5
Disserth .......48 D2
Distington ......98 B2
Ditchampton ....25 F5
Ditcheat .......23 F8
Ditchingham ....69 E6
Ditchling ......17 C7
Ditherington ...60 C5
Dittisham .......7 D6
Ditton Halton ...86 F2
  Kent ..........29 D8
Ditton Green ....55 D7
Ditton Priors ...61 F6
Divach ........137 B7
Divlyn .........47 F6
Dixton Glos .....50 F4
  Mon ..........36 C2
Dobcross .......87 D7
Dobwalls ........5 C7
Doccombe .......10 F2
Dochfour House .151 H9
Dochgarroch ...151 G9
Docking ........80 D3
Docklow ........49 D7
Dockray ........99 B5
Dockroyd .......94 F3
Doc Penfro
  =Pembroke Dock..44 E4
Dodburn .......115 D7
Doddinghurst ...42 E1
Doddington Cambs 66 E3
  Kent ..........30 D3
  Lincs..........78 B2
  Northum........123 F5
  Shrops ........49 B8
Doddiscombsleigh 10 F3
Dodford
  W Nhants.......52 C4
  Worcs .........50 B4
Dodington ......24 A2
Dodleston ......73 C7
Dods Leigh .....75 F7
Dodworth ......88 D4
Doe Green ......86 F3
Doe Lea ........76 C4
Dogdyke ........78 D5
Dogmersfield ...27 D5
Dogridge .......37 F7
Dogsthorpe .....65 D8
Dog Village ....10 E4
Dolanog ........59 C7
Dolau Powys ....48 C3
  Rhondda........34 F3
Dolbenmaen .....71 C6
Dolfach ........59 D8
Dolfor .........59 F8
Dol-fôr ........58 D5
Dolgarrog ......83 E7
Dolgellau .......58 C4
Dolgran ........46 F3
Dolhendre ......72 F2
Doll ..........157 J11
Dollar .........127 E8
Dolley Green ....48 C4
Dollwen ........58 F3
Dolphin ........73 B5
Dolphinholme ...92 D5
Dolphinton ....120 E4
Dolton .........9 C7
Dolwen Conwy ...83 D8
  Powys .........59 D6
Dolwyd .........83 D7
Dolwyddelan ....83 F7
Dôl-y-Bont .....58 F3
Dol-y-cannau ...48 E4
Dolyhir ........48 D4
Doncaster ......89 D6
Dones Green ....74 B3
Donhead St
  Andrew.........13 B7
Donhead St Mary .13 B7
Donibristle ...128 F3
Donington ......78 F5
Donington on Bain 91 F6
Donington South
  Ing ...........78 F5
Donisthorpe ....63 C7
Donkey Town ....27 C7

Donnington Glos.. 38 B1
  Hereford ......50 F2
  Shrops ........61 D5
  Telford .......61 C7
  W Berks ........26 C2
  W Sus .........16 D2
Donnington Wood.61 C7
Donyatt ........11 C8
Doonfoot ......112 C3
Dorback Lodge .139 C6
Dorchester Dorset..12 E4
  Oxon..........39 E5
Dordon .........63 D6
Dore ...........88 F4
Dores .........151 H8
Dorking ........28 E2
Dormansland ....28 E5
Dormanstown ..102 B3
Dormington .....49 E7
Dormston ......50 D4
Dornal .........105 B6
Dornie .......149 F13
Dornoch ......151 C10
Dornock .......108 C2
Dorrery .......158 E2
Dorridge .......51 B6
Dorrington Lincs .78 D3
  Shrops ........60 D4
Dorsington......51 E6
Dorstone .......48 E5
Dorton .........39 C6
Dorusduain ....136 B2
Dosthill ........63 E6
Dottery ........12 E2
Doublebois ......5 C6
Dougarie ......143 E9
Doughton .......37 E5
Douglas IoM .....84 E3
  S Lanark ......119 F8
Douglas & Angus 134 F4
Douglastown ...134 E4
Douglas Water ..119 F8
Douglas West ...119 F8
Doulting .......23 E8
Dounby ........159 F3
Doune Highld ...156 J7
  Stirling ......127 D6
Doune Park ....153 B7
Douneside .....140 D3
Dounie ........151 B8
Dounreay .....157 C12
Dousland ........6 C3
Dovaston .......60 B3
Dove Holes .....75 B7
Dovenby .......107 F7
Dover ..........31 E7
Dovercourt .....57 F6
Doverdale ......50 C3
Doveridge ......75 F8
Doversgreen ....28 E3
Dowally .......133 E7
Dowbridge ......92 F4
Dowdeswell .....37 C6
Dowlais ........34 D4
Dowland .........9 C7
Dowlish Wake ...11 C8
Down Ampney ...37 E8
Downcraig
  Ferry ........145 H10
Downderry .......5 D8
Downe ..........28 C5
Downend IoW ....15 F6
  S Glos .........23 B8
  W Berks ........26 B2
Downfield .....134 F3
Downgate .......5 B8
Downham Essex ..42 E3
  Lancs .........93 E7
  Northumb.......123 F5
Downham Market .67 D6
Down Hatherley ..37 B5
Downhead .......23 E8
Downhill Perth .133 F7
  T&W ..........111 D6
Downholland
  Cross .........85 D4
Downholme ....101 E6
Downies .......141 E8
Downley ........39 E8
Down St Mary ...10 D2
Downside Som ...23 E8
  Sur ...........28 D2
Down Thomas .....6 D3
Downton Hants ..14 E3
  Wilts .........14 B2
Downton on the
  Rock ..........49 B6
Dowsby .........65 B8
Dowsdale .......66 C2
Dowthwaitehead. 99 B5
Doxey ..........62 B3
Doxford .......117 B7
Doxford Park ...111 D6
Doynton ........24 B2
Draffan .......119 E7
Dragonby .......90 C3
Drakeland Corner ..6 D3
Drakemyre .....118 D2
Drake's Broughton 50 E4
Drakes Cross ...51 B5
Drakewalls ......6 B2
Draughton N Yorks.94 D3
  W Nhants.......53 B5
Drax ...........89 B7
Draycote .......52 B2
Draycott Derbys .76 F4
  Glos ..........51 F6
  Som ..........23 D6
Draycott in the
  Clay ..........63 B5
Draycott in the
  Moors .........75 E6
Drayford .......10 C2
Drayton Leics ...64 E5
  Lincs..........78 F5
  Norf ..........68 C4
  Oxon..........38 E4
  Oxon..........52 E2
  Ptsmth ........15 D7
  Som ..........12 B2
  Worcs .........50 B3
Drayton Bassett .63 D5
Drayton
  Beauchamp .....40 C2
Drayton Parslow .39 B8

Drayton St Leonard 39 E5
Drebley 94 D3
Dreemskerry 84 C4
Dreenhill 44 D4
Drefach Carms 33 C6
Carms 46 F2
Dre-fach Carms 33 C7
Ceredig 46 E4
Drefelin 46 F2
Dreghorn 118 F3
Drellingore 31 E6
Drem 121 B8
Dresden 75 E6
Dreumasdal 148 E2
Drewsteignton 10 E2
Driby 79 B6
Driffield E Yorks 97 D6
Glos 37 E7
Drigg 98 E2
Drighlington 88 B3
Drimnin 147 F8
Drimpton 12 D2
Drimsynie 125 E7
Drinisiadar 154 H6
Drinkstone 56 C3
Drinkstone Green 56 C3
Drishaig 125 D7
Drissaig 124 D5
Drochil 120 E4
Drointon 62 B4
Droitwich Spa 50 C3
Droman 156 D4
Dron 128 C3
Dronfield 76 B3
Dronfield Woodhouse 76 B3
Drongan 112 C4
Dronley 134 F3
Droxford 15 C7
Droylsden 87 E7
Druid 72 E4
Druidston 44 D3
Druimarbin 130 B4
Druimavuic 130 E4
Druimdrishaig 144 F6
Druimindarroch 147 C9
Druimyeon More 143 C7
Drum Argyll 145 F8
Perth 128 D2
Drumbeg 156 F4
Drumblade 152 D5
Drumblair 153 D6
Drumbuie Dumfries 113 F5
Highld 149 E12
Drumburgh 108 D2
Drumburn 107 C6
Drumchapel 118 B5
Drumchardine 151 G8
Drumchork 155 J13
Drumclog 119 F6
Drumderfit 151 F9
Drumeldrie 129 D6
Drumelzier 120 F4
Drumfearn 149 G11
Drumgask 138 E2
Drumgley 134 D4
Drumguish 138 E3
Drumin 152 E1
Drumlasie 140 D5
Drumlemble 143 G7
Drumligair 141 C8
Drumlithie 141 F6
Drummoddie 105 E7
Drummond 151 E9
Drummore 104 F5
Drummuir 152 D3
Drummuir Castle 152 D3
Drumnadrochit 137 B8
Drumnagorrach 152 C5
Drumoak 141 E6
Drumpark 107 A5
Drumphail 105 C6
Drumrash 106 B3
Drumrunie 156 J4
Drums 141 B8
Drumsallie 130 B3
Drumstinchall 107 D5
Drumsturdy 134 F4
Drumtochty Castle 135 B6
Drumtroddan 105 E7
Drumuie 149 D9
Drumuillie 138 B5
Drumvaich 127 D5
Drumwhindle 153 E9
Drunkendub 135 E6
Drury 73 C6
Drury Square 68 C2
Drybeck 100 C1
Drybridge Moray 152 B4
N Ayrs 118 F3
Drybrook 36 C3
Dryburgh 121 F8
Dry Doddington 77 E8
Dry Drayton 54 C4
Dryhope 115 B5
Drylaw 120 B5
Drym 2 C5
Drymen 126 F3
Drymuir 153 D9
Drynoch 149 E9
Dryslwyn 33 B6
Dryton 61 D5
Dubford 153 B8
Dubton 135 D5
Duchally 156 H6
Duchlage 126 F2
Duck Corner 57 E7
Duckington 73 D8
Ducklington 38 D3
Duckmanton 76 B4
Duck's Cross 54 D2
Duddenhoe End 55 F5
Duddingston 121 B5
Duddington 65 D6
Duddleswell 17 B8
Duddo 122 E5
Duddon 74 C2
Duddon Bridge 98 F4
Dudleston 73 F7
Dudleston Heath 73 F7
Dudley T&W 111 B5
W Mid 62 E3
Dudley Port 62 E3
Duffield 76 E3
Duffryn Neath 34 E2
Newport 35 F6
Dufftown 152 E3
Duffus 152 B1
Dufton 100 B1
Duggleby 96 C4
Duirinish 149 E12
Duisdalemore 149 G12
Duisky 130 B4
Dukestown 35 C5
Dukinfield 87 E7
Dulas 82 C4
Dulcote 23 E7
Dulford 11 D5
Dull 133 E5
Dullatur 119 B7
Dullingham 55 D7
Dulnain Bridge 139 B5
Duloe Bedford 54 C2
Corn 5 D7
Dulsie 151 G12
Dulverton 10 B4
Dulwich 28 B4
Dumbarton 118 B3
Dumbleton 50 F5
Dumcrieff 114 D4
Dumfries 107 B6
Dumgoyne 126 F4
Dummer 26 E3
Dumpford 16 B2
Dumpton 31 C7
Dun 135 D6
Dunain House 151 G9
Dunalastair 132 D4
Dunan 149 F10
Dunans 145 D9
Dunball 22 E5
Dunbar 122 B2
Dunbeath 158 H3
Dunbeg 124 B4
Dunblane 127 D6
Dunbog 128 C4
Duncanston 151 F8
Duncanstone 140 B4
Dun Charlabhaigh 154 C6
Dunchurch 52 B2
Duncote 52 D4
Duncow 114 F2
Duncraggan 126 D4
Duncrievie 128 D3
Duncton 16 C3
Dundas House 159 K5
Dundee 134 F4
Dundeugh 113 F5
Dundon 23 F6
Dundonald 118 F3
Dundonnell 150 C3
Dundonnell Hotel 150 C3
Dundonnell House 150 C4
Dundraw 108 E2
Dundreggan 137 C6
Dundreggan Lodge 137 C6
Dundrennan 106 E4
Dundry 23 C7
Dunecht 141 D6
Dunfermline 128 F2
Dunfield 37 E8
Dunford Bridge 88 D2
Dungworth 88 F3
Dunham 77 B8
Dunham-on-the-Hill 73 B8
Dunhampton 50 C3
Dunham Town 86 F5
Dunholme 78 B3
Dunino 129 C7
Dunipace 127 F7
Dunira 127 B6
Dunkeld 133 E7
Dunkerton 24 D2
Dunkeswell 11 D6
Dunkeswick 95 E6
Dunkirk Kent 30 D4
Norf 81 E8
Dunk's Green 29 D7
Dunlappie 135 C5
Dunley Hants 26 D2
Worcs 50 C2
Dunlichity Lodge 151 H9
Dunlop 118 E4
Dunmaglass Lodge 137 B8
Dunmore Argyll 144 G6
Falk 127 F7
Dunnet 158 C4
Dunnichen 135 E5
Dunninald 135 D7
Dunning 128 C2
Dunnington E Yorks 97 D7
Warks 51 D5
York 96 D2
Dunnockshaw 87 B6
Dunollie 124 B4
Dunoon 145 F10
Dunragit 105 D5
Dunrostan 144 E6
Duns 122 D3
Dunsby 65 B8
Dunscore 113 F8
Dunscroft 89 D7
Dunsdale 102 C4
Dunsden Green 26 B5
Dunsfold 27 F8
Dunsford 10 F3
Dunshalt 128 C4
Dunshillock 153 D9
Dunskey House 104 D4
Dunsley 103 C6
Dunsmore 40 D1
Dunsop Bridge 93 D6
Dunstable 40 B3
Dunstall 63 B5
Dunstall Common 50 E3
Dunstall Green 55 C8
Dunstan 117 C8
Dunstan Steads 117 B8
Dunster 21 E8
Duns Tew 38 B4
Dunston Lincs 78 C3
Norf 68 D5
Staffs 62 C3
T&W 110 C5
Dunsville 89 D7
Dunswell 97 F6
Dunsyre 120 E3
Dunterton 5 B8
Duntisbourne Abbots 37 D6
Duntisbourne Leer 37 D6
Duntisbourne Rouse 37 D6
Duntish 12 D4
Duntocher 118 B4
Dunton Bucks 39 B8
C Beds 54 E3
Norf 80 D4
Dunton Bassett 64 E2
Dunton Green 29 D6
Dunton Wayletts 42 E2
Duntulm 149 A9
Dunure 112 C2
Dunvant 33 E6
Dunvegan 148 D7
Dunwich 57 B8
Dunwood 75 D6
Dupplin Castle 128 C2
Durdar 108 D4
Durgates 18 B3
Durham 111 E5
Durisdeer 113 D8
Durisdeermill 113 D8
Durkar 88 C4
Durleigh 22 F4
Durley Hants 15 C6
Wilts 25 C7
Durnamuck 150 B3
Durness 156 C7
Durno 141 B6
Duror 130 D3
Durran Argyll 125 E5
Highld 158 D3
Durrington Wilts 25 E6
W Sus 16 D5
Dursley 36 E4
Durston 11 B7
Durweston 13 D6
Dury 160 G6
Duston 52 C5
Duthil 138 B5
Dutlas 48 B4
Duton Hill 42 B2
Dutson 8 F5
Dutton 74 B2
Duxford Cambs 55 E5
Oxon 38 E3
Dwygyfylchi 83 D7
Dwyran 82 E4
Dyce 141 C7
Dye House 110 D2
Dyffryn Bridgend 34 F2
Carms 32 B4
Pembs 44 B4
Dyffryn Ardudwy 71 E6
Dyffryn Castell 58 F4
Dyffryn Ceidrych 33 B8
Dyffryn Cellwen 34 D2
Dyke Lincs 65 B8
Moray 151 F12
Dykehead Angus 134 C3
N Lanark 119 D8
Stirling 126 E4
Dykelands 135 C7
Dykends 134 D2
Dykeside 153 D7
Dykesmains 118 E2
Dylife 59 E5
Dymchurch 19 C7
Dymock 50 F2
Dyrham 24 B2
Dysart 128 E5
Dyserth 72 B4


## E


Eadar Dha Fhadhail 154 D5
Eagland Hill 92 E4
Eagle 77 C8
Eagle Barnsdale 77 C8
Eagle Moor 77 C8
Eaglescliffe 102 C2
Eaglesfield Cumb 98 B2
Dumfries 108 B2
Eaglesham 119 D5
Eaglethorpe 65 E7
Eairy 84 E2
Eakley Lanes 53 D6
Eakring 77 C6
Ealand 89 C8
Ealing 40 F4
Eals 109 D6
Eamont Bridge 99 B7
Earby 94 E2
Earcroft 86 B4
Eardington 61 E7
Eardisland 49 D6
Eardisley 48 E5
Eardiston Shrops 60 B3
Worcs 49 C8
Earith 54 B4
Earle 117 B5
Earley 27 B5
Earlham 68 D5
Earlish 149 B8
Earls Barton 53 C6
Earls Colne 42 B4
Earl's Croome 50 E3
Earlsdon 51 B8
Earlsferry 129 E6
Earlsfield 78 F2
Earlsford 153 E8
Earl's Green 56 C4
Earlsheaton 88 B3
Earl Shilton 63 E8
Earlsmill 151 F12
Earl Soham 57 C6
Earl Sterndale 75 C7
Earlston Borders 121 F8
E Ayrs 118 F4
Earl Stonham 56 D5
Earlswood Mon 36 E1
Sur 28 E3
Warks 51 B6
Earnley 16 E2
Earsairidh 148 J2
Earsdon 111 B6
Earsham 69 F6
Earswick 96 D2
Eartham 16 D3
Easby N Yorks 101 D6
N Yorks 102 D3
Easdale 124 D3
Easebourne 16 B2
Easenhall 52 B2
Eashing 27 E7
Easington Bucks 39 C6
Durham 111 E7
E Yorks 91 C7
Northumb 123 F7
Oxon 39 E6
Oxon 52 F2
Redcar 103 C5
Easington Colliery 111 E7
Easington Lane 111 E6
Easingwold 95 C8
Easole Street 31 D6
Eassie 134 E3
East Aberthaw 22 C2
East Adderbury 52 F2
East Allington 7 E5
East Anstey 10 B3
East Appleton 101 E7
East Ardsley 88 B4
East Ashling 16 D2
East Auchronie 141 D7
East Ayton 103 F7
East Bank 35 D6
East Barkwith 91 F5
East Barming 29 D8
East Barnby 103 C6
East Barnet 41 E5
East Barns 122 B3
East Barsham 80 D5
East Beckham 81 D7
East Bedfont 27 B8
East Bergholt 56 F4
East Bilney 68 C2
East Blatchington 17 D8
East Boldre 14 D4
Eastbourne 18 F3
East Brent 22 D5
Eastbridge 57 C8
East Bridgford 77 E6
East Buckland 21 F5
East Budleigh 11 F5
Eastburn 94 E3
East Burrafirth 160 H5
East Burton 13 F6
Eastbury London 40 E3
W Berks 25 B8
East Butsfield 110 E4
East Butterwick 90 D2
Eastby 94 D3
East Cairnbeg 135 B7
East Calder 120 C3
East Carleton 68 D4
East Carlton N Nhants 64 F5
W Yorks 94 E5
East Chaldon 13 F5
East Challow 38 F3
East Chiltington 17 C7
East Chinnock 12 C2
East Chisenbury 25 D6
Eastchurch 30 B3
East Clandon 27 D8
East Claydon 39 B7
East Clyne 157 J12
East Coker 12 C3
Eastcombe 37 D5
East Combe 22 F3
East Common 96 F2
East Compton 23 E8
Eastcote London 40 F4
N Nhants 52 D4
W Mid 51 B6
Eastcott Corn 8 C4
Wilts 24 D5
East Cottingwith 96 E3
Eastcourt Wilts 25 C7
Wilts 37 E6
East Cowes 15 E6
East Cowick 89 B7
East Cowton 101 D8
East Cramlington 111 B5
East Cranmore 23 E8
East Creech 13 F7
East Croachy 138 B2
East Croftmore 139 C5
East Curthwaite 108 E3
East Dean E Sus 18 F2
Hants 14 B3
W Sus 16 C3
East Down 20 E5
East Drayton 77 B7
East Ella 90 B4
East End Dorset 13 E7
E Yorks 91 B6
Hants 14 E4
Hants 15 B7
Hants 26 C2
Herts 41 B7
Kent 18 B5
N Som 23 B6
Oxon 38 C3
Easter Ardross 151 D9
Easter Balmoral 139 E8
Easter Boleskine 137 B8
Easter Compton 36 F2
Easter Cringate 127 F6
Easter Davoch 140 D3
Easter Earshaig 114 D3
Easter Fearn 151 C9
Easter Galcantray 151 G11
Eastergate 16 D3
Easterhouse 119 C6
Easter Howgate 120 C5
Easter Howlaws 122 E3
Easter Kinkell 151 F8
Easter Lednathie 134 C3
Easter Milton 151 F12
Easter Moniack 151 G8
Eastern Green 63 F6
Easter Ord 141 D7
Easter Quarff 160 K6
Easter Rhynd 128 C3
Easter Row 127 E6
Easter Silverford 153 B7
Easter Skeld 160 J5
Easterton 24 D5
Eastertown 22 D5
Eastertown of Auchleuchries 153 E10
Easter Whyntie 152 B6
East Farleigh 29 D8
East Farndon 64 F4
East Ferry 90 E2
Eastfield N Lanark 119 C8
N Yorks 103 F8
Eastfield Hall 117 D8
East Fortune 121 B8
East Garston 25 B8
Eastgate Durham 110 F2
Norf 81 E7
East Ginge 38 F4
East Goscote 64 C3
East Grafton 25 C7
East Grimstead 14 B3
East Grinstead 28 F4
East Guldeford 19 C6
East Haddon 52 C4
East Hagbourne 39 F5
East Halton 90 C5
Eastham 85 F4
East Ham 41 F7
Eastham Ferry 85 F4
Easthampstead 27 C6
East Hanney 38 E4
East Hanningfield 42 D3
East Hardwick 89 C5
East Harling 68 F2
East Harlsey 102 E2
East Harnham 14 B2
East Harptree 23 D7
East Hartford 111 B5
East Harting 15 C8
East Hatley 54 D3
East Hauxwell 101 E6
East Haven 135 F5
Eastheath 27 C6
East Heckington 78 E4
East Hedleyhope 110 E4
East Hendred 38 F4
East Herrington 111 D6
East Heslerton 96 B5
East Hoathly 18 D2
Easthope 61 E5
Easthorpe Essex 43 B5
Leics 77 F8
Notts 77 D7
East Horrington 23 E7
East Horsley 27 D8
East Horton 123 F6
Easthouses 121 C6
East Huntspill 22 E5
East Hyde 40 C4
East Ilkerton 21 E6
East Ilsley 38 F4
Eastington Devon 10 D2
Glos 36 D4
Glos 37 C8
East Keal 79 C6
East Kennett 25 C6
East Keswick 95 E6
East Kilbride 119 D6
East Kirkby 79 C6
East Knapton 96 B4
East Knighton 13 F6
East Knoyle 24 F3
East Kyloe 123 F6
East Lambrook 12 C2
East Lamington 151 D10
East Langdon 31 E7
East Langton 64 E4
East Langwell 157 J10
East Lavant 16 D2
East Lavington 16 C3
East Layton 101 D6
Eastleach Martin 38 D2
Eastleach Turville 38 D1
East Leake 64 B2
East Learmouth 122 F4
Eastleigh Devon 9 B6
Hants 14 C5
East Leigh 9 D8
East Lexham 67 C8
East Lilburn 117 B6
Eastling 30 D3
East Linton 121 B8
East Liss 15 B8
East Looe 5 D7
East Lound 89 E8
East Lulworth 13 F6
East Lutton 96 C5
East Lydford 23 F7
East Mains 141 E5
East Malling 29 D8
East March 134 F4
East Marden 16 C2
East Markham 77 B7
East Marton 94 D2
East Meon 15 B7
East Mere 10 C4
East Mersea 43 C6
East Mey 158 C5
East Molesey 28 C2
Eastmoor Derbys 76 B3
Norf 67 D7
East Morden 13 E7
East Morton 94 E3
East Ness 96 B2
East Newton 97 F8
Eastney 15 E7
Eastnor 50 F2
East Norton 64 D4
East Nynehead 11 B6
East Oakley 26 D3
Eastoft 90 C2
East Ogwell 7 B6
Eastoke 15 E8
Easton Cambs 54 B2
Cumb 108 B4
Cumb 108 D2
Devon 10 F2
Dorset 12 G4
Hants 26 F3
Lincs 65 B6
Norf 68 C4
Som 23 E7
Suff 57 D6
Wilts 24 B3
Easton Grey 37 F5
Easton-in-Gordano 23 B7
Easton Maudit 53 D6
Easton on the Hill 65 D7
Easton Royal 25 C7
East Orchard 13 C6
East Ord 123 D5
East Panson 9 E5
Eastpark 107 C7
East Peckham 29 E7
East Pennard 23 F7
East Perry 54 C2
East Portlemouth 6 F5
East Prawle 7 F5
East Preston 16 D4
East Putford 9 C5
East Quantoxhead 22 E3
East Rainton 111 E6
East Ravendale 91 E6
East Raynham 80 E4
Eastrea 66 E2
East Rhidorroch Lodge 150 B5
Eastriggs 108 C2
East Rigton 95 E6
Eastrington 89 B8
East Rounton 102 D2
East Row 103 C6
East Rudham 80 E4
East Runton 81 C7
East Ruston 69 B6
Eastry 31 D7
East Saltoun 121 C7
East Sleekburn 117 F8
East Somerton 69 C7
East Stockwith 89 E8
East Stoke Dorset 13 F6
Notts 77 E7
East Stour 13 B6
East Stourmouth 31 C6
East Stowford 9 B8
East Stratton 26 F3
East Studdal 31 E7
East Suisnish 149 E10
East Taphouse 5 C6
East-the-Water 9 B6
East Thirston 117 E7
East Tilbury 29 B7
East Tisted 26 F5
East Torrington 90 F5
East Tuddenham 68 C3
East Tytherley 14 B3
East Tytherton 24 B4
East Village 10 D3
Eastville Bristol 23 B8
Lincs 79 D7
East Wall 60 E5
East Walton 67 C7
Eastwell 64 B4
East Wellow 14 B4
East Wemyss 128 E5
East Whitburn 120 C2
Eastwick Herts 41 C7
Shetland 160 F5
East Williamston 32 D1
East Winch 67 C6
East Winterslow 25 F7
East Wittering 15 E8
East Witton 101 F6
Eastwood Notts 76 E4
Southend 42 F4
W Yorks 87 B7
East Woodburn 116 F5
East Woodhay 26 C2
East Worldham 26 F5
East Worlington 10 C2
East Worthing 17 D5
Eathorpe 51 C8
Eaton Ches E 75 C5
Ches W 74 C2
Leics 64 B4
Norf 68 D5
Notts 77 B7
Oxon 38 D4
Shrops 60 F3
Shrops 60 F5
Eaton Bishop 49 F6
Eaton Bray 40 B2
Eaton Constantine 61 D5
Eaton Green 40 B2
Eaton Hastings 38 E2
Eaton on Tern 61 B6
Eaton Socon 54 D2
Eavestone 94 C5
Ebberston 103 F6
Ebbesbourne Wake 13 B7
Ebbw Vale = Glyn Ebwy 35 D5
Ebchester 110 D4
Ebford 10 F4
Ebley 37 D5
Ebnal 73 E8
Ebrington 51 F6
Ecchinswell 26 D2
Ecclaw 122 C3
Ecclefechan 107 B8
Eccles Borders 122 E3
Gtr Man 87 E5
Kent 29 C8
Ecclesall 88 F4
Ecclesfield 88 E4
Ecclesgreig 135 C7
Eccleshall 62 B2
Eccleshill 94 F4
Ecclesmachan 120 B3
Eccles on Sea 69 B7
Eccles Road 68 E3
Eccleston Ches W 73 C8
Lancs 86 C3
Mers 86 E2
Eccleston Park 86 E2
Eccup 95 E5
Echt 141 D6
Eckford 116 B3
Eckington Derbys 76 B4
Worcs 50 E4
Ecton 53 C6
Edale 88 F2
Edburton 17 C6
Edderside 107 E7
Edderton 151 C10
Eddistone 8 B4
Eddleston 120 E5
Edenbridge 28 E5
Edenfield 87 C5
Edenhall 109 F5
Edenham 65 B7
Eden Park 28 C4
Edensor 76 C2
Edentaggart 126 E2
Edenthorpe 89 D7
Edentown 108 D3
Ederline 124 E4
Edern 70 D3
Edgarley 23 F7
Edgbaston 62 F4
Edgcott Bucks 39 B6
Som 21 F7
Edge 60 D3
Edgebolton 61 B5
Edge End 36 C2
Edgefield 81 D6
Edgefield Street 81 D6
Edge Green 73 D8
Edge Hill 85 F4
Edgeside 87 B6
Edgeworth 37 D6
Edgmond 61 C7
Edgmond Marsh 61 B7
Edgton 60 F3
Edgware 40 E4
Edgworth 86 C5
Edinample 126 B4
Edinbane 149 C8
Edinburgh 121 B5
Edingale 63 C6
Edingight House 152 C5
Edingley 77 D6
Edingthorpe 69 A6
Edingthorpe Green 69 A6
Edington Som 23 F5
Wilts 24 D4
Edintore 152 D4
Edithmead 22 E5
Edith Weston 65 D6
Edlesborough 40 C2
Edlingham 117 D7
Edlington 78 B5
Edmondsham 13 C8
Edmondsley 110 E5
Edmondthorpe 65 C5
Edmonstone 159 F6
Edmonton 41 E6
Edmundbyers 110 D3
Ednam 122 F3
Ednaston 76 E2
Edradynate 133 D5
Edrom 122 D4
Edstaston 74 F2
Edstone 51 C6
Edvin Loach 49 D8
Edwalton 77 F5
Edwardstone 56 E3
Edwinsford 46 F5
Edwinstowe 77 C6
Edworth 54 E3
Edwyn Ralph 49 D8
Edzell 135 C5
E Eachwick 110 B4
Efail Isaf 34 F4
Efailnewydd 70 D4
Efailwen 32 B2
Efenechtyd 72 D5
Effingham 28 D2
Effirth 160 H5
Efford 10 D3
Egdon 50 D4
Egerton Gtr Man 86 C5
Kent 30 E3
Egerton Forstal 30 E2
Eggborough 89 B6
Eggbuckland 6 D3
Eggington 40 B2
Egginton 63 B6
Egglescliffe 102 C2
Eggleston 100 B4
Egham 27 B8
Egleton 65 D5
Eglingham 117 C7
Egloshayle 4 B5
Egloskerry 8 F4
Eglwysbach 83 D8
Eglwys-Brewis 22 C2
Eglwys Cross 73 E8
Eglwys Fach 58 E3
Eglwyswen 45 F3
Eglwyswrw 45 F3
Egmanton 77 C7
Egremont Cumb 98 C2
Mers 85 E4
Egton 103 D6
Egton Bridge 103 D6
Eight Ash Green 43 B5
Eignaig 130 E1
Eil 138 C4
Eilanreach 149 G13
Eileanach Lodge 151 E8
Eilean Darach 150 C4
Einacleite 154 E6
Eisgean 155 F8
Eisingrug 71 D7
Elan Village 47 C8
Elberton 36 F3
Elburton 6 D3
Elcho 128 B3
Elcombe 37 F8
Eldernell 66 E3
Eldersfield 50 F3
Elderslie 118 C4
Eldon 101 B7
Eldrick 112 F2
Eldroth 93 C7
Eldwick 94 E4
Elfhowe 99 E6
Elford Northumb 123 F7
Staffs 63 C5
Elgin 152 B2
Elgol 149 G10
Elham 31 E5
Elie 129 D6
Elim 82 C3
Eling 14 C4
Elishader 149 B10
Elishaw 116 E4
Elkesley 77 B6
Elkstone 37 C6
Ellan 138 B4
Elland 88 B2
Ellary 144 F6
Ellastone 75 E8
Ellemford 122 C3
Ellenbrook 84 E3
Ellenhall 62 B2
Ellen's Green 27 F8
Ellerbeck 102 E2
Ellerburn 103 F6
Ellerby 103 C5
Ellerdine Heath 61 B6
Ellerhayes 10 D4
Elleric 130 E4
Ellerker 90 B3
Ellerton E Yorks 96 F3
Shrops 61 B7
Ellesborough 39 D8
Ellesmere 73 F8
Ellesmere Port 73 B8
Ellingham Norf 69 E6
Northumb 117 B7
Ellingstring 101 F6
Ellington Cambs 54 B2
Northumb 117 E8
Elliot 135 F6
Ellisfield 26 E4
Ellistown 63 C8
Ellon 153 E9
Ellonby 108 F4
Ellough 69 F7
Elloughton 90 B3
Ellwood 36 D2
Elm 66 D4
Elmbridge 50 C4
Elmdon Essex 55 F5
W Mid 63 F5
Elmdon Heath 63 F5
Elmers End 28 C4
Elmesthorpe 63 E8
Elmfield 15 E7
Elm Hill 13 B6
Elmhurst 62 C5
Elmley Castle 50 E4
Elmley Lovett 50 C3
Elmore 36 C4
Elmore Back 36 C4
Elm Park 41 F8
Elmscott 8 B4
Elmsett 56 E4
Elmstead Market 43 B6
Elmsted 30 E5
Elmstone 31 C6
Elmstone Hardwicke 37 B6
Elmswell E Yorks 97 D5
Suff 56 C3
Elmton 76 B5
Elphin 156 H5
Elphinstone 121 B6
Elrick 141 D7
Elrig 105 E7
Elsdon 117 E5
Elsecar 88 E4
Elsenham 41 B8
Elsfield 39 C5
Elsham 90 C4
Elsing 68 C3
Elslack 94 E2
Elson 73 F7
Elsrickle 120 E3
Elstead 27 E7
Elsted 16 C2
Elsthorpe 65 B7
Elstob 101 B8
Elston Notts 77 E7
Wilts 25 E5
Elstone 9 C8
Elstow 53 E8
Elstree 40 E4
Elstronwick 97 F8
Elswick 92 F4
Elsworth 54 C4
Elterwater 99 D5
Eltham 28 B5
Eltisley 54 D3
Elton Cambs 65 E7
Ches W 73 B8
Derbys 76 C2
Glos 36 C4
Hereford 49 B6
Notts 77 F7
Stockton 102 C2
Elton Green 73 B8
Elvanfoot 114 C2
Elvaston 76 F4
Elveden 56 B2
Elvingston 121 B7
Elvington Kent 31 D6
York 96 E2
Elwick Hrtlpl 111 F7
Northumb 123 F7
Elworth 74 C4
Elworthy 22 F2
Ely Cambs 66 F5
Cardiff 22 B3
Emberton 53 E6
Embleton Cumb 107 F8
Northumb 117 B8
Embo 151 B11
Emborough 23 D8
Embo Street 151 B11
Embsay 94 D3
Emersons Green 23 B8
Emery Down 14 D3
Emley 88 C3
Emmbrook 27 C5
Emmer Green 26 B5
Emmington 39 D7
Emneth 66 D4
Emneth Hungate 66 D5
Empingham 65 D6
Empshott 27 F5
Emstrey 60 C5
Emsworth 15 D8
Enborne 26 C2
Enchmarsh 60 E5
Enderby 64 E2
Endmoor 99 F7
Endon 75 D6
Endon Bank 75 D6
Enfield 41 E6
Enfield Wash 41 E6
Enford 25 D6
Engamoor 160 H4
Engine Common 36 F3
Englefield 26 B4
Englefield Green 27 B7
Englesea-brook 74 D4
English Bicknor 36 C2
Englishcombe 24 C2
English Frankton 60 B4
Enham Alamein 25 E8
Enmore 22 F4
Ennerdale Bridge 98 C2
Enoch 113 D8
Enochdhu 133 C7
Ensay 146 G6
Ensbury 13 E8
Ensdon 60 C4
Ensis 9 B7
Enstone 38 B3
Enterkinfoot 113 D8
Enterpen 102 D2
Enville 62 F2
Eolaigearraidh 148 H2
Eorabus 146 J6
Eòropaidh 155 A10
Epperstone 77 E6
Epping 41 D7
Epping Green Essex 41 D7
Herts 41 D5
Epping Upland 41 D7
Eppleby 101 C6
Eppleworth 97 F6
Epsom 28 C3
Epwell 51 E8
Epworth 89 D8
Epworth Turbary 89 D8
Erbistock 73 E7
Erbusaig 149 F12
Erchless Castle 150 G7
Erdington 62 E5
Eredine 125 E5
Eriboll 156 D7
Ericstane 114 C3
Eridge Green 18 B2
Erines 145 F7
Eriswell 55 B8
Erith 29 B6
Erlestoke 24 D4
Ermine 78 B2
Ermington 6 D4
Erpingham 81 D7
Errogie 137 B8
Errol 128 B4
Erskine 118 B4
Erskine Bridge 118 B4
Ervie 104 C4
Erwarton 57 F6
Erwood 48 E2
Eryholme 101 D8
Eryrys 73 D6
Escomb 101 B6
Escrick 96 E2
Esgairdawe 46 E5
Esgairgeiliog 58 D4
Esh 110 E4
Esher 28 C2
Esholt 94 E4
Eshott 117 E8
Eshton 94 D2
Esh Winning 110 E4
Eskadale 150 H7
Eskbank 121 C6
Eskdale Green 98 D3
Eskdalemuir 115 E5
Eske 97 E6
Eskham 91 E7
Esk Valley 103 D6
Esprick 92 F4
Essendine 65 C7
Essendon 41 D5
Essich 151 H9
Essington 62 D3
Esslemont 141 B8
Eston 102 C3
Eswick 160 H6
Etal 122 F5
Etchilhampton 24 C5
Etchingham 18 C4
Etchinghill Kent 19 B8
Staffs 62 C4
Ethie Castle 135 E6
Ethie Mains 135 E6
Etling Green 68 C3
Eton 27 B7
Eton Wick 27 B7
Etteridge 138 E2
Ettersgill 100 B3
Ettingshall 62 E3
Ettington 51 E7
Etton E Yorks 97 E5
Pboro 65 D8
Ettrick 115 C5
Ettrickbridge 115 B6
Ettrickhill 115 C5
Etwall 76 F2
Euston 56 B2
Euximoor Drove 66 E4
Euxton 86 C3
Evanstown 34 F3
Evanton 151 E9
Evedon 78 E3
Evelix 151 B10
Evenjobb 48 C4
Evenley 52 F3
Evenlode 38 B2
Evenwood 101 B6
Evenwood Gate 101 B6
Everbay 159 F7
Evercreech 23 F8
Everdon 52 D3
Everingham 96 E4
Everleigh 25 D7
Everley 103 F7
Eversholt 53 F7
Evershot 12 D3
Eversley 27 C5
Eversley Cross 27 C5
Everthorpe 96 F5
Everton C Beds 54 D3
Hants 14 E3
Mers 85 E4
Notts 89 E7
Evertown 108 B3
Evesbatch 49 E8
Evesham 50 E5
Evington 64 D3
Ewden Village 88 E3
Ewell 28 C3
Ewell Minnis 31 E6
Ewelme 39 E6
Ewen 37 E7
Ewenny 21 B8
Ewerby 78 E4
Ewerby Thorpe 78 E4
Ewes 115 E6
Ewesley 117 E6
Ewhurst 27 E8
Ewhurst Green E Sus 18 C4
Sur 27 F8
Ewloe 73 C7
Ewloe Green 73 C6
Ewood 86 B4
Eworthy 9 F6
Ewshot 27 E6
Ewyas Harold 35 B7
Exbourne 9 D8
Exbury 14 E5
Exebridge 10 B4
Exelby 101 F7
Exeter 10 E4
Exford 21 F7
Exhall 51 D6
Exley Head 94 F3
Exminster 10 F4
Exmouth 10 F5
Exnaboe 160 M5
Exning 55 C7
Exton Devon 10 F4
Hants 15 B7

**Exton** continued
Rutland . . . . . . 65 C6
Som . . . . . . 21 F8
Exwick . . . . . . 10 E4
Eyam . . . . . . 76 B2
Eydon . . . . . . 52 D3
Eye Hereford . . . . . . 49 C6
Pboro . . . . . . 66 D2
Suff . . . . . . 56 B5
Eye Green . . . . . . 66 D2
Eyemouth . . . . . . 122 C5
Eyeworth . . . . . . 54 E3
Eyhorne Street . . . . . . 30 D2
Eyke . . . . . . 57 D7
Eynesbury . . . . . . 54 C2
Eynort . . . . . . 149 F8
Eynsford . . . . . . 29 C6
Eynsham . . . . . . 38 D4
Eype . . . . . . 12 E2
Eyre Highld . . . . . . 149 C9
Highld . . . . . . 149 E10
Eythorne . . . . . . 31 E6
Eyton Hereford . . . . . . 49 C6
Shrops . . . . . . 60 F3
Wrex . . . . . . 73 E7
Eyton upon the Weald
Moors . . . . . . 61 C6

**F**

Faceby . . . . . . 102 D2
Facit . . . . . . 87 C6
Faddiley . . . . . . 74 D2
Fadmoor . . . . . . 102 F4
Faerdre . . . . . . 33 D7
Failand . . . . . . 23 B7
Failford . . . . . . 112 B4
Failsworth . . . . . . 87 D6
Fain . . . . . . 150 D4
Fairbourne . . . . . . 58 C3
Fairburn . . . . . . 89 B5
Fairfield Derbys . . . . . . 75 B7
Stockton . . . . . . 102 C2
Worcs . . . . . . 50 B4
Worcs . . . . . . 50 E5
Fairford . . . . . . 38 D1
Fair Green . . . . . . 67 C6
Fairhaven . . . . . . 85 B4
Fair Hill . . . . . . 108 F5
Fairlie . . . . . . 118 D2
Fairlight . . . . . . 19 D5
Fairlight Cove . . . . . . 19 D5
Fairmile . . . . . . 11 E5
Fairmilehead . . . . . . 120 C5
Fairoak . . . . . . 74 F4
Fair Oak . . . . . . 15 C5
Fair Oak Green . . . . . . 26 C4
Fairseat . . . . . . 29 C7
Fairstead Essex . . . . . . 42 C3
Norf . . . . . . 67 C6
Fairwarp . . . . . . 17 B8
Fairy Cottage . . . . . . 84 D4
Fairy Cross . . . . . . 9 B6
Fakenham . . . . . . 80 E5
Fakenham Magna . 56 B3
Fala . . . . . . 121 C7
Fala Dam . . . . . . 121 C7
Falahill . . . . . . 121 D6
Falcon . . . . . . 49 F8
Faldingworth . . . . . . 90 F4
Falfield . . . . . . 36 E3
Falkenham . . . . . . 57 F6
Falkirk . . . . . . 119 B8
Falkland . . . . . . 128 D4
Falla . . . . . . 116 C3
Fallgate . . . . . . 76 C3
Fallowfield . . . . . . 87 E6
Fallsidehill . . . . . . 122 E2
Falmer . . . . . . 17 D7
Falmouth . . . . . . 3 C7
Falsgrave . . . . . . 103 F8
Falstone . . . . . . 116 F3
Fanagmore . . . . . . 156 E4
Fangdale Beck . 102 E3
Fangfoss . . . . . . 96 D3
Fankerton . . . . . . 127 F6
Fanmore . . . . . . 146 G7
Fannich Lodge . 150 E5
Fans . . . . . . 122 E2
Far Bank . . . . . . 89 C7
Far Bletchley . . . . . . 53 F6
Farcet . . . . . . 66 E2
Far Cotton . . . . . . 52 D5
Farden . . . . . . 49 B7
Fareham . . . . . . 15 D6
Farewell . . . . . . 62 C4
Far Forest . . . . . . 50 B2
Farforth . . . . . . 79 B6
Faringdon . . . . . . 38 E2
Farington . . . . . . 86 B3
Farlam . . . . . . 109 D5
Farlary . . . . . . 157 J10
Far Laund . . . . . . 76 E3
Farleigh N Som . 23 C6
Sur . . . . . . 28 C4
Farleigh
Hungerford . . 24 D3
Farleigh Wallop . 26 E4
Farlesthorpe . . . . . . 79 B7
Farleton Lancs . . 93 C5
W&F . . . . . . 99 F7
Farley Shrops . . 60 D3
Staffs . . . . . . 75 E7
Wilts . . . . . . 14 B3
Farley Green . . . . . . 27 E8
Farley Hill Luton . 40 B3
Wokingham . . 26 C5
Farleys End . . . . . . 36 C4
Farlington . . . . . . 96 C2
Farlow . . . . . . 61 F6
Farmborough . . 23 C8
Farmcote Glos . . 37 B7
Shrops . . . . . . 61 E7
Farmington . . . . . . 37 C8
Farmoor . . . . . . 38 D4
Farmtown . . . . . . 152 C5
Farnborough Hants 28 C5
London . . . . . . 28 C5
Warks . . . . . . 52 E2
W Berks . . . . . . 38 F4
Farnborough
Green . . . . . . 27 D6
Farncombe . . . . . . 27 E7
Farndish . . . . . . 53 C7
Farndon Ches W . 73 D8
Notts . . . . . . 77 D7
Farnell . . . . . . 135 D6

Farnham Dorset . . 13 C7
Essex . . . . . . 41 B7
N Yorks . . . . . . 95 C6
Suff . . . . . . 57 C7
Sur . . . . . . 27 E6
Farnham Common 40 F2
Farnham Green . 41 B7
Farnham Royal . 40 F2
Farnhill . . . . . . 94 E3
Farningham . . . . . . 29 C6
Farnley N Yorks . 94 E5
W Yorks . . . . . . 95 F5
Farnley Tyas . . 88 C2
Farnsfield . . . . . . 77 D6
Farnworth Gtr Man . 86 D5
Halton . . . . . . 86 F3
Farr Highld . . . . . . 138 D4
Highld . . . . . . 151 H9
Highld . . . . . . 157 C10
Farr House . . . . . . 151 H9
Farringdon . . . . . . 10 E5
Farrington Gurney . 23 D8
Far Sawrey . . . . . . 99 E5
Farsley . . . . . . 94 F5
Farthinghoe . . 52 F3
Farthingloe . . . . . . 31 E6
Farthingstone . . 52 D4
Fartown . . . . . . 88 C2
Farway . . . . . . 11 E6
Fasag . . . . . . 149 C13
Fascadale . . . . . . 147 D8
Faslane Port . . . . . . 145 E11
Fasnacloich . . . . . . 130 E4
Fasnakyle Ho . . 137 B6
Fassfern . . . . . . 130 B4
Fatfield . . . . . . 111 D6
Fattahead . . . . . . 153 C6
Faugh . . . . . . 108 D5
Fauldhouse . . . . . . 120 C2
Faulkbourne . . . . . . 42 C3
Faulkland . . . . . . 24 D2
Fauls . . . . . . 74 F2
Faversham . . . . . . 30 C4
Favillar . . . . . . 152 E2
Fawdington . . . . . . 95 B7
Fawfieldhead . . 75 C7
Fawkham Green . 29 C6
Fawler . . . . . . 38 C3
Fawley Bucks . . 39 F7
Hants . . . . . . 15 D5
W Berks . . . . . . 38 F3
Fawley Chapel . 36 B2
Fawley Waterside . 15 D5
Faxfleet . . . . . . 90 B2
Faygate . . . . . . 28 F3
Fazakerley . . . . . . 85 E4
Fazeley . . . . . . 63 D6
Fearby . . . . . . 101 F6
Fearn . . . . . . 151 D11
Fearnan . . . . . . 132 E4
Fearnbeg . . . . . . 149 C12
Fearnhead . . . . . . 86 E4
Fearn Lodge . . . . . . 151 C9
Fearnmore . . . . . . 149 B12
Fearn Station . . 151 D11
Featherstone Staffs 62 D3
W Yorks . . . . . . 88 B5
Featherwood . . 116 D4
Feckenham . . . . . . 50 C5
Feering . . . . . . 42 B4
Feetham . . . . . . 100 E4
Feizor . . . . . . 93 C7
Felbridge . . . . . . 28 F4
Felbrigg . . . . . . 81 D8
Felcourt . . . . . . 28 E4
Felden . . . . . . 40 D3
Felin-Crai . . . . . . 34 B2
Felindre Carms . . 33 B6
Carms . . . . . . 46 F2
Carms . . . . . . 47 F5
Ceredig . . . . . . 46 D4
Powys . . . . . . 59 F8
Swansea . . . . . . 33 D7
Felindre Farchog . 45 F3
Felinfach Ceredig . 46 D4
Powys . . . . . . 48 F2
Felinfoel . . . . . . 33 D6
Felingwmisaf . . 33 B6
Felingwmuchaf . 33 B6
Felinwynt . . . . . . 45 D4
Felixkirk . . . . . . 102 F2
Felixstowe . . . . . . 57 F6
Felixstowe Ferry . 57 F7
Felkington . . . . . . 122 E5
Felkirk . . . . . . 88 C4
Felling . . . . . . 111 C5
Fell Side . . . . . . 108 F3
Felmersham . . 53 D7
Felmingham . . 81 E8
Felpham . . . . . . 16 E3
Felsham . . . . . . 56 D3
Felsted . . . . . . 42 B2
Feltham . . . . . . 28 B2
Felthorpe . . . . . . 68 C4
Felton Hereford . 49 E7
Northumb . . . . . . 117 D7
N Som . . . . . . 23 C7
Felton Butler . . 60 C3
Feltwell . . . . . . 67 E7
Fenay Bridge . . 88 C2
Fence . . . . . . 93 F8
Fence Houses . . 111 D6
Fen Ditton . . . . . . 55 C5
Fen Drayton . . 54 C4
Fen End . . . . . . 51 B7
Fengate Norf . . 81 E7
Pboro . . . . . . 66 E2
Fenham . . . . . . 123 E6
Fenhouses . . . . . . 79 E5
Feniscliffe . . . . . . 86 B4
Feniscowles . . 86 B4
Feniton . . . . . . 11 E6
Fenlake . . . . . . 53 E8
Fenny Bentley . 75 D8
Fenny Bridges . 11 E6
Fenny Compton . 52 D2
Fenny Drayton . 63 E7
Fenny Stratford . 53 F6
Fenrother . . . . . . 117 E7
Fen Side . . . . . . 79 D6
Fenstanton . . . . . . 54 C4
Fenton Cambs . . 54 B4
Lincs . . . . . . 77 B8
Lincs . . . . . . 77 D8
Stoke . . . . . . 75 E5
Fenton Barns . . 129 F7
Fenton Town . . 123 F5
Fenwick E Ayrs . 118 E4

**Fenwick** continued
Northumb . . . . . . 110 B3
Northumb . . . . . . 123 E6
S Yorks . . . . . . 89 C6
Feochaig . . . . . . 143 G8
Feock . . . . . . 3 C7
Feolin Ferry . . . . . . 144 G3
Ferindonald . . . . . . 149 H11
Feriniquarrie . . 148 C6
Ferlochan . . . . . . 130 E3
Fern . . . . . . 134 C4
Ferndale . . . . . . 34 E4
Ferndown . . . . . . 13 D8
Ferness . . . . . . 151 G12
Ferney Green . . 99 E6
Fernham . . . . . . 38 E2
Fernhill Heath . . 50 D3
Fernhurst . . . . . . 16 B2
Fernie . . . . . . 128 C5
Ferniegair . . . . . . 119 D7
Fernilea . . . . . . 149 E8
Fernilee . . . . . . 75 B7
Ferrensby . . . . . . 95 C6
Ferring . . . . . . 16 D4
Ferrybridge . . . . . . 89 B5
Ferryden . . . . . . 135 D7
Ferryhill Aberdeen . 141 D8
Durham . . . . . . 111 F5
Ferry Hill . . . . . . 66 F3
Ferryhill Station . 111 F6
Ferry Point . . . . . . 151 C10
Ferryside . . . . . . 32 C4
Fersfield . . . . . . 68 F3
Fersit . . . . . . 131 B7
Ferwig . . . . . . 45 E3
Feshiebridge . . 138 D4
Fetcham . . . . . . 28 D2
Fetterangus . . . . . . 153 C9
Fettercairn . . . . . . 135 B6
Fettes . . . . . . 151 F8
Fewcott . . . . . . 39 B5
Fewston . . . . . . 94 D4
F Faccombe . . 25 D8
Ffairfach . . . . . . 33 B7
Ffald-y-Brenin . 47 C6
Ffaldybrenin . . 46 E5
Ffarmers . . . . . . 47 E5
Ffawyddog . . . . . . 35 C6
Fforest . . . . . . 33 D6
Fforest-fach . . 33 E7
Ffostrasol . . . . . . 46 E2
Ffos-y-ffin . . . . . . 46 C3
Ffridd-Uchaf . . 83 F5
Ffrith . . . . . . 73 D6
Ffrwd . . . . . . 82 F4
Ffynnon ddrain . 33 B5
Ffynnongroyw . 85 F2
Ffynnon-oer . . 46 D4
Fidden . . . . . . 146 J6
Fiddes . . . . . . 141 F7
Fiddington Glos . 50 F4
Som . . . . . . 22 E4
Fiddleford . . . . . . 13 C6
Fiddlers Hamlet . 41 D7
Field . . . . . . 75 F7
Field Broughton . 99 F5
Field Dalling . . 81 D6
Field Head . . . . . . 63 D8
Fifehead
Magdalen . . . . . . 13 B5
Fifehead Neville . 13 C5
Fifield Oxon . . 38 C2
Wilts . . . . . . 25 D6
Windsor . . . . . . 27 B7
Fifield Bavant . 13 B8
Figheldean . . . . . . 25 E6
Filands . . . . . . 37 F6
Filby . . . . . . 69 C7
Filey . . . . . . 97 A7
Filgrave . . . . . . 53 E6
Filkins . . . . . . 38 D2
Filleigh Devon . . 9 B8
Devon . . . . . . 10 C2
Fillingham . . . . . . 90 F3
Fillongley . . . . . . 63 F6
Filton . . . . . . 23 B8
Fimber . . . . . . 96 C4
Finavon . . . . . . 134 D4
Finchairn . . . . . . 124 E5
Fincham . . . . . . 67 D6
Finchampstead . 27 C5
Finchdean . . . . . . 15 C8
Finchingfield . . 55 F7
Finchley . . . . . . 41 E5
Findern . . . . . . 76 F3
Findhorn . . . . . . 151 E13
Findhorn Bridge . 138 B4
Findochty . . . . . . 152 B4
Findo Gask . . . . . . 128 B2
Findon Aberds . . 141 E8
W Sus . . . . . . 16 D5
Findon Mains . . 151 E9
Findrack House . 140 D5
Finedon . . . . . . 53 B7
Fingal Street . . 57 C6
Fingask . . . . . . 141 B6
Fingerpost . . . . . . 50 B2
Fingest . . . . . . 39 F7
Finghall . . . . . . 101 F6
Fingland Cumb . 108 D2
Dumfries . . . . . . 113 C7
Finglesham . . . . . . 31 D7
Fingringhoe . . 43 B6
Finlarig . . . . . . 132 F2
Finmere . . . . . . 52 F4
Finnart . . . . . . 132 D2
Finningham . . 56 C4
Finningley . . . . . . 89 E7
Finnygaud . . . . . . 152 C5
Finsbury . . . . . . 41 F6
Finstall . . . . . . 50 C4
Finsthwaite . . 99 F5
Finstock . . . . . . 38 C3
Finstown . . . . . . 159 G4
Fintry Aberds . . 153 C7
Dundee . . . . . . 134 F4
Stirling . . . . . . 126 F5
Finzean . . . . . . 140 E5
Fionnphort . . . . . . 146 J6
Fionnsbhagh . . 154 J5
Firbeck . . . . . . 89 F6
Firby N Yorks . . 96 C3
N Yorks . . . . . . 101 F7
Firgrove . . . . . . 87 C7
Firsby . . . . . . 79 C7
Firsdown . . . . . . 25 F7
First Coast . . . . . . 150 B2
Fir Tree . . . . . . 110 F4
Fishbourne IoW . 15 E6

**Fishbourne** continued
W Sus . . . . . . 16 D2
Fishburn . . . . . . 111 F6
Fishcross . . . . . . 127 E7
Fisherford . . . . . . 153 E6
Fisher Place . . 99 C5
Fisherstreet . . 27 F7
Fisher's Pond . . 15 B5
Fisherton Highld . 151 F10
S Ayrs . . . . . . 112 C2
Fishguard
= Abergwaun . . 44 B4
Fishlake . . . . . . 89 C7
Fishleigh Barton . 9 B7
Fishponds . . . . . . 23 B8
Fishpool . . . . . . 36 B3
Fishtoft . . . . . . 79 E6
Fishtoft Drove . 79 E6
Fishtown of Usan . 135 D7
Fishwick . . . . . . 122 D5
Fiskavaig . . . . . . 149 E8
Fiskerton Lincs . 78 B3
Notts . . . . . . 77 D7
Fitling . . . . . . 97 F8
Fittleton . . . . . . 25 E6
Fittleworth . . 16 C4
Fitton End . . . . . . 66 C4
Fitz . . . . . . 60 C4
Fitzhead . . . . . . 11 B6
Fitzwilliam . . 88 C5
Fiunary . . . . . . 147 G9
Five Acres . . . . . . 36 C2
Five Ashes . . . . . . 18 C2
Fivecrosses . . 74 B2
Fivehead . . . . . . 11 B8
Five Oak Green . 29 E7
Five Oaks Jersey . 17 I3
W Sus . . . . . . 16 B4
Five Roads . . 33 D5
Flack's Green . 42 C3
Flackwell Heath . 40 F1
Fladbury . . . . . . 50 E4
Fladdabister . . 160 K6
Flagg . . . . . . 75 C8
Flamborough . . 97 B8
Flamstead . . . . . . 40 C3
Flamstead End . 41 D6
Flansham . . . . . . 16 D3
Flanshaw . . . . . . 88 B4
Flasby . . . . . . 94 D2
Flash . . . . . . 75 C7
Flashader . . . . . . 149 C8
Flask Inn . . . . . . 103 D7
Flaunden . . . . . . 40 D3
Flawborough . . 77 E7
Flawith . . . . . . 95 C7
Flax Bourton . . 23 C7
Flaxby . . . . . . 95 D6
Flaxholme . . . . . . 76 E3
Flaxley . . . . . . 36 C3
Flaxpool . . . . . . 22 F3
Flaxton . . . . . . 96 C2
Fleckney . . . . . . 64 E3
Flecknoe . . . . . . 52 C3
Fledborough . . 77 B8
Fleet Hants . . 15 D8
Hants . . . . . . 27 D6
Lincs . . . . . . 66 B3
Fleetham . . . . . . 117 B7
Fleet Hargate . . 66 B3
Fleetlands . . . . . . 15 D6
Fleetville . . . . . . 40 D4
Fleetwood . . . . . . 92 E3
Flemingston . . 22 B2
Flemington . . . . . . 119 D6
Flempton . . . . . . 56 C2
Fleoideabhagh . 154 J5
Fletchertown . . 108 E2
Fletching . . . . . . 17 B8
Fleuchary . . . . . . 8 D4
Flexbury . . . . . . 27 E7
Flexford . . . . . . 18 B4
Flimby . . . . . . 107 F7
Flimwell . . . . . . 18 B4
Flint = Y Fflint . . 73 B6
Flintham . . . . . . 77 E7
Flint Mountain . 73 B6
Flinton . . . . . . 97 F8
Flintsham . . . . . . 48 D5
Flitcham . . . . . . 80 E3
Flitton . . . . . . 53 F8
Flitwick . . . . . . 53 F8
Flixborough . . 90 C2
Flixborough
Stather . . . . . . 90 C2
Flixton Gtr Man . 86 E5
N Yorks . . . . . . 97 B6
Suff . . . . . . 69 F6
Flockton . . . . . . 88 C3
Flodaigh . . . . . . 148 C3
Flodden . . . . . . 122 F5
Flodigarry . . . . . . 149 A9
Flood's Ferry . . 66 E3
Flookburgh . . 92 B3
Florden . . . . . . 68 E4
Flore . . . . . . 52 C4
Flotterton . . . . . . 117 D5
Flowton . . . . . . 56 E4
Flush House . . 88 D2
Flushing Aberds . 153 D10
Corn . . . . . . 3 C7
Flyford Flavell . 50 D4
Foals Green . . 57 B6
Fobbing . . . . . . 42 F3
Fochabers . . . . . . 152 C3
Fochriw . . . . . . 35 D5
Fockerby . . . . . . 90 C2
Fodderletter . . 139 B7
Fodderty . . . . . . 151 F8
Foel . . . . . . 59 C6
Foel-gastell . . 33 C6
Foffarty . . . . . . 134 E4
Foggathorpe . . 96 F3
Fogo . . . . . . 122 E3
Fogorig . . . . . . 122 E3
Foindle . . . . . . 156 E4
Folda . . . . . . 134 C1
Fole . . . . . . 75 F7
Foleshill . . . . . . 63 F7
Folke . . . . . . 12 C4
Folkestone . . 31 F6
Folkingham . . 78 F3
Folkington . . . . . . 18 E2
Folksworth . . 65 F8
Folkton . . . . . . 97 B6
Folla Rule . . . . . . 153 E7
Follifoot . . . . . . 95 D6
Folly Gate . . . . . . 9 E7
Fonthill Bishop . 24 F4
Fonthill Gifford . 24 F4

Fontmell Magna . 13 C6
Fontwell . . . . . . 16 D3
Foolow . . . . . . 75 B8
Foots Cray . . . . . . 29 B5
Forbestown . . 140 C2
Force Mills . . . . . . 99 E5
Forcett . . . . . . 101 C6
Ford Argyll . . . . . . 124 E4
Bucks . . . . . . 39 D7
Devon . . . . . . 9 B6
Glos . . . . . . 37 B7
Northumb . . . . . . 122 F5
Shrops . . . . . . 60 C4
Staffs . . . . . . 75 D7
Wilts . . . . . . 24 B3
W Sus . . . . . . 16 D3
Fordcombe . . 29 E6
Fordell . . . . . . 128 F3
Forden . . . . . . 60 D2
Ford End . . . . . . 42 C2
Forder Green . . 7 C5
Fordham Cambs . 55 B7
Essex . . . . . . 43 B5
Norf . . . . . . 67 E6
Fordhouses . . 62 D3
Fordingbridge . 14 C2
Fordon . . . . . . 97 B6
Fordoun . . . . . . 135 B7
Ford's Green . . 56 C4
Fordstreet . . . . . . 43 B5
Ford Street . . . . . . 11 C6
Fordwells . . . . . . 38 C3
Fordwich . . . . . . 31 D5
Fordyce . . . . . . 152 B5
Forebridge . . . . . . 62 B3
Forest . . . . . . 109 F8
Forest Becks . . 93 D7
Forestburn Gate . 117 E6
Foresterseat . . 152 C1
Forest Gate . . 41 F7
Forest Green . . 28 E2
Forest Hall . . . . . . 99 D7
Forest Head . . 109 D5
Forest Hill . . . . . . 39 D5
Forest Lane Head . 95 D6
Forest Lodge
Argyll . . . . . . 131 E6
Highld . . . . . . 139 C6
Perth . . . . . . 133 B6
Forest Mill . . . . . . 127 E8
Forest Row . . 28 F5
Forestside . . . . . . 15 C8
Forest Town . . 77 C5
Forfar . . . . . . 134 D4
Forgandenny . . 128 C2
Forge . . . . . . 58 E4
Forge Side . . . . . . 35 D6
Forgewood . . 119 D7
Forgie . . . . . . 152 C3
Forglen House . 153 C6
Formby . . . . . . 85 D4
Forncett End . . 68 E4
Forncett St Mary . 68 E4
Forncett St Peter . 68 E4
Forneth . . . . . . 133 E7
Fornham All
Saints . . . . . . 56 C2
Fornham St
Martin . . . . . . 56 C2
Forres . . . . . . 151 F13
Forrestfield . . 119 C8
Forrest Lodge . 113 F5
Forsbrook . . . . . . 75 E6
Forse . . . . . . 158 G4
Forse House . . 158 G4
Forsinain . . . . . . 157 E12
Forsinard . . . . . . 157 E11
Forsinard
Station . . . . . . 157 E11
Forston . . . . . . 12 E4
Fort Augustus . 137 D6
Forteviot . . . . . . 128 C2
Fort George Guern . 16 I2
Highld . . . . . . 151 F10
Forth . . . . . . 120 D2
Forthampton . . 50 F3
Forth Road
Bridge . . . . . . 120 B4
Fortingall . . . . . . 132 E4
Forton Hants . . 26 E2
Lancs . . . . . . 92 D4
Shrops . . . . . . 60 C4
Som . . . . . . 11 D8
Staffs . . . . . . 61 B7
Forton Heath . . 60 C4
Fortrie . . . . . . 153 D6
Fortrose . . . . . . 151 F10
Fortuneswell . . 12 G4
Fort William . . 131 B5
Forty Green . . 40 E2
Forty Hill . . . . . . 41 E6
Forward Green . 56 D4
Fosbury . . . . . . 25 D8
Fosdyke . . . . . . 79 F6
Foss . . . . . . 132 D4
Foss Cross . . . . . . 37 D7
Fossebridge . . 37 C7
Fosterhouses . . 89 C7
Foster Street . . 41 D7
Foston Derbys . . 75 F8
Lincs . . . . . . 77 E8
N Yorks . . . . . . 96 C2
Foston on the
Wolds . . . . . . 97 D7
Fotherby . . . . . . 91 E7
Fotheringhay . . 65 E7
Foubister . . . . . . 159 H6
Foulby . . . . . . 88 C4
Foulden Borders . 122 D5
Norf . . . . . . 67 E7
Foulis Castle . . 151 E8
Foul Mile . . . . . . 18 D3
Foulridge . . . . . . 93 E8
Foulsham . . . . . . 81 E6
Fountainhall . . 121 E7
Four Ashes Staffs . 62 F2
Suff . . . . . . 56 B4
Four Crosses
Powys . . . . . . 59 D7
Powys . . . . . . 60 C2
Wrex . . . . . . 73 D6
Four Elms . . . . . . 29 E5
Four Forks . . . . . . 22 F4
Four Gotes . . . . . . 66 C4
Four Lane Ends . 74 C2
Four Lanes . . 3 C5
Fourlanes End . 74 D5

Four Mile Bridge . 82 D2
Four Oaks E Sus . 19 C5
W Mid . . . . . . 62 E5
W Mid . . . . . . 63 F6
Fourpenny . . . . . . 151 B11
Four Roads Carms . 33 D5
IoM . . . . . . 84 F2
Fourstones . . 109 C8
Four Throws . . 18 C4
Fovant . . . . . . 13 B8
Foveran . . . . . . 141 B8
Fowey . . . . . . 5 D6
Fowley Common . 86 E4
Fowlis . . . . . . 134 F3
Fowlis Wester . 127 B8
Fowlmere . . . . . . 54 E5
Fownhope . . . . . . 49 F7
Foxbar . . . . . . 118 C4
Foxcombe Hill . 38 D4
Fox Corner . . . . . . 27 D7
Foxdale . . . . . . 84 E2
Foxearth . . . . . . 56 E2
Foxfield . . . . . . 98 F4
Foxham . . . . . . 24 B4
Foxhole Corn . . 4 D4
Swansea . . . . . . 33 E7
Foxholes . . . . . . 97 B6
Foxhunt Green . 18 D2
Fox Lane . . . . . . 27 D6
Foxley Norf . . 81 E6
Wilts . . . . . . 37 F5
Fox Street . . . . . . 43 B6
Foxt . . . . . . 75 E7
Foxton Cambs . 54 E5
Durham . . . . . . 102 B1
Leics . . . . . . 64 E4
Foxup . . . . . . 93 B8
Foxwist Green . 74 C3
Foxwood . . . . . . 49 B8
Foy . . . . . . 36 B2
Foyers . . . . . . 137 B7
Fraddam . . . . . . 2 C4
Fraddon . . . . . . 4 D4
Fradley . . . . . . 63 C5
Fradswell . . . . . . 75 F6
Fraisthorpe . . . . . . 97 C7
Framfield . . . . . . 17 B8
Framingham Earl . 69 D5
Framingham Pigot 69 D5
Framlingham . . 57 C6
Frampton Dorset . 12 E4
Lincs . . . . . . 79 F6
Frampton
Cotterell . . . . . . 36 F3
Frampton Mansell . 37 D6
Frampton on
Severn . . . . . . 36 D4
Frampton West
End . . . . . . 79 E6
Framsden . . . . . . 57 D5
Framwellgate
Moor . . . . . . 111 E5
Franche . . . . . . 50 B3
Frankby . . . . . . 85 F3
Frankley . . . . . . 62 F3
Frank's Bridge . 48 D3
Frankton . . . . . . 52 B2
Frant . . . . . . 18 B2
Fraserburgh . . 153 B9
Frating Green . 43 B6
Fratton . . . . . . 15 E7
Freathy . . . . . . 5 D8
Freckenham . . 55 B7
Freckleton . . . . . . 86 B2
Freeby . . . . . . 64 B5
Freehay . . . . . . 75 E7
Freeland . . . . . . 38 C4
Freester . . . . . . 160 H6
Freethorpe . . . . . . 69 D7
Freiston . . . . . . 79 E6
Fremington Devon . 20 F4
N Yorks . . . . . . 101 E5
Frenchay . . . . . . 23 B8
Frenchbeer . . . . . . 9 F8
French . . . . . . 126 D3
Frensham . . . . . . 27 E6
Fresgoe . . . . . . 157 C12
Freshfield . . . . . . 85 D3
Freshford . . . . . . 24 C2
Freshwater . . 14 F4
Freshwater Bay . 14 F4
Freshwater East . 32 E1
Fressingfield . . 57 B6
Freston . . . . . . 57 F5
Freswick . . . . . . 158 D5
Fretherne . . . . . . 36 D4
Frettenham . . 68 C5
Freuchie . . . . . . 128 D4
Freuchies . . . . . . 134 C2
Freystrop . . . . . . 44 D4
Friar's Gate . . 29 F5
Friarton . . . . . . 128 B3
Friday Bridge . 66 D4
Friday Street . . 18 E3
Fridaythorpe . . 96 D4
Friern Barnet . . 41 E5
Friesland . . . . . . 146 F4
Friesthorpe . . 90 F4
Frieston . . . . . . 78 E2
Frieth . . . . . . 39 E7
Frilford . . . . . . 38 E4
Frilsham . . . . . . 26 B3
Frimley . . . . . . 27 D6
Frimley Green . 27 D6
Frindsbury . . . . . . 29 B8
Fring . . . . . . 80 D3
Fringford . . . . . . 39 B6
Frinsted . . . . . . 30 D2
Frinton-on-Sea . 43 B8
Friockheim . . 135 E5
Friog . . . . . . 58 C3
Frisby on the
Wreake . . . . . . 64 C3
Friskney . . . . . . 79 D7
Friskney Eaudike . 79 D7
Friskney Tofts . 79 D7
Friston E Sus . . 18 F2
Suff . . . . . . 57 C8
Fritchley . . . . . . 76 D3
Frith Bank . . . . . . 79 E6
Frith Common . 49 C8
Frithelstock . . 9 C6
Frithelstock Stone . 9 C6
Frithville . . . . . . 79 D6
Frittenden . . . . . . 30 E2
Frittiscombe . . 7 E6
Fritton Norf . . 68 E5
Norf . . . . . . 69 D7

Fritwell . . . . . . 39 B5
Frizinghall . . . . . . 94 F4
Frizington . . . . . . 98 C2
Frocester . . . . . . 36 D4
Frodesley . . . . . . 60 D5
Frodingham . . 90 C2
Frodsham . . . . . . 74 B2
Frogden . . . . . . 116 B3
Froggatt . . . . . . 76 B2
Froghall . . . . . . 75 E7
Frogmore Devon . 7 E5
Hants . . . . . . 27 D6
Frognall . . . . . . 65 C8
Frogshall . . . . . . 81 D8
Frogwell . . . . . . 5 C8
Frolesworth . . . . . . 64 E2
Frome . . . . . . 24 E2
Frome St Quintin . 12 D3
Fromes Hill . . . . . . 49 E8
Fron Denb . . . . . . 72 C4
Gwyn . . . . . . 70 D3
Gwyn . . . . . . 82 F5
Powys . . . . . . 59 E8
Powys . . . . . . 60 D2
Froncysyllte . . . . . . 73 E3
Frongoch . . . . . . 72 F3
Frostenden . . . . . . 69 F7
Frosterley . . . . . . 110 F3
Frotoft . . . . . . 159 F5
Froxfield . . . . . . 25 C7
Froxfield Green . 15 B8
Froyle . . . . . . 27 E5
Fryerning . . . . . . 42 D2
Fryton . . . . . . 96 B2
Fulbeck . . . . . . 78 D2
Fulbourn . . . . . . 55 D6
Fulbrook . . . . . . 38 C2
Fulford Som . . 11 B7
Staffs . . . . . . 75 F6
York . . . . . . 96 E2
Fulham . . . . . . 28 B3
Fulking . . . . . . 17 C6
Fullarton Glasgow . 119 C6
N Ayrs . . . . . . 118 F3
Fuller's Moor . . 73 D8
Fuller Street . . 42 C3
Fullerton . . . . . . 25 F8
Fulletby . . . . . . 79 B5
Full Sutton . . . . . . 96 D3
Fullwood . . . . . . 118 D4
Fulmer . . . . . . 40 F2
Fulmodestone . . 81 D5
Fulnetby . . . . . . 78 B3
Fulstow . . . . . . 91 E7
Fulwell . . . . . . 111 D6
Fulwood Lancs . 92 F5
S Yorks . . . . . . 88 F4
Fundenhall . . . . . . 68 E4
Fundenhall Street . 68 E4
Funtington . . . . . . 15 D8
Funtley . . . . . . 15 D6
Funtullich . . . . . . 127 B6
Funzie . . . . . . 160 D8
Furley . . . . . . 11 D7
Furnace Argyll . 125 E6
Carms . . . . . . 33 D6
Furnace End . . 63 E6
Furneaux Pelham . 41 B7
Furness Vale . . 87 F8
Furzehill . . . . . . 21 E6
Furze Platt . . . . . . 40 F1
Fyfett . . . . . . 11 C7
Fyfield Essex . . 42 D1
Glos . . . . . . 38 D2
Hants . . . . . . 25 E7
Oxon . . . . . . 38 E4
Wilts . . . . . . 25 C6
Fylingthorpe . . 103 D7
Fyvie . . . . . . 153 E7

**G**

Gabhsann bho
Dheas . . . . . . 155 B9
Gabhsann bho
Thuath . . . . . . 155 B9
Gablon . . . . . . 151 B10
Gabroc Hill . . . . . . 118 D4
Gaddesby . . . . . . 64 C3
Gadebridge . . . . . . 40 D3
Gaer . . . . . . 35 B5
Gaerllwyd . . . . . . 35 E8
Gaerwen . . . . . . 82 D4
Gagingwell . . . . . . 38 B4
Gaick Lodge . . . . . . 138 F3
Gailey . . . . . . 62 C3
Gainford . . . . . . 101 C6
Gainsborough Lincs 90 E2
Som . . . . . . 11 B7
Gainsford End . 55 F8
Gairloch . . . . . . 149 A13
Gairlochy . . . . . . 136 F4
Gairney Bank . 128 E3
Gairnshiel Lodge . 139 D8
Gaisgill . . . . . . 99 D8
Gaitsgill . . . . . . 108 E3
Galashiels . . . . . . 121 F7
Galgate . . . . . . 92 D4
Galhampton . . 12 B4
Gallaberry . . . . . . 114 F2
Gallachoille . . 144 E6
Gallanach Argyll . 124 C4
Argyll . . . . . . 146 E5
Gallantry Bank . 74 D2
Gallatown . . . . . . 128 E4
Galley Common . 63 E7
Galleyend . . . . . . 42 D3
Galley Hill . . . . . . 54 C4
Galleywood . . 42 D3
Gallin . . . . . . 132 E2
Gallowfauld . . 134 E4
Gallows Green . 75 E7
Galltair . . . . . . 149 F13
Galmisdale . . . . . . 146 C7
Galmpton Devon . 6 E4
Torbay . . . . . . 7 D6
Galphay . . . . . . 95 B5
Galston . . . . . . 118 F5
Galtrigill . . . . . . 148 C6
Gamblesby . . . . . . 109 F6
Gamesley . . . . . . 87 E8
Gamlingay . . . . . . 54 D3
Gammersgill . . 101 F5
Gamston . . . . . . 77 B7
Ganarew . . . . . . 36 C2
Ganavan . . . . . . 124 B4
Gang . . . . . . 5 C8
Ganllwyd . . . . . . 71 E8

Gayles . . . . . . 101 D6
Gay Street . . . . . . 16 B4
Gayton Mers . . 85 F3
Norf . . . . . . 67 C7
Staffs . . . . . . 62 B3
W Nhants . . . . . . 52 D5
Gayton le Marsh . 91 F8
Gayton le Wold . 91 F6
Gayton Thorpe . 67 C7
Gaywood . . . . . . 67 B6
Gazeley . . . . . . 55 C8
Gearraidh
Bhailteas . . . . 148 F2
Gearraidh Bhaird . 155 E8
Gearraidh na h-
Aibhne . . . . . 154 D7
Gearraidh na
Monadh . . . . 148 G2
Geary . . . . . . 148 B7
Geddes House . 151 F11
Gedding . . . . . . 56 D3
Geddington . . . . . . 65 F5
Gedintailor . . . . . . 149 E10
Gedling . . . . . . 77 E6
Gedney . . . . . . 66 B4
Gedney Broadgate . 66 B4
Gedney Drove End . 66 B4
Gedney Dyke . 66 B4
Gedney Hill . . . . . . 66 C3
Gee Cross . . . . . . 87 E7
Geilston . . . . . . 118 B3
Geirinis . . . . . . 148 D2
Geise . . . . . . 158 D3
Geisiadar . . . . . . 154 D6
Geldeston . . . . . . 69 E6
Gell . . . . . . 83 E8
Gelli Pembs . . 32 C1
Rhondda . . . . . . 34 E3
Gellideg . . . . . . 34 D4
Gellifor . . . . . . 72 C5
Gelligaer . . . . . . 35 E5
Gellilydan . . . . . . 71 D7
Gellinudd . . . . . . 33 D8
Gellyburn . . . . . . 133 F7
Gellywen . . . . . . 32 B3
Gelston Dumfries . 106 D4
Lincs . . . . . . 78 E2
Gembling . . . . . . 97 D7
Gentleshaw . . . . . . 62 C4
Geocrab . . . . . . 154 H6
Georgefield . . . . . . 115 E5
George Green . 40 F3
Georgeham . . . . . . 20 F3
George Nympton . 10 B2
Georgetown . . . . . . 35 D5
Gerlan . . . . . . 83 E6
Germansweek . . 9 E6
Germoe . . . . . . 2 D4
Gerrans . . . . . . 3 C7
Gerrards Cross . 40 F3
Gestingthorpe . 56 F2
Geuffordd . . . . . . 60 C2
Gibbet Hill . . . . . . 64 F2
Gibbshill . . . . . . 106 B4
Gib Hill . . . . . . 74 B3
Gidea Park . . . . . . 41 F8
Gidleigh . . . . . . 9 F8
Giffnock . . . . . . 119 D5
Gifford . . . . . . 121 C8
Giffordland . . . . . . 118 E2
Giffordtown . . . . . . 128 C4
Giggleswick . . . . . . 93 C8
Gilberdyke . . . . . . 90 B2
Gilchriston . . . . . . 121 C7
Gilcrux . . . . . . 107 F8
Gildersome . . . . . . 88 B3
Gildingwells . . 89 F6
Gileston . . . . . . 22 C2
Gilfach . . . . . . 35 E5
Gilfach Goch . . 34 F3
Gilfachrheda . . 46 D3
Gillamoor . . . . . . 102 F4
Gillar's Green . . 86 E2
Gillen . . . . . . 148 C7
Gilling East . . . . . . 96 B2
Gillingham Dorset . 13 B6
Medway . . . . . . 29 C8
Norf . . . . . . 69 E7
Gilling West . . . . . . 101 D6
Gillock . . . . . . 158 E4
Gillow Heath . . 75 D5
Gills . . . . . . 158 C5
Gill's Green . . 18 B4
Gilmanscleuch . 115 B6
Gilmerton Edin . 121 C5
Perth . . . . . . 127 B7
Gilmonby . . . . . . 100 C4
Gilmorton . . . . . . 64 F2
Gilmourton . . . . . . 119 E6
Gilsland . . . . . . 109 C6
Gilsland Spa . . 109 C6
Gilston Borders . 121 D7
Herts . . . . . . 41 C7
Gilwern . . . . . . 35 C6
Gimingham . . . . . . 81 D8
Giosla . . . . . . 154 F6
Gipping . . . . . . 56 C4
Gipsey Bridge . 79 E5
Girdle Toll . . . . . . 118 E3
Girlsta . . . . . . 160 H6
Girsby . . . . . . 102 D1
Girtford . . . . . . 54 D2
Girthon . . . . . . 106 D3
Girton Cambs . . 54 C5
Notts . . . . . . 77 C8
Girvan . . . . . . 112 E1
Gisburn . . . . . . 93 E8
Gisleham . . . . . . 69 F8
Gislingham . . . . . . 56 B4
Gissing . . . . . . 68 F4
Gittisham . . . . . . 11 E6
Gladestry . . . . . . 48 D4
Gladsmuir . . . . . . 121 B7
Glais . . . . . . 33 D8
Glaisdale . . . . . . 103 D5
Glame . . . . . . 149 D10
Glamis . . . . . . 134 E3
Glan Adda . . . . . . 83 D5
Glanaman . . . . . . 33 C7
Glan Conwy Conwy . 83 F8
Conwy . . . . . . 83 D8
Glandford . . . . . . 81 C6
Glan-Duar . . . . . . 46 E4
Glandwr . . . . . . 32 B2
Glan-Dwyfach . 71 C5

Glandy Cross . . . . . 32 B2
Glandyfi . . . . . . . . 58 E3
Glan Gors . . . . . . . 82 D4
Glangrwyney . . . . . 35 C6
Glanmule . . . . . . . 59 E8
Glanrafon . . . . . . . 58 F3
Glanrhyd Gwyn. . . . 70 D3
Pembs . . . . . . . . 45 E3
Glan-rhyd . . . . . . . 82 F4
Glanton . . . . . . . . 117 C6
Glanton Pike . . . . 117 C6
Glan-traeth . . . . . . 82 D2
Glanvilles
Wootton . . . . . . 12 D4
Glan-y-don . . . . . . 73 B5
Glan-y-nant . . . . . 59 F6
Glan-yr-afon
Anglesey . . . . . . 83 C6
Gwyn . . . . . . . . 72 E3
Gwyn . . . . . . . . 72 E4
Glan-y-wern . . . . . 71 D7
Glapthorn . . . . . . . 65 E7
Glapwell . . . . . . . 76 C4
Glas-allt Shiel . . . 139 F8
Glasbury . . . . . . . 48 F3
Glaschoil . . . . . . 151 H13
Glascoed Denb. . . . 72 B3
Mon . . . . . . . . . 35 D7
Powys . . . . . . . 59 C8
Glascorrie . . . . . . 140 E2
Glascote . . . . . . . 63 D6
Glascwm . . . . . . . 48 D3
Glasdrum . . . . . . 130 E4
Glasfryn . . . . . . . 72 D3
Glasgow . . . . . . . 119 C5
Glashvin . . . . . . . 149 B9
Glasinfryn . . . . . . 83 E5
Glasnacardoch . . . 147 B9
Glasnakille . . . . . 149 G10
Glasphein . . . . . . 148 D6
Glaspwll . . . . . . . 58 E4
Glassburn . . . . . . 150 H6
Glasserton . . . . . . 105 F8
Glassford . . . . . . . 119 E7
Glasshouse Hill . . . 36 B4
Glasshouses . . . . . 94 C4
Glasslie . . . . . . . 128 D4
Glasson Cumb . . . . 108 C2
Lancs . . . . . . . . 92 D4
Glassonby . . . . . . 109 F5
Glasterlaw . . . . . 135 D5
Glaston . . . . . . . . 65 D5
Glastonbury . . . . . 23 F7
Glatton . . . . . . . . 65 F8
Glazebury . . . . . . 86 E4
Glazeley . . . . . . . 61 F7
Gleadless . . . . . . . 88 F4
Gleadsmoss . . . . . 74 C5
Gleann
Tholàstaidh . . . 155 C10
Gleaston . . . . . . . 92 B2
Gleiniant . . . . . . . 59 E6
Glemsford . . . . . . 56 E2
Glen Dumfries . . . 106 B5
Dumfries . . . . . 106 D2
Glenamachrie . . . 124 C5
Glen Auldyn . . . . . 84 C4
Glenbarr . . . . . . . 143 E7
Glenbeg Highld . . . 139 B6
Highld . . . . . . . 147 E8
Glen Bernisdale . . 149 D8
Glenbervie . . . . . . 141 F6
Glenboig . . . . . . . 119 C7
Glenborrodale . . . 147 E9
Glenbranter . . . . . 125 F7
Glenbreck . . . . . . 114 B3
Glenbrein Lodge . . 137 C7
Glenbrittle House . 149 F9
Glenbuchat
Lodge . . . . . . . 140 C2
Glenbuck . . . . . . . 113 B7
Glenburn . . . . . . . 118 C4
Glencalvie Lodge . 150 C7
Glencanisp
Lodge . . . . . . . 156 G4
Glencaple . . . . . . 107 C6
Glencarron
Lodge . . . . . . . 150 F3
Glencarse . . . . . . 128 B3
Glencassley
Castle . . . . . . . 156 J7
Glenceitlein . . . . . 131 E5
Glencoe . . . . . . . 130 D4
Glencraig . . . . . . 128 E3
Glencripesdale . . . 147 F9
Glencrosh . . . . . . 113 F7
Glendavan House . 140 D3
Glendevon . . . . . . 127 D8
Glendoebeg . . . . . 137 D7
Glendoe Lodge . . . 137 D7
Glendoick . . . . . . 128 B4
Glendoll Lodge . . . 134 B2
Glendoune . . . . . . 112 E1
Glenduckie . . . . . . 128 C4
Glendye Lodge . . . 140 F5
Gleneagles Hotel . 127 C8
Gleneagles
House . . . . . . . 127 D8
Glenegedale . . . . 142 C4
Glenelg . . . . . . . 149 G13
Glenernie . . . . . . 151 G13
Glenfarg . . . . . . . 128 C3
Glenfarquhar
Lodge . . . . . . . 141 F6
Glenferness
House . . . . . . . 151 G12
Glenfeshie Lodge 138 E4
Glenfield . . . . . . . 64 D2
Glenfinnan . . . . . 147 C11
Glenfoot . . . . . . . 128 C3
Glenfyne Lodge . . 125 D8
Glengap . . . . . . . 106 D3
Glengarnock . . . . . 118 D3
Glengorm Castle . 146 F7
Glengrasco . . . . . 149 D9
Glenhead Farm . . 134 C2
Glen Ho . . . . . . . 121 F5
Glenhoul . . . . . . . 113 F6
Glenhurich . . . . . 130 C2
Glenkerry . . . . . . 115 C5
Glenkiln . . . . . . . 106 B5
Glenkindie . . . . . . 140 C3
Glenlatterach . . . 152 C1
Glenlee . . . . . . . . 113 F6
Glenlichorn . . . . . 127 C6

Glenlivet . . . . . . . 139 B7
Glenlochsie . . . . . 133 B7
Glenloig . . . . . . . 143 E10
Glenluce . . . . . . . 105 D6
Glenmallan . . . . . 125 F8
Glenmarksie . . . . 150 F6
Glenmassan . . . . 145 E10
Glenmavis . . . . . . 119 C7
Glenmidge . . . . . . 113 F8
Glen Mona . . . . . . 84 D4
Glenmore Argyll . . 124 D4
Highld . . . . . . . 149 D9
Glenmore Lodge . 139 D5
Glenmoy . . . . . . . 134 C4
Glen Nevis House . 131 B5
Glenogil . . . . . . . 134 C4
Glenprosen
Village . . . . . . 134 C2
Glenprosen
Village . . . . . . 134 C3
Glenquiech . . . . . 134 C4
Glenreasdell
Mains . . . . . . . 145 H7
Glenree . . . . . . . 143 F10
Glenridding . . . . . 99 C5
Glenrossal . . . . . . 156 J7
Glenrothes . . . . . 128 D4
Glensanda . . . . . . 130 E2
Glensaugh . . . . . . 135 B6
Glenshero Lodge . 137 E8
Glen Sluain . . . . . 125 F6
Glenstockadale . . 104 C4
Glenstriven . . . . . 145 F9
Glentaggart . . . . . 113 B8
Glen Tanar
House . . . . . . . 140 F3
Glentham . . . . . . . 90 E4
Glentirranmuir . . 127 E5
Glenton . . . . . . . . 140 B5
Glentress . . . . . . 121 F5
Glentromie
Lodge . . . . . . . 138 E3
Glen Trool Lodge . 112 F4
Glentrool Village . 105 B7
Glentruan . . . . . . 84 B4
Glentruim House . 138 E2
Glentworth . . . . . . 90 F3
Glenuig . . . . . . . . 147 D9
Glenurquhart . . . 151 E10
Glen Village . . . . 119 B8
Glen Vine . . . . . . 84 E3
Glespin . . . . . . . 113 B8
Gletness . . . . . . 160 H6
Glewstone . . . . . . 36 B2
Glinton . . . . . . . . 65 D8
Glooston . . . . . . . 64 E4
Glororum . . . . . . 123 F7
Glossop . . . . . . . 87 E8
Gloster Hill . . . . . 117 D8
Gloucester . . . . . . 37 C5
Gloup . . . . . . . . 160 C7
Glusburn . . . . . . . 94 E3
Glutt Lodge . . . . 157 F12
Glympton . . . . . . 38 B4
Glynarthen . . . . . . 46 E2
Glynbrochan . . . . 59 F6
Glyn-Ceiriog . . . . 73 F6
Glyncoch . . . . . . 34 E4
Glyncorrwg . . . . . 34 E2
Glyn-cywarch . . . . 71 D7
Glynde . . . . . . . . 17 D8
Glyndebourne . . . . 17 C8
Glyndyfrdwy . . . . . 72 E5
Glyn Ebwy
= Ebbw Vale . . . 35 D5
Glynedd
= Glynneath . . . 34 D2
Glyn-neath . . . . . . 34 D2
Glynogwr . . . . . . . 34 F3
Glyntaff . . . . . . . . 34 F4
Glyntawe . . . . . . . 34 C2
Gnosall . . . . . . . . 62 B2
Gnosall Heath . . . . 62 B2
Goadby . . . . . . . . 64 E4
Goadby Marwood . 64 B4
Goatacre . . . . . . . 24 B5
Goathill . . . . . . . . 12 C4
Goathland . . . . . 103 D6
Goathurst . . . . . . . 22 F4
Goat Lees . . . . . . 30 E4
Gobernuisgach
Lodge . . . . . . . 156 E7
Gobhaig . . . . . . . 154 G5
Gobowen . . . . . . . 73 F7
Godalming . . . . . . 27 E7
Godley . . . . . . . . 87 E7
Godmanchester . . 54 B3
Godmanstone . . . . 12 E4
Godmersham . . . . 30 D4
Godney . . . . . . . . 23 E6
Godolphin Cross . . 2 C5
Godre'r-graig . . . . 34 D1
Godshill Hants . . . 14 C2
IoW . . . . . . . . 15 F6
Godstone . . . . . . . 28 D4
Godwinscroft . . . . 14 E2
Goetre Hereford . . 49 F6
N Yorks . . . . . . 95 C7
Goff's Oak . . . . . . 41 D6
Gogar . . . . . . . 120 B4
Goginan . . . . . . . 58 F3
Golan . . . . . . . . . 71 C6
Golant . . . . . . . . . 5 D6
Golberdon . . . . . . 5 B8
Golborne . . . . . . . 86 E4
Golcar . . . . . . . . 88 C2
Goldcliff . . . . . . . 35 F7
Golden Cross . . . . 18 D2
Golden Green . . . . 29 E7
Golden Grove . . . . 33 C6
Goldenhill . . . . . . 75 D5
Golden Hill . . . . . . 14 E3
Golden Pot . . . . . . 26 E5
Golden Valley . . . . 37 B6
Golders Green . . . . 41 F5
Goldhanger . . . . . 43 D5
Gold Hill . . . . . . . 66 E5
Golding . . . . . . . . 60 D5
Goldington . . . . . . 53 D8
Goldsborough
N Yorks . . . . . . 95 D6
N Yorks . . . . . . 103 C6
Goldsithney . . . . . 2 C4
Goldsworthy . . . . . 9 B5
Goldthorpe . . . . . . 89 D5

Gollanfield . . . . . 151 F11
Golspie . . . . . . . 157 J11
Golval . . . . . . . . 157 C11
Gomeldon . . . . . . 25 F6
Gomersal . . . . . . . 88 B3
Gomshall . . . . . . . 27 E8
Gonalston . . . . . . 77 E6
Gonfirth . . . . . . . 160 G5
Good Easter . . . . . 42 C2
Gooderstone . . . . 67 D7
Goodleigh . . . . . . 20 F5
Goodmanham . . . . 96 E4
Goodnestone Kent . 30 C4
Kent . . . . . . . . 31 D6
Goodrich . . . . . . . 36 C2
Goodrington . . . . . 7 D6
Goodshaw . . . . . . 87 B6
Goodwick = Wdig. . 44 B4
Goodworth
Clatford . . . . . 25 E8
Goole . . . . . . . . 89 B8
Goonbell . . . . . . . 3 B6
Goonhavern . . . . . 4 D2
Goose Eye . . . . . . 94 E3
Goose Green
Gtr Man . . . . . 86 D3
Norf . . . . . . . . 68 F4
W Sus . . . . . . 16 C5
Gooseham . . . . . . 8 C4
Goosey . . . . . . . . 38 E3
Goosnargh . . . . . . 93 F5
Goostrey . . . . . . . 74 B4
Gorcott Hill . . . . . 51 C5
Gord . . . . . . . . 160 L6
Gordon . . . . . . . 122 E2
Gordonbush . . . . 157 J11
Gordonsburgh . . . 152 B4
Gordonstoun . . . . 152 B1
Gordonstown
Aberds . . . . . . 152 C5
Aberds . . . . . . 153 E7
Gore . . . . . . . . . 31 D7
Gorebridge . . . . . 121 C6
Gore Cross . . . . . 24 D5
Gorefield . . . . . . . 66 C4
Gore Pit . . . . . . . 42 C4
Gorey . . . . . . . . 17 I3
Gorgie . . . . . . . 120 B5
Goring . . . . . . . . 39 F6
Goring-by-Sea . . . 16 D5
Goring Heath . . . . 26 B4
Gornalwood . . . . . 62 E3
Gorrachie . . . . . 153 C7
Gorran Churchtown 3 B8
Gorran Haven . . . . 3 C9
Gorrenberry . . . . 115 E7
Gors . . . . . . . . . 46 B5
Gorsedd . . . . . . . 73 B5
Gorse Hill . . . . . . 38 F1
Gorseinon . . . . . . 33 E6
Gorseness . . . . . 159 G5
Gorslas . . . . . . . 33 C6
Gorsley . . . . . . . 36 B3
Gorstan . . . . . . . 150 E6
Gorstanvorran . . 130 B2
Gorsteyhill . . . . . . 74 D4
Gorsty Hill . . . . . 62 B5
Gortantaoid . . . . 142 A4
Gorton . . . . . . . . 87 E6
Gosbeck . . . . . . . 57 D5
Gosberton . . . . . . 78 F5
Gosberton Clough . 65 B8
Gosfield . . . . . . . 42 B3
Gosford . . . . . . . 49 C7
Gosforth Cumb . . . 98 D2
T&W . . . . . . . . 110 C5
Gosmore . . . . . . . 40 B4
Gosport . . . . . . . 15 E7
Gossabrough . . . 160 E7
Gossington . . . . . 36 D4
Goswick . . . . . . 123 E6
Gotham . . . . . . . 76 F5
Gotherington . . . . 37 B6
Gott . . . . . . . . 160 J6
Goudhurst . . . . . . 18 B4
Goulceby . . . . . . . 79 B5
Gourdas . . . . . . 153 D7
Gourdon . . . . . . 135 B8
Gourock . . . . . . 118 B2
Govan . . . . . . . 119 C5
Govanhill . . . . . . 119 C5
Goveton . . . . . . . 7 E5
Govilon . . . . . . . 35 C6
Gowanhill . . . . . 153 B10
Gowdall . . . . . . . 89 B7
Gowerton . . . . . . 33 E6
Gowkhall . . . . . . 128 F2
Gowthorpe . . . . . 96 D3
Goxhill E Yorks . . . 97 F7
N Lincs . . . . . . 90 B5
Goxhill Haven . . . . 90 B5
Goytre . . . . . . . . 34 F1
Grabhair . . . . . . 155 F8
Graby . . . . . . . . 65 B7
Grade . . . . . . . . 3 E6
Graffham . . . . . . . 16 C3
Grafham Cambs . . 54 C2
Sur . . . . . . . . 27 E8
Grafton Hereford . . 49 F6
N Yorks . . . . . . 95 C7
Oxon . . . . . . . 38 D2
Shrops . . . . . . 60 C4
Worcs . . . . . . . 49 C7
Grafton Flyford . . . 50 D4
Grafton Regis . . . . 53 E5
Grafton
Underwood . . . 65 F6
Grafty Green . . . . 30 E2
Graianrhyd . . . . . 73 D6
Graig Conwy . . . . 83 D8
Denb . . . . . . . 72 B4
Graig-fechan . . . . 72 D5
Grain . . . . . . . . . 30 B2
Grainsby . . . . . . . 91 E6
Grainthorpe . . . . . 91 E7
Grampound . . . . . 3 B8
Grampound Road . 4 D4
Gramsdal . . . . . 148 C3
Granborough . . . . 39 B7
Granby . . . . . . . . 77 F7
Grandborough . . . 52 C2
Grandtully . . . . . 133 D6
Grange Cumb . . . 98 C4
E Ayrs . . . . . . 118 F4
Medway . . . . . 29 C8
Perth . . . . . . 128 B4

Grange
Crossroads . . . 152 C4
Grange Hall . . . . 151 E13
Grange Hill . . . . . 41 E7
Grangemill . . . . . 76 D2
Grange Moor . . . . 88 C3
Grangemouth . . . 127 F8
Grange of
Lindores . . . . 128 C4
Grange-over-
Sands . . . . . . 92 B4
Grangepans . . . . 128 F2
Grangetown Cardiff 22 B3
Redcar . . . . . . 102 B3
Grange Villa . . . . 110 D5
Granish . . . . . . 138 C5
Gransmoor . . . . . 97 D7
Granston . . . . . . 44 B3
Grantchester . . . . 54 D5
Grantham . . . . . . 78 F2
Grantlodge . . . . 141 C6
Granton Dumfries . 114 D3
Edin . . . . . . . 120 B5
Grantown-on-
Spey . . . . . . 139 B6
Grantshouse . . . 122 C4
Grappenhall . . . . 86 F4
Grasby . . . . . . . 90 D4
Grasmere . . . . . . 99 D5
Grasscroft . . . . . 87 D7
Grassendale . . . . 85 F4
Grassholme . . . . 100 B4
Grassington . . . . 94 C3
Grassmoor . . . . . 76 C4
Grassthorpe . . . . 77 C7
Grateley . . . . . . . 25 E7
Gratwich . . . . . . . 75 F7
Graveley Cambs . . 54 C3
Herts . . . . . . . 41 B5
Gravelly Hill . . . . 62 E5
Gravels . . . . . . . 60 D3
Graven . . . . . . . 160 F6
Graveney . . . . . . 30 C4
Gravesend Herts . . 41 B7
Kent . . . . . . . 29 B7
Grayingham . . . . . 90 E3
Grayrigg . . . . . . . 99 E7
Grays . . . . . . . . 29 B7
Grayshott . . . . . . 27 F6
Grayswood . . . . . 27 F7
Graythorp . . . . . 102 B3
Grazeley . . . . . . . 26 C4
Greasbrough . . . . 88 E5
Greasby . . . . . . . 85 F3
Great Abington . . . 55 E6
Great Addington . . 53 B7
Great Alne . . . . . . 51 D6
Great Altcar . . . . . 85 D4
Great Amwell . . . . 41 C6
Great Asby . . . . . 100 C1
Great Ashfield . . . 56 C3
Great Ayton . . . . 102 C3
Great Baddow . . . 42 D3
Great Bardfield . . . 55 F7
Great Barford . . . . 54 D2
Great Barr . . . . . . 62 E4
Great Barrington . . 38 C2
Great Barrow . . . . 73 C8
Great Barton . . . . 56 C2
Great Barugh . . . . 96 B3
Great Bavington . 117 F5
Great Bealings . . . 57 E6
Great Bedwyn . . . 25 C7
Great Bentley . . . . 43 B7
Great Billing . . . . 53 C6
Great Bircham . . . 80 D3
Great Blakenham . 56 D5
Great Blencow . . 108 F4
Great Bolas . . . . . 61 B6
Great Bookham . . 28 D2
Great Bourton . . . 52 E2
Great Bowden . . . 64 F4
Great Bradley . . . 55 D7
Great Braxted . . . 42 C4
Great Bricett . . . . 56 D4
Great Brickhill . . . 53 F7
Great Bridge . . . . 62 E3
Great Bridgeford . 62 B2
Great Brington . . . 52 C4
Great Bromley . . . 43 B6
Great Broughton
Cumb . . . . . . 107 F7
N Yorks . . . . . 102 D3
Great Budworth . . 74 B3
Great Burdon . . . 101 C8
Great Burgh . . . . . 28 D3
Great Burstead . . . 42 E2
Great Busby . . . . 102 D3
Great Canfield . . . 42 C1
Great Carlton . . . . 91 F8
Great Casterton . . 65 D7
Great Chart . . . . . 30 E3
Great Chatwell . . . 61 C7
Great Chesterford . 55 E6
Great Cheverell . . 24 D4
Great Chishill . . . . 54 F5
Great Clacton . . . . 43 C7
Great Cliff . . . . . . 88 C4
Great Clifton . . . . 98 B2
Great Coates . . . . 91 D6
Great Comberton . 50 E4
Great Corby . . . . 108 D4
Great Cornard . . . 56 E2
Great Cowden . . . 97 E8
Great Coxwell . . . 38 E2
Great Crakehall . . 101 E7
Great Cransley . . . 53 B6
Great
Cressingham . . 67 D8
Great Crosby . . . . 85 E4
Great Cubley . . . . 75 F8
Great Dalby . . . . . 64 C4
Great Denham . . . 53 E8
Great Doddington . 53 C6
Great Dunham . . . 67 C8
Great Dunmow . . . 42 B2
Great Durnford . . . 25 F6
Great Easton Essex . 42 B2
Leics . . . . . . . 64 E5
Great Eccleston . . 92 E4
Great Edstone . . 103 F5
Great Ellingham . . 68 E3
Great Elm . . . . . . 24 E2
Greater Doward . . 36 C2
Greater Eversden . 54 D4
Great Fencote . . . 101 E7
Great Finborough . 56 D4
Greatford . . . . . . 65 C7

Great Fransham . . 67 C8
Great Gaddesden . 40 C3
Greatgate . . . . . . 75 E7
Great Gidding . . . 65 F8
Great Givendale . . 96 D4
Great Glemham . . 57 C7
Great Glen . . . . . . 64 E3
Great Gonerby . . . 77 F8
Great Gransden . . 54 D3
Great Green Norf . 69 F5
Suff . . . . . . . 56 D3
Great Habton . . . . 96 B3
Great Hale . . . . . . 78 E4
Great Hallingbury . 41 C8
Greatham Hants . . 27 F5
Hrtlpl . . . . . . 102 B2
W Sus . . . . . . 16 C4
Great Hampden . . 39 D8
Great Harrowden . 53 B6
Great Harwood . . . 93 F7
Great Haseley . . . 39 D6
Great Hatfield . . . 97 E7
Great Haywood . . 62 B4
Great Heath . . . . . 63 F7
Great Heck . . . . . 89 B6
Great Henny . . . . . 56 F2
Great Hinton . . . . 24 D4
Great Hockham . . 68 E2
Great Holland . . . 43 C8
Great Horkesley . . 56 F3
Great Hormead . . . 41 B6
Great Horton . . . . 94 F4
Great Horwood . . . 53 F5
Great Houghton
S Yorks . . . . . 88 D5
W Nhants . . . . 53 D5
Great Hucklow . . . 75 B8
Great Kelk . . . . . . 97 D7
Great Kimble . . . . 39 D8
Great Kingshill . . . 40 E1
Great Langton . . 101 E7
Great Leighs . . . . 42 C3
Great Lever . . . . . 86 D5
Great Limber . . . . 90 D5
Great Linford . . . . 53 E6
Great Livermere . . 56 B2
Great Longstone . . 76 B2
Great Lumley . . . 111 E5
Great Lyth . . . . . . 60 D4
Great Malvern . . . 50 E2
Great Maplestead . 56 F2
Great Marton . . . . 92 F3
Great Massingham 80 C3
Great Melton . . . . 68 D4
Great Milton . . . . 39 D6
Great Missenden . . 40 D1
Great Mongeham . 31 D7
Great Moulton . . . 68 E4
Great Munden . . . 41 B6
Great Musgrave . 100 C2
Great Ness . . . . . 60 C3
Great Notley . . . . 42 B3
Great Oakley Essex . 43 B7
N Nhants . . . . 65 F5
Great Offley . . . . . 40 B4
Great Ormside . . 100 C2
Great Orton . . . . 108 D3
Great Ouseburn . . 95 C7
Great Oxendon . . . 64 F4
Great Oxney
Green . . . . . . . 42 D2
Greatoworth . . . . . 52 E3
Great Palgrave . . . 67 C8
Great Parndon . . . 41 D7
Great Paxton . . . . 54 C3
Great Plumpton . . 92 F3
Great Plumstead . . 69 C6
Great Ponton . . . . 78 F2
Great Preston . . . . 88 B5
Great Raveley . . . . 66 F2
Great Rissington . . 38 C1
Great Rollright . . . 51 F8
Great Ryburgh . . . 81 E5
Great Ryle . . . . . 117 C6
Great Ryton . . . . . 60 D4
Great Saling . . . . 42 B3
Great Salkeld . . . 109 F5
Great Sampford . . 55 F7
Great Sankey . . . . 86 F3
Great Saxham . . . 55 C8
Great Shefford . . . 25 B8
Great Shelford . . . 54 D5
Great Smeaton . . 101 D8
Great Snoring . . . . 80 D5
Great Somerford . 37 F6
Great Stainton . . 101 B8
Great Stambridge . 42 E4
Great Staughton . . 54 C2
Great Steeping . . . 79 C7
Great Stonar . . . . 31 D7
Greatstone on Sea 19 C7
Great Strickland . 99 B7
Great Stukeley . . . 54 B3
Great Sturton . . . . 78 B5
Great Sutton
Ches W . . . . . 73 B7
Shrops . . . . . . 60 F5
Great Swinburne . 110 B2
Great Tew . . . . . . 38 B3
Great Tey . . . . . . 42 B4
Great Thurkleby . . 95 B7
Great Thurlow . . . 55 D7
Great Torrington . . 9 C6
Great Tosson . . . 117 D6
Great Totham . . . 42 C4
Great Tows . . . . . 91 E6
Great Urswick . . . 92 B2
Great Wakering . . 43 F5
Great Waldingfield 56 E3
Great Walsingham . 80 D5
Great Waltham . . . 42 C2
Great Warley . . . . 42 E1
Great Washbourne . 50 F4
Great Weldon . . . . 65 F6
Great Welnetham . 56 D2
Great Wenham . . . 56 F4
Great
Whittington . . 110 B3
Great Wigborough . 43 C5
Great Wilbraham . 55 D6
Great Wishford . . . 25 F5
Great Witcombe . . 37 C6
Great Witley . . . . 50 C2
Great Wolford . . . 51 F7
Greatworth . . . . . 52 E3
Great Wratting . . . 55 E7
Great Wymondley . 41 B5
Great Wyrley . . . . 62 D3
Great Wytheford . 61 C5

Great Yarmouth . . 69 D8
Great Yeldham . . . 55 F8
Greave . . . . . . . . 87 B6
Greeba . . . . . . . . 84 D3
Green . . . . . . . . . 72 C4
Greenbank . . . . . 160 C7
Greenburn . . . . . 120 C2
Greendikes . . . . . 117 B6
Green End . . . . . . 54 D2
Greenfield C Beds . 53 F8
Flint . . . . . . . . 73 B5
Gtr Man . . . . . 87 D7
Highld . . . . . . 136 D5
Oxon . . . . . . . 39 E7
Greenford . . . . . . 40 F4
Greengairs . . . . . 119 B7
Greenham . . . . . . 26 C2
Green
Hammerton . . . 95 D7
Greenhaugh . . . . 116 F3
Greenhead . . . . . 109 C6
Greenhill Falk . . . 119 B8
Kent . . . . . . . 31 C5
Leics . . . . . . . 63 C8
London . . . . . . 40 F4
Greenhills . . . . . 118 D3
Greenhithe . . . . . 29 B6
Greenholm . . . . . 118 F5
Greenholme . . . . . 99 D7
Greenhouse . . . . 115 B8
Greenhow Hill . . . 94 C4
Greenigoe . . . . . 159 H5
Greenland . . . . . 158 D4
Greenlands . . . . . 39 F7
Greenlaw Aberds . 153 C6
Borders . . . . . 122 E3
Greenlea . . . . . . 107 B7
Greenloaning . . . 127 D7
Greenmount . . . . 87 C5
Greenmow . . . . . 160 L6
Greenock . . . . . . 118 B2
Greenock West . . 118 B2
Greenodd . . . . . . 99 F5
Green Ore . . . . . . 23 D7
Greenrow . . . . . 107 D8
Greens Norton . . . 52 E4
Greenstead
Green . . . . . . . 42 B4
Greensted . . . . . . 41 D8
Green Street . . . . 40 E4
Greenway . . . . . . 14 B4
Greenwich . . . . . . 28 B4
Greet . . . . . . . . . 50 F5
Greete . . . . . . . . 49 B7
Greetham Lincs . . 79 B6
Rutland . . . . . 65 C6
Greetland . . . . . . 87 B8
Gregg Hall . . . . . . 99 E6
Gregson Lane . . . . 86 B3
Greinetobht . . . . 148 A3
Greinton . . . . . . . 23 F6
Gremista . . . . . . 160 J6
Grenaby . . . . . . . 84 E2
Grendon N Nhants . 53 C6
Warks . . . . . . 63 D6
Grendon Green . . . 49 D7
Grendon
Underwood . . . 39 B6
Grenofen . . . . . . . 6 B2
Grenoside . . . . . . 88 E4
Greosabhagh . . . 154 H6
Gresford . . . . . . . 73 D7
Gresham . . . . . . . 81 D7
Greshornish . . . . 149 C8
Gressenhall . . . . . 68 C2
Gressingham . . . . 93 C5
Gresty Green . . . . 74 D4
Greta Bridge . . . . 101 C5
Gretna . . . . . . . 108 C3
Gretna Green . . . 108 C3
Gretton Glos . . . . 50 F5
N Nhants . . . . 65 E5
Shrops . . . . . . 60 E5
Grewelthorpe . . . . 94 B5
Greygarth . . . . . . 94 B4
Grey Green . . . . . 89 D8
Greynor . . . . . . . 33 D6
Greysouthen . . . . 98 B2
Greystoke . . . . . 108 F4
Greystone Angus . 135 E5
Dumfries . . . . 107 B6
Greywell . . . . . . . 26 D5
Griais . . . . . . . 155 C9
Grianan . . . . . . 155 D9
Gribthorpe . . . . . 96 F3
Gridley Corner . . . 9 E5
Griff . . . . . . . . . 63 F7
Griffithstown . . . . 35 E6
Grimbister . . . . . 159 G4
Grimblethorpe . . . 91 F6
Grimeford Village . 86 C4
Grimethorpe . . . . 88 D5
Griminis . . . . . . 148 C2
Grimister . . . . . 160 D6
Grimley . . . . . . . 50 C3
Grimness . . . . . 159 J5
Grimoldby . . . . . . 91 F7
Grimpo . . . . . . . . 60 B3
Grimsargh . . . . . . 93 F5
Grimsbury . . . . . . 52 E2
Grimsby . . . . . . . 91 C6
Grimscote . . . . . . 52 D4
Grimscott . . . . . . 8 D4
Grimsthorpe . . . . . 65 B7
Grimston E Yorks . 97 F8
Leics . . . . . . . 64 B3
Norf . . . . . . . 80 E3
York . . . . . . . 96 D2
Grimstone . . . . . . 12 E4
Grinacombe Moor . 9 E6
Grindale . . . . . . . 97 B7
Grindigar . . . . . 159 H6
Grindiscol . . . . . 160 K6
Grindle . . . . . . . . 61 D7
Grindleford . . . . . 76 B2
Grindleton . . . . . . 93 E7
Grindley . . . . . . . 62 B4
Grindley Brook . . . 74 E2
Grindlow . . . . . . . 75 B8
Grindon Northumb . 122 E5
Staffs . . . . . . 75 D7
Gringley on
the Hill . . . . . 89 E8

Grinsdale . . . . . 108 D3
Grinshill . . . . . . . 60 B5
Grinton . . . . . . . 101 E5
Griomsidar . . . . 155 E8
Grishipoll . . . . . 146 F4
Grisling Common . 17 B8
Gristhorpe . . . . . 103 F8
Griston . . . . . . . . 68 E2
Gritley . . . . . . . 159 H6
Grittenham . . . . . 37 F7
Grittleton . . . . . . 37 F5
Grizebeck . . . . . . 98 A4
Grizedale . . . . . . 99 E5
Grobister . . . . . 159 F7
Groby . . . . . . . . 64 D2
Groes Conwy . . . . 72 C4
Neath . . . . . . 34 F1
Groes-faen . . . . . 34 F4
Groesffordd Marli . 72 B4
Groeslon Gwyn . . 82 F4
Gwyn . . . . . . . 82 E4
Groes-lwyd . . . . . 60 C2
Grogport . . . . . . 143 D9
Gromford . . . . . . 57 D7
Gronant . . . . . . . 72 A4
Groombridge . . . . 18 B2
Grosmont Mon . . . 35 B8
N Yorks . . . . . 103 D6
Groton . . . . . . . . 56 E3
Grougfoot . . . . . 120 B3
Grove Dorset . . . . 12 G5
Kent . . . . . . . 31 C6
Notts . . . . . . . 77 B7
Oxon . . . . . . . 38 E4
Grove Park . . . . . 28 B5
Grovesend . . . . . 33 D6
Grove Vale . . . . . 62 E4
Grudie . . . . . . . 150 E6
Gruids . . . . . . . 157 J8
Gruinard House . 150 B2
Grula . . . . . . . 149 F8
Gruline . . . . . . . 147 G8
Grunasound . . . . 160 K5
Grundisburgh . . . 57 D6
Grunsagill . . . . . 93 D7
Gruting . . . . . . 160 J4
Grutness . . . . . 160 N6
Gualachulain . . . 131 E5
Gualin House . . . 156 D6
Guardbridge . . . 129 C6
Guarlford . . . . . . 50 E3
Guay . . . . . . . 133 E7
Guestling Green . . 19 D5
Guestling Thorn . . 19 D5
Guestwick . . . . . . 81 E6
Guestwick Green . 81 E6
Guide . . . . . . . . 86 B5
Guide Post . . . . 117 F8
Guilden Morden . . 54 E3
Guilden Sutton . . . 73 C8
Guildford . . . . . . 27 E7
Guildtown . . . . . 133 F8
Guilsborough . . . . 52 B4
Guilsfield . . . . . . 60 C2
Guilton . . . . . . . 31 D6
Guineaford . . . . . 20 F4
Guisborough . . . 102 C4
Guiseley . . . . . . . 94 E4
Guist . . . . . . . . 81 E5
Guith . . . . . . . 159 E6
Guiting Power . . . 37 B7
Gulberwick . . . . 160 K6
Gullane . . . . . . 129 F6
Gulval . . . . . . . . 2 C3
Gulworthy . . . . . . 6 B2
Gumfreston . . . . . 32 D2
Gumley . . . . . . . 64 E3
Gummow's Shop . 4 D3
Gunby E Yorks . . . 96 F3
Lincs . . . . . . . 65 B6
Gundleton . . . . . . 26 F4
Gun Hill . . . . . . . 18 D2
Gunn . . . . . . . . 20 F5
Gunnerside . . . . 100 E4
Gunnerton . . . . . 110 B2
Gunness . . . . . . . 90 C2
Gunnislake . . . . . 6 B2
Gunnista . . . . . 160 J7
Gunthorpe Norf . . 81 D6
Notts . . . . . . . 77 E6
Pboro . . . . . . . 65 D8
Gunville . . . . . . . 15 F5
Gunwalloe . . . . . . 3 D5
Gurnard . . . . . . . 15 E5
Gurnett . . . . . . . 75 B6
Gurney Slade . . . . 23 E8
Gurnos . . . . . . . 34 D1
Gussage
All Saints . . . . 13 C8
Gussage
St Michael . . . 13 C7
Guston . . . . . . . 31 E7
Gutcher . . . . . . 160 D7
Guthrie . . . . . . 135 D5
Guyhirn . . . . . . . 66 D3
Guyhirn Gull . . . . 66 D3
Guy's Head . . . . . 66 B4
Guy's Marsh . . . . 13 B6
Guyzance . . . . . 117 D8
Gwaenysgor . . . . 72 A4
Gwalchmai . . . . . 82 D3
Gwaun-Cae-
Gurwen . . . . . 33 C8
Gwaun-Leision . . . 33 C8
Gwbert . . . . . . . 45 E3
Gweek . . . . . . . . 3 D6
Gwehelog . . . . . . 35 D7
Gwenddwr . . . . . 48 E2
Gwennap . . . . . . 3 C6
Gwenter . . . . . . . 3 E6
Gwernaffield . . . . 73 C6
Gwernesney . . . . 35 D8
Gwernogle . . . . . 46 F4
Gwernymynydd . . 73 C6
Gwersyllt . . . . . . 73 D7
Gwespyr . . . . . . . 72 A5
Gwithian . . . . . . . 2 B4
Gwredog . . . . . . . 82 C4
Gwyddelwern . . . 72 E4
Gwyddgrug . . . . . 46 F3
Gwydyr Uchaf . . . 83 E7
Gwynfryn . . . . . . 73 D6
Gwystre . . . . . . . 48 C2
Gwytherin . . . . . . 83 E8
Gyfelia . . . . . . . 73 E7
Gyffin . . . . . . . . 83 D7
Gyre . . . . . . . . 159 H4
Gyrn-goch . . . . . . 70 C5

**H**

Habberley . . . . . . 60 D3
Habergham . . . . . 93 F8
Habrough . . . . . . 90 C5
Haceby . . . . . . . 78 F3
Hacheston . . . . . 57 D7
Hackbridge . . . . . 28 C3
Hackenthorpe . . . . 88 F5
Hackford . . . . . . . 68 D3
Hackforth . . . . . 101 E7
Hackland . . . . . 159 F4
Hackleton . . . . . . 53 D6
Hackness N Yorks . 103 E7
Orkney . . . . . 159 J4
Hackney . . . . . . . 41 F6
Hackthorn . . . . . . 90 F3
Hackthorpe . . . . . 99 B7
Haconby . . . . . . . 65 B8
Hacton . . . . . . . . 41 F8
Hadden . . . . . . . 122 F3
Haddenham Bucks . 39 D7
Cambs . . . . . . 55 B5
Haddington
E Loth . . . . . . 121 B8
Lincs . . . . . . . 78 C2
Haddiscoe . . . . . . 69 E7
Haddon Cambs . . . 65 E8
Ches E . . . . . . 75 C6
Hade Edge . . . . . 88 D2
Hademore . . . . . . 63 D5
Hadfield . . . . . . . 87 E8
Hadham Cross . . . 41 C7
Hadham Ford . . . . 41 B7
Hadleigh Essex . . . 42 F4
Suff . . . . . . . 56 E4
Hadley . . . . . . . . 61 C6
Hadley End . . . . . 62 B5
Hadlow . . . . . . . 29 E7
Hadlow Down . . . . 18 C2
Hadnall . . . . . . . 60 C5
Hadstock . . . . . . 55 E6
Hady . . . . . . . . 76 B3
Hadzor . . . . . . . 50 C4
Haffenden Quarter 30 E2
Hafod-Dinbych . . . 83 F8
Hafod-Iom . . . . . . 83 D8
Haggate . . . . . . . 93 F8
Haggbeck . . . . . 108 B4
Haggerston . . . . 123 E6
Haghmond Hill . . . 60 C5
Hagley Hereford . . 49 F7
Worcs . . . . . . 62 F3
Hagworthingham . 79 C6
Haigh Gtr Man . . . 86 D4
S Yorks . . . . . 88 C3
Haigh Moor . . . . . 88 B3
Haighton Green . . 93 F5
Haile . . . . . . . . . 98 D2
Hailes . . . . . . . . 50 F5
Hailey Herts . . . . . 41 C6
Oxon . . . . . . . 38 C3
Hailsham . . . . . . 18 E2
Hail Weston . . . . . 54 C2
Haimer . . . . . . . 158 D3
Hainault . . . . . . . 41 E7
Hainford . . . . . . . 68 C5
Hainton . . . . . . . 91 F5
Hairmyres . . . . . 119 D6
Haisthorpe . . . . . 97 C7
Hakin . . . . . . . . 44 E3
Halam . . . . . . . . 77 D6
Halbeath . . . . . 128 F3
Halberton . . . . . . 10 C5
Halcro . . . . . . . 158 D4
Hale Gtr Man . . . . 87 F5
Halton . . . . . . . 86 F2
Hale Bank . . . . . . 86 F2
Halebarns . . . . . . 87 F5
Hales Norf . . . . . . 69 E6
Staffs . . . . . . 74 F4
Halesfield . . . . . . 61 D7
Halesgate . . . . . . 66 B3
Halesowen . . . . . 62 F3
Hales Place . . . . . 30 D5
Hale Street . . . . . 29 E7
Halesworth . . . . . 57 B7
Halewood . . . . . . 86 F2
Halford Shrops . . . 60 F4
Warks . . . . . . 51 E7
Halfpenny Furze . . 32 C3
Halfpenny Green . . 62 E2
Halfway Carms . . . 46 F5
Carms . . . . . . 47 F7
W Berks . . . . . 26 C2
Halfway Bridge . . . 16 B3
Halfway House . . . 60 C3
Halfway Houses . . 30 B3
Halifax . . . . . . . . 87 B8
Halket . . . . . . . 118 D4
Halkirk . . . . . . . 158 E3
Halkyn . . . . . . . . 73 B6
Halland . . . . . . . 18 D2
Hallatrow . . . . . . 23 D8
Hallaton . . . . . . . 64 E4
Hallatrow . . . . . . 23 D8
Hallbankgate . . . 109 D5
Hall Dunnerdale . . 98 E4
Hallen . . . . . . . . 36 F2
Hall Green W Mid . 62 F5
W Yorks . . . . . 88 C4
Hall Grove . . . . . . 41 C5
Halliburton . . . . 122 E2
Hallin . . . . . . . 148 C7
Halling . . . . . . . 29 C8
Hallington Lincs . . 91 F7
Northumb . . . 110 B2
Halliwell . . . . . . . 86 C5
Hall of
Tankerness . . 159 H6
Hall of the Forest . 60 F2
Halloughton . . . . 77 D6
Hallow . . . . . . . . 50 D3
Hallrule . . . . . . 115 C8
Halls . . . . . . . . 122 B2
Hall's Green . . . . 41 B5
Hallsands . . . . . . 7 F6
Hallthwaites . . . . 98 F3
Hallworthy . . . . . . 8 F3
Hallyburton
House . . . . . . 134 F2
Hallyne . . . . . . 120 E4
Halmer End . . . . . 74 E4
Halmore . . . . . . . 36 D3
Halmyre Mains . . 120 E4
Halnaker . . . . . . 16 D3
Halsall . . . . . . . . 85 C4
Halse Som . . . . . . 11 B6

Halse continued
W Nhants . . . . 52 E3
Halsetown . . . . . . 2 C4
Halsham . . . . . . . 91 B6
Halsinger . . . . . . 20 F4
Halstead Essex . . 56 F2
Kent . . . . . . . 29 C5
Leics . . . . . . . 64 D4
Halstock . . . . . . . 12 D3
Haltham . . . . . . . 78 C5
Haltoft End . . . . . 79 E6
Halton Bucks . . . . 40 C1
Halton Halton . . . 86 F3
Lancs . . . . . . 92 C5
Halton Northumb . 110 C2
Wrex . . . . . . . 73 F7
W Yorks . . . . . 95 F6
Halton East . . . . . 94 D3
Halton Gill . . . . . . 93 B8
Halton Holegate . . 79 C7
Halton Lea Gate . 109 D6
Halton West . . . . 93 D8
Haltwhistle . . . . 109 C7
Halvergate . . . . . 69 D7
Halwell . . . . . . . . 7 D5
Halwill . . . . . . . . 9 E6
Halwill Junction . . 9 D6
Ham Devon . . . . . 11 D7
Glos . . . . . . . 36 E3
Highld . . . . . . 158 C4
Kent . . . . . . . 31 D7
London . . . . . . 28 B2
Shetland . . . . 160 K1
Wilts . . . . . . . 25 C8
Hambleden . . . . . 39 F7
Hambledon Hants . 15 C7
Sur . . . . . . . . 27 F7
Hamble-le-Rice . . 15 D5
Hambleton Lancs . 92 E3
N Yorks . . . . . 95 F8
Hambridge . . . . . 11 B8
Hambrook S Glos . 23 B8
W Sus . . . . . . 15 D8
Ham Common . . . 13 B6
Hameringham . . . 79 C6
Hamerton . . . . . . 54 B2
Hametoun . . . . . 160 K1
Ham Green
Hereford . . . . . 50 E2
Kent . . . . . . . 19 C5
Kent . . . . . . . 30 C2
N Som . . . . . . 23 B7
Worcs . . . . . . 50 C5
Hamilton . . . . . 119 D7
Hammer . . . . . . . 27 F6
Hammerpot . . . . . 16 D4
Hammersmith . . . 28 B3
Hammerwich . . . . 62 D4
Hammerwood . . . 28 F5
Hammond Street . 41 D6
Hammoon . . . . . . 13 C6
Hamnavoe
Shetland . . . . 160 E4
Shetland . . . . 160 F6
Shetland . . . . 160 F6
Shetland . . . . 160 K5
Hampden Park . . . 18 E3
Hamperden End . . 55 F6
Hampnett . . . . . . 37 C7
Hampole . . . . . . . 89 C6
Hampreston . . . . . 13 E8
Hampstead . . . . . 41 F5
Hampstead
Norreys . . . . . 26 B3
Hampsthwaite . . . 95 D5
Hampton Pboro . . 65 E8
Lundun . . . . . . 28 C2
Shrops . . . . . . 61 F7
Worcs . . . . . . 50 E5
Hampton Bishop . . 49 F7
Hampton Heath . . 73 E8
Hampton in Arden . 63 F6
Hampton Loade . . 61 F7
Hampton Lovett . . 50 C3
Hampton Lucy . . . 51 D7
Hampton on the
Hill . . . . . . . 51 C7
Hampton Poyle . . . 39 C5
Hamrow . . . . . . . 80 E5
Hamsey . . . . . . . 17 C8
Hamsey Green . . . 28 D4
Hamstall Ridware . 62 C5
Hamstead IoW . . . 14 E5
W Mid . . . . . . 62 E4
Hamstead
Marshall . . . . 26 C2
Hamsterley
Durham . . . . . 110 D4
Durham . . . . . 110 F4
Hamstreet . . . . . . 19 B7
Ham Street . . . . . 23 F7
Hamworthy . . . . . 13 E7
Hanbury Staffs . . . 63 B5
Worcs . . . . . . 50 C4
Hanbury Woodend 63 B5
Hanby . . . . . . . . 78 F3
Hanchurch . . . . . 74 E5
Handbridge . . . . . 73 C8
Handcross . . . . . . 17 B6
Handforth . . . . . . 87 F6
Handley . . . . . . . 73 D8
Handsacre . . . . . . 62 C4
Handsworth
S Yorks . . . . . 88 F5
W Mid . . . . . . 62 E4
Handy Cross . . . . 9 B6
Hanford . . . . . . . 75 E5
Hanging Langford . 24 F5
Hangleton . . . . . . 16 D4
Hanham . . . . . . . 23 B8
Hankelow . . . . . . 74 E3
Hankerton . . . . . . 37 E6
Hankham . . . . . . 18 E3
Hanley . . . . . . . . 75 E5
Hanley Castle . . . 50 E3
Hanley Child . . . . 49 C8
Hanley Swan . . . . 50 E3
Hanley William . . 49 C8
Hanlith . . . . . . . . 94 C2
Hanmer . . . . . . . 73 F8
Hannah . . . . . . . 79 B8
Hannington Hants . 26 D3
Swindon . . . . . 38 E1
W Nhants . . . . 53 B6
Hannington Wick . 38 E1
Hansel Village . . 118 F3
Hanslope . . . . . . 53 E6
Hanthorpe . . . . . . 65 B7
Hanwell London . . 40 F4

Hanwell *continued*
Oxon 52 E2
Hanwood 60 D4
Hanworth London 28 B2
Norf 81 D7
Happendon 119 F8
Happisburgh 69 A6
Happisburgh Common 69 B6
Hapsford 73 B8
Hapton Lancs 93 F7
Norf 68 E4
Harberton 7 D5
Harbertonford 7 D5
Harbledown 30 D5
Harborne 62 F4
Harborough Magna 52 B2
Harbottle 117 D5
Harbury 51 D8
Harby Leics 77 F7
Notts 77 B8
Harcombe 11 E6
Harden W Mid 62 D4
W Yorks 94 F3
Hardenhuish 24 B4
Hardgate 141 D6
Hardham 16 C4
Hardingham 68 D3
Hardingstone 53 D5
Hardington 24 D2
Hardington Mandeville 12 C3
Hardington Marsh 12 D3
Hardley 14 D5
Hardley Street 69 D6
Hardmead 53 E7
Hardrow 100 E3
Hardstoft 76 C4
Hardway Hants 15 D7
Som 24 F2
Hardwick Bucks 39 C8
Cambs 54 D4
N Nhants 53 C6
Norf 67 C6
Norf 68 F5
Notts 77 B6
Oxon 38 D3
Oxon 39 B5
W Mid 62 E4
Hardwicke Glos 36 C4
Glos 37 B6
Hereford 48 E4
Hardy's Green 43 B5
Hareby 79 C6
Hareden 93 D6
Harefield 40 E3
Hare Green 43 B6
Hare Hatch 27 B6
Harehills 95 F6
Harehope 117 B6
Haresceugh 109 E6
Harescombe 37 C5
Haresfield 37 C5
Hareshaw 119 C8
Hareshaw Head 116 F4
Hare Street 41 B6
Harewood 95 E6
Harewood End 36 B2
Harford Carms 46 E5
Devon 6 D4
Hargate 68 E4
Hargatewall 75 B8
Hargrave Ches W 73 C8
N Nhants 53 B8
Suff 55 D8
Harker 108 C3
Harkland 160 E6
Harkstead 57 F5
Harlaston 63 C6
Harlaw House 141 B6
Harlaxton 77 F8
Harlech 71 D6
Harlequin 77 F6
Harlescott 60 C5
Harlesden 41 F5
Harleston Devon 7 E5
Norf 68 F5
Suff 56 D4
Harlestone 52 C5
Harle Syke 93 F8
Harley Shrops 61 D5
S Yorks 88 E4
Harleyholm 120 F2
Harlington C Beds 53 F8
London 27 B8
S Yorks 89 D5
Harlosh 149 D7
Harlow 41 C7
Harlow Hill
Northumb 110 C3
N Yorks 95 D5
Harlthorpe 96 F3
Harlton 54 D4
Harman's Cross 13 F7
Harmby 101 F6
Harmer Green 41 C5
Harmer Hill 60 B4
Harmondsworth 27 B8
Harmston 78 C2
Harnham 110 B3
Harnhill 37 D7
Harold Hill 41 E8
Haroldston West 44 D3
Haroldswick 160 B8
Harold Wood 41 E8
Harome 102 F4
Harpenden 40 C4
Harpford 11 E5
Harpham 97 C6
Harpley Norf 80 E3
Worcs 49 C8
Harpole 52 C4
Harpsdale 158 E3
Harpsden 39 F7
Harpswell 90 F3
Harpurhey 87 D6
Harpur Hill 75 B7
Harraby 108 D4
Harrapool 149 F11
Harrier 160 J1
Harrietfield 127 B8
Harrietsham 30 D2
Harrington Cumb 98 B1
Lincs 79 B6
N Nhants 64 F4
Harringworth 65 E6
Harris 146 B6
Harrogate 95 D6
Harrold 53 D7
Harrow 40 F4
Harrowbarrow 5 C8
Harrowden 53 E8
Harrowgate Hill 101 C7
Harrow on the Hill 40 F4
Harrow Street 56 F3
Harrow Weald 40 E4
Harston Cambs 54 D5
Leics 77 F8
Harswell 96 E4
Hart 111 F7
Hartburn
Northumb 117 F6
Stockton 102 C2
Hart Common 86 D4
Hartest 56 D2
Hartfield 29 F5
Hartford Cambs 54 B3
Ches W 74 B3
Hartfordbridge 27 D5
Hartford End 42 C2
Hartforth 101 D6
Harthill Ches W 74 D2
N Lanark 120 C2
S Yorks 89 F5
Hart Hill 40 B4
Hartington 75 C8
Hartland 8 B4
Hartlebury 50 B3
Hartlepool 111 F8
Hartley Kent 18 B4
Kent 29 C7
Northumb 111 B6
W&F 100 D2
Hartley Westpall 26 D4
Hartley Wintney 27 D5
Hartlip 30 C2
Hartoft End 103 E5
Harton N Yorks 96 C3
Shrops 60 F4
T&W 111 C6
Hartpury 36 B4
Hartshead 88 B2
Hartshill 63 E7
Hartshorne 63 B7
Hartsop 99 C6
Hart Station 111 F7
Hartwell 53 D5
Hartwood 119 D8
Harvieston 126 F4
Harvington 51 E5
Harvington Cross 51 E5
Harwell 38 F4
Harwich 57 F6
Harwood Durham 109 F8
Gtr Man 86 C5
Harwood Dale 103 E7
Harworth 89 E7
Hasbury 62 F3
Hascombe 27 E7
Haselbech 52 B5
Haselbury Plucknett 12 C2
Haseley 51 C7
Haselor 51 D6
Hasfield 37 B5
Hasguard 44 E3
Haskayne 85 D4
Hasketon 57 D6
Hasland 76 C3
Haslemere 27 F7
Haslingden 87 B5
Haslingfield 54 D5
Haslington 74 D4
Hassall 74 D4
Hassall Green 74 D4
Hassell Street 30 E4
Hassendean 115 B8
Hassingham 69 D6
Hassocks 17 C6
Hassop 76 B2
Hastigrow 158 D4
Hastingleigh 30 E4
Hastings 18 E5
Hastingwood 41 D7
Hastoe 40 D2
Haswell 111 E6
Haswell Plough 111 E6
Hatch C Beds 54 E2
Hants 26 D4
Wilts 13 B7
Hatch Beauchamp 11 B8
Hatch End 40 E4
Hatchet Gate 14 D4
Hatch Green 11 C8
Hatching Green 40 C4
Hatchmere 74 B2
Hatcliffe 91 D6
Hatfield Hereford 49 D7
Herts 41 D5
S Yorks 89 D7
Worcs 50 D3
Hatfield Broad Oak 41 C8
Hatfield Garden Village 41 D5
Hatfield Heath 41 C8
Hatfield Hyde 41 C5
Hatfield Peverel 42 C3
Hatfield Woodhouse 89 D7
Hatford 38 E3
Hatherden 25 D8
Hatherleigh 9 D7
Hathern 63 B8
Hatherop 38 D1
Hathersage 88 F3
Hathershaw 87 D7
Hatherton Ches E 74 E3
Staffs 62 C3
Hatley St George 54 D3
Hatt 5 C8
Hattingley 26 F4
Hatton Aberds 153 E10
Derbys 63 B6
Lincs 78 B4
Shrops 60 E4
Warks 51 C7
Warr 86 F3
Hatton Castle 153 D7
Hattoncrook 141 B7
Hatton Heath 73 C8
Hatton of Fintray 141 C7
Haugh E Ayrs 112 B4
Gtr Man 87 C7
Lincs 79 B7
Haugham 91 F7
Haugh Head 117 B6
Haughley 56 C4
Haughley Green 56 C4
Haugh of Glass 152 E4
Haugh of Urr 106 C5
Haughs of Clinterty 141 C7
Haughton Notts 77 B6
Shrops 60 B3
Shrops 61 C5
Shrops 61 D7
Shrops 61 E6
Staffs 62 B2
Haughton Castle 110 B2
Haughton Green 87 E7
Haughton Moss 74 D2
Haultwick 41 B6
Haunn Argyll 146 G6
W Isles 148 G2
Haunton 63 C6
Hauxley 117 D8
Hauxton 54 D5
Havant 15 D8
Haven 49 D6
Haven Bank 78 D5
Haven Side 91 B5
Havenstreet 15 E6
Havercroft 88 C4
Haverfordwest
= *Hwlffordd* 44 D4
Haverhill 55 E7
Haverigg 92 B1
Havering-atte-Bower 41 E8
Haveringland 81 E7
Haversham 53 E6
Haverthwaite 99 F5
Haverton Hill 102 B2
Hawarden
= *Penarlâg* 73 C7
Hawcoat 92 B2
Hawen 46 E2
Hawes 100 F3
Hawes' Green 68 E5
Hawes Side 92 F3
Hawford 50 C3
Hawick 115 C8
Hawkchurch 11 D8
Hawkedon 55 D8
Hawkenbury Kent 18 B2
Kent 30 E2
Hawkeridge 24 D3
Hawkerland 11 F5
Hawkesbury S Glos 36 F4
Warks 63 F7
Hawkesbury Upton 36 F4
Hawkes End 63 F7
Hawk Green 87 F7
Hawkhill 117 C8
Hawkhurst 18 B4
Hawkinge 31 F6
Hawkley 15 B8
Hawkridge 21 F7
Hawkshead 99 E5
Hawkshead Hill 99 E5
Hawksland 119 F8
Hawkswick 94 B2
Hawksworth Notts 77 E7
W Yorks 94 E4
W Yorks 95 F5
Hawkwell 42 E4
Hawley Hants 27 D6
Kent 29 B6
Hawling 37 B7
Hawnby 102 F3
Haworth 94 F3
Hawstead 56 D2
Hawthorn Durham 111 E7
Rhondda 35 F5
Wilts 24 C3
Hawthorn Hill
Brack 27 B6
Lincs 78 D5
Hawthorpe 65 B7
Hawton 77 D7
Haxby 96 D2
Haxey 89 D8
Haydock 86 E3
Haydon 12 C4
Haydon Bridge 109 C8
Haydon Wick 37 F8
Haye 5 C8
Hayes London 28 C5
London 40 F4
Hayfield Derbys 87 F8
Fife 128 E4
Hay Green 66 C5
Hayhill 112 C4
Hayhillock 135 E5
Hayle 2 C4
Haynes 53 E8
Haynes Church End 53 E8
Hay-on-Wye
= *Y Gelli Gandryll* 48 E4
Hayscastle 44 C3
Hayscastle Cross 44 C4
Hayshead 135 E6
Hay Street 41 B6
Hayton Aberdeen 141 D8
Cumb 107 E8
Cumb 108 D5
E Yorks 96 E4
Notts 89 F8
Hayton's Bent 60 F5
Haytor Vale 7 B5
Haywards Heath 17 B7
Haywood 89 C6
Haywood Oaks 77 D6
Hazelbank 119 E8
Hazelbury Bryan 12 D5
Hazeley 26 D5
Hazel Grove 87 F7
Hazelhurst 87 D7
Hazelslade 62 C4
Hazel Street 18 B3
Hazelton 37 C7
Hazelton Walls 128 B5
Hazelwood 76 E3
Hazlemere 40 E1
Hazlerigg 110 B5
Hazlewood 94 D3
Hazon 117 D7
Heacham 80 D2
Headbourne Worthy 26 F2
Headbrook 48 D5
Headcorn 30 E2
Headingley 95 F5
Headington 39 D5
Headlam 101 C6
Headless Cross 50 C5
Headley Hants 26 C3
Hants 27 F6
Sur 28 D3
Head of Muir 127 F7
Headon 77 B7
Heads 119 E7
Heads Nook 108 D4
Heage 76 D3
Healaugh N Yorks 95 E7
N Yorks 101 E5
Heald Green 87 F6
Heale Devon 20 E5
Som 23 E8
Healey Gtr Man 87 C6
Northumb 110 D3
N Yorks 101 F6
Healing 91 C6
Heamoor 2 C3
Heanish 146 G3
Heanor 76 E4
Heanton Punchardon 20 F4
Heapham 90 F2
Hearthstane 114 B4
Heasley Mill 21 F6
Heast 149 G11
Heath Cardiff 22 B3
Derbys 76 C4
Heath and Reach 40 B2
Heathcote 75 C8
Heath End Hants 26 C3
Sur 27 E6
Warks 51 C7
Heather 63 C7
Heatherfield 149 D9
Heathfield Devon 7 B6
E Sus 18 C2
Som 11 B6
Heathhall 107 B6
Heath Hayes 62 C4
Heath Hill 61 C7
Heath House 23 E6
Heathrow Airport 27 B8
Heathstock 11 D7
Heathton 62 E2
Heath Town 62 E3
Heatley 86 F5
Heaton Lancs 92 C4
Staffs 75 C6
T&W 111 C5
W Yorks 94 F4
Heaton Moor 87 E6
Heaverham 29 D6
Heaviley 87 F7
Heavitree 10 E4
Hebburn 111 C6
Hebden 94 C3
Hebden Bridge 87 B7
Hebron Anglesey 82 C4
Carms 32 B2
Northumb 117 F7
Heck 114 F3
Heckfield 26 C5
Heckfield Green 57 B5
Heckfordbridge 43 B5
Heckington 78 E4
Heckmondwike 88 B3
Heddington 24 C4
Heddle 159 G4
Heddon-on-the-Wall 110 C4
Hedenham 69 E6
Hedge End 15 C5
Hedgerley 40 F2
Hedging 11 B8
Hedley on the Hill 110 D3
Hednesford 62 C4
Hedon 91 B5
Hedsor 40 F2
Hedworth 111 C6
Hegdon Hill 49 D7
Heggerscales 100 C3
Heglibister 160 H5
Heighington Darl 101 B7
Lincs 78 C3
Heights of Brae 151 E8
Heights of Kinlochewe 150 E3
Heilam 156 C7
Heiton 122 F3
Hele Devon 10 D4
Devon 20 E4
Helensburgh 145 E11
Helford 3 D6
Helford Passage 3 D6
Helhoughton 80 E4
Helions Bumpstead 55 E7
Hellaby 89 E6
Helland 5 B5
Hellesdon 68 C5
Hellidon 52 D3
Hellifield 93 D8
Hellingly 18 D2
Hellington 69 D6
Hellister 160 J5
Helm 117 E7
Helmdon 52 E3
Helmingham 57 D5
Helmington Row 110 F4
Helmsdale 157 H13
Helmshore 87 B5
Helmsley 102 F4
Helperby 95 C7
Helperthorpe 97 B5
Helpringham 78 E4
Helpston 65 D8
Helsby 73 B8
Helsey 79 B8
Helston 3 D5
Helstone 8 F2
Helton 99 B7
Helwith Bridge 93 C8
Hemblington 69 C6
Hemel Hempstead 40 D3
Hemingbrough 96 F2
Hemingby 78 B5
Hemingford Abbots 54 B3
Hemingford Grey 54 B3
Hemingstone 57 D5
Hemington Leics 63 B8
N Nhants 65 F7
Som 24 D2
Hemley 57 E6
Hemlington 102 C3
Hemp Green 57 C7
Hempholme 97 D6
Hempnall 68 E5
Hempnall Green 68 E5
Hempriggs House 158 F5
Hempstead Essex 55 F7
Medway 29 C8
Norf 69 B7
Norf 81 D7
Hempsted 37 C5
Hempton Norf 80 E5
Oxon 52 F2
Hemsby 69 C7
Hemswell 90 E3
Hemswell Cliff 90 F3
Hemsworth 88 C5
Hemyock 11 C6
Henbury Bristol 23 B7
Ches E 75 B5
Hendon London 41 F5
T&W 111 D7
Hendre 73 C5
Hendre-ddu 83 E8
Hendreforgan 34 F3
Hendy 33 D6
Heneglwys 82 D4
Hen-feddau fawr 45 F4
Henfield 17 C6
Henford 9 E5
Henghurst 19 B6
Hengoed Caerph 35 E5
Powys 48 D4
Shrops 73 F6
Hengrave 56 C2
Henham 41 B8
Heniarth 59 D8
Henlade 11 B7
Henley Shrops 49 B7
Som 23 F6
Suff 57 D5
W Sus 16 B2
Henley-in-Arden 51 C6
Henley-on-Thames 39 F7
Henley's Down 18 D4
Henllan Ceredig 46 E2
Denb 72 C4
Henllan Amgoed 32 B2
Henllys 35 E6
Henlow 54 F2
Hennock 10 F3
Henny Street 56 F2
Henryd 83 D7
Henry's Moat 32 B1
Hensall 89 B6
Henshaw 109 C7
Hensingham 98 C1
Henstead 69 F7
Henstridge 12 C5
Henstridge Ash 12 B5
Henstridge Marsh 12 B5
Henton Oxon 39 D7
Som 23 E6
Henwood 5 B7
Heogan 160 J6
Heol-las 33 E7
Heol Senni 34 B3
Heol-y-Cyw 34 F3
Hepburn 117 B6
Hepple 117 D5
Hepscott 117 F8
Heptonstall 87 B7
Hepworth Suff 56 B3
W Yorks 88 D2
Herbrandston 44 E3
Hereford 49 E7
Heriot 121 D6
Hermiston 120 B4
Hermitage
Borders 115 E8
Dorset 12 D4
W Berks 26 B3
W Sus 15 D8
Hermon Anglesey 82 E3
Carms 33 B7
Carms 46 F2
Pembs 45 F4
Herne 31 C5
Herne Bay 31 C5
Herner 9 B7
Hernhill 30 C4
Herodsfoot 5 C7
Herongate 42 E2
Heronsford 104 A5
Herriard 26 E4
Herringfleet 69 E7
Herringswell 55 B8
Hersden 31 C6
Hersham Corn 8 D4
Sur 28 C2
Herstmonceux 18 D3
Herston 159 J5
Hertford 41 C6
Hertford Heath 41 C6
Hertingfordbury 41 C6
Hesketh Bank 86 B2
Hesketh Lane 93 E6
Hesket Newmarket 108 F3
Heskin Green 86 C3
Hesleden 111 F7
Hesleyside 116 F4
Heslington 96 D2
Hessay 95 D8
Hessenford 5 D8
Hessett 56 C3
Hessle 90 B4
Hest Bank 92 C4
Heston 28 B2
Hestwall 159 G3
Heswall 85 F3
Hethe 39 B5
Hethersett 68 D4
Hethersgill 108 C4
Hethpool 116 B4
Hett 111 F5
Hetton 94 D2
Hetton-le-Hole 111 E6
Hetton Steads 123 F6
Heugh 110 B3
Heugh-head 140 C2
Heveningham 57 B7
Hever 29 E5
Heversham 99 F6
Hevingham 81 E7
Hewas Water 3 B8
Hewelsfield 36 D2
Hewish N Som 23 C6
Hewish *continued*
Som 12 D2
Heworth 96 D2
Hexham 110 C2
Hextable 29 B6
Hexton 54 F2
Hexworthy 6 B4
Hey 93 E8
Heybridge Essex 42 D4
Essex 42 E2
Heybridge Basin 42 D4
Heybrook Bay 6 E3
Heydon Cambs 54 E5
Norf 81 E7
Heydour 78 F3
Heyford Park Oxon 39 B5
Heylipol 146 G2
Heylor 160 E4
Heysham 92 C4
Heyshott 16 C2
Heyside 87 D7
Heytesbury 24 E4
Heythrop 38 B3
Heywood Gtr Man 87 C6
Wilts 24 D3
Hibaldstow 90 D3
Hickleton 89 D5
Hickling Norf 69 B7
Notts 64 B3
Hickling Green 69 B7
Hickling Heath 69 B7
Hickstead 17 B6
Hidcote Boyce 51 E6
High Ackworth 88 C5
Higham Derbys 76 D3
Kent 29 B8
Lancs 93 F8
Suff 55 C8
Suff 56 F4
Higham Dykes 110 B4
Higham Ferrers 53 C7
Higham Gobion 54 F2
Higham on the Hill 63 E7
Highampton 9 D6
Higham Wood 29 E6
High Angerton 117 F6
High Bankhill 109 E5
High Barnes 111 D6
High Beach 41 E7
High Bentham 93 C6
High Bickington 9 B8
High Birkwith 93 B7
High Blantyre 119 D6
High Bonnybridge 119 B8
High Bradfield 88 E3
High Bray 21 F5
Highbridge Highld 136 F4
Som 22 E5
Highbrook 28 F4
High Brooms 29 E6
High Bullen 9 B7
Highburton 88 C2
Highbury 23 E8
High Buston 117 D8
High Callerton 110 B4
High Catton 96 D3
Highclere 26 C2
Highcliffe 14 E3
High Cogges 38 D3
High Coniscliffe 101 C7
High Cross Hants 15 B8
Herts 41 C6
High Easter 42 C2
High Eggborough 89 B6
High Ellington 101 F6
Higher Ansty 13 D5
Higher Ashton 10 F3
Higher Ballam 92 F3
Higher Bartle 92 F5
Higher Boscaswell 2 C2
Higher Burwardsley 74 D2
High Ercall 61 C5
Higher Clovelly 8 B5
Higher End 86 D3
Higher Kinnerton 73 C7
Higher Penwortham 86 B3
Higher Town 2 E4
Higher Walreddon 6 B2
Higher Walton
Lancs 86 B3
Warr 86 F3
Higher Wheelton 86 B4
Higher Whitley 86 F4
Higher Wincham 74 B3
Higher Wych 73 E8
High Etherley 101 B6
Highfield E Yorks 96 F3
Gtr Man 86 D5
N Ayrs 118 D3
Oxon 39 B5
S Yorks 88 F4
T&W 110 D4
Highfields Cambs 54 D4
Northumb 123 D5
High Garrett 42 B3
Highgate 41 F5
High Grange 110 F4
High Green Norf 68 D4
S Yorks 88 E4
Worcs 50 E3
High Halden 19 B5
High Halstow 29 B8
High Ham 23 F6
High Harrington 98 B2
High Hatton 61 B6
High Hawsker 103 D7
High Hesket 108 E4
High Hesleden 111 F7
High Hoyland 88 C3
High Hunsley 97 F5
High Hurstwood 17 B8
High Hutton 96 C3
High Ireby 108 F2
High Kelling 81 C7
High Kilburn 95 B8
High Lands 101 B6
Highlane Ches E 75 C5
Derbys 88 F5
High Lane Gtr Man 87 F7
Worcs 49 C8
High Laver 41 D8
Highlaws 107 E8
Highleadon 36 B4
High Legh 86 F5
Highleigh 16 E2
High Leven 102 C2
Highley 61 F7
High Littleton 23 D8
High Lorton 98 B3
High Marishes 96 B4
High Marnham 77 B8
High Melton 89 D6
High Mickley 110 C3
High Mindork 105 D7
Highmoor Cross 39 F7
Highmoor Hill 36 F1
Highnam 36 C4
Highnam Green 36 B4
High Newton 99 F6
High Newton-by-the-Sea 117 B8
High Nibthwaite 98 F4
High Offley 61 B7
High Ongar 42 D1
High Onn 62 C2
High Roding 42 C2
High Row 108 F3
High Salvington 16 D5
High Sellafield 98 D2
High Shaw 100 E3
High Spen 110 D4
Highsted 30 C3
High Stoop 110 E4
High Street Corn 4 D4
Kent 18 B4
Suff 56 E2
Suff 57 B8
Suff 57 D8
Highstreet Green 55 F8
High Street Green 56 D4
Hightae 107 B7
High Throston 111 F7
Hightown Ches E 75 C5
Mers 85 D4
Hightown Green 56 D3
High Toynton 79 C5
High Trewhitt 117 D6
High Valleyfield 128 F2
Highway 24 B5
Highweek 7 B6
High Westwood 110 D4
Highworth 38 E2
High Wray 99 E5
High Wych 41 C7
High Wycombe 40 E1
Hilborough 67 D8
Hilcote 76 D4
Hilcott 25 D6
Hildenborough 29 E6
Hilden Park 29 E6
Hildersham 55 E6
Hilderstone 75 F6
Hilderthorpe 97 C7
Hilfield 12 D4
Hilgay 67 E6
Hill Pembs 32 D2
S Glos 36 E3
W Mid 62 E5
Hillam 89 B6
Hillbeck 100 C2
Hillborough 31 C6
Hillbrae Aberds 141 B6
Aberds 152 D6
Hill Brow 15 B8
Hillbutts 13 D7
Hillcliffane 76 E2
Hillcommon 11 B6
Hill Dale 86 C2
Hill Dyke 79 E6
Hillend 128 F3
Hill End Durham 110 F3
Fife 128 E2
N Yorks 94 D3
Hillerton 10 E2
Hillesden 39 B6
Hillesley 36 F4
Hillfarance 11 B6
Hillhead Aberds 152 E5
Devon 7 D7
S Ayrs 112 C4
Hill Head Hants 15 D6
Northumb 110 C2
Hillhead of Auchentumb 153 C9
Hillhead of Cocklaw 153 D10
Hillhouse 121 D8
Hilliclay 158 D3
Hillingdon 40 F3
Hillington Glasgow 118 C5
Norf 80 E3
Hillmorton 52 B3
Hill Mountain 44 E4
Hillockhead
Aberds 140 C3
Aberds 140 D2
Hill of Beath 128 E3
Hill of Fearn 151 D11
Hill of Mountblairy 153 C6
Hill Ridware 62 C4
Hillside Aberds 141 E8
Angus 135 C7
Mers 85 C4
Orkney 159 J5
Shetland 160 G6
Hillswick 160 F4
Hill Top Durham 100 B4
Hants 14 D5
W Mid 62 E3
W Yorks 88 C4
Hill View 13 E7
Hillway 15 F7
Hillwell 160 M5
Hilmarton 24 B5
Hilperton 24 D3
Hilsea 15 D7
Hilston 97 F8
Hilton Aberds 153 E9
Cambs 54 C3
Derbys 76 F2
Dorset 13 D5
Durham 101 B6
Highld 151 C10
Shrops 61 E7
Stockton 102 C2
W&F 100 B2
Hilton of Cadboll 151 D11
Himbleton 50 D4
Himley 62 E2
Hincaster 99 F7
Hinckley 63 F8
Hinderclay 56 B4
Hinderton 73 B7
Hinderwell 103 C5
Hindford 73 F7
Hindhead 27 F6
Hindley 86 D4
Hindley Green 86 D4
Hindlip 50 D3
Hindolveston 81 E6
Hindon 24 F4
Hindringham 81 D5
Hingham 68 D3
Hinstock 61 B6
Hintlesham 56 E4
Hinton Hants 14 E3
Hereford 48 F5
S Glos 24 B2
Shrops 60 D4
W Nhants 52 D3
Hinton Ampner 15 B6
Hinton Blewett 23 D7
Hinton Charterhouse 24 D2
Hinton-in-the-Hedges 52 F3
Hinton Martell 13 D8
Hinton on the Green 50 E5
Hinton Parva 38 F2
Hinton St George 12 C2
Hinton St Mary 13 C5
Hinton Waldrist 38 E3
Hints Shrops 49 B8
Staffs 63 D5
Hinwick 53 C7
Hinxhill 30 E4
Hinxton 55 E5
Hinxworth 54 E3
Hipperholme 88 B2
Hipswell 101 E6
Hirael 83 D5
Hiraeth 32 B2
Hirn 141 D6
Hirnant 59 B7
Hirst N Lanark 119 C8
Northumb 117 F8
Hirst Courtney 89 B7
Hirwaen 72 C5
Hirwaun 34 D3
Hiscott 9 B7
Histon 54 C5
Hitcham 56 D3
Hitchin 40 B4
Hither Green 28 B4
Hittisleigh 10 E2
Hive 96 F4
Hixon 62 B4
Hoaden 31 D6
Hoaldalbert 35 B7
Hoar Cross 62 B5
Hoarwithy 36 B2
Hoath 31 C6
Hobarris 48 B5
Hobbister 159 H4
Hobkirk 115 C8
Hobson 110 D4
Hoby 64 C3
Hockering 68 C3
Hockerton 77 D7
Hockley 42 E4
Hockley Heath 51 B6
Hockliffe 40 B2
Hockwold cum Wilton 67 F7
Hockworthy 10 C5
Hoddesdon 41 D6
Hoddlesden 86 B5
Hoddomcross 107 B8
Hoddom Mains 107 B8
Hodgeston 32 E1
Hodley 59 E8
Hodnet 61 B6
Hodthorpe 76 B5
Hoe Hants 15 C6
Norf 68 C2
Hoe Gate 15 C7
Hoff 100 C1
Hoggard's Green 56 D2
Hoggeston 39 B8
Hogha Gearraidh 148 A2
Hoghton 86 B4
Hognaston 76 D2
Hog Patch 27 E6
Hogsthorpe 79 B8
Holbeach 66 B3
Holbeach Bank 66 B3
Holbeach Clough 66 B3
Holbeach Drove 66 C3
Holbeach Hurn 66 B3
Holbeach St Johns 66 C3
Holbeach St Marks 79 F6
Holbeach St Matthew 79 F7
Holbeck Notts 76 B5
W Yorks 95 F5
Holbeck Woodhouse 76 B5
Holberrow Green 50 D5
Holbeton 6 D4
Holborn 41 F6
Holbrook Derbys 76 E3
Suff 57 F5
S Yorks 88 F5
Holburn 123 F6
Holbury 14 D5
Holcombe Devon 7 B7
Som 23 E8
Holcombe Rogus 11 C5
Holcot 53 C5
Holden 93 E7
Holdenby 52 C4
Holdenhurst 14 E2
Holdgate 61 F5
Holdingham 78 E3
Holditch 11 D8
Holefield 122 F4
Holehouses 74 B4
Hole-in-the-Wall 36 B3
Holemoor 9 D6
Holestane 113 E8
Holford 22 E3
Holgate 95 D8
Holker 92 B3
Holkham 80 C4
Hollacombe 9 D5
Holland Orkney 159 C5
Orkney 159 F7
Holland Fen 78 E5
Holland-on-Sea 43 C8
Hollandstoun 159 C8
Hollee 108 C2
Hollesley 57 E7
Hollicombe 7 C6
Hollingbourne 30 D2
Hollington Derbys 76 F2
E Sus 18 D4
Staffs 75 F7
Hollington Grove 76 F2
Hollingworth 87 E8
Hollins 87 D6
Hollinsclough 75 C7
Hollins Green 86 E4
Hollins Lane 92 D4
Hollinwood
Gtr Man 87 D7
Shrops 74 F2
Hollocombe 9 C8
Holloway 76 D3
Hollowell 52 B4
Hollow Meadows 88 F3
Hollybush Caerph 35 D5
E Ayrs 112 C3
Worcs 50 F2
Holly End 66 D4
Holly Green 50 E3
Hollym 91 B7
Hollywood 51 B5
Holmbridge 88 D2
Holmbury St Mary 28 E2
Holmbush 4 D5
Holmcroft 62 B3
Holme Cambs 65 F8
Notts 77 D8
N Yorks 102 F1
W&F 92 B5
W Yorks 88 D2
Holme Chapel 87 B6
Holme Green 95 E8
Holme Hale 67 D8
Holme Lacy 49 F7
Holme Marsh 48 D5
Holme next the Sea 80 C3
Holme-on-Spalding-Moor 96 F4
Holme on the Wolds 97 E5
Holme Pierrepont 77 F6
Holmer 49 E7
Holmer Green 40 E2
Holme St Cuthbert 107 E8
Holmes Chapel 74 C4
Holmesfield 76 B3
Holmeswood 86 C2
Holmewood 76 C4
Holme Wood 94 F4
Holmfirth 88 D2
Holmhead
Dumfries 113 F7
E Ayrs 113 B5
Holmisdale 148 D6
Holmpton 91 B7
Holmrook 98 E2
Holmsgarth 160 J6
Holmwrangle 108 E5
Holne 6 C5
Holnest 12 D4
Holsworthy 8 D5
Holsworthy Beacon 9 D5
Holt Dorset 13 D8
Norf 81 D6
Wilts 24 C3
Worcs 50 C3
Wrex 73 D8
Holtby 96 D2
Holt End Hants 26 F4
Worcs 51 C5
Holt Fleet 50 C3
Holt Heath 50 C3
Holton Oxon 39 D6
Som 12 B4
Suff 57 B7
Holton cum Beckering 90 F5
Holton Heath 13 E7
Holton le Clay 91 D6
Holton le Moor 90 E4
Holton St Mary 56 F4
Holt Park 95 E5
Holwell Dorset 12 C5
Herts 54 F2
Leics 64 B4
Oxon 38 D2
Holwick 100 B4
Holworth 13 F5
Holybourne 26 E5
Holy Cross 50 B4
Holyhead
= *Caergybi* 82 C2
Holy Island 123 E7
Holymoorside 76 C3
Holyport 27 B6
Holystone 117 D5
Holytown 119 C7
Holywell Cambs 54 B4
Corn 4 D2
Dorset 12 D3
E Sus 18 F2
Northumb 111 B6
Holywell
= *Treffynnon* 73 B5
Holywell Green 87 C8
Holywell Lake 11 B6
Holywell Row 55 B8
Holywood 114 F2
Homer 61 D6
Homersfield 69 F5
Hom Green 36 B2
Homington 14 B2
Honeyborough 44 E4
Honeybourne 51 E6
Honeychurch 9 D8
Honey Hill 30 C5
Honey Street 25 C6
Honey Tye 56 F3
Honiley 51 B7
Honing 69 B6
Honingham 68 C4
Honington Lincs 78 E2
Suff 56 B3
Warks 51 E7
Honiton 11 D6
Honley 88 C2
Hood Green 88 D4
Hooe E Sus 18 E3
Plym 6 D3

Hoo Common .... 18 D3
Hoo Green .... 86 F5
Hook E Yorks .... 89 B8
  Hants .... 26 D5
  London .... 28 C2
  Pembs .... 44 D4
  Wilts .... 37 F7
Hooke .... 12 E3
Hookgate .... 74 F4
Hook Green Kent . 18 B3
  Kent .... 29 C7
Hook Norton .... 51 F8
Hookway .... 10 E3
Hookwood .... 28 E3
Hoole .... 73 C8
Hooley .... 28 D3
Hoop .... 36 D2
Hoo St Werburgh . 29 B8
Hooton .... 73 B7
Hooton Levitt .... 89 E6
Hooton Pagnell .... 89 D5
Hooton Roberts .... 89 E5
Hope Derbys .... 88 F2
  Devon. .... 6 F4
  Highld .... 156 B7
  Powys .... 60 D2
  Shrops .... 60 D3
  Staffs .... 74 E5
Hope = Yr Hôb . 73 D7
Hope Bagot .... 49 B7
Hope Bowdler .... 60 E4
Hope End Green . 42 B1
Hope Green .... 87 F7
Hopeman .... 152 B1
Hope Mansell .... 36 C3
Hopesay .... 60 F3
Hope's Green .... 42 F3
Hope under
  Dinmore .... 49 D7
Hopley's Green .... 48 D5
Hopperton .... 95 D7
Hop Pole .... 65 C8
Hopstone .... 61 E7
Hopton Shrops .... 60 B3
  Shrops .... 61 B5
  Staffs .... 62 B3
  Suff .... 56 B3
Hopton Cangeford . 60 F5
Hopton Castle .... 49 B5
Hoptonheath .... 49 B5
Hopton on Sea .... 69 D8
Hopton Wafers .... 49 B8
Hopwas .... 63 D5
Hopwood Gtr Man . 87 D6
  Worcs .... 50 B5
Horam .... 18 D2
Horbling .... 78 F4
Horbury .... 88 C3
Horden .... 111 E7
Horderley .... 60 F4
Hordle .... 14 E3
Hordley .... 73 F7
Horeb Carms .... 33 B6
  Carms .... 33 D5
  Ceredig .... 46 E2
Horfield .... 23 B8
Horham .... 57 B6
Horkesley Heath. . 43 B5
Horkstow .... 90 C3
Horley Oxon. .... 52 E2
  Sur .... 28 E3
Hornblotton Green 23 F7
Hornby Lancs .... 93 C5
  N Yorks .... 101 E7
  N Yorks .... 102 D1
Horncastle .... 79 C5
Hornchurch .... 41 F8
Horncliffe .... 122 E5
Horndean Borders. 122 E4
  Hants .... 15 C8
Horndon .... 6 B3
Horndon on the
  Hill .... 42 F2
Horne .... 28 E4
Hornichaugh .... 134 C4
Horning .... 69 C6
Horninghold .... 64 E5
Horninglow .... 63 B6
Horningsea .... 55 C5
Horningsham .... 24 E3
Horningtoft .... 80 E5
Hornsby .... 108 D5
Horns Corner .... 18 C4
Horns Cross Devon . 8 B5
  E Sus .... 18 C5
Hornsea .... 97 E8
Hornsea Bridge .... 97 E8
Hornsey .... 41 F6
Hornton .... 51 E8
Horrabridge .... 6 C3
Horringer .... 56 C2
Horringford .... 15 F6
Horsebridge Devon. . 6 B2
  Hants .... 25 F8
Horse Bridge .... 75 D6
Horsebrook .... 62 C2
Horsehay .... 61 D6
Horseheath .... 55 E7
Horsehouse .... 101 F5
Horsell .... 27 D7
Horseman's Green 73 E8
Horseway .... 66 F4
Horsey .... 69 B7
Horsford .... 68 C4
Horsforth .... 94 F5
Horsham Worcs .... 50 D2
  W Sus .... 28 F2
Horsham St Faith . 68 C5
Horsington Lincs . 78 C4
  Som .... 12 B5
Horsley Derbys .... 76 E3
  Glos. .... 37 E5
  Northumb. .... 110 C3
  Northumb. .... 116 E4
Horsley Cross .... 43 B7
Horsleycross
  Street .... 43 B7
Horsleyhill .... 115 C8
Horsleyhope .... 110 E3
Horsley
  Woodhouse.... 76 E3
Horsmonden.... 18 B4
Horspath .... 39 D5
Horstead.... 69 C5
Horsted Keynes . 17 B7

Horton Bucks .... 40 C2
  Dorset .... 13 D8
  Lancs .... 93 D8
  S Glos .... 36 F4
  Shrops .... 60 B4
  Som .... 11 C8
  Staffs .... 75 D6
  Swansea .... 33 F5
  Wilts .... 25 C5
  Windsor .... 27 B8
  W Nhants .... 53 D6
Horton-cum-
  Studley .... 39 C5
Horton Green .... 73 E8
Horton Heath .... 15 C5
Horton in
  Ribblesdale . 93 B8
  Northumb. .... 117 B5
Horton Kirby .... 29 C6
Hortonlane .... 60 C4
Horwich .... 86 C4
Horwich End .... 87 F8
Horwood .... 9 B7
Hose .... 64 B4
Hoselaw .... 122 F4
Hoses .... 98 E4
Hosh .... 127 B7
Hosta .... 148 A2
Hoswick .... 160 L6
Hotham .... 96 F4
Hothfield .... 30 E3
Hoton .... 64 B2
Houbie .... 160 D8
Houdston .... 112 E1
Hough Ches E .... 74 D4
  Ches E .... 75 B5
Hougham .... 77 E8
Hough Green .... 86 F2
Hough-on-the-
  Hill .... 78 E2
Houghton Cambs .... 54 B3
  Cumb .... 108 D4
  Hants .... 25 F8
  Pembs .... 44 E4
  W Sus .... 16 C4
Houghton
  Conquest .... 53 E8
Houghton Green
  E Sus .... 19 C6
  Warr. .... 86 E4
Houghton-le-
  Side .... 101 B7
Houghton-le-
  Spring .... 111 E6
Houghton on the
  Hill .... 64 D3
Houghton Regis . 40 B3
Houghton St Giles. 80 E5
Houlland Shetland . 160 H6
Houll .... 15 D5
Hound Green .... 26 D5
Houndslow .... 122 E2
Houndwood .... 122 C4
Hounslow .... 28 B2
Hounslow Green . 42 C2
Housay .... 160 F8
House of Daviot .151 G10
House of
  Glenmuick .... 140 E2
Housetter .... 160 E5
Houss .... 160 K5
Houston .... 118 C4
Houstry .... 158 G3
Houton .... 159 H4
Hoveringham .... 77 E6
Hoveton .... 69 C6
Hovingham .... 96 B2
How .... 108 D5
Howbrook .... 88 E4
How Caple .... 49 F8
Howden Borders . 116 B2
  E Yorks .... 89 B8
Howden-le-Wear 110 F4
Howe Highld .... 158 D5
  Norf .... 69 D5
  N Yorks .... 101 F8
Howe Bridge .... 86 D4
Howe Green .... 42 D3
Howell .... 78 E4
Howe of Teuchar .153 D7
Howe Street Essex . 42 C2
  Essex .... 55 F7
Howey .... 48 D2
Howgate .... 120 D5
How Green .... 29 E5
Howick .... 117 C8
Howle Durham .... 101 B5
  Telford .... 61 B6
Howlett End .... 55 F6
Howley .... 11 D7
Hownam .... 116 C3
Hownam Mains .. 116 B3
Howpasley .... 115 D6
Howsham N Lincs . 90 D4
  N Yorks .... 96 C3
Howslack .... 114 D3
Howtel .... 122 F4
Howton .... 35 B8
Howtown .... 99 C6
Howwood .... 118 C3
Hoxne .... 57 B5
Hoy .... 159 H3
Hoylake .... 85 F3
Hoyland .... 88 D4
Hoylandswaine .. 88 D3
Hubberholme .... 94 B2
Hubbert's Bridge . 79 E5
Huby N Yorks .... 95 C8
  N Yorks .... 95 E5
Hucclecote .... 37 C5
Hucking .... 30 D2
Hucknall .... 76 E5
Huddersfield .... 88 C2
Huddington .... 50 D4
Hudswell .... 101 D6
Huggate .... 96 D4
Hugglescote .... 63 C8
Hughenden Valley . 40 E1
Hughley .... 61 E5
Hugh Town .... 2 E4
Huish Devon .... 9 C7
  Wilts .... 25 C6
Huish
  Champflower... 11 B5
Huish Episcopi .... 12 B2

Huisinis .... 154 F4
Hulcott .... 40 C1
Hulland .... 76 E2
Hulland Ward .... 76 E2
Hullavington .... 37 F5
Hullbridge .... 42 E4
Hulme .... 87 E6
Hulme End .... 75 D8
Hulme Walfield.. 74 C5
Hulverstone .... 14 F4
Hulver Street .... 69 F7
Humber .... 49 D7
Humber Bridge... 90 B4
Humberston .... 91 D7
Humbie .... 121 C7
Humbleton E Yorks . 97 F8
  Northumb. .... 117 B5
Humby .... 78 F3
Hume .... 122 E3
Humshaugh .... 110 B2
Huna .... 158 C5
Huncoat .... 93 F7
Huncote .... 64 E2
Hundalee .... 116 C2
Hunderthwaite .. 100 B4
Hundleby .... 79 C6
Hundle Houses .... 79 D5
Hundleton .... 44 E4
Hundon .... 55 E8
Hundred Acres .... 15 C6
Hundred End .... 86 B2
Hundred House .. 48 D3
Hungarton .... 64 D3
Hungerford Hants . 14 C2
  W Berks. .... 25 C8
Hungerford
  Newtown .... 25 B8
Hungerton .... 65 B5
Hunglader .... 149 A8
Hunmanby .... 97 B6
Hunmanby Moor . 97 B7
Hunningham .... 51 C8
Hunny Hill .... 15 F5
Hunsdon .... 41 C7
Hunsingore .... 95 D7
Hunslet .... 95 F6
Hunsonby .... 109 F5
Hunspow .... 158 C4
Hunstanton .... 80 C2
Hunstanworth. 110 E2
Hunsterson .... 74 E3
Hunston Suff. .... 56 C3
  W Sus .... 16 D2
Hunstrete .... 23 C8
Hunt End .... 50 C5
Hunter's Quay . 145 F10
Huntham Lodge . 134 B4
Huntingdon .... 54 B3
Huntingfield .... 57 B7
Huntingford .... 24 F2
Huntington E Loth . 121 B7
  Hereford .... 48 D4
  Staffs .... 62 C3
  York .... 96 D2
Huntingtower .... 128 B2
Huntley .... 36 C4
Huntly .... 152 E5
Huntlywood .... 122 E2
Hunton Kent .... 29 E8
  N Yorks. .... 101 E6
Hunt's Corner .... 68 F3
Hunt's Cross .... 86 F2
Huntsham .... 10 B5
Huntspill .... 22 E5
Huntworth .... 22 F5
Hunwick .... 110 F4
Hunworth .... 81 D6
Hurdsfield .... 75 B6
Hurley Warks .... 63 E6
  Windsor .... 39 F8
Hurlford .... 118 F4
Hurliness .... 159 K3
Hurn .... 14 E2
Hurn's End .... 79 E7
Hursley .... 14 B5
Hurst N Yorks .... 101 D5
  Som .... 12 C2
  Wokingham .... 27 B5
Hurstbourne
  Priors .... 26 E2
Hurstbourne
  Tarrant .... 25 D8
Hurst Green E Sus . 18 C4
  Lancs .... 93 F6
Hurstpierpoint .... 17 C6
Hurst Wickham .... 17 C6
Hurstwood .... 93 F8
Hurtmore .... 27 E7
Hurworth Place .... 101 D7
Hury .... 100 C4
Husabost .... 148 C7
Husbands
  Bosworth... 64 F3
Husborne Crawley. 53 F7
Husthwaite .... 95 B8
Hutchwns.... 21 B7
Huthwaite .... 76 D4
Huttoft .... 79 B8
Hutton Borders .... 122 D5
  Essex .... 42 E2
  E Yorks .... 97 D6
  Lancs .... 86 B2
  N Som .... 22 D5
  W&F .... 99 B6
Hutton Buscel .... 103 F7
Hutton Conyers .... 95 B6
Hutton Cranswick . 97 D6
Hutton End .... 108 F4
Hutton Gate .... 102 C3
Hutton Henry .... 111 F7
Hutton-le-Hole . 103 E5
Hutton Magna .... 101 C6
Hutton Roof W&F . 93 B5
  W&F .... 100 F1
Hutton Rudby .... 102 D2
Hutton Sessay .... 95 B7
Hutton Village .... 102 C3
Hutton Wandesley. 95 D8
Huxley .... 74 C2
Huxter Shetland .... 160 G7
  Shetland .... 160 H5
Huxton.... 122 C4
Huyton .... 86 E2
Hwlffordd
  = Haverfordwest.. 44 D4
Hycemoor .... 98 F2
Hyde Glos... 37 D5
  Gtr Man... 87 E7
  Hants .... 14 C2

Hyde Heath .... 40 D2
Hyde Park .... 89 D6
Hydestile .... 27 E7
Hylton Castle .... 111 D6
Hyndford Bridge . 120 E2
Hynish .... 146 H2
Hyssington .... 60 E3
Hythe Hants. .... 14 D5
  Kent .... 19 B8
Hythe End .... 27 B8
Hythie .... 153 C10

**I**

Ibberton .... 13 D5
Ible .... 76 D2
Ibsley .... 14 C2
Ibstock .... 63 C8
Ibstone .... 39 E7
Ibthorpe .... 25 D8
Ibworth .... 26 D3
Ichrachan .... 125 B6
Ickburgh .... 67 E8
Ickenham .... 40 F3
Ickford .... 39 D6
Ickham .... 31 D6
Ickleford .... 54 F2
Icklesham .... 19 D5
Ickleton .... 55 E5
Icklingham .... 55 B8
Ickwell Green .... 54 E2
Icomb .... 38 B2
Idbury .... 38 C2
Ide .... 10 E3
Ideford .... 7 B6
Ide Hill .... 29 D5
Iden .... 19 C6
Iden Green Kent .... 18 B4
  Kent .... 18 B5
Idle .... 94 F4
Idlicote .... 51 E7
Idmiston .... 25 F6
Idole .... 33 C5
Idridgehay .... 76 E2
Idrigill .... 149 B8
Idstone .... 38 F2
Idvies .... 135 E5
Iffley .... 39 D5
Ifield .... 28 F3
Ifold .... 27 F8
Iford .... 17 D8
Ifton Heath .... 73 F7
Ightfield .... 74 F3
Ightham .... 29 D6
Iken .... 57 D8
Ilam .... 75 D8
Ilchester .... 12 B3
Ilderton .... 117 B6
Ilford .... 41 F7
Ilfracombe .... 20 E4
Ilkeston .... 76 E4
Ilketshall St
  Andrew .... 69 F6
Ilketshall St
  Lawrence .... 69 F6
Ilketshall St
  Margaret .... 69 F6
Ilkley .... 94 E4
Illey .... 62 F3
Illingworth .... 87 B8
Illogan .... 3 B5
Illston on the Hill . 64 E4
Ilmer .... 39 D7
Ilmington .... 51 E7
Ilminster .... 11 C8
Ilsington .... 7 B5
Ilston .... 33 E6
Ilton N Yorks .... 94 B4
  Som .... 11 C8
Imachar .... 143 D9
Imeraval .... 142 D4
Immingham .... 91 C5
Impington .... 54 C5
Ince .... 73 B8
Ince Blundell .... 85 D4
Ince in Makerfield . 86 D3
Inchbare .... 135 C6
Inchberry .... 152 C3
Inchbraoch .... 135 D7
Incheril .... 150 E3
Inchgrundle .... 134 B4
Inchina .... 150 B2
Inchinnan .... 118 C4
Inchkinloch .... 157 E8
Inchlaggan .... 136 D4
Inchlumpie .... 151 D8
Inchmore .... 150 G6
Inchnacardoch
  Hotel .... 137 C6
Inchnadamph .... 156 G5
Inch of Arnhall .. 135 B6
Inchree .... 130 C4
Inchture .... 128 B4
Indian Queens .. 4 D4
Inerval .... 142 D4
Ingatestone .... 42 E2
Ingbirchworth... 88 D3
Ingestre .... 62 B3
Ingham Lincs .... 90 F3
  Norf .... 69 B6
  Suff .... 56 B2
Ingham Corner .... 69 B6
Ingleborough .... 66 C4
Ingleby Derbys .... 63 B7
  Lincs... 77 B8
Ingleby Arncliffe .102 D2
Ingleby Barwick .102 C2
Ingleby
  Greenhow .... 102 D3
Inglemire .... 97 F6
Inglesbatch .... 24 C2
Ingleton Durham . 101 B6
  N Yorks. .... 93 B6
Inglewhite .... 92 E5
Ingliston .... 120 B4
Ingoe .... 110 B3
Ingol .... 92 F5
Ingoldisthorpe .... 80 D2
Ingoldmells .... 79 C8
Ingoldsby .... 78 F3
Ingon .... 51 D7
Ingram .... 117 C6
Ingrow .... 94 F3
Ings .... 99 E6
Ingst .... 36 F2

Ingworth .... 81 E7
Inham's End .... 66 E2
Inkberrow .... 50 D5
Inkpen .... 25 C8
Inkstack .... 158 C4
Inn .... 99 D6
Innellan .... 145 F10
Innerleithen .... 121 F6
Innerleven .... 129 D5
Innermessan .... 104 C4
Innerwick E Loth . 122 B3
  Perth .... 132 E2
Innis Chonain .... 125 C7
Insch .... 140 B5
Insh .... 138 D4
Inshore .... 156 C6
Inskip .... 92 F4
Instoneville .... 89 C6
Instow .... 20 F3
Intake .... 89 D6
Inver Aberds .... 139 E8
  Highld .... 151 C11
  Perth .... 133 E7
Inverailort .... 147 C10
Inveraldie .... 134 F4
Inverallign .... 149 C13
Inverallochy .... 153 B10
Inveran .... 151 B8
Inveraray .... 125 E6
Inverarish .... 149 E10
Inverarity .... 134 E4
Inverarnan .... 126 C2
Inverasdale .... 155 J13
Inverbeg .... 126 E2
Inverbervie .... 135 B8
Inverboyndie .... 153 B6
Invercassley .... 156 J7
Invercauld House .139 E7
Inverchaolain .... 145 F9
Invercharnan .... 131 E5
Inverchoran .... 150 F5
Invercreran .... 130 E4
Inverdruie .... 138 C5
Inverebrie .... 153 E9
Invereck .... 145 E10
Inverernan
  House .... 140 C2
Invereshie House .138 D4
Inveresk .... 121 B6
Inverey .... 139 F6
Inverfarigaig .... 137 B8
Invergarry .... 137 D6
Invergelder .... 139 E8
Invergeldie .... 127 B6
Invergordon .... 151 E10
Invergowrie .... 134 F3
Inverguseran .... 149 H12
Inverhadden .... 132 D3
Inverharroch .... 152 E3
Inverherive .... 126 B2
Inverie .... 147 B10
Inverinan .... 125 C5
Inverinate .... 136 B2
Inverkeilor .... 135 E6
Inverkeithing .... 128 F3
Inverkeithny .... 153 D6
Inverkip .... 118 B2
Inverkirkaig .... 156 H3
Inverlael .... 150 C4
Inverlochlarig .... 126 C3
Inverlochy Argyll . 125 C7
  Highld .... 131 B5
Inverlussa .... 144 E5
Inver Mallie .... 136 F4
Invermark Lodge . 140 F3
Invermoidart .... 147 D9
Invermoriston .... 137 C7
Invernaver .... 157 C10
Inverneill .... 145 E7
Inverness .... 151 G9
Invernettie .... 153 D11
Invernoaden .... 125 F7
Inveroran Hotel . 131 E6
Inverpolly Lodge .156 H3
Inverquharity .... 134 D4
Inverquhomery .153 D10
Inverroy .... 137 F5
Inversanda .... 130 D3
Invershiel .... 136 C2
Invershin .... 151 B8
Inversnaid Hotel. 126 D2
Inveruglas .... 126 D2
Inveruglass .... 138 D4
Inverurie .... 141 B6
Invervar .... 132 E3
Inverythan .... 153 D7
Inwardleigh .... 9 E7
Inworth .... 42 C4
Iochdar .... 148 D2
Iping .... 16 B2
Ipplepen .... 7 C6
Ipsden .... 39 F6
Ipsley .... 51 C5
Ipstones .... 75 D7
Ipswich .... 57 E5
Irby .... 85 F3
Irby in the Marsh . 79 C7
Irby upon Humber . 91 D5
Irchester .... 53 C7
Ireby Cumb. .... 108 F2
  Lancs .... 93 B6
Ireland Orkney .. 159 H4
  Shetland... 160 L5
Ireland's Cross .. 74 E4
Ireleth .... 92 B2
Ireshopeburn .... 109 F8
Irlam .... 86 E5
Irnham .... 65 B7
Iron Acton .... 36 F3
Ironbridge .... 61 D6
Iron Cross .... 51 D5
Irongray .... 107 B6
Ironmacannie .... 106 B3
Ironside .... 153 C8
Ironville .... 76 D4
Irstead .... 69 B6
Irthington .... 108 C4
Irthlingborough . 53 B7
Irton .... 103 F8
Irvine .... 118 F3
Isauld .... 157 C12
Isbister Orkney .... 159 D5
  Orkney .... 159 G4
  Shetland .... 160 D5
  Shetland .... 160 G7
Isfield .... 17 C8
Isham .... 53 B6

Isle Abbotts .... 11 B8
Isle Brewers .... 11 B8
Isleham .... 55 B7
Isle of Whithorn . 105 F8
Isleornsay .... 149 G12
Islesburgh .... 160 G5
Islesteps .... 107 B6
Isleworth .... 28 B2
Isley Walton .... 63 B8
Islibhig .... 154 E4
Islington .... 41 F6
Islip N Nhants. .... 53 B7
  Oxon. .... 39 C5
Istead Rise .... 29 C7
Isycoed .... 73 D8
Itchen .... 14 C5
Itchen Abbas .... 26 F3
Itchen Stoke .... 26 F3
Itchingfield .... 16 B5
Itchington .... 36 F3
Itteringham .... 81 D7
Itton .... 9 E8
Itton Common .... 36 E1
Ivegill .... 108 E4
Iver .... 40 F3
Iver Heath .... 40 F3
Iveston .... 110 D4
Ivinghoe .... 40 C2
Ivinghoe Aston .... 40 C2
Ivington .... 49 D6
Ivington Green .... 49 D6
Ivybridge .... 6 D4
Ivy Chimneys .... 41 D7
Ivychurch .... 19 C7
Ivy Cross .... 13 B6
Ivy Hatch .... 29 D6
Iwade .... 30 C3
Iwerne Courtney or
  Shroton .... 13 C6
Iwerne Minster .... 13 C6
Ixworth .... 56 B3
Ixworth Thorpe .... 56 B3

**J**

Jack Hill .... 94 D5
Jack in the Green. 10 E5
Jacksdale .... 76 D4
Jackstown .... 153 E7
Jacobstow .... 8 E3
Jacobstowe .... 9 D7
Jameston .... 32 E1
Jamestown
  Dumfries .... 115 E6
  Highld .... 150 F7
  W Dunb .... 126 F2
Jarrow .... 111 C6
Jarvis Brook .... 18 C2
Java .... 124 B3
Jawcraig .... 119 B8
Jaywick .... 43 C7
Jealott's Hill .... 27 B6
Jedburgh .... 116 B2
Jeffreyston .... 32 D1
Jellyhill .... 119 B6
Jemimaville .... 151 E10
Jersey Farm .... 40 D4
Jesmond .... 111 C5
Jevington .... 18 E2
Jockey End .... 40 C3
Johnby .... 108 F4
John o'Groats .... 158 C5
John's Cross .... 18 C4
Johnshaven .... 135 C7
Johnston Renfs . 118 C4
  Pembs .... 44 D4
Johnstonebridge. 114 E3
Johnstown Carms . 33 C5
  Wrex .... 73 E7
Joppa Edin. .... 121 B6
  S Ayrs. .... 112 C4
Jordans .... 40 E2
Jordanthorpe .... 88 F4
Jump .... 88 D4
Jumpers Green .... 14 E2
Juniper Green .... 120 C4
Jurby East .... 84 C3
Jurby West .... 84 C3

**K**

Kaber .... 100 C2
Kaimend .... 120 E2
Kaimes .... 121 C5
Kalemouth .... 116 B3
Kames Argyll .... 124 D4
  Argyll .... 145 F8
  E Ayrs. .... 113 B6
Kea .... 3 B7
Keadby .... 90 C2
Keal Cotes .... 79 C6
Kearsley .... 87 D5
Kearstwick .... 99 F8
Kearton .... 100 E4
Kearvaig .... 156 B5
Keasden .... 93 C7
Keckwick .... 86 F3
Keddington .... 91 F7
Kedington .... 55 E8
Kedleston .... 76 E3
Keelby .... 91 C5
Keele .... 74 E5
Keeley Green .... 53 E8
Keeston .... 44 D4
Keevil .... 24 D4
Kegworth .... 63 B8
Kehelland .... 2 B5
Keig .... 140 C5
Keighley .... 94 E3
Keil .... 130 D3
Keilarsbrae .... 127 E7
Keillhill .... 153 C7
Keillmore .... 144 E5
Keillor .... 134 E2
Keillour .... 127 B8
Keills .... 142 B5
Keils .... 144 G4
Keinton
  Mandeville .... 23 F7
Keir Mill .... 113 E8
Keisby .... 65 B7
Keiss .... 158 D5
Keith .... 152 C4
Keith Inch .... 153 D11
Keithock .... 135 C6
Kelbrook .... 94 E2

Kelby .... 78 E3
Keld N Yorks .... 100 D3
  W&F .... 99 C7
Keldholme .... 103 F5
Kelfield N Lincs .... 90 D2
  N Yorks. .... 95 F8
Kelham .... 77 D7
Kellan .... 147 G8
Kellas Angus .... 134 F4
  Moray... 152 C1
Kellaton .... 7 F6
Kelleth .... 100 D1
Kelleythorpe .... 97 D5
Kelling .... 81 C6
Kellingley .... 89 B6
Kellington .... 89 B6
Kelloe .... 111 F6
Kelloholm .... 113 C7
Kelly .... 9 F5
Kelly Bray .... 5 B8
Kelmarsh .... 52 B5
Kelmscot .... 38 E2
Kelsale .... 57 C7
Kelsall .... 74 C2
Kelsall Hill .... 74 C2
Kelshall .... 54 F4
Kelsick .... 107 D8
Kelso .... 122 F3
Kelstedge .... 76 C3
Kelstern .... 91 E6
Kelston .... 24 C2
Keltneyburn .... 132 E4
Kelton .... 107 B6
Kelty .... 128 E3
Kelvedon .... 42 C4
Kelvedon Hatch .... 42 E1
Kelvin .... 119 D6
Kelvinside .... 119 C5
Kelynack .... 2 C2
Kemback .... 129 C6
Kemberton .... 61 D7
Kemble .... 37 E6
Kemerton .... 50 F4
Kemeys
  Commander .... 35 D7
Kemnay .... 141 C6
Kempley .... 36 B3
Kempsey .... 50 E3
Kempsford .... 38 E1
Kemps Green... 51 B6
Kempshott .... 26 D4
Kempston .... 53 E8
Kempston
  Hardwick .... 53 E8
Kempton .... 60 F3
Kemp Town .... 17 D7
Kemsing .... 29 D6
Kemsley .... 30 C3
Kenardington .... 19 B6
Kenchester .... 49 E6
Kencot .... 38 D2
Kendal .... 99 E7
Kendoon .... 113 F6
Kendray .... 88 D4
Kenfig .... 34 F2
Kenfig Hill .... 34 F2
Kenilworth .... 51 B7
Kenknock .... 132 F1
Kenley London... 28 D4
  Shrops .... 61 D5
Kenmore Highld . 149 C12
  Perth .... 132 E4
Kenn Devon .... 10 F4
  N Som .... 23 C6
Kennacley .... 154 H6
Kennacraig .... 145 G7
Kennerleigh .... 10 D3
Kennet .... 127 E8
Kennethmont .... 140 B4
Kennett .... 55 C7
Kennford .... 10 F4
Kenninghall .... 68 F3
Kenninghall Heath 68 F3
Kennington Kent . 30 E4
  Oxon. .... 39 D5
Kennoway .... 129 D5
Kenny Hill .... 55 B7
Kennythorpe .... 96 C3
Kenovay .... 146 G2
Kensaleyre .... 149 C9
Kensington .... 28 B3
Kensworth .... 40 C3
Kensworth
  Common .... 40 C3
Kentallen .... 130 D4
Kentchurch .... 35 B8
Kentford .... 55 C8
Kentisbeare .... 11 D5
Kentisbury .... 20 E5
Kentisbury Ford . 20 E5
Kentmere .... 99 D6
Kenton Devon .... 10 F4
  Suff .... 57 C5
  T&W. .... 110 C5
Kenton Bankfoot .110 C5
Kentra .... 147 E9
Kents Bank .... 92 B3
Kent's Green .... 36 B4
Kent's Oak .... 14 B4
Kent Street E Sus . 18 D4
  Kent .... 29 D7
  W Sus .... 17 B6
Kenwick .... 73 F8
Kenwyn .... 3 B7
Keoldale .... 156 C6
Keppanach .... 130 C4
Keppoch .... 136 B2
Keprigan .... 143 G7
Kepwick .... 102 E2
Kerchesters .... 122 F3
Keresley .... 63 F7
Kernborough .... 7 E5
Kerne Bridge .... 36 C2
Kerris .... 2 D3
Kerry .... 59 F8
Kerrycroy .... 145 G10
Kerrysdale .... 149 A13
Kerry's Gate .... 49 F5
Kersall .... 77 C7
Kersey .... 56 E4
Kershopefoot .... 115 F7
Kersoe .... 50 F4
Kerswell .... 11 D5
Kerswell Green .... 50 E3
Kesgrave .... 57 E6
Kessingland .... 69 F8
Kessingland Beach 69 F8
Kessington .... 119 B5
Kestle .... 3 B8

Kestle Mill .... 4 D3
Keston .... 28 C5
Keswick Cumb .... 98 B4
  Norf .... 68 D5
  Norf .... 81 D9
Ketley .... 61 C6
Ketley Bank .... 61 C6
Ketsby .... 79 B6
Kettering .... 53 B6
Ketteringham .... 68 D4
Kettins .... 134 F2
Kettlebaston .... 56 D3
Kettlebridge .... 128 D5
Kettleburgh .... 57 C6
Kettlehill .... 128 D5
Kettleholm .... 107 B8
Kettleness .... 103 C6
Kettleshulme .... 75 B6
Kettlesing Bottom 94 D5
Kettlesing Head .. 94 D5
Kettlestone .... 81 D5
Kettlethorpe .... 77 B8
Kettletoft .... 159 E7
Kettlewell .... 94 B2
Ketton .... 65 D6
Kew .... 28 B2
Kew Bridge .... 28 B2
Kewstoke .... 22 C5
Kexbrough .... 88 D4
Kexby Lincs .... 90 F2
  York .... 96 D3
Key Green .... 75 C5
Keyham .... 64 D3
Keyhaven .... 14 E4
Keyingham .... 91 B6
Keymer .... 17 C7
Keynsham .... 23 C8
Keysoe .... 53 C8
Keysoe Row .... 53 C8
Keyston .... 53 B8
Keyworth .... 77 F6
Kibblesworth .... 110 D5
Kibworth
  Beauchamp... 64 E3
Kibworth Harcourt 64 E3
Kidbrooke .... 28 B5
Kiddemore Green . 62 D2
Kidderminster .... 50 B3
Kiddington .... 38 B4
Kidlington .... 38 C4
Kidmore End .... 26 B4
Kidsgrove .... 74 D5
Kidstones .... 100 F4
Kidwelly
  = Cydweli .... 33 D5
Kiel Crofts .... 124 B5
Kielder .... 116 E2
Kierfiold Ho .... 159 G3
Kilbagie .... 127 F8
Kilbarchan .... 118 C4
Kilbeg .... 149 H11
Kilberry .... 144 G6
Kilbirnie .... 118 D3
Kilbride Argyll .... 124 C4
  Argyll .... 124 C5
  Highld .... 149 F10
Kilburn Angus . 134 C3
  Derbys .... 76 E3
  London .... 41 F5
  N Yorks. .... 95 B8
Kilby .... 64 E3
Kilchamaig .... 145 G7
Kilchattan .... 144 D2
Kilchattan Bay . 145 H10
Kilchenzie .... 143 F7
Kilcheran .... 124 B4
Kilchiaran .... 142 B3
Kilchoan Argyll .. 124 D3
  Highld .... 146 E7
Kilchoman .... 142 B3
Kilchrenan .... 125 C6
Kilconquhar .... 129 D6
Kilcot .... 36 B3
Kilcoy .... 151 F8
Kilcreggan .... 145 E11
Kildale .... 102 D4
Kildalloig .... 143 G8
Kildary .... 151 D10
Kildermorie
  Lodge .... 151 D8
Kildonan .... 143 F11
Kildonan Lodge .157 G12
Kildonnan .... 146 C7
Kildrummy .... 140 C3
Kildwick .... 94 E3
Kilfinan .... 145 F8
Kilfinnan .... 137 E5
Kilgetty .... 32 D2
Kilgwrrwg
  Common .... 36 E1
Kilham E Yorks .... 97 C6
  Northumb. .... 122 F4
Kilkenneth .... 146 G2
Kilkerran .... 143 G8
Kilkhampton .... 9 E6
Killamarsh .... 89 F5
Killay .... 33 E7
Killbeg .... 147 G9
Killean .... 143 D7
Killearn .... 126 F4
Killen .... 151 F9
Killerby .... 101 C6
Killichonan .... 132 D2
Killiechonate .... 136 F5
Killiechronan .... 147 G8
Killiecrankie .... 133 C6
Killiemor .... 146 H7
Killilan .... 150 H2
Killimster .... 158 E5
Killin .... 132 F2
Killinallan .... 142 A4
Killinghall .... 95 D5
Killington .... 99 F8
Killingworth .... 111 B5
Killmahumaig .... 144 D6
Killochyett .... 121 E7
Killocraw .... 143 E7
Killundine .... 147 G8
Kilmacolm .... 118 C3
Kilmaha .... 124 E5
Kilmahog .... 126 D5
Kilmalieu .... 130 D2
Kilmaluag .... 149 A9
Kilmany .... 129 B5
Kilmarie .... 149 G10
Kilmarnock .... 118 F4
Kilmaron Castle . 129 C5

Kilmartin .... 124 E4
Kilmaurs .... 118 E4
Kilmelford .... 124 D4
Kilmeny .... 142 B4
Kilmersdon .... 23 D8
Kilmeston .... 15 B6
Kilmichael .... 143 F7
Kilmichael
  Glassary .... 145 D7
Kilmichael of
  Inverlussa .... 144 E6
Kilmington Devon . 11 E7
  Wilts .... 24 F2
Kilmonivaig .... 136 F4
Kilmorack .... 150 G7
Kilmore Argyll .... 124 C4
  Highld .... 149 H11
Kilmory Argyll .... 144 F6
  Highld .... 147 D8
  Highld .... 149 H8
  N Ayrs .... 143 F10
Kilmuir Highld... 148 D7
  Highld .... 149 A8
  Highld .... 151 D10
  Highld .... 151 G9
Kilmun Argyll .... 124 D5
  Argyll .... 145 E10
Kilncadzow .... 119 E8
Kilndown .... 18 B4
Kilnhurst .... 89 E5
Kilninian .... 146 G6
Kilninver .... 124 C4
Kiln Pit Hill .... 110 D3
Kilnsea .... 91 C8
Kilnsey .... 94 C2
Kilnwick .... 97 E5
Kilnwick Percy .... 96 D4
Kiloran .... 144 D2
Kilpatrick .... 143 F10
Kilpeck .... 49 F6
Kilphedir .... 157 H12
Kilpin .... 89 B8
Kilpin Pike .... 89 B8
Kilrenny .... 129 D7
Kilsby .... 52 B3
Kilspindie .... 128 B4
Kilsyth .... 119 B7
Kiltarlity .... 151 G8
Kilton Notts .... 77 B5
  Som .... 22 E3
Kilton Thorpe .... 102 C4
Kilvaxter .... 149 B8
Kilve .... 22 E3
Kilvington .... 77 E7
Kilwinning .... 118 E3
Kimberley Norf .... 68 D3
  Notts .... 76 E5
Kimberworth .... 88 E5
Kimble Wick .... 39 D8
Kimbolton Cambs . 53 C8
  Hereford .... 49 C7
Kimcote .... 64 F2
Kimmeridge .... 13 G7
Kimmerston .... 123 F5
Kimpton Hants .... 25 E7
  Herts .... 40 C4
Kinbrace .... 157 F11
Kinbuck .... 127 D6
Kincaple .... 129 C6
Kincardine Fife . 127 F8
  Highld .... 151 C9
Kincardine
  Bridge .... 127 F8
Kincardine O'Neil 140 E4
Kinclaven .... 134 F1
Kincorth .... 141 D8
Kincorth House . 151 E13
Kincraig .... 138 D4
Kincraigie .... 133 E6
Kindallachan .... 133 E6
Kineton Glos. .... 37 B7
  Warks .... 51 D8
Kinfauns .... 128 B3
Kingairloch .... 130 D2
Kingarth .... 145 H9
Kingcoed .... 35 D8
King Edward .... 153 C7
Kingerby .... 90 E4
Kingham .... 38 B2
Kingholm Quay .. 107 B6
Kinghorn .... 128 F4
Kingie .... 136 D4
Kinglassie .... 128 E4
Kingoodie .... 128 B5
King's Acre .... 49 E6
Kingsand .... 6 D2
Kingsbarns .... 129 C7
Kingsbridge Devon . 6 E5
  Som .... 21 F8
King's Bromley .... 62 C5
Kingsburgh .... 149 C8
Kingsbury London . 41 F5
  Warks .... 63 E6
Kingsbury
  Episcopi .... 12 B2
King's Caple .... 36 B2
Kingsclere .... 26 D3
King's Cliffe .... 65 E7
Kingscote .... 37 E5
Kingscott .... 9 C7
King's Coughton . 51 D5
Kingscross .... 143 F11
Kingsdon .... 12 B3
Kingsdown .... 31 E7
Kingseat .... 128 E3
Kingsey .... 39 D7
Kingsfold .... 28 F2
Kingsford E Ayrs . 118 E4
  Worcs .... 62 F2
Kingsforth .... 90 C4
King's Green .... 50 F2
Kingshall Street . 56 C3
Kingsheanton .... 20 F4
King's Heath .... 62 F4
Kings Hedges .... 55 C5
King's Hill .... 29 D7
Kingshouse
  Hotel .... 131 D6
Kingside Hill .... 107 D8
Kingskerswell .... 7 C6
Kingskettle .... 128 D5
Kingsland Anglesey. 82 C2
  Hereford .... 49 C6
Kings Langley .... 40 D3
Kingsley Ches W . 74 B2
  Hants .... 27 F5
  Staffs .... 75 E7
Kingsley Green .... 27 F6
Kingsley Holt .... 75 E7

Kingsley Park . . . . . 53 C5
King's Lynn . . . . . 67 B6
King's Meaburn . . 99 B8
King's Mills . . . . 73 E7
Kingsmuir Angus . . 134 E4
  Fife . . . . . . . . . 129 D7
Kings Muir . . . . . 121 F5
King's Newnham . . 52 B2
King's Newton . . . 63 B7
Kingsnorth . . . . . 19 B7
King's Norton Leics 64 D3
  W Mid . . . . . . . . 51 B5
King's Nympton . . . 9 C8
King's Pyon . . . . 49 D6
King's Ripton . . . . 54 B3
King's Somborne . 25 F8
King's Stag . . . . . 12 C5
King's Stanley . . . 37 D5
King's Sutton . . . 52 F2
Kingstanding . . . . 62 E4
Kingsteignton . . . . 7 B6
King Sterndale . . . 75 B7
King's Thorn . . . . 49 F7
Kingsthorpe . . . . . 53 C5
Kingston Cambs . . 54 D4
  Devon . . . . . . . . . . 6 E4
  Dorset . . . . . . . . 13 D5
  Dorset . . . . . . . . 13 G7
  E Loth . . . . . . . 129 F7
  Hants . . . . . . . . 14 D2
  IoW . . . . . . . . . . 15 F5
  Kent . . . . . . . . . 31 D5
  Moray . . . . . . . . 152 B3
Kingston Bagpuize 38 E4
Kingston Blount . . 39 E7
Kingston by Sea . . 17 D6
Kingston Deverill . 24 F3
Kingstone Hereford . 49 F6
  Som . . . . . . . . . 11 C8
  Staffs . . . . . . . . 62 B4
Kingston Gorse . . . 16 D4
Kingston Lisle . . . 38 F3
Kingston
  Maurward . . . . 12 E5
Kingston near
  Lewes . . . . . . . . 17 D7
Kingston on Soar . 64 B2
Kingston Russell . 12 E3
Kingston St Mary . 11 B7
Kingston Seymour . 23 C6
Kingston upon
  Hull . . . . . . . . . 90 B4
Kingston upon
  Thames . . . . . . 28 C2
Kingston Vale . . . 28 B3
Kingstown . . . . . 108 D3
King's Walden . . . 40 B4
Kingswear . . . . . . 7 D6
Kingswells . . . . . 141 D7
Kingswinford . . . 62 F2
Kingswood Bucks . 39 C6
  Glos . . . . . . . . . 36 E4
  Hereford . . . . . . 48 D4
  Kent . . . . . . . . . 30 D2
  Powys . . . . . . . . 60 D2
  S Glos . . . . . . . . 23 B8
  Sur . . . . . . . . . . 28 D3
  Warks . . . . . . . . 51 B6
Kings Worthy . . . 26 F2
Kingthorpe . . . . . 78 B4
Kington Hereford . 48 D4
  Worcs . . . . . . . . 50 D4
Kington Langley . 24 B4
Kington Magna . . 13 B5
Kington St
  Michael . . . . . . 24 B4
Kingussie . . . . . 138 D3
Kingweston . . . . 23 F7
Kininvie House . . 152 D3
Kinkell Bridge . . 127 C8
Kinknockie . . . . 153 D10
Kinlet . . . . . . . . 61 F7
Kinloch Fife . . . . 128 C4
  Highld . . . . . . . 146 B6
  Highld . . . . . . . 149 G11
  Highld . . . . . . . 156 F6
  Perth . . . . . . . . 133 E8
  Perth . . . . . . . . 134 E2
Kinlochan . . . . . 130 C2
Kinlochard . . . . 126 D3
Kinlochbeoraid . 147 C11
Kinlochbervie . . 156 D5
Kinlocheil . . . . . 130 B3
Kinlochewe . . . . 150 E3
Kinloch Hourn . . 136 D2
Kinloch Laggan . 137 F8
Kinlochleven . . . 131 C5
Kinloch Lodge . . 157 D8
Kinlochmoidart . 147 D10
Kinlochmorar . . 147 B11
Kinloch Rannoch . 132 D3
Kinlochspelve . . 124 C2
Kinloid . . . . . . . 147 C9
Kinloss . . . . . . . 151 E13
Kinmel Bay . . . . 72 A3
Kinmuck . . . . . . 141 C7
Kinmundy . . . . . 141 C7
Kinnadie . . . . . . 153 D9
Kinnaird . . . . . . 128 B4
Kinnaird Castle . 135 D6
Kinneff . . . . . . . 135 B8
Kinnelhead . . . . 114 D3
Kinnell . . . . . . . 135 D6
Kinnerley . . . . . 60 B3
Kinnersley Hereford 48 E5
  Worcs . . . . . . . . 50 E3
Kinnerton . . . . . 48 C4
Kinnesswood . . . 128 D3
Kinninvie . . . . . 101 B5
Kinnordy . . . . . 134 D3
Kinoulton . . . . . 77 F6
Kinross . . . . . . . 128 D3
Kinrossie . . . . . . 134 F1
Kinsbourne Green . 40 C4
Kinsey Heath . . . 74 E3
Kinsham Hereford . 49 C5
  Worcs . . . . . . . . 50 F4
Kinsley . . . . . . . 88 C5
Kinson . . . . . . . 13 E8
Kintbury . . . . . . 25 C8
Kintessack . . . . 151 E12
Kintillo . . . . . . 128 C3
Kintocher . . . . . 140 D4
Kinton Hereford . 49 B6
  Shrops . . . . . . . . 60 C3
Kintour . . . . . . 142 C5
Kintra Argyll . . . 142 D4

Kintra continued
  Argyll . . . . . . . . 146 J6
Kintraw . . . . . . 124 E4
Kinuachdrachd . . 124 F3
Kinveachy . . . . . 138 C5
Kinver . . . . . . . 62 F2
Kippax . . . . . . . 95 F7
Kippen . . . . . . . 127 E5
Kippford or
  Scaur . . . . . . 106 D5
Kirbister Orkney . 159 F7
  Orkney . . . . . . 159 H4
Kirby Bedon . . . 69 D5
Kirby Bellars . . . 64 C4
Kirby Cane . . . . 69 E6
Kirby Cross . . . . 43 B8
Kirby Grindalythe . 96 C5
  N Yorks . . . . . . 101 D6
Kirby Knowle . . . 102 F2
Kirby-le-Soken . . 43 B8
Kirby Misperton . 96 B3
Kirby Muxloe . . . 64 D2
Kirby Row . . . . 69 E6
Kirby Sigston . . 102 E2
Kirby Underdale . 96 D4
Kirby Wiske . . . 102 F1
Kirdford . . . . . . 16 B4
Kirk . . . . . . . . 158 E4
Kirkabister . . . 160 K6
Kirkandrews . . 106 E3
Kirkandrews upon
  Eden . . . . . . . 108 D3
Kirkbampton . . . 108 D3
Kirkbean . . . . . 107 D6
Kirk Bramwith . . 89 C7
Kirkbride . . . . . 108 D2
Kirkbuddo . . . . 135 E5
Kirkburn E Yorks . 97 D5
  Borders . . . . . . 121 F5
Kirkburton . . . . 88 C2
Kirkby Lincs . . . 90 E4
  Mers . . . . . . . . 86 E2
  N Yorks . . . . . . 102 D3
Kirkby Fleetham . 101 E7
Kirkby Green . . . 78 D3
Kirkby-in-Ashfield 76 D5
Kirkby-in-Furness 98 F4
Kirkby la Thorpe . 78 E3
Kirkby Lonsdale . 93 B6
Kirkby Malham . . 93 C8
Kirkby Mallory . . 63 D8
Kirkby Malzeard . 94 B5
Kirkby Mills . . . 103 F5
Kirkbymoorside . 102 F4
Kirkby on Bain . . 78 C5
Kirkby Overblow . 95 E6
Kirkby Stephen . . 100 D2
Kirkby Thore . . . 99 B8
Kirkby Underwood 65 B7
Kirk Yetholm . . . 116 B4
Kirkcaldy . . . . . 128 E4
Kirkcambeck . . . 108 C5
Kirkcarswell . . . 106 E4
Kirkcolm . . . . . 104 C4
Kirkconnel . . . . 113 C7
Kirkconnell . . . . 107 C6
Kirkcowan . . . . 105 C7
Kirkcudbright . . 106 D3
Kirkdale . . . . . . 85 E4
Kirk Deighton . . 95 D6
Kirk Ella . . . . . . 90 B4
Kirkfieldbank . . 119 E8
Kirkgunzeon . . . 107 C5
Kirk Hallam . . . 76 E4
Kirkham Lancs . . 92 F4
  N Yorks . . . . . . 96 C3
Kirkhamgate . . . 88 B3
Kirk Hammerton . 95 D7
Kirkharle . . . . . 117 F6
Kirkheaton
  Northumb . . . . . 110 B3
  W Yorks . . . . . . 88 C2
Kirkhill Angus . . 135 C6
  Highld . . . . . . 151 G8
  Midloth . . . . . . 120 C5
  Moray . . . . . . . 152 E2
Kirkhope . . . . . 115 B6
Kirkhouse . . . . 121 F6
Kirkiboll . . . . . 157 D8
Kirkibost . . . . . 149 G10
Kirkinch . . . . . 134 E3
Kirkinner . . . . . 105 D8
Kirkintilloch . . . 119 B6
Kirkland Cumb . . 98 C2
  Dumfries . . . . . 113 C7
  Dumfries . . . . . 113 E8
  W&F . . . . . . . . 109 F6
Kirkleatham . . . 102 B3
Kirklevington . . 102 D2
Kirkley . . . . . . . 69 E8
Kirklington Notts . 77 D6
  N Yorks . . . . . . 101 F8
Kirklinton . . . . 108 C4
Kirkliston . . . . 120 B4
Kirkmaiden . . . 104 F5
Kirk Merrington . 111 F5
Kirkmichael Perth . 133 D7
  S Ayrs . . . . . . . 112 D3
Kirk Michael . . . 84 C3
Kirkmuirhill . . . 119 E7
Kirknewton
  Northumb . . . . . 122 F5
  W Loth . . . . . . 120 C4
Kirkney . . . . . . 152 E5
Kirk of Shotts . . 119 C8
Kirkoswald
  S Ayrs . . . . . . . 112 D2
  W&F . . . . . . . . 109 E5
Kirkpatrick
  Durham . . . . . 106 B4
Kirkpatrick-
  Fleming . . . . . 108 B2
Kirk Sandall . . . 89 D7
Kirksanton . . . . 98 F3
Kirk Smeaton . . 89 C6
Kirkstall . . . . . . 95 F5
Kirkstead . . . . . 78 C4
Kirkstile . . . . . 152 E5
Kirkstyle . . . . . 158 C5
Kirkton Aberds . 140 B5
  Aberds . . . . . . 153 D6
  Angus . . . . . . . 134 E4
  Borders . . . . . . 115 C8
  Dumfries . . . . . 114 F2

Kirkton continued
  Fife . . . . . . . . . 129 B5
  Highld . . . . . . 149 F13
  Highld . . . . . . 150 G2
  Highld . . . . . . 151 B10
  Highld . . . . . . 151 F10
  Perth . . . . . . . 127 C8
  S Lanark . . . . . 114 B2
  Stirling . . . . . . 126 D4
Kirktonhill . . . . 121 D7
Kirkton Manor . . 121 F5
Kirkton of Airlie . 134 D3
Kirkton of
  Auchterhouse . 134 F3
Kirkton of
  Auchterless . . 153 D7
Kirkton of
  Barevan . . . . 151 G11
Kirkton of
  Bourtie . . . . . 141 B7
Kirkton of
  Collace . . . . . 134 F1
Kirkton of Craig . 135 D7
Kirkton of
  Culsalmond . . 153 E6
Kirkton of Durris 141 E6
Kirkton of
  Glenbuchat . . 140 C2
Kirkton of
  Glenisla . . . . 134 C2
Kirkton of
  Kingoldrum . . 134 D3
Kirkton of Largo . 129 D6
Kirkton of
  Lethendy . . . 133 E8
Kirkton of Logie
  Buchan . . . . . 141 B8
Kirkton of
  Maryculter . . 141 E7
Kirkton of
  Menmuir . . . 135 C5
Kirkton of
  Monikie . . . . 135 F5
Kirkton of Oyne . 141 B5
Kirkton of Rayne . 153 F6
Kirkton of Skene . 141 D7
Kirkton of Tough . 140 C5
Kirktown . . . . 153 C10
Kirktown of
  Alvah . . . . . . 153 B6
Kirktown of
  Deskford . . . 152 B5
Kirktown of
  Fetteresso . . 141 F7
Kirktown of
  Mortlach . . . 152 E3
Kirktown of
  Slains . . . . . 141 B9
Kirkurd . . . . . 120 E4
Kirkwall . . . . . 159 G5
Kirkwhelpington . 117 F6
Kirk Yetholm . . . 116 B4
Kirmington . . . . 90 C5
Kirmond le Mire . 91 E5
Kirn . . . . . . . 145 F10
Kirriemuir . . . . 134 D3
Kirstead Green . . 69 E5
Kirtlebridge . . . 108 B2
Kirtleton . . . . . 115 F5
Kirtling . . . . . . 55 D7
Kirtling Green . . 55 D7
Kirtlington . . . . 38 C4
Kirtomy . . . . . 157 C10
Kirton Lincs . . . 79 F6
  Notts . . . . . . . 77 C6
  Suff . . . . . . . . 57 F6
Kirton End . . . . 79 E5
Kirton Holme . . 79 E5
Kirton in Lindsey . 90 E3
Kislingbury . . . 52 D4
Kites Hardwick . 52 C2
Kittisford . . . . . 11 B5
Kittle . . . . . . . 33 F6
Kitt's Green . . . 63 F5
Kitt's Moss . . . 87 F6
Kittybrewster . . 141 D8
Kitwood . . . . . 26 F4
Kivernoll . . . . . 49 F6
Kiveton Park . . . 89 F5
Knaith . . . . . . 90 F2
Knaith Park . . . 90 F2
Knap Corner . . . 13 B6
Knaphill . . . . . 27 D7
Knapp Perth . . . 134 F2
  Som . . . . . . . . 11 B8
Knapthorpe . . . 77 D7
Knapton Norf . . 81 D9
  York . . . . . . . 95 D8
Knapton Green . 49 D6
Knapwell . . . . . 54 C4
Knaresborough . 95 D6
Knarsdale . . . . 109 D6
Knauchland . . . 152 C5
Knaven . . . . . . 153 D8
Knayton . . . . . 102 F2
Knebworth . . . . 41 B5
Knedlington . . . 89 B8
Kneesall . . . . . 77 C7
Kneesworth . . . 54 E4
Kneeton . . . . . 77 E7
Knelston . . . . . 33 F5
Knenhall . . . . . 75 F6
Knettishall . . . . 68 F2
Knightacott . . . 21 F5
Knightcote . . . . 51 D8
Knightley Dale . . 62 B2
Knighton Devon . . 6 E3
  Leicester . . . . . 64 D2
  Staffs . . . . . . . 61 B7
  Staffs . . . . . . . 74 F4
Knighton
  = Tref-y-Clawdd . 48 B4
Knightswood . . 118 C5
Knightwick . . . 50 D2
Knill . . . . . . . 48 C4
Knipton . . . . . 77 F8
Knitsley . . . . . 110 E4
Kniveton . . . . . 76 D2
Knock Argyll . . . 147 H4
  Moray . . . . . . . 152 C5
  W&F . . . . . . . . 100 B1
Knockally . . . . 158 H3
Knockan . . . . . 156 H5
Knockando . . . 152 D1
Knockando
  House . . . . . 152 D2
Knockbain . . . . 151 F9
Knockbreck . . . 148 B7

Knockbrex . . . . 106 E2
Knockdee . . . . . 158 D3
Knockdolian . . . 104 A5
Knockenkelly . . . 143 F11
Knockentiber . . 118 F3
Knockespock
  House . . . . . 140 B4
Knockfarrel . . . 151 F8
Knockglass . . . 104 D4
Knockholt . . . . 29 D5
Knockholt Pound . 29 D5
Knockie Lodge . . 137 C7
Knockin . . . . . . 60 B3
Knockinlaw . . . 118 F4
Knocklearn . . . 106 B4
Knocknaha . . . 143 G7
Knocknain . . . 104 C3
Knockrome . . . 144 F4
Knocksharry . . 84 D2
Knodishall . . . . 57 C8
Knolls Green . . 74 B5
Knolton . . . . . 73 F7
Knolton Bryn . . 73 F7
Knook . . . . . . 24 E4
Knossington . . 64 D5
Knott End-on-Sea. 92 E3
Knotting . . . . . 53 C8
Knotting Green . 53 C8
Knottingley . . . 89 B6
Knotts Lancs . . . 93 D7
  W&F . . . . . . . 99 B6
Knotty Ash . . . 86 E2
Knotty Green . . 40 E2
Knowbury . . . . 49 B7
Knowe . . . . . . 105 B7
Knowehead . . . 113 E6
Knowesgate . . . 117 F5
Knowes of Elrick . 152 C6
Knoweton . . . . 119 D7
Knowhead . . . 153 C9
Knowle Bristol . . 23 B8
  Devon . . . . . . 10 D2
  Devon . . . . . . 11 F5
  Devon . . . . . . 20 F3
  Shrops . . . . . . 49 B7
  W Mid . . . . . . 51 B6
Knowle Green . . 93 F6
Knowle Park . . . 94 E3
Knowl Hill . . . . 27 B6
Knowlton Dorset . 13 C8
  Kent . . . . . . . 31 D6
Knowsley . . . . 86 E2
Knowstone . . . 10 B3
Knox Bridge . . . 29 E8
Knucklas . . . . . 48 B4
Knuston . . . . . 53 C7
Knutsford . . . . 74 B4
Knutton . . . . . 74 E5
Knypersley . . . . 75 D5
Kuggar . . . . . . 3 E6
Kyleakin . . . . . 149 F12
Kyle of Lochalsh . 149 F12
Kylerhea . . . . . 149 F12
Kylesknoydart . 147 B11
Kylesku . . . . . 156 F5
Kylesmorar . . . 147 B11
Kylestrome . . . 156 F5
Kyllachy House . 138 B3
Kynaston . . . . 60 B3
Kynnersley . . . 61 C6
Kyre Magna . . . 49 C8

**L**

Labost . . . . . 155 C7
Lacasaidh . . . 155 E8
Lacasdal . . . . 155 D9
Laceby . . . . . . 91 D6
Lacey Green . . . 39 E8
Lach Dennis . . . 74 B4
Lackford . . . . . 55 B8
Lacock . . . . . . 24 C4
Ladbroke . . . . 52 D2
Laddingford . . . 29 E7
Lade Bank . . . . 79 D6
Ladock . . . . . . 4 D3
Lady . . . . . . . 159 D7
Ladybank . . . . 128 C5
Ladykirk . . . . . 122 E4
Ladysford . . . . 153 B9
La Fontenelle . . 16 I2
Laga . . . . . . . 147 E9
Lagalochan . . . 124 D4
Lagavulin . . . . 142 D5
Lagg Argyll . . . 144 F4
  N Ayrs . . . . . . 143 F10
Laggan Argyll . . 142 C3
  Highld . . . . . . 137 E5
  Highld . . . . . . 138 E2
  Highld . . . . . . 147 D10
  S Ayrs . . . . . . 112 F2
Lagganulva . . . 146 G7
Laide . . . . . . 155 H13
Laigh Fenwick . . 118 E4
Laigh Glengall . . 112 C3
Laighmuir . . . . 118 E4
Laindon . . . . . 42 F2
Lair . . . . . . . . 150 G3
Lairg . . . . . . . 157 J8
Lairg Lodge . . . 157 J8
Lairgmore . . . . 151 H8
Lairg Muir . . . . 157 J8
Laisterdyke . . . 94 F4
Laithes . . . . . . 108 F4
Lake IoW . . . . . 15 F6
  Wilts . . . . . . . 25 F6
Lakenham . . . . 68 D5
Lakenheath . . . 67 F7
Lakesend . . . . 66 E5
Lakeside . . . . . 99 F5
Laleham . . . . . 27 C8
Laleston . . . . . 21 B7
Lamarsh . . . . . 56 F2
Lamas . . . . . . 81 E8
Lambden . . . . 122 E3
Lamberhurst . . 18 B3
Lamberhurst
  Quarter . . . . 18 B3
Lambeth . . . . 28 B4
Lambhill . . . . 119 C5
Lambley Northumb . 109 D6
  Notts . . . . . . . 77 E6
Lamborough Hill . 38 D4
Lambourn . . . . 25 B8
Lambourne End . 41 E7
Lambs Green . . 28 F3
Lambston . . . . 44 D4

Lambton . . . . . 111 D5
Lamerton . . . . . 6 B2
Lamesley . . . . . 111 D5
Laminess . . . . . 159 E7
Lamington
  Highld . . . . . 151 D10
  S Lanark . . . . . 120 F2
Lamlash . . . . . 143 E11
Lamloch . . . . . 112 E5
Lamonby . . . . . 108 F4
Lamorna . . . . . . 2 D3
Lamorran . . . . . . 3 B7
Lampardbrook . . 57 C6
Lampeter = Llanbedr
  Pont Steffan . . 46 E4
Lampeter Velfrey . 32 C2
Lamphey . . . . . 32 D1
Lamplugh . . . . . 98 B2
Lamport . . . . . 53 B5
Lamyatt . . . . . 23 F8
Lana . . . . . . . . 8 E5
Lanark . . . . . . 119 E8
Lancaster . . . . 92 C4
Lanchester . . . 110 E4
Lancing . . . . . 17 D5
Landbeach . . . . 55 C5
Landcross . . . . . 9 B6
Landerberry . . . 141 D6
Landford . . . . . 14 C3
Landford Manor . 14 B3
Landimore . . . . 33 E5
Landkey . . . . . 20 F4
Landore . . . . . 33 E7
Landrake . . . . . 5 C8
Landscove . . . . 7 C5
Landshipping . . 32 C1
Landshipping
  Quay . . . . . . 32 C1
Landulph . . . . . 6 C2
Landwade . . . . 55 C7
Lane . . . . . . . . 4 C3
Laneast . . . . . . 8 F4
Lane End Bucks . 39 E8
  Cumb . . . . . . . 98 E3
  Dorset . . . . . . 13 E6
  Hants . . . . . . . 15 B6
  IoW . . . . . . . . 15 F7
  Lancs . . . . . . . 93 D7
Lane Ends Lancs . 93 D7
  N Yorks . . . . . . 94 E2
Laneham . . . . . 77 B8
Lanehead Durham . 109 E8
  Northumb . . . . . 116 F3
Lane Head Derbys . 75 B8
  Durham . . . . . 101 C6
  Gtr Man . . . . . . 86 E4
  W Yorks . . . . . . 88 D2
Lanercost . . . . 109 C5
Laneshaw Bridge . 94 E2
Lane Side . . . . 87 B5
Lanfach . . . . . 35 E6
Langar . . . . . . 77 F7
Langbank . . . . 118 B3
Langbar . . . . . 94 D3
Langburnshiels . 115 D8
Langcliffe . . . . 93 C8
Langdale . . . . 157 E9
Langdale End . . 103 E7
Langdon . . . . . 8 F5
Langdon Beck . . 109 F8
Langdon Hills . . 42 F2
Langdyke . . . . 128 D5
Langenhoe . . . . 43 C6
Langford C Beds . 54 E2
  Devon . . . . . . 10 D5
  Essex . . . . . . . 42 D4
  Notts . . . . . . . 77 D8
  Oxon . . . . . . . 38 D2
Langford Budville . 11 B6
Langham Essex . 56 F4
  Norf . . . . . . . . 81 C6
  Rutland . . . . . . 64 C5
  Suff . . . . . . . . 56 C3
Langhaugh . . . 120 F5
Langho . . . . . . 93 F7
Langholm . . . . 115 F6
Langleeford . . . 117 B5
Langley Ches E . . 75 B6
  Hants . . . . . . . 14 D5
  Herts . . . . . . . 41 B5
  Kent . . . . . . . 30 D2
  Northumb . . . . . 109 C8
  Slough . . . . . . 27 B8
  Warks . . . . . . . 51 C6
  W Sus . . . . . . . 16 B2
Langley Burrell . 24 B4
Langley Common . 76 F2
Langley Heath . . 30 D2
Langley Lower
  Green . . . . . 54 F5
Langley Marsh . . 11 B5
Langley Park . . 110 E5
Langley Street . . 69 D6
Langley Upper
  Green . . . . . 54 F5
Langney . . . . . 18 E3
Langold . . . . . 89 F6
Langore . . . . . . 8 F5
Langport . . . . . 12 B2
Langrick . . . . . 79 E5
Langridge . . . . 24 C2
Langridge Ford . . 9 B7
Langrigg . . . . . 107 E8
Langrish . . . . . 15 B8
Langsett . . . . . 88 D3
Langshaw . . . . 121 F8
Langside . . . . . 127 C6
Langskaill . . . . 159 D5
Langstone Hants . 15 D8
  Newport . . . . . 35 E7
Langthorne . . . 101 E7
Langthorpe . . . 95 C6
Langthwaite . . . 101 E5
Langtoft E Yorks . 97 C6
  Lincs . . . . . . . 65 C8
Langton Durham . 101 C6
  Lincs . . . . . . . 78 C5
  Lincs . . . . . . . 79 B6
  N Yorks . . . . . . 96 C3
Langton by
  Wragby . . . . 78 B4
Langton Green
  Kent . . . . . . . 18 B2
  Suff . . . . . . . . 56 B5
Langton Herring . 12 F4
Langton
  Matravers . . . 13 G8
Langtree . . . . . . 9 C6

Langwathby . . . 109 F5
Langwell House . 158 H3
Langwell Lodge . 156 J4
Langwith . . . . . 76 C5
Langwith Junction 76 C5
Langworth . . . . 78 B3
Lanivet . . . . . . . 4 C5
Lanjeth . . . . . . . 4 D4
Lanlivery . . . . . . 5 D5
Lanner . . . . . . . . 3 C6
Lanreath . . . . . . 5 D6
Lansallos . . . . . . 5 D6
Lansdown . . . . . 37 B6
Lanteglos Highway . 5 D6
Lanton Borders . . 116 B2
  Northumb . . . . . 122 F5
Lapford . . . . . . 10 D2
Laphroaig . . . . 142 D4
Lapley . . . . . . . 62 C2
Lapworth . . . . . 51 B6
Larachbeg . . . . 147 G9
Larbert . . . . . . 127 F7
Larden Green . . . 74 D2
Largie . . . . . . 152 E6
Largiemore . . . 145 E8
Largoward . . . . 129 D6
Largs . . . . . . . 118 D2
Largybeg . . . . 143 F11
Largymore . . . 143 F11
Larkfield . . . . . 118 B2
Larkhall . . . . . 119 D7
Larkhill . . . . . . 25 E6
Larling . . . . . . 68 F2
Larriston . . . . . 115 E8
Lartington . . . . 101 C5
Lary . . . . . . . 140 D2
Lasham . . . . . . 26 E4
Lashenden . . . . 30 E2
Lassington . . . . 36 B4
Lassodie . . . . . 128 E3
Lastingham . . . 103 E5
Latcham . . . . . 23 E6
Latchford Herts . 41 B6
  Warr . . . . . . . 86 F4
Latchingdon . . . 42 D4
Latchley . . . . . . 6 B2
Lately Common . 86 E4
Lathbury . . . . . 53 E6
Latheron . . . . . 158 G3
Latheronwheel . 158 G3
Latheronwheel
  House . . . . . 158 G3
Lathones . . . . 129 D6
Latimer . . . . . . 40 E3
Latteridge . . . . 36 F3
Lattiford . . . . . 12 B4
Latton . . . . . . 37 E7
Latton Bush . . . 41 D7
Lauchintilly . . . 141 C6
Lauder . . . . . . 121 E8
Laugharne . . . . 32 C4
Laughterton . . . 77 B8
Laughton E Sus . . 18 D2
  Leics . . . . . . . 64 F3
  Lincs . . . . . . . 78 F3
  Lincs . . . . . . . 90 E2
Laughton Common 89 F6
Laughton en le
  Morthen . . . . 89 F6
Launcells . . . . . 8 D4
Launceston . . . . 8 F5
Launton . . . . . 39 B6
Laurencekirk . . 135 B7
Laurieston
  Dumfries . . . . 106 C3
  Falk . . . . . . . 120 B2
Lavendon . . . . 53 D7
Lavenham . . . . 56 E3
Laverhay . . . . . 114 E4
Laversdale . . . 108 C4
Laverstock . . . 25 F6
Laverstoke . . . 26 E2
Laverton Glos . . 51 F5
  N Yorks . . . . . . 94 B5
  Som . . . . . . . 24 D2
Lavister . . . . . 73 D7
Law . . . . . . . 119 D8
Lawers Perth . . 127 B6
  Perth . . . . . . 132 F3
Lawford . . . . . 56 F4
Lawhitton . . . . 9 F5
Lawkland . . . . 93 C7
Lawley . . . . . . 61 D6
Lawnhead . . . . 62 B2
Lawrenny . . . . 32 D1
Lawshall . . . . . 56 D2
Lawton . . . . . . 49 D6
Laxey . . . . . . 84 D4
Laxfield . . . . . 57 B6
Laxfirth Shetland . 160 H6
  Shetland . . . . . 160 J6
Laxford Bridge . 156 E5
Laxo . . . . . . . 160 G6
Laxobigging . . . 160 F6
Laxton E Yorks . . 89 B8
  N Hants . . . . . . 65 E6
  Notts . . . . . . . 77 C7
Laycock . . . . . 94 E3
Layer Breton . . . 43 C5
Layer de la Haye . 43 C5
Layer Marney . . 43 C5
Layham . . . . . 56 E4
Laylands Green . 25 C8
Laytham . . . . . 96 F3
Layton . . . . . . 92 F3
Lazenby . . . . . 102 B3
Lazonby . . . . . 108 F5
Lea Derbys . . . . 76 D3
  Hereford . . . . . 36 B3
  Lincs . . . . . . . 90 F2
  Shrops . . . . . . 60 D4
  Shrops . . . . . . 60 F3
  Wilts . . . . . . . 37 F6
Leabrooks . . . . 76 D4
Leac a Li . . . . . 154 H6
Leachkin . . . . . 151 G9
Leadburn . . . . 120 D5
Leaden Roding . 42 C1
Leadgate Durham . 110 D4
  T&W . . . . . . . 110 D4
  W&F . . . . . . . . 109 E7
Leadhills . . . . . 113 C8
Leafield . . . . . 38 C3
Leagrave . . . . 40 B3
Leake . . . . . . 102 E2
Leake
  Commonside . 79 D6
Lealholm . . . . 103 D5

Lealt Argyll . . . . 144 D5
  Highld . . . . . . 149 B10
Lea Marston . . . 63 E6
Leamington
  Hastings . . . . 52 C2
Leamonsley . . . 62 D5
Leamside . . . . 111 E6
Leanaig . . . . . 151 F8
Leargybreck . . . 144 F4
Leasgill . . . . . . 99 F6
Leasingham . . . 78 E3
Leasingthorne . 101 B7
Leasowe . . . . . 85 E3
Leatherhead . . . 28 D2
Leatherhead
  Common . . . . 28 D2
Leathley . . . . . 94 E5
Leaton . . . . . . 60 C4
Lea Town . . . . . 92 F4
Leaveland . . . . 30 D4
Leavening . . . . 96 C3
Leaves Green . . 28 C5
Leazes . . . . . . 110 D4
Lebberston . . . 103 F8
Lechlade-on-
  Thames . . . . 38 E2
Leck . . . . . . . 93 B6
Leckford . . . . . 25 F8
Leckfurin . . . . 157 D10
Leckgruinart . . 142 B3
Leckhampstead
  Bucks . . . . . . 52 F5
  W Berks . . . . . . 26 B2
Leckhampstead
  Thicket . . . . 26 B2
Leckhampton . . 37 C6
Leckie . . . . . . 150 E3
Leckmelm . . . . 150 B4
Leckwith . . . . . 22 B3
Leconfield . . . . 97 E6
Ledaig . . . . . . 124 B5
Ledburn . . . . . 40 B2
Ledbury . . . . . . 50 F2
Ledcharrie . . . . 126 B4
Ledgemoor . . . . 49 D6
Ledicot . . . . . . 49 C6
Ledmore . . . . . 156 H5
Lednagullin . . . 157 C10
Ledsham Ches W . 73 B7
  W Yorks . . . . . . 89 B5
Ledston . . . . . 88 B5
Ledston Luck . . . 95 F7
Ledwell . . . . . 38 B4
Lee Argyll . . . . 146 J7
  Devon . . . . . . 20 E3
  Hants . . . . . . 14 C4
  Lancs . . . . . . . 93 D5
  Shrops . . . . . . 73 F8
Leeans . . . . . . 160 J5
Leebotten . . . . 160 L6
Leebotwood . . . 60 E4
Lee Brockhurst . 60 B5
Leece . . . . . . . 92 C2
Leechpool . . . . 44 D4
Lee Clump . . . . 40 D2
Leeds Kent . . . . 30 D2
  W Yorks . . . . . . 95 F5
Leedstown . . . . 2 C5
Leek . . . . . . . 75 D6
Leekbrook . . . . 75 D6
Leek Wootton . . 51 C7
Lee Mill . . . . . . 6 D4
Leeming . . . . . 101 F7
Leeming Bar . . . 101 E7
Lee Moor . . . . . 6 C3
Lee-on-the-
  Solent . . . . . 15 D6
Lees Derbys . . . 76 F2
  Gtr Man . . . . . . 87 D7
  W Yorks . . . . . . 94 F3
Leeswood . . . . 73 C6
Legbourne . . . . 91 F7
Legerwood . . . 121 E8
Legsby . . . . . . 90 F5
Leicester . . . . . 64 D2
Leicester Forest
  East . . . . . . 64 D2
Leigh Dorset . . . 12 D4
  Glos . . . . . . . 37 B5
  Gtr Man . . . . . . 86 D4
  Kent . . . . . . . 29 E6
  Shrops . . . . . . 60 D3
  Sur . . . . . . . . 28 E3
  Wilts . . . . . . . 37 E7
  Worcs . . . . . . . 50 D2
Leigh Beck . . . . 42 F4
Leigh Common . . 12 B5
Leigh Delamere . 24 B3
Leigh Green . . . 19 B6
Leigh on Sea . . . 42 F4
Leigh Park . . . . 15 D8
Leigh Sinton . . . 50 D2
Leighswood . . . 62 D4
Leighterton . . . 37 E5
Leighton N Yorks . 94 B4
  Powys . . . . . . 60 D2
  Shrops . . . . . . 61 D6
  Som . . . . . . . 24 E2
Leighton
  Bromswold . . 54 B2
Leighton Buzzard . 40 B2
Leigh upon
  Mendip . . . . 23 E8
Leigh Woods . . . 23 B7
Leinthall Earls . . 49 C6
Leinthall Starkes . 49 C6
Leintwardine . . . 49 B6
Leire . . . . . . . 64 E2
Leirinmore . . . 156 C7
Leiston . . . . . . 57 C8
Leitfie . . . . . . 134 E2
Leith . . . . . . . 121 B5
Leitholm . . . . . 122 E3
Lelant . . . . . . . 2 C4
Lelley . . . . . . . 97 F8
Lem Hill . . . . . . 50 B2
Lemmington Hall . 117 C7
Lempitlaw . . . . 122 F3
Lenchwick . . . . 50 E5
Lendalfoot . . . . 112 F1
Lendrick Lodge . 126 D4
Lenham . . . . . 30 D2
Lenham Heath . . 30 E3
Lennel . . . . . . 122 E4
Lennoxtown . . . 119 B6
Lenton Lincs . . . 78 F3
  Nottingham . . . 77 F5
Lentran . . . . . 151 G8
Lenwade . . . . . 68 C3

Leny House . . . 126 D5
Lenzie . . . . . . 119 B6
Leoch . . . . . . . 134 F3
Leochel-Cushnie. 140 C4
Leominster . . . . 49 D6
Leonard Stanley . 37 D5
Leorin . . . . . . 142 D4
Lepe . . . . . . . 15 E5
Lephin . . . . . . 148 D6
Lephinchapel . . 145 D8
Lephinmore . . . 145 D8
Le Planel . . . . . 16 I2
Leppington . . . . 96 C3
Lepton . . . . . . 88 C3
Lerryn . . . . . . . 5 D6
Lerwick . . . . . 160 J6
Lesbury . . . . . 117 C8
Leslie Aberds . . . 140 B4
  Fife . . . . . . . 128 D4
Lesmahagow . . 119 F8
Lesnewth . . . . . 8 E3
Lessendrum . . . 152 D5
Lessingham . . . 69 B6
Lessonhall . . . . 108 D2
Leswalt . . . . . . 104 C4
Letchmore Heath . 40 E4
Letchworth Garden
  City . . . . . . 54 F3
Letcombe Bassett . 38 F3
Letcombe Regis . 38 F3
Letham Angus . . 135 E5
  Falk . . . . . . . 127 F7
  Fife . . . . . . . 128 C5
  Perth . . . . . . 128 B2
Letham Grange . 135 E6
Lethenty . . . . . 153 D8
Letheringham . . 57 D6
Letheringsett . . 81 D6
Lettaford . . . . . 10 F2
Lettan . . . . . . 159 D8
Letterewe . . . . 150 D2
Letterfearn . . . 149 F13
Letterfinlay . . . 137 E5
Lettermorar . . . 147 C10
Lettermore . . . 146 G7
Letters . . . . . . 150 C4
Letterston . . . . 44 C4
Lettoch Highld . . 139 C6
  Highld . . . . . . 151 H13
Letton Hereford . 48 E5
  Hereford . . . . . 49 B5
Letton Green . . 68 D2
Letty Green . . . 41 C5
Letwell . . . . . . 89 F6
Leuchars . . . . . 129 B6
Leuchars House . 152 B2
Leumrabhagh . . 155 F8
Levan . . . . . . 118 B2
Levaneap . . . . 160 G6
Levedale . . . . . 62 C2
Leven E Yorks . . 97 E7
  Fife . . . . . . . 129 D5
Levencorroch . . 143 F11
Levens . . . . . . 99 F6
Levens Green . . 41 B6
Levenshulme . . 87 E6
Levenwick . . . . 160 L6
Leverburgh
  = An t-Ob . . . 154 J5
Leverington . . . 66 C4
Leverton . . . . . 79 E7
Leverton Highgate 79 E7
Leverton
  Lucasgate . . . 79 E7
Leverton Outgate. 79 E7
Le Villocq . . . . 16 I2
Levington . . . . 57 F6
Levisham . . . . . 103 E6
Levishie . . . . . 137 C7
Lew . . . . . . . . 38 D3
Lewannick . . . . . 8 F4
Lewdown . . . . . 9 F6
Lewes . . . . . . 17 C8
Leweston . . . . 44 C4
Lewisham . . . . 28 B4
Lewiston . . . . . 137 B8
Lewistown . . . . 34 F3
Lewknor . . . . . 39 E7
Leworthy Devon . 9 D5
  Devon . . . . . . 21 F5
Lewtrenchard . . 9 F6
Lexden . . . . . . 43 B5
Ley Aberds . . . . 140 C4
  Corn . . . . . . . 5 C7
Leybourne . . . . 29 D7
Leyburn . . . . . 101 E6
Leyfields . . . . . 63 D6
Leyhill . . . . . . 40 D2
Leyland . . . . . . 86 B3
Leylodge . . . . . 141 C6
Leys Aberds . . . 153 C10
  Perth . . . . . . 134 F2
Leys Castle . . . 151 G9
Leysdown-on-Sea 30 B4
Leysmill . . . . . 135 E6
Leys of Cossans . 134 E3
Leysters Pole . . 49 C7
Leyton . . . . . . 41 F6
Leytonstone . . . 41 F6
Lezant . . . . . . . 5 B8
Leziate . . . . . . 67 C6
Lhanbryde . . . . 152 B2
Liatrie . . . . . . 150 H5
Libanus . . . . . 34 B3
Libberton . . . . 120 E2
Liberton . . . . . 121 C5
Liceasto . . . . . 154 H6
Lichfield . . . . . 62 D5
Lickey . . . . . . 50 B4
Lickey End . . . . 50 B4
Lickfold . . . . . 16 B3
Liddel . . . . . . 159 K5
Liddesdale . . . . 130 D1
Liddington . . . . 38 F2
Lidgate . . . . . . 55 D8
Lidget . . . . . . 89 D7
Lidget Green . . 94 F4
Lidgett . . . . . . 77 C6
Lidstone . . . . . 38 B3
Lieurary . . . . . 158 D2
Liff . . . . . . . . 134 F3
Lifton . . . . . . . 9 F5
Liftondown . . . . 9 F5
Lighthorne . . . . 51 D8
Lightwater . . . . 27 C7

Lightwood . . . . 75 E6
Lightwood Green
  Ches E . . . . . 74 E3
  Wrex . . . . . . . 73 E7
Lilbourne . . . . 52 B3
Lilburn Tower . . 117 B6
Lilleshall . . . . . 61 C7
Lilley Herts . . . 40 B4
  W Berks . . . . . . 26 B2
Lilliesleaf . . . . 115 B8
Lillingstone
  Dayrell . . . . . 52 F5
Lillingstone Lovell . 52 E5
Lillington Dorset . 12 C4
  Warks . . . . . . . 51 C8
Lilliput . . . . . . 13 E8
Lilstock . . . . . . 22 E3
Lilyhurst . . . . . 61 C7
Limbury . . . . . 40 B3
Limebrook . . . . 49 C5
Limefield . . . . . 87 C6
Limekilnburn . . 119 D7
Limekilns . . . . 128 F2
Limerigg . . . . . 119 B8
Limerstone . . . 14 F5
Limington . . . . 12 B3
Limpenhoe . . . 69 D6
Limpley Stoke . . 24 C2
Limpsfield . . . . 28 D5
Limpsfield Chart . 28 D5
Linby . . . . . . . 76 D5
Linchmere . . . . 27 F6
Lincluden . . . . 107 B6
Lincoln . . . . . . 78 B2
Lincomb . . . . . 50 C3
Lindale . . . . . . 99 F6
Lindal in Furness . 92 B2
Lindean . . . . . 121 F7
Lindfield . . . . . 17 B7
Lindford . . . . . 27 F6
Lindifferon . . . 128 C5
Lindley . . . . . . 88 C2
Lindley Green . . 94 E5
Lindores . . . . . 128 C4
Lindridge . . . . 49 C8
Lindsell . . . . . 42 B2
Lindsey . . . . . 56 E3
Linford Hants . . 14 D2
  Thurrock . . . . . 29 B7
Lingague . . . . . 84 E2
Lingards Wood . 87 C8
Lingbob . . . . . 94 F3
Lingdale . . . . . 102 C4
Lingen . . . . . . 49 C5
Lingfield . . . . . 28 E4
Lingreabhagh . . 154 J5
Lingwood . . . . 69 D6
Linicro . . . . . . 149 B8
Linkenholt . . . . 25 C8
Linkhill . . . . . . 18 C5
Linkinhorne . . . 5 B8
Linklater . . . . . 159 K5
Linksness . . . . 159 H3
Linktown . . . . 128 E4
Linley . . . . . . . 60 E3
Linley Green . . . 49 D8
Linlithgow
  Bridge . . . . . 120 B2
Linshiels . . . . . 116 D4
Linsiadar . . . . 154 D7
Linsidemore . . . 151 B8
Linslade . . . . . 40 B2
Linstead Parva . 57 B7
Linstock . . . . . 108 D4
Linthwaite . . . . 88 C2
Lintlaw . . . . . . 122 D4
Lintmill . . . . . 152 B5
Linton Borders . . 116 B3
  Cambs . . . . . . 55 E6
  Derbys . . . . . . 63 C6
  Hereford . . . . . 36 B3
  Kent . . . . . . . 29 E8
  Northumb . . . . . 117 E8
  W Yorks . . . . . . 95 E6
Linton-on-Ouse . 95 C7
Linwood Hants . . 14 D2
  Lincs . . . . . . . 90 F5
  Renfs . . . . . . . 118 C4
Lionacleit . . . . 148 D2
Lional . . . . . . 155 A10
Liphook . . . . . 27 F6
Liscard . . . . . . 85 E4
Liscombe . . . . 21 F7
Liskeard . . . . . . 5 C7
L'Islet . . . . . . 16 I2
Liss . . . . . . . . 15 B8
Lissett . . . . . . 97 D7
Liss Forest . . . . 15 B8
Lissington . . . . 90 F5
Lisvane . . . . . . 35 F5
Liswerry . . . . . 35 F7
Litcham . . . . . 67 C8
Litchborough . . 52 D4
Litchfield . . . . 26 D2
Litherland . . . . 85 E4
Litlington Cambs . 54 E4
  E Sus . . . . . . . 18 E2
Little Abington . 55 E6
Little Addington . 53 B7
Little Alne . . . . 51 C6
Little Altcar . . . 85 D4
Little Asby . . . . 100 D1
Little Assynt . . . 156 G4
Little Aston . . . 62 D4
Little Atherfield . 15 F5
Little Ayre . . . . 159 J4
Little-ayre . . . . 160 G5
Little Ayton . . . 102 C3
Little Baddow . . 42 D3
Little Badminton . 37 F5
Little Ballinluig . 133 D6
Little Bampton . 108 D2
Little Bardfield . 55 F7
Little Barford . . 54 D2
Little Barningham 81 D7
Little Barrow . . 73 B8
Little Barugh . . 96 B3
Little Bavington . 110 B2
Little Bealings . . 57 E6
Little Bedwyn . . 25 C7
Little Bentley . . 43 B7

**Little**
Berkhamsted . . . . 41 D5
Little Billing. . . . . . . 53 C6
Little Birch . . . . . . . . 49 F7
Little Blakenham . . . 56 E5
Little Blencow . . . . 108 F4
Little Bollington. . . . 86 F5
Little Bookham . . . . 28 D2
**Littleborough**
Gtr Man . . . . . . . 87 C7
Notts . . . . . . . . . . 90 F2
Littlebourne . . . . . . 31 D6
Little Bowden . . . . . 64 F4
Little Bradley. . . . . . 55 D7
Little Brampton . . . . 60 F3
Little Brechin . . . . 135 C5
Littlebredy . . . . . . . . 12 F3
Little Brickhill. . . . . 53 F7
Little Brington . . . . 52 C4
Little Bromley . . . . . 43 B6
Little Broughton . . 107 F7
Little Budworth . . . 74 C2
Little Burstead . . . . 42 E2
Littlebury . . . . . . . . 55 F6
Littlebury Green. . . . 55 F5
Little Bytham. . . . . . 65 C7
Little Carlton Lincs . 91 F7
Notts . . . . . . . . . . 77 D7
Little Casterton . . . . 65 D7
Little Cawthorpe . . . 91 F7
Little Chalfont. . . . . 40 E2
Little Chart. . . . . . . . 30 E3
Little Chesterford . . 55 F5
Little Cheverell. . . . 24 D4
Little Chishill . . . . . 54 F5
Little Clacton . . . . . 43 C7
Little Clifton . . . . . . 98 B2
Little Colp. . . . . . . 153 D7
Little Comberton . . 50 E4
Little Common . . . . 18 E4
Little Compton . . . . 51 F7
Little Cornard . . . . . 56 F2
Little Cowarne . . . . 49 D8
Little Coxwell . . . . . 38 E2
Little Crakehall . . . 101 E7
Little Cressingham 67 D8
Little Crosby . . . . . . 85 D4
Little Dalby . . . . . . . 64 C4
Little Dawley . . . . . . 61 D6
Littledean. . . . . . . . . 36 C3
Little Dens . . . . . . . 153 D9
Little Dewchurch . . 49 F7
Little Downham . . . 66 F5
Little Driffield . . . . . 97 D6
Little Dunham . . . . . 67 C8
Little Dunkeld . . . . 133 E7
Little Dunmow . . . . 42 B2
Little Easton . . . . . . 42 B2
Little Eaton . . . . . . . 76 E3
Little Eccleston . . . . 92 E4
Little Ellingham . . . 68 E3
Little End . . . . . . . . 41 D8
Little Eversden . . . . 54 D4
Little Faringdon . . . 38 D2
Little Fencote . . . . 101 E7
Little Fenton . . . . . . 95 F8
Littleferry . . . . . . . 151 B11
Little Finborough . . 56 D4
Little Fransham . . . . 68 C2
Little Gaddesden . . 40 C2
Little Gidding . . . . . 65 F8
Little Glemham . . . . 57 D7
Little Glenshee . . . 133 F6
Little Gransden . . . . 54 D3
Little Green . . . . . . 24 E2
Little Grimsby . . . . . 91 E7
Little Gruinard . . . 150 C2
Little Habton . . . . . 96 B3
Little Hadham . . . . . 41 B7
Little Hale. . . . . . . . 78 E4
Little Hallingbury . 41 C7
Littleham Devon. . . . 9 B6
Devon. . . . . . . . . . 10 F5
Little Hampden . . . . 40 D1
Littlehampton. . . . . 16 D4
Little Harrowden . . 53 B6
Little Haseley . . . . . 39 D6
Little Hatfield . . . . . 97 E7
Little Hautbois . . . . 81 E8
Little Haven . . . . . . 44 D3
Little Hay . . . . . . . . 62 D5
Little Hayfield . . . . . 87 F8
Little Haywood . . . . 62 B4
Little Heath . . . . . . 63 F7
Littlehempston . . . . 7 C6
Little Hereford . . . . 49 C7
Little Horkesley . . . 56 F3
Little Horsted . . . . . 17 C8
Little Horton . . . . . . 94 F4
Little Horwood . . . . 53 F6
Littlehoughton . . . 117 C8
**Little Houghton**
S Yorks . . . . . . . . 88 D5
W Nhants. . . . . . . 53 D6
Little Hucklow . . . . 75 B8
Little Hulton . . . . . . 86 D5
Little Humber . . . . . 91 B5
Little Hungerford . . 26 B3
Little Irchester . . . . 53 C7
Little Kimble . . . . . . 39 D8
Little Kineton . . . . . 51 D8
Little Kingshill . . . . 40 E1
Little Langdale . . . . 99 D5
Little Langford . . . . 25 F5
Little Laver . . . . . . . 41 D8
Little Leigh . . . . . . . 74 B3
Little Leighs . . . . . . 42 C3
Little Lever . . . . . . . 87 D5
Little London Bucks 39 C6
E Sus . . . . . . . . . . 18 D2
Hants . . . . . . . . . 25 E8
Hants . . . . . . . . . 26 D4
Lincs. . . . . . . . . . 66 B4
Norf . . . . . . . . . . 81 E7
Powys . . . . . . . . . 59 F7
Little
Longstone. . . . 75 B8
Little Lynturk. . . . . 140 C4
Little Malvern . . . . . 50 E2
Little Maplestead . . 56 F2
Little Marcle . . . . . . 49 F8
Little Marlow . . . . . 40 F1
Little Marsden . . . . 93 F8
Little Massingham. 80 E3
Little Melton . . . . . . 68 D4
Littlemill Aberds . . . 140 E2

**Littlemill** continued
E Ayrs. . . . . . . . . 112 C4
Highld . . . . . . . . 151 F12
Northumb. . . . . . 117 C8
Little Mill . . . . . . . . 35 D7
Little Milton . . . . . . 39 D6
Little Missenden . . . 40 E2
Littlemoor . . . . . . . . 12 F4
Littlemore . . . . . . . . 39 D5
Little Musgrave . . . 100 C2
Little Ness . . . . . . . 60 C4
Little Neston . . . . . . 73 B6
Little Newcastle . . . 44 C4
Little Newsham . . . 101 C6
Little Oakley Essex . 43 B8
N Nhants . . . . . . 65 F5
Little Orton . . . . . . 108 D3
Little Ouseburn . . . . 95 C7
Littleover . . . . . . . . 76 F3
Little Paxton . . . . . . 54 C2
Little Petherick . . . . . 4 B4
Little Pitlury . . . . . 152 D4
Little Plumpton . . . . 92 F3
Little Plumstead . . . 69 C6
Little Ponton . . . . . . 78 F2
**Llanbedr-**
y-cennin . . . . . . 83 E7
Llanberis . . . . . . . . . 83 E5
Llanbethery . . . . . . 22 C2
Llanbister . . . . . . . . 48 B3
Llanblethian . . . . . . 21 B8
Llanboidy . . . . . . . . 32 B3
Llanbradach . . . . . . 35 E5
Llanbrynmair . . . . . 59 D5
Llancarfan . . . . . . . . 22 B2
Llancayo . . . . . . . . . 35 D7
Llancloudy . . . . . . . 36 B1
Llancynfelyn . . . . . . 58 E3
Llandaff . . . . . . . . . 22 B3
Llandanwg . . . . . . . 71 E6
Llandarcy . . . . . . . . 33 E8
Llandawke . . . . . . . 32 C3
Llanddaniel Fab . . . 82 E4
Llanddarog . . . . . . . 33 C6
Llanddeiniol . . . . . . 46 B4
Llanddeiniolen . . . . 82 E5
Llandderfel . . . . . . . 72 F3
**Llanddeusant**
Anglesey . . . . . . 82 C3
Carms . . . . . . . . . 34 B1
Llanddew . . . . . . . . 48 F2
Llanddewi . . . . . . . . 33 F5
Llanddewi-Brefi . . . 47 D5
**Llanddewi**
Rhydderch . . . . 35 C7
Llanddewi Velfrey . 32 C2
Llanddoged . . . . . . 83 E8
Llanddona . . . . . . . 83 D5
Llanddowror . . . . . . 32 C3
Llanddulas . . . . . . . 72 B3
Llanddwywe . . . . . . 71 E6
Llanddyfnan . . . . . . 82 D5
Llandefaelog Fach 48 F2
Llandefaelog-
tre'r-graig. . . . . 35 B8
Llandefalle . . . . . . . 48 F3
Llandegai . . . . . . . . 83 D5
Llandegfan . . . . . . . 83 D5
Llandegla . . . . . . . . 73 D5
Llandegley . . . . . . . 48 C3
Llandegveth . . . . . . 35 E7
Llandegwning . . . . . 70 D3
Llandeilo . . . . . . . . 33 B7
Llandeilo Graban . . 48 E2
Llandeilo'r Fan . . . . 47 F7
Llandeloy . . . . . . . . 44 C3
Llandenny . . . . . . . . 35 D8
Llandevenny . . . . . . 35 F8
Llandewednock . . . . 3 E6
**Llandewi**
Ystradenny . . . . 48 C3
Llandinabo . . . . . . . 36 B2
Llandinam . . . . . . . . 59 F7
Llandissilio . . . . . . . 32 B2
Llandogo . . . . . . . . 36 D2
Llandough V Glam . 22 B1
V Glam . . . . . . . . 22 B3
**Llandovery**
= Llanymddyfri. . 47 F6
Llandow . . . . . . . . . 21 B8
Llandre Carms . . . . 47 E5
Ceredig . . . . . . . 58 F3
Llandrillo . . . . . . . . 72 F4
**Llandrillo-yn-**
Rhos . . . . . . . . . 83 C8
**Llandrindod** =
Llandrindod Wells. 48 C2
**Llandrindod Wells**
= Llandrindod. . 48 C2
Llandrinio . . . . . . . . 60 C2
Llandudno . . . . . . . 83 C7
**Llandudno Junction**
= Cyffordd
Llandudno . . . . 83 D7
Llandwrog . . . . . . . 82 F4
Llandybie . . . . . . . . 33 C7
Llandyfaelog . . . . . . 33 C5
Llandyfan . . . . . . . . 33 C7
Llandyfriog . . . . . . . 46 E2
Llandyfrydog . . . . . 82 C4
Llandygai . . . . . . . . 83 D5
Llandygwydd . . . . . 45 E4
Llandynan . . . . . . . . 73 E5
Llandyrnog . . . . . . . 72 C5
Llandysilio . . . . . . . 60 C2
Llandyssil . . . . . . . . 59 E8
Llandysul . . . . . . . . 46 E3
Llanedeyrn . . . . . . . 35 F6
Llanedi . . . . . . . . . . 33 D6
Llaneglwys . . . . . . . 48 F2
Llanegryn . . . . . . . . 58 D2
Llanegwad . . . . . . . 33 B6
Llaneilian . . . . . . . . 82 B4
**Llanelian-**
yn-Rhos . . . . . . 83 D8
Llanelidan . . . . . . . 72 D5
Llanelieu . . . . . . . . 35 C7
Llanellen . . . . . . . . 35 C7
Llanelltyd . . . . . . . . 58 C4
Llanelly . . . . . . . . . . 35 C6
Llanelly Hill . . . . . . 35 C6
Llanelwedd . . . . . . . 48 D2
Llanelwy = StAsaph 72 B4
Llanenddwyn . . . . . 71 E6
Llanengan . . . . . . . . 70 E3
Llanerchymedd . . . . 82 C4
Llanerfyl . . . . . . . . . 59 D7
Llanfachraeth . . . . . 82 C3
Llanfachreth . . . . . . 71 E8
Llanfaelog . . . . . . . . 82 D3

Llanfaelrhys . . . . . . 70 E3
Llanfaenor . . . . . . . 35 C8
Llanfaes Anglesey . . 83 D6
Powys . . . . . . . . . 34 B4
Llanfaethlu . . . . . . . 82 C3
Llanfaglan . . . . . . . . 82 E4
Llanfair . . . . . . . . . . 71 E6
Llanfair-ar-y-bryn 47 F7
**Llanfair**
Caereinion . . . . 59 D8
Llanfair Clydogau . 46 D5
**Llanfair-Dyffryn-**
Clwyd . . . . . . . . 72 D5
Llanfairfechan . . . . 83 D6
**Llanfair**
Kilgheddin . . . . 35 D7
**Llanfair-Nant-**
Gwyn . . . . . . . . 45 F3
Llanfairpwllgwyngyll
. . . . . . . . . . . . . . 82 D5
Llanfair Talhaiarn . 72 B3
Llanfair Waterdine 48 B4
**Llanfair-ym-Muallt**
= Builth Wells . . 48 D2
Llanfairynghornwy 82 B3
Llanfallteg . . . . . . . . 32 C2
Llanfaredd . . . . . . . . 48 D2
Llanfarian . . . . . . . . 46 B4
Llanfechain . . . . . . . 59 B8
Llanfechan . . . . . . . 47 D8
Llanfechell . . . . . . . 82 B3
Llanfendigaid . . . . . 58 D2
Llanferres . . . . . . . . 73 C5
Llan Ffestiniog . . . . 71 C8
Llanfflewyn . . . . . . . 82 C3
**Llanfihangel-**
ararth . . . . . . . . 46 F3
**Llanfihangel-**
Crucorney . . . . 35 B7
**Llanfihangel Glyn**
Myfyr . . . . . . . . 72 E3
**Llanfihangel Nant**
Bran. . . . . . . . . . 47 F8
**Llanfihangel-nant-**
Melan . . . . . . . . 48 D3
**Llanfihangel**
Rhydithon . . . . 48 C3
**Llanfihangel**
Rogiet. . . . . . . . 35 F8
Llanfihangel Tal-y-
llyn. . . . . . . . . . . 35 B5
**Llanfihangel-uwch-**
Gwili . . . . . . . . 33 B5
**Llanfihangel-y-**
Creuddyn . . . . . 47 B5
**Llanfihangel-yn-**
Ngwynfa . . . . . . 59 C7
**Llanfihangel yn**
Nhowyn . . . . . . 82 D3
**Llanfihangel-y-**
pennant
Gwyn . . . . . . . . . 58 D3
Gwyn . . . . . . . . . 71 C6
**Llanfihangel-y-**
traethau . . . . . . 71 D6
Llanfilo . . . . . . . . . . 48 F3
Llanfoist . . . . . . . . . 35 C6
Llanfor . . . . . . . . . . 72 F3
Llanfrechfa . . . . . . . 35 E7
Llanfrothen . . . . . . . 71 C7
Llanfrynach . . . . . . . 34 B4
Llanfwrog Anglesey 82 C3
Denb . . . . . . . . . . 72 D5
Llanfyllin . . . . . . . . 59 C8
Llanfynydd Carms . 33 B6
Flint . . . . . . . . . . 73 D6
Llanfyrnach . . . . . . . 45 F4
Llangadfan . . . . . . . 59 C7
Llangadog . . . . . . . . 33 B8
**Llangadwaladr**
Anglesey . . . . . . 82 E3
Powys . . . . . . . . . 73 F5
Llangaffo . . . . . . . . 82 E4
Llangain . . . . . . . . . 32 C4
**Llangammarch**
Wells . . . . . . . . 47 E8
Llangan . . . . . . . . . . 21 B8
Llangarron . . . . . . . 36 B2
Llangasty Talyllyn . 35 B5
Llangathen . . . . . . . 33 B6
Llangattock . . . . . . . 35 C6
Llangattock
Lingoed . . . . . . 35 B7
Llangattock nigh
Usk. . . . . . . . . . . 35 D7
Llangattock-Vibon-
Avel . . . . . . . . . 36 C1
Llangedwyn . . . . . . 59 B8
Llangefni . . . . . . . . . 82 D4
Llangeinor . . . . . . . . 34 F3
Llangeitho . . . . . . . . 46 D5
Llangeler . . . . . . . . . 46 F2
Llangelynin . . . . . . . 58 D2
Llangendeirne . . . . . 33 C5
Llangennech . . . . . . 33 D6
Llangennith . . . . . . . 33 E5
Llangenny . . . . . . . . 35 C6
Llangernyw . . . . . . . 83 E8
Llangian . . . . . . . . . 70 E3
Llanglydwen . . . . . . 32 B2
Llangoed . . . . . . . . . 83 D6
Llangoedmor . . . . . 45 E3
Llangollen . . . . . . . . 73 E6
Llangolman . . . . . . . 32 B2
Llangors . . . . . . . . . 35 B5
Llangovan . . . . . . . . 36 D1
Llangower . . . . . . . . 72 F3
Llangranog . . . . . . . 46 D2
Llangristiolus . . . . . 82 D4
Llangrove . . . . . . . . 36 C2
Llangua . . . . . . . . . . 35 B7
Llangunllo . . . . . . . . 48 B4
Llangunnor . . . . . . . 33 C5
Llangurig . . . . . . . . 47 B8
Llangwm Conwy . . 72 E3
Mon . . . . . . . . . . 35 D8
Pembs . . . . . . . . . 44 E4
Llangwnnadl . . . . . . 70 D3
Llangwyfan . . . . . . . 72 C5
Llangwyfan-isaf . . . 82 E3
Llangwyllog . . . . . . 82 D4
Llangwyryfon . . . . . 46 B4
Llangybi Ceredig . . 46 D5
Gwyn . . . . . . . . . 70 C5
Mon . . . . . . . . . . 35 E7
Llangyfelach . . . . . . 33 E7
Llangynhafal . . . . . . 72 C5

Llangynidr . . . . . . . . 35 C5
Llangynin . . . . . . . . 32 C3
Llangynog Carms. . . 32 C4
Powys . . . . . . . . . 59 B7
Llangynwyd . . . . . . 34 F2
Llanhamlach . . . . . . 34 B4
Llanharan . . . . . . . . 34 F4
Llanharry . . . . . . . . 34 F4
Llanhennock . . . . . . 35 E7
**Llanhilleth**
= Llanhilleth . . 35 D6
Llanhilleth . . . . . . . 35 D6
Llanidloes . . . . . . . . 59 F6
Llaniestyn . . . . . . . . 70 D3
Llanifyny . . . . . . . . . 59 F5
Llanigon . . . . . . . . . 48 F4
Llanilar . . . . . . . . . . 46 B5
Llanilid . . . . . . . . . . 34 F3
**Llanilltud Fawr**
= Llantwit Major. 21 C8
Llanishen Cardiff . . 35 F5
Mon . . . . . . . . . . 36 D1
Llanllawddog . . . . . 33 B5
Llanllechid. . . . . . . . 83 E6
Llanllowell . . . . . . . 35 E7
Llanllugan . . . . . . . . 59 D7
Llanllwch . . . . . . . . 32 C4
Llanllwchaiarn . . . . 59 E8
Llanllwni . . . . . . . . . 46 F3
Llanllyfni . . . . . . . . 82 F4
Llanmadoc . . . . . . . 33 E5
Llanmaes . . . . . . . . 21 C8
Llanmartin . . . . . . . 35 F7
Llanmihangel . . . . . 21 B8
Llanmorlais . . . . . . . 33 E6
Llannefydd . . . . . . . 72 B3
Llannon . . . . . . . . . . 33 D6
Llannor . . . . . . . . . . 70 D4
Llanon . . . . . . . . . . . 46 C4
Llanover . . . . . . . . . 35 D7
Llanpumsaint . . . . . 33 B5
Llanreithan . . . . . . . 44 C3
Llanrhaeadr. . . . . . . 72 C4
**Llanrhaeadr-ym-**
Mochnant . . . . 59 B8
Llanrhian . . . . . . . . 44 B3
Llanrhidian . . . . . . . 33 E5
Llanrhos . . . . . . . . . 83 C7
Llanrhyddlad . . . . . . 82 C3
Llanrhystud . . . . . . 46 C4
Llanrosser . . . . . . . . 48 F4
Llanrothal . . . . . . . . 36 C1
Llanrug . . . . . . . . . . 82 E5
Llanrumney . . . . . . . 35 F6
Llanrwst . . . . . . . . . 83 E8
Llansadurnen . . . . . 32 C3
Llansadwrn
Anglesey . . . . . . 83 D5
Carms . . . . . . . . . 47 F5
Llansaint . . . . . . . . . 32 D4
Llansamlet . . . . . . . 33 E7
**Llansanffraid-ym-**
Mechain . . . . . 60 B2
Llansannan . . . . . . . 72 C3
Llansannor . . . . . . . 21 B8
**Llansantffraed**
Ceredig . . . . . . . 46 C4
Powys . . . . . . . . . 35 B5
**Llansantffraed**
Cwmdeuddwr. . 47 C8
**Llansantffraed-in-**
Elvel . . . . . . . . . 48 D2
Llansantffraid . . . . . 46 F5
Llansilin . . . . . . . . . 60 B2
Llansoy . . . . . . . . . . 35 D8
Llanspyddid. . . . . . . 34 B4
Llanstadwell . . . . . . 44 E4
Llansteffan . . . . . . . 32 C4
Llanstephan . . . . . . 48 B3
Llantarnam . . . . . . . 35 E7
Llanteg . . . . . . . . . . 32 C2
Llanthony . . . . . . . . 35 B6
**Llantilio**
Crossenny . . . . 35 C7
Llantilio Pertholey. 35 C7
Llantood . . . . . . . . . 45 E3
**Llantrisant**
Anglesey . . . . . . 82 C3
Mon . . . . . . . . . . 35 E7
Rhondda . . . . . . 34 F4
**Llantrithyd** . . . . . 22 B2
Llantwit Fardre. . . . 34 F4
Llantwit Major
= Llanilltud Fawr. 21 C8
Llanuwchllyn. . . . . . 72 F2
Llanvaches . . . . . . . 35 E8
Llanvair Discoed . . 35 E8
Llanvapley . . . . . . . 35 C7
Llanvetherine . . . . . 35 C7
Llanveynoe. . . . . . . . 48 F5
**Llanvihangel**
Gobion . . . . . . . 35 C7
Llanvihangel-Ystern-
Llewern . . . . . . 35 C8
Llanwarne . . . . . . . . 36 B2
Llanwddyn . . . . . . . 59 C7
Llanweddyn . . . . . . 59 C7
Llanwenog . . . . . . . 46 E3
Llanwern . . . . . . . . 35 F7
Llanwinio . . . . . . . . 32 B3
Llanwnda Gwyn . . . 82 F4
Pembs . . . . . . . . . 44 B4
Llanwnnen . . . . . . . 46 E4
Llanwnog . . . . . . . . 59 E7
Llanwrda . . . . . . . . . 47 F6
Llanwrin . . . . . . . . . 58 D4
Llanwrthwl. . . . . . . . 47 C8
**Llanwrtud**
= Llanwrtyd Wells. 47 E7
**Llanwrtyd Wells**
. . . . . . . . . . . . . . 47 E7
Llanwyddelan . . . . . 59 D7
Llanyblodwel. . . . . . 60 B2
Llanybri . . . . . . . . . . 32 C4
Llanybydder . . . . . . 46 E4
Llanycefn . . . . . . . . 32 B1
Llanychaer . . . . . . . 44 B4
Llanycil . . . . . . . . . . 72 F3
Llanycrwys . . . . . . . 46 E5
Llanymawddwy . . . 59 C6
Llanymddyfri
= Llandovery. . . 47 F6
Llanymynech . . . . . 60 B2
Llanynghenedl . . . . 82 C3
Llanynys . . . . . . . . . 72 C5
Llan-y-pwll . . . . . . . 73 D7
Llanyre . . . . . . . . . . 48 C2
Llanystumdwy . . . . 71 D5

Llanywern . . . . . . . . 35 B5
Llawhaden. . . . . . . . 32 C1
Llawnt . . . . . . . . . . . 73 F6
Llawr Dref . . . . . . . . 70 E3
Llawryglyn. . . . . . . . 59 E6
Llay . . . . . . . . . . . . . 73 D7
Llechcynfarwy . . . . 82 C3
Llecheiddior . . . . . . 71 C5
Llechfaen . . . . . . . . 34 B4
Llechryd Caerph. . . 35 D5
Ceredig . . . . . . . 45 E4
Llechrydau . . . . . . . 73 F6
Lledrod . . . . . . . . . . 46 B5
Llenmerewig . . . . . . 59 E8
Llethrid. . . . . . . . . . 33 E6
Llidiad Nenog . . . . 46 F4
Llidiardau . . . . . . . . 72 F2
Llidiart-y-parc . . . . 72 E5
Llithfaen . . . . . . . . . 70 C4
Llong . . . . . . . . . . . . 73 C6
Llowes . . . . . . . . . . 48 E3
Llundain-fach. . . . . 46 D4
Llwydcoed . . . . . . . 34 D3
Llwyn . . . . . . . . . . . 60 F2
Llwyncelyn. . . . . . . . 46 D3
Llwyndafydd . . . . . 46 D2
Llwynderw . . . . . . . 60 D2
Llwyn-du . . . . . . . . . 35 C6
Llwyndyrys . . . . . . . 70 C4
Llwyn-hendy . . . . . . 33 E6
Llwynmawr . . . . . . . 73 F6
Llwyn-têg . . . . . . . . 33 D6
Llwyn-y-brain . . . . . 32 C2
Llwyn-y-groes. . . . . 46 D4
Llwynypia . . . . . . . . 34 E3
Llynclys . . . . . . . . . 60 B2
Llynfaes . . . . . . . . . 82 D4
Llysfaen . . . . . . . . . 83 D8
Llyswen . . . . . . . . . 48 F3
Llysworney . . . . . . . 21 B8
Llys-y-frân . . . . . . . 32 B1
Llywel . . . . . . . . . . . 47 F7
Loan . . . . . . . . . . . 120 B2
Loanend . . . . . . . . 122 D5
Loanhead . . . . . . . 121 C5
Loans . . . . . . . . . . 118 F3
Loans ofTullich. . 151 D11
Lobb. . . . . . . . . . . . 20 F3
Loch a Charnain. . 148 D3
Loch a'
Ghainmhich. . . 155 E7
Lochailort . . . . . . . 147 C10
Lochaline. . . . . . . . 147 G9
Lochans . . . . . . . . . 104 D4
Lochassynt
Lodge . . . . . . . 156 G4
Lochavich House. 124 D5
Lochawe . . . . . . . . 125 C7
Loch Baghasdail
= Lochboisdale. 148 G2
Lochboisdale =
Loch Baghasdail. 148 G2
Lochbuie . . . . . . . . 124 C2
Lochcarron. . . . . . 149 E13
Loch Choire
Lodge . . . . . . . 157 H9
Lochdhu . . . . . . . . 157 E13
Lochdochart
House . . . . . . . 126 B3
Lochdon . . . . . . . . 124 B3
Lochdrum . . . . . . . 150 D5
Lochearnhead . . . 126 B4
Lochee . . . . . . . . . 134 F3
Lochend Highld . . 151 H8
Highld . . . . . . . . 158 D4
Locherben . . . . . . . 114 E2
Loch Euphoirt . . . 148 B3
Lochfoot . . . . . . . . 107 B5
Lochgair. . . . . . . . . 145 D8
Lochgarthside . . . . 137 C8
Lochgelly . . . . . . . 128 E3
Lochgilphead. . . . . 145 E7
Lochgoilhead. . . . . 125 E8
Loch Head . . . . . . . 105 E7
Lochhill . . . . . . . . . 152 B2
Lochindorb
Lodge . . . . . . . 151 H12
Lochinver. . . . . . . . 156 G3
Lochlane. . . . . . . . . 127 B7
Loch Loyal Lodge. 157 E9
Lochluichart . . . . . 150 E6
Lochmaben . . . . . . 114 F3
Lochmaddy =
Loch nam Madadh 148 B4
Lochmore
Cottage . . . . . . 158 F2
Lochmore Lodge . 156 F5
Loch nam Madadh
= Lochmaddy. . 148 B4
Lochore . . . . . . . . . 128 E3
Lochportain . . . . . 148 A4
Lochranza . . . . . . . 143 C10
Lochs Crofts . . . . . 152 B3
Loch Sgioport . . . 148 E3
Lochside Aberds . . 135 C7
Highld . . . . . . . . 151 F11
Highld . . . . . . . . 156 D7
Highld . . . . . . . . 157 F11
Lochslin . . . . . . . . 151 C11
Lochstack Lodge . 156 F5
Lochton . . . . . . . . . 141 E6
Lochty Angus. . . . . 135 C5
Fife. . . . . . . . . . . 129 D7
Perth . . . . . . . . . 128 B2
Lochuisge . . . . . . . 130 D1
Lochurr . . . . . . . . . 113 F7
Lochwinnoch . . . . 118 D3
Lochwood . . . . . . . 114 E3
Lochyside. . . . . . . . 131 B5
Lockengate . . . . . . . 4 C5
Lockerbie . . . . . . . 114 F4
Lockeridge . . . . . . 25 C6
Lockerley . . . . . . . 14 B3
Locking. . . . . . . . . 23 D5
Lockinge. . . . . . . . 38 F4
Lockington E Yorks 97 E5
Leics. . . . . . . . . . 63 B8
Lockleywood . . . . . 61 B6
Locks Heath . . . . . 15 D6
Lockton . . . . . . . . . 103 E6
Lockwood . . . . . . . 88 C2
Loddington Leics. . 64 D4
N Nhants . . . . . . 53 B6
Loddiswell . . . . . . . 6 E5
Loddon . . . . . . . . . 69 E6

Lode. . . . . . . . . . . . 55 C6
Loders . . . . . . . . . . 12 E2
Lodsworth . . . . . . . 16 B3
Lofthouse N Yorks . 94 B4
W Yorks. . . . . . . . 88 B4
Loftus . . . . . . . . . . 103 C5
Logan. . . . . . . . . . 113 B5
Loganlea. . . . . . . . 120 C2
Logan Mains . . . . 104 E4
Loggerheads . . . . . 74 F4
**Logie** Angus. . . . 135 C6
Fife. . . . . . . . . . . 129 B6
Moray. . . . . . . . . 151 F13
Logiealmond
Lodge . . . . . . . 133 F6
Logie Coldstone . 140 D3
Logie Hill . . . . . . . 151 D10
Logie Newton . . . 153 E6
Logie Pert . . . . . . 135 C6
Logierait . . . . . . . 133 D6
Login . . . . . . . . . . 32 B2
Lolworth . . . . . . . . 54 C4
Lonbain. . . . . . . . 149 C11
Londesborough . . 96 E4
London Colney . . . 40 D4
Londonderry . . . . 101 F8
Londonthorpe. . . . 78 F2
Londubh . . . . . . . . 155 J13
Lonemore. . . . . . . 151 C10
Long Ashton . . . . 23 B7
Longbar. . . . . . . . . 118 D3
Long Bennington. . 77 E8
Longbenton . . . . . 111 C5
Longborough . . . . 38 B1
Long Bredy. . . . . . 12 E3
Longbridge Warks . 51 C7
W Mid . . . . . . . . . 50 B5
Longbridge
Deverill . . . . . . 24 E3
Long Buckby . . . . 52 C4
Longburton . . . . . . 12 C4
Long Clawson . . . 64 B4
Longcliffe. . . . . . . 76 D2
Long Common . . . 15 C6
**Long Compton**
Staffs . . . . . . . . 62 B2
Warks . . . . . . . . 51 F7
Longcot. . . . . . . . . 38 E2
Long Crendon . . . 39 D6
Long Crichel . . . . . 13 C7
Longcroft . . . . . . . 119 B7
Longden . . . . . . . . 60 D4
Long Ditton. . . . . . 28 C2
**Longdon** Staffs . . 62 C4
Worcs . . . . . . . . . 50 F3
Longdon on Tern . 61 C6
**Longdown** . . . . . . 10 E3
Longdowns. . . . . . . 3 C6
Long Drax . . . . . . 89 B7
Long Duckmanton. 76 B4
Long Eaton. . . . . . 76 F4
**Longfield** Kent . . 29 C7
Shetland. . . . . . 160 M5
**Longford** Derbys . 76 F3
Glos . . . . . . . . . . 37 B5
London. . . . . . . . 27 B8
Shrops . . . . . . . . 74 F3
Telford. . . . . . . . 61 C7
W Mid . . . . . . . . 63 F7
Longfordlane . . . . 76 F2
Longforgan. . . . . . 128 B5
Longformacus . . . 122 D3
Longframlington . 117 D7
Long Green . . . . . . 50 F3
Longham Dorset . . 13 E8
Norf . . . . . . . . . . 68 C2
Long Hanborough . 38 C4
Longhaven . . . . . 153 E11
Longhill. . . . . . . . 153 C9
Longhirst . . . . . . 117 F8
Longhope Glos . . . 36 C3
Orkney . . . . . . . 159 J4
Longhorsley . . . . 117 E7
Longhoughton . . 117 C8
Long Itchington . . 52 C2
Long Lane . . . . . . 61 C6
Longlane Derbys . . 76 F2
W Berks. . . . . . . 26 B2
Long Lawford . . . . 52 B2
Longlevens . . . . . 37 B5
Longley. . . . . . . . . 88 D2
Longley Green . . . 50 D2
Long Load. . . . . . . 12 B2
Long Marston
Herts . . . . . . . . . 40 C1
N Yorks . . . . . . . 95 D8
Warks . . . . . . . . 51 E6
Long Marton . . . . 100 B1
Long Melford . . . . 56 E2
Longmoor Camp . 27 F5
Longmorn . . . . . . 152 C2
Long Newnton . . . 37 E6
Longnewton
Borders . . . . . . 115 B8
Stockton. . . . . . 102 C1
Long Newton. . . . 121 C8
Longney . . . . . . . . 36 C4
Longniddry . . . . . . 121 B7
**Longnor** Shrops . . 60 D4
Staffs . . . . . . . . . 75 C7
Longparish . . . . . . 26 E2
Longport. . . . . . . . 75 E5
Long Preston . . . . 93 D8
Longridge Lancs . . 93 F6
Staffs . . . . . . . . . 62 C3
W Loth . . . . . . . 120 C2
Longriggend . . . . 119 B8
Long Riston . . . . . 97 E7
Longsdon. . . . . . . 75 D6
Longshaw . . . . . . . 86 D3
Longside. . . . . . . 153 D10
Long Sight . . . . . . 87 D7
Longstanton . . . . 54 C4
Longstock . . . . . . 25 F8
Longstone. . . . . . . 44 E5
Longstowe . . . . . . 54 D4
Long Stratton . . . 68 E4
Long Street . . . . . 53 E5
Long Sutton Hants 26 E5
Lincs. . . . . . . . . . 66 B4
Somerset. . . . . . 12 B2
Longthorpe . . . . . 65 E8
Long Thurlow . . . . 56 C4
Longthwaite . . . . . 99 B6
Longton Lancs . . . 86 B2
Stoke. . . . . . . . . 75 E6
Longtown Cumb. . 108 C3
Hereford . . . . . . 35 B7

Longview . . . . . . . 86 E2
Longville in the
Dale. . . . . . . . . 60 E5
Long Whatton . . . . 63 B8
Longwick . . . . . . . 39 D7
Long Wittenham . 39 E5
Longwitton . . . . . 117 F6
Longwood . . . . . . 61 D6
Longworth . . . . . . 38 E3
Longyester . . . . . . 121 C8
Lonmay . . . . . . . . 153 C10
Lonmore . . . . . . . 148 D7
Lonton . . . . . . . . . 100 C4
Loose . . . . . . . . . . 29 D8
Loosley Row . . . . . 39 D8
Lopcombe Corner . 25 F7
Lopen . . . . . . . . . . 12 C2
Loppington . . . . . 60 B4
Lopwell. . . . . . . . . 6 C2
Lorbottle . . . . . . . 117 D6
Lorbottle Hall . . . 117 D6
Lornty . . . . . . . . . 134 E1
Loscoe. . . . . . . . . 76 E4
Losgaintir . . . . . . 154 H5
Lossiemouth . . . . 152 A2
Lossit . . . . . . . . . . 142 C2
Lostford . . . . . . . . 74 F3
Lostock Gralam . . 74 B3
Lostock Green. . . . 74 B3
Lostock Hall. . . . . 86 B3
Lostock Junction . 86 D4
Lostwithiel. . . . . . 5 D6
Loth . . . . . . . . . . 159 E7
Lothbeg . . . . . . . 157 H12
Lothersdale . . . . . 94 E2
Lothmore . . . . . . 157 H12
Loudwater . . . . . . 40 E2
Loughborough . . . 64 C2
Loughor . . . . . . . . 33 E6
Loughton Essex . . 41 E7
Shrops . . . . . . . . 61 F6
Lound Lincs . . . . . 65 C7
Notts . . . . . . . . . 89 F7
Suff. . . . . . . . . . . 69 E8
Lount . . . . . . . . . . 63 C7
Louth . . . . . . . . . . 91 F7
Love Clough. . . . . 87 B6
Lovedean . . . . . . . 15 C7
Lover . . . . . . . . . . 14 B3
Loversall . . . . . . . 89 E6
Loves Green . . . . . 42 D2
Lovesome Hill . . . 102 E1
Loveston. . . . . . . . 32 D1
Lovington. . . . . . . 23 F7
Low Ackworth . . . 89 C5
Low Barlings . . . . 78 B3
Low Bentham . . . . 93 C6
Low Bradfield . . . . 88 E3
Low Bradley. . . . . 94 E3
Low Braithwaite. 108 E4
Low Brunton . . . . 110 B2
Low Burnham . . . . 89 D8
Low Burton . . . . . 101 F7
Low Buston . . . . . 117 D8
Low Catton . . . . . 96 D3
Low Clanyard . . . . 104 F5
Low Coniscliffe . . 101 C7
Low Crosby . . . . . 108 D4
Low Dalby . . . . . . 103 F6
Lowdham . . . . . . . 77 E6
Low Dinsdale . . . . 101 C8
Lowe . . . . . . . . . . 74 F2
Low Ellington. . . . 101 F7
Lower Aisholt . . . . 22 F4
Lower Arncott. . . . 39 C6
Lower Ashton . . . . 10 F3
Lower Assendon . 39 F7
Lower Badcall . . . 156 E4
Lower Bartle . . . . 92 F4
Lower Basildon . . 26 B4
Lower Beeding . . . 17 B6
Lower Benefield . . 65 F6
Lower Boddington 52 D2
Lower Brailes . . . . 51 F8
Lower Breakish . . 149 F11
Lower Broadheath 50 D3
Lower Bullingham 49 F7
Lower Cam. . . . . . 36 D4
Lower Chapel . . . . 48 F2
Lower Chute . . . . 25 D8
Lower Cragabus . 142 D4
Lower Crossings . 87 F8
Lower
Cumberworth. . 88 D3
Lower Darwen . . . 86 B4
Lower Dean . . . . . 53 C8
Lower Diabaig . . . 149 B12
Lower Dicker . . . . 18 D2
Lower Dinchope. . 60 F4
Lower Down . . . . 60 F3
Lower Drift. . . . . . 2 D3
Lower Dunsforth . 95 C7
Lower Egleton . . . 49 E8
Lower Elkstone. . . 75 D7
Lower End . . . . . . 40 B2
Lower Everleigh. . 25 D6
Lower Farringdon 26 F5
Lower Foxdale . . . 84 E2
Lower Frankton . . 73 F7
Lower Froyle. . . . . 27 E5
Lower Gledfield . . 151 B8
Lower Green . . . . 81 D5
Lower Hacheston . 57 D7
Lower Halistra . . . 148 C7
Lower Halstow . . . 30 C2
Lower Hardres . . . 31 D5
Lower Hawthwaite 98 F4
Lower Heath . . . . 75 C5
Lower
Hempriggs . . . 151 E14
Lower Hergest . . . 48 D4
Lower Heyford . . . 38 B4
Lower Higham . . . 29 B8
Lower Holbrook . . 57 F5
Lower Hordley . . . 60 B3
Lower
Horsebridge . . 18 D2
Lower Killeyan. . . 142 D3
Lower Kingswood 28 D3
Lower Kinnerton . 73 C7
Lower Langford . . 23 C6
Lower Largo . . . . 129 D6
Lower Leigh. . . . . 75 F7
Lower Lemington . 51 F7
Lower Lenie . . . . 137 B8

Lower Lydbrook . . 36 C2
Lower Lye. . . . . . . 49 C6
Lower Machen . . . 35 F6
Lower Maes-coed 48 F5
Lower Mayland . . 43 D5
Lower Midway . . . 63 B7
Lower Milovaig. . 148 C6
Lower Moor . . . . . 50 E4
Lower Nazeing . . . 41 D6
Lower Netchwood 61 E6
Lower Ollach . . . 149 E10
Lower Penarth . . . 22 B3
Lower Penn . . . . . 62 E2
Lower Pennington 14 E4
Lower Peover . . . . 74 B4
Lower Pexhill . . . . 75 B5
Lower Place. . . . . . 87 C7
Lower Quinton . . . 51 E6
Lower Rochford . . 49 C8
Lower Seagry . . . . 37 F6
Lower Shelton . . . 53 E7
Lower Shiplake . . 27 B5
Lower
Shuckburgh . . 52 C2
Lower Slaughter . 38 B1
Lower Stanton St
Quintin . . . . . . 37 F6
Lower Stoke . . . . . 30 B2
Lower Stondon . . 54 F2
Lower Stow Bedon 68 E2
Lower Street Norf . 69 C6
Norf . . . . . . . . . . 81 D8
Lower Strensham . 50 E4
Lower Stretton . . . 86 F4
Lower Sundon . . . 40 B3
Lower Swanwick . 15 D5
Lower Swell . . . . . 38 B1
Lower Tean. . . . . . 75 F7
Lower Thurlton. . . 69 E7
Lower Tote . . . . . 149 B10
Lower Town . . . . . 44 B4
Lower Tysoe . . . . 51 E8
Lower Upham . . . 15 C6
Lower Vexford . . . 22 F3
Lower Weare . . . . 23 D6
Lower Welson . . . 48 D4
Lower Whitley . . . 74 B3
Lower Wield . . . . 26 E4
Lower
Winchendon . . 39 C7
Lower Withington 74 C5
Lower Woodend . . 39 F8
Lower Woodford . 25 F6
Lower Wyche . . . . 50 E2
Lowestoft . . . . . . 69 E8
Loweswater . . . . . 98 B3
Low Etherley . . . 101 B6
Low Fell . . . . . . . 111 D5
Lowford . . . . . . . . 15 C5
Low Fulney. . . . . . 66 B2
Low Garth. . . . . . 103 D5
Low Gate. . . . . . . 110 C2
Lowgill Lancs . . . . 93 C6
W&F. . . . . . . . . . 99 E8
Low Grantley . . . . 94 B5
Low Habberley . . . 50 B3
Low Ham . . . . . . . 12 B2
Low Hesket . . . . . 108 E4
Low Hesleyhurst . 117 E6
Low Hutton . . . . . 96 C3
Lowick N Nhants . . 65 F6
Northumb. . . . . 123 F6
Lowick Bridge. . . . 98 F4
Lowick Green . . . . 98 F4
Low Laithe . . . . . . 94 C4
Lowlands . . . . . . . 35 E6
Low Leighton . . . . 87 F8
Low Lorton. . . . . . 98 B3
Low Marishes . . . . 96 B4
Low Marnham . . . 77 C8
Low Mill . . . . . . . 102 E4
Low Moor Lancs . . 93 E7
W Yorks. . . . . . . . 88 B3
Lowmoor Row . . . 99 B8
Low Moorsley . . . 111 E6
Low Newton . . . . 99 F6
Low Newton-by-the-
Sea . . . . . . . . . 117 B8
Lownie Moor . . . 134 E4
Low Row Cumb . . 108 F3
Cumb. . . . . . . . 109 C5
N Yorks. . . . . . . 100 E4
Low Salchrie . . . . 104 C4
Low Smerby. . . . . 143 F8
Lowsonford . . . . . 51 C6
Lowther . . . . . . . . 99 B7
Lowthorpe . . . . . . 97 C6
Lowton . . . . . . . . 86 E4
Lowton Common . 86 E4
Low Torry . . . . . . 128 F2
Low Worsall . . . . 102 D1
Low Wray . . . . . . 99 D5
Loxbeare. . . . . . . . 10 C4
Loxhill. . . . . . . . . 27 F8
Loxhore . . . . . . . . 20 F5
Loxley . . . . . . . . . 51 D7
Loxton . . . . . . . . . 23 D5
Loxwood . . . . . . . 27 F8
Lubcroft. . . . . . . 156 J6
Lubenham . . . . . . 64 F4
Luccombe . . . . . . 21 E8
Luccombe Village . 15 G6
Lucker. . . . . . . . . 123 F7
Luckett . . . . . . . . 5 B8
Luckington . . . . . 37 F5
Lucklawhill . . . . 129 B6
Luckwell Bridge . 21 F8
Lucton . . . . . . . . 49 C6
Ludag. . . . . . . . . 148 G2
Ludborough . . . . . 91 E6
Ludchurch . . . . . . 32 C2
Luddenden . . . . . 87 B8
Luddenden Foot . 87 B8
Luddesdown . . . . 29 C7
Luddington N Lincs 90 C2
Warks . . . . . . . . 51 D6
Luddington in the
Brook . . . . . . . 65 F8
Lude House . . . . 133 C5
Ludford Lincs . . . . 91 F6
Shrops . . . . . . . . 49 B7
Ludgershall Bucks . 39 C6
Wilts . . . . . . . . . 25 D7
Ludgvan . . . . . . . 2 C4
Ludham . . . . . . . . 69 C6
Ludlow . . . . . . . . 49 B7
Ludwell. . . . . . . . 13 B7
Ludworth . . . . . . 111 E6

Luffincott....8 E5
Lugar....113 B5
Luggate Burn....122 B2
Lugg Green....49 C6
Luggiebank....119 B7
Lugton....118 D4
Lugwardine....49 E7
Luib....149 F10
Lulham....49 E6
Lullenden....28 E5
Lullington Derbys....63 C6
Som....24 D2
Lulsgate Bottom....23 C7
Lulsley....50 D2
Lumb....87 B8
Lumby....95 F7
Lumloch....119 C6
Lumphanan....140 D4
Lumphinnans....128 E3
Lumsdaine....122 C4
Lumsden....140 B3
Lunan....135 D6
Lunanhead....134 D4
Luncarty....128 B2
Lund E Yorks....97 E5
N Yorks....96 F2
Shetland....160 C7
Lunderton....153 D11
Lundie Angus....134 F2
Highld....136 C4
Lundin Links....129 D6
Lunga....124 E3
Lunna....160 G6
Lunning....160 G7
Lunnon....33 F6
Lunsford's Cross....18 E4
Lunt....85 D4
Luntley....49 D5
Luppitt....11 D6
Lupset....88 C4
Lupton....99 F7
Lurgashall....16 B3
Lusby....79 C6
Luson....6 E4
Luss....126 E2
Lussagiven....144 E5
Lusta....149 C7
Lustleigh....10 F2
Luston....49 C6
Luthermuir....135 C6
Luthrie....128 C5
Luton Devon....7 B7
Luton....40 B3
Medway....29 C8
Lutterworth....64 F2
Lutton Devon....6 D3
Lincs....66 B4
N Nhants....65 F8
Lutworthy....10 C2
Luxborough....21 F8
Luxulyan....5 D5
Lybster....158 G4
Lydbury North....60 F3
Lydcott....21 F5
Lydd....19 C7
Lydden....31 E6
Lyddington....65 E5
Lydd on Sea....19 C7
Lydeard St Lawrence....22 F3
Lyde Green....26 D5
Lydford....9 F7
Lydford-on-Fosse....23 F7
Lydgate....87 B7
Lydham....60 E3
Lydiard Green....37 F7
Lydiard Millicent....37 F7
Lydiate....85 D4
Lydlinch....12 C5
Lydney....36 D3
Lydstep....32 E1
Lye....62 F3
Lye Green Bucks....40 D2
E Sus....18 B2
Lyford....38 E3
Lymbridge Green....30 E5
Lyme Regis....11 E8
Lyminge....31 E5
Lymington....14 E4
Lyminster....16 D4
Lymm....86 F4
Lymore....14 E3
Lympne....19 B8
Lympsham....22 D5
Lympstone....10 F4
Lynchat....138 D3
Lyndale House....149 C8
Lyndhurst....14 D4
Lyndon....65 D6
Lyne....27 C8
Lyneal....73 F8
Lyne Down....49 F8
Lyneham Oxon....38 B2
Wilts....24 B5
Lynemore....139 B6
Lynemouth....117 E8
Lyne of Gorthleck....137 B8
Lyne of Skene....141 C6
Lyness....159 J4
Lyng Norf....68 C3
Som....11 B8
Lynmouth....21 E6
Lynsted....30 C3
Lynton....21 E6
Lyon's Gate....12 D4
Lyonshall....48 D5
Lytchett Matravers 13 E7
Lytchett Minster....13 E7
Lyth....158 D4
Lytham....85 B4
Lytham St Anne's....85 B4
Lythe....103 C6
Lythes....159 K5

**M**

Mabe Burnthouse....3 C6
Mabie....107 B6
Mablethorpe....91 F9
Macclesfield....75 B6
Macclesfield Forest....75 B6
Macduff....153 B7
Mace Green....56 E5
Machan....35 F6
Machrihanish....143 F7

Machynlleth....58 D4
Machynys....33 E6
Mackerel's Common....16 B4
Mackworth....76 F3
Macmerry....121 B7
Madderty....127 B8
Maddiston....120 B2
Madehurst....16 C3
Madeley Staffs....74 E4
Telford....61 D6
Madeley Heath....74 E4
Madeley Park....74 E4
Madingley....54 C4
Madley....49 F6
Madresfield....50 E3
Madron....2 C3
Maen-y-groes....46 D2
Maenaddwyn....82 C4
Maenclochog....32 B1
Maendy....22 B2
Maentwrog....71 C7
Maer....74 F4
Maerdy Conwy....72 E4
Rhondda....34 E3
Maesbrook....60 B2
Maesbury....60 B3
Maesbury Marsh....60 B3
Maesgwyn-Isaf....59 C8
Maesgwynne....32 B3
Maeshafn....73 C6
Maesllyn....46 E2
Maesmynis....48 E2
Maesteg....34 E2
Maes-Treylow....48 C4
Maesybont....33 C6
Maesycrugiau....46 E3
Maesy cwmmer....35 E5
Maesymeillion....46 E3
Magdalen Laver....41 D8
Maggieknockater 152 D3
Magham Down....18 D3
Maghull....85 D4
Magor....35 F8
Magpie Green....56 B4
Maiden Bradley....24 F3
Maidencombe....7 C7
Maidenhall....57 E5
Maidenhead....40 F1
Maiden Law....110 E4
Maiden Newton....12 E3
Maidens....112 D2
Maidensgrave....57 E6
Maiden's Green....27 B6
Maidenwell Corn....5 B6
Lincs....79 B6
Maiden Wells....44 F4
Maidford....52 E4
Maids Moreton....52 F5
Maidstone....29 D8
Maidwell....52 B5
Mail....160 L6
Main....59 C8
Maindee....35 F7
Mainsforth....111 F6
Mains of Airies....104 C3
Mains of Allardice....135 B8
Mains of Annochie....153 D9
Mains of Ardestie 135 F5
Mains of Balhall....135 C5
Mains of Ballindarg....134 D4
Mains of Balnakettle....135 B6
Mains of Birness....153 E9
Mains of Burgie....151 F13
Mains of Clunas....151 G11
Mains of Crichie....153 D9
Mains of Dalvey....151 H14
Mains of Dellavaird....141 F6
Mains of Drum....141 E7
Mains of Edingight....152 C5
Mains of Fedderate....153 D8
Mains of Inkhorn....153 E9
Mains of Mayen....152 D5
Mains of Melgund....135 D5
Mains of Thornton....135 B6
Mains of Watten....158 D4
Mainsriddle....107 D6
Mainstone....60 F2
Maisemore....37 B5
Malacleit....148 A2
Malborough....6 F5
Malcoff....87 F8
Maldon....42 D4
Malham....94 C2
Maligar....149 B9
Mallaig....147 B9
Malleny Mills....120 C4
Malling....126 D4
Malltraeth....42 E3
Mallwyd....59 C5
Malmesbury....37 F6
Malmsmead....21 E6
Malpas Ches W....73 E8
Corn....3 B7
Newport....35 E7
Malswick....36 B4
Maltby Stockton....102 C2
S Yorks....89 E6
Maltby le Marsh....91 F8
Malting Green....43 B5
Maltman's Hill....30 E3
Malton....96 B3
Malvern Link....50 E2
Malvern Wells....50 E2
Mamble....49 B8

Mamhilad....35 D7
Manaccan....3 D6
Manafon....59 D8
Manais....154 J6
Manar House....141 B6
Manaton....10 F2
Manby....91 F7
Mancetter....63 E7
Manchester....87 E6
Manchester Airport....87 F6
Mancot....73 C7
Mandally....137 D5
Manea....66 F4
Manfield....101 C7
Mangaster....160 F5
Mangotsfield....23 B8
Mangurstadh....154 D5
Mankinholes....87 B7
Manley....74 B2
Manmoel....35 D5
Mannal....146 G2
Mannerston....120 B3
Manningford Bohune....25 D6
Manningford Bruce....25 D6
Manningham....94 F4
Mannings Heath....17 B6
Mannington....13 D8
Manningtree....56 F4
Mannofield....141 D8
Manor....41 F7
Manorbier....32 E1
Manordeilo....33 B7
Manor Estate....88 F4
Manorhill....122 F2
Manorowen....44 B4
Mansell Lacy....49 E6
Mansell Gamage....49 E5
Mansergh....99 F8
Mansfield E Ayrs....113 C6
Notts....76 C5
Mansfield Woodhouse....76 C5
Mansriggs....98 F4
Manston Dorset....13 C6
Kent....31 C7
W Yorks....95 F6
Manswood....13 D7
Manthorpe Lincs....65 C7
Lincs....78 F2
Manton N Lincs....90 D3
Notts....77 B5
Rutland....65 D5
Wilts....25 C6
Manuden....41 B7
Maperton....12 B4
Maplebeck....77 C7
Maple Cross....40 E3
Mapledurham....26 B4
Mapledurwell....26 D4
Maplehurst....17 B5
Maplescombe....29 C6
Mapleton....75 E8
Mapperley....76 E4
Mapperley Park....77 E5
Mapperton....12 E3
Mappleborough Green....51 C5
Mappleton....97 E8
Mappowder....12 D5
Maraig....154 G6
Marazanvose....4 D3
Marazion....2 C4
Marbhig....155 F9
Marbury....74 E2
March Cambs....66 E4
S Lanark....114 C2
Marcham....38 E4
Marchamley....61 B5
Marchington....75 F8
Marchington Woodlands....62 B5
Marchroes....70 E4
Marchwiel....73 E7
Marchwood....14 C4
Marcross....21 C8
Marden Hereford....49 E7
Kent....29 E8
T&W....111 B6
Wilts....25 D5
Marden Beech....29 E8
Marden Thorn....29 E8
Mardy....35 C7
Marefield....64 D4
Mareham le Fen....79 C5
Mareham on the Hill....79 C5
Marehay....76 E3
Marehill....16 C4
Maresfield....17 B8
Marfleet....90 B5
Marford....73 D7
Margam....34 F1
Margaret Marsh....13 C6
Margaret Roding....42 C1
Margaretting....42 D2
Margate....31 B7
Margnaheglish....143 E11
Margrove Park....102 C4
Marham....67 C7
Marhamchurch....8 D4
Marholm....65 D8
Mariandyrs....83 C6
Marianglas....82 C5
Mariansleigh....10 B2
Marionburgh....141 D6
Marishader....149 B9
Marjoriebanks....114 F3
Mark Dumfries....104 D5
S Ayrs....104 B4
Som....23 E5
Markbeech....29 E5
Markby....79 B7
Mark Causeway....23 E5
Mark Cross E Sus....17 C8
E Sus....18 B2
Market Bosworth....63 D8
Market Deeping....65 D8
Market Drayton....74 F3
Market Harborough....64 F4
Markethill....134 F2
Market Lavington 24 D5
Market Overton....65 C5
Market Rasen....90 F5
Market Stainton....78 B5
Market Warsop....77 C5
Market Weighton....96 E4
Markfield....63 C8
Markham....35 D5
Markham Moor....77 B7
Markinch....128 D4
Markington....95 C5
Marks Tey....43 B5
Markyate....40 C3

Marlcliff....51 D5
Marldon....7 C6
Marlesford....57 D7
Marley Green....74 E2
Marley Hill....110 D5
Marley Mount....14 E3
Marlingford....68 D4
Mar Lodge....139 E6
Marloes....44 E2
Marlow Bucks....39 F8
Hereford....49 B6
Marlow Bottom....40 F1
Marlpit Hill....28 E5
Marlpool....76 E4
Marnhull....13 C5
Marnock....152 C5
Marnock....119 C7
Marple....87 F7
Marple Bridge....87 F7
Marr....89 D6
Marrel....157 H13
Marrick....101 E5
Marrister....160 G7
Marros....32 D3
Marsden T&W....111 C6
W Yorks....87 C8
Marsett....100 F4
Marsh Devon....11 C7
W Yorks....94 F3
Marshall's Heath....40 C4
Marshalsea....11 D8
Marshalswick....40 D4
Marsham....81 E7
Marshaw....93 D5
Marsh Baldon....39 E5
Marshborough....31 D7
Marshbrook....60 F4
Marshchapel....91 E7
Marshfield Newport 35 F6
S Glos....24 B2
Marshgate....8 E3
Marsh Gibbon....39 B6
Marsh Green Devon 10 E5
Kent....28 E5
Staffs....75 D5
Marshland St James....66 D5
Marsh Lane....76 B4
Marshside....85 C4
Marsh Street....21 E8
Marshwood....11 E8
Marske....101 D6
Marske-by-the-Sea....102 B4
Marston Ches W....74 B3
Hereford....49 D5
Lincs....77 E8
Oxon....39 D5
Staffs....62 C2
Warks....63 E6
Wilts....24 D4
Marston Doles....52 D2
Marston Green....63 F5
Marston Magna....12 B3
Marston Meysey....37 E8
Marston Montgomery....75 F8
Marston Moretaine....53 E7
Marston on Dove....63 B6
Marston St Lawrence....52 E3
Marston Stannett....49 D7
Marston Trussell....64 F3
Marstow....36 C2
Marsworth....40 C2
Marten....25 D7
Marthall....74 B5
Martham....69 C7
Martin Hants....13 C8
Kent....31 E7
Lincs....78 C5
Lincs....78 D4
Martin Dales....78 C4
Martin Drove End....13 B8
Martinhoe....21 E5
Martinhoe Cross....21 E5
Martin Hussingtree....50 C3
Martin Mill....31 E7
Martinscroft....86 F4
Martinstown....12 F4
Martlesham....57 E6
Martlesham Heath 57 E6
Martletwy....32 C1
Martley....50 D2
Martock....12 C2
Marton Ches E....75 C5
E Yorks....97 F7
Lincs....90 F2
Mbro....102 C3
N Yorks....95 C7
N Yorks....103 F5
Shrops....60 D2
Shrops....60 D2
Warks....52 C2
Marton-le-Moor....95 B6
Martyr's Grcen....27 D8
Martyr Worthy....26 F3
Marwick....159 F3
Marwood....20 F4
Marybank....151 F8
Maryburgh....151 F8
Maryhill....119 C5
Marykirk....135 C6
Marylebone....86 D3
Marypark....152 E1
Maryport Cumb....107 F7
Dumfries....104 F5
Mary Tavy....9 F7
Maryton....135 D6
Marywell Aberds....140 E4
Aberds....141 E8
Angus....135 E6
Masham....101 F7
Mashbury....42 C2
Masongill....93 B6
Masonhill....112 B3
Mastin Moor....76 B4
Mastrick....141 D7
Matching....41 C8
Matching Green....41 C8
Matching Tye....41 C8
Matfen....110 B3
Matfield....29 E7
Mathern....36 E2
Mathon....50 E2
Mathry....44 B3

Matlaske....81 D7
Matlock....76 C2
Matlock Bath....76 D2
Matson....37 C5
Matterdale End....99 B5
Mattersey....89 F7
Mattersey Thorpe....89 F7
Mattingley....26 D5
Mattishall....68 C3
Mattishall Burgh....68 C3
Mauchline....112 B4
Maud....153 D9
Maugersbury....38 B2
Maughold....84 C4
Mauld....150 H7
Maulden....53 F8
Maulds Meaburn....99 C8
Maunby....102 F1
Maund Bryan....49 D7
Maundown....11 B5
Mautby....69 C7
Mavis Enderby....79 C6
Mawbray....107 E7
Mawdesley....86 C2
Mawdlam....34 F2
Mawgan....3 D6
Mawgan Porth....4 C3
Maw Green....74 D4
Mawla....3 B6
Mawnan....3 D6
Mawnan Smith....3 D6
Mawsley....53 B6
Maxey....65 D8
Maxstoke....63 F6
Maxton Borders....122 F2
Kent....31 E7
Maxwellheugh....122 F3
Maxwelltown....107 B6
Maxworthy....8 E4
Mayals....33 E7
May Bank....75 E5
Maybole....112 D3
Mayfield E Sus....18 C2
Midloth....121 C6
Staffs....75 E8
W Loth....120 C2
Mayford....27 D7
Mayland....43 D5
Maynard's Green....18 D2
Maypole Mon....36 C1
Scilly....2 E4
Maypole Green Essex....43 B6
Norf....69 E7
Suff....57 C6
Maywick....160 L5
Meadle....39 D8
Meadowtown....60 D3
Meaford....75 F5
Mealabost....155 D9
Mealabost Bhuirgh....155 B9
Meal Bank....99 E7
Mealsgate....108 E2
Meanwood....95 F5
Mearbeck....93 C8
Meare....23 E6
Meare Green....11 B8
Mears Ashby....53 C6
Measham....63 C7
Meath Green....28 E3
Meathop....99 F6
Meaux....97 F6
Meavy....6 C3
Medbourne....64 E4
Medburn....110 B4
Meddon....8 C4
Meden Vale....77 C5
Medlam....79 D6
Medmenham....39 F8
Medomsley....110 D4
Medstead....26 F4
Meerbrook....75 C6
Meer End....51 B7
Meers Bridge....91 F8
Meesden....54 F5
Meeth....9 D7
Meggethead....114 B4
Meidrim....32 B3
Meifod Denb....72 D4
Powys....59 C8
Meigle N Ayrs....118 C1
Perth....134 E2
Meikle Earnock....119 D7
Meikle Ferry....151 C10
Meikle Forter....134 C1
Meikle Gluich....151 C9
Meikleour....134 F1
Meikle Pinkerton 122 B3
Meikle Strath....135 B6
Meikle Tarty....141 B8
Meikle Wartle....153 E7
Meinciau....33 C5
Meir....75 E6
Meir Heath....75 E6
Melbourn....54 E4
Melbourne Derbys....63 B7
E Yorks....96 E3
S Lanark....120 E3
Melbury Abbas....13 B6
Melbury Bubb....12 D3
Melbury Osmond....12 D3
Melbury Sampford 12 D3
Melby....160 H3
Melchbourne....53 C8
Melcombe Bingham....13 D5
Melcombe Regis....12 F4
Meldon Devon....9 E7
Northumb....117 F7
Meldreth....54 E4
Meldrum House....141 B7
Melfort....124 D4
Melgarve....137 E7
Meliden....72 A4
Melinbyrhedyn....58 D5
Melincourt....34 D2
Melin-y-coed....83 E8
Melin-y-ddôl....59 D7
Melin-y-grug....59 D7
Melin-y-Wig....72 E4
Melkinthorpe....99 B7
Melkridge....109 C7
Melksham....24 C4
Melldalloch....145 E8
Melling Lancs....93 B5
Mers....85 D4
Melling Mount....86 D2
Mellis....56 B5

Mellon Charles....155 H13
Mellon Udrigle....155 H13
Mellor Gtr Man....87 F7
Lancs....93 F6
Mellor Brook....93 F6
Mells....24 E2
Melmerby N Yorks....95 B6
N Yorks....101 F5
W&F....109 F6
Melplash....12 E2
Melrose....121 F8
Melsetter....159 K3
Melsonby....101 D6
Meltham....88 C2
Melton....57 D6
Meltonby....96 D3
Melton Constable....81 D6
Melton Mowbray....64 C4
Melton Ross....90 C4
Melvaig....155 J12
Melverley....60 C3
Melverley Green....60 C3
Melvich....157 C11
Membury....11 D7
Memsie....153 B9
Memus....134 D4
Menabilly....5 D5
Menai Bridge = Porthaethwy....83 D5
Mendham....69 F5
Mendlesham....56 C5
Mendlesham Green....56 C4
Menheniot....5 C7
Mennock....113 D8
Menston....94 E4
Menstrie....127 E7
Menthorpe....96 F2
Mentmore....40 C2
Meoble....147 C10
Meole Brace....60 C4
Meols....85 E3
Meonstoke....15 C7
Meopham....29 C7
Meopham Station 29 C7
Mepal....66 F4
Meppershall....54 F2
Merbach....48 E5
Mere Ches E....86 F5
Wilts....24 F3
Mere Brow....86 C2
Mereclough....93 F8
Mere Green....62 E5
Mereside....92 F3
Mereworth....29 D7
Mergie....141 F6
Meriden....63 F6
Merkadale....149 E8
Merkland Dumfries 106 B4
S Ayrs....112 E2
Merkland Lodge....156 G7
Merley....13 E8
Merlin's Bridge....44 D4
Merrington....60 B4
Merrion....44 F4
Merriott....12 C2
Merrivale....6 B3
Merrow....27 D8
Merrymeet....5 C7
Mersham....19 B7
Merstham....28 D3
Merston....16 D2
Merstone....15 F6
Merther....3 B7
Merthyr....32 B4
Merthyr Cynog....47 F8
Merthyr-Dyfan....22 C3
Merthyr Mawr....21 B7
Merthyr Tudful = Merthyr Tydfil 34 D4
Merthyr Tydfil = Merthyr Tudful....34 D4
Merthyr Vale....34 E4
Merton Devon....9 C7
London....28 B3
Norf....68 E2
Oxon....39 C5
Mervinslaw....116 C2
Meshaw....10 C2
Messing....42 C4
Messingham....90 D2
Metfield....69 F5
Metheringham....78 C3
Methil....129 E5
Methlem....70 D2
Methley....88 B4
Methlick....153 E8
Methven....128 B2
Methwold....67 E7
Methwold Hythe....67 E7
Mettingham....69 F6
Mevagissey....3 B9
Mewith Head....93 C7
Mexborough....89 D5
Mey....158 C4
Meysey Hampton....37 E8
Miabhag W Isles....154 G5
W Isles....154 H6
Miabhig....154 D5
Michaelchurch....36 B2
Michaelchurch Escley....48 F5
Michaelchurch on Arrow....48 D4
Michaelston-le-Pit....22 B3
Michaelston-y-Fedw....35 F6
Michaelstow....8 F3
Michealston-super-Ely....22 B3
Micheldever....26 F3
Michelmersh....14 B4
Mickfield....56 C5
Micklebring....89 E6
Mickleby....103 C6
Micklefield....95 F7
Micklefield Green....40 E3
Mickleham....28 D2
Mickleover....76 F3
Micklethwaite....94 E4
Mickleton Durham....100 B4
Glos....51 E6
Mickletown....88 B4
Mickle Trafford....73 C8
Mickley....95 B5
Mickley Square....110 C3
Mid Ardlaw....153 B9
Mid Auchinleck....118 B3
Mid Beltie....140 D5
Mid Calder....120 C3
Mid Cloch Forbie....153 C7
Mid Clyth....158 G4
Middle Assendon....39 F7
Middle Aston....38 B4
Middle Barton....38 B4
Middlebie....108 B2
Middle Cairncake....153 D7
Middle Claydon....39 B7
Middle Drums....135 D5
Middleforth Green 86 B3
Middleham....101 F6
Middle Handley....76 B4
Middlehope....60 F4
Middle Littleton....51 E5
Middle Maes-coed 48 F5
Middlemarsh....12 D4
Middle Mill....44 C3
Middlemuir....141 B8
Middle Rasen....90 F4
Middle Rigg....128 D2
Middlesbrough....102 B2
Middleshaw....107 B8
Middlesmoor....94 B3
Middlestone....111 F5
Middlestone Moor 110 F5
Middlestown....88 C3
Middlethird....122 E2
Middleton Aberds....141 C7
Argyll....146 G2
Derbys....75 C8
Derbys....76 D2
Essex....56 F2
Gtr Man....87 D6
Hants....26 E2
Hereford....49 C7
Lancs....92 D4
Midloth....121 D6
N Nhants....64 F5
Norf....67 C6
Northumb....117 F6
Northumb....123 F7
N Yorks....94 E4
N Yorks....103 F5
Perth....128 D3
Perth....133 E8
Shrops....49 B7
Shrops....60 B3
Suff....56 B4
W&F....109 F6
W Yorks....88 B3
Middleton Cheney....52 E2
Middleton Green....75 F6
Middleton Hall....117 B5
Middleton-in-Teesdale....100 B4
Middleton Moor....57 C8
Middleton One Row....102 C1
Middleton-on-Leven....102 D2
Middleton-on-Sea 16 D3
Middleton on the Hill....49 C7
Middleton-on-the-Wolds....96 E5
Middleton Priors....61 E6
Middleton Quernhow....95 B6
Middleton St George....102 C1
Middleton Scriven....61 F6
Middleton Stoney....39 B5
Middleton Tyas....101 D7
Middletown Cumb....98 D1
Powys....60 C3
Middle Tysoe....51 E8
Middle Wallop....25 F7
Middlewich....74 C3
Middle Winterslow....25 F7
Middle Woodford....25 F6
Middlewood Green....56 C4
Middlezoy....23 F5
Middridge....101 B7
Midfield....157 C8
Midge Hall....86 B3
Midgeholme....109 D6
Midgham....26 C3
Midgley W Yorks....87 B8
W Yorks....88 C3
Midhopestones....88 E3
Midhurst....16 B2
Mid Lavant....16 D2
Midlem....115 B8
Mid Main....150 H7
Midmar....141 D5
Midsomer Norton 23 D8
Midton....118 B2
Midtown Highld....155 J13
Highld....157 C8
Midtown of Buchromb....152 D3
Mid Urchany....151 G11
Midville....79 D6
Mid Walls....160 H4
Midway....87 F7
Mid Yell....160 D7
Migdale....151 B9
Migvie....140 D3
Milarrochy....126 E3
Milborne Port....12 C4
Milborne St Andrew....13 E6
Milborne Wick....12 B4
Milbourne....110 B4
Milburn....100 B1
Milbury Heath....36 E3
Milcombe....52 F2
Milden....56 E3
Mildenhall Suff....55 B8
Wilts....25 C7
Milebrook....48 B5
Milebush....29 E8
Mile Cross....68 C5
Mile Elm....24 C4
Mile End Essex....43 B5
Glos....36 C2
Mileham....68 C2
Mile Oak....17 D6
Milesmark....128 F2

Milfield....122 F5
Milford Derbys....76 E3
Devon....8 B4
Powys....59 E7
Staffs....62 B3
Sur....27 E7
Wilts....14 B2
Milford Haven = Aberdaugleddau 44 E4
Milford on Sea....14 E3
Milkwall....36 D2
Milkwell....13 B7
Milland....16 B2
Millarston....118 C4
Millbank Aberds....153 D11
Highld....158 D3
Mill Bank....87 B8
Millbeck....98 B4
Millbounds....159 E6
Millbreck....153 D10
Millbrook C Beds....53 F8
Corn....6 D2
Soton....14 C4
Millburn....112 B4
Millcombe....7 E6
Mill Common....69 F7
Millcorner....18 C5
Milldale....75 D8
Millden Lodge....135 B5
Milldens....135 D5
Mill End Bucks....39 F7
Herts....54 F4
Millerhill....121 C6
Miller's Dale....75 B8
Miller's Green....76 D2
Millgreen....61 B6
Mill Green Essex....42 D2
Norf....68 F4
Suff....56 E3
Millhalf....48 E4
Millhayes....11 D7
Millheugh....119 D7
Mill Hill....41 E5
Millholme....99 E7
Millhouse Argyll....145 F8
W&F....108 F3
Millhousebridge....114 F4
Millhouse Green....88 D3
Millhouses....88 F4
Millikenpark....118 C4
Millin Cross....44 D4
Millington....96 D4
Mill Lane....27 D5
Millmeece....74 F5
Mill of Kingoodie....141 B7
Mill of Muiresk....153 D6
Mill of Sterin....140 E2
Mill of Uras....141 F7
Millom....98 F3
Millook....8 E3
Mill Place....90 D3
Millpool....5 B6
Millport....145 H10
Millquarter....113 F6
Mill Side....99 F6
Mill Street....68 C3
Millthorpe....78 F4
Millthrop....100 E1
Milltimber....141 D7
Milltown Corn....5 D6
Devon....20 F4
Dumfries....108 B3
Milltown of Aberdalgie....128 B2
Milltown of Auchindoun....152 D3
Milltown of Craigston....153 C7
Milltown of Edinvillie....152 D2
Milltown of Kildrummy....140 C3
Milltown of Rothiemay....152 D5
Milltown of Towie....140 C3
Milnathort....128 D3
Milner's Heath....73 C8
Milngavie....119 B5
Milnrow....87 C7
Milnshaw....87 B5
Milnthorpe....99 F6
Milo....33 C6
Milson....49 B8
Milstead....30 D3
Milston....25 E6
Milton Angus....134 E3
Cambs....55 C5
Cumb....109 C5
Derbys....63 B7
Dumfries....105 D6
Dumfries....106 B5
Dumfries....113 F8
Highld....150 F6
Highld....151 D10
Highld....151 G8
Highld....158 E3
Moray....152 B5
N Som....22 C5
Notts....77 B7
Oxon....38 E4
Oxon....52 F2
Pembs....32 D1
Perth....127 C8
Ptsmth....15 E7
Stirling....126 D4
Stoke....75 D6
W Dunb....118 B4
Milton Abbas....13 D6
Milton Abbot....6 B2
Milton Bridge....120 C5
Milton Bryan....53 F7
Milton Clevedon....23 F8
Milton Coldwells....153 E9
Milton Combe....6 C2
Milton Damerel....9 C5
Milton End....37 D8
Milton Ernest....53 D8
Milton Green....73 D8
Milton Hill....38 E4
Milton Keynes....53 F6

Milton Keynes Village....53 F6
Milton Lilbourne....25 C6
Milton Malsor....52 D5
Milton Morenish....132 F3
Milton of Auchinhove....140 D4
Milton of Balgonie....128 D5
Milton of Buchanan....126 E3
Milton of Campfield....140 D5
Milton of Campsie....119 B6
Milton of Corsindae....141 D5
Milton of Cushnie....140 C4
Milton of Dalcapon....133 D6
Milton of Edradour....133 D6
Milton of Gollanfield....151 F10
Milton of Lesmore....140 B3
Milton of Logie....140 D3
Milton of Murtle....141 D7
Milton of Noth....140 B4
Milton of Tullich....140 E2
Milton on Stour....13 B5
Milton Regis....30 C3
Milton under Wychwood....38 C2
Milverton Som....11 B6
Warks....51 C8
Milwich....75 F6
Minard....125 F5
Minchinhampton....37 D5
Mindrum....122 F4
Minehead....21 E8
Minera....73 D6
Minety....37 E7
Minffordd Gwyn....58 C3
Gwyn....71 D6
Gwyn....83 D5
Miningsby....79 C6
Minions....5 B7
Minishant....112 C3
Minllyn....59 C5
Minnes....141 B8
Minngearraidh....148 F2
Minnigaff....105 C8
Minnonie....153 B7
Minskip....95 C6
Minstead....14 C3
Minsted....16 B2
Minster Kent....30 B3
Kent....31 C7
Minsterley....60 D3
Minster Lovell....38 C3
Minsterworth....36 C4
Minterne Magna....12 D4
Minting....78 B4
Mintlaw....153 D9
Minto....115 B8
Minton....60 E4
Minwear....32 C1
Minworth....63 E5
Mirbister....159 F4
Mirehouse....98 C1
Mireland....158 D5
Mirfield....88 C3
Miserden....37 D6
Miskin....34 F4
Misson....89 E7
Misterton Leics....64 F2
Notts....89 E8
Som....12 D2
Mistley....56 F5
Mitcham....28 C3
Mitcheldean....36 C3
Mitchell....4 D3
Mitchel Troy....36 C1
Mitcheltroy Common....36 C1
Mitford....117 F7
Mithian....4 D2
Mitton....62 C2
Mixbury....52 F4
Moat....108 B4
Moats Tye....56 D4
Mobberley Ches E....74 B4
Staffs....75 E7
Moccas....49 E5
Mochdre Conwy....83 D8
Powys....59 F7
Mochrum....105 E7
Mockbeggar....14 D2
Mockerkin....98 B2
Modbury....6 D4
Moddershall....75 F6
Moelfre Anglesey....82 C5
Powys....59 B8
Moffat....114 D3
Moggerhanger....54 E2
Moira....63 C7
Molash....30 D4
Mol-chlach....149 G9
Mold = Yr Wyddgrug....73 C6
Moldgreen....88 C2
Molehill Green....42 B1
Molescroft....97 E6
Molesden....117 F7
Molesworth....53 B8
Moll....149 E10
Molland....10 B3
Mollington Ches W....73 B7
Oxon....52 E2
Mollinsburn....119 B7
Monachty....46 C4
Monachylemore....126 C3
Monar Lodge....150 G5
Monaughty....48 C4
Mondynes....135 B7
Monevechadan....125 E7
Monewden....57 D6
Moneydie....128 B2
Moniaive....113 E7
Monifieth....135 F5
Monikie....135 F5
Monimail....128 C4
Monington....45 E3

Monk Bretton.....88 D4
Monken Hadley...41 E5
Monk Fryston....89 B6
Monkhopton....61 E6
Monkland....49 D6
Monkleigh....9 B6
Monknash....21 B8
Monkokehampton..9 D7
Monkseaton....111 B6
Monks Eleigh....56 E3
Monk's Gate....17 B6
Monks Heath....74 B5
Monk Sherborne..26 D4
Monkshill....153 D7
Monksilver....22 F2
Monks Kirby....63 F8
Monk Soham....57 C6
Monkspath....51 B6
Monks Risborough 39 D8
Monk Street....42 B2
Monkswood....35 D7
Monkton Devon...11 D6
  Kent....31 C6
  Pembs....44 E4
  S Ayrs....112 B3
Monkton Combe..24 C2
Monkton Deverill..24 F3
Monkton Farleigh.24 C3
Monkton
  Heathfield....11 B7
Monkton Up
  Wimborne....13 C8
Monkwearmouth.111 D6
Monkwood....26 F4
Monmouth
  =Trefynwy....36 C2
Monmouth Cap...35 B7
Monnington on
  Wye....49 E5
Monreith....105 E7
Monreith Mains..105 E7
Montacute....12 C2
Montcoffer
  House....153 B6
Montford Argyll..145 G10
  Shrops....60 C4
Montford Bridge..60 C4
Montgarrie....140 C4
Montgomery
  =Trefaldwyn....60 E2
Montrave....129 D5
Montrose....135 D7
Mont Saint....16 I2
Montsale....43 E6
Monxton....25 E8
Monyash....75 C8
Monymusk....141 C5
Monzie....127 B7
Moodiesburn....119 B6
Moonzie....128 C5
Moor Allerton....95 F5
Moorby....79 C5
Moor Crichel....13 D8
Moordown....13 E8
Moore....86 F3
Moorend E Yorks...96 F4
  York....96 D2
Moorends....89 C7
Moorgate....88 E5
Moorgreen....76 E4
Moorhall....76 B3
Moorhampton....49 E5
Moorhead....94 F4
Moorhouse Cumb.108 D3
  Notts....77 C7
Moorlinch....23 F5
Moorby....95 D8
Moor of Granary.151 F13
Moor of
  Ravenstone....105 E7
Moor Row....98 C2
Moorsholm....102 C4
Moorside....87 D7
Moor Street....30 C2
Moorthorpe....89 C5
Moortown Hants..14 D2
  IoW....14 F5
  Lincs....90 E4
Morangie....151 C10
Morar....147 B9
Morborne....65 E8
Morchard Bishop..10 D2
Morcombelake....12 E2
Morcott....65 D6
Morda....60 B2
Morden Dorset...13 E7
  London....28 C3
Mordiford....49 F7
Mordon....101 B8
More....60 E3
Morebath....10 B4
Morebattle....116 B3
Morecambe....92 C4
Morefield....150 B4
Moreleigh....7 D5
Morenish....132 F2
Moresby....98 B1
Moresby Parks....98 C1
Morestead....15 B6
Moreton Dorset...13 F6
  Essex....41 D8
  Mers....85 E3
  Oxon....39 D6
  Staffs....61 C7
Moreton Corbet..61 B5
Moretonhampstead
  ....10 F2
Moreton-in-Marsh 51 F7
Moreton Jeffries..49 E8
Moreton Morrell..51 D8
Moreton on Lugg.49 E7
Moreton Pinkney..52 E3
Moreton Say....74 F3
Moreton Valence..36 D4
Morfa Carms....33 C6
  Carms....33 E6
Morfa Bach....32 C4
Morfa Bychan....71 D6
Morfa Dinlle....82 F4
Morfa Glas....34 D2
Morfa Nefyn....70 C3
Morfydd....72 E5
Morgan's Vale....14 B2
Moriah....46 B5

Morland....99 B7
Morley Derbys....76 E3
  Durham....101 B6
  W Yorks....88 B3
Morley Green....87 F6
Morley St Botolph.68 E3
Morningside Edin.120 B5
  N Lanark....119 D8
Morningthorpe....68 E5
Morpeth....117 F8
Morphie....135 C7
Morrey....62 C5
Morris Green....55 F8
Morriston....33 E7
Morston....81 C6
Mortehoe....20 E3
Mortimer....26 C4
Mortimer's Cross..49 C6
Mortimer West
  End....26 C4
Mortlake....28 B3
Morton Cumb....108 D3
  Derbys....76 C4
  Lincs....65 B7
  Lincs....77 C8
  Lincs....90 E2
  Norf....68 C4
  Notts....77 D7
  S Glos....36 E3
  Shrops....60 B2
Morton Bagot....51 C6
Morton-on-
  Swale....101 E8
Morvah....2 C3
Morval....5 D7
Morvich Highld...136 B2
  Highld....157 J10
Morville....61 E6
Morville Heath....61 E6
Morwenstow....8 C4
Mosborough....88 F5
Moscow....118 E4
Mosedale....108 F3
Moseley W Mid...62 E3
  W Mid....62 F4
  Worcs....50 D3
Moss Argyll....146 G2
  Highld....147 E9
  S Yorks....89 C6
  Wrex....73 D7
Mossat....140 C3
Mossbank....160 F6
Moss Bank....86 E3
Mossblown....112 B4
Mossbrow....86 F5
Mossburnford....116 C2
Mossdale....119 D7
Moss Edge....92 E4
Mossgiel....112 B4
Mosside....134 D4
Mossley Ches E...75 C5
  Gtr Man....87 D7
Mossley Hill....85 F4
Moss of
  Barmuckity....152 B2
Moss Pit....62 B3
Moss-side....151 F11
Mosstodloch....152 B3
Mosston....135 E5
Mossy Lea....86 C3
Mosterton....12 D2
Moston Gtr Man..87 D6
  Shrops....61 B5
Moston Green....74 C4
Mostyn....85 F2
Mostyn Quay....85 F2
Motcombe....13 B6
Mothecombe....6 E4
Motherby....99 B6
Motherwell....119 D7
Mottingham....28 B5
Mottisfont....14 B4
Mottistone....14 F5
Mottram in
  Longdendale....87 E7
Mottram St
  Andrew....75 B5
Mouilpied....16 I2
Mouldsworth....74 B2
Moulin....133 D6
Moulsecoomb....17 D7
Moulsford....39 F5
Moulsoe....53 E7
Moulton Ches W..74 C3
  Lincs....66 B3
  N Yorks....101 D7
  Suff....55 C7
  V Glam....22 B2
  W Nhants....53 C5
Moulton Chapel..66 C2
Moulton Eaugate..66 C2
Moulton St Mary..69 D6
Moulton Seas End.66 B3
Mounie Castle....141 B6
Mount Corn....4 D2
  Corn....5 C6
  Highld....151 G12
Mountain....94 F3
Mountain Ash
  =Aberpennar....34 E4
Mountain Cross..120 E4
Mountain Water..44 C4
Mountbenger....115 B6
Mount Bures....56 F3
Mount Canisp....151 D10
Mountfield....18 C4
Mountgerald....151 E8
Mount Hawke....3 B6
Mountjoy....4 C3
Mountnessing....42 E2
Mounton....36 E2
Mount Pleasant
  Ches E....74 D5
  Derbys....63 C6
  Derbys....76 E3
  Flint....73 B6
  Hants....14 E3
  W Yorks....88 B3
Mountsorrel....64 C2
Mount Sorrel....13 B8
Mount Tabor....87 B8
Mousehole....2 D3
Mousen....123 F7

Mouswald....107 B7
Mow Cop....75 D5
Mowhaugh....116 B4
Mowsley....64 F3
Moxley....62 E3
Moy Highld....137 F7
  Highld....151 H10
Moy Hall....151 H10
Moy House....151 E13
Moyles Court....14 D2
Moylgrove....45 E3
Moy Lodge....137 F7
Muasdale....143 D7
Muchalls....141 E8
Much Birch....49 F7
Much Cowarne....49 E8
Much Dewchurch..49 F6
Muchelney....12 B2
Much Hadham....41 C7
Much Hoole....86 B2
Muchlarnick....5 D7
Much Marcle....49 F8
Muchrachd....150 H5
Much Wenlock....61 D6
Muckernich....151 F8
Mucking....42 F2
Muckleford....12 E4
Mucklestone....74 F4
Muckleton....61 B5
Muckletown....140 B4
Muckley Corner....62 D4
Muckton....91 F7
Mudale....157 F8
Muddiford....20 F4
Mudeford....14 E2
Mudford....12 C3
Mugdock....119 B5
Mugeary....149 E9
Mugginton....76 E2
Muggleswick....110 E3
Muie....157 J9
Muir....139 F6
Muirden....153 C7
Muirdrum....135 F5
Muirhead Angus..134 F3
  Fife....128 D4
  N Lanark....119 C6
  S Ayrs....118 F3
Muirhouselaw....116 B2
Muirhouses....128 F2
Muirkirk....113 B6
Muirmill....127 F6
Muir of Fairburn.150 F7
Muir of Fowlis....140 C4
Muir of Ord....151 F8
Muir of Pert....134 F4
Muirshearlich....136 F4
Muirskie....141 E7
Muirtack....153 E10
Muirton Highld...151 E10
  Perth....127 C8
  Perth....128 B3
Muirton Mains....150 F7
Muirton of
  Ardblair....134 E1
Muirton of
  Ballochy....135 C6
Muiryfold....153 C7
Muker....100 E4
Mulbarton....68 D4
Mulben....152 C3
Mulindry....142 C4
Mullardoch
  House....150 H5
Mullion....3 E5
Mullion Cove....3 E5
Mumby....79 B8
Munderfield Row..49 D8
Munderfield
  Stocks....49 D8
Mundesley....81 D9
Mundford....67 E8
Mundham....69 E6
Mundon....42 D4
Mundurno....141 C8
Munerigie....137 D5
Muness....160 C8
Mungasdale....150 B2
Mungrisdale....108 F3
Munlochy....151 F9
Munsley....49 E8
Munslow....60 F5
Murcott....39 C5
Murkle....158 D3
Murlaggan Highld.136 E3
  Highld....137 F6
Murra....159 H3
Murrayfield....120 B5
Murrow....66 D3
Mursley....39 B8
Murthill....134 D4
Murthly....133 F7
Murton Durham..111 E6
  Northumb....123 E5
  W&F....100 B2
  York....96 D2
Musbury....11 E7
Muscoates....102 F4
Musdale....124 C5
Musselburgh....121 B6
Muston Leics....77 F8
  N Yorks....97 B6
Mustow Green....50 B3
Mutehill....106 E3
Mutford....69 F7
Muthill....127 C7
Mutterton....10 D5
Muxton....61 C7
Mybster....158 E3
Myddfai....34 B1
Myddle....60 B4
Mydroilyn....46 D3
Myerscough....92 F4
Mylor Bridge....3 C7
Mynachlog-ddu..45 F3
Myndtown....60 F3
Mynydd Bach....47 B6
Mynydd-bach....36 E1
Mynydd Bodafon..82 C4
Mynydd Isa....73 B6
Mynyddygarreg....33 D5
Mynytho....70 D4
Myrebird....141 E6
Myrelandhorn....158 E4
Myreside....128 B4
Myrtle Hill....47 F6
Mytchett....27 D6

Mytholm....87 B7
Mytholmroyd....87 B8
Myton-on-Swale..95 C7
Mytton....60 C4

# N

Naast....155 J13
Naburn....95 E8
Nackington....31 D5
Nacton....57 E6
Nafferton....97 D6
Na Gearrannan..154 C6
Nailbridge....36 C3
Nailsbourne....11 B7
Nailsea....23 B6
Nailstone....63 D8
Nailsworth....37 E5
Nairn....151 F11
Nalderswood....28 E3
Nancegollan....2 C5
Nancledra....2 C3
Nanhoron....70 D3
Nannau....71 E8
Nannerch....73 C5
Nanpantan....64 C2
Nanpean....4 D4
Nansledan....4 C3
Nanstallon....4 C5
Nant-ddu....34 C4
Nantgaredig....33 B5
Nantgarw....35 F5
Nant-glas....47 C8
Nantglyn....72 C4
Nantgwyn....47 B8
Nantlle....82 F5
Nantmawr....60 B2
Nantmel....48 C2
Nantmor....71 C7
Nant Peris....83 F6
Nant Uchaf....72 D4
Nantwich....74 D3
Nant-y-Bai....47 E6
Nant-y-cafn....34 D2
Nantycaws....33 C5
Nant-y-derry....35 D7
Nant-y-ffin....46 F4
Nantyffyllon....34 E2
Nantyglo....35 C5
Nant-y-moel....34 E3
Nant-y-pandy....83 D6
Naphill....39 E8
Nappa....93 D8
Napton on the
  Hill....52 C2
Narberth
  =Arberth....32 C2
Narborough Leics.64 E2
  Norf....67 C7
Nasareth....82 F4
Naseby....52 B4
Nash Bucks....53 F5
  Hereford....48 C5
  Newport....35 F7
  Shrops....49 B8
Nash Lee....39 D8
Nassington....65 E7
Nasty....41 B6
Nateby Lancs....92 E4
  W&F....100 D2
Natland....99 F7
Naughton....56 E4
Naunton Glos....37 B8
  Worcs....50 F3
Naunton
  Beauchamp....50 D4
Navenby....78 D2
Navestock Heath..41 E8
Navestock Side....42 E1
Navidale....157 H13
Nawton....102 F4
Nayland....56 F3
Nazeing....41 D7
Neacroft....14 E2
Neal's Green....63 F7
Neap....160 H7
Near Sawrey....99 E5
Neasham....101 C8
Neath
  =Castell-Nedd...33 E8
Neath Abbey....33 E8
Neatishead....69 B6
Nebo Anglesey....82 B4
  Ceredig....46 C4
  Conwy....83 F8
  Gwyn....82 F4
Necton....67 D8
Nedd....156 F4
Nedderton....117 F8
Nedging Tye....56 E4
Needham....68 F5
Needham Market..56 D4
Needingworth....54 B4
Needwood....63 B5
Neen Savage....49 B8
Neen Sollars....49 B8
Neenton....61 F6
Nefyn....70 C4
Neilston....118 D4
Neinthirion....59 D6
Neithrop....52 E2
Nelly Andrews
  Green....60 D2
Nelson Caerph....35 E5
  Lancs....93 F8
Nelson Village....111 B5
Nemphlar....119 E8
Nempnett
  Thrubwell....23 C7
Nene Terrace....66 D2
Nenthall....109 E7
Nenthead....109 E7
Nenthorn....122 F2
Nerabus....142 C3
Nercwys....73 C6
Nerston....119 D6
Nesbit....123 F5
Ness....73 B7
Nesscliffe....60 C3
Neston Ches W...73 B6
  Wilts....24 C3
Nether Alderley....74 B5
Netheravon....25 E6
Nether Blainslie..121 E8
Nether Booth....88 F2
Netherbrae....153 C7
Netherbrough....159 G4
Nether Broughton.64 B3

Netherburn....119 E8
Nether Burrow....93 B6
Netherbury....12 E2
Netherby Cumb....108 B3
  N Yorks....95 E6
Nether Cerne....12 E4
Nether Compton..12 C3
Nethercote....52 C3
Nethercott....20 F3
Nether Crimond..141 B7
Nether Dalgliesh.115 D5
Nether Dallachy..152 B3
Netherend....36 D2
Nether Exe....10 D4
Netherfield....18 D4
Nether Glasslaw..153 C8
Netherhampton....14 B2
Nether Handwick.134 E3
Nether Haugh....88 E5
Nether Heage....76 D3
Nether Heyford....52 D4
Nether Hindhope.116 C3
Nether
  Howcleuch....114 C3
Nether Kellet....92 C5
Nether
  Kinmundy....153 D10
Nether Langwith..76 B5
Netherlaw....106 E4
Nether Leask....153 E10
Nether Lenshie..153 D6
Netherley Aberds.141 E7
  Mers....86 F2
Nethermill....114 F3
Nether Monynut..122 C3
Nethermuir....153 D9
Nether Padley....76 B3
Nether Park....153 C10
Netherplace....118 D5
Nether Poppleton.95 D8
Netherseal....63 C6
Nether Silton....102 E2
Nether Stowey....22 F3
Netherthird....113 C5
Netherthong....88 D2
Netherthorpe....89 F5
Netherton Angus..135 D5
  Devon....7 B6
  Hants....25 D8
  Mers....85 D4
  Northumb....117 D5
  Oxon....38 E4
  Perth....133 D8
  Staffs....75 D5
  W Mid....62 F3
  W Yorks....88 C2
  Worcs....50 E4
Nethertown Highld
  ....158 C5
Nether Urquhart.128 D3
Nether Wallop....25 F8
Nether Whitacre..63 E6
Netherwitton....117 E7
Netherwood....113 B6
Nether Worton....52 F2
Nethy Bridge....139 B6
Netley....15 D5
Netley Marsh....14 C4
Nettacott....11 C7
Nettlebed....39 F7
Nettlebridge....23 E8
Nettlecombe....12 E3
Nettleden....40 C3
Nettleham....78 B3
Nettlestead....29 D7
Nettlestead Green.29 D7
Nettlesworth....111 E5
Nettleton Lincs....90 D5
  Wilts....24 B3
Neuadd....33 B7
Nevendon....42 E3
Nevern....45 E2
New Abbey....107 C6
New Aberdour....153 B8
New Addington....28 C4
New Alresford....26 F3
New Alyth....134 E2
Newark Orkney...159 D8
  Pboro....66 D2
Newark-on-Trent.77 D7
New Arley....63 F6
Newarthill....119 D7
New Ash Green....29 C7
New Barn....29 C7
New Barnetby....90 C4
Newbarns....92 B2
New Barton....53 C6
New Bewick....117 B6
Newbiggin Cumb..98 B2
  Cumb....100 B4
  Cumb....108 F4
  Durham....100 B4
  N Yorks....100 E4
  N Yorks....100 F4
New Bilton....52 B2
Newbold Derbys...76 B3
  Leics....63 C8
Newbold on Avon.52 B2
Newbold on Stour 51 E7
Newbold Pacey....51 D7
Newbold Verdon..63 D8
New Bolingbroke.79 D6
Newborough
  Anglesey....82 E4
  Pboro....66 D2
  Staffs....62 B5
Newbottle T&W....111 D6
  W Nhants....52 F3
New Boultham....78 B2
New Bradwell....53 E6
New Brancepeth..110 E5
Newbridge Caerph.35 E6
  Ceredig....46 D4
  Corn....2 C2

Newbridge continued
  Corn....5 C8
  Dumfries....107 B6
  Edin....120 B4
  Hants....14 C3
  IoW....14 F5
  Pembs....44 B4
New Bridge....73 E6
Newbridge Green..50 F3
Newbridge-on-
  Usk....35 E7
Newbridge on
  Wye....48 D2
New Brighton Flint.73 C6
  Mers....85 E4
New Brinsley....76 D4
Newbrough....109 C8
New Broughton....73 D7
New Buckenham..68 E3
Newbuildings....10 D2
Newburgh Aberds.141 B8
  Aberds....153 C9
  Borders....115 C6
  Fife....128 C4
  Lancs....86 C2
Newburn....110 C4
Newbury....26 C2
Newbury Park....41 F7
Newby Lancs....93 E8
  N Yorks....93 B7
  N Yorks....102 C3
  N Yorks....103 E8
  W&F....99 B7
Newby Bridge....99 F5
Newby East....108 D4
New Byth....153 C8
Newby West....108 D3
Newby Wiske....102 F1
Newcastle Mon...35 C8
  Shrops....60 F2
Newcastle Emlyn
  =Castell Newydd
  Emlyn....46 E2
Newcastleton or
  Copshaw Holm..115 F7
Newcastle-under-
  Lyme....74 E5
Newcastle upon
  Tyne....110 C5
New Catton....68 C5
Newchapel Pembs.45 F1
  Powys....59 F6
  Staffs....75 D5
  Sur....28 E4
Newchurch Carms.32 B4
  IoW....15 F6
  Kent....19 B7
  Lancs....93 F8
  Mon....36 E1
  Powys....48 D4
  Staffs....62 B5
Newcott....11 D7
New Cowper....107 E8
Newcraighall....121 B6
New Cross Ceredig..46 B5
  London....28 B4
New Cumnock....113 C6
New Deer....153 D8
New Delaval....111 B5
Newdigate....28 E2
New Duston....52 C5
New Earswick....96 D2
New Edlington....89 E6
New Elgin....152 B2
New Ellerby....97 F7
Newell Green....27 B6
New Eltham....28 B5
Newenden....18 C5
Newent....36 B4
Newerne....36 D3
New Farnley....94 F5
New Ferry....85 F4
Newfield Durham..110 F5
  Highld....151 D10
Newford....2 E4
Newfound....26 D3
New Fryston....89 B5
Newgale....44 C3
New Galloway....106 B3
Newgate....81 C6
Newgate Street....41 D6
New Gilston....129 D6
New Grimsby....2 E3
New Hainford....68 C5
Newhall Ches E...74 E3
  Derbys....63 B6
Newhall House....151 E9
Newhall Point....151 E10
Newham....117 B7
Newham Hall....117 B7
Newhaven Derbys..75 D8
  Edin....121 B5
  E Sus....17 D8
New Haw....27 C8
New Hedges....32 D2
New Herrington..111 D6
Newhey....87 C7
New Hinksey....39 D5
New Holkham....80 D4
New Holland....90 B4
Newholm....103 C6
New Houghton
  Derbys....76 C4
  Norf....80 E3
Newhouse....119 C7
New Houses....93 B8
New Humberstone.64 D3
New Hutton....99 E7
New Hythe....29 D8
Newick....17 B8
Newingreen....19 B8
Newington Kent...30 C2
  Kent....31 C7
  Notts....89 E7
  Oxon....39 E6
  Shrops....60 F4
New Inn Carms....46 F3
  Mon....36 D1
  Pembs....44 C5
  Torf....35 E7
New Invention
  Shrops....48 B4
  W Mid....62 D3
New Kelso....150 G2

New Kingston....64 B2
New Lanark....119 E8
Newland Glos....36 D2
  Hull....97 F6
  N Yorks....89 B7
  Worcs....50 E2
Newlandrig....121 C6
Newlands Borders.115 E8
  Highld....151 G10
  Moray....152 C3
  Northumb....110 D3
Newlands Park....82 C2
New Lane....86 C2
New Lane End....86 E4
New Leake....79 D7
New Leeds....153 C9
New Longton....86 B3
Newlot....159 G6
New Luce....105 C5
Newlyn....2 D3
Newmachar....141 C7
Newmains....119 D8
New Malden....28 C3
Newmarket Suff...55 C7
  W Isles....155 D9
New Marske....102 B4
New Marton....73 F7
New Micklefield....95 F7
Newmill Borders..115 C7
  Corn....2 C3
  Moray....152 C5
New Mill Aberds..141 F6
  Herts....40 C2
  Wilts....25 C6
  W Yorks....88 D2
Newmill of
  Inshewan....134 C4
New Mills Ches E..87 F5
  Corn....4 D3
  Derbys....87 F7
  Powys....59 D7
Newmills of
  Boyne....152 C5
Newmiln....133 F8
Newmilns....118 F5
New Mistley....56 F5
New Moat....32 B1
Newnham Glos....36 C3
  Hants....26 D5
  Herts....54 F3
  Kent....30 D3
  W Nhants....52 D3
Newnham Bridge..49 C8
New Ollerton....77 C6
New Oscott....62 E4
Newpark....129 C6
New Park....95 D5
New Pitsligo....153 C8
New Polzeath....4 B4
Newpound
  Common....16 B4
Newport Devon....20 F4
  Essex....55 F6
  E Yorks....96 F4
  Highld....158 H3
  IoW....15 F6
  Norf....69 C8
  Telford....61 C7
Newport
  =Casnewydd....35 F7
Newport
  =Trefdraeth....45 F2
Newport-on-Tay.129 B6
Newport Pagnell..53 E6
Newpound
  Common....16 B4
Newquay....4 C3
New Quay
  =Ceinewydd....46 D2
New Rackheath....69 C5
New Radnor....48 C4
New Rent....108 F4
New Ridley....110 D3
New Road Side....94 E2
New Romney....19 C7
New Rossington..89 E7
New Row Ceredig..47 B6
  Lancs....93 F6
  N Yorks....102 C4
New Sarum....25 F6
Newsbank....74 C5
Newseat Aberds..153 D10
  Aberds....153 E7
Newsham Northumb.111 B6
  N Yorks....101 C6
  N Yorks....102 F1
Newsholme
  E Yorks....89 B8
  Lancs....93 D8
New Silksworth..111 D6
Newsome....88 C2
Newstead Borders.121 F8
  Northumb....117 B7
  Notts....76 D5
New Stevenston..119 D7
New Street....75 D7
New Street Lane...74 F3
New Swanage....13 F8
Newthorpe....95 F7
Newton Argyll....125 F6
  Borders....116 B2
  Bridgend....21 B7
  Cambs....54 E5
  Cambs....66 C4
  Cardiff....22 B4
  Ches W....73 C8
  Ches W....74 B2
  Ches W....74 D2
  Cumb....92 B2
  Derbys....76 D4
  Dorset....13 C6
  Dumfries....108 B2
  Dumfries....114 E4
  Gtr Man....87 E7
  Hereford....48 F5
  Hereford....49 E7
  Highld....151 G10
  Highld....151 H10
  Highld....151 B10
  Highld....158 F5
  IoW....14 E4
  Lancs....86 F3
  Lancs....92 E4
  Lancs....93 B5
  Lancs....93 D6
  Lancs....78 F3

Newton continued
  Moray....152 B1
  N Nhants....65 F5
  Norf....67 C8
  Northumb....110 C3
  Notts....77 E6
  Perth....133 F5
  S Lanark....119 C6
  S Lanark....120 F2
  Staffs....62 B4
  Suff....56 E3
  Swansea....33 F7
  S Yorks....89 D6
  Warks....52 B3
  W&F....92 B2
  Wilts....14 B3
  W Loth....120 B3
Newton Abbot....7 B6
Newtonairds....113 F8
Newton Arlosh....107 D8
Newton Aycliffe..101 B7
Newton Bewley..102 B2
Newton
  Blossomville....53 D7
Newton
  Bromswold....53 C7
Newton
  Burgoland....63 D7
Newton by Toft....90 F4
Newton Ferrers....6 E3
Newton Flotman..68 E5
Newtongrange....121 C6
Newton Hall....110 C3
Newton Harcourt..64 E3
Newton Heath....87 D6
Newtonhill Aberds.141 E8
  Highld....151 G8
Newton House....141 B5
Newton Kyme....95 E7
Newton-le-Willows
  Mers....86 E3
  N Yorks....101 F7
Newton Longville.53 F6
Newton Mearns..118 D5
Newtonmill....135 C6
Newtonmore....138 E3
Newton Morrell..101 D7
Newton
  Mulgrave....103 C5
Newton of
  Ardtoe....147 D9
Newton of
  Balcanquhal....128 C3
Newton of
  Falkland....128 D4
Newton on Ayr....112 B3
Newton-on-
  Rawcliffe....103 E6
Newton-on-the-
  Moor....117 D7
Newton on Trent..77 B8
Newton
  Poppleford....11 F5
Newton Purcell....52 F4
Newton Regis....63 D6
Newton Reigny....108 F4
Newton St Cyres..10 E3
Newton St Faith...68 C5
Newton St Loe....24 C2
Newton St Petrock.9 C6
Newton Solney....63 B6
Newton Stacey....26 E2
Newton Stewart..105 C8
Newton Tony....25 E7
Newton Tracey....9 B7
Newton under
  Roseberry....102 C3
Newton upon
  Derwent....96 E3
Newton Valence..26 F5
New Totley....76 B3
Newtown Argyll..125 E6
  BCP....13 E8
  Ches W....74 B2
  Corn....3 D6
  Cumb....107 E7
  Cumb....108 C5
  Derbys....87 F7
  Devon....10 B2
  Glos....36 D3
  Glos....50 F4
  Hants....14 C3
  Hants....15 C7
  Hants....15 D7
  Hants....26 C2
  Hereford....49 E8
  Highld....137 D7
  IoW....14 E4
  IoW....14 F5
  Northumb....111 B6
  Northumb....117 B6
  Northumb....117 D6
  Northumb....123 F5
  Shrops....60 F4
  Staffs....75 C6
  Staffs....75 D7
  Wilts....13 B7
Newtown
  =Y Drenewydd...59 E8
Newtown Linford..64 D2
Newtown St
  Boswells....121 F8
Newtown Unthank.63 D8
New Tredegar
  =Tredegar Newydd..35 D5
New Trows....119 F8
Newtyle....134 E2
New Ulva....144 E6
New Walsoken....66 D4
New Waltham....91 D6
New Whittington..76 B3
New Wimpole....54 E4
New Winton....121 B7

Nigg continued
  Highld....151 D11
Nigg Ferry....151 E10
Nightcott....10 B3
Nilig....72 D4
Nine Ashes....42 D1
Ninebanks....109 D7
Nine Mile Burn..120 D4
Nine Wells....44 C2
Ninfield....18 D4
Ningwood....14 F4
Nisbet....116 B2
Nisthouse Orkney.159 G4
  Shetland....160 G7
Niton....15 G6
Nitshill....118 C5
Noak Hill....41 E8
Noblethorpe....88 D3
Nobottle....52 C4
Nocton....78 C3
Noke....39 C5
Nolton....44 D3
Nolton Haven....44 D3
No Man's Heath
  Ches W....74 E2
  Warks....63 D6
Nomansland Devon..10 C3
  Wilts....14 C3
Noneley....60 B4
Nonikiln....151 D9
Nonington....31 D6
Noonsbrough....160 H4
Norbreck....92 E3
Norbridge....50 E2
Norbury Ches E....74 E2
  Derbys....75 E8
  Shrops....60 E3
  Staffs....61 B7
Nordelph....67 D5
Norden....87 C6
Norden Heath....13 F7
Nordley....61 E6
Norham....122 E5
Norley....74 B2
Norleywood....14 E4
Normanby N Lincs..90 C2
  N Yorks....103 F5
  Redcar....102 C3
Normanby-by-
  Spital....90 F4
Normanby by Stow.90 F2
Normanby le Wold..90 E4
Norman Cross....65 E8
Normandy....27 D7
Norman's Bay....18 E3
Norman's Green..11 D5
Normanston....69 E8
Normanton Derby..76 F3
  Leics....77 E8
  Lincs....78 E2
  Notts....77 D7
  Rutland....65 D6
  W Yorks....88 B4
Normanton le
  Heath....63 C7
Normanton on
  Soar....64 B2
Normanton-on-the-
  Wolds....77 F6
Normanton on
  Trent....77 C7
Normoss....92 F3
Norney....27 E7
Norrington
  Common....24 C3
Norris Green....85 E4
Norris Hill....63 C7
Northacre....68 E2
Northallerton....102 E1
Northam Devon....9 B6
  Soton....14 C5
Northampton....53 C5
North Anston....89 F6
North Aston....38 B4
Northaw....41 D5
North Baddesley..14 C4
North
  Ballachulish....130 C4
North Barrow....12 B4
North Barsham....80 D5
Northbeck....78 E3
North Benfleet....42 F3
North Bersted....16 D3
North Berwick....129 F7
North Boarhunt....15 C7
Northborough....65 D8
North Bovey....10 F2
North Bradley....24 D3
North Brentor....9 F6
North Brewham..24 F2
Northbridge
  Street....18 C4
North Buckland..20 E3
North Burlingham.69 C6
North Cadbury....12 B4
North Cairn....104 B3
North Carlton....78 B2
North Carrine....143 H7
North Cave....96 F4
North Cerney....37 D7
North
  Cockerington..91 E7
North Coker....12 C3
Northcott....8 E5
North Collafirth..160 E5
North Common....17 B7
North Connel....124 B5
North Cornelly....34 F2
North Cotes....91 D7
Northcourt....38 E5
North Cove....69 F7
North Cowton....101 D7
North Crawley....53 E7
North Cray....29 B5
North Creake....80 D4
North Curry....11 B8
North Dalton....96 D5
North Dawn....159 H5
North Deighton..95 D6
Northdown....31 B7
North Duffield....96 F2

Northdyke . . . . . . . 159 F3
North Elkington . . 91 E6
North Elmham . . . 81 E5
North Elmshall . . . 89 C5
Northend Bath . . . 24 C2
Bucks . . . . . . . . . . 39 E7
Warks . . . . . . . . . . 51 D8
North End Bucks . . 39 B8
Essex . . . . . . . . . 42 C2
E Yorks . . . . . . . . 97 F8
Hants . . . . . . . . . 26 C2
Lincs . . . . . . . . . 78 E5
N Som . . . . . . . . 23 C6
Ptsmth . . . . . . . . 15 D7
Som . . . . . . . . . 11 B7
W Sus . . . . . . . . 16 D5
Northenden . . . . . 87 E6
North Erradale . . . 155 J12
North Fambridge . 42 E4
North Fearns . . . 149 E10
North
Featherstone . . . 88 B5
North Ferriby . . . 90 B3
Northfield
Aberdeen . . . . . . 141 D8
Borders . . . . . . . 122 C5
E Yorks . . . . . . . 90 B4
W Mid . . . . . . . . 50 B5
Northfields . . . . . . 65 D7
Northfleet . . . . . . 29 B7
North Frodingham 97 D7
Northgate . . . . . . . 65 B8
North Gluss . . . . 160 F5
North Gorley . . . . 14 C2
North Green Norf . 68 F5
Suff . . . . . . . . . . 57 C7
North Greetwell . . 78 B3
North Grimston . . 96 C4
North Halley . . . . 159 H6
North Halling . . . . 29 C8
North Hayling . . . . 15 D8
North Hazelrigg . 123 F6
North Heasley . . . 21 F6
North Heath . . . . . 16 B4
North Hill Cambs . . 55 B5
Corn . . . . . . . . . . 5 B7
North Hinksey . . . 38 D4
North Holmwood . . 28 E2
Northhouse . . . . 115 D7
North Howden . . . 96 F3
North Huish . . . . . 6 D5
North Hykeham . . 78 C2
Northiam . . . . . . . 18 C5
Northill . . . . . . . . . 54 E2
Northington . . . . . 26 F3
North Johnston . . 44 D4
North Kelsey . . . . 90 D4
North Kelsey Moor 90 D4
North Kessock . . 151 G9
North
Killingholme . . . 90 C5
North Kilvington . 102 F2
North Kilworth . . . 64 F3
North Kirkton . . . 153 C11
North Kiscadale . 143 F11
North Kyme . . . . 78 D4
North Lancing . . . 17 D5
Northlands . . . . . . 79 D6
Northlea . . . . . . . 111 D7
Northleach . . . . . . 37 C8
North Lee . . . . . . 39 D8
Northleigh . . . . . . 11 E6
North Leigh . . . . . 38 C3
North Leverton with
Habblesthorpe . . 89 F8
Northlew . . . . . . . . 9 E7
North Littleton . . . 51 E5
North Lopham . . . 68 F3
North Luffenham . 65 D6
North Marden . . . 16 C2
North Marston . . . 39 B7
North Middleton
Midloth . . . . . . . 121 D6
Northumb . . . . . . 117 B6
North Molton . . . . 10 B2
Northmoor . . . . . . 38 D4
Northmoor Green or
Moorland . . . . . . 22 F5
North Moreton . . . 39 F5
Northmuir . . . . . . 134 D3
North Mundham . 16 D2
North Muskham . . 77 D7
North Newbald . . 96 F5
North Newington . 52 F2
North Newnton . . 25 D6
North Newton . . . 22 F4
Northney . . . . . . . 15 D8
North Nibley . . . . 36 E4
North Oakley . . . . 26 D3
North Ockendon . . 42 F1
Northolt . . . . . . . . 40 F4
Northop . . . . . . . . 73 C6
Northop Hall . . . . 73 C6
North Ormesby . . 102 B3
North Ormsby . . . 91 E6
Northorpe Lincs . . 65 C7
Lincs . . . . . . . . . 78 F5
Lincs . . . . . . . . . 90 E2
North
Otterington . . . . 102 F1
Northover Som . . . 12 B3
Som . . . . . . . . . 23 F6
North Owersby . . 90 E4
Northowram . . . . 88 B2
North Perrott . . . . 12 D2
North Petherton . 22 F4
North Petherwin . . 8 F4
North Pickenham . 67 D8
North Piddle . . . . 50 D4
North Poorton . . . 12 E3
Northport . . . . . . . 13 F7
North Port . . . . . 125 C6
Northpunds . . . . 160 L6
North
Queensferry . . . 128 F3
North Radworthy . 21 F6
North Rauceby . . 78 E3
North Threaps . . . 91 D8
North Reston . . . . 91 F7
North Rigton . . . . 95 C5
North Rode . . . . . 75 C5
North Roe . . . . . 160 E5
North Runcton . . 67 C6
North Sandwick . 160 D7
North Scale . . . . . 92 C1
North Scarle . . . . 77 C8
North Seaton . . . 117 F8
North Shian . . . . 130 E3
North Shields . . . 111 C6

North Shoebury . . 43 F5
North Shore . . . . . 92 F3
North Side Cumb . 98 B2
Pboro . . . . . . . . 66 E2
North Skelton . . 102 C4
North Somercotes . 91 E8
North Stainley . . . 95 B5
North Stainmore . 100 C3
North Stifford . . . 42 F2
North Stoke Bath . 24 C2
Oxon . . . . . . . . . 39 F6
W Sus . . . . . . . . 16 C4
Northstowe . . . . . 54 C5
North Street Hants . 26 F4
Kent . . . . . . . . . . 30 D4
Medway . . . . . . . 30 B2
W Berks . . . . . . . 26 B4
North
Sunderland . . . . 123 F8
North Tamerton . . 8 E5
North Tawton . . . . 9 D8
North Thoresby . . 91 E6
North Tidworth . . 25 E7
North Togston . . . 117 D8
Northtown . . . . . 159 J5
North Tuddenham . 68 C3
North Walbottle . 110 C4
North Walsham . . 81 D8
North Waltham . . 26 E3
North
Warnborough . . 26 D5
North Water
Bridge . . . . . . . 135 C6
North Watten . . . 158 E4
Northway . . . . . . . 50 F4
North Weald
Bassett . . . . . . . 41 D7
North Wheatley . . 89 F8
North Whilborough . 7 C6
Northwich . . . . . . 74 B3
Northwick . . . . . . 36 F2
North Wick . . . . . 23 C7
North Willingham . 91 F5
North Wingfield . . 76 C4
North Witham . . . 65 B6
Northwold . . . . . . 67 E7
Northwood Derbys . 76 C2
IoW . . . . . . . . . . 15 E5
Kent . . . . . . . . . 31 C7
London . . . . . . . 40 E3
Shrops . . . . . . . . 73 F8
Northwood Green . 36 C4
North Woolwich . . 28 B5
North Wootton
Dorset . . . . . . . . 12 C4
Norf . . . . . . . . . . 67 B6
Som . . . . . . . . . 23 E7
North Wraxall . . . 24 B3
North Wroughton . 38 F1
Norton E Sus . . . . 17 D8
Glos . . . . . . . . . 37 B5
Halton . . . . . . . . 86 F3
Herts . . . . . . . . 54 F3
IoW . . . . . . . . . 14 F4
Mon . . . . . . . . . 35 C8
Notts . . . . . . . . . 77 B5
Powys . . . . . . . . 48 C5
Shrops . . . . . . . . 60 F4
Shrops . . . . . . . . 61 D5
Shrops . . . . . . . . 61 D7
Stockton . . . . . . 102 B2
Suff . . . . . . . . . . 56 C3
S Yorks . . . . . . . 89 C6
Wilts . . . . . . . . . 37 F5
W Nhants . . . . . . 52 D4
Worcs . . . . . . . . 50 D3
Worcs . . . . . . . . 50 E5
W Sus . . . . . . . . 16 D3
Norton Bavant . . . 24 E4
Norton Bridge . . . 75 F5
Norton Canes . . . 62 D4
Norton Canon . . . 49 E5
Norton Corner . . . 81 E6
Norton Disney . . . 77 D8
Norton East . . . . . 62 D4
Norton Ferris . . . . 24 F2
Norton Fitzwarren . 11 B6
Norton Green . . . 14 F4
Norton Hawkfield . 23 C7
Norton Heath . . . 42 D2
Norton in Hales . . 74 F4
Norton-in-the-
Moors . . . . . . . 75 D5
Norton-Juxta-
Twycross . . . . . 63 D7
Norton-le-Clay . . 95 B7
Norton Lindsey . . 51 C7
Norton Malreward . 23 C8
Norton Mandeville 42 D1
Norton-on-
Derwent . . . . . . 96 B3
Norton St Philip . 24 D2
Norton sub
Hamdon . . . . . . 12 C2
Norton Woodseats 88 F4
Norwell . . . . . . . . 77 C7
Norwell
Woodhouse . . . . 77 C7
Norwich . . . . . . . . 68 D5
Norwick . . . . . . . 160 B8
Norwood . . . . . . . 89 F5
Norwood Hill . . . . 28 E3
Norwoodside . . . . 66 E4
Noseley . . . . . . . . 64 E4
Noss . . . . . . . . . 160 M5
Noss Mayo . . . . . . 6 E3
Nosterfield . . . . . 101 F7
Nosterfield End . . 55 E7
Notgrove . . . . . . . 37 B8
Nottage . . . . . . . . 21 B7
Nottingham . . . . . 77 F5
Notton Wilts . . . . 24 C4
W Yorks . . . . . . . 88 C4
Nounsley . . . . . . . 42 C3
Noutard's Green . . 50 C2
Novar House . . . 151 E9
Nox . . . . . . . . . . 60 C4
Nuffield . . . . . . . . 39 F6
Nunburnholme . . . 96 E4
Nuncargate . . . . . 76 D5
Nuneaton . . . . . . 63 E7
Nuneham
Courtenay . . . . . 39 E5
Nun Hills . . . . . . . 87 B6
Nun Monkton . . . . 95 D8
Nunney . . . . . . . . 24 E2
Nunnington . . . . . 96 B3

Nunnykirk . . . . . . 117 E6
Nunsthorpe . . . . . 91 D6
Nunthorpe Mbro . 102 C3
York . . . . . . . . . 96 D2
Nunton . . . . . . . . 14 B2
Nunwick . . . . . . . 95 B6
Nupend . . . . . . . . 36 D4
Nursling . . . . . . . 14 C4
Nursted . . . . . . . . 15 B8
Nutbourne W Sus . 15 D8
W Sus . . . . . . . . 16 C4
Nutfield . . . . . . . . 28 D4
Nuthall . . . . . . . . 76 F5
Nuthampstead . . . 54 F5
Nuthurst . . . . . . . 17 B5
Nutley E Sus . . . . . 17 B8
Hants . . . . . . . . 26 E4
Nutwell . . . . . . . . 89 D7
Nybster . . . . . . . 158 D5
Nyetimber . . . . . . 16 E2
Nyewood . . . . . . . 16 B2
Nymet Rowland . . 10 D2
Nymet Tracey . . . 10 D2
Nympsfield . . . . . . 37 D5
Nynehead . . . . . . 11 B6
Nyton . . . . . . . . . 16 D3

## O

Oadby . . . . . . . . . 64 D3
Oad Street . . . . . . 30 C2
Oakamoor . . . . . . 75 E7
Oakbank . . . . . . . 120 C3
Oak Cross . . . . . . . 9 E7
Oakdale . . . . . . . . 35 E5
Oake . . . . . . . . . . 11 B6
Oaken . . . . . . . . . 62 D2
Oakenclough . . . . 92 E5
Oakengates . . . . . 61 C7
Oakenholt . . . . . . 73 B6
Oakenshaw
Durham . . . . . . 110 F5
W Yorks . . . . . . . 88 B2
Oakerthorpe . . . . 76 D3
Oakes . . . . . . . . . 88 C2
Oakfield . . . . . . . . 35 E7
Oakford Ceredig . . 46 D3
Devon . . . . . . . . 10 B4
Oakfordbridge . . . 10 B4
Oakgrove . . . . . . . 75 C6
Oakham . . . . . . . 65 D5
Oakhanger . . . . . . 27 F5
Oakhill . . . . . . . . 23 E8
Oakhurst . . . . . . . 29 D6
Oakington . . . . . . 54 C5
Oaklands Herts . . . 41 C5
Powys . . . . . . . . 48 D2
Oakle Street . . . . 36 C4
Oakley BCP . . . . . 13 E8
Bedford . . . . . . . 53 D8
Bucks . . . . . . . . 39 C6
Fife . . . . . . . . . 128 F2
Hants . . . . . . . . 26 D3
Oxon . . . . . . . . . 39 D7
Suff . . . . . . . . . . 57 B5
Oakley Green . . . . 27 B7
Oakley Park . . . . . 59 F6
Oakmere . . . . . . . 74 C2
Oakridge Glos . . . 37 D6
Hants . . . . . . . . 26 D4
Oaks . . . . . . . . . . 60 D4
Oaksey . . . . . . . . 37 E6
Oaks Green . . . . . 75 F8
Oakthorpe . . . . . . 63 C7
Oakwoodhill . . . . 28 F2
Oakworth . . . . . . . 94 F3
Oape . . . . . . . . . 156 J7
Oare Kent . . . . . . 30 C4
Som . . . . . . . . . . 21 E7
W Berks . . . . . . . 26 B3
Wilts . . . . . . . . . 25 C6
Oasby . . . . . . . . . 78 F3
Oathlaw . . . . . . . 134 D4
Oatlands . . . . . . . 95 D6
Oban Argyll . . . . 124 C4
Highld . . . . . . . 147 C11
Oborne . . . . . . . . 12 C4
Obthorpe . . . . . . . 65 C7
Occlestone Green . 74 C3
Occold . . . . . . . . 57 B5
Ochiltree . . . . . . 112 B5
Ochtermuthill . . . 127 C7
Ochtertyre . . . . . 127 B7
Ockbrook . . . . . . . 76 F4
Ockham . . . . . . . . 27 D8
Ockle . . . . . . . . . 147 D8
Ockley . . . . . . . . . 28 F2
Ocle Pychard . . . 49 E7
Octon . . . . . . . . . 97 C6
Octon Cross
Roads . . . . . . . . 97 C6
Odcombe . . . . . . . 12 C3
Odd Down . . . . . . 24 C2
Oddendale . . . . . . 99 C7
Odder . . . . . . . . . 78 B2
Oddingley . . . . . . 50 D4
Oddington Glos . . 38 B2
Oxon . . . . . . . . . 39 C5
Odell . . . . . . . . . 53 D7
Odie . . . . . . . . . 159 F7
Odiham . . . . . . . . 26 D5
Odstock . . . . . . . 14 B2
Odstone . . . . . . . 63 D7
Offchurch . . . . . . 51 C8
Offenham . . . . . . 51 E5
Offham E Sus . . . . 17 C7
Kent . . . . . . . . . 29 D7
W Sus . . . . . . . . 16 D4
Offord Cluny . . . . 54 C3
Offord Darcy . . . . 54 C3
Offton . . . . . . . . . 56 E4
Offwell . . . . . . . . 11 E6
Ogbourne Maizey . 25 B6
Ogbourne St
Andrew . . . . . . . 25 B6
Ogbourne St
George . . . . . . . 25 B7
Ogil . . . . . . . . . . 134 C4
Ogle . . . . . . . . . 110 B4
Ogmore . . . . . . . . 21 B7
Ogmore-by-Sea . . 21 B7
Ogmore Vale . . . . 34 E3
Okeford Fitzpaine . 13 C6
Okehampton . . . . . 9 E7
Okehampton Camp . 9 E7
Okraquoy . . . . . 160 K6
Old . . . . . . . . . . 53 B5
Old Aberdeen . . 141 D8

Old Alresford . . . 26 F3
Oldany . . . . . . . 156 F4
Old Arley . . . . . . 63 E6
Old Basford . . . . 76 E5
Old Basing . . . . . 26 D4
Oldberrow . . . . . 51 C6
Old Bewick . . . . 117 B6
Old Bolingbroke . 79 C6
Oldborough . . . . 10 D2
Old Bramhope . . 94 E5
Old Brampton . . . 76 B3
Old Bridge of Tilt 133 C5
Old Bridge of Urr 106 C4
Old Buckenham . 68 E3
Old Burghclere . . 26 D2
Oldbury Shrops . . 61 E7
Warks . . . . . . . 63 E7
W Mid . . . . . . . . 62 F3
Oldbury-on-
Severn . . . . . . . 36 E3
Oldbury on the Hill 37 F5
Old Byland . . . . 102 F3
Old Cassop . . . . 111 F6
Oldcastle Bridgend . 21 B8
Mon . . . . . . . . . 35 B7
Old Castleton . . 115 E8
Old Catton . . . . . 68 C5
Old Clee . . . . . . . 91 D6
Old Cleeve . . . . . 22 E2
Old Clipstone . . . 77 C6
Old Colwyn . . . . . 83 D8
Oldcotes . . . . . . 89 F6
Old Coulsdon . . . 28 D4
Old Crombie . . . 152 C5
Old Dailly . . . . . 112 E2
Old Dalby . . . . . . 64 B3
Old Deer . . . . . 153 D9
Old Denaby . . . . 89 E5
Old Edlington . . . 89 E6
Old Eldon . . . . . 101 B7
Old Ellerby . . . . . 97 F7
Oldfallow . . . . . . 62 C3
Old Felixstowe . . 57 F7
Oldfield . . . . . . . 50 C3
Old Fletton . . . . . 65 E8
Oldford . . . . . . . 24 D2
Old Glossop . . . . 87 E8
Old Goole . . . . . 89 B8
Old Hall . . . . . . . 59 F6
Oldham . . . . . . . 87 D7
Oldhamstocks . . 122 B3
Old Heath . . . . . 43 B6
Old Heathfield . . 18 C2
Old Hill . . . . . . . 62 F3
Old Hunstanton . 80 C2
Old Hurst . . . . . . 54 B3
Old Hutton . . . . . 99 F7
Old Kea . . . . . . . . 3 B7
Old Kilpatrick . . 118 B4
Old Kinnernie . . 141 D6
Old Knebworth . . 41 B5
Oldland . . . . . . . 23 B8
Old Langho . . . . . 93 F7
Old Laxey . . . . . . 84 D4
Old Leake . . . . . . 79 D7
Old Malton . . . . . 96 B3
Oldmeldrum . . . 141 B7
Old Micklefield . . 95 F7
Old Milton . . . . . 14 E3
Old Milverton . . . 51 C7
Old Monkland . . 119 C7
Old Netley . . . . . 15 D5
Old Philpstoun . . 120 B3
Old Quarrington . 111 F6
Old Radnor . . . . 48 D4
Old Rattray . . . . 153 C10
Old Rayne . . . . . 141 B5
Old Romney . . . . 19 C7
Oldshore Beg . . . 156 D4
Oldshoremore . . 156 D5
Old Sodbury . . . . 36 F4
Old Somerby . . . 78 F2
Oldstead . . . . . . 102 F3
Old Stratford . . . 53 E5
Old Thirsk . . . . . 102 F2
Oldtown . . . . . . 140 B4
Old Town
Northumb . . . . . 116 E4
N Yorks . . . . . . 93 D8
Scilly . . . . . . . . . 2 E4
W&F . . . . . . . . . 99 F7
W&F . . . . . . . . 108 E4
Oldtown of Ord . . 152 C6
Old Trafford . . . . 87 E6
Old Tupton . . . . . 76 C3
Old Warden . . . . 54 E2
Oldway . . . . . . . . 33 F6
Oldways End . . . 10 B3
Old Weston . . . . 53 B8
Oldwhat . . . . . . 153 C8
Old Whittington . 76 B3
Old Wick . . . . . 158 E5
Old Windsor . . . . 27 B7
Old Wives Lees . . 30 D4
Old Woking . . . . 27 D8
Old Woodhall . . . 78 C5
Olgrinmore . . . . 158 E2
Oliver's Battery . . 15 B5
Ollaberry . . . . . 160 E5
Ollerton Ches E . . 74 B4
Notts . . . . . . . . 77 C6
Shrops . . . . . . . 61 B6
Olmarch . . . . . . . 46 D5
Olney . . . . . . . . . 53 D6
Olrig House . . . . 158 D3
Olton . . . . . . . . . 62 F5
Olveston . . . . . . 36 F3
Olwen . . . . . . . . 46 E4
Ombersley . . . . . 50 C3
Ompton . . . . . . . 77 C6
Onchan . . . . . . . 84 E3
Onecote . . . . . . . 75 D7
Onen . . . . . . . . . 35 C8
Ongar Hill . . . . . 67 B5
Ongar Street . . . . 49 C5
Onibury . . . . . . . 49 B6
Onich . . . . . . . 130 C4
Onllwyn . . . . . . . 34 C2
Onneley . . . . . . . 74 E4
Onslow Village . . 27 E7
Onthank . . . . . . 118 E4
Openwoodgate . . 76 E3
Opinan Highld . . 149 A12
Highld . . . . . . . 155 H13
Orange Lane . . . 122 E3
Orange Row . . . . 66 B5
Orasaigh . . . . . . 155 F8
Orbliston . . . . . 152 C3
Orbost . . . . . . . 148 D7
Orby . . . . . . . . . 79 C7

Orchard Hill . . . . . 9 B6
Orchard Portman . 11 B7
Orcheston . . . . . . 25 E5
Orcop . . . . . . . . . 36 B1
Orcop Hill . . . . . . 36 B1
Ord . . . . . . . . . 149 G11
Ordhead . . . . . . 141 C5
Ordie . . . . . . . . . 140 D3
Ordiequish . . . . 152 C3
Ordsall . . . . . . . . 89 F7
Ore . . . . . . . . . . 18 D5
Oreton . . . . . . . . 61 F6
Orford Suff . . . . . 57 E8
Warr . . . . . . . . . 86 E4
Orgreave . . . . . . 63 C5
Orlestone . . . . . . 19 B6
Orleton Hereford . 49 C6
Worcs . . . . . . . . 49 C8
Orlingbury . . . . . . 53 B6
Ormesby . . . . . . 102 C3
Ormesby St
Margaret . . . . . . 69 C7
Ormesby St
Michael . . . . . . . 69 C7
Ormiclate Castle . 148 E2
Ormiscaig . . . . . 155 H13
Ormiston . . . . . . 121 C7
Ormsaigbeg . . . 146 E7
Ormsaigmore . . 146 E7
Ormsary . . . . . . 144 F6
Ormsgill . . . . . . . 92 B1
Ormskirk . . . . . . 86 D2
Orpington . . . . . . 29 C5
Orrell Gtr Man . . . 86 D3
Mers . . . . . . . . 85 E4
Orrisdale . . . . . . 84 C3
Orroland . . . . . 106 E4
Orsett . . . . . . . . 42 F2
Orslow . . . . . . . . 62 C2
Orston . . . . . . . . 77 E7
Orthwaite . . . . . 108 F2
Ortner . . . . . . . . 92 D5
Orton N Nhants . . 53 B6
W&F . . . . . . . . . 99 D8
Orton Longueville . 65 E8
Orton-on-the-Hill 63 D7
Orton Waterville . 65 E8
Orwell . . . . . . . . 54 D4
Osbaldeston . . . . 93 F6
Osbaldwick . . . . . 96 D2
Osbaston . . . . . . 60 B3
Osbournby . . . . . 78 F3
Oscroft . . . . . . . 74 C2
Ose . . . . . . . . . 149 D8
Osgathorpe . . . . 63 C8
Osgodby Lincs . . 90 E4
N Yorks . . . . . . . 96 F2
N Yorks . . . . . . 103 F8
Oskaig . . . . . . . 149 E10
Oskamull . . . . . 146 G7
Osmaston Derby . 76 F3
Derbys . . . . . . . 76 E2
Osmington . . . . . 12 F5
Osmington Mills . 12 F5
Osmotherley . . . 102 E2
Ospisdale . . . . . 151 C10
Ospringe . . . . . . 30 C4
Ossett . . . . . . . . 88 B3
Ossington . . . . . 77 C7
Ostend . . . . . . . . 43 E5
Oswaldkirk . . . . . 96 B2
Oswaldtwistle . . . 86 B5
Oswestry . . . . . . 60 B2
Otford . . . . . . . . 29 D6
Otham . . . . . . . . 29 D8
Othery . . . . . . . . 23 F5
Otley Suff . . . . . . 57 D6
W Yorks . . . . . . 94 E5
Otterburn
Northumb . . . . 116 E4
N Yorks . . . . . . . 93 D8
Otterburn Camp . 116 E4
Otter Ferry . . . . 145 E8
Otterham . . . . . . . 8 E3
Otterhampton . . . 22 E4
Ottershaw . . . . . 27 C8
Otterswick . . . . 160 E7
Otterton . . . . . . . 11 E6
Ottery St Mary . . 11 E6
Ottinge . . . . . . . 31 E5
Ottringham . . . . 91 B6
Oughterby . . . . . 108 D2
Oughtershaw . . 100 F3
Oughterside . . . 107 E8
Oughtibridge . . . 88 E4
Oughtrington . . . 86 F4
Oulston . . . . . . . 95 B8
Oulton Cumb . . . 108 D2
Norf . . . . . . . . . 81 E7
Staffs . . . . . . . . 75 F6
Suff . . . . . . . . . 69 E8
W Yorks . . . . . . . 88 B4
Oulton Broad . . . 69 E8
Oulton Street . . . 81 E7
Oundle . . . . . . . 65 F7
Ousby . . . . . . . 109 F6
Ousdale . . . . . . 158 H2
Ousden . . . . . . . 55 D8
Ousefleet . . . . . . 90 B2
Ouston Durham . 111 D5
Northumb . . . . . 110 B3
Outertown . . . . 159 G3
Outgate . . . . . . . 99 E5
Outhgill . . . . . . 100 D2
Outlane . . . . . . . 87 C8
Out Newton . . . . 91 B7
Out Rawcliffe . . . 92 E4
Outwell . . . . . . . 66 D5
Outwick . . . . . . . 14 C2
Outwood Sur . . . . 28 E4
W Yorks . . . . . . . 88 B4
Outwoods . . . . . 121 F7
Ovenden . . . . . . 87 B8
Over Cambs . . . . 54 B4
Ches W . . . . . . . 74 C3
S Glos . . . . . . . 36 F2
Overbister . . . . . 159 D7
Overbury . . . . . . 50 F4
Overcombe . . . . 12 F4
Over Compton . . 12 C3
Over Green . . . . 63 E5
Over Haddon . . . 76 C2
Over Hulton . . . . 86 D4
Over Kellet . . . . . 92 B5
Over Kiddington . 38 B4
Over Knutsford . . 74 B4

Overleigh . . . . . . 23 F6
Overley Green . . . 51 D5
Over Monnow . . . 36 C2
Over Norton . . . . 38 B3
Over Peover . . . . 74 B4
Overpool . . . . . . 73 B7
Overseal . . . . . . 63 C6
Over Silton . . . . 102 E2
Oversland . . . . . 30 D4
Overstone . . . . . 53 C6
Over Stowey . . . . 22 F3
Over Stratton . . . 12 C2
Overstrand . . . . 81 C8
Over Tabley . . . . 86 F5
Overthorpe . . . . 52 E2
Overton = Owrtyn . 73 E7
Overton Aberdeen 141 C7
Ches W . . . . . . . 74 B2
Dumfries . . . . . 107 C6
Hants . . . . . . . . 26 E3
Lancs . . . . . . . . 92 D4
N Yorks . . . . . . . 95 D8
Shrops . . . . . . . 49 B7
Swansea . . . . . . 33 F5
W Yorks . . . . . . . 88 C3
Overton = Owrtyn . 73 E7
Overton Bridge . . 73 E7
Overtown . . . . . 119 D8
Over Wallop . . . . 25 F7
Over Whitacre . . . 63 E6
Over Worton . . . . 38 B4
Oving Bucks . . . . 39 B7
W Sus . . . . . . . . 16 D3
Ovingdean . . . . . 17 D7
Ovingham . . . . . 110 C3
Ovington Durham . 101 C6
Essex . . . . . . . . 55 E8
Hants . . . . . . . . 26 F3
Norf . . . . . . . . . 68 D2
Northumb . . . . . 110 C3
Ower . . . . . . . . . 14 C4
Owermoigne . . . . 13 F5
Owlbury . . . . . . . 60 E3
Owler Bar . . . . . 76 B2
Owlerton . . . . . . 88 F4
Owl's Green . . . . 57 C6
Owlswick . . . . . . 39 D7
Owmby . . . . . . . 90 D4
Owmby-by-Spital . 90 F4
Owrtyn = Overton . 73 E7
Owslebury . . . . . 15 B6
Owston Leics . . . . 64 D4
S Yorks . . . . . . . 89 C6
Owston Ferry . . . 90 D2
Owstwick . . . . . . 97 F8
Owthorne . . . . . . 91 B7
Owthorpe . . . . . . 77 F6
Oxborough . . . . . 67 D7
Oxcombe . . . . . . 79 B6
Oxen End . . . . . . 55 F7
Oxenholme . . . . . 99 F7
Oxenhope . . . . . . 94 F3
Oxen Park . . . . . . 99 F5
Oxenton . . . . . . . 50 F4
Oxenwood . . . . . 25 D8
Oxford . . . . . . . . 39 D5
Oxhey . . . . . . . . 40 E4
Oxhill . . . . . . . . . 51 E8
Oxley . . . . . . . . . 62 D3
Oxley Green . . . . 43 C5
Oxley's Green . . . 18 C3
Oxnam . . . . . . . 116 C2
Oxshott . . . . . . . 28 C2
Oxspring . . . . . . 88 D3
Oxted . . . . . . . . 28 D4
Oxton Borders . . 121 D7
Notts . . . . . . . . 77 D6
Oxwich . . . . . . . 33 F5
Oxwick . . . . . . . 80 E5
Oykel Bridge . . . 156 J6
Oyne . . . . . . . . 141 B5

## P

Pabail larach . . . 155 D10
Pabail Uarach . . 155 D10
Pace Gate . . . . . 94 D4
Packington . . . . 63 C7
Padanaram . . . . 134 D4
Padbury . . . . . . . 52 F5
Paddington . . . . 41 F5
Paddlesworth . . . 19 B8
Paddockhaugh . . 152 C2
Paddockhole . . . 115 F5
Paddock Wood . . 29 E7
Padfield . . . . . . 87 E8
Padiham . . . . . . . 93 F7
Padog . . . . . . . . 83 F8
Padside . . . . . . . 94 D4
Padstow . . . . . . . 4 B4
Padworth . . . . . . 26 C4
Page Bank . . . . 110 F5
Pagham . . . . . . . 16 E2
Paglesham
Churchend . . . . 43 E5
Paglesham
Eastend . . . . . . 43 E5
Paibeil . . . . . . . 148 B2
Paible . . . . . . . 154 H5
Paignton . . . . . . . 7 C6
Pailton . . . . . . . . 63 F8
Painscastle . . . . 48 E3
Painshawfield . . 110 C3
Painsthorpe . . . . 96 D4
Painswick . . . . . 37 D5
Pairc Shiaboist . 154 C7
Paisley . . . . . . . 118 C4
Pakefield . . . . . . 69 E8
Pakenham . . . . . 56 C3
Pale . . . . . . . . . 72 F3
Palestine . . . . . . 25 E7
Paley Street . . . . 27 B6
Palfrey . . . . . . . 62 E4
Palgowan . . . . . 112 F3
Palgrave . . . . . . 56 B5
Pallion . . . . . . . 111 D6
Palmarsh . . . . . . 19 B8
Palnackie . . . . . 106 D5
Palnure . . . . . . 105 C8
Palterton . . . . . . 76 C4
Pamber End . . . . 26 D4
Pamber Green . . 26 D4
Pamber Heath . . 26 C4
Pamphill . . . . . . 13 D7
Pampisford . . . . 55 E5
Pan . . . . . . . . 159 J4
Panbride . . . . . 135 F5
Pancrasweek . . . . 8 D4
Pandy Gwyn . . . . 58 D3

Pandy continued
Mon . . . . . . . . . 35 B7
Powys . . . . . . . . 59 D6
Wrex . . . . . . . . 73 F5
Pandy Tudur . . . . 83 E8
Panfield . . . . . . . 42 B3
Pangbourne . . . . 26 B4
Pannal . . . . . . . . 95 D6
Panshanger . . . . 41 C5
Pant . . . . . . . . . . 60 B2
Pant-glas Carms . . 33 B6
Gwyn . . . . . . . . 71 C5
Pant-glàs . . . . . . 58 E4
Pant-glas . . . . . . 73 F6
Pantgwyn Carms . . 33 B6
Ceredig . . . . . . . 45 E4
Pant-lasau . . . . . 33 E7
Pant Mawr . . . . . 59 F5
Panton . . . . . . . . 78 B4
Pantperthog . . . . 58 D4
Pant-teg . . . . . . . 33 B5
Pant-y-Caws . . . . 32 B2
Pant-y-dwr . . . . . 47 B8
Pant-y-ffridd . . . 59 D8
Pantyffynnon . . . 33 C7
Pantymwyn . . . . . 73 C5
Pant-yr-awel . . . . 34 F3
Pant-y-Wacco . . . 72 B5
Panxworth . . . . . 69 C6
Papcastle . . . . . 107 F8
Papigoe . . . . . . 158 E5
Papil . . . . . . . . 160 K5
Papley . . . . . . . 159 J5
Papple . . . . . . . 121 B8
Papplewick . . . . . 76 D5
Papworth Everard 54 C3
Papworth St
Agnes . . . . . . . 54 C3
Par . . . . . . . . . . . 5 D5
Parbold . . . . . . . 86 C2
Parbrook Som . . . 23 F7
W Sus . . . . . . . . 16 B4
Parc . . . . . . . . . 72 F2
Parclylln . . . . . . . 45 D4
Parc-Seymour . . . 35 E8
Parc-y-rhôs . . . . 46 E4
Pardshaw . . . . . . 98 B2
Parham . . . . . . . 57 C7
Park . . . . . . . . . 114 E2
Park Corner Oxon . 39 F6
Windsor . . . . . . . 40 F1
Parkend . . . . . . . 36 D3
Park End Mbro . . 102 C3
Northumb . . . . . 109 B8
Parkeston . . . . . . 57 F6
Parkgate Ches W . 73 B6
Dumfries . . . . . 114 F3
Kent . . . . . . . . . 19 B5
Sur . . . . . . . . . . 28 E3
Park Gate . . . . . . 15 D6
Parkham . . . . . . . . 9 B5
Parkham Ash . . . . 9 B5
Park Hill Notts . . . 77 D6
N Yorks . . . . . . . 95 C6
Parkhill House . . 141 C7
Parkhouse . . . . . 36 D1
Parkhouse Green . 76 C4
Parkhurst . . . . . . 15 E5
Parkmill . . . . . . . 33 F6
Parkneuk . . . . . . 135 B7
Parkstone . . . . . . 13 E8
Park Street . . . . . 28 F2
Parley Cross . . . . 13 E8
Parracombe . . . . 21 E5
Parrog . . . . . . . . 45 F2
Parsley Hay . . . . 75 C8
Parsonage Green . 42 D3
Parsonby . . . . . 107 F8
Parson Cross . . . 88 E4
Parson Drove . . . 66 D3
Parson's Heath . . 43 B6
Partick . . . . . . . 119 C5
Partington . . . . . 86 E5
Partney . . . . . . . 79 C7
Parton Cumb . . . . 98 B1
Dumfries . . . . . 106 B3
Glos . . . . . . . . . 37 B5
Partridge Green . 17 C5
Parwich . . . . . . . 75 D8
Passenham . . . . 53 F5
Paston . . . . . . . . 81 D9
Patchacott . . . . . . 9 E6
Patcham . . . . . . . 17 D7
Patchetts Green . 40 E4
Patching . . . . . . 16 D4
Patchole . . . . . . 20 E5
Pateley Bridge . . 94 C4
Paternoster Heath 43 C5
Path of Condie . . 128 C2
Pathhead Aberds . 135 C7
E Ayrs . . . . . . . 113 C6
Fife . . . . . . . . . 128 E4
Midloth . . . . . . 121 C6
Path of Condie . . 128 C2
Pathstruie . . . . . 128 C2
Patna . . . . . . . . 112 C4
Patney . . . . . . . . 25 D5
Patrick . . . . . . . . 84 D2
Patrick
Brompton . . . . 101 E7
Patrington . . . . . 91 B7
Patrixbourne . . . 31 D5
Patterdale . . . . . 99 C5
Pattingham . . . . 62 E2
Pattishall . . . . . . 52 D4
Pattiswick Green . 42 B4
Patton Bridge . . . 99 E7
Paul . . . . . . . . . . 2 D3
Paulerspury . . . . 52 E5
Paull . . . . . . . . . 91 B5
Paulton . . . . . . . 23 D8
Pavenham . . . . . 53 D7
Pawlett . . . . . . . 22 E5
Pawston . . . . . . 122 F4
Paxford . . . . . . . 51 F6
Paxton . . . . . . . 122 D5
Payhembury . . . . 11 D5
Paythorne . . . . . 93 D8
Peacehaven . . . . 17 D8
Peak Dale . . . . . 75 B8
Peak Forest . . . . 75 B8
Peakirk . . . . . . . 65 D8
Pearsie . . . . . . 134 D3
Peasedown St
John . . . . . . . . 24 D2
Peasemore . . . . . 26 B2
Peasenhall . . . . . 57 C7
Pease Pottage . . 28 F3
Peaslake . . . . . . 27 E8
Peasley Cross . . . 86 E3

Peasmarsh . . . . . 19 C5
Peaston . . . . . . 121 C7
Peastonbank . . . 121 C7
Peathill . . . . . . 153 B9
Peat Inn . . . . . . 129 D6
Peatling Magna . 64 E2
Peatling Parva . . 64 F2
Peaton . . . . . . . 60 F5
Pebmarsh . . . . . 56 F2
Pebworth . . . . . . 51 E6
Pecket Well . . . . 87 B7
Peckforton . . . . . 74 D2
Peckham . . . . . . 28 B4
Peckleton . . . . . . 63 D8
Pedlinge . . . . . . 19 B8
Pedmore . . . . . . 62 F3
Pedwell . . . . . . . 23 F6
Peebles . . . . . . 121 E5
Peel . . . . . . . . . . 84 D2
Peel Common . . . 15 D6
Peel Park . . . . . 119 D6
Peening Quarter . 19 C5
Pegsdon . . . . . . 54 F2
Pegswood . . . . . 117 F8
Pegwell . . . . . . . 31 C7
Peinchorran . . . 149 E10
Peinlich . . . . . . 149 C9
Pelaw . . . . . . . . 111 C5
Pelcomb Bridge . . 44 D4
Pelcomb Cross . . 44 D4
Peldon . . . . . . . 43 C5
Pellon . . . . . . . . 87 B8
Pelsall . . . . . . . . 62 D4
Pelton . . . . . . . 111 D5
Pelutho . . . . . . 107 E8
Pelynt . . . . . . . . . 5 D7
Pemberton . . . . . 86 D3
Pembrey . . . . . . 33 D5
Pembridge . . . . . 49 D5
Pembroke
= Penfro . . . . . . 44 E4
Pembroke Dock
= Doc Penfro . . . 44 E4
Pembury . . . . . . 29 E7
Penallt . . . . . . . . 36 C2
Penally . . . . . . . 32 E2
Penalt . . . . . . . . 36 B2
Penare . . . . . . . . 3 B8
Penarlâg
= Hawarden . . . 73 C7
Penarth . . . . . . . 22 B3
Pen-bont
Rhydybeddau . . 58 F3
Penbryn . . . . . . 45 D4
Pencader . . . . . . 46 F3
Pencaenewydd . . 70 C5
Pencaitland . . . . 121 C7
Pencarnisiog . . . 82 D3
Pencarreg . . . . . 46 E4
Pencelli . . . . . . . 34 B4
Pen-clawdd . . . . 33 E6
Pencoed . . . . . . 34 F3
Pencombe . . . . . 49 D7
Pencoyd . . . . . . 36 B2
Pencraig Hereford . 36 B2
Powys . . . . . . . . 59 B7
Pendeen . . . . . . . 2 C2
Penderyn . . . . . . 34 D3
Pendine . . . . . . . 32 D3
Pendlebury . . . . . 87 D5
Pendleton . . . . . 93 F7
Pendock . . . . . . 50 F2
Pendoggett . . . . . 4 B5
Pendomer . . . . . 12 C3
Pendoylan . . . . . 22 B2
Pendre . . . . . . . . 34 F3
Penegoes . . . . . 58 D4
Pen-ffordd . . . . . 32 B1
Penfro
= Pembroke . . . 44 E4
Pengam . . . . . . . 35 E5
Penge . . . . . . . . 28 B4
Pengenffordd . . . 48 F3
Pengorffwysfa . . 82 B4
Pengover Green . . 5 C7
Pen-groes-oped . 35 D7
Penhale Corn . . . . 3 E5
Corn . . . . . . . . . . 4 D4
Penhalvaen . . . . . 3 C6
Penhill . . . . . . . . 38 F1
Penhow . . . . . . . 35 E8
Penhurst . . . . . . 18 D3
Peniarth . . . . . . . 58 D3
Penicuik . . . . . . 120 C5
Peniel Carms . . . 33 B5
Denb . . . . . . . . . 72 C4
Penifiler . . . . . . 149 D9
Peninver . . . . . . 143 F8
Penisarwaun . . . 83 E5
Penistone . . . . . 88 D3
Penjerrick . . . . . . 3 C6
Penketh . . . . . . . 86 F3
Penkill . . . . . . . 112 E2
Penkridge . . . . . 62 C3
Penley . . . . . . . . 73 F8
Penllergaer . . . . 33 E7
Penllyn . . . . . . . 21 B8
Pen-llyn . . . . . . 82 C3
Pen-lon . . . . . . . 82 E4
Penmachno . . . . 83 F7
Penmaen . . . . . . 33 F6
Penmaenan . . . . 83 D7
Penmaenmawr . . 83 D7
Penmaenpool . . . 58 C3
Penmark . . . . . . 22 C2
Penmarth . . . . . . 3 C6
Penmon . . . . . . . 83 C6
Penmorfa Ceredig . 46 D2
Gwyn . . . . . . . . 71 C6
Penmynydd . . . . 82 D5
Penn Bucks . . . . . 40 E2
W Mid . . . . . . . . 62 E2
Pennal . . . . . . . 58 D4
Pennan . . . . . . 153 B8
Pennant Ceredig . . 46 C4
Denb . . . . . . . . . 72 D4
Denb . . . . . . . . . 72 F4
Powys . . . . . . . . 59 E5
Pennant Melangell 59 B7
Pennar . . . . . . . . 44 E4
Pennard . . . . . . . 33 F6
Pennerley . . . . . . 60 E3
Pennington
Gtr Man . . . . . . . 86 E4
Hants . . . . . . . . 14 E4
W&F . . . . . . . . . 92 B2
Penn Street . . . . 40 E2

Penny Bridge . . . . 99 F5
Pennycross . . . . 147 J8
Pennygate . . . . . 69 B6
Pennygown . . . . 147 G8
Pennymoor . . . . 10 C3
Pennywell . . . . . 111 D6
Penparc Ceredig . 45 E4
Pembs . . . . . . . . 44 B3
Penparcau . . . . . 58 F2
Penperlleni . . . . 35 D7
Penpillick . . . . . . . 5 D5
Penpol . . . . . . . . . 3 C7
Penpoll . . . . . . . . 5 D6
Penpont Dumfries 113 E8
Powys . . . . . . . . 34 B3
Penrherber . . . . . 45 F4
Penrhiwceiber . . . 34 E4
Penrhiw goch . . . 33 C6
Penrhiw-llan . . . . 46 E2
Penrhiw-pâl . . . . 46 E2
Penrhos . . . . . . . 70 D4
Penrhôs . . . . . . . 35 C8
Penrhos . . . . . . . 34 C1
Penrhosfeilw . . . . 82 C2
Penrhyn Bay . . . . 83 C8
Penrhyn-coch . . . 58 F3
Penrhyndeudraeth 71 D7
Penrhynside . . . . 83 C8
Penrice . . . . . . . 33 F5
Penrith . . . . . . . 108 F5
Penrose . . . . . . . . 4 B3
Penruddock . . . . 99 B6
Penryn . . . . . . . . . 3 C6
Pensarn Carms . . 33 D5
Conwy . . . . . . . . 72 B3
Pen-sarn Gwyn . . 70 C5
Gwyn . . . . . . . . 71 E6
Pensax . . . . . . . . 50 C2
Pensby . . . . . . . . 85 F3
Penselwood . . . . 24 F2
Pensford . . . . . . 23 C8
Penshaw . . . . . 111 D6
Penshurst . . . . . 29 E6
Pensilva . . . . . . . 5 C7
Penston . . . . . . 121 B7
Pentewan . . . . . . . 3 B9
Pentir . . . . . . . . 83 E5
Pentire . . . . . . . . 4 C2
Pentlow . . . . . . . 56 E2
Pentney . . . . . . . 67 C7
Penton Mewsey . . 25 E8
Pentraeth . . . . . . 82 D5
Pentre Carms . . . 33 C6
Powys . . . . . . . . 59 F7
Powys . . . . . . . . 60 E2
Rhondda . . . . . . 34 E3
Shrops . . . . . . . 60 C3
Wrex . . . . . . . . 72 F5
Wrex . . . . . . . . 73 E6
Pentrebach M Tydf . 34 D4
Swansea . . . . . . 33 D7
Pentre-bâch . . . . 46 E4
Pentre-bach . . . . 47 E8
Pentrebeirdd . . . 59 C8
Pentre Berw . . . . 82 D4
Pentre-bont . . . . 83 F7
Pentrecagal . . . . 46 E2
Pentre-celyn Denb 72 D5
Powys . . . . . . . . 59 D5
Pentre-chwyth . . 33 E7
Pentre-cwrt . . . . 46 F2
Pentre Dolau-
Honddu . . . . . . 47 E8
Pentredwr . . . . . 73 E5
Pentre-dwr . . . . . 33 E7
Pentrefelin Carms . 33 B6
Ceredig . . . . . . . 46 E5
Conwy . . . . . . . . 83 D8
Gwyn . . . . . . . . 71 D6
Pentrefoelas . . . . 83 F8
Pentre-galar . . . . 45 F3
Pentregat . . . . . . 46 D2
Pentre-Gwenlais . 33 C7
Pentre-Gwynfryn . 71 E6
Pentre Halkyn . . . 73 B6
Pentreheyling . . . 60 E2
Pentre-Isaf . . . . . 47 F8
Pentre
Llanrhaeadr . . . 72 C4
Pentre-llwyn-
ll yd . . . . . . . . . 47 D8
Pentre-llyn . . . . . 46 B5
Pentre-llyn
cymmer . . . . . . 72 D3
Pentre Meyrick . . 21 B8
Pentre-piod . . . . 35 F6
Pentre'r Felin . . . 47 F8
Pentre'r-felin . . . 47 D5
Pentre-tafarn-
yfedw . . . . . . . 83 E7
Pentre-ty-gwyn . . 47 F7
Pentrich . . . . . . . 76 D3
Pentridge . . . . . . 13 C8
Pen-twyn . . . . . . 36 D2
Pentyrch . . . . . . 35 F5
Penuchadre . . . . 21 B7
Penuwch . . . . . . 46 C4
Penwithick . . . . . . 4 D5
Penwyllt . . . . . . . 34 C2
Penybanc . . . . . . 33 C7
Pen-y-banc . . . . . 33 B7
Pen-y-bont Carms 32 B4
Gwyn . . . . . . . . 58 D4
Gwyn . . . . . . . . 71 E7
Powys . . . . . . . . 60 B2
Pen-y-Bont Ar Ogwr
= Bridgend . . . . 21 B8
Penybontfawr . . . 59 B7
Pen-y-bryn Gwyn . 58 C3
Pembs . . . . . . . . 45 E3
Penycae . . . . . . . 73 E6
Pen-y-cae . . . . . . 34 C2
Pen-y-cae-mawr . 35 E8
Pen-y-cefn . . . . . 72 B5
Pen-y-clawdd . . . 36 D1
Pen-y-coedcae . . 34 F4
Penycwm . . . . . . 44 C3
Pen-y-fai . . . . . . 34 F2
Penyffordd . . . . . 73 C7
Penyffridd . . . . . 82 F5
Pen-y-garn Carms 46 F4
Ceredig . . . . . . . 58 F3
Penygarnedd . . . 59 B8
Pen-y-garnedd . . 82 D5

Pen-y-gop...72 E3
Penygraig...34 E3
Pen-y-graig...70 D2
Penygroes Gwyn...82 F4
  Pembs...45 F3
Pen-y-groes...33 C6
Pen-y-groeslon...70 D3
Pen-y-Gwryd
Hotel...83 F6
Penyrheol...35 F5
Pen-yr-heol...35 C8
Pen-yr-
Heolgerrig...34 D4
Penysarn...82 B4
Pen-y-stryt...73 D5
Penywaun...34 D3
Penzance...2 C3
Peopleton...50 D4
Peover Heath...74 B4
Peper Harow...27 E7
Perceton...118 E3
Percie...140 E4
Percyhorner...153 B9
Periton...21 E8
Perivale...40 F4
Perkinsville...111 D5
Perlethorpe...77 B6
Perranarworthal...3 C6
Perranporth...4 D2
Perranuthnoe...2 D4
Perranzabuloe...4 D2
Perry Barr...62 E4
Perryfoot...88 F2
Perry Green Herts...41 C7
  Wilts...37 F6
Perry Street...29 B7
Pershall...74 F5
Pershore...50 E4
Pert...135 C6
Pertenhall...53 C8
Perth...128 B3
Perthy...73 F7
Perton...62 E2
Pertwood...24 F3
Peterborough...65 E8
Peterburn...155 J12
Peterchurch...48 F5
Peterculter...141 D7
Peterhead...153 D11
Peterlee...111 E7
Petersfield...15 B8
Peter's Green...18 C4
Peters Marland...9 C6
Peterstone
Wentlooge...35 F6
Peterston super
Ely...22 B2
Peterstow...36 B2
Peter Tavy...6 B3
Petertown...159 H4
Petham...30 D5
Petrockstow...9 D7
Pett...57 D5
Pettaugh...57 D5
Petteridge...29 E7
Pettinain...120 E2
Pettistree...57 D6
Petton Devon...10 B5
  Shrops...60 B4
Petts Wood...28 C5
Petty...153 E7
Pettycur...128 F4
Pettymuick...141 B8
Petworth...16 B3
Pevensey...18 E3
Pevensey Bay...18 E3
Pewsey...25 C6
Philham...8 B4
Philiphaugh...115 B7
Phillack...2 C4
Philleigh...3 C7
Philpstoun...120 B3
Phocle Green...36 B3
Phoenix Green...27 D5
Pica...98 B2
Piccotts End...40 D3
Pickering...103 F5
Picket Piece...25 E8
Picket Post...14 D2
Pickhill...101 F8
Picklescott...60 E4
Pickletillem...129 B6
Pickmere...74 B3
Pickney...11 B6
Pickstock...61 B7
Pickwell Devon...20 E3
  Leics...64 C4
Pickworth Lincs...78 F3
  Rutland...65 C7
Picton Ches W...73 B8
  Flint...85 F2
  N Yorks...102 D2
Piddinghoe...17 D8
Piddington Oxon...39 C6
  W Nhants...53 D6
Piddlehinton...12 E5
Piddletrenthide...12 E5
Pidley...54 B4
Piercebridge...101 C7
Pierowall...159 D5
Pigdon...117 F7
Pikehall...75 C8
Pilgrims Hatch...42 E1
Pilham...90 E2
Pill...23 B7
Pillaton...5 C8
Pillerton Hersey...51 E8
Pillerton Priors...51 E7
Pilleth...48 C4
Pilley Hants...14 E4
  S Yorks...88 D4
Pilling...92 E4
Pilling Lane...92 E3
Pillowell...36 D3
Pillwell...13 C5
Pilning...36 F2
Pilsbury...75 C8
Pilsdon...12 E2
Pilsgate...65 D7
Pilsley Derbys...76 B2
  ...76 C4
Pilton Devon...20 F4
  N Hants...65 E7
  Rutland...65 D6
  Som...23 E7
Pilton Green...33 F5

Pimperne...13 D7
Pinchbeck...66 B2
Pinchbeck Bars...65 B8
Pinchbeck West...66 B2
Pincheon Green...89 C7
Pinehurst...38 F1
Pinfold...85 C4
Pinged...33 D5
Pinhoe...10 E4
Pinkneys Green...40 F1
Pinley...51 B8
Pin Mill...57 F6
Pinminnoch...112 C1
Pinmore...112 C2
Pinmore Mains...112 C2
Pinner...40 F4
Pinvin...50 E4
Pinwherry...112 F1
Pinxton...76 D4
Pipe and Lyde...49 E7
Pipe Gate...74 E4
Piperhill...151 F11
Piper's Pool...8 F4
Pipewell...64 F5
Pippacott...20 F4
Pipton...48 F3
Pirbright...27 D7
Pirnmill...143 D9
Pirton Herts...54 F2
  Worcs...50 E3
Pisgah Ceredig...47 B5
  Stirling...127 D6
Pishill...39 F7
Pistyll...70 C4
Pitagowan...133 C5
Pitblae...153 B9
Pitcairngreen...128 B2
Pitcalnie...151 D11
Pitcaple...141 B6
Pitchcombe...37 D5
Pitchcott...39 B7
Pitchford...60 D5
Pitch Green...39 D7
Pitch Place...27 D7
Pitcombe...23 F8
Pitcorthie...129 D7
Pitcox...122 B2
Pitcur...134 F2
Pitfichie...141 C5
Pitforthie...135 B8
Pitgrudy...151 B10
Pitkennedy...135 D5
Pitkevy...128 D4
Pitkierie...129 D7
Pitlessie...128 D5
Pitlochry...133 D6
Pitmachie...141 B5
Pitmain...138 E3
Pitmedden...141 B7
Pitminster...11 C7
Pitmuies...135 D5
Pitmunie...141 C5
Pitney...12 B2
Pitscottie...129 C6
Pitsea...42 F3
Pitsford...53 C5
Pitsmoor...88 F4
Pitstone...40 C2
Pitstone Green...40 C2
Pittendreich...152 B1
Pittentrail...157 J10
Pittenweem...129 D7
Pittington...111 E6
Pittodrie...141 B5
Pitton...25 F7
Pittswood...29 E7
Pittulie...153 B9
Pityme...4 B4
Pity Me...111 E5
Pityoulish...138 C5
Pixey Green...57 B6
Pixham...28 D2
Pixley...49 F8
Place Newton...96 B4
Plaidy...153 C7
Plains...119 C7
Plaish...60 E5
Plaistow...27 F8
Plaitford...14 C3
Plank Lane...86 E4
Plas Gogerddan...58 F3
Plas Llwyngwern...58 D4
Plas Nantyr...73 F5
Plastow Green...26 C3
Plas-yn-Cefn...72 B4
Platt...29 D7
Platt Bridge...86 D4
Platts Common...88 D4
Plawsworth...111 E5
Plaxtol...29 D7
Playden...19 C6
Playford...57 E6
Play Hatch...26 B5
Playing Place...3 B7
Playley Green...50 F2
Plealey...60 D4
Plean...127 F7
Pleasington...86 B4
Pleasley...76 C5
Pleckgate...93 F6
Plenmeller...109 C7
Pleshey...42 C2
Plockton...149 E13
Ploughfield...49 E5
Plowden...60 F3
Ploxgreen...60 D3
Pluckley...30 E3
Pluckley Thorne...30 E3
Plumbland...107 F8
Plumley...74 B4
Plumpton E Sus...17 C7
  W&F...108 F4
Plumpton Green...17 C7
Plumpton Head...108 F5
Plumtree...77 F6
Plungar...77 F7
Plush...12 D5
Plwmp...46 D2
Plymouth...6 D2
Plympton...6 D3
Plymstock...6 D3
Plymtree...11 D5
Pockley...102 F4
Pocklington...96 E4
Pode Hole...66 B2

Podimore...12 B3
Podington...53 C7
Podmore...74 F4
Point Clear...43 C6
Pointon...78 F4
Pokesdown...14 E2
Pol a Charra...148 G2
Polbae...105 B6
Polbain...156 H2
Polbathic...5 D8
Polbeth...120 C3
Polchar...138 D4
Polebrook...65 F7
Pole Elm...50 E3
Polegate...18 E2
Poles...151 B10
Polesworth...63 D6
Polgigga...2 D2
Polglass...156 J3
Polgooth...4 D4
Polkerris...5 D5
Polla...156 D6
Pollington...89 C7
Polloch...130 C1
Pollok...118 C5
Pollokshields...119 C5
Polmassick...3 B8
Polmont...120 B2
Polnessan...112 C4
Polnish...147 C10
Polperro...5 D7
Polruan...5 D6
Polsham...23 E7
Polstead...56 F3
Poltalloch...124 F4
Poltimore...10 E4
Polton...121 C5
Polwarth...122 D3
Polyphant...8 F4
Polzeath...4 B4
Pondersbridge...66 E2
Ponders End...41 E6
Pondtail...27 D6
Ponsanooth...3 C6
Ponsworthy...6 B5
Pont Aber...33 B8
Pont Aber-Geirw...71 E8
Pontamman...33 C7
Pontantwn...33 C5
Pontardawe...33 D8
Pontarddulais...33 D6
Pont-ar-gothi...33 B6
Pont-ar-llechau...33 B8
Pontarsais...33 B5
Pontblyddyn...73 C6
Pont Cwm Pydew...72 F4
Pont Cyfyng...83 F7
Pont Cysyllte...73 E6
Pont Dolydd
  Prysor...71 D8
Pontefract...89 B5
Ponteland...110 B4
Ponterwyd...58 F4
Pontesbury...60 D3
Pontfadog...73 F6
Pontfaen...45 F2
Pont-faen...48 F2
Pont Fronwydd...58 B5
Pont-gareg...45 E3
Pontgarreg...46 D2
Ponthir...35 E7
Ponthirwaun...45 E4
Pontllanfraith...35 E5
Pontlliw...33 D7
Pont-Llogel...59 C7
Pontllyfni...82 F4
Pontlottyn...35 D5
Pontneddfechan...34 D3
Pontnewydd...35 E6
Pont Pen-y-
  benglog...83 F6
Pontrhydfendigaid...47 C6
Pont Rhyd-goch...83 E6
Pont-Rhyd-sarn...59 B5
Pont Rhyd-y-cyff...34 F2
Pontrhydyfen...34 E1
Pont-rhyd-y-
  groes...47 B6
Pontrilas...35 B8
Pontrobert...59 C8
Pont-rug...82 E5
Pont Senni
  =Sennybridge...34 B3
Ponts Green...18 D3
Pontshill...36 B3
Pont-siân...46 E3
Pontsticill...34 C4
Pontwgan...83 D7
Pontyates...33 D5
Pontyberem...33 C6
Pontyclun...34 F4
Pontycymer...34 E3
Pontyglasier...45 F3
Pont-y-gwaith...34 E4
Pont-y-pant...83 F7
Pont y Pennant...59 B6
Pontypool
  =Pont-y-pŵl...35 D6
Pontypridd...34 F4
Pont-y-pŵl
  =Pontypool...35 D6
Pont yr Afon-Gam...71 C8
Pont-yr-hafod...44 C4
Pontywaun...35 E6
Pooksgreen...14 C4
Pool Corn...3 B5
  W Yorks...94 E5
Poole...13 E8
Poole Keynes...37 E6
Poolend...75 C6
Pooley Bridge...99 B6
Poolfold...75 D5
Poolhill...36 B4
Pool o'Muckhart...128 D2
Pool Quay...60 C2
Poolsbrook...76 B4
Pootings...29 E5
Pope Hill...44 D4
Popeswood...27 C6
Popham...26 E3
Poplar...41 F6
Porchester...77 E5

Porchfield...14 E5
Porin...150 F6
Poringland...69 D5
Porkellis...3 C5
Porlock...21 E7
Porlock Weir...21 E7
Portachoillan...144 H6
Port Ann...145 E8
Port Appin...130 E3
Port Arthur...160 K5
Port Askaig...142 B5
Portavadie...145 G8
Port Bannatyne...145 G9
Portbury...23 B7
Port Carlisle...108 C2
Port Charlotte...142 C3
Portchester...15 D7
Portclair...137 C7
Port Clarence...102 B2
Port Driseach...145 F8
Port Ellen...142 D4
Port Elphinstone...141 C6
Portencalzie...104 B4
Portencross...118 E1
Port Erin...84 F1
Port Erroll...153 E10
Portesham...12 F4
Portessie...152 B4
Port e Vullen...84 C4
Port-Eynon...33 F5
Portfield Gate...44 D4
Portgate...9 F6
Port Gaverne...8 F2
Port Glasgow...118 B3
Portgordon...152 B3
Portgower...157 H13
Porth Corn...4 C3
  Rhondda...34 E4
Porthaethwy
  =Menai Bridge...83 D5
Porthallow Corn...3 D6
  Corn...5 D7
Porthcawl...21 B7
Porthcothan...4 B3
Porthcurno...2 D2
Port Henderson...149 A12
Porthgain...44 B3
Porthill...60 C4
Porthkerry...22 C2
Porthleven...2 D5
Porthllechog...82 B4
Porthmadog...71 D6
Porthmeor...1 C3
Porth Navas...3 D6
Portholland...3 B8
Porthoustock...4 D5
Porthpean...4 D5
Porthtowan...3 B5
Porthyrhyd Carms...33 C6
  Carms...47 F6
Porth-y-waen...60 B2
Portincaple...145 D11
Portington...96 F3
Portinnisherrich...125 D5
Portinscale...98 B4
Port Isaac...4 A4
Portishead...23 B6
Portkil...145 E11
Portknockie...152 B4
Port Lamont...145 F9
Portlethen...141 E8
Portling...107 D5
Port Lion...44 E4
Portloe...3 C8
Port Logan...104 E4
Portmahomack...151 C12
Portmeirion...71 D6
Portmellon...3 B9
Port Mor...146 D7
Portmore...14 E4
Port Mulgrave...103 C5
Portnacroish...130 E3
Portnahaven...142 C2
Portnalong...149 E8
Portnaluchaig...147 C9
Portnancon...156 C7
Port Nan
  Giùran...155 D10
Port nan Long...148 A3
Portnellan...126 B3
Port Nis...155 A10
Portobello...121 B6
Port of Menteith...126 D4
Porton...25 F7
Portpatrick...104 D4
Port Quin...4 A4
Port Ramsay...130 E2
Portreath...3 B5
Portree...149 D9
Port St Mary...84 F2
Portscatho...3 C7
Portsea...15 D7
Portskerra...157 C11
Portskewett...36 F2
Portslade...17 D6
Portslade-by-Sea...17 D6
Portsmouth Ptsmth...15 D7
  W Yorks...87 B7
Portsonachan...125 C6
Portsoy...152 B5
Port Sunlight...85 F4
Portswood...14 C5
Port Talbot...34 E1
Porttanachy...152 B3
Port Tennant...33 E7
Portuairk...146 E7
Portway Hereford...49 E6
  Worcs...51 B5
Port Wemyss...142 C2
Port William...105 E7
Portwrinkle...5 D8
Poslingford...55 E8
Postbridge...6 B4
Postcombe...39 E7
Posting...19 B8
Postwick...69 D5
Potholm...115 F6
Potsgrove...40 B2
Potten End...40 D3
Potter Brompton...97 B5
Potterhanworth...78 C3
Potterhanworth
  Booths...78 C3
Potter Heigham...69 C7
Potterne...24 D4
Potterne Wick...24 D5

Potternewton...95 F6
Potters Bar...41 D5
Potter's Cross...62 F2
Prittlewell...42 F4
Potterspury...53 E5
Potter Street...41 D7
Potterton Aberds...141 C8
  W Yorks...95 F7
Potto...102 D2
Potton...54 E3
Pott Row...80 E3
Pott Shrigley...75 B6
Poughill Corn...8 D4
  Devon...10 D3
Poulshot...24 D4
Poulton Glos...37 D8
  Mers...85 E4
Poulton-le-Fylde...92 F3
Pound Bank...50 B2
Poundbury...12 E4
Poundfield...18 B2
Pound Green
  E Sus...18 C2
  IoW...14 F4
  Worcs...50 B2
Pound Hill...28 F3
Poundon...39 B6
Poundsgate...6 B5
Poundstock...8 E4
Powburn...117 C6
Powderham...10 F4
Powerstock...12 E3
Powfoot...107 C8
Powick...50 D3
Powmill...128 E2
Poxwell...12 F5
Poyle...27 B8
Poynings...17 C6
Poyntington...12 C4
Poynton...87 F7
Poynton Green...61 C5
Poystreet Green...56 D3
Praa Sands...2 D4
Pratt's Bottom...29 C5
Praze...2 C4
Praze-an-Beeble...2 C5
Predannack Wollas...3 E5
Prees...74 F2
Preesall...92 E3
Prees Green...74 F2
Preesgweene...73 F6
Prees Heath...74 F2
Prees Higher
  Heath...74 F2
Prees Lower Heath...74 F2
Prendergast...44 D4
Prendwick...117 C6
Pren-gwyn...46 E3
Prenteg...71 C6
Prenton...85 F4
Prescot...86 E2
Prescott...60 B4
Pressen...122 F4
Prestatyn...72 A4
Prestbury Ches E...75 B6
  Glos...37 B6
Presteigne
  =Llanandras...48 C5
Presthope...61 E5
Prestleigh...23 E8
Preston Borders...122 D3
  Brighton...17 D7
  Devon...7 B6
  Dorset...12 F5
  E Loth...121 B8
  E Yorks...97 F7
  Glos...37 D7
  Glos...49 F8
  Herts...40 B4
  Kent...30 C4
  Kent...31 C6
  Lancs...86 B3
  Northumb...117 B7
  Rutland...65 D5
  Shrops...60 C5
  Wilts...24 B5
  Wilts...25 B7
Preston Bagot...51 C6
Preston Bissett...39 B6
Preston Bowyer...11 B6
Preston
  Brockhurst...60 B5
Preston Brook...86 F3
Preston Candover...26 E4
Preston Capes...52 D3
Preston
  Crowmarsh...39 E6
Preston Gubbals...60 C4
Prestonmill...107 D6
Preston on Stour...51 E7
Preston on the Hill...86 F3
Preston on Wye...49 E5
Prestonpans...121 B6
Preston Plucknett...12 C3
Preston St Mary...56 D3
Preston-under-
  Scar...101 E5
Preston upon the
  Weald Moors...61 C6
Preston Wynne...49 E7
Prestwich...87 D6
Prestwick
  Northumb...110 B4
  S Ayrs...112 B3
Prestwood...40 D1
Price Town...34 E3
Prickwillow...67 F5
Priddy...23 D7
Priesthaugh...115 D7
Priest Hutton...92 B5
Priest Weston...60 E2
Primethorpe...64 E2
Primrose Green...68 C4
Primrosehill...40 D3
Primrose Valley...97 B7
Princes Gate...32 C2
Princes
  Risborough...39 D8
Princethorpe...52 B2
Princetown Caerph...35 C5
  Devon...6 B3
Prion...72 C4
Prior Muir...129 C7
Prior Park...123 D5
Priors Frome...49 F7
Priors Hardwick...52 D2
Priorslee...61 C7
Priors Marston...52 D2
Priory Wood...48 E4

Priston...23 C8
Pristow Green...68 F4
Prittlewell...42 F4
Privett...15 B7
Prixford...20 F4
Probus...3 B7
Proncy...151 B10
Prospect...107 E8
Prudhoe...110 C3
Ptarmigan Lodge...126 D2
Pubil...132 E1
Puckeridge...41 B6
Puckington...11 C8
Pucklechurch...23 B8
Pucknall...14 B4
Puckrup...50 F3
Puddinglake...74 C4
Puddington
  Ches W...73 B7
  Devon...10 C3
Puddledock...68 E3
Puddletown...13 E5
Pudleston...49 D7
Pudsey...94 F5
Pulborough...16 C4
Puleston...61 B7
Pulford...73 D7
Pulham...12 D5
Pulham Market...68 F4
Pulham St Mary...68 F5
Pulloxhill...53 F8
Pumpherston...120 C3
Pumsaint...47 E5
Puncheston...32 B1
Puncknowle...12 F3
Punnett's Town...18 C3
Purbrook...15 D7
Purewell...14 E2
Purfleet...29 B6
Puriton...22 E5
Purleigh...42 D4
Purley London...28 C4
  W Berks...26 B4
Purlogue...48 B4
Purls Bridge...66 F4
Purse Caundle...12 C4
Purslow...60 F3
Purston Jaglin...88 C5
Purton Glos...36 D3
  Wilts...37 F7
Purton Stoke...37 E7
Pury End...52 E5
Pusey...38 E3
Putley...49 F8
Putney...28 B3
Putsborough...20 E3
Puttenham Herts...40 C1
  Sur...27 E7
Puxton...23 C6
Pwll...33 D5
Pwllcrochan...44 E4
Pwll-glas...72 D5
Pwllgloyw...48 F2
Pwllheli...70 D4
Pwllmeyric...36 E2
Pwll-trap...32 C3
Pwll-y-glaw...34 E1
Pyecombe...17 C6
Pye Corner...35 F7
Pye Green...62 C3
Pyewipe...91 C6
Pyle...15 G5
Pyle = Y Pîl...34 F2
Pylle...23 E8
Pymoor...66 F4
Pyrford...27 D8
Pyrton...39 E6
Pytchley...53 B6
Pyworthy...8 D5

**Q**

Quabbs...60 F2
Quadring...78 F5
Quainton...39 C7
Quarley...25 E7
Quarndon...76 E3
Quarrier's
  Homes...118 C3
Quarrington...78 E3
Quarrington Hill...111 F6
Quarry Bank...62 F3
Quarryford...121 C8
Quarryhill...151 C10
Quarrywood...152 B1
Quarter...119 D7
Quatford...61 E7
Quatt...61 F7
Quebec...110 E4
Quedgeley...37 C5
Queen Adelaide...67 F5
Queen Camel...12 B3
Queen Charlton...23 C8
Queen Dart...10 C3
Queenhill...50 F3
Queen Oak...24 F2
Queensbury...94 F4
Queensferry Edin...120 B4
  Flint...73 C7
Queensferry
  Crossing...120 B4
Queen's Head...60 B3
Queen's Park
  Bedford...53 E8
  W Nhants...53 C5
Queenstown...92 F3
Queen Street Kent...29 E7
  Wilts...37 F7
Queenzieburn...119 B6
Quemerford...24 C5
Quendale...160 M5
Quendon...55 F6
Queniborough...64 C3
Quenington...37 D8
Quernhead...92 B5
Quethiock...5 C8
Quholm...159 G3
Quicks Green...26 B3
Quidenham...68 F3
Quidhampton
  Hants...26 D3
  Wilts...25 F6
Quilquox...153 E9
Quina Brook...74 F2
Quindry...159 J5
Quinton W Mid...62 F3
  W Nhants...53 D5

Quintrell Downs...4 C3
Quixhill...75 E8
Quoditch...9 E6
Quoig...127 B7
Quorndon...64 C2
Quothquan...120 E2
Quoyloo...159 F3
Quoyness...159 H3
Quoys Shetland...160 B8
  Shetland...160 G6

**R**

Raasay House...149 E10
Rabbit's Cross...29 E8
Raby...73 B7
Rachan Mill...120 F4
Rachub...83 E6
Rackenford...10 C3
Rackham...16 C4
Rackheath...69 C5
Racks...107 B7
Rackwick Orkney...159 D5
  Orkney...159 J3
Radbourne...76 F2
Radcliffe Gtr Man...87 D5
  Northumb...117 D8
Radcliffe on Trent...77 F6
Radclive...52 F4
Radcot...38 E2
Raddery...151 F10
Radernie...129 D6
Radford Semele...51 C8
Radipole...12 F4
Radlett...40 E4
Radley...39 E5
Radmanthwaite...76 C5
Radmoor...61 B6
Radmore Green...74 D2
Radnage...39 E7
Radstock...23 D8
Radstone...52 E3
Radway...51 E8
Radway Green...74 D4
Radwell Bedford...53 D8
  Herts...54 F3
Radwinter...55 F7
Radyr...35 F5
Rafford...151 F13
Ragdale...64 C3
Raglan...35 D8
Ragnall...77 B7
Rahane...145 E11
Rainford...86 D2
Rainford Junction...86 D2
Rainham London...41 F8
  Medway...30 C2
Rainhill...86 E2
Rainhill Stoops...86 E3
Rainow...75 B6
Rainton...95 B6
Rainworth...77 D5
Raisbeck...99 D8
Raise...109 E7
Rait...128 B4
Raithby Lincs...79 C6
  Lincs...91 F7
Rake...16 B2
Rakewood...87 C7
Ram...59 A4
Ramasaig...148 D6
Rame Corn...3 C6
  Corn...6 E2
Rameldry Mill
  Bank...128 D5
Ram Lane...30 E3
Ramnageo...160 C8
Rampisham...12 D3
Rampside...92 C2
Rampton Cambs...54 C5
  Notts...77 B7
Ramsbottom...87 C5
Ramsbury...25 B7
Ramscraigs...158 H3
Ramsdean...15 B8
Ramsdell...26 D3
Ramsden...38 C3
Ramsden
  Bellhouse...42 E3
Ramsden Heath...42 E3
Ramsey Cambs...66 F2
  Essex...57 F6
  IoM...84 C4
Ramsey Forty Foot...66 F3
Ramsey Heights...66 F2
Ramsey Island...43 D5
Ramsey Mereside...66 F2
Ramsey St Mary's...66 F2
Ramsgate...31 C7
Ramsgill...94 B4
Ramshorn...75 E7
Ramsnest
  Common...27 F7
Ranais...155 E9
Ranby Lincs...78 B5
  Notts...89 F7
Randwick...37 D5
Ranfurly...118 C3
Rangag...158 F3
Rangemore...63 B5
Rangeworthy...36 F3
Rankinston...112 C4
Ranmoor...88 F4
Ranmore Common...28 D2
Rannerdale...98 C3
Rannoch Station...131 D8
Ranochan...147 C11
Ranskill...89 F7
Ranton...62 B2
Ranworth...69 C6
Raploch...127 E6
Rapness...159 D6
Rascal Moor...96 F4
Rascarrel...106 E4
Rashiereive...141 B8
Raskelf...95 B7
Rassau...35 C5
Ratagan...136 C2
Ratby...64 D2
Ratcliffe Culey...63 E7
Ratcliffe on Soar...63 B8
Ratcliffe on the
  Wreake...64 C3
Rathen...153 B10
Rathillet...129 B5

Rathmell...93 D8
Ratho...120 B4
Ratho Station...120 B4
Rathven...152 B4
Ratley...51 E8
Ratlinghope...60 E4
Rattar...158 C4
Ratten Row...92 E4
Rattery...6 C5
Rattlesden...56 D3
Rattray...134 E1
Raughton Head...108 E3
Raunds...53 B7
Ravenfield...89 E5
Ravenglass...98 E2
Raveningham...69 E6
Ravenscar...103 D7
Ravenscraig...118 B2
Ravensdale...84 C3
Ravenseat...100 D3
Ravenshead...77 D5
Ravensmoor...74 D3
Ravensthorpe
  W Nhants...52 B4
  W Yorks...88 B3
Ravenstone Leics...63 C8
  M Keynes...53 D6
Ravenstonedale...100 D2
Ravenstown...92 B3
Ravenstruther...120 E2
Ravensworth...101 D6
Raw...103 D7
Rawcliffe E Yorks...89 B7
  York...95 D8
Rawcliffe Bridge...89 B7
Rawdon...94 F5
Rawmarsh...88 E5
Rawreth...42 E3
Rawridge...11 D7
Rawtenstall...87 B6
Raxton...153 E8
Raydon...56 F4
Raylees...117 E5
Rayleigh...42 E4
Rayne...42 B3
Rayners Lane...40 F4
Raynes Park...28 C3
Reach...55 C6
Read...93 F7
Reading...26 B5
Reading Street...19 B6
Readymoney...5 D6
Reagill...99 C8
Rearquhar...151 B10
Rearsby...64 C3
Reaster...158 D4
Reaulay...160 J1
Reawick...160 J5
Reay...157 C12
Rechullin...149 C13
Reculver...31 C6
Redberth...32 D1
Redbourn...40 C4
Redbourne...90 E3
Redbrook Mon...36 C2
  Wrex...74 E2
Redburn Highld...151 E8
  Highld...151 G12
  Northumb...109 C7
Redcar...102 B4
Redcastle Angus...135 D6
  Highld...151 G8
Redcliff Bay...23 B6
Red Dial...108 E2
Redding...120 B2
Reddingmuirhead...120 B2
Reddish...87 E6
Redditch...50 C5
Rede...56 D2
Redenhall...69 F5
Redesdale Camp...116 E4
Redesmouth...116 F4
Redford Aberds...135 B7
  Angus...135 E5
  Durham...110 F3
Redfordgreen...115 C6
Redgorton...128 B2
Redgrave...56 B4
Redhill Aberds...141 D6
  Aberds...153 E6
  N Som...23 C7
  Sur...28 D3
Red Hill...50 D3
Redhouse...145 G7
Redhouses...142 B4
Redisham...69 F7
Redland Bristol...23 B7
  Orkney...159 F4
Redlingfield...57 B5
Red Lodge...55 B7
Redlynch Som...24 F2
  Wilts...14 B3
Redmarley
  D'Abitot...50 F2
Redmarshall...102 B1
Redmile...77 F7
Redmire...101 E5
Redmoor...5 C5
Rednal...60 B3
Redpath...121 F8
Redpoint...149 B12
Red Rail...36 B2
Red Rock...86 D3
Red Roses...32 C2
Red Row...117 E8
Redruth...3 B5
Red Street...74 D5
Redvales...87 D6
Redwick Newport...35 F8
  S Glos...36 F2
Redworth...101 B7
Reed...54 F4
Reedham...69 D7
Reedness...89 B8
Reeds Beck...78 C5
Reepham Lincs...78 B3
  Norf...81 E6
Reeth...101 E5
Regaby...84 C4
Regoul...151 F11
Reiff...156 H2
Reigate...28 D3
Reighton...97 B7
Reighton Gap...97 B7
Reinigeadal...154 G7
Reiss...158 E5
Rejerrah...4 D2

Releath...3 C5
Relubbus...2 C4
Relugas...151 G12
Remenham...39 F7
Remenham Hill...39 F7
Remony...132 E4
Rempstone...64 B2
Rendcomb...37 D7
Rendham...57 C7
Rendlesham...57 D7
Renfrew...118 C5
Renhold...53 D8
Renishaw...76 B4
Rennington...117 C8
Renton...118 B3
Renwick...109 E5
Repps...69 C7
Repton...63 B7
Reraig...149 E13
Rescobie...135 D5
Resipole...147 E10
Resolis...151 E9
Resolven...34 D2
Reston...122 C4
Reswallie...135 D5
Retew...4 D4
Retford...89 F8
Rettendon...42 E3
Rettendon Place...42 E3
Revesby...79 C5
Revesby Bridge...79 C6
Rewe...10 E4
New Street...15 E5
Reydon...57 B8
Reydon Smear...57 B8
Reymerston...68 D3
Reynalton...32 D1
Reynoldston...33 E5
Rezare...5 B8
Rhaeadr Gwy
  =Rhayader...47 C8
Rhandirmwyn...47 E6
Rhayader
  =Rhaeadr Gwy...47 C8
Rhedyn...70 D3
Rhemore...147 F8
Rhencullen...84 C3
Rhes-y-cae...73 B5
Rhewl Denb...72 C5
  Denb...73 E5
Rhian...157 H8
Rhicarn...156 H3
Rhiconich...156 D5
Rhicullen...151 D9
Rhidorroch
  House...150 B4
Rhifail...157 E10
Rhigos...34 D3
Rhilochan...157 J10
Rhiroy...150 C4
Rhisga =Risca...35 E6
Rhiw...70 E3
Rhiwabon
  =Ruabon...73 E7
Rhiwbina...35 F5
Rhiwbryfdir...71 C7
Rhiwderin...35 F6
Rhiwlas Gwyn...72 F3
  Gwyn...83 E5
  Powys...73 F5
Rhodes...87 D6
Rhodesia...77 B5
Rhodes Minnis...31 E5
Rhodiad...44 C2
Rhondda...34 E3
Rhonehouse or
  Kelton Hill...106 D4
Rhoose =Y Rhws...22 C2
Rhôs Carms...46 F2
  Neath...33 D8
Rhosaman...33 C8
Rhosbeirio...82 B3
Rhoscefnhir...82 D5
Rhoscolyn...82 D2
Rhoscrowther...44 E4
Rhosesmor...73 C6
Rhos-fawr...70 D4
Rhosgadfan...82 F5
Rhosgoch...82 C4
Rhos-goch...48 E3
Rhos-hill...45 E3
Rhoshirwaun...70 E2
Rhoslan...71 C5
Rhoslefain...58 D2
Rhosllanerchrugog...73 E6
Rhosmaen...33 B7
Rhosmeirch...82 D4
Rhosneigr...82 D3
Rhosnesni...73 D7
Rhos-on-Sea...83 C8
Rhosrobin...73 D7
Rhossili...33 F5
Rhosson...44 C2
Rhostryfan...82 F4
Rhostyllen...73 E7
Rhosybol...82 C4
Rhos-y-brithdir...59 B8
Rhos-y-garth...46 B5
Rhos-y-gwaliau...72 F3
Rhos-y-llan...70 D3
Rhos-y-Madoc...73 E7
Rhos-y-meirch...48 C4
Rhu Argyll...145 E11
  Argyll...145 G7
Rhuallt...72 B4
Rhuddall Heath...74 C2
Rhuddlan Ceredig...46 E3
  Denb...72 B4
Rhue...150 B3
Rhulen...48 E3
Rhunahaorine...143 D8
Rhuthun
  =Ruthin...72 D5
Rhyd Gwyn...71 C7
  Powys...59 D6
Rhydaman
  =Ammanford...33 C7
Rhydargaeau...33 B5
Rhydcymerau...46 F4
Rhydd...50 E3
Rhyd-Ddu...83 F5
Rhydding...33 E8
Rhydfudr...46 C4
Rhydlewis...46 E2
Rhydlios...70 D2
Rhydlydan...83 F8
Rhyd-moel-ddu...48 B2
Rhydness...48 E3
Rhydowen...46 E3

Rhyd-Rosser . . . . . . 46 C4
Rhydspence. . . . . . . 48 E4
Rhydtalog. . . . . . . . 73 D6
Rhyd–uchaf . . . . . . 72 F3
Rhyd-wen . . . . . . . 58 C4
Rhydwyn. . . . . . . . 82 C3
Rhydycroesau . . . . 73 F6
Rhydyfelin Ceredig . 46 B4
Rhondda. . . . . . . . 34 F4
Rhyd-y-foel. . . . . . 72 B3
Rhyd-y-fro. . . . . . . 33 D8
Rhyd-y-gwin. . . . . . 33 D7
Rhydymain. . . . . . . 58 B5
Rhyd-y-meirch . . . 35 D7
Rhyd-y-meudwy . . 72 D5
Rhydymwyn . . . . . . 73 C6
Rhyd-y-pandy . . . . 33 D7
Rhyd-yr-onen . . . . 58 D3
Rhyd-y-sarn . . . . . 71 C7
Rhyl = Y Rhyl . . . . . 72 A4
Rhymney
= Rhymni . . . . . . 35 D5
Rhymni
= Rhymney . . . . . 35 D5
Rhynd Fife . . . . . . 129 B6
Perth . . . . . . . . 128 B3
Rhynie Aberds. . . 140 B3
Highld . . . . . . . . . 151 D11
Ribbesford . . . . . . 50 B2
Ribblehead . . . . . . 93 B7
Ribbleton . . . . . . . 93 F5
Ribchester . . . . . . 93 F6
Ribigill. . . . . . . . . 157 D8
Riby . . . . . . . . . . 91 D5
Riby Cross Roads . 91 D5
Riccall. . . . . . . . . 96 F2
Riccarton . . . . . . 118 F4
Richards Castle . . 49 C6
Richings Park . . . 27 B8
Richmond London . 28 B2
N Yorks. . . . . . . 101 D6
Rickarton . . . . . . 141 F7
Rickinghall . . . . . . 56 B4
Rickleton . . . . . . 111 D5
Rickling. . . . . . . . 55 F5
Rickmansworth . . 40 E3
Riddings Cumb . . 108 B4
Derbys . . . . . . . . 76 D4
Riddlecombe. . . . . . 9 C8
Riddlesden . . . . . . 94 E3
Riddrie . . . . . . . 119 C6
Ridge Dorset . . . . 13 F7
Hants . . . . . . . . . 14 C4
Wilts . . . . . . . . . 24 F4
Ridgebourne . . . . 48 C2
Ridge Green . . . . . 28 E4
Ridgehill. . . . . . . 23 C7
Ridge Lane . . . . . 63 E6
Ridgeway Cross . . 50 E2
Ridgewell. . . . . . . 55 E8
Ridgewood . . . . . . 17 C8
Ridgmont . . . . . . 53 F7
Riding Mill . . . . . 110 C3
Ridleywood . . . . . 73 D8
Ridlington Norf . . 69 A6
Rutland . . . . . . . 64 D5
Ridsdale . . . . . . 116 F5
Riechip . . . . . . . 133 E7
Riemore . . . . . . . 133 E7
Rienachait . . . . . 156 F3
Rievaulx . . . . . . 102 F3
Rift House . . . . . 111 F7
Rigg . . . . . . . . 108 C2
Riggend . . . . . . 119 B7
Rigsby . . . . . . . . 79 B7
Rigside . . . . . . . 119 F8
Riley Green . . . . . 86 B4
Rileyhill. . . . . . . . 62 C5
Rilla Mill . . . . . . . 5 B7
Rillington . . . . . . 96 B4
Rimington . . . . . . 93 E8
Rimpton . . . . . . . 12 B4
Rimswell. . . . . . . 91 B7
Rinaston . . . . . . 44 C4
Ringasta . . . . . . 160 M5
Ringford . . . . . . 106 D3
Ringinglow . . . . . 88 F3
Ringland . . . . . . 68 C4
Ringles Cross . . . 17 B8
Ringmer . . . . . . . 17 C8
Ringmore . . . . . . . 6 E4
Ringorm . . . . . . 152 D2
Ring's End . . . . . 66 D3
Ringsfield . . . . . . 69 F7
Ringsfield Corner . 69 F7
Ringshall Herts . . 40 C2
Suff . . . . . . . . . 56 D4
Ringshall Stocks . 56 D4
Ringstead N Nhants. 53 B7
Norf . . . . . . . . . 80 C3
Ringwood . . . . . . 14 D2
Ringwould . . . . . . 31 E7
Rinmore . . . . . . 140 C3
Rinnigill . . . . . . 159 J4
Rinsey . . . . . . . . . 2 D4
Riof . . . . . . . . . 154 D6
Ripe . . . . . . . . . 18 D2
Ripley Derbys . . . 76 D3
Hants . . . . . . . . 14 E2
N Yorks. . . . . . . 95 C5
Sur . . . . . . . . . . 27 D8
Riplingham . . . . . 97 F5
Ripon . . . . . . . . 95 B6
Rippingale . . . . . 65 B7
Ripple Kent . . . . . 31 E7
Worcs . . . . . . . . 50 F3
Ripponden . . . . . 87 C8
Rireavach . . . . . 150 B3
Risabus . . . . . . 142 D4
Risbury . . . . . . . 49 D7
Risby . . . . . . . . 55 C8
Risca = Rhisga . . . 35 E6
Rise . . . . . . . . . 97 E7
Riseden. . . . . . . . 18 B3
Risegate . . . . . . . 66 B2
Riseholme . . . . . . 78 B2
Riseley Bedford. . . 53 C8
Wokingham . . . . 26 C5
Rishangles . . . . . 57 C5
Rishton . . . . . . . 93 F7
Rishworth. . . . . . 87 C8
Rising Bridge . . . . 87 B5
Risley Derbys. . . . 76 F4
Warr. . . . . . . . . 86 E4
Risplith . . . . . . . 94 C5
Rispond . . . . . . 156 C7
Rivar . . . . . . . . 25 C8
Rivenhall End . . . 42 C4

River Bank . . . . . . 55 C6
Riverhead. . . . . . 29 D6
Rivington . . . . . . 86 C4
Roachill. . . . . . . 10 B3
Roade . . . . . . . . 53 D5
Road Green . . . . 69 E5
Roadhead. . . . . 108 B5
Roadmeetings . . 119 E8
Roadside . . . . . 158 D3
Roadside of
Catterline . . . 135 B8
Roadside of
Kinneff . . . . . 135 B8
Roadwater . . . . . 22 F2
Roag. . . . . . . . 149 D7
Roa Island . . . . . 92 C2
Roath . . . . . . . . 22 B3
Roberton Borders . 115 C7
S Lanark. . . . . 114 B2
Robertsbridge . . 18 C4
Roberttown . . . . 88 B2
Robeston Cross . . 44 E3
Robeston Wathen . 32 C1
Robin Hood . . . . 88 B4
Robin Hood's
Bay. . . . . . . . 103 D7
Roborough Devon . . 6 C3
Devon. . . . . . . . . 9 C7
Roby . . . . . . . . 86 E2
Roby Mill . . . . . . 86 D3
Rocester . . . . . . 75 F8
Roch. . . . . . . . . 44 C3
Rochdale . . . . . . 87 C6
Roche . . . . . . . . . 4 C4
Rochester Medway . 29 C8
Northumb. . . . . 116 E4
Rochford . . . . . . 42 E4
Roch Gate. . . . . 44 C3
Rock Corn . . . . . . 4 B4
Northumb. . . . 117 B8
Worcs . . . . . . . 50 B2
W Sus . . . . . . . 16 C5
Rockbeare . . . . . 10 E5
Rockbourne. . . . . 14 C2
Rockcliffe Cumb. . 108 C3
Dumfries . . . . 107 D5
Rock Ferry . . . . . 85 F4
Rockfield Highld. . 151 C12
Mon . . . . . . . . 36 C1
Rockford. . . . . . 14 D2
Rockhampton. . . 36 E3
Rockingham . . . . 65 E5
Rockland All
Saints . . . . . . 68 E2
Rockland St Mary . 69 D6
Rockland St Peter . 68 E2
Rockley . . . . . . . 25 B6
Rockwell End . . . 39 F7
Rockwell Green . . 11 B6
Rodborough . . . . 37 D5
Rodbourne Swindon 37 F8
Wilts . . . . . . . . 37 F6
Rodbourne Cheney 37 F8
Rodd . . . . . . . . 48 C5
Roddam . . . . . . 117 B6
Rodden . . . . . . . 12 F4
Rode . . . . . . . . 24 D3
Rodeheath . . . . . 75 C5
Rode Heath . . . . 74 D5
Roden . . . . . . . 61 C5
Rodhuish . . . . . . 22 F2
Rodington . . . . . 61 C5
Rodley Glos . . . . 36 C4
W Yorks . . . . . . 94 F5
Rodmarton. . . . . 37 E6
Rodmell . . . . . . 17 D8
Rodmersham . . . 30 C3
Rodney Stoke . . . 23 D6
Rodsley . . . . . . . 76 E2
Rodway . . . . . . . 22 F4
Rodwell. . . . . . . 12 G4
Roecliffe. . . . . . 95 C6
Roe Green . . . . . 54 F4
Roehampton . . . 28 B3
Roesound . . . . 160 G5
Roffey . . . . . . . 28 F2
Rogart . . . . . . 157 J10
Rogart Station . . 157 J10
Rogate. . . . . . . . 16 B2
Rogerstone . . . . 35 F6
Roghadal . . . . . 154 J5
Rogiet . . . . . . . 36 F1
Rogue's Alley . . . 66 D3
Roke . . . . . . . . 39 E6
Roker . . . . . . . 111 D7
Rollesby . . . . . . 69 C7
Rolleston Leics. . . 64 D4
Notts . . . . . . . . 77 D7
Rolleston-on-
Dove . . . . . . . 63 B6
Rolston . . . . . . . 97 E8
Rolvenden . . . . . 18 B5
Rolvenden Layne . 19 B5
Romaldkirk . . . . 100 B4
Romanby . . . . . 102 E1
Romannobridge . 120 E4
Romansleigh. . . . 10 B2
Romford . . . . . . 41 F8
Romiley . . . . . . . 87 E7
Romsey . . . . . . 14 B4
Romsey Town . . . 55 D5
Romsley Shrops . . 61 F7
Worcs . . . . . . . 50 B4
Ronague . . . . . . 84 E2
Rookhope. . . . . 110 E2
Rookley . . . . . . . 15 F6
Rooks Bridge . . . 23 D5
Roos . . . . . . . . 97 F8
Roosebeck . . . . . 92 C2
Rootham's Green . 54 D2
Rootpark . . . . . 120 D2
Ropley . . . . . . . 26 F4
Ropley Dean . . . . 26 F4
Ropsley . . . . . . 78 F2
Rora . . . . . . . 153 C10
Rorandle . . . . . 141 C5
Rorrington . . . . . 60 D3
Roscroggan . . . . . 3 B5
Rose . . . . . . . . . 4 D2
Roseacre Kent . . . 29 D8
Lancs. . . . . . . . 92 F4
Rose Ash . . . . . 10 B2
Rosebank . . . . . 119 E8
Rosebrough. . . . 117 B7
Rosebush . . . . . 32 B1
Rosecare . . . . . . 8 E3
Rosedale Abbey . 103 E5
Roseden . . . . . 117 B6
Rosefield . . . . . 151 F11

Rose Green . . . . . 16 E3
Rose Grove. . . . . 93 F8
Rosehall . . . . . 156 J7
Rosehaugh Mains 151 F9
Rosehearty . . . . 153 B9
Rosehill. . . . . . . 74 F3
Rose Hill E Sus . . 17 C8
Lancs . . . . . . . 93 F8
Suff . . . . . . . . . 57 E5
Roseisle . . . . . 152 B1
Roselands . . . . . 18 E3
Rosemarket . . . . 44 E4
Rosemarkie . . . 151 F10
Rosemary Lane. . . 11 C6
Rosemount . . . . 134 E1
Rosenannon . . . . 4 C4
Rosewell . . . . . 121 C5
Roseworth . . . . 102 B2
Roseworthy . . . . . 2 C5
Rosgill . . . . . . . 99 C7
Roshven . . . . . 147 D10
Roskhill. . . . . . 149 D7
Roskill House . . 151 F9
Rosley . . . . . . 108 E3
Roslin . . . . . . 121 C5
Rosliston . . . . . 63 C6
Rosneath . . . . . 145 E11
Ross Dumfries . . 106 E3
Northumb. . . . . 123 F7
Perth . . . . . . . 127 B6
Rossett . . . . . . 73 D7
Rossett Green . . 95 D6
Rossie Ochill . . 128 C2
Rossie Priory . . 134 F2
Rossington . . . . 89 E7
Rosskeen . . . . 151 E9
Rossland. . . . . 118 B4
Ross-on-Wye . . . 36 B3
Roster . . . . . . 158 G4
Rostherne . . . . 86 F5
Rosthwaite . . . . 98 C4
Roston . . . . . . 75 E8
Rosyth . . . . . . 128 F3
Rothbury . . . . . 117 D6
Rotherby . . . . . 64 C3
Rotherfield . . . . 18 C2
Rotherfield Greys. . 39 F7
Rotherfield
Peppard . . . . . 39 F7
Rotherham. . . . . 88 E5
Rothersthorpe . . 52 D5
Rotherwick . . . . 26 D5
Rothes. . . . . . . 152 D2
Rothesay. . . . . 145 G9
Rothiebrisbane . . 153 E7
Rothienorman . . 153 E7
Rothiesholm . . . 159 F7
Rothley Leics. . . . 64 C2
Northumb. . . . . 117 F6
Rothley Shield
East . . . . . . . 117 E6
Rothmaise . . . . 153 E6
Rothwell Lincs . . 91 E5
N Nhants . . . . . 64 F5
W Yorks. . . . . . 88 B4
Rothwell Haigh. . 88 B4
Rotsea . . . . . . . 97 D6
Rottal. . . . . . . 134 C3
Rotten End. . . . . 57 C7
Rottingdean . . . . 17 D7
Rottington . . . . . 98 C1
Roud . . . . . . . . 15 F6
Rougham Norf . . . 80 E4
Suff . . . . . . . . . 56 C3
Rougham Green. . 56 C3
Roughburn. . . . 137 F6
Rough Close . . . . 75 F6
Rough Common . 30 D5
Roughlee . . . . . . 93 E8
Roughley . . . . . . 62 E5
Roughsike . . . . 108 B5
Roughton Lincs . . 78 C5
Norf . . . . . . . . 81 D8
Shrops . . . . . . . 61 E7
Roughton Moor . . 78 C5
Roundhay. . . . . . 95 F6
Roundstonefoot. 114 D4
Roundstreet
Common . . . . 16 B4
Roundway . . . . . 24 C5
Rousdon . . . . . . 11 E7
Rous Lench . . . . 50 D5
Routenburn . . . 118 C1
Routh . . . . . . . 97 E6
Row Corn . . . . . . . 5 B5
W&F. . . . . . . . 99 F6
Rowanburn . . . 108 B4
Rowardennan . . 126 E2
Rowde . . . . . . . 24 C4
Rowen . . . . . . . 83 D7
Rowfoot . . . . . 109 C6
Row Heath . . . . 43 C7
Rowhedge . . . . . 43 B6
Rowhook . . . . . . 28 F2
Rowington . . . . . 51 C7
Rowland . . . . . . 76 B2
Rowlands Castle . 15 C8
Rowlands Gill . . 110 D4
Rowledge . . . . . 27 E6
Rowlestone . . . . 35 B7
Rowley E Yorks . . 97 F5
Shrops . . . . . . . 60 D3
Rowley Hill. . . . . 88 C2
Rowley Regis . . . 62 F3
Rowly. . . . . . . . 27 E8
Rowney Green . . 50 B5
Rownhams. . . . . 14 C4
Rowrah . . . . . . 98 C2
Rowsham . . . . . 39 C8
Rowsley . . . . . . 76 C2
Rowstock . . . . . 38 F4
Rowston . . . . . . 78 D3
Rowton Ches W . . 73 C8
Shrops . . . . . . . 60 C3
Telford . . . . . . 61 C6
Roxburgh . . . . 122 F3
Roxby N Lincs . . 90 C3
N Yorks. . . . . . 103 C5
Roxton . . . . . . . 54 D2
Roxwell . . . . . . 42 D2
Royal Leamington
Spa . . . . . . . . 51 C8
Royal Oak Darl . . 101 B7
Lancs . . . . . . . 86 D2
Royal Tunbridge
Wells . . . . . . . 18 B2
Royal Wootton
Bassett . . . . . . 37 F7
Royston-on-
Dunsmore . . . . 51 B8

Roydhouse. . . . . 88 C3
Roydon Essex . . 41 D7
Norf . . . . . . . . 68 F3
Norf . . . . . . . . 80 E3
Roydon Hamlet. . 41 D7
Royston Herts. . . 54 E4
S Yorks . . . . . . 88 C4
Royton . . . . . . . 87 D7
Rozel . . . . . . . . 17 I3
Ruabon = Rhiwabon 73 E7
Ruaig . . . . . . . 146 G3
Ruan Lanihorne . . 3 B7
Ruan Minor . . . . . 3 E6
Ruarach . . . . . 136 B2
Ruardean . . . . . 36 C3
Ruardean
Woodside . . . 36 C3
Rubery. . . . . . . 50 B4
Ruckcroft . . . . 108 E5
Ruckhall . . . . . . 49 F6
Ruckinge . . . . . . 19 B7
Ruckland . . . . . 79 B6
Ruckley . . . . . . 60 D5
Rudbaxton . . . . 44 C4
Rudby . . . . . . 102 D2
Ruddington . . . . 77 F5
Rudford . . . . . . 36 B4
Rudge Shrops . . 62 E2
Som . . . . . . . . 24 D3
Rudgeway . . . . . 36 F3
Rudgwick . . . . . 27 F8
Rudhall . . . . . . 36 B3
Rudheath . . . . . 74 B3
Rudley Green . . . 42 D4
Rudry . . . . . . . 35 F5
Rudston . . . . . . 97 C6
Rudyard . . . . . . 75 D6
Rufford . . . . . . 86 C2
Rufforth . . . . . . 95 D8
Rugby . . . . . . . 52 B3
Rugeley . . . . . . 62 C4
Ruglen. . . . . . 112 D2
Ruilick. . . . . . 151 G8
Ruishton . . . . . 11 B7
Ruisigearraidh . . 154 J4
Ruislip. . . . . . . 40 F3
Ruislip Common . 40 F3
Rumbling Bridge . 128 E2
Rumburgh . . . . . 69 F6
Rumford . . . . . . . 4 B3
Rumney . . . . . . 22 B4
Runcorn . . . . . . 86 F3
Runcton . . . . . . 16 D2
Runcton Holme . 67 D6
Rundlestone . . . . 6 B3
Runfold . . . . . . 27 E6
Runhall . . . . . . 68 D3
Runham Norf . . . 69 C7
Norf . . . . . . . . 69 D8
Runnington . . . . 11 B6
Runsell Green . . 42 D3
Runswick Bay . . 103 C6
Runwell. . . . . . 42 E3
Ruscombe . . . . . 27 B5
Rushall Hereford . 49 F8
Norf . . . . . . . . 68 F4
Wilts . . . . . . . . 25 D6
W Mid . . . . . . . 62 D4
Rushbrooke . . . . 56 C2
Rushbury . . . . . 60 E5
Rushden Herts . . 54 F4
N Nhants . . . . . 53 C7
Rushenden. . . . . 30 B3
Rushford. . . . . . 68 F2
Rush Green . . . . 41 F8
Rush-head. . . . 153 D8
Rushlake Green . . 18 D3
Rushmere. . . . . 69 F7
Rushmere St
Andrew . . . . . 57 E6
Rushmoor . . . . . 27 E6
Rushock . . . . . . 50 B3
Rusholme . . . . . 87 E6
Rushton Ches W . 74 C2
N Nhants . . . . . 64 F5
Rushton Spencer . 75 C6
Rushwick . . . . . 50 D3
Rushyford. . . . 101 B7
Ruskie . . . . . . 126 D5
Ruskington . . . . 78 D3
Rusland . . . . . . 99 F5
Rusper . . . . . . . 28 F3
Ruspidge . . . . . 36 C3
Russell's Water . . 39 F7
Russel's Green . . 57 B6
Rusthall . . . . . . 18 B2
Rustington. . . . . 16 D4
Ruston Parva . . . 97 C6
Ruswarp . . . . . 103 D6
Rutherford. . . . 122 F2
Rutherglen. . . . 119 C6
Ruthernbridge . . . 4 C5
Ruthin = Rhuthun . 72 D5
Ruthrieston . . . 141 D8
Ruthven Aberds . . 152 D5
Angus. . . . . . . 134 E2
Highld . . . . . . 138 E3
Highld . . . . . . . 151 H11
Ruthven House . 134 E3
Ruthvoes . . . . . . 4 C4
Ruthwell. . . . . 107 C7
Ruyton-XI-Towns . 60 B3
Ryal . . . . . . . 110 B3
Ryal Fold. . . . . 86 B4
Ryall . . . . . . . . 12 E2
Ryarsh . . . . . . . 29 D7
Rydal . . . . . . . 99 D5
Ryde . . . . . . . . 15 E6
Rye . . . . . . . . . 19 C6
Ryecroft Gate . . 75 C6
Rye Foreign . . . . 19 C5
Rye Harbour . . . 19 D6
Ryehill . . . . . . . 91 B6
Rye Park . . . . . . 41 C6
Rye Street. . . . . 50 F2
Ryhall . . . . . . . 65 C7
Ryhill. . . . . . . . 88 C4
Ryhope . . . . . 111 D7
Rylstone . . . . . . 94 D2
Ryme Intrinseca . 12 C3
Ryther . . . . . . . 95 F8
Ryton Glos . . . . 50 F2
N Yorks. . . . . . 96 B3
Shrops . . . . . . 61 D7
T&W . . . . . . . 110 C4
Ryton-on-
Dunsmore . . . . 51 B8

S

Sabden . . . . . . . 93 F7
Sacombe . . . . . . 41 C6
Sacriston . . . . . 110 E5
Sadberge . . . . . 101 C8
Saddell . . . . . . 143 E8
Saddington . . . . 64 E3
Saddle Bow . . . . 67 C6
Saddlescombe. . . 17 C6
Sadgill. . . . . . . . 99 D6
Saffron Walden . . 55 F6
Sageston . . . . . . 32 D1
Saham Hills . . . . 68 D2
Saham Toney . . . 68 D2
Saighdinis . . . . 148 B3
Saighton . . . . . . 73 C8
St Abbs . . . . . . 122 C5
St Abb's Haven . . 122 C5
St Agnes Corn. . . . 4 D2
Scilly . . . . . . . . 2 F3
St Albans . . . . . . 40 D4
St Allen . . . . . . . 4 D3
St Andrews. . . . 129 C6
St Andrew's
Major . . . . . . 22 B3
St Anne. . . . . . . 16 I1
St Annes . . . . . . 85 B4
St Ann's . . . . . . 114 E3
St Ann's Chapel
Corn . . . . . . . . 6 B2
Devon. . . . . . . . 6 E4
St Anthony-in-
Meneage . . . . . 3 D6
St Anthony's Hill . 18 E3
St Arvans . . . . . . 36 E2
St Asaph
= Llanelwy. . . . 72 B4
St Athan . . . . . . 22 C2
St Aubin . . . . . . 17 I3
St Austell . . . . . . 4 D5
St Bees . . . . . . . 98 C1
St Blazey . . . . . . . 5 D5
St Boswells . . . . 121 F8
St Brelade . . . . . 17 I3
St Breock . . . . . . 4 B4
St Breward . . . . . 5 B5
St Briavels . . . . . 36 D2
St Bride's . . . . . . 44 D3
St Brides Major. . 21 B7
St Bride's
Netherwent. . . 35 F8
St Brides-
super-Ely. . . . 22 B2
St Brides
Wentlooge. . . . 35 F6
St Budeaux . . . . . 6 D2
St Buryan . . . . . . 2 D3
St Catherine . . . . 24 B2
St Catherine's . . 125 E7
St Clears
= Sanclêr. . . . . 32 C3
St Cleer . . . . . . . 5 C7
St Clement . . . . . 3 B7
St Clements . . . . 17 I3
St Clether. . . . . . 8 F4
St Colmac. . . . . 145 G9
St Columb Major . 4 C4
St Columb Minor . 4 C3
St Columb Road . 4 D4
St Combs . . . . 153 B10
St Cross South
Elmham . . . . . 69 F5
St Cyrus. . . . . . 135 C7
St David's
= Tyddewi . . . . 44 C2
St Day . . . . . . . . 3 B6
St Dennis . . . . . . 4 D4
St Devereux . . . . 49 F6
St Dogmaels . . . 45 E3
St Dogwells . . . . 44 C4
St Dominick. . . . . 6 C2
St Donat's . . . . . 21 C8
St Edith's . . . . . 24 C4
St Endellion. . . . . 4 B4
St Enoder . . . . . . 4 D3
St Erme . . . . . . . 4 D3
St Erney . . . . . . . 5 D8
St Erth . . . . . . . . 2 C4
St Ervan . . . . . . . 4 B4
St Eval . . . . . . . . 4 C3
St Ewe . . . . . . . . 3 B8
St Fagans . . . . . 22 B3
St Fergus . . . . . 153 C10
St Fillans . . . . . 127 B5
St Florence . . . . 32 D1
St Genny's . . . . . 8 E3
St George . . . . . 72 B3
St George's . . . . 22 B2
St Germans . . . . . 5 D8
St Giles . . . . . . . 78 B2
St Giles in the
Wood . . . . . . . 9 C7
St Giles on the
Heath . . . . . . . 9 E5
St Harmon . . . . . 47 B8
St Helena . . . . . 63 D6
St Helen
Auckland . . . . 101 B6
St Helens IoW . . . 15 F7
Mers . . . . . . . . 86 E3
St Helen's . . . . . 18 E4
St Helier Jersey . . 17 I3
London . . . . . . 28 C3
St Hilary Corn . . . 2 C4
V Glam. . . . . . . 22 B2
Saint Hill . . . . . . 28 F4
St Illtyd . . . . . . . 35 D6
St Ippollytts . . . . 40 B4
St Ishmael's . . . . 44 E3
St Issey . . . . . . . 4 B4
St Ive . . . . . . . . . 5 C8
St Ives Cambs . . 54 B4
Corn . . . . . . . . . 2 B4
Dorset . . . . . . . 14 D2
St James South
Elmham . . . . . 69 F6
St Jidgey . . . . . . 4 C4
St John . . . . . . . . 6 D2
St John's IoM. . . 84 D2
Jersey . . . . . . . 17 I3
Sur . . . . . . . . . 27 D7
Worcs . . . . . . . 50 D3
St John's Chapel . 109 F8
St John's Fen End . 66 C5
St John's Highway . 66 C5

St John's Town of
Dalry . . . . . . . 113 F6
St Judes . . . . . . 84 C3
St Just . . . . . . . . 2 C2
St Just in
Roseland . . . . . 3 C7
St Katherine's . . 153 E7
St Keverne . . . . . 3 D6
St Kew . . . . . . . . 4 B5
St Kew Highway . . 4 B5
St Keyne . . . . . . . 5 C7
St Lawrence Corn . 4 C5
Essex . . . . . . . 43 D5
IoW . . . . . . . . 15 G6
St Leonards Dorset . 14 D2
E Sus . . . . . . . 18 E4
S Lanark. . . . . 119 D6
St Leonard's . . . 40 D2
St Levan . . . . . . . 2 D2
St Lythans . . . . . 22 B3
St Mabyn . . . . . . 4 B5
St Madoes . . . . 128 B3
St Margarets . . . 41 C6
St Margaret's . . . 49 F5
St Margaret's at
Cliffe . . . . . . . 31 E7
St Margaret's
Hope . . . . . . . 159 J5
St Margaret South
Elmham . . . . . 69 F6
St Mark's . . . . . . 84 E2
St Martin . . . . . . 5 D7
St Martins Corn . . 3 E6
Perth . . . . . . . 134 F1
St Martin's Jersey . 17 I3
Shrops . . . . . . . 73 F7
St Mary Bourne . . 26 D2
St Mary Church. . 22 B2
St Mary Cray . . . 29 C5
St Mary Hill . . . . 21 B8
St Mary Hoo. . . . 30 B2
St Mary in the
Marsh . . . . . . 19 C7
St Mary's Jersey. . 17 I3
Orkney . . . . . . 159 H5
St Mary's Bay. . . 19 C7
St Maughans . . . 36 C1
St Mawes . . . . . . 3 C7
St Mawgan . . . . . 4 C3
St Mellion . . . . . . 5 C8
St Mellons . . . . . 35 F6
St Merryn . . . . . . 4 B3
St Mewan . . . . . . 4 D4
St Michael
Caerhays . . . . . 3 B8
St Michael
Penkevil . . . . . 3 B7
St Michaels . . . . 49 C7
St Michael's . . . . 19 B5
St Michael's on
Wyre . . . . . . . 92 E4
St Michael South
Elmham . . . . . 69 F6
St Minver . . . . . . 4 B4
St Monans . . . . 129 D7
St Neot . . . . . . . 5 C6
St Neots . . . . . . 54 C2
St Newlyn East . . 4 D3
St Nicholas Pembs. . 44 B3
V Glam. . . . . . . 22 B2
St Nicholas at
Wade. . . . . . . 31 C6
St Ninians . . . . 127 E6
St Osyth . . . . . . 43 C7
St Osyth Heath . . 43 C7
St Ouens . . . . . . 17 I3
St Owens Cross. . 36 B2
St Paul's Cray . . . 29 C5
St Paul's Walden . 40 B4
St Peter Port . . . 16 I2
St Peter's Jersey . . 17 I3
Kent . . . . . . . . 31 C7
St Petrox . . . . . . 44 F4
St Pinnock . . . . . 5 C7
St Quivox . . . . . 112 B3
St Ruan . . . . . . . 3 E6
St Sampson . . . . 16 I2
St Stephen . . . . . 4 D4
St Stephens Corn . 6 D2
Herts . . . . . . . 40 D4
St Stephen's . . . . 8 F5
St Teath . . . . . . . 8 F2
St Thomas . . . . . 10 E4
St Tudy. . . . . . . . 5 B5
St Twynnells . . . 44 F4
St Veep. . . . . . . . 5 D6
St Vigeans . . . . 135 E6
St Wenn . . . . . . . 4 C4
St Weonards . . . . 36 B1
Salcombe. . . . . . 6 F5
Salcombe Regis . 11 F6
Salcott . . . . . . . 43 C5
Sale . . . . . . . . . 87 E5
Saleby . . . . . . . 79 B7
Sale Green . . . . . 50 D4
Salehurst . . . . . 18 C4
Salem Carms . . . 33 B7
Ceredig . . . . . . 58 F3
Salen Argyll . . . 147 G8
Highld . . . . . . 147 E9
Salesbury . . . . . 93 F6
Salford C Beds. . . 53 F7
Gtr Man . . . . . 87 E6
Oxon . . . . . . . . 38 B2
Salford Priors . . 51 D5
Salfords . . . . . . 28 E3
Salhouse . . . . . 69 C6
Saline . . . . . . . 128 E2
Salisbury . . . . . 14 B2
Sallachan . . . . . 130 C3
Sallachy Highld . . 150 H2
Highld . . . . . . . 157 J8
Salle . . . . . . . . 81 E7
Salmonby . . . . . 79 B6
Salmond's Muir . 135 F5
Salperton . . . . . 37 B7
Salph End. . . . . . 53 D8
Salsburgh . . . . 119 C8
Salt. . . . . . . . . 62 B3
Saltaire . . . . . . 94 F4
Saltash . . . . . . . 6 D2
Saltburn . . . . . 151 E10
Saltburn-by-
the-Sea . . . . 102 B4
Saltby . . . . . . . 65 B5
Saltcoats Cumb . . 98 E2
N Ayrs . . . . . . 118 E2
Saltdean . . . . . . 17 D7
Salt End. . . . . . . 91 B5

Salter. . . . . . . . 93 C6
Salterforth. . . . . 93 E8
Salterswall. . . . . 74 C3
Saltfleet . . . . . . 91 E8
Saltfleetby All
Saints . . . . . . 91 E8
Saltfleetby St
Clements . . . . 91 E8
Saltfleetby St
Peter. . . . . . . 91 F8
Salford . . . . . . . 23 C8
Salthouse. . . . . . 81 C6
Saltmarshe . . . . 89 B8
Saltney . . . . . . . 73 C7
Salton . . . . . . . 96 B3
Saltwick . . . . . 110 B4
Saltwood . . . . . . 19 B8
Salum . . . . . . . 146 G3
Salvington . . . . . 16 D5
Salwarpe . . . . . . 50 C3
Salwayash . . . . . 12 E2
Sambourne . . . . 51 C5
Sambrook . . . . . 61 B7
Samhla . . . . . . 148 B2
Samlesbury . . . . 93 F5
Samlesbury
Bottoms . . . . . 86 B4
Sampford Arundel 11 C6
Sampford Brett. . 22 E2
Sampford
Courtenay . . . . 9 D8
Sampford Peverell 10 C5
Sampford Spiney . 6 B3
Sampool Bridge . 99 F6
Samuelston . . . 121 B7
Sanachan . . . . 149 D13
Sanaigmore. . . 142 A3
Sanclêr
= St Clears . . . . 32 C3
Sancreed . . . . . . 2 D3
Sancton . . . . . . 96 F5
Sand Highld . . . . 150 B2
Shetland. . . . . 160 J5
Sandaig . . . . . 149 H12
Sandale . . . . . . 108 E2
Sandal Magna. . . 88 C4
Sandbach. . . . . . 74 C4
Sandbank. . . . . 145 E10
Sandbanks . . . . 13 F8
Sandend . . . . . 152 B5
Sanderstead . . . . 28 C4
Sandfields . . . . . 37 B6
Sandford Devon . . 10 D3
Dorset . . . . . . . 13 F7
IoW . . . . . . . . 15 F6
N Som . . . . . . . 23 D6
Shrops . . . . . . 74 F2
S Lanark. . . . . 119 E7
W&F. . . . . . . 100 C2
Sandfordhill . . . 153 D11
Sandford on
Thames . . . . . 39 D5
Sandford Orcas. . 12 B4
Sandford St
Martin. . . . . . 38 B4
Sandgate . . . . . . 19 B8
Sandgreen . . . . 106 D2
Sandhaven . . . . 153 B9
Sandhead. . . . . 104 E4
Sandhills . . . . . . 27 F7
Sandhoe . . . . . 110 C2
Sand Hole . . . . . 96 F4
Sandholme E Yorks. 96 F4
Lincs. . . . . . . . 79 F6
Sandhurst Brack . . 27 C6
Glos . . . . . . . . 37 B5
Kent . . . . . . . . 18 C4
Sandhurst Cross . 18 C4
Sandhutton . . . 102 F1
Sand Hutton . . . 96 D2
Sandiacre. . . . . 76 F4
Sandilands Lincs . 91 F9
S Lanark. . . . . 119 F8
Sandiway . . . . . 74 B3
Sandleheath . . . . 14 C2
Sandling . . . . . . 29 D8
Sandlow Green . . 74 C4
Sandness . . . . . 160 H3
Sandon Essex . . . 42 D3
Herts . . . . . . . 54 F4
Staffs . . . . . . . 75 F6
Sandown . . . . . . 15 F6
Sandplace . . . . . 5 D7
Sandridge Herts . . 40 C4
Wilts . . . . . . . . 24 C4
Sandringham . . . 67 B6
Sandsend . . . . 103 C6
Sandside House . 157 C12
Sandsound . . . . 160 J5
Sandtoft . . . . . . 89 D8
Sandway . . . . . . 30 D2
Sandwell. . . . . . 62 F4
Sandwich . . . . . 31 D7
Sandwick Orkney. . 159 K5
Shetland. . . . . 160 L6
W&F. . . . . . . . 99 C6
Sandwith . . . . . . 98 C1
Sandy Carms . . . 33 D5
C Beds . . . . . . 54 E2
Sandy Bank . . . . 79 D5
Sandycroft . . . . 73 C7
Sandyford
Dumfries . . . . 114 E5
Stoke . . . . . . . 75 D5
Sandygate . . . . . 84 C3
Sandy Haven . . . 44 E3
Sandyhills . . . . 107 D5
Sandylands . . . . 92 C4
Sandy Lane Wilts. . 24 C4
Wrex . . . . . . . . 73 E7
Sandypark . . . . . 10 F2
Sandysike . . . . 108 C3
Sangobeg. . . . . 156 C7
Sangomore . . . 156 C7
Sanna . . . . . . 146 E7
Sanndabhaig
W Isles . . . . . . 148 D3
W Isles . . . . . . 155 D9
Sannox . . . . . 143 D11
Sanquhar . . . . 113 D7
Santon . . . . . . . 90 C3
Santon Bridge . . 98 D3
Santon Downham . 67 F8
Sapcote . . . . . . 63 E8
Sapey Common . . 50 C2
Sapiston . . . . . . 56 B3
Sapley . . . . . . . 54 B3
Sapperton Glos . . 37 D6
Lincs . . . . . . . 78 F3

Saracen's Head . . 66 B3
Sarclet. . . . . . . 158 F5
Sardis . . . . . . . 33 D6
Sarn Bridgend . . 34 F3
Powys . . . . . . . 60 E2
Sarnau Carms . . . 32 C4
Ceredig . . . . . . 46 D2
Gwyn . . . . . . . 72 F3
Powys . . . . . . . 48 F2
Powys . . . . . . . 60 C2
Sarn Bach. . . . . 70 E4
Sarnesfield . . . . 49 D5
Sarn Meyllteyrn . 70 D3
Saron Carms . . . 33 C7
Carms . . . . . . . 46 F2
Denb . . . . . . . . 72 C4
Gwyn . . . . . . . 82 E5
Gwyn . . . . . . . 82 F4
Sarratt. . . . . . . 40 E3
Sarre . . . . . . . . 31 C6
Sarsden . . . . . . 38 B2
Sarsgrum . . . . . 156 C6
Satley . . . . . . . 110 E4
Satron . . . . . . 100 E4
Satterleigh. . . . . . 9 B8
Satterthwaite . . . 99 E5
Satwell . . . . . . . 39 F7
Sauchen . . . . . 141 C5
Saucher . . . . . . 134 F1
Sauchie. . . . . . 127 E7
Sauchieburn . . . 135 C6
Saughall . . . . . . 73 B7
Saughtree . . . . 115 E8
Saul . . . . . . . . 36 D4
Saundby . . . . . . 89 F8
Saundersfoot . . . 32 D2
Saunderton . . . . 39 D7
Saunton . . . . . . 20 F3
Sausthorpe . . . . 79 C6
Saval . . . . . . . 157 J8
Savary . . . . . . 147 G9
Savile Park. . . . . 87 B8
Sawbridge . . . . 52 C3
Sawbridgeworth . 41 C7
Sawdon . . . . . 103 F7
Sawley Derbys . . 76 F4
Lancs . . . . . . . 93 E7
N Yorks. . . . . . 94 C5
Sawston . . . . . . 55 E5
Sawtry . . . . . . . 65 F8
Saxby Leics . . . . 64 C5
Lincs . . . . . . . . 90 F4
Saxby All Saints . 90 C3
Saxelbye . . . . . . 64 B4
Saxham Street . . 56 C4
Saxilby. . . . . . . 77 B8
Saxlingham . . . . 81 D6
Saxlingham Green. 68 E5
Saxlingham
Nethergate . . . 68 E5
Saxlingham
Thorpe . . . . . 68 E5
Saxmundham . . . 57 C7
Saxondale . . . . . 77 F6
Saxon Street . . . 55 D7
Saxtead . . . . . . 57 C6
Saxtead Green . . 57 C6
Saxthorpe . . . . . 81 D7
Saxton . . . . . . . 95 F7
Sayers Common . 17 C6
Scackleton. . . . . 96 B2
Scadabhagh . . . 154 H6
Scaftworth. . . . . 89 E7
Scagglethorpe . . 96 B4
Scaitcliffe. . . . . . 87 B5
Scalasaig . . . . 144 D2
Scalby E Yorks . . 90 B2
N Yorks. . . . . . 103 E8
Scaldwell . . . . . 53 B5
Scaleby . . . . . . 108 C4
Scaleby Hill . . . 108 C4
Scale Houses . . 109 E5
Scales Lancs . . . 92 F4
W&F. . . . . . . 92 B2
W&F. . . . . . . . 99 B5
Scalford . . . . . . 64 B4
Scaling . . . . . . 103 C5
Scallastle . . . . . 124 B2
Scalloway . . . . 160 K6
Scalpay. . . . . . 154 H7
Scalpay House . 149 F11
Scalpsie . . . . . 145 H9
Scamadale . . . . 147 B10
Scamblesby . . . . 79 B5
Scamodale . . . . 130 B2
Scampston . . . . 96 B4
Scampton . . . . . 78 B2
Scapa . . . . . . . 159 H5
Scapegoat Hill . . 87 C8
Scar . . . . . . . 159 D7
Scarborough . . . 103 F8
Scarcliffe . . . . . 76 C4
Scarcroft . . . . . 95 E6
Scarcroft Hill . . . 95 E6
Scardroy . . . . . 150 F5
Scarff . . . . . . . 160 E4
Scarfskerry . . . . 158 C4
Scargill . . . . . 101 C5
Scarinish . . . . . 146 G3
Scarisbrick . . . . 85 C4
Scarning . . . . . . 68 C2
Scarrington . . . . 77 E7
Scartho . . . . . . 91 D6
Scarwell . . . . . 159 F3
Scatness . . . . . 160 M5
Scatraig . . . . . 151 H10
Scawby . . . . . . 90 D3
Scawsby . . . . . . 89 D6
Scawton . . . . . 102 F3
Scayne's Hill . . . 17 B7
Scethrog. . . . . . 35 B5
Scholar Green . . 74 D5
Scholes W Yorks . . 88 B2
W Yorks . . . . . 88 D2
W Yorks . . . . . 95 F6
School Green . . . 74 C3
Scleddau . . . . . . 44 B4
Scofton . . . . . . 89 F7
Scole . . . . . . . . 56 B5
Scolpaig . . . . . 148 A2
Scone . . . . . . . 128 B3
Sconser . . . . . 149 E10
Scoonie . . . . . . 129 D5
Scoor . . . . . . 146 K7
Scopwick . . . . . 78 D3
Scoraig . . . . . . 150 B3
Scorborough . . . 97 E6
Scorrier . . . . . . . 3 B6
Scorton Lancs. . . 92 E5

Rhy–Sel 179

Scorton continued
N Yorks. . . . . . 101 D7
Sco Ruston. . . . . 81 E8
Scotbheinn . . . . 148 C3
Scotby . . . . . . 108 D4
Scotch Corner . . 101 D7
Scotforth . . . . . . 92 D4
Scothern. . . . . . 78 B3
Scotland Gate . . 117 F8
Scotlandwell . . . 128 D3
Scotsburn. . . . . 151 D10
Scotscalder
Station . . . . . 158 E2
Scotscraig . . . . 129 B6
Scots' Gap . . . . 117 F6
Scotston Aberds. . 135 B7
Perth . . . . . . . 133 E6
Scotstoun . . . . 118 C5
Scotstown . . . . 130 C2
Scotswood . . . . 110 C4
Scottas . . . . . . 149 H12
Scotter . . . . . . . 90 D2
Scotterthorpe. . . 90 D2
Scottlethorpe . . . 65 B7
Scotton Lincs . . . 90 E2
N Yorks. . . . . . 95 D6
N Yorks. . . . . . 101 E6
Scottow . . . . . . 81 E8
Scoughall . . . . 129 F8
Scoulag . . . . . 145 H10
Scoulton . . . . . . 68 D2
Scourie . . . . . . 156 E4
Scourie More . . 156 E4
Scousburgh . . . 160 M5
Scrabster . . . . 158 C2
Scrafield. . . . . . 79 C6
Scrainwood . . . 117 D6
Scrane End . . . . 79 E6
Scraptoft . . . . . 64 D3
Scratby . . . . . . 69 C8
Scrayingham . . . 96 C3
Scredington . . . . 78 E3
Scremby . . . . . 79 C7
Scremerston . . . 123 E6
Screveton. . . . . 77 E7
Scrivelsby . . . . . 79 C5
Scriven . . . . . . 95 D6
Scrooby . . . . . . 89 E7
Scropton . . . . . . 75 F8
Scrub Hill . . . . . 78 D5
Scruton . . . . . 101 E7
Sculcoates . . . . 97 F6
Sculthorpe. . . . . 80 D4
Scunthorpe . . . . 90 C2
Scurlage . . . . . . 33 F5
Seaborough . . . . 12 D2
Seacombe . . . . . 85 E4
Seacroft Lincs. . . 79 C8
W Yorks . . . . . 95 F6
Seadyke . . . . . . 79 F6
Seafield S Ayrs . . 112 B3
W Loth . . . . . . 120 C3
Seaford . . . . . . 18 E2
Seaforth . . . . . . 85 E4
Seagrave . . . . . 64 C3
Seaham . . . . . 111 E7
Seahouses . . . . 123 F8
Seal . . . . . . . . 29 D6
Sealand . . . . . . 73 C7
Seale . . . . . . . 27 E6
Seamer N Yorks. . 102 C2
N Yorks. . . . . . 103 F8
Seamill . . . . . . 118 E2
Sea Palling . . . . 69 B7
Searby . . . . . . . 90 D4
Seasalter . . . . . 30 C4
Seascale . . . . . . 98 D2
Seathorne . . . . . 79 C8
Seathwaite Cumb . 98 C4
W&F. . . . . . . . 98 E4
Seatoller . . . . . . 98 C4
Seaton Corn . . . . . 5 D8
Cumb . . . . . . 107 F7
Devon. . . . . . . 11 F7
Durham . . . . . 111 D6
E Yorks. . . . . . 97 E7
Northumb. . . . 111 B6
Rutland . . . . . 65 E6
Seaton Burn . . . 110 B5
Seaton Carew . . 102 B3
Seaton Delaval . . 111 B6
Seaton Ross . . . 96 E3
Seaton Sluice . . 111 B6
Seatown Aberds . . 152 B5
Dorset . . . . . . . 12 E2
Seave Green . . . 102 D3
Seaview . . . . . . 15 E7
Seaville . . . . . 107 D8
Seavington St
Mary . . . . . . 12 C2
Seavington St
Michael . . . . . 12 C2
Sebergham . . . . 108 E3
Seckington . . . . 63 D6
Second Coast . . 150 B2
Sedbergh . . . . 100 E1
Sedbury . . . . . . 36 E2
Sedbusk . . . . . 100 E3
Sedgeberrow . . . 50 F5
Sedgebrook . . . . 77 F8
Sedgefield . . . . 102 B1
Sedgeford . . . . . 80 D3
Sedgehill . . . . . 13 B6
Sedgley . . . . . . 62 E3
Sedgwick . . . . . 99 F7
Sedlescombe . . . 18 D4
Sedlescombe
Street . . . . . 18 D4
Seend . . . . . . . 24 C4
Seend Cleeve . . . 24 C4
Seer Green . . . . 40 E2
Seething . . . . . . 69 E6
Sefton . . . . . . . 85 D4
Seghill . . . . . . 111 B5
Seifton . . . . . . . 60 F4
Seighford . . . . . 62 B2
Seilebost . . . . . 154 H5
Seion . . . . . . . 82 E5
Seisdon . . . . . . 62 E2
Seisiadar . . . . . 155 D10
Selattyn . . . . . . 73 F6
Selborne . . . . . . 26 F5
Selby . . . . . . . . 96 F2
Selham . . . . . . . 16 B3
Selhurst . . . . . . 28 C4
Selkirk . . . . . . 115 B7

Sellack .... 36 B2
Sellafirth .... 160 D7
Sellibister .... 159 D8
Sellindge .... 19 B7
Sellindge Lees .... 19 B8
Selling .... 30 D4
Sells Green .... 24 C4
Selly Oak .... 62 F4
Selmeston .... 18 E2
Selsdon .... 28 C4
Selsey .... 16 E2
Selsfield Common .... 28 F4
Selsted .... 31 E6
Selston .... 76 D4
Selworthy .... 21 E8
Semblister .... 160 H5
Semer .... 56 E3
Semington .... 24 C3
Semley .... 13 B6
Send .... 27 D8
Send Marsh .... 27 D8
Senghenydd .... 35 E5
Sennen .... 2 D2
Sennen Cove .... 2 D2
Sennybridge
  = Pont Senni .... 34 B3
Serlby .... 89 F7
Sessay .... 95 B7
Setchey .... 67 C6
Setley .... 14 D4
Setter Shetland .... 160 E6
  Shetland .... 160 H5
  Shetland .... 160 J7
Settiscarth .... 159 G4
Settle .... 93 C8
Settrington .... 96 B4
Sevenhampton .... 37 B7
Seven Kings .... 41 F7
Sevenoaks .... 29 D6
Sevenoaks Weald .... 29 E6
Seven Sisters .... 34 D2
Severn Beach .... 36 F2
Severnhampton .... 38 E2
Severn Stoke .... 50 E3
Sevington .... 30 E4
Sewards End .... 55 F6
Sewardstone .... 41 E6
Sewardstonebury .... 41 E6
Sewerby .... 97 C7
Seworgan .... 3 C6
Sewstern .... 65 B5
Sezincote .... 51 F6
Sgarasta Mhòr .... 154 H5
Sgiogarstaigh .... 155 A10
Shabbington .... 39 D6
Shackerstone .... 63 D7
Shackleford .... 27 E7
Shade .... 87 B7
Shadforth .... 111 E6
Shadingfield .... 69 F7
Shadoxhurst .... 19 B6
Shadsworth .... 86 B5
Shadwell Norf .... 68 F2
  W Yorks .... 95 F6
Shaftesbury .... 13 B6
Shafton .... 88 C4
Shalbourne .... 25 C8
Shalcombe .... 14 F4
Shalden .... 26 E4
Shaldon .... 7 B7
Shalfleet .... 14 F5
Shalford Essex .... 42 B3
  Sur .... 27 E8
Shalford Green .... 42 B3
Shallowford .... 21 E6
Shalmsford Street .... 30 D4
Shalstone .... 52 F4
Shamley Green .... 27 E8
Shandon .... 145 E11
Shandwick .... 151 D11
Shangton .... 64 E4
Shankhouse .... 111 B5
Shanklin .... 15 F6
Shanquhar .... 152 E5
Shanzie .... 134 D2
Shap .... 99 C7
Shapwick Dorset .... 13 D7
  Som .... 23 F6
Shardlow .... 76 F4
Shareshill .... 62 D3
Sharlston .... 88 C4
Sharlston
  Common .... 88 C4
Sharnbrook .... 53 D7
Sharnford .... 63 E8
Sharoe Green .... 92 F5
Sharow .... 95 B6
Sharpenhoe .... 53 F8
Sharperton .... 117 D5
Sharpness .... 36 D3
Sharp Street .... 69 B6
Sharpthorne .... 28 F4
Sharrington .... 81 D6
Shatterford .... 61 F7
Shaugh Prior .... 6 C3
Shavington .... 74 D4
Shaw Gtr Man .... 87 D7
  W Berks .... 26 C2
  Wilts .... 24 C3
Shawbury .... 61 B5
Shawdon Hall .... 117 C6
Shawell .... 64 F2
Shawford .... 15 B5
Shawforth .... 87 B6
Shaw Green .... 86 C3
Shawhead .... 107 B5
Shawhill .... 108 C2
Shaw Mills .... 95 C5
Shawton .... 119 E6
Shawtonhill .... 119 E6
Shear Cross .... 24 E3
Shearington .... 107 C7
Shearsby .... 64 E3
Shebbear .... 9 D6
Shebdon .... 61 B7
Shebster .... 157 C13
Sheddens .... 119 D5
Shedfield .... 15 C6
Sheen .... 75 C8
Sheepscar .... 95 C5
Sheepscombe .... 37 C5
Sheepstor .... 6 C3
Sheepwash .... 9 D6
Sheepway .... 23 B6
Sheepy Magna .... 63 D7
Sheepy Parva .... 63 D7

Sheering .... 41 C8
Sheerness .... 30 B3
Sheet .... 15 B8
Sheffield .... 88 F4
Sheffield Bottom .... 26 C4
Sheffield Green .... 17 B8
Shefford .... 54 F2
Shefford
  Woodlands .... 25 B8
Sheigra .... 156 C4
Sheinton .... 61 D6
Shelderton .... 49 B6
Sheldon Derbys .... 75 C8
  Devon .... 11 D6
  W Mid .... 63 F5
Sheldwich .... 30 D4
Shelf .... 88 B2
Shelfanger .... 68 F4
Shelfield Warks .... 51 C5
  W Mid .... 62 D4
Shelford .... 77 E6
Shellacres .... 122 E4
Shelley Essex .... 42 D1
  Suff .... 56 F4
  W Yorks .... 88 C3
Shellingford .... 38 E3
Shellow Bowells .... 42 D2
Shelsley
  Beauchamp .... 50 C2
Shelsley Walsh .... 50 C2
Shelthorpe .... 64 C2
Shelton Bedford .... 53 C8
  Norf .... 68 E5
  Notts .... 77 E7
  Shrops .... 60 C4
Shelton Green .... 68 E5
Shelve .... 60 E3
Shelwick .... 49 E7
Shenfield .... 42 E2
Shenington .... 51 E8
Shenley .... 40 D4
Shenley Brook End 53 F6
Shenleybury .... 40 D4
Shenley Church
  End .... 53 F6
Shenmore .... 49 F5
Shennanton .... 105 C7
Shenstone Staffs .... 62 D5
  Worcs .... 50 B3
Shenton .... 63 D7
Shenval Highld .... 137 B7
  Moray .... 139 B8
Shepeau Stow .... 66 C3
Shephall .... 41 B5
Shepherd's Green .... 39 F7
Shepherd's Port .... 80 D2
Shepherdswell .... 31 E6
Shepley .... 88 D2
Shepperdine .... 36 E2
Shepperton .... 27 C8
Shepreth .... 54 E4
Shepshed .... 63 C8
Shepton
  Beauchamp .... 12 C2
Shepton Mallet .... 23 E8
Shepton Montague .... 23 F8
Shepway .... 29 D8
Sheraton .... 111 F7
Sherborne Dorset .... 12 C4
  Glos .... 38 C1
Sherborne St
  John .... 26 D4
Sherbourne .... 51 C7
Sherburn Durham .... 111 E6
  N Yorks .... 97 B5
Sherburn Hill .... 111 E6
Sherburn in Elmet .... 95 F7
Shere .... 27 E8
Shereford .... 80 E4
Sherfield English .... 14 B3
Sherfield on
  Loddon .... 26 D4
Sherford .... 7 E5
Sheriffhales .... 61 C7
Sheriff Hutton .... 96 C2
Sheringham .... 81 C7
Sherington .... 53 E6
Shernal Green .... 50 C4
Shernborne .... 80 D3
Sherrington .... 24 F4
Sherston .... 37 F5
Sherwood Green .... 9 B7
Shettleston .... 119 C6
Shevington .... 86 D3
Shevington Moor .... 86 C3
Shevington Vale .... 86 C3
Sheviock .... 5 D8
Shide .... 15 F5
Shiel Bridge .... 136 C2
Shieldaig Highld. .... 149 A13
  Highld .... 149 C13
Shieldhill Dumfries 114 F3
  Falk .... 119 B8
  S Lanark .... 120 E3
Shielfoot .... 147 E9
Shielhill Angus .... 134 D4
  Invclyd .... 118 B2
Shifford .... 38 D3
Shifnal .... 61 D7
Shilbottle .... 117 D7
Shildon .... 101 B7
Shillingford Devon .... 10 B4
  Oxon .... 39 E5
Shillingford St
  George .... 10 F4
Shillingstone .... 13 C6
Shillington .... 54 F2
Shillmoor .... 116 D4
Shilton Oxon .... 38 D2
  Warks .... 63 F8
Shilvington .... 117 F7
Shimpling Norf .... 68 F4
  Suff .... 56 D2
Shimpling Street .... 56 D2
Shincliffe .... 111 E5
Shiney Row .... 111 D6
Shinfield .... 26 C5
Shingham .... 67 D7
Shingle Street .... 57 E7
Shinner's Bridge .... 7 C5
Shinness .... 157 H8
Shipbourne .... 29 D6
Shipdham .... 68 D2
Shipham .... 23 D6
Shiphay .... 7 C6
Shiplake .... 27 B5
Shipley Derbys .... 76 E4
  Northumb .... 117 C7
  Shrops .... 62 E2

Shipley continued
  W Sus .... 16 B5
  W Yorks .... 94 F4
Shipley Shiels .... 116 E3
Shipmeadow .... 69 F6
Shippea Hill
  Station .... 67 F6
Shippon .... 38 E4
Shipston-on-
  Stour .... 51 E7
Shipton Glos .... 37 C7
  N Yorks .... 95 D8
  Shrops .... 61 E5
Shipton Bellinger .... 25 E7
Shipton Gorge .... 12 E2
Shipton Green .... 16 D2
Shipton Moyne .... 37 F5
Shipton on
  Cherwell .... 38 C4
Shipton Solers .... 37 C7
Shiptonthorpe .... 96 E4
Shipton-under-
  Wychwood .... 38 C2
Shirburn .... 39 E6
Shirdley Hill .... 85 C4
Shirebrook .... 76 C5
Shiregreen .... 88 E4
Shirehampton .... 23 B7
Shiremoor .... 111 B6
Shirenewton .... 36 E1
Shireoaks .... 89 F6
Shirkoak .... 19 B6
Shirland .... 76 D3
Shirley Derbys .... 76 E2
  London .... 28 C4
  Soton .... 14 C5
  W Mid .... 51 B6
Shirl Heath .... 49 D6
Shirrell Heath .... 15 C6
Shirwell .... 20 F4
Shirwell Cross .... 20 F4
Shiskine .... 143 F10
Shobdon .... 49 C6
Shobnall .... 63 B6
Shobrooke .... 10 D3
Shoby .... 64 C3
Shocklach .... 73 E8
Shoeburyness .... 43 F5
Sholden .... 31 D7
Sholing .... 14 C5
Shoot Hill .... 60 C4
Shop Corn .... 4 B3
  Corn .... 8 C4
Shop Corner .... 57 F6
Shoreditch .... 41 F6
Shoreham .... 29 C6
Shoreham by Sea 17 D6
Shore Mill .... 151 E10
Shoresdean .... 123 E5
Shoreswood .... 122 E5
Shoreton .... 151 E9
Shorncote .... 37 E7
Shorne .... 29 B7
Shortacombe .... 9 F7
Shortgate .... 17 C8
Short Heath .... 62 D3
Shortlanesend .... 3 B7
Shortlees .... 118 F4
Shortstown .... 53 E8
Shorwell .... 15 F5
Shoscombe .... 24 D2
Shotesham .... 69 E5
Shotgate .... 42 E3
Shotley .... 57 F6
Shotley Bridge .... 110 D3
Shotleyfield .... 110 D3
Shotley Gate .... 57 F6
Shottenden .... 30 D4
Shottermill .... 27 F6
Shottery .... 51 D6
Shotteswell .... 52 E2
Shottisham .... 57 E7
Shottle .... 76 E3
Shottlegate .... 76 E3
Shotton Durham .... 111 F7
  Flint .... 73 C7
  Northumb .... 122 F4
Shotton Colliery .... 111 E6
Shotts .... 119 C8
Shotwick .... 73 B7
Shouldham .... 67 D6
Shouldham
  Thorpe .... 67 D6
Shoulton .... 50 D3
Shover's Green .... 18 B3
Shrawardine .... 60 C4
Shrawley .... 50 C3
Shrewley Common 51 C7
Shrewsbury .... 60 C4
Shrewton .... 25 E5
Shripney .... 16 D3
Shropham .... 68 E2
Shrub End .... 43 B5
Shucknall .... 49 E7
Shudy Camps .... 55 E7
Shulishadermor .... 149 D9
Shurdington .... 37 C6
Shurlock Row .... 27 B6
Shurrery .... 157 D13
Shurrery Lodge .... 157 D13
Shurton .... 22 E4
Shustoke .... 63 E6
Shute Devon .... 10 D3
  Devon .... 11 E7
Shuthonger .... 50 F3
Shutlanger .... 52 E5
Shuttington .... 63 D6
Shuttlewood .... 76 B4
Siabost bho
  Dheas .... 154 C7
Siabost bho
  Thuath .... 154 C7
Siadar .... 155 B8
Siadar Iarach .... 155 B8
Siadar Uarach .... 155 B8
Sibbaldbie .... 114 F4
Sibbertoft .... 64 F3
Sibdon Carwood .... 60 F4
Sibford Ferris .... 51 F8
Sibford Gower .... 51 F8
Sible Hedingham .... 55 F8
Sibsey .... 79 D6
Sibson Cambs .... 65 E7
  Leics .... 63 D7
Sibthorpe .... 77 E7
Sibton .... 57 C7

Sibton Green .... 57 B7
Sicklesmere .... 56 C2
Sicklinghall .... 95 E6
Sid .... 11 F6
Sidbury Devon .... 11 E6
  Shrops .... 61 F6
Sidcot .... 23 D6
Sidcup .... 29 B5
Siddick .... 107 F7
Siddington Ches E .... 74 B5
  Glos .... 37 E7
Sidemoor .... 50 B4
Sidestrand .... 81 D8
Sidford .... 11 E6
Sidlesham .... 16 E2
Sidley .... 18 E4
Sidlow .... 28 E3
Sidmouth .... 11 F6
Sigford .... 7 B5
Sigglesthorne .... 97 E7
Sighthill .... 120 B4
Sigingstone .... 21 B8
Signet .... 38 C2
Silchester .... 26 C4
Sildinis .... 155 F7
Sileby .... 64 C2
Silecroft .... 98 F3
Silfield .... 68 E4
Silian .... 46 D4
Silkstone .... 88 D3
Silkstone
  Common .... 88 D3
Silk Willoughby .... 78 E3
Silloth .... 107 D8
Sills .... 116 D4
Sillyearn .... 152 C5
Siloh .... 47 F6
Silpho .... 103 E7
Silsden .... 94 E3
Silsoe .... 53 F8
Silverburn .... 120 C5
Silverdale Lancs .... 92 B4
  Staffs .... 74 E5
Silver End .... 42 C4
Silvergate .... 81 E7
Silverhill .... 18 D4
Silverley's Green .... 57 B6
Silverstone .... 52 E4
Silverton .... 10 D4
Silvington .... 49 B8
Silwick .... 160 J4
Simm's Lane
  End .... 86 D3
Simm's Cross .... 86 F3
Simonburn .... 109 B8
Simonsbath .... 21 F6
Simonstone .... 93 F7
Simprim .... 122 E4
Simpson .... 53 F6
Simpson Cross .... 44 D3
Sinclair's Hill .... 122 D4
Sinclairston .... 112 C4
Sinderby .... 101 F8
Sinderhope .... 109 D8
Sindlesham .... 27 C5
Singdean .... 115 D8
Singleborough .... 53 F5
Singleton Lancs .... 92 F3
  W Sus .... 16 C2
Singlewell .... 29 B7
Sinkhurst Green .... 30 E2
Sinnahard .... 140 C3
Sinnington .... 103 F5
Sinton Green .... 50 C3
Sipson .... 27 B8
Sirhowy .... 35 C5
Sisland .... 69 E6
Sissinghurst .... 18 B4
Sisterpath .... 122 E3
Siston .... 23 B8
Sithney .... 2 D5
Sittingbourne .... 30 C2
Six Ashes .... 61 F7
Sixhills .... 91 F5
Six Hills .... 64 B3
Six Mile Bottom .... 55 D6
Sixpenny Handley .... 13 C7
Sizewell .... 57 C8
Skail .... 157 E10
Skaill Orkney .... 159 E5
  Orkney .... 159 G3
  Orkney .... 159 H6
Skares .... 113 C5
Skateraw .... 122 B3
Skaw .... 160 G7
Skeabost .... 149 D9
Skeabrae .... 159 F3
Skeeby .... 101 D7
Skeffington .... 64 D4
Skeffling .... 91 C7
Skegby .... 76 C4
Skegness .... 79 C8
Skelberry .... 160 M5
Skelbo .... 151 B10
Skelbrooke .... 89 C6
Skeldyke .... 79 F6
Skellingthorpe .... 78 B2
Skellister .... 160 H6
Skellow .... 89 C6
Skelmanthorpe .... 88 C3
Skelmersdale .... 86 D2
Skelmonae .... 153 E8
Skelmorlie .... 118 C1
Skelmuir .... 153 D9
Skelpick .... 157 D10
Skelton E Yorks .... 89 B8
  N Yorks .... 101 D6
  Redcar .... 102 C4
  W&F .... 108 F4
  York .... 95 D8
Skelton-on-Ure .... 95 C6
Skelwick .... 159 D5
Skelwith Bridge .... 99 D5
Skendleby .... 79 C7
Skene House .... 141 D6
Skenfrith .... 36 B1
Skerne .... 97 D6
Skeroblingarry .... 143 F8
Skerray .... 157 C9
Skerton .... 92 C4
Sketchley .... 63 E8
Sketty .... 33 F7
Skewen .... 33 E8
Skewsby .... 96 B2
Skeyton .... 81 E8
Skiag Bridge .... 156 G5
Skibo Castle .... 151 C10
Skidbrooke .... 91 E8
Skidbrooke North
  End .... 91 E8
Skidby .... 97 F6

Skilgate .... 10 B4
Skillington .... 65 B5
Skinburness .... 107 D8
Skinflats .... 127 F8
Skinidin .... 148 D7
Skinnet .... 157 C8
Skinningrove .... 103 B5
Skipness .... 145 H7
Skippool .... 92 E3
Skipsea .... 97 D7
Skipsea Brough .... 97 D7
Skipton .... 94 D2
Skipton-on-Swale 95 B6
Skipwith .... 96 F2
Skirbeck .... 79 E6
Skirbeck Quarter .... 79 E6
Skirlaugh .... 97 F7
Skirling .... 120 F3
Skirmett .... 39 F7
Skirpenbeck .... 96 D3
Skirwith .... 109 F6
Skirza .... 158 D5
Skulamus .... 149 F11
Skullomie .... 157 C9
Skyborry Green .... 48 B4
Skye of Curr .... 139 B5
Skyreholme .... 94 C3
Slackhall .... 87 F8
Slackhead .... 152 B4
Slad .... 37 D5
Slade Devon .... 20 E4
  Pembs .... 44 D4
Slade Green .... 29 B6
Slaggyford .... 109 D6
Slaidburn .... 93 D7
Slaithwaite .... 87 C8
Slaley .... 110 D2
Slamannan .... 119 B8
Slapton Bucks .... 40 B2
  Devon .... 7 E6
  Northants .... 52 E4
Slatepit Dale .... 76 C3
Slattocks .... 87 D6
Slaugham .... 17 B6
Slaughterford .... 24 B3
Slawston .... 64 E4
Sleaford Hants .... 27 F6
  Lincs .... 78 E3
Sleagill .... 99 C7
Sleapford .... 61 C6
Sledge Green .... 50 F3
Sledmere .... 96 C5
Sleightholme .... 100 C4
Sleights .... 103 D6
Slepe .... 13 E7
Slickly .... 158 D4
Sliddery .... 143 F10
Sligachan Hotel .... 149 F10
Slimbridge .... 36 D4
Slindon Staffs .... 74 F5
  W Sus .... 16 D3
Slinfold .... 28 F2
Sling .... 83 E6
Slingsby .... 96 B2
Slioch .... 152 E5
Slip End C Beds .... 40 C3
  Herts .... 54 F3
Slipton .... 53 B7
Slitting Mill .... 62 C4
Slochd .... 138 B4
Slockavullin .... 124 F4
Sloley .... 81 E8
Sloothby .... 79 B7
Slough .... 27 B7
Slough Green .... 17 B6
Sluggan .... 138 B4
Slumbay .... 149 E13
Slyfield .... 27 D7
Slyne .... 92 C4
Smailholm .... 122 F2
Smallbridge .... 87 C7
Smallburgh .... 69 B6
Smallburn
  Aberds .... 153 D10
  E Ayrs .... 113 B6
Small Dole .... 17 C6
Smalley .... 76 E4
Smallfield .... 28 E4
Small Hythe .... 19 B5
Smallridge .... 11 D8
Smannell .... 25 E8
Smardale .... 100 D2
Smarden .... 30 E2
Smarden Bell .... 30 E2
Smeatharpe .... 11 C6
Smeeth .... 19 B7
Smeeton Westerby 64 E3
Smercleit .... 148 G2
Smerral .... 158 G3
Smethcote .... 62 F4
Smethwick .... 62 F4
Smirisary .... 147 D9
Smisby .... 63 C7
Smithfield .... 108 C4
Smith Green .... 92 D4
Smithincott .... 11 C5
Smith's Green .... 42 B1
Smithstown .... 149 A12
Smithton .... 151 G10
Smithy Green .... 74 B4
Smockington .... 63 F8
Smoogro .... 159 H4
Smythe's Green .... 43 C5
Snaigow House .... 133 E7
Snailbeach .... 60 D3
Snailwell .... 55 C7
Snainton .... 103 F7
Snaith .... 89 B7
Snape N Yorks .... 101 F7
  Suff .... 57 D7
Snape Green .... 85 C4
Snarestone .... 63 D7
Snarford .... 90 F4
Snargate .... 19 C7
Snave .... 19 C7
Snead .... 60 E3
Sneath Common .... 68 F4
Sneaton .... 103 D6
Sneatonthorpe .... 103 D7
Snelland .... 90 F4
Snelston .... 75 E8
Snettisham .... 80 D2
Sniseabhal .... 148 E2
Snitter .... 117 D6
Snitterby .... 90 E3
Snitterfield .... 51 D7
Snitton .... 49 B7
Snodhill .... 48 E5
Snodland .... 29 C7
Snowden Hill .... 88 D3

Snowdown .... 31 D6
Snowshill .... 51 F5
Snydale .... 88 C5
Soar Anglesey .... 82 D3
  Carms .... 33 B7
  Devon .... 6 F5
Soar-y-Mynydd .... 47 D6
Soberton .... 15 C7
Soberton Heath .... 15 C7
Sockbridge .... 99 B7
Sockburn .... 101 D8
Soham .... 55 B6
Soham Cotes .... 55 B6
Solas .... 148 A3
Soldon Cross .... 8 C5
Soldridge .... 26 F4
Sole Street Kent .... 29 C7
  Kent .... 30 E4
Solihull .... 51 B6
Sollers Dilwyn .... 49 D6
Sollers Hope .... 49 F8
Sollom .... 86 C2
Solva .... 44 C2
Somerby Leics .... 64 C4
  Lincs .... 90 D4
Somercotes .... 76 D4
Somerford .... 14 E2
Somerford Keynes .... 37 E7
Somerley .... 16 E2
Somerleyton .... 69 E7
Somersal Herbert .... 75 F8
Somersby .... 79 B6
Somersham Cambs .... 54 B4
  Suff .... 56 E4
Somerton Oxon .... 38 B4
  Som .... 12 B2
Sompting .... 17 D5
Sonning .... 27 B5
Sonning Common .... 39 F7
Sonning Eye .... 27 B5
Sontley .... 73 E7
Sopley .... 14 E2
Sopwell .... 40 D4
Sopworth .... 37 F5
Sorbie .... 105 E8
Sordale .... 158 D3
Sorisdale .... 146 E5
Sorn .... 113 B5
Sornhill .... 118 F5
Sortat .... 158 D4
Sotby .... 78 B5
Sots Hole .... 78 C4
Sotterley .... 69 F7
Soudley .... 61 B7
Soughton .... 73 C6
Soulbury .... 40 B1
Soulby .... 100 C2
Souldern .... 52 F3
Souldrop .... 53 C7
Sound Ches E .... 74 E3
  Shetland .... 160 H5
  Shetland .... 160 J6
Sound Heath .... 74 E3
Soundwell .... 23 B8
Sourhope .... 116 B4
Sourin .... 159 E5
Sourton .... 9 E7
Soutergate .... 98 F4
South Acre .... 67 C8
South Allington .... 7 F5
South Alloa .... 127 E7
Southam Glos .... 37 B6
  Warks .... 52 C2
South Ambersham .... 16 B3
Southampton .... 14 C5
South Anston .... 89 F6
South Ascot .... 27 C7
South
  Ballachulish .... 130 D4
South Balloch .... 112 E3
South Bank .... 102 B3
South Barrow .... 12 B4
South Beach .... 70 D4
South Benfleet .... 42 F3
South Bersted .... 16 D3
Southborough .... 29 E6
Southbourne BCP .... 14 E2
  W Sus .... 15 D8
South Brent .... 6 C4
South Brewham .... 24 F2
South Broomhill .... 117 E8
Southburgh .... 68 D2
South Burlingham .... 99 D5
Southburn .... 97 D5
South Cadbury .... 12 B4
South Cairn .... 104 C3
South Carlton .... 78 B2
South Cave .... 96 F5
South Cerney .... 37 E7
South Chard .... 11 D8
South Charlton .... 117 B7
South Cheriton .... 12 B4
Southchurch .... 43 F5
South Cliffe .... 96 F4
South Clifton .... 77 B8
South
  Cockerington .... 91 F7
South Cornelly .... 34 F2
Southcott .... 25 D6
Southcourt .... 39 C8
South Cove .... 69 F7
South Creagan .... 130 E3
South Creake .... 80 D4
South Croxton .... 64 C3
South Croydon .... 28 C4
South Dalton .... 97 E5
South Darenth .... 29 C6
Southdean .... 116 D2
South Duffield .... 96 F2
Southease .... 17 D8
South Elkington .... 91 F6
South Elmsall .... 89 C5
South End Bucks .... 40 B1
  N Lincs .... 90 B5
  W&F .... 92 C2
Southend Argyll .... 143 H7
  W Berks .... 26 B2
  Wilts .... 25 D7
Southend-on-Sea .... 42 F4
Southernden .... 30 E2
Southerndown .... 21 B7
Southerness .... 107 D6
Southery .... 67 E6
South Erradale .... 149 A12
Southerton .... 11 E6
South Fambridge .... 42 E4
South Fawley .... 38 F3
South Ferriby .... 90 B4

Southfield .... 111 B5
Southfleet .... 29 B7
South Garth .... 160 D7
South Garvan .... 130 B3
Southgate Ceredig .... 46 B4
  London .... 41 E5
  Norf .... 81 E7
  Swansea .... 33 F6
South Glendale .... 148 G2
South Godstone .... 28 E4
South Gorley .... 14 C2
South Green Essex .... 42 E2
  Kent .... 30 C2
South-haa .... 160 E5
South Ham .... 26 D4
South
  Hanningfield .... 42 E3
South Harting .... 15 C8
South Hatfield .... 41 D5
South Hayling .... 15 E8
South Hazelrigg .... 123 F6
South Heath .... 40 D2
South Heighton .... 17 D8
South Hetton .... 111 E6
South Hiendley .... 88 C4
South Hill .... 5 B8
South Hinksey .... 39 D5
South Hole .... 8 B4
South Holme .... 96 B2
South Holmwood .... 28 E2
South Hornchurch .... 41 F8
South Hykeham .... 78 C2
South Hylton .... 111 D6
South Kelsey .... 90 E4
South Kessock .... 151 G9
South
  Killingholme .... 91 C5
South Kilvington .... 102 F2
South Kilworth .... 64 F3
South Kirkby .... 88 C5
South Kirkton .... 141 D6
South Kiscadale .... 143 F11
South Kyme .... 78 E4
South Lancing .... 17 D5
South Leigh .... 38 D3
South Leverton .... 89 F8
South Littleton .... 51 E5
South Lopham .... 68 F3
South Luffenham .... 65 D6
South Malling .... 17 C8
South Marston .... 38 F1
South Middleton .... 117 B5
South Milford .... 95 F7
South Millbrook .... 153 D8
South
  Molton .... 10 B2
South Moreton .... 39 F5
South Mundham .... 16 D2
South Muskham .... 77 D7
South Newbald .... 96 F5
South Newington .... 52 F2
South Newton .... 25 F5
South Normanton .... 76 D4
South Norwood .... 28 C4
South Nutfield .... 28 E4
South Ockendon .... 42 F1
South Ormsby .... 79 B6
Southorpe .... 65 D7
South
  Otterington .... 102 F1
South Owersby .... 90 E4
Southowram .... 88 B2
South Oxhey .... 40 E4
South Perrott .... 12 D2
South Petherton .... 12 C2
South Petherwin .... 8 F5
South Pickenham .... 67 D8
South Pool .... 7 E5
Southport .... 85 C4
South Port .... 125 C6
Southpunds .... 160 L6
South Radworthy .... 21 F6
South Rauceby .... 78 E3
South Raynham .... 80 E4
Southrepps .... 81 D8
South Reston .... 91 F8
Southrey .... 78 C4
South Runcton .... 67 D6
South Scarle .... 77 C8
Southsea .... 15 E7
South Shian .... 130 E3
South Shields .... 111 C6
South Shore .... 92 F3
South Somercotes 91 E8
South Stainley .... 95 C6
South Stainmore .... 100 C3
South Stifford .... 29 B7
Southstoke .... 24 C2
South Stoke Oxon .... 39 F5
  W Sus .... 16 D4
South Street E Sus .... 17 C7
  Kent .... 30 C4
  London .... 28 D5
South Tawton .... 9 E8
South Thoresby .... 79 B7
South Tidworth .... 25 E7
Southtown Norf .... 69 D8
  Orkney .... 159 J5
South Town .... 26 F4
South View .... 26 D4
Southwaite .... 108 E4
South Walsham .... 69 C6
Southwark .... 28 B4
South
  Warnborough .... 26 E5
South Weald .... 42 E1
South Weston .... 39 E7
South Wheatley
  Corn .... 8 E4
  Notts .... 89 F8
South Whiteness .... 160 J5
Southwick Hants .... 15 D7
  Northants .... 65 E7
  T&W .... 111 D6

Southwick continued
  Wilts .... 24 D3
  W Sus .... 17 D6
South Widcombe .... 23 D7
South Wigston .... 64 E2
South Willingham .... 91 F5
South Wingfield .... 76 D3
South Witham .... 65 C6
Southwold .... 57 B9
South Wonston .... 26 F2
Southwood Norf .... 69 D6
  Som .... 23 F7
South Woodham
  Ferrers .... 42 E4
South Wootton .... 67 B6
South Wraxall .... 24 C3
South Zeal .... 9 E8
Soval Lodge .... 155 E8
Sowber Gate .... 102 F1
Sowerby N Yorks .... 102 F1
  W Yorks .... 87 B8
Sowerby Bridge .... 87 B8
Sowerby Row .... 108 F3
Sowood .... 87 C8
Sowton .... 10 E4
Soyal .... 151 B8
Spacey Houses .... 95 D6
Spa Common .... 81 D8
Spadeadam Farm 109 B5
Spalding .... 66 B2
Spaldington .... 96 F3
Spaldwick .... 54 B2
Spalford .... 77 C8
Spanby .... 78 F3
Sparham .... 68 C3
Spark Bridge .... 99 F5
Sparkford .... 12 B4
Sparkhill .... 62 F4
Sparkwell .... 6 D3
Sparrow Green .... 68 C2
Sparrowpit .... 87 F8
Sparsholt Hants .... 26 F2
  Oxon .... 38 F3
Spartylea .... 109 E8
Spaunton .... 103 F5
Spaxton .... 22 F4
Spean Bridge .... 136 F5
Spear Hill .... 16 C5
Speen Bucks .... 39 E7
  W Berks .... 26 C2
Speeton .... 97 B7
Speke .... 86 F2
Speldhurst .... 29 E6
Spellbrook .... 41 C7
Spelsbury .... 38 B3
Spencers Wood .... 26 C5
Spennithorne .... 101 F6
Spennymoor .... 111 F5
Spetchley .... 50 D3
Spetisbury .... 13 D7
Spexhall .... 69 F6
Spey Bay .... 152 B3
Speybridge .... 139 B6
Speyview .... 152 D2
Spilsby .... 79 C7
Spindlestone .... 123 F7
Spinkhill .... 76 B4
Spinningdale .... 151 C9
Spirthill .... 24 B4
Spital Hill .... 89 E7
Spital in the Street 90 F3
Spithurst .... 17 C8
Spittal Dumfries .... 105 D7
  E Loth .... 121 B7
  Highld .... 158 E3
  Northumb .... 123 D6
  Pembs .... 44 C4
  Stirling .... 126 D4
Spittalfield .... 133 E8
Spittal of
  Glenmuick .... 140 F2
Spittal of
  Glenshee .... 133 B8
Spixworth .... 68 C5
Splayne's Green .... 17 B8
Spofforth .... 95 D6
Spondon .... 76 F4
Spon End .... 51 B8
Spon Green .... 73 C6
Spooner Row .... 68 E3
Sporle .... 67 C8
Spott .... 122 B2
Spratton .... 52 B5
Spreakley .... 27 E6
Spreyton .... 9 E8
Spridlington .... 90 F4
Springburn .... 119 C6
Springfield
  Dumfries .... 108 C3
  Essex .... 42 D3
  Fife .... 128 C5
  Moray .... 151 F13
  W Mid .... 62 D3
Springhill .... 62 D3
Springkell .... 108 B2
Springside .... 118 F3
Springthorpe .... 90 F2
Spring Vale .... 88 D2
Spring Valley .... 84 E3
Springwell .... 111 D5
Sproatley .... 97 F7
Sproston Green .... 74 C4
Sprotbrough .... 89 D6
Sproughton .... 56 E5
Sprouston .... 122 F3
Sprowston .... 68 C5
Sproxton Leics .... 65 B5
  N Yorks .... 102 F4
Spurstow .... 74 D2
Spynie .... 152 B2
Squires Gate .... 92 F3
Srannda .... 154 J5
Sronphadruig
  Lodge .... 132 B4
Stableford Shrops .... 61 E7
  Staffs .... 74 F5
Stacey Bank .... 88 E3
Stackhouse .... 93 C8
Stackpole .... 44 F4
Staddiscombe .... 6 D3
Staddlethorpe .... 90 B2
Stadhampton .... 39 E6
Stadhlaigearraidh .... 148 E2
Staffield .... 108 E5
Stafford .... 62 B3

Stagsden .... 53 E7
Stainburn Cumb .... 98 B2
  N Yorks .... 94 E5
Stainby .... 65 B6
Staincross .... 88 C4
Staindrop .... 101 B6
Staines-upon-
  Thames .... 27 B8
Stainfield Lincs .... 65 B7
  Lincs .... 78 B4
Stainforth N Yorks .... 93 C8
  S Yorks .... 89 C7
Staining .... 92 F3
Stainland .... 87 C8
Stainsacre .... 103 D7
Stainsby .... 76 C4
Stainton Durham .... 101 C5
  Mbro .... 102 C2
  N Yorks .... 101 E6
  S Yorks .... 89 E5
  W&F .... 99 B6
  W&F .... 99 F7
Stainton by
  Langworth .... 78 B3
Staintondale .... 103 E7
Stainton le Vale .... 91 E5
Stainton with
  Adgarley .... 92 B2
Stair Cumb .... 98 B4
  E Ayrs .... 112 B4
Stairhaven .... 105 D6
Staithes .... 103 C5
Stakeford .... 117 F8
Stake Pool .... 92 E4
Stalbridge .... 12 C5
Stalbridge Weston 12 C5
Stalham .... 69 B6
Stalham Green .... 69 B6
Stalisfield Green .... 30 D3
Stallingborough .... 91 C5
Stalling Busk .... 100 F4
Stalmine .... 92 E3
Stalybridge .... 87 E7
Stambourne .... 55 F8
Stambourne Green 55 F8
Stamford .... 65 D7
Stamford Bridge
  Ches W .... 73 C8
  E Yorks .... 96 D3
Stanah .... 92 E3
Stanborough .... 41 C5
Stanbridge C Beds .... 40 B2
  Dorset .... 13 D8
Stanbrook .... 50 E3
Stanbury .... 94 F3
Stand Gtr Man .... 87 D5
  N Lanark .... 119 C7
Standburn .... 120 B2
Standeford .... 62 D3
Standen .... 30 E2
Standford .... 27 F6
Standingstone .... 107 F7
Standish .... 86 C3
Standlake .... 38 D3
Standon Hants .... 14 B5
  Herts .... 41 B6
  Staffs .... 74 F5
Stane .... 119 D8
Stanfield .... 80 E5
Stanford C Beds .... 54 E2
  Kent .... 19 B8
Stanford Bishop .... 49 D8
Stanford Bridge .... 50 C2
Stanford Dingley .... 26 B3
Stanford in the
  Vale .... 38 E3
Stanford-le-Hope .... 42 F2
Stanford on Avon .... 52 B3
Stanford on Soar .... 64 B2
Stanford on Teme .... 50 C2
Stanford Rivers .... 41 D8
Stanfree .... 76 B4
Stanghow .... 102 C4
Stanground .... 66 E2
Stanhoe .... 80 D4
Stanhope Borders .... 114 B4
  Durham .... 110 F2
Stanion .... 65 F6
Stanley Derbys .... 76 E4
  Durham .... 110 D4
  Lancs .... 86 D2
  Perth .... 133 F8
  Staffs .... 75 D6
  W Yorks .... 88 B4
Stanley Common .... 76 E4
Stanley Gate .... 86 D2
Stanley Hill .... 49 E8
Stanlow .... 73 B8
Stanmer .... 17 D7
Stanmore Hants .... 15 B5
  London .... 40 E4
  W Berks .... 26 B2
Stanningley .... 94 F5
Stannington
  Northumb .... 110 B5
  S Yorks .... 88 F4
Stansbatch .... 48 C5
Stansfield .... 55 D8
Stanstead .... 56 E2
Stanstead Abbotts 41 C6
Stansted .... 29 C7
Stansted Airport .... 42 B1
Stansted
  Mountfitchet .... 41 B8
Stanton Glos .... 51 F5
  Mon .... 35 B7
  Northumb .... 117 E7
  Staffs .... 75 E8
  Suff .... 56 B3
Stanton by Bridge .... 63 B7
Stanton-by-Dale .... 76 F4
Stanton Drew .... 23 C7
Stanton
  Fitzwarren .... 38 E1
Stanton Harcourt .... 38 D4
Stanton Hill .... 76 C4
Stanton in Peak .... 76 C2
Stanton Lacy .... 49 B6
Stanton Long .... 61 E5
Stanton-on-the-
  Wolds .... 77 F6
Stanton Prior .... 23 C8
Stanton St
  Bernard .... 25 C6
Stanton St John .... 39 D5
Stanton St Quintin .... 24 B4
Stanton Street .... 56 C3

Stanton under Bardon.....63 C8
Stanton upon Hine Heath.....61 B5
Stanton Wick.....23 C8
Stanwardine in the Fields.....60 B4
Stanwardine in the Wood.....60 B4
Stanway Essex.....43 B5
Glos.....51 F5
Stanway Green.....57 B6
Stanwell.....27 B8
Stanwell Moor.....27 B8
Stanwick.....53 B7
Stanwick-St-John.....101 C6
Stanwix.....108 D4
Stanydale.....160 H4
Staoinebrig.....148 E2
Stape.....103 E5
Stapehill.....13 D8
Stapeley.....74 E3
Stapenhill.....63 B6
Staple Kent.....31 D6
Som.....22 E3
Staple Cross.....18 C4
Staplefield.....17 B6
Staple Fitzpaine.....11 C7
Stapleford Cambs...55 D5
Herts.....41 C6
Leics.....64 C5
Lincs.....77 D8
Notts.....76 F4
Wilts.....25 F7
Stapleford Abbotts 41 E8
Stapleford Tawney.41 E8
Staplegrove.....11 B7
Staplehay.....11 B7
Staplehurst.....29 E8
Staplers.....15 F6
Stapleton Bristol....23 B8
Cumb.....108 B5
Hereford.....48 C5
Leics.....63 E8
N Yorks.....101 C7
Shrops.....60 D4
Som.....12 B2
Stapley.....11 C6
Staploe.....54 C2
Staplow.....49 E8
Star Anglesey.....82 D5
Fife.....128 D5
Pembs.....45 F4
Som.....23 D6
Stara.....159 F3
Starbeck.....95 D6
Starbotton.....94 B2
Starcross.....10 F4
Stareton.....51 B8
Starkholmes.....76 D3
Starlings Green.....55 F5
Starston.....68 F5
Startforth.....101 C5
Startley.....37 F6
Stathe.....11 B8
Stathern.....77 F7
Station Town.....111 F7
Staughton Green..54 C2
Staughton Highway.....54 C2
Staunton Glos....36 B4
Glos.....36 C2
Staunton in the Vale.....77 E8
Staunton on Arrow.....49 C5
Staunton on Wye.49 E5
Staveley Derbys...76 B4
N Yorks.....95 C6
W&F.....99 E6
W&F.....99 F5
Staverton Devon...7 C5
Glos.....37 B5
Wilts.....24 C3
W Nhants.....52 C3
Staverton Bridge..37 B5
Stawell.....23 F5
Staxigoe.....158 E5
Staxton.....97 B6
Staylittle.....59 E5
Staynall.....92 E3
Staythorpe.....77 D7
Stean.....94 B3
Stearsby.....96 B2
Steart.....22 E4
Stebbing.....42 B2
Stebbing Green.....42 B2
Stedham.....16 B2
Steele Road.....115 E8
Steen's Bridge.....49 D7
Steep.....15 B8
Steeple Dorset....13 F7
Essex.....43 D5
Steeple Ashton....24 D4
Steeple Aston.....38 B4
Steeple Barton....38 B4
Steeple Bumpstead..55 E7
Steeple Claydon.39 B6
Steeple Gidding..65 F8
Steeple Langford.24 F5
Steeple Morden.54 E3
Steep Marsh.....15 B8
Steeton.....94 E3
Stein.....148 C7
Steinmanhill.....153 D7
Stelling Minnis..30 E5
Stemster.....158 D3
Stemster House.158 D3
Stenalees.....4 D5
Stenhousemuir.127 F7
Stenigot.....91 F6
Stenness.....160 F4
Stenso.....159 F4
Stenson.....63 B7
Stenton E Loth....122 B2
Fife.....128 E4
Stenwith.....77 F8
Stepaside.....32 D2
Stepping Hill.....87 F7
Steppingley.....53 F8
Stepps.....119 C6
Sterndale Moor..75 C8
Sternfield.....57 C7
Sterridge.....20 E4
Stert.....24 D5
Stetchworth.....55 D7

Stevenage.....41 B5
Stevenston.....118 E2
Steventon Hants...26 E3
Oxon.....38 E4
Stevington.....53 D7
Stewartby.....53 E8
Stewarton Argyll..143 G7
E Ayrs.....118 E4
Stewkley.....40 B1
Stewton.....91 F7
Steyne Cross.....15 F7
Steyning.....17 C5
Steynton.....44 E4
Stibb.....8 C4
Stibbard.....81 E5
Stibb Cross.....9 C6
Stibb Green.....25 C7
Stibbington.....65 E7
Stichill.....122 F3
Sticker.....4 D4
Stickford.....79 D6
Sticklepath.....9 E8
Stickney.....79 D6
Stiffkey.....81 C5
Stifford's Bridge..50 E2
Stillingfleet.....95 E8
Stillington N Yorks..95 C8
Stockton.....102 B1
Stilton.....65 F8
Stinchcombe.....36 E4
Stinsford.....12 E5
Stirchley.....61 D7
Stirkoke House...158 E5
Stirling Aberds...153 D11
Stirling.....127 E6
Stisted.....42 B3
Stithians.....3 C6
Stittenham.....151 D9
Stivichall.....51 B8
Stixwould.....78 C4
Stoak.....73 B8
Stobieside.....119 F6
Stobo.....120 F4
Stoborough.....13 F7
Stoborough Green..13 F7
Stobshiel.....121 C7
Stobswood.....117 E8
Stock.....42 E2
Stockbridge.....25 F8
Stockbury.....30 C2
Stockcross.....26 C2
Stockdalewath...108 E3
Stockerston.....64 E5
Stock Green.....50 D4
Stockheath.....15 D8
Stockiemuir.....126 F4
Stockingford.....63 E7
Stocking Pelham..41 B7
Stockland.....11 D7
Stockland Bristol...22 E4
Stockleigh English 10 D3
Stockleigh Pomeroy.....10 D3
Stockley.....24 C5
Stocklinch.....11 C8
Stockport.....87 E6
Stocksbridge.....88 E3
Stocksfield.....110 C3
Stockton Hereford...49 C7
Norf.....69 E6
Shrops.....60 D2
Shrops.....61 E7
Warks.....52 C2
Wilts.....24 F4
Stockton Heath...86 F4
Stockton-on-Tees.....102 C2
Stockton on Teme..50 C2
Stockton on the Forest.....96 D2
Stock Wood.....50 D5
Stodmarsh.....31 C6
Stody.....81 D6
Stoer.....156 G3
Stoford Som.....12 C3
Wilts.....25 F5
Stogumber.....22 F2
Stogursey.....22 E4
Stoke Devon.....8 B4
Hants.....15 D8
Hants.....26 D2
Medway.....30 B2
Suff.....57 E5
Stoke Abbott.....12 D2
Stoke Albany.....64 F5
Stoke Ash.....56 B5
Stoke Bardolph....77 E6
Stoke Bliss.....49 C8
Stoke Bruerne.....52 E5
Stoke by Clare....55 E8
Stoke-by-Nayland 56 F3
Stoke Canon.....10 E4
Stoke Charity.....26 F2
Stoke Climsland....5 B8
Stoke D'Abernon..28 D2
Stoke Doyle.....65 F7
Stoke Dry.....65 E5
Stoke Farthing....13 B8
Stoke Ferry.....67 E7
Stoke Fleming.....7 E6
Stokeford.....13 F6
Stoke Gabriel.....7 D6
Stoke Gifford.....23 B8
Stoke Golding.....63 E7
Stoke Goldington.53 E6
Stoke Green.....40 F2
Stokeham.....77 B7
Stoke Hammond..40 B1
Stoke Heath.....61 B6
Stoke Holy Cross.68 D5
Stokeinteignhead..7 B7
Stoke Lacy.....49 E8
Stoke Lyne.....39 B5
Stoke Mandeville..39 C8
Stokenchurch.....39 E7
Stoke Newington..41 F6
Stokenham.....7 E6
Stoke on Tern....61 B6
Stoke-on-Trent...75 E5
Stoke Orchard....37 B6
Stoke Poges.....40 F2
Stoke Prior Hereford..49 D7
Worcs.....50 C4
Stoke Rivers.....20 F5
Stoke Rochford...65 B6
Stoke Row.....39 F6
Stoke St Gregory..11 B8
Stoke St Mary.....11 B7

Stoke St Michael..23 E8
Stoke St Milborough.....61 F5
Stokesay.....60 F4
Stokesby.....69 C7
Stokesley.....102 D3
Stoke sub Hamdon.....12 C2
Stoke Talmage....39 E6
Stoke Trister.....12 B5
Stoke Wake.....13 D5
Stolford.....22 E4
Stondon Massey..42 D1
Stone Bucks.....39 C7
Glos.....36 E3
Kent.....19 C6
Kent.....29 B6
Staffs.....75 F6
S Yorks.....89 F6
Worcs.....50 B3
Stone Allerton...23 D6
Ston Easton.....23 D8
Stone Bridge Corner.....66 D2
Stonebroom.....76 D4
Stone Chair.....88 B2
Stone Cross E Sus...18 E3
Kent.....31 D7
Stone-edge Batch..23 B6
Stoneferry.....97 F7
Stonefield.....119 D6
Stonegate E Sus....18 C3
N Yorks.....103 D5
Stonegrave.....96 B2
Stonehaugh.....109 B7
Stonehaven.....141 F7
Stonehouse Glos....37 D5
Northumb.....109 D6
S Lanark.....119 E7
Stone House.....100 F2
Stoneleigh.....51 B8
Stonely.....54 C2
Stoner Hill.....15 B8
Stonesby.....64 B5
Stonesfield.....38 C3
Stone's Green.....43 B7
Stone Street Kent..29 D6
Suff.....56 F3
Suff.....69 F6
Stonethwaite.....98 C4
Stoneybreck.....160 N8
Stoneyburn.....120 C2
Stoney Cross.....14 C3
Stoneygate Aberds....153 E10
Leicester.....64 D3
Stoneyhills.....43 E5
Stoneykirk.....104 D4
Stoney Middleton.76 B2
Stoney Stanton...63 E8
Stoney Stoke.....24 F2
Stoney Stratton...23 F8
Stoney Stretton...60 D3
Stoneywood Aberdeen....141 C7
Falk.....127 F6
Stonganess.....160 C7
Stonham Aspal....56 D5
Stonnall.....62 D4
Stonor.....39 F7
Stonton Wyville...64 E4
Stony Cross.....50 E2
Stonyfield.....151 D9
Stony Stratford...53 E5
Stoodleigh.....10 C4
Stopes.....88 F3
Stopham.....16 C4
Stopsley.....40 B4
Stores Corner....57 E7
Storeton.....85 F4
Stornoway.....155 D9
Storridge.....50 E2
Storrington.....16 C4
Storrs.....99 E5
Storth.....99 F6
Storwood.....96 E3
Stotfield.....152 A2
Stotfold.....54 F3
Stottesdon.....61 F6
Stoughton Leics...64 D3
Sur.....27 D7
W Sus.....16 C2
Stoul.....147 B10
Stoulton.....50 E4
Stourbridge.....62 F3
Stourpaine.....13 D6
Stourport on Severn.....50 B3
Stour Provost....13 B5
Stour Row.....13 B6
Stourton Staffs....62 F2
Warks.....51 F7
Wilts.....24 F2
Stourton Caundle..12 C5
Stove Orkney.....159 E7
Shetland.....160 L6
Stoven.....69 F7
Stow Borders....121 E7
Lincs.....78 F3
Lincs.....90 F2
Stow Bardolph....67 D6
Stow Bedon.....68 E2
Stowbridge.....67 D6
Stow cum Quy....55 C6
Stowe.....48 B5
Stowe-by-Chartley.....62 B4
Stowe Green.....36 D2
Stowell.....12 B4
Stowford.....9 F6
Stowlangtoft.....56 C3
Stow Longa.....54 B2
Stow Maries.....42 E4
Stowmarket.....56 D4
Stow-on-the-Wold.....38 B1
Stowting.....30 E5
Stowupland.....56 D4
Straad.....145 G9
Strachan.....141 E5
Stradbroke.....57 B6
Stradishall.....55 D8
Stradsett.....67 D6
Stragglethorpe....78 D2
Straid.....112 E1
Straith.....113 F8
Straiton Edin.....121 C5
S Ayrs.....112 D3
Straloch Aberds....141 B7

Straloch continued
Perth.....133 C7
Stramshall.....75 F7
Strang.....84 E3
Stranraer.....104 C4
Stratfield Mortimer.....26 C4
Stratfield Saye....26 C4
Stratfield Turgis..26 D4
Stratford.....41 F6
Stratford St Andrew.....57 C7
Stratford St Mary..56 F4
Stratford Sub Castle.....25 F6
Stratford Tony....13 B8
Stratford-upon-Avon.....51 D6
Strath Highld.....149 A12
Highld.....158 E4
Strathan Highld....156 G3
Highld.....157 C8
Strathaven.....119 E7
Strathblane.....119 B5
Strathcanaird....156 J4
Strathcarron.....150 G2
Strathcoil.....124 B2
Strathdon.....140 C2
Strathellie.....153 B10
Strathkinness....129 C6
Strathmashie House.....137 E8
Strathmiglo.....128 C4
Strathmore Lodge.....158 F3
Strathpeffer.....150 F7
Strathrannoch...150 D6
Strathtay.....133 D6
Strathvaich Lodge.....150 D6
Strathwhillan....143 E11
Strathy.....157 C11
Strathyre.....126 C4
Stratton Corn.....8 D4
Dorset.....12 E4
Glos.....37 D7
Stratton Audley....39 B6
Stratton on the Fosse.....23 D8
Stratton St Margaret.....38 F1
Stratton St Michael.....68 E5
Stratton Strawless 81 E8
Stravithie.....129 C7
Streat.....17 C7
Streatham.....28 B4
Streatley C Beds....40 B3
W Berks.....39 F5
Street Lancs.....92 D5
N Yorks.....103 D5
Som.....23 F6
Street End Kent....30 D5
W Sus.....16 E2
Street Gate.....110 D5
Streethay.....62 C5
Streetlam.....101 E8
Streetly.....62 E4
Street Lydan.....73 F8
Streetly End.....55 E7
Strefford.....60 F4
Strelley.....76 E5
Strensall.....96 C2
Stretcholt.....22 E4
Strete.....7 E6
Stretford.....87 E6
Strethall.....55 F5
Stretham.....55 B6
Strettington.....16 D2
Stretton Ches W....73 D8
Derbys.....76 C3
Rutland.....65 C6
Staffs.....62 C2
Staffs.....63 B6
Warr.....86 F4
Stretton Grandison.....49 E8
Stretton-on-Dunsmore.....52 B2
Stretton-on-Fosse 51 F7
Stretton Sugwas..49 E6
Stretton under Fosse.....63 F8
Stretton Westwood.....61 E5
Strichen.....153 C9
Strines.....87 F7
Stringston.....22 E3
Strixton.....53 C7
Stroat.....36 E2
Stromeferry.....149 E13
Stromemore.....149 E13
Stromness.....159 H3
Stronaba.....136 F5
Stronachlachar...126 C3
Stronchreggan...130 B4
Stronchrubie.....156 H5
Strone Argyll.....145 E10
Highld.....136 F4
Highld.....137 B8
Invclyd.....145 F11
Stronmilchan....125 C7
Strontian.....130 C2
Strood.....29 C8
Strood Green Sur...28 E3
W Sus.....16 B4
W Sus.....28 F2
Stroud Glos.....37 D5
Hants.....15 B8
Stroud Green.....42 E4
Stroxton.....78 F2
Struan Highld.....149 E8
Perth.....133 C5
Strubby.....91 F8
Strumpshaw.....69 D6
Strutherhill.....119 E7
Struy.....150 H6
Stryt-issa.....73 E6
Stuartfield.....153 D9
Stubbington.....15 D6
Stubbins.....87 C5
Stubbs Cross.....19 B6
Stubbs Green.....69 E6
Stubb's Green....69 E5
Stubhampton.....13 C7
Stub Place.....98 E2
Stubton.....77 E8

Stuckgowan.....126 D2
Stuckton.....14 C2
Stud Green.....27 B6
Studham.....40 C3
Studland.....13 F8
Studley Warks.....51 C5
Wilts.....24 B4
Studley Roger....95 B5
Stump Cross.....55 E6
Stuntney.....55 B6
Sturbridge.....74 F5
Sturmer.....55 E7
Sturminster Marshall.....13 D7
Sturminster Newton.....13 C5
Sturry.....31 C5
Sturton.....90 D2
Sturton by Stow..90 F2
Sturton le Steeple.89 F8
Stuston.....56 B5
Stutton N Yorks....95 E7
Suff.....57 F5
Styal.....87 F6
Styrrup.....89 E7
Suainebost.....155 A10
Suardail.....155 D9
Succoth Aberds....152 E4
Argyll.....125 E8
Suckley.....50 D2
Suckquoy.....159 K5
Sudborough.....65 F6
Sudbourne.....57 D8
Sudbrook Lincs....78 E2
Mon.....36 F2
Sudbrooke.....78 B3
Sudbury Derbys....75 F8
London.....40 F4
Suff.....56 E2
Suddie.....151 F9
Sudgrove.....37 D6
Suffield Norf.....81 D8
N Yorks.....103 E7
Sugnall.....74 F4
Suladale.....149 C8
Sulaisiadar.....155 D10
Sulby.....84 C3
Sulgrave.....52 E3
Sulham.....26 B4
Sulhamstead.....26 C4
Sulland.....159 D6
Sullington.....16 C4
Sullom.....160 F5
Sullom Voe Oil Terminal.....160 F5
Sully.....22 C3
Sumburgh.....160 N6
Summer Bridge...94 C5
Summercourt.....4 D3
Summerfield.....80 D3
Summergangs....97 F7
Summer-house...101 C7
Summerleaze....35 F8
Summersdale.....16 D2
Summerseat.....87 C5
Summertown.....39 D5
Summit.....87 D7
Sunbury-on-Thames.....28 C2
Sundaywell.....113 F8
Sunderland Argyll..142 B3
Cumb.....107 F8
T&W.....111 D6
Sunderland Bridge.....111 F5
Sundhope.....115 B6
Sundon Park....40 B3
Sundridge.....29 D5
Sunipol.....146 F6
Sunk Island.....91 C6
Sunningdale.....27 C7
Sunninghill.....27 C7
Sunningwell.....38 D4
Sunniside Durham.110 F4
T&W.....110 D5
Sunnyhurst.....86 B4
Sunnylaw.....127 E6
Sunnyside.....28 F4
Sunton.....25 D7
Surbiton.....28 C2
Surby.....84 E2
Surfleet.....66 B2
Surfleet Seas End.66 B2
Surlingham.....69 D6
Sustead.....81 D7
Susworth.....90 D2
Sutcombe.....8 C5
Suton.....68 E3
Sutors of Cromarty.....151 E11
Sutterby.....79 B6
Sutterton.....79 F5
Sutton Cambs.....54 B5
C Beds.....54 E3
Kent.....31 E7
London.....28 C3
Mers.....86 E3
Norf.....69 B6
Notts.....77 F7
N Yorks.....89 B5
Oxon.....38 D4
Pboro.....65 E8
Shrops.....61 F7
Shrops.....74 F3
Som.....23 F8
Staffs.....61 B7
Suff.....57 E7
Sur.....27 E8
S Yorks.....89 C6
W Sus.....16 C3
Sutton at Hone...29 B6
Sutton Bassett....64 E4
Sutton Benger....24 B4
Sutton Bonington.64 B2
Sutton Bridge....66 B4
Sutton Cheney....63 D8
Sutton Coldfield...62 E5
Sutton Courtenay.39 E5
Sutton Crosses....66 B4
Sutton Grange....95 B5
Sutton Green.....27 D8
Sutton Howgrave.95 B6
Sutton in Ashfield.76 D4
Sutton-in-Craven 94 E3
Sutton Ings.....97 F7
Sutton in the Elms.64 E2
Sutton Lane Ends..75 B6
Sutton Leach.....86 E3

Sutton Maddock...61 D7
Sutton Mallet....23 F5
Sutton Mandeville.13 B7
Sutton Manor....86 E3
Sutton Montis....12 B4
Sutton on Hull....97 F7
Sutton on Sea....91 F9
Sutton-on-the-Forest.....95 C8
Sutton on the Hill.76 F2
Sutton on Trent...77 C7
Sutton St Edmund.66 C3
Sutton St James..66 C3
Sutton St Nicholas 49 E7
Sutton Scarsdale..76 C4
Sutton Scotney....26 F2
Sutton under Brailes.....51 F8
Sutton-under-Whitestonecliffe 102 F2
Sutton upon Derwent.....96 E3
Sutton Valence...30 E2
Sutton Veny.....24 E3
Sutton Waldron...13 C6
Sutton Weaver....74 B2
Sutton Wick.....23 D7
Swaby.....79 B6
Swadlincote.....63 C7
Swaffham.....67 D8
Swaffham Bulbeck 55 C6
Swaffham Prior...55 C6
Swafield.....81 D8
Swainby.....102 D2
Swainshill.....49 E6
Swainsthorpe....68 D5
Swainswick.....24 C2
Swalcliffe.....51 F8
Swalecliffe.....30 C5
Swallow.....91 D5
Swallowcliffe....13 B7
Swallowfield.....26 C5
Swallownest.....89 F5
Swallows Cross...42 E2
Swanage.....13 G8
Swanbister.....159 H4
Swanbourne.....39 B8
Swan Green Ches W...74 B4
Suff.....57 B6
Swanland.....90 B3
Swanley.....29 C6
Swanley Village...29 C6
Swanmore.....15 C6
Swannington Leics..63 C8
Norf.....68 C4
Swanscombe.....29 B7
Swansea = Abertawe.....33 E7
Swanton Abbott..81 E8
Swanton Morley..68 C3
Swanton Novers..81 D6
Swanton Street...30 D2
Swanwick Derbys..76 D4
Hants.....15 D6
Swarby.....78 E3
Swardeston.....68 D5
Swarister.....160 E7
Swarkestone.....63 B7
Swarland.....117 D7
Swarland Estate..117 D7
Swarthmoor.....92 B2
Swathwick.....76 C3
Swaton.....78 F4
Swavesey.....54 C4
Sway.....14 E3
Swayfield.....65 B6
Swaythling.....14 C5
Sweet Green....49 C8
Sweetham.....10 E3
Sweethouse.....5 C5
Sweffling.....57 C7
Swepstone.....63 C7
Swerford.....51 F8
Swettenham.....74 C5
Swetton.....94 B4
Swffryd.....35 E6
Swiftsden.....18 C4
Swilland.....57 D5
Swillington.....95 F6
Swimbridge.....9 B8
Swimbridge Newland.....20 F5
Swinbrook.....38 C2
Swinderby.....77 C8
Swindon Glos.....37 B6
Staffs.....62 E2
Swindon.....38 F1
Swine.....97 F7
Swinefleet.....89 B8
Swineshead Bedford.....53 C8
Lincs.....78 E5
Swineside.....101 F5
Swiney.....158 G4
Swinford Leics....52 B3
Oxon.....38 D4
Swingate.....76 E5
Swingfield Minnis.31 E6
Swingfield Street..31 E6
Swinhoe.....117 B8
Swinhope.....91 E6
Swining.....160 G6
Swinithwaite.....101 F5
Swinnie.....116 C2
Swinnow Moor....94 F5
Swinscoe.....75 E8
Swinside Hall....116 C3
Swinstead.....65 B7
Swinton Borders...122 E4
Gtr Man.....87 D5
N Yorks.....94 B5
N Yorks.....96 B3
S Yorks.....88 E5
Swintonmill.....122 E4
Swithland.....64 C2
Swordale.....151 E8
Swordland.....147 B10
Swordly.....157 C10
Sworton Heath...86 F4
Swydd-ffynnon...47 C5
Swynnerton.....75 F5
Swyre.....12 F3
Sychdyn.....59 D6
Syde.....37 C6
Sydenham London..28 B4
Oxon.....39 D7
Sydenham Damerel.....6 B2

Syderstone.....80 D4
Sydling St Nicholas.....12 E4
Sydmonton.....26 D2
Syerston.....77 E7
Syke.....87 C6
Sykehouse.....89 C7
Sykes.....93 D6
Syleham.....57 B6
Sylen.....33 D6
Symbister.....160 G7
Symington S Ayrs..118 F3
S Lanark.....120 F2
Symondsbury....12 E2
Symonds Yat....36 C2
Synod Inn.....46 D3
Syre.....157 E9
Syreford.....37 B7
Syresham.....52 E4
Syston Leics.....64 C3
Lincs.....78 E2
Sytchampton.....50 C3
Sywell.....53 C6

## T

Taagan.....150 E3
Tábost.....155 A10
Tabost.....155 F8
Tackley.....38 B4
Tacleit.....154 D6
Tacolneston.....68 E4
Tadcaster.....95 E7
Taddington.....75 B8
Taddiport.....9 C6
Tadley.....26 C4
Tadlow.....54 E3
Tadmarton.....51 F8
Tadworth.....28 D3
Tafarnau-bach....35 C5
Tafarn-y-gelyn...73 C5
Tafolwern.....59 D5
Tai.....83 E7
Taibach.....34 F1
Tai-bach.....59 B8
Taigh a Ghearraidh.148 A2
Tai-mawr.....72 E3
Tain Highld.....151 C10
Highld.....158 D4
Tainant.....73 E6
Tainlon.....82 F4
Tairbeart = Tarbert.....154 G6
Tai'r-Bull.....34 B3
Tairgwaith.....33 C8
Tai-Ucha.....72 D4
Takeley.....42 B1
Takeley Street....41 B8
Talachddu.....48 F2
Talacre.....85 F2
Talardd.....59 B5
Talaton.....11 E5
Talbenny.....44 D3
Talbot Green.....34 F4
Talbot Village....13 E8
Tale.....11 D5
Talerddig.....59 D6
Talgarreg.....46 D3
Talgarth.....48 F3
Taliesin.....58 E3
Talke.....74 D5
Talkin.....109 D5
Talladale.....150 D2
Talla Linnfoots...114 B4
Tallarn Green....73 E8
Tallentire.....107 F8
Talley.....46 F5
Tallington.....65 D7
Talmine.....157 C8
Talog.....32 B4
Talsarn.....34 B1
Tal-sarn.....46 D4
Talsarnau.....71 D7
Talskiddy.....4 C4
Talwrn Anglesey...82 D4
Wrex.....73 E6
Tal-y-bont Ceredig...32 F6
Conwy.....83 E7
Gwyn.....71 E6
Gwyn.....83 D6
Talybont-on-Usk..35 B5
Tal-y-cafn.....83 D7
Talygarn.....34 F4
Talyllyn.....35 B5
Tal-y-llyn.....58 D4
Talysarn.....82 F4
Talywain.....35 D6
Tal-y-wern.....58 D5
Tame Bridge....102 D3
Tamerton Foliot..6 C2
Tamworth.....63 D6
Tandem.....88 C2
Tanden.....19 B6
Tandridge.....28 D4
Tanerdy.....33 B5
Tanfield.....110 D4
Tanfield Lea....110 D4
Tangasdal.....148 J1
Tangiers.....44 D4
Tangley.....25 D8
Tanglwst.....46 F2
Tangmere.....16 D3
Tangwick.....160 F4
Tan Hinon.....59 F5
Tankersley.....88 D4
Tankerton.....30 C5
Tan-lan Conwy....83 E7
Gwyn.....71 C7
Tannach.....158 F5
Tannachie.....141 F6
Tannadice.....134 D4
Tannington.....57 C6
Tansley.....76 D3
Tansley Knoll....76 C3
Tansor.....65 E7
Tantobie.....110 D4
Tanton.....102 C3
Tanworth-in-Arden.....51 B6
Tan-y-bwlch.....71 C7
Tan-y-fron.....72 C3
Tan-y-graig Anglesey.....82 D5
Gwyn.....70 D4
Tanygrisiau.....71 C7
Tan-y-groes.....45 E4

Tan-y-pistyll.....59 B7
Tan-yr-allt.....82 F4
Tanyrhydiau.....47 C6
Taobh a Chaolais.148 G2
Taobh a'Ghlinne..155 F8
Taobh a Thuath Loch Aineort.....148 F2
Taobh a Tuath Loch Baghasdail.148 F2
Taobh Tuath.....154 J4
Taplow.....40 F2
Tapton.....76 B3
Tarbat House.....151 D10
Tarbert Argyll.....143 C7
Argyll.....144 E5
Argyll.....145 G7
Tarbert = Tairbeart.....154 G6
Tarbet Argyll.....126 D2
Highld.....147 B10
Highld.....156 F4
Tarbock Green....86 F2
Tarbolton.....112 B4
Tarbrax.....120 D3
Tardebigge.....50 C5
Tarfside.....134 B4
Tarland.....140 D3
Tarleton.....86 B2
Tarlogie.....151 C10
Tarlscough.....86 C2
Tarlton.....37 E6
Tarnbrook.....93 D5
Tarporley.....74 C2
Tarr.....22 F3
Tarrant Crawford..13 D7
Tarrant Gunville..13 C7
Tarrant Hinton....13 C7
Tarrant Keyneston.13 D7
Tarrant Launceston.....13 D7
Tarrant Monkton..13 D7
Tarrant Rawston..13 D7
Tarrant Rushton..13 D7
Tarrel.....151 C11
Tarring Neville....17 D8
Tarrington.....49 E8
Tarsappie.....128 B3
Tarskavaig.....149 H10
Tarves.....153 E8
Tarvie Highld.....150 F7
Perth.....133 C7
Tarvin.....73 C8
Tasburgh.....68 E5
Tasley.....61 E6
Taston.....38 B3
Tatenhill.....63 B6
Tathall End.....53 E6
Tatham.....93 C6
Tathwell.....91 F7
Tatling End.....40 F3
Tatsfield.....28 D5
Tattenhall.....73 D8
Tattenhoe.....53 F6
Tatterford.....80 E4
Tattersett.....80 D4
Tattershall.....78 D5
Tattershall Bridge.78 D4
Tattershall Thorpe.78 D5
Tattingstone.....56 F5
Tatworth.....11 D8
Taunton.....11 B7
Taverham.....68 C4
Tavernspite.....32 C2
Tavistock.....6 B2
Taw Green.....9 E8
Tawstock.....9 B7
Taxal.....75 B7
Tay Bridge.....129 B6
Tayinloan.....143 D7
Taymouth Castle.132 E4
Taynish.....144 E6
Taynton Glos.....36 B4
Oxon.....38 C2
Taynuilt.....125 B6
Tayport.....129 B6
Tayvallich.....144 E6
Tealby.....91 E5
Tealing.....134 F4
Teangue.....149 H11
Teanna Mhachair.148 B2
Tebay.....99 D8
Tebworth.....40 B2
Tedburn St Mary..10 E3
Teddington Glos...50 F4
London.....28 B2
Tedstone Delamere.....49 D8
Tedstone Wafre...49 D8
Teeton.....52 B4
Teffont Evias....24 F4
Teffont Magna...24 F4
Tegryn.....45 F4
Teigh.....65 C5
Teigncombe.....9 F8
Teigngrace.....7 B6
Teignmouth.....7 B7
Telford.....61 D6
Telham.....18 D4
Tellisford.....24 D3
Telscombe.....17 D8
Telscombe Cliffs..17 D7
Templand.....114 F3
Temple Corn.....5 B6
Glasgow.....118 C5
Midloth.....121 D6
Temple Balsall...51 B7
Temple Bar Carms..33 C6
Ceredig.....46 D4
Temple Cloud....23 D8
Temple Combe....12 B5
Temple Ewell....31 E6
Temple Grafton...51 D6
Temple Guiting...37 B7
Templehall.....128 E4
Temple Herdewyke.51 D8
Temple Hirst....89 B7
Temple Normanton.....76 C4
Temple Sowerby...99 B8
Templeton Devon..10 C3
Pembs.....32 C2
Templeton Bridge.10 C3
Templetown.....110 D4
Tempsford.....54 D2
Tenbury Wells....49 C7
Tenby = Dinbych-y-Pysgod.....32 D2
Tendring.....43 B7

Tendring Green...43 B7
Ten Mile Bank...67 E6
Tenston.....159 G3
Tenterden.....19 B5
Terling.....42 C3
Ternhill.....74 F3
Terregles Banks..107 B6
Terrick.....39 D8
Terrington.....96 B2
Terrington St Clement.....66 C5
Terrington St John.....66 C5
Teston.....29 D8
Testwood.....14 C4
Tetbury.....37 E5
Tetbury Upton....37 E5
Tetchill.....73 F7
Tetcott.....8 E5
Tetford.....79 B6
Tetney.....91 D7
Tetney Lock.....91 D7
Tetsworth.....39 D6
Tettenhall.....62 E2
Teuchan.....153 E10
Teversal.....76 C4
Teversham.....55 D5
Teviothead.....115 D7
Tewel.....141 F7
Tewin.....41 C5
Tewkesbury.....50 F3
Teynham.....30 C3
Thackthwaite....98 B3
Thainston.....135 B6
Thakeham.....16 C5
Thame.....39 D7
Thames Ditton...28 C2
Thames Haven...42 F3
Thamesmead.....41 F7
Thanington.....30 D5
Thankerton.....120 F2
Tharston.....68 E4
Thatcham.....26 C3
Thatto Heath....86 E3
Thaxted.....55 F7
The Aird.....149 C9
Theakston.....101 F8
Thealby.....90 C2
Theale Som.....23 E6
W Berks.....26 B4
The Arms.....67 E8
The Bage.....48 E4
The Balloch.....127 C7
The Barony.....159 F3
Theberton.....57 C8
The Bog.....60 E3
The Bourne.....27 E6
The Braes.....149 E10
The Broad.....49 C6
The Butts.....24 E2
The Camp Glos....37 D6
Herts.....40 D4
The Chequer.....73 E8
The City.....39 E7
The Common.....25 F7
The Craigs.....150 B7
The Cronk.....84 C3
Theddingworth...64 F3
Theddlethorpe All Saints.....91 F8
Theddlethorpe St Helen.....91 F8
The Dell.....69 E7
The Den.....118 D3
The Eals.....116 F3
The Eaves.....36 D3
The Flatt.....109 B5
The Four Alls....74 F3
The Garths.....160 B8
The Green Cumb...98 F3
Wilts.....24 F3
The Grove.....107 B6
The Hall.....160 D8
The Haven.....27 F8
The Heath Norf....81 E7
Suff.....56 F5
The Hill.....98 F3
The Howe IoM....84 F1
W&F.....99 F6
The Hundred....49 C7
Thelbridge Barton.10 C2
The Lee.....40 D2
The Lhen.....84 B3
Thelnetham.....56 B4
Thelveton.....68 F4
Thelwall.....86 F4
The Marsh Powys...60 E3
Wilts.....37 F7
Themelthorpe...81 E6
The Middles.....110 D5
The Moor.....18 C4
The Mumbles = Y Mwmbwls....33 F7
The Murray.....119 D6
The Neuk.....141 E6
Thenford.....52 E3
The Oval.....24 C2
The Pole of Itlaw.153 C6
The Quarry.....36 E4
Therfield.....54 F4
The Rhos.....32 C1
The Rock.....61 D6
The Ryde.....41 D5
The Sands.....27 E6
The Stocks.....19 C6
Thetford Lincs....65 C8
Norf.....67 F8
The Throat.....27 C6
The Vauld.....49 E7
The Wyke.....61 D7
Theydon Bois....41 E7
Thickwood.....24 B3
Thimbleby Lincs....78 C5
N Yorks.....102 E2
Thingwall.....85 F3
Thirdpart.....118 E1
Thirlby.....102 F2
Thirlestane.....121 E8
Thirn.....101 F7
Thirsk.....102 F2
Thirtleby.....97 F7
Thistleton Lancs....92 F4
Rutland.....65 C6
Thistley Green....55 B7
Thixendale.....96 C4

Thockrington ..... 110 B2
Tholomas Drove .. 66 D3
Tholthorpe ........ 95 C7
Thomas Chapel ... 32 D2
Thomas Close .... 108 E4
Thomastown ..... 152 E5
Thompson ........ 68 E2
Thomshill ....... 152 C2
Thong ........... 29 B7
Thongsbridge .... 88 D2
Thoralby ........ 101 F5
Thoresway ....... 91 E5
Thorganby Lincs .. 91 E6
  N Yorks ......... 96 E2
Thorgill ......... 103 E5
Thorington ....... 57 B8
Thorington Street . 56 F4
Thorlby .......... 94 D2
Thorley .......... 41 C7
Thorley Street
  Herts ........... 41 C7
  IoW ............ 14 F4
Thormanby ....... 95 B7
Thornaby-on-
  Tees .......... 102 C2
Thornage ........ 81 D6
Thornborough
  Bucks .......... 52 F5
  N Yorks ........ 95 B5
Thornbury Devon ... 9 D6
  Hereford ....... 49 D8
  S Glos ......... 36 E3
  W Yorks ........ 94 F4
Thornby ......... 52 B4
Thorncliffe ..... 75 D7
Thorncombe
  Dorset ......... 11 D8
  Dorset ......... 13 D6
Thorncombe
  Street ......... 27 E8
Thorncote Green .. 54 E2
Thorncross ...... 14 F5
Thorndon ........ 56 C5
Thorndon Cross ... 9 E7
Thorne .......... 89 C7
Thorner ......... 95 E6
Thorne St
  Margaret ....... 11 B5
Thorney Notts .... 77 B8
  Pboro .......... 66 D2
Thorney Crofts ... 91 B6
Thorney Green ... 56 C4
Thorney Hill .... 14 E2
Thorney Toll .... 66 D3
Thornfalcon ..... 11 B7
Thornford ....... 12 C3
Thorngumbald ... 91 B6
Thornham ........ 80 C3
Thornham Magna .. 56 B5
Thornham Parva .. 56 B5
Thornhaugh ...... 65 D7
Thornhill Cardiff .. 35 F5
  Cumb ........... 98 D2
  Derbys ......... 88 F2
  Dumfries ...... 113 E8
  Soton .......... 15 C5
  Stirling ...... 127 E5
  W Yorks ........ 88 C3
Thornhill Edge ... 88 C3
Thornhill Lees ... 88 C3
Thornholme ...... 97 C7
Thornley Durham . 110 F4
  Durham ........ 111 F6
Thornliebank ... 118 D5
Thorns .......... 55 D8
Thornsett ....... 87 F8
Thorns Green .... 87 F5
Thornthwaite
  Cumb ........... 98 B4
  N Yorks ........ 94 D4
Thornton Angus .. 134 F3
  Bucks .......... 53 F5
  E Yorks ........ 96 E3
  Fife .......... 128 E4
  Lancs .......... 92 C3
  Leics .......... 63 D8
  Lincs .......... 78 C5
  Mbro .......... 102 C2
  Mers ........... 85 D4
  Northumb ...... 123 E5
  Pembs .......... 44 E4
  W Yorks ........ 94 F4
Thornton Curtis .. 90 C4
Thornton Heath .. 28 C4
Thornton Hough .. 85 F4
Thornton in
  Craven ......... 94 E2
Thornton-le-
  Beans ......... 102 E1
Thornton-le-Clay . 96 C2
Thornton-le-
  Dale .......... 103 F6
Thornton le Moor . 90 E4
Thornton-le-
  Moor .......... 102 F1
Thornton-le-
  Moors .......... 73 B8
Thornton-le-
  Street ........ 102 F2
Thorntonloch ... 122 B3
Thorntonpark ... 122 E5
Thornton Rust .. 100 F4
Thornton
  Steward ....... 101 F6
Thornton Watlass 101 F7
Thornwood
  Common ........ 41 D7
Thornydykes ... 122 E2
Thoroton ........ 77 E7
Thorp Arch ...... 95 E7
Thorpe Derbys ... 75 D8
  E Yorks ........ 97 E5
  Lincs .......... 91 F8
  Norf ........... 69 E7
  Notts .......... 77 E7
  N Yorks ........ 94 C3
  Sur ............ 27 C8
Thorpe Abbotts .. 57 B5
Thorpe Acre ..... 64 B2
Thorpe Arnold ... 64 B4
Thorpe Audlin ... 89 C5
Thorpe Bassett .. 96 B4
Thorpe Bay ...... 43 F5
Thorpe by Water . 65 E5
Thorpe Common .. 57 F6

Thorpe
  Constantine .... 63 D6
Thorpe Culvert ... 79 C7
Thorpe End ...... 69 C5
Thorpe Fendykes . 79 C7
Thorpe Green
  Essex .......... 43 B7
  Suff ........... 56 D3
Thorpe Hesley ... 88 E4
Thorpe in Balne .. 89 C6
Thorpe in the
  Fallows ........ 90 F3
Thorpe Langton .. 64 E4
Thorpe Larches .. 102 B1
Thorpe-le-Soken . 43 B7
Thorpe le Street .. 96 E4
Thorpe Malsor ... 53 B6
Thorpe Mandeville 52 E3
Thorpe Market ... 81 D8
Thorpe Marriot .. 68 C4
Thorpe Morieux .. 56 D3
Thorpeness ...... 57 D8
Thorpe on the Hill 78 C2
Thorpe St Andrew 69 D5
Thorpe St Peter .. 79 C7
Thorpe Salvin ... 89 F6
Thorpe Satchville 64 C4
Thorpe Thewles . 102 B2
Thorpe Tilney ... 78 D4
Thorpe
  Underwood ..... 95 D7
Thorpe Waterville 65 F7
Thorpe Willoughby 95 F8
Thorrington ..... 43 C6
Thorverton ...... 10 D4
Thrandeston ..... 56 B5
Thrapston ....... 53 B7
Thrashbush ..... 119 C7
Threapland Cumb . 107 F8
  N Yorks ........ 94 C2
Threapwood
  Ches W ......... 73 E8
  Staffs ......... 75 E7
Three Ashes ..... 36 B2
Three Bridges ... 28 F3
Three Burrows .... 3 B6
Three Chimneys .. 18 B5
Three Cocks ..... 48 F3
Three Crosses ... 33 E6
Three Cups
  Corner ......... 18 C3
Threehammer
  Common ........ 69 C6
Three Holes ..... 66 D5
Threekingham .... 78 F3
Three Leg Cross . 18 B3
Three Legged Cross 13 D8
Threemilestone ... 3 B6
Threemiletown .. 120 B3
Three Oaks ...... 18 D5
Threlkeld ....... 99 B5
Threshfield ..... 94 C2
Thrigby ......... 69 C7
Thringarth ..... 100 B4
Thringstone ..... 63 C8
Thrintoft ...... 101 E8
Thriplow ........ 54 E5
Throckenholt .... 66 D3
Throcking ....... 54 F4
Throckley ...... 110 C4
Throckmorton ... 50 E4
Throphill ...... 117 F7
Thropton ....... 117 D6
Throwleigh ...... 9 E8
Throwley ........ 30 D3
Thrumpton ...... 76 F5
Thrumster ...... 158 F5
Thrunton ....... 117 C6
Thrupp Glos ..... 37 D5
  Oxon ........... 38 C4
Thrushelton ...... 9 F6
Thrussington .... 64 C3
Thruxton Hants .. 25 E7
  Hereford ....... 49 F6
Thrybergh ....... 89 E5
Thulston ........ 76 F4
Thundergay .... 143 D9
Thundersley ..... 42 F3
Thundridge ..... 41 C6
Thurcaston ..... 64 C2
Thurcroft ....... 89 F5
Thurgarton Norf . 81 D7
  Notts .......... 77 E6
Thurgoland ...... 88 D3
Thurlaston Leics . 64 E2
  Warks .......... 52 B2
Thurlbear ....... 11 B7
Thurlby Lincs .... 65 C8
  Lincs .......... 78 C2
Thurleigh ....... 53 D8
Thurlestone ...... 6 E4
Thurloxton ...... 22 F4
Thurlstone ...... 88 D3
Thurlton ........ 69 E7
Thurlwood ....... 74 D5
Thurmaston ..... 64 D3
Thurnby ......... 64 D3
Thurne .......... 69 C7
Thurnham Kent .. 30 D2
  Lancs .......... 92 D4
Thurning N Nhants 65 F7
  Norf ........... 81 E6
Thurnscoe ....... 89 D5
Thurnscoe East .. 89 D5
Thursby ........ 108 D3
Thursford ....... 81 D5
Thursley ........ 27 F7
Thurso ......... 158 D3
Thurso East .... 158 D3
Thurstaston ..... 85 F3
Thurston ........ 56 C3
Thurstonfield .. 108 D3
Thurstonland .... 88 C2
Thurton ......... 69 D6
Thuxton ......... 68 D3
Thwaite N Yorks . 100 E3
  Suff ........... 56 C5
Thwaites ........ 94 E3
Thwaite St Mary . 69 E6
Thwaites Brow ... 94 E3
Thwing .......... 97 B6
Tibbermore .... 128 B2
Tibberton Glos ... 36 B4
  Telford ........ 61 B6
  Worcs .......... 50 D4

Tibenham ........ 68 F4
Tibshelf ........ 76 C4
Tibthorpe ....... 97 D5
Ticehurst ....... 18 B3
Tichborne ....... 26 F3
Tickencote ...... 65 D6
Tickenham ....... 23 B6
Tickhill ........ 89 E6
Ticklerton ...... 60 E4
Ticknall ........ 63 B7
Tickton ......... 97 E6
Tidcombe ........ 25 D7
Tiddington Oxon . 39 D6
  Warks .......... 51 D7
Tidebrook ....... 18 C3
Tideford ......... 5 D8
Tideford Cross ... 5 C8
Tidenham ........ 36 E2
Tideswell ....... 75 B8
Tidmarsh ........ 26 B4
Tidmington ...... 51 F7
Tidpit .......... 13 C8
Tidworth ........ 25 E7
Tiers Cross ..... 44 D4
Tiffield ........ 52 D4
Tifty .......... 153 D7
Tigerton ....... 135 C5
Tigh-na-Blair .. 127 C6
Tighnabruaich .. 145 F8
Tighnafiline ... 155 J13
Tigley ........... 7 C5
Tilbrook ........ 53 C8
Tilbury ......... 43 D5
Tilbury Juxta Clare 55 E8
Tile Cross ...... 63 F5
Tile Hill ....... 51 B7
Tilehurst ....... 26 B4
Tilford ......... 27 E6
Tilgate ......... 28 F3
Tilgate Forest Row 28 F3
Tillathrowie ... 152 E4
Tilley .......... 60 B5
Tillicoultry ... 127 E8
Tillingham ...... 43 D5
Tillington Hereford 49 E6
  W Sus .......... 16 B3
Tillington
  Common ........ 49 E6
Tillyarblet .... 135 C5
Tillybirloch ... 141 D5
Tillycorthie ... 141 B8
Tillydrine ..... 141 E5
Tillyfour ...... 140 C4
Tillyfourie .... 140 C5
Tillygarmond .. 140 E5
Tillygreig ..... 141 B7
Tillykerrie .... 141 B7
Tillyminnate .. 152 E5
Tillyrie ....... 128 C3
Tilmanstone ..... 31 D7
Tilney All Saints 79 C6 (?)
Tilney Fen End .. 66 C5
Tilney High End . 67 C5
Tilney St
  Lawrence ...... 66 C5
Tilshead ........ 24 E5
Tilstock ........ 74 F2
Tilston ......... 73 D8
Tilstone Fearnall 74 C2
Tilsworth ....... 40 B2
Tilton on the Hill 64 D4
Timberland ...... 78 D4
Timbersbrook ... 75 C5
Timberscombe ... 21 E8
Timble .......... 94 D4
Timperley ....... 87 F5
Timsbury Bath ... 23 D8
  Hants .......... 14 B4
Timsgearraidh .. 154 D5
Timworth Green .. 56 C2
Tincleton ....... 13 E5
Tindale ........ 109 D6
Tingewick ....... 52 F4
Tingley ......... 88 B3
Tingrith ........ 53 F8
Tingwall ....... 159 F4
Tinhay ........... 9 F5
Tinshill ........ 95 F5
Tinsley ......... 88 E5
Tintagel ......... 8 F2
Tintern Parva ... 36 D2
Tintinhull ...... 12 C3
Tintwistle ...... 87 E8
Tinwald ........ 114 F3
Tinwell ......... 65 D7
Tipperty ....... 141 B8
Tipsend ......... 66 E5
Tipton .......... 62 E3
Tipton St John .. 11 E5
Tiptree ......... 42 C4
Tirabad ......... 47 E7
Tiraghoil ...... 146 J6
Tirley .......... 37 B5
Tirphil ......... 35 D5
Tir-y-dail ...... 33 C7
Tisbury ......... 13 B7
Tisman's Common 27 F8
Tissington ...... 75 D8
Titchberry ....... 8 B4
Titchfield ...... 15 D6
Titchmarsh ...... 53 B8
Titchwell ....... 80 C3
Tithby .......... 77 F6
Titley .......... 48 C5
Titlington ..... 117 C7
Titsey .......... 28 D5
Tittensor ....... 75 F5
Tittleshall ..... 80 E4
Tiverton Ches W . 74 C2
  Devon .......... 10 C4
Tivetshall St
  Margaret ....... 68 F4
Tivetshall St Mary 68 F4
Tividale ........ 62 E3
Tivy Dale ....... 88 D3
Tixall .......... 62 B3
Tixover ......... 65 D6
Toab Orkney .... 159 H6
  Shetland ...... 160 M5
Toadmoor ........ 76 D3
Toberonochy ... 124 E3
Tobha Mor ..... 148 E2
Tobhtarol ...... 154 D6
Tobson ......... 154 D6
Tocher ......... 153 E6
Tockenham ...... 24 B5
Tockenham Wick . 37 F7
Tockholes ....... 86 B4
Tockington ...... 36 F3
Tockwith ........ 95 D7

Todber .......... 13 B6
Todding ......... 49 B6
Toddington C Beds 40 B3
  Glos ........... 50 F5
Todenham ........ 51 F7
Todhills ....... 108 C3
Todlachie ...... 141 C5
Todmorden ....... 87 B7
Todrig ......... 115 C2
Todwick ......... 89 F5
Toft Cambs ...... 54 D4
  Lincs .......... 65 C7
Toft Hill Durham 101 B6
  Lincs .......... 78 C5
Toft Monks ...... 69 E7
Toft next Newton 90 F4
Toftrees ........ 80 E4
Tofts .......... 158 D5
Toftwood ........ 68 C2
Togston ........ 117 D8
Tokavaig ...... 149 G11
Tokers Green .... 26 B5
Tolastadh a
  Chaolais ...... 154 D6
Tolastadh bho
  Thuath ....... 155 C10
Tolland ......... 22 F3
Tollard Royal ... 13 C7
Tollbar End ..... 51 B8
Toll End ........ 62 E3
Toller Fratrum .. 12 E3
Toller Porcorum . 12 E3
Tollerton Notts . 77 F6
  N Yorks ........ 95 C8
Tollesbury ...... 43 C5
Tolleshunt D'Arcy 43 C5
Tolleshunt Major 43 C5
Toll of Birness 153 E10
Tolm .......... 155 D9
Tolpuddle ....... 13 E5
Tolvah ......... 138 E4
Tolworth ........ 28 C2
Tomatin ....... 138 B4
Tombreck ...... 151 H9
Tomchrasky .... 137 C5
Tomdoun ....... 136 D4
Tomich Highld .. 137 B5
  Highld ........ 151 D9
Tomich House .. 151 G8
Tomintoul Aberds 139 E7
  Moray ......... 139 D7
Tomnaven ...... 152 E4
Tomnavoulin ... 139 B8
Tonbridge ....... 29 E6
Tondu ........... 34 F2
Tonfanau ........ 58 D2
Tong Shrops ..... 61 D7
  W Yorks ........ 94 F5
Tonge ........... 63 B8
Tongham ......... 27 E6
Tongland ...... 106 D3
Tong Norton .... 61 D7
Tongue ........ 157 D8
Tongue End ...... 65 C8
Tongwynlais ..... 35 F5
Tonna ........... 34 E1
Ton-Pentre ...... 34 E3
Tonwell ......... 41 C6
Tonypandy ...... 34 E3
Tonyrefail ...... 34 F4
Toot Baldon ..... 39 D5
Toothill ........ 14 C4
Toot Hill ....... 41 D8
Topcliffe ....... 95 B7
Topcroft ........ 69 E5
Topcroft Street . 69 E5
Top of Hebers .. 87 D6
Toppesfield ..... 55 F8
Toppings ........ 86 C5
Topsham ......... 10 F4
Torbay ........... 7 D7
Torbeg ........ 143 F10
Torboll Farm .. 151 B10
Torbrex ....... 127 E6
Torbryan ......... 7 C6
Torcross ......... 7 E6
Tore .......... 151 F9
Torinturk ..... 145 G7
Torksey ......... 77 B8
Torlum ........ 148 C2
Torlundy ...... 131 B5
Tormarton ....... 24 B2
Tormisdale .... 142 C2
Tormitchell ... 112 E2
Tormore ....... 143 E9
Tornagrain .... 151 G10
Tornahaish .... 139 D8
Tornaveen ..... 140 D5
Torness ....... 138 B8
Toronto ....... 110 F4
Torpenhow ..... 108 F2
Torphichen .... 120 B2
Torphins ...... 140 D5
Torpoint ......... 6 D2
Torquay .......... 7 C7
Torquhan ...... 121 E7
Torran Argyll .. 124 E4
  Highld ....... 149 D10
  Highld ....... 151 D10
Torrance ...... 119 B6
Torrans ....... 146 J7
Torranyard .... 118 E3
Torre ............ 7 C7
Torridon ...... 149 C13
Torridon House 149 C13
Torrin ........ 149 F10
Torrisdale .... 157 C9
Torrish ....... 157 H12
Torrisholme .... 92 C4
Torroble ...... 157 J8
Torry Aberdeen . 141 D8
  Aberds ........ 152 E4
Torryburn ..... 128 F2
Torterston .... 153 D10
Torthorwald ... 107 B7
Tortington ...... 16 D4
Tortworth ....... 36 E4
Torvaig ....... 149 D9
Torver .......... 98 E4
Torwood ....... 127 F7
Torworth ........ 89 F7
Tosberry ......... 8 B4
Toscaig ....... 149 E12
Toseland ........ 54 C3
Tosside .......... 93 D7
Tostock ......... 56 C3

Totaig Highld .. 148 C7
  Highld ........ 149 F13
Tote .......... 149 D9
Totegan ....... 157 C11
Tothill ......... 91 F8
Totland ......... 14 F4
Totnes ........... 7 C6
Toton ........... 76 F5
Totronald ..... 146 F4
Totscore ...... 149 B8
Tottenham ....... 41 E6
Tottenhill ...... 67 C6
Tottenhill Row .. 67 C6
Totteridge ...... 41 E5
Totternhoe ...... 40 B2
Tottington ...... 87 C5
Totton .......... 14 C4
Touchen End ..... 27 B6
Tournaig ...... 155 J13
Toux .......... 153 C9
Tovil ........... 29 D8
Toward ........ 145 G10
Towcester ....... 52 E4
Towednack ........ 2 C3
Tower End ....... 67 C6
Towersey ........ 39 D7
Towie Aberds ... 140 C3
  Aberds ........ 153 B8
Towiemore ..... 152 D3
Tow Law ....... 110 F4
Townend ....... 118 B4
Town End Cambs . 66 E4
  W&F ............ 99 F6
Towngate ........ 65 C8
Townhead
  Dumfries ...... 106 E3
  S Ayrs ........ 112 D2
  S Yorks ........ 88 D2
  W&F ........... 108 F5
Townhead of
  Greenlaw ...... 106 C4
Townhill ....... 128 F3
Town Row ........ 18 B2
Townsend Bucks . 39 D7
  Herts .......... 40 D4
Townshend ........ 2 C4
Town Yetholm .. 116 B4
Towthorpe ....... 96 D2
Towton .......... 95 F7
Towyn ........... 72 B3
Toxteth ......... 85 F4
Toynton All Saints 79 C6
Toynton Fen Side 79 C6
Toynton St Peter 79 C7
Toy's Hill ...... 29 D5
Trabboch ...... 112 C4
Trabbochburn .. 112 C4
Traboe ........... 3 D6
Tradespark Highld 151 F11
  Orkney ........ 159 H4
Trafford Park ... 87 E5
Trallong ........ 34 B3
Tranent ....... 121 B7
Tranmere ........ 85 F4
Trantlebeg .... 157 D11
Trantlemore ... 157 D11
Tranwell ...... 117 F7
Trapp ........... 33 C7
Traprain ...... 121 B8
Traquair ...... 121 F6
Trawden ......... 94 F2
Trawsfynydd ..... 71 D8
Trealaw ......... 34 E4
Treales ......... 92 F4
Trearddur ....... 82 D2
Treaslane ..... 149 C8
Trebanog ........ 34 E4
Trebanos ........ 33 D8
Trebartha ........ 5 B7
Trebarwith ....... 8 F2
Trebetherick ..... 4 B4
Treborough ...... 22 F2
Trebudannon ...... 4 C3
Trebullett ....... 5 B8
Treburley ........ 5 B8
Trebyan .......... 5 C5
Trecastle ....... 34 B2
Trecenydd ....... 35 F5
Trecwn .......... 44 B4
Trecynon ........ 34 D3
Tredavoe ......... 2 D3
Treddiog ........ 44 C3
Tredegar ........ 35 D5
Tredegar =Newydd
  New Tredegar .. 35 D5
Tredington Glos . 37 B6
  Warks .......... 51 E7
Tredinnick ....... 4 B4
Tredomen ........ 48 F3
Tredunnock ...... 35 E7
Tredustan ....... 48 F3
Treen ............ 2 D2
Treeton ......... 88 F5
Trefaldwyn
  =Montgomery .. 60 E2
Trefasser ....... 44 B3
Trefdraeth ...... 82 D4
Trefdraeth
  =Newport ....... 45 F2
Trefecca ........ 48 F3
Trefechan ....... 58 F3
Trefeglwys ...... 59 E6
Trefenter ....... 46 C5
Treffgarne ...... 44 C4
Treffynnon ...... 44 C3
Treffynnon
  =Holywell ..... 73 B5
Trefgarn Owen .. 44 C3
Trefil .......... 35 C5
Trefilan ........ 46 D4
Trefin .......... 44 B3
Treflach ........ 60 B2
Trefnanney ...... 60 C2
Trefnant ........ 72 B4
Trefonen ........ 60 B2
Trefor Anglesey . 82 C3
  Gwyn .......... 70 C4
Treforest ....... 34 F4
Trefriw ......... 83 E7
Tref-y-Clawdd
  =Knighton ..... 48 B4
Trefynwy
  =Monmouth .... 36 C2
Tregadillett ..... 5 C8
Tregaian ........ 82 D4
Tregare ......... 35 C8
Tregaron ........ 47 D5
Tregarth ........ 83 E6
Tregeare ......... 8 F4

Tregeiriog ...... 73 F5
Tregele ......... 82 B3
Tre-Gibbon ...... 34 D3
Tregidden ........ 3 D6
Treglemais ...... 44 C3
Tregole .......... 8 E3
Tregonetha ....... 4 C4
Tregony .......... 3 B8
Tregoss .......... 4 C4
Tregoyd ......... 48 F4
Tregroes ........ 46 E3
Tregurrian ....... 4 C3
Tregynon ........ 59 E7
Trehafod ........ 34 E4
Treharris ....... 34 E4
Treherbert ...... 34 E3
Trekenner ........ 5 B8
Treknow .......... 8 F2
Trelan ........... 3 E6
Trelash .......... 8 E3
Trelassick ....... 4 D3
Trelawnyd ....... 72 B4
Trelech ......... 45 F4
Treleddyd-fawr .. 44 C2
Trelewis ........ 35 E5
Treligga ......... 8 F2
Trelights ........ 4 B4
Trelill .......... 4 B5
Trelissick ....... 3 C7
Trellech ........ 36 D2
Trelleck Grange . 36 D1
Trelogan ........ 85 F2
Trelystan ....... 60 D2
Tremadog ........ 71 C6
Tremail .......... 8 F3
Tremain ......... 45 E4
Tremaine ......... 8 F4
Tremar ........... 5 C7
Trematon ......... 5 D8
Tremeirchion ... 72 B4
Trenance ......... 4 C3
Trenarren ........ 3 B9
Trench .......... 61 C6
Treneglos ........ 8 F4
Trenewan ......... 5 D6
Trent ........... 12 C3
Trentham ........ 75 E5
Trentishoe ...... 20 E5
Trent Vale ...... 75 E5
Treoes .......... 21 B8
Treorchy =Treorci 34 E3
Treorci =Treorchy 34 E3
Tre-Taliesin .... 58 E3
Trethurgy ........ 4 D5
Tretio .......... 44 C2
Tretire ......... 36 B2
Tretower ........ 35 B5
Treuddyn ........ 73 D6
Trevalga ......... 8 F2
Trevalyn ........ 73 D7
Trevanson ........ 4 B4
Trevarren ........ 4 C4
Trevarrian ....... 4 C3
Trevarrick ....... 3 B8
Trevaughan ...... 32 C2
Tre-vaughan ..... 32 B4
Trevellas ........ 4 D2
Treverva ......... 3 C6
Trevethin ....... 35 D6
Trevigro ......... 5 C8
Treviscoe ........ 4 D4
Trevone .......... 4 B3
Trevor .......... 73 E6
Trewarmett ....... 8 F2
Trewassa ......... 8 F3
Trewellard ....... 2 C2
Trewen ........... 8 F4
Trewennack ....... 3 D5
Trewern ......... 60 C2
Trewethern ....... 4 B5
Trewidland ....... 5 D7
Trewint Corn ..... 8 E4
  Corn ............ 5 B7
Trewithian ....... 3 C7
Trewoofe ......... 2 D3
Trewoon .......... 4 D4
Treworga ......... 3 B7
Treworlas ........ 3 C7
Tre-wyn ......... 35 B7
Treyarnon ........ 4 C3
Treyford ........ 16 C2
Trezaise ......... 4 D4
Triangle ........ 87 B8
Trickett's Cross 13 D8
Triffleton ...... 44 C4
Trimdon ....... 111 F6
Trimdon Colliery 111 F6
Trimdon Grange 111 F6
Trimingham ..... 81 D8
Trimley Lower
  Street ......... 57 F6
Trimley St Martin 57 F6
Trimley St Mary . 57 F6
Trimpley ........ 50 B2
Trimsaran ....... 33 D5
Trimstone ....... 20 E3
Trinafour ..... 132 C4
Trinant ......... 35 D6
Tring ........... 40 C2
Tring Wharf ..... 40 C2
Trinity Angus .. 135 C6
  Jersey ......... 17 I3
Trisant ......... 47 B6
Triscombe ....... 22 F3
Trislaig ...... 130 B4
Trispen .......... 4 D3
Tritlington ... 117 E8
Trochry ....... 133 E6
Trodigal ...... 143 F7
Troed-rhiwdalar 47 D8
Troedyraur .... 46 E2
Troedyrhiw .... 34 D4

Tromode ......... 84 E3
Trondavoe ..... 160 F5
Troon Corn ....... 3 C5
  S Ayrs ........ 118 F3
Trosaraidh .... 148 G2
Trossachs Hotel . 126 D4
Troston ......... 56 B2
Trottiscliffe ... 29 D7
Trotton ......... 16 B2
Troutbeck W&F ... 99 B5
  W&F ............ 99 D6
Troutbeck Bridge 99 D6
Trowbridge ...... 24 D3
Trowell ......... 76 F4
Trow Green ...... 36 D2
Trowle Common .. 24 D3
Trowley Bottom .. 40 C3
Trows ......... 122 F2
Trowse Newton .. 68 D5
Trudoxhill ...... 24 E2
Trull ........... 11 B7
Trumaisgearraidh 148 A3
Trumpan ....... 148 B7
Trumpet ......... 49 F8
Trumpington .... 54 D5
Trunch .......... 81 D8
Trunnah ......... 92 E3
Truro ............ 3 B7
Trusham ......... 10 F3
Trusley ......... 76 F2
Trusthorpe ...... 91 F9
Trysull ......... 62 E2
Tubney .......... 38 E4
Tuckenhay ........ 7 D6
Tuckhill ........ 61 F7
Tuckingmill ...... 3 B5
Tuddenham ...... 55 B8
Tuddenham
  St Martin ..... 57 E5
Tudeley ......... 29 E7
Tudhoe ........ 111 F5
Tudorville ...... 36 B2
Tudweiliog ...... 70 D3
Tuesley ......... 27 E7
Tuffley ......... 37 C5
Tufton Hants .... 26 E2
  Pembs .......... 32 B1
Tugby ........... 64 D4
Tugford ......... 61 F5
Tullibardine ... 127 C8
Tullibody ..... 127 E7
Tullich Argyll .. 125 D7
  Highld ........ 138 B2
Tullich Muir .. 151 D10
Tulliemet ..... 133 D7
Tulloch Aberds . 153 E8
  Highld ........ 130 B2
  Perth ......... 128 B2
Tulloch Castle . 151 E8
Tullochgorm ... 125 F5
Tulloes ....... 135 E5
Tullybannocher 127 B6
Tullybelton ... 133 F7
Tullyfergus ... 134 E2
Tullymurdoch .. 134 D1
Tullynessle ... 140 C4
Tumble .......... 33 C6
Tumby
  Woodside ...... 79 D5
Tummel Bridge . 132 D4
Tunga ......... 155 D9
Tunstall E Yorks . 97 F9
  Kent ........... 30 C2
  Lancs .......... 93 B6
  N Yorks ....... 101 E7
  Norf ........... 69 D7
  Stoke .......... 75 D5
  Suff ........... 57 D7
  T&W ........... 111 D6
Tunstead Derbys . 75 B8
  Gtr Man ........ 87 D8
  Norf ........... 81 E8
Tunworth ........ 26 E4
Tupsley ......... 49 E7
Tupton .......... 76 C3
Turgis Green .... 26 D4
Turin ......... 135 D5
Turkdean ........ 37 C7
Tur Langton ..... 64 E4
Turleigh ........ 24 C3
Turn ............ 87 C6
Turnastone ...... 48 F5
Turnberry ..... 112 D2
Turnditch ....... 76 E2
Turners Hill .... 28 F4
Turners Puddle . 13 E6
Turnford ........ 41 D6
Turnhouse ..... 120 B4
Turnworth ....... 13 D6
Turriff ....... 153 D7
Turton Bottoms .. 86 C5
Turves .......... 66 E3
Turvey .......... 53 D7
Turville ........ 39 E7
Turville Heath .. 39 E7
Turweston ....... 52 F4
Tushielaw ..... 115 C6
Tutbury ......... 63 B6
Tutnall ......... 50 B4
Tutshill ........ 36 E2
Tuttington ...... 81 E8
Tutts Clump ..... 26 B3
Tuxford ......... 77 B7
Twatt Orkney .. 159 F3
  Shetland ...... 160 H5
Twechar ....... 119 B7
Tweedmouth ... 123 D5
Tweedsmuir .... 114 B3
Twelve Heads ..... 3 B6
Twemlow Green .. 74 C4
Twenty .......... 65 B8
Twerton ......... 24 C2
Twickenham ..... 28 B2
Twigworth ....... 37 B5
Twineham ........ 17 C6
Twinhoe ......... 24 D2
Twinstead ....... 56 F2
Twinstead Green . 56 F2
Twiss Green ..... 86 E4
Twiston ......... 93 E8
Twitchen Devon .. 21 F6
  Shrops ......... 49 B5
Two Bridges ...... 6 B4
Two Dales ....... 76 C2
Two Mills ....... 73 B7
Twycross ........ 63 D7
Twyford Bucks ... 39 B6
  Derbys ......... 63 B7

Twyford continued
  Leics .......... 64 C4
  Lincs .......... 65 B6
  Norf ........... 81 E6
  Wokingham ..... 27 B5
Twyford Common . 49 F7
Twynholm ...... 106 D3
Twyning ......... 50 F3
Twyning Green .. 50 F4
Twynllanan ...... 34 B1
Twynmynydd .... 33 C7
Twyn-y-Sheriff . 35 D8
Twywell ......... 53 B7
Tyberton ........ 49 F5
Tyburn .......... 62 E5
Tycroes ......... 33 C7
Tycrwyn ......... 59 C8
Tyddewi
  =St David's ... 44 C2
Tydd Gote ....... 66 C4
Tydd St Giles ... 66 C4
Tydd St Mary .... 66 C4
Tyddyn-mawr .... 71 C6
Ty-draw ......... 83 F8
Tye Green Essex . 41 D7
  Essex .......... 42 B3
  Essex .......... 55 F6
Ty-hen Carms .... 32 B4
  Gwyn .......... 70 D2
Tyldesley ....... 86 D4
Tyler Hill ...... 30 C5
Tylers Green .... 40 E2
Tylorstown ...... 34 E4
Tylwch .......... 59 F6
Ty-mawr ......... 46 E4
Ty Mawr ......... 72 E3
Ty-mawr Conwy .. 72 E3
Ty-nant Conwy .. 72 E3
  Gwyn .......... 59 B6
Tyncelyn ........ 46 C5
Tyndrum ....... 131 F7
Tyneham ......... 13 F6
Tynehead ...... 121 D6
Tynemouth .... 111 C6
Tyne Tunnel ... 111 C6
Tynewydd ........ 34 E3
Tyninghame .... 122 B2
Tynron ........ 113 E8
Tyn-y-celyn .... 73 F5
Tyn-y-coed ...... 60 B2
Tyn-y-fedwen ... 72 F5
Tyn-y-ffridd ... 72 F5
Tyn-y-graig ..... 47 D8
Tynygongl ....... 82 C5
Tyn-y-groes ..... 83 E6
Ty'n-y-pwll ..... 82 C4
Tyr-felin-isaf .. 83 E8
Tyrie ......... 153 B9
Tyringham ....... 53 E6
Tythecott ........ 9 C6
Tytherington
  Ches E ......... 75 B6
  S Glos ......... 36 F3
  Som ............ 24 E2
  Wilts .......... 24 E4
Tytherleigh ..... 11 D8
Ty-uchaf ........ 59 B7
Tywardreath ...... 5 D5
Tywyn Conwy .... 83 D7
  Gwyn .......... 58 D2

**U**

Uachdar ....... 148 C2
Uags .......... 149 E12
Ubbeston Green .. 57 B7
Ubley ........... 23 D7
Uckerby ....... 101 D7
Uckfield ........ 17 B8
Uckington ....... 37 D6
Uddingston .... 119 C6
Uddington ..... 119 F8
Udimore ......... 19 D5
Udny Green .... 141 B7
Udny Station .. 141 B8
Udston ........ 119 D6
Udstonhead .... 119 E7
Uffcott ......... 25 B6
Uffculme ........ 11 C5
Uffington Lincs . 65 D7
  Oxon ........... 38 F3
  Shrops ......... 60 C5
Ufford Pboro .... 65 D7
  Suff ........... 57 D6
Ufton ........... 51 C8
Ufton Nervet .... 26 C4
Ugadale ....... 143 F8
Ugborough ........ 6 D4
Uggeshall ....... 69 F7
Ugglebarnby ... 103 D6
Ughill .......... 88 E3
Ugley ........... 41 B8
Ugley Green ..... 41 B8
Ugthorpe ...... 103 C5
Uidh .......... 148 J1
Uig Argyll .... 145 E10
  Highld ........ 148 C6
  Highld ........ 149 B8
Uigen ......... 154 D5
Uigshader ..... 149 D9
Uisken ........ 146 K6
Ulbster ....... 158 F5
Ulceby Lincs .... 79 B7
  N Lincs ........ 90 C5
Ulceby Skitter .. 90 C5
Ulcombe ......... 30 E2
Uldale ........ 108 F2
Uley ............ 36 D4
Ulgham ........ 117 E8
Ullapool ...... 150 B4
Ullenhall ....... 51 C6
Ullenwood ....... 37 C6
Ulleskelf ....... 95 E8
Ullesthorpe ..... 64 F2
Ulley ........... 89 F5
Ullingswick ..... 49 E7
Ullinish ...... 149 E8
Ullock .......... 98 B2
Ulnes Walton .... 86 C3
Ulpha ........... 98 E3
Ulrome .......... 97 D7
Ulsta ......... 160 E6
Ulva House .... 146 H7
Ulverston ....... 92 B2

Ulwell .......... 13 F8
Umberleigh ....... 9 B8
Unapool ....... 156 F5
Unasary ....... 148 F2
Underbarrow ..... 99 E6
Undercliffe ..... 94 F4
Underhoull .... 160 C7
Underriver ...... 29 D6
Underwood ....... 76 D4
Undy ............ 35 F8
Unifirth ...... 160 H4
Union Cottage . 141 E7
Union Mills ..... 84 E3
Union Street .... 18 B4
Unstone ......... 76 B3
Unstone Green .. 76 B3
Unthank W&F ... 108 F4
  W&F ........... 109 E6
Unthank End ... 108 F4
Upavon .......... 25 D6
Up Cerne ........ 12 D4
Upchurch ........ 30 C2
Upcott .......... 48 D5
Upend ........... 55 D7
Up Exe .......... 10 D4
Upgate .......... 68 C4
Uphall ......... 120 B3
Uphall Station . 120 B3
Upham Devon ..... 10 D3
  Hants .......... 15 B6
Uphampton ....... 50 C3
Up Hatherley .... 37 B6
Uphill .......... 22 D5
Up Holland ...... 86 D3
Uplawmoor .... 118 D4
Upleadon ........ 36 B4
Upleatham ..... 102 C4
Uplees .......... 30 C3
Uploders ........ 12 E3
Uplowman ........ 10 C5
Uplyme .......... 11 E8
Up Marden ....... 15 C8
Upminster ....... 42 F1
Up Nately ....... 26 D4
Upnor ........... 29 B8
Upottery ........ 11 D7
Upper Affcott ... 60 F4
Upper
  Ardchronie ... 151 C9
Upper Arley ..... 61 F7
Upper Arncott ... 39 C6
Upper Astrop .... 52 F3
Upper Badcall .. 156 E4
Upper Basildon .. 26 B3
Upper Beeding ... 17 C5
Upper Bighouse 157 D11
Upper
  Boddington .... 52 D2
Upper Borth ..... 58 F3
Upper Boyndlie . 153 B9
Upper Brailes ... 51 F8
Upper Breinton .. 49 E6
Upper Broadheath 50 D3
Upper Broughton 64 B3
Upper Bucklebury 26 C3
Upper
  Burnhaugh .... 141 E7
Upper Caldecote . 54 E2
Upper Catesby ... 52 D3
Upper Chapel .... 48 E2
Upper Church
  Village ........ 34 F4
Upper Chute ..... 25 D7
Upper Clatford .. 25 E8
Upper Clynnog ... 71 C5
Upper
  Cumberworth .. 88 D3
Upper Cwmbran .. 35 E6
Upper Dallachy . 152 B3
Upper Dean ...... 53 C8
Upper Denby ..... 88 D3
Upper Denton .. 109 C6
Upper Derraid . 151 H13
Upper Dicker .... 18 E2
Upper Dovercourt 57 F6
Upper Druimfin . 147 F8
Upper Dunsforth 95 C7
Upper Eathie .. 151 E10
Upper Elkstone .. 75 D7
Upper End ....... 75 B7
Upper Farringdon 26 F5
Upper Framilode . 36 C4
Upper
  Glenfintaig .. 137 F5
Upper Gornal .... 62 E3
Upper Gravenhurst 54 F2
Upper Green Mon . 35 C7
  W Berks ........ 25 C8
Upper Grove
  Common ........ 36 B2
Upper Hackney .. 76 C2
Upper Hale ...... 27 E6
Upper Halistra . 148 C7
Upper Halling ... 29 C7
Upper Hambleton 65 D6
Upper Hardres
  Court .......... 31 D5
Upper Hartfield . 29 F5
Upper Haugh ..... 88 E5
Upper Heath ..... 61 F5
Upper Hellesdon . 68 C5
Upper Helmsley .. 96 D2
Upper Hergest ... 48 D4
Upper Heyford
  Oxon ........... 38 B4
  W Nhants ....... 52 D4
Upper Hill ...... 49 D6
Upper Hopton ... 88 C2
Upper
  Horsebridge ... 18 D2
Upper Hulme ..... 75 C7
Upper Inglesham . 38 E2
Upper
  Inverbrough .. 151 H11
Upper Killay .... 33 E6
Upper
  Knockando .... 152 D1
Upper Lambourn . 38 F3
Upper Leigh ..... 75 F7
Upper Lenie ... 137 B8
Upper Lochton . 141 E5
Upper Longdon .. 62 C4
Upper Lybster . 158 G4
Upper Lydbrook . 36 C3
Upper Maes-coed 48 F5
Upper Midway ... 63 B6

Uppermill.........87 D7
Upper Hale......148 D6
Upper Minety.....37 E7
Upper Mitton.....50 B3
Upper North Dean. 39 E8
Upper Obney.....133 F7
Upper Ollach...149 E10
Upper Padley....76 B2
Upper Pollicott...39 C7
Upper Poppleton..95 D8
Upper Quinton...51 E6
Upper Ratley....14 B4
Upper Rissington. 38 C2
Upper Rochford...49 C8
Upper Sandaig..149 G12
Upper Sanday...159 H6
Upper Sapey.....49 C8
Upper Saxondale..77 F6
Upper Seagry....37 F6
Upper Shelton...53 E7
Upper Sheringham....81 C7
Upper Skelmorlie...118 C2
Upper Slaughter..38 B1
Upper Soudley....36 C3
Uppersound.....160 J6
Upper Stondon...54 F2
Upper Stowe.....52 D4
Upper Stratton...38 F1
Upper Street Hants. 14 C2
  Norf.........69 C6
  Suff.........56 F5
Upper Strensham..50 F4
Upper Sundon....40 B3
Upper Swell.....38 B1
Upper Tean......75 F7
Upperthong.....88 D2
Upperthorpe.....89 D8
Upper Tillyrie...128 D3
Upperton.......16 B3
Upper Tooting...28 B3
Upper Tote.....149 C10
Uppertown
  Derbys.......76 C3
  Highld.......158 C5
  Orkney.......159 J5
Upper Town......23 C7
Upper Treverward. 48 B4
Upper Tysoe.....51 E8
Upper Upham....25 B7
Upper Wardington 52 E2
Upper Weald....53 F5
Upper Weedon....52 D4
Upper Wield.....26 F4
Upper Winchendon...39 C7
Upper Witton....62 E4
Upper Woodend..141 C5
Upper Woodford. 25 F6
Upper Wootton...26 D3
Upper Wyche.....50 E2
Uppingham.....65 E5
Uppington......61 D6
Upsall.........102 F2
Upshire.........41 D7
Up Somborne....25 F8
Upstreet.......31 C6
Up Sydling......12 D4
Upthorpe.......56 B3
Upton Cambs.....54 B2
  Ches W.......73 C8
  Corn..........8 C4
  Dorset........12 F5
  Dorset........13 E7
  Hants........14 C4
  Hants........25 D8
  Leics.........63 E7
  Lincs.........90 F2
  Mers.........85 F3
  Norf.........69 C6
  Notts.........77 B7
  Notts.........77 D7
  Oxon..........39 F5
  Pboro.........65 D8
  Slough........27 B7
  Som...........10 B4
  W Nhants.....52 C5
  W Yorks......89 C5
Upton Bishop....36 B3
Upton Cheyney...23 C8
Upton Cressett...61 E6
Upton Cross......5 B7
Upton Grey......26 E4
Upton Hellions...10 D3
Upton Lovell....24 E4
Upton Magna....61 C5
Upton Noble.....24 F2
Upton Pyne.....10 E4
Upton St
  Leonard's.....37 C5
Upton Scudamore. 24 E3
Upton Snodsbury..50 D4
Upton upon
  Severn.......50 E3
Upton Warren....50 C4
Upwaltham......16 C3
Upware.........55 B6
Upwell.........66 D4
Upwey.........12 F4
Upwood.........66 F2
Uradale.......160 K6
Urafirth......160 F5
Urchfont.......24 D5
Urdimarsh......49 E7
Ure...........160 F4
Ure Bank.......95 B6
Urgha.........154 H6
Urishay Common.. 48 F5
Urlay Nook.....102 C1
Urmston.........87 E5
Urpeth.........110 D5
Urquhart Highld.. 151 F8
  Moray........152 B2
Urra...........102 D3
Urray.........151 F8
Ushaw Moor....110 E5
Usk = Brynbuga... 35 D7
Usselby.........90 E4
Usworth.......111 D6
Utkinton.......74 C2
Utley.........94 E3
Uton..........10 E3
Utterby.........91 E7
Uttoxeter......75 F7
Uwchmynydd.....70 E2
Uxbridge........40 F3
Uyeasound.....160 C7
Uzmaston......44 D4

**V**

Valley.........82 D2
Valleyfield....106 D3
Valley Truckle.....8 F2
Valsgarth......160 B8
Valtos........149 B10
Van............59 F6
Vange..........42 F3
Varteg.........35 D6
Vatten........149 D7
Vaul...........146 G3
Vaynor.........34 C4
Veensgarth.....160 J6
Velindre.......48 F3
Vellow.........22 F2
Veness........159 F6
Venn Green......9 C5
Vennington.....60 D3
Venn Ottery....11 E5
Venny Tedburn...10 E3
Ventnor........15 G6
Vernham Dean...25 D8
Vernham Street.. 25 D8
Vernolds Common. 60 F4
Verwood........13 D8
Veryan..........3 C8
Vicarage.......11 F7
Vickerstown....92 C1
Victoria Corn....4 C4
  S Yorks.......88 D2
Vidlin.........160 G6
Viewpark.......119 C7
Vigo Village....29 C7
Vinehall Street..18 C4
Vine's Cross....18 D2
Viney Hill......36 D3
Virginia Water...27 C8
Virginstow......9 E5
Vobster........24 E2
Voe Shetland...160 E5
  Shetland.....160 G6
Vowchurch......49 F5
Voxter........160 F5
Voy...........159 G3

**W**

Wackerfield....101 B6
Wacton.........68 E4
Wadbister.....160 J6
Wadborough.....50 E4
Waddesdon......39 C7
Waddingham.....90 E3
Waddington Lancs 93 E7
  Lincs........78 C2
Wadebridge......4 B4
Wadeford.......11 C8
Wadenhoe.......65 F7
Wadesmill......54 F3
Wadhurst.......18 B3
Wadshelf.......76 B3
Wadsley.........88 E4
Wadsley Bridge.. 88 E4
Wadworth.......89 E6
Waen Denb......72 C3
  Denb........72 C3
Waen Fach......60 C2
Waen Goleugoed..72 B4
Wag..........157 G13
Wainfleet All
  Saints........79 D7
Wainfleet Bank...79 D7
Wainfleet St Mary. 79 D8
Wainfleet Tofts...79 D7
Wainhouse Corner..8 E3
Wainscott......29 B8
Wainstalls.....87 B8
Waitby.........100 D2
Waithe.........91 D6
Wakefield......88 B4
Wake Lady Green. 102 E4
Wakerley.......65 E6
Wakes Colne....42 B4
Walberton......16 D3
Walbottle.....110 C4
Walcot Lincs....78 F3
  N Lincs......90 B2
  Shrops.......60 D3
  Swindon......38 F1
  Telford......61 C5
  Warks........51 D7
Walcote Leics...64 F2
  Warks........51 D6
Walcot Green....68 F4
Walcott Lincs....78 D5
  Norf.........69 A6
Walden.........101 F5
Walden Head...100 F4
Walden Stubbs.. 89 C6
Waldersey......66 D4
Walderslade....29 C8
Walderton.......15 C8
Walditch.......12 E2
Waldley........75 F8
Waldridge.....111 D5
Waldringfield
  Heath........57 E6
Waldron........18 D2
Wales..........89 F5
Walesby Lincs....90 E5
  Notts.........77 B6
Walford Hereford. 36 B2
  Hereford.....49 B5
  Shrops.......60 B4
Walford Heath...60 C4
Walgherton.....74 E3
Walgrave.......53 B6
Walhampton....14 E4
Walk............111 C5
Walker.........111 C5
Walker Barn.....75 B6
Walkden.........87 D5
Walker Fold.....93 E6
Walkeringham... 89 E8
Walkerith......89 E8
Walkern........41 C6
Walker's Green... 49 E7
Walkerville.....101 E7
Walkford........14 E3
Walkhampton.....6 C3
Walkington......97 F5
Walkley.........88 F4
Walk Mill.......93 F8
Wall Northumb...110 C2
  Staffs........62 D5

Wallaceton.....113 F8
Wallacetown
  S Ayrs.......112 B3
  S Ayrs.......112 D2
Wallands Park....17 C8
Wallasey........85 E4
Wall Bank......60 E5
Wallcrouch......18 B3
Wall Heath......62 F2
Wallingford.....39 F6
Wallington Hants. 15 D6
  Herts........54 F3
  London.......28 C3
Wallis.........32 B1
Walliswood......28 F2
Walls.........160 J4
Wallsend......111 C5
Wallston.......22 B3
Wall under
  Heywood......60 E5
Wallyford......121 B6
Walmer........31 D7
Walmer Bridge...86 B2
Walmersley.....87 C6
Walmley........62 E5
Walpole........57 B7
Walpole Cross
  Keys.........66 C5
Walpole Highway. 66 C5
Walpole Marsh...66 C4
Walpole St
  Andrew.......66 C5
Walpole St Peter. 66 C5
Walsall........62 E4
Walsall Wood....62 D4
Walsden........87 B7
Walsgrave on
  Sowe.........63 F7
Walsham le
  Willows......56 B3
Walshaw........87 C5
Walshford......95 D7
Walsoken.......66 C4
Walston.......120 E3
Walsworth......54 F3
Walters Ash....39 E8
Walterston......22 B2
Walterstone.....35 B7
Waltham Kent....30 E5
  NE Lincs......91 D6
Waltham Abbey...41 D6
Waltham Chase...15 C6
Waltham Cross...41 D6
Waltham on the
  Wolds.........64 B5
Waltham St
  Lawrence.....27 B6
Walthamstow....41 F6
Walton Cumb...108 C5
  Derbys........76 C3
  Leics.........64 F2
  Mers.........85 E4
  M Keynes......53 F6
  Pboro.........65 D8
  Powys........48 D4
  Som...........23 F6
  Staffs........75 F5
  Suff..........57 F6
  Telford.......61 C5
  Warks........51 D7
  W Yorks......88 C4
  W Yorks......95 E6
Walton Cardiff...50 F4
Walton East.....32 B1
Walton-in-
  Gordano......23 B6
Walton-le-Dale.. 86 B3
Walton-on-
  Thames......28 C2
Walton on the Hill
  Staffs........62 B3
  Sur..........28 D3
Walton-on-the-
  Naze.........43 B8
Walton on the
  Wolds.........64 C2
Walton-on-Trent. 63 C6
Walton West....44 D3
Walwen.........73 B6
Walwick.......110 B2
Walworth.......101 C7
Walworth Gate...101 B7
Walwyn's Castle.. 44 D3
Wambrook.......11 D8
Wanborough Sur.. 27 E7
  Swindon......38 F2
Wandsworth.....28 B3
Wangford.......57 B8
Wanlockhead....113 C8
Wansford E Yorks. 97 D6
  Pboro.........65 E7
Wanstead.......41 F7
Wanstrow.......24 E2
Wanswell.......36 D3
Wantage........38 F3
Wapley.........24 B2
Wappenbury.....51 C8
Wappenham.....52 E4
Warbleton......18 D3
Warblington.....15 D8
Warborough.....39 E5
Warboys.........66 F3
Warbreck.......92 F3
Warbstow........8 E4
Warburton......86 F5
Warcop........100 C2
Ward End.......62 F5
Ward Green....56 C4
Wardhill......159 F7
Wardington.....52 E2
Wardlaw.......115 C5
Wardle Ches E...74 D3
  Gtr Man......87 C7
Wardley.........64 D5
Wardlow........75 B8
Wardy Hill......66 F4
Ware Herts......41 C6
  Kent..........31 C6
Wareham........13 F7
Warehorne......19 B6
Warenford.....117 B7
Waren Mill.....123 F7
Warenton.....123 F7
Wareside........41 C6
Waresley Cambs.. 54 D3

Warfleet.........7 D6
Wargrave.......27 B5
Warham........80 C5
Wark Northumb..109 B8
  Northumb.....122 F4
Warkleigh........9 B8
Warkton........53 B6
Warkworth
  Northumb.....117 D0
  W Nhants......52 E2
Warlaby.......101 E8
Warland........87 B7
Warleggan.......5 C6
Warlingham.....28 D4
Warmfield......88 B4
Warmingham.....74 C4
Warmington
  N Nhants......65 E7
  Warks........52 E2
Warminster......24 E3
Warmlake.......30 D2
Warmley........23 B8
Warmley Tower... 23 B8
Warmonds Hill... 53 C7
Warmsworth.....89 D6
Warmwell.......13 F5
Warndon........50 D3
Warnford.......15 B7
Warnham........28 F2
Warninglid......17 B6
Warren Ches E...75 B5
  Pembs.........44 F4
Warren Heath...57 E6
Warren Row.....39 F8
Warren Street...30 D3
Warrington
  M Keynes......53 D6
  Warr..........86 F4
Warsash........15 D5
Warslow.........75 D7
Warsop Vale.....76 C4
Warter.........96 D4
Warthermarske.. 94 B5
Warthill.......96 D2
Wartling.......18 E3
Wartnaby.......64 B4
Warton Lancs....86 B2
  Lancs........92 B4
  Northumb....117 D6
  Warks........63 D6
Warwick.........51 C7
Warwick Bridge. 108 D4
Warwick on Eden. 108 D4
Wasbister.....159 E4
Wasdale Head....98 D3
Washaway........4 C5
Washbourne......7 D5
Wash Common...26 C2
Washfield.......10 C4
Washfold......101 D5
Washford........22 E2
Washford Pyne...10 C3
Washingborough. 78 B3
Washington T&W. 111 D6
  W Sus........16 C5
Wasing.........26 C3
Waskerley......110 E3
Wasperton......51 D7
Wasps Nest.....78 C3
Wass...........95 B8
Watchet........22 E2
Watchfield Oxon.. 38 E2
  Som..........22 E5
Watchgate.......99 E7
Watchhill......107 E8
Watcombe........7 C7
Watendlath......98 C4
Water Devon.....10 F2
  Lancs........87 B6
Waterbeach
  Cambs........55 C5
  W Sus........16 D4
Waterbeck.....108 B2
Waterden.......80 D4
Water End E Yorks. 96 F3
  Herts........40 C3
  Herts........41 D5
Waterfall.......75 D7
Waterfoot E Renf. 119 D5
  Lancs........87 B6
Waterford Hants. 14 E4
  Herts........41 C6
Waterhead
  Dumfries.....114 E4
  W&F..........99 D5
Waterheads....120 D5
Waterhouses
  Durham......110 E4
  Staffs........75 D7
Wateringbury....29 D7
Waterloo BCP....13 E8
  Gtr Man......87 D7
  Highld.....149 F11
  Mers........85 E4
  N Lanark....119 D8
  Norf.........68 C5
  Perth........133 F7
  Shrops.......74 F2
Waterloo Port...82 E4
Waterlooville...15 D7
Watermeetings.. 114 C2
Watermillock....99 B6
Water Newton....65 E8
Water Orton....63 E5
Waterperry......39 D6
Waterrow.......11 B5
Watersfield....16 C4
Waterside Aberds. 141 B9
  Blackburn....86 B5
  Cumb........108 E2
  E Ayrs.......112 D4
  E Ayrs.......118 E4
  E Renf........118 D5
Water's Nook....86 D4
Waterstock......39 D6
Waterston......44 E4
Water Stratford. 52 F4
Waters Upton....61 C6
Water Yeat.....98 F4
Watford Herts...40 E4
  W Nhants......52 C4
Watford Gap....62 D5
Wath N Yorks....94 C4
  N Yorks......95 B6
Wath Brow......98 C2
Wath upon
  Dearne.......88 D5
Watlington Norf.. 67 C6
  Oxon.........39 E6

Watnall.........76 E5
Watten........158 E4
Wattisfield......56 B4
Wattisham......56 D4
Wattlesborough
  Heath........60 C3
Watton E Yorks...97 D6
  Norf.........68 D2
Watton at Stone. 41 C6
Wattston.......119 B7
Wattstown.......34 E4
Wauchan.......136 F2
Waulkmill Lodge.159 H4
Waun...........59 D5
Waunarlwydd.....33 E7
Waunclunda.....47 F5
Waunfawr.......82 F5
Waungron.......33 D6
Waunlwyd.......35 D5
Wavendon.......53 F7
Waverbridge...108 E2
Waverley S Yorks..88 F5
Waverton Ches W. 73 C8
  Cumb........108 E2
Wavertree......85 F4
Wawne..........97 F6
Waxham.........69 B7
Waxholme......91 F7
Way............31 C7
Wayfield.......29 C8
Wayford........12 D2
Waymills.......74 E2
Wayne Green....35 C8
Way Village.....10 C3
Wdig = Goodwick. 44 B4
Weachyburn.....153 C6
Weald..........38 D3
Wealdstone......40 F4
Weardley.......95 E5
Weare..........23 D6
Weare Giffard....9 B6
Wearhead......109 F8
Weasdale......100 D1
Weasenham All
  Saints........80 E4
Weasenham St
  Peter........80 E4
Weatherhill.....28 E4
Weaverham......74 B3
Weaverthorpe...97 B5
Webheath.......50 C5
Wedderlairs....153 E8
Wedderlie.....122 D2
Weddington.....63 E7
Wedhampton.....25 D5
Wedmore.........23 E6
Wednesbury.....62 E3
Wednesfield....62 D3
Weedon.........39 C8
Weedon Bec.....52 D4
Weedon Lois.....52 E4
Weeford........62 D5
Week...........10 C2
Weeke..........26 F2
Weekley.........65 F5
Week St Mary.....8 E4
Weel...........97 F6
Weeley.........43 B7
Weeley Heath....43 B7
Weem..........133 E5
Weeping Cross... 62 B3
Weethley Gate...51 D5
Weeting........67 F7
Weeton E Yorks...91 B7
  Lancs........92 F3
  N Yorks......95 E5
Weetwood Hall.. 117 B6
Weir...........87 B6
Weir Quay.......6 C2
Welborne.......68 D3
Welbourn.......78 D2
Welburn N Yorks.. 96 C2
  N Yorks......102 F4
Welbury.......102 D1
Welby..........78 F2
Welches Dam.....66 F4
Welcombe........8 C4
Weld Bank......86 C3
Weldon........117 E7
Welford W Berks.. 26 B2
  W Nhants......52 B4
Welford-on-Avon. 51 D6
Welham Leics....64 E4
  Notts.........89 F8
Welham Green...41 D5
Well Hants......27 E5
  Lincs........79 B7
  N Yorks......101 F7
Welland........50 E2
Wellbank......134 F4
Welldale......107 C8
Well End......40 F1
Wellesbourne...51 D7
Well Heads......94 F3
Well Hill.......29 C5
Welling........29 B5
Wellingborough. 53 C6
Wellingham.....80 E4
Wellingore......78 D2
Wellington Cumb. 98 D2
  Hereford.....49 E6
  Som..........11 B6
  Telford.......61 C6
Wellington Heath. 50 E2
Wellington Hill... 95 F6
Wellow Bath....24 D2
  IoW..........14 F4
  Notts.........77 C6
Wellpond Green.. 41 B7
Wells..........23 E7
Wellsborough...63 D7
Wells Green....74 D3
Wells-next-the-
  Sea..........80 C5
Wellswood.......7 C7
Well Town......10 D4
Wellwood......128 F2
Welney..........66 E5
Welsh Bicknor...36 C2
Welsh End......74 F2
Welsh Frankton.. 73 F7
Welsh Hook......44 C4
Welsh Newton...36 C1
Welshpool
  = Y Trallwng.. 60 D2
Welsh St Donats. 22 B2
Welton Cumb....108 E3

Welton continued
  E Yorks.......90 B3
  Lincs.........78 B3
  W Nhants......52 C3
Welton Hill......90 F4
Welton le Marsh. 79 C7
Welton le Wold.. 91 F6
Welwick........91 B7
Welwyn.........41 C5
Welwyn Garden
  City..........41 C5
Wembdon........22 F4
Wembley........40 F4
Wembury.........6 E3
Wembworthy....9 D8
Wemyss Bay....118 C1
Wenallt Ceredig.. 47 B5
  Gwyn.........72 E3
Wendens Ambo.. 55 F6
Wendlebury.....39 C5
Wendling.......68 C2
Wendover.......40 D1
Wendron........3 C5
Wendy..........54 E4
Wenfordbridge....5 B5
Wenhaston......57 B8
Wennington Cambs. 54 B3
  Lancs........93 B6
  London.......41 F8
Wensley Derbys.. 76 C2
  N Yorks......101 F5
Wentbridge.....89 C5
Wentnor........60 E3
Wentworth Cambs. 55 B5
  S Yorks.......88 E4
Wenvoe.........22 B3
Weobley.........49 D6
Weobley Marsh.. 49 D6
Wereham........67 D6
Wergs..........62 D2
Wern Powys.....59 C6
  Powys........60 C2
Wernffrwd.......33 E6
Wernyrheolydd.. 35 C7
Werrington Corn.. 8 F5
  Pboro........65 D8
  Staffs........75 E6
Wervin.........73 B8
Wesham.........92 F4
Wessington.....76 D3
West Acre......67 C7
West Adderbury. 52 F2
West Allerdean.. 123 E5
West Alvington...6 E5
West Amesbury.. 25 E6
West Anstey....10 B3
West Ashby.....79 B5
West Ashling....16 D2
West Ashton....24 D3
West Auckland..101 B6
West Ayton.....103 F7
West Bagborough.22 F3
West Barkwith.. 91 F5
West Barnby....103 C6
West Barns.....122 B2
West Barsham....80 D5
West Bay........12 E2
West Beckham...81 D7
West Bedfont....27 B8
West Benhar....119 C8
West Bergholt...43 B5
West Bexington.. 12 F3
West Bilney.....67 C7
West Blatchington. 17 D6
West Bourne BCP. 13 E8
  Suff..........56 E5
  W Sus........15 D8
West Bowling....94 F4
West Bradford...93 E7
West Bradley....23 F7
West Bretton....88 C3
West Bridgford.. 77 F5
West Bromwich.. 62 E4
Westbrook......26 B2
West Buckland
  Devon........21 F5
  Som..........11 B6
West Burrafirth. 160 H4
West Burton
  N Yorks......101 F5
  W Sus........16 C3
Westbury Bucks.. 52 F4
  Shrops.......60 D3
  Wilts........24 D3
Westbury Leigh.. 24 D3
Westbury-on-
  Severn.......36 C4
Westbury on Trym 23 B7
Westbury-sub-
  Mendip.......23 E7
West Butterwick. 90 D2
West Byfleet....27 C8
West Caister....69 C8
West Calder....120 C3
West Camel.....12 B3
West Challow....38 F3
West Chelborough 12 D3
West Chevington. 117 E8
West Chiltington. 16 C4
West Chiltington
  Common......16 C4
West Chinnock... 12 C2
West Chisenbury. 25 D6
West Clandon....27 D8
West Cliffe......31 E7
Westcliff-on-Sea. 42 F4
West Clyne....157 J11
West Clyth.....158 G4
West Coker.....12 C3
Westcombe......23 F8
West Compton
  Dorset........12 E3
  Som..........23 E7
Westcote.......38 B2
Westcott Bucks... 39 C7
  Devon........10 D5
  Sur..........28 E2
Westcott Barton. 38 B4
West Cowick....89 B7
West Cranmore.. 23 E8
West Cross.....33 F7
West Cullery...141 D6
West Curry.......8 E4
West Curthwaite. 108 E3

West Darlochan.. 143 F7
Westdean.......18 F2
West Dean Wilts.. 14 B3
  W Sus........16 C2
West Deeping....65 D8
Westdene.......17 D6
West Derby......85 E4
West Dereham... 67 D6
West Didsbury.. 87 E6
West Ditchburn.. 117 B7
West Down......20 E4
West Drayton
  London.......27 B8
  Notts.........77 B7
West Ella.......90 B4
West End Bedford. 53 D8
  E Yorks.......96 F5
  E Yorks.......97 F7
  Hants........15 C5
  Lancs........86 B5
  Norf.........68 D2
  Norf.........69 C8
  N Som........23 C6
  Oxon.........38 D4
  S Lanark.....120 E2
  Suff..........69 F7
  Sur..........27 C7
  S Yorks.......89 D7
  Wilts........13 B7
  Wilts........24 B4
  W Sus........17 C6
West End Green.. 26 C4
Wester
  Aberchalder.. 137 B8
Wester Balgedie. 128 D3
Wester
  Culbeuchly.. 153 B6
Westerdale Highld. 158 E3
  N Yorks......102 D4
Wester
  Dechmont... 120 C3
Wester Denoon.. 134 E3
Westerfield
  Shetland.....160 H5
  Suff..........57 E5
Westergate.....16 D3
Wester Fintray. 141 C7
Wester Gruinards 151 B8
Westerham......28 D5
Westerhope....110 C4
Wester Leith...151 D9
Westerleigh.....23 B9
Wester Milton.. 151 F12
Wester Newburn 129 D6
Wester Quarff.. 160 K6
Wester Skeld...160 J4
Westerton Angus. 135 D6
  Durham......110 F5
  W Sus........16 D2
Westerwick....160 J4
West Farleigh...29 D8
West Felton....60 B3
West Fenton....129 F6
West Ferry.....134 F4
Westfield Cumb.. 98 B1
  E Sus........18 D5
  Hereford.....50 E2
  Highld......158 D2
  N Lanark....119 B7
  Norf.........68 D2
  W Loth......120 B2
Westfields.....12 D5
Westfields of
  Rattray.....134 E1
West Firle.....17 D8
Westgate Durham. 110 F2
  N Lincs......89 D8
  Norf.........80 C4
  Norf.........81 C5
Westgate on Sea. 31 B7
West Ginge.....38 F4
West Grafton....25 C7
West Green......26 D5
West
  Greenskares.. 153 B7
West Grimstead. 14 B3
West Grinstead.. 17 B5
West Haddlesey.. 89 B6
West Haddon....52 B4
West Hagbourne. 39 F5
West Hagley.....62 F3
West Hall.....109 C5
West Hallam....76 E4
West Halton.....90 B3
West Ham.......41 F7
Westhampnett... 16 D2
West Handley....76 B3
West Hanney....38 E4
West Hanningfield. 42 E3
West Hardwick.. 88 C5
West Harnham....14 B2
West Harptree.. 23 D7
West Hatch......11 B7
Westhay.........23 E6
Westhead.......86 D2
West Head......67 D6
West Heath Ches E. 74 C5
  Hants........26 D3
  Hants........27 D6
West Helmsdale.157 H13
West Hendred... 38 F4
West Heslerton.. 96 B5
Westhide.......49 E7
Westhill Aberds.. 141 D7
West Hill Devon.. 11 E5
  E Yorks.......97 C7
  N Som........23 B6
West Hoathly....17 B7
West Holme.....13 F6
Westhope Hereford. 49 D6
  Shrops.......60 F4
West Horndon...42 F2
Westhorpe Lincs.. 78 F5
  Suff..........56 C4
West Horrington. 23 E7
West Horsley....27 D8
West Horton....123 F6
West Hougham.. 31 E6
West Houlland.. 160 H4
West Orchard....13 C6
West Overton....25 C6

Westhumble......28 D2
West Huntington 96 D2
West Hythe.....19 B8
West Ilsley.....38 F4
West Itchenor...15 D8
West Keal......79 C6
West Kennett....25 C6
West Kilbride.. 118 E2
West Kingsdown. 29 C6
West Kington....24 B3
West
  Kinharrachie.. 153 E9
West Kirby......85 F3
West Knapton... 96 B4
West Knighton.. 12 F5
West Knoyle....24 F3
West Kyloe....123 E6
West Lambrook.. 12 C2
West Langdon....31 E7
West Langwell.. 157 J9
West Lavington
  Wilts........24 D5
  W Sus........16 B2
West Layton...101 D6
West Lea......111 E7
West Leake.....64 B2
West Learmouth. 122 F4
Westleigh Devon.. 9 B6
  Devon.........11 C5
  Gtr Man......86 D4
West Leigh......9 D8
Westleton......57 C8
West Lexham....67 C8
Westley Shrops... 60 D3
  Suff..........56 C2
Westley Waterless 55 D7
West Lilling....96 C2
Westlington.....39 C7
West Linton...120 D4
West Liss......15 B8
West Littleton.. 24 B2
West Looe........5 D7
West Luccombe. 21 E7
West Lulworth.. 13 F6
West Lutton....96 C5
West Lydford...23 F7
West Lyng......11 B8
West Lynn......67 B6
West Malling....29 D7
West Malvern....50 E2
West Marden....15 C8
West Markham... 77 B7
West Marsh......91 C6
West Marton....93 D8
West Meon.......15 B7
West Mersea....43 C6
Westmeston.....17 C7
West Milton....12 E3
Westmill........41 B6
West Minster....30 B3
West Molesey....28 C2
West Monkton....11 B7
West Moors......13 D8
West Morriston.. 122 E2
Westmuir......134 D3
West Muir.....135 C5
Westness......159 F4
West Ness......96 B2
West Newham...110 B3
Westnewton Cumb 107 E8
  Northumb....122 F5
West Newton
  E Yorks.......97 F7
  Norf.........67 B6
West Norwood....28 B4
Westoe.........111 C6
West Ogwell......7 B6
Weston Bath....24 C2
  Ches E........74 D4
  Devon........11 F6
  Dorset........12 G4
  Halton........86 F3
  Hants........15 B8
  Herts........54 F3
  Lincs........66 B2
  Notts.........77 C7
  N Yorks......94 E4
  Shrops.......60 B5
  Shrops.......61 E5
  Staffs........62 B3
  W Berks......26 B2
  W Nhants......52 E3
Weston Beggard. 49 E7
Weston by
  Welland......64 E4
Weston Colville. 55 D7
Westoncommon.. 60 B4
Weston Coyney.. 75 E6
Weston Favell...53 C5
Weston Green
  Cambs........55 D7
  Norf.........68 C4
Weston Heath...61 C7
Weston Hills....66 B2
Westoning......53 F8
Weston-in-
  Gordano......23 B6
Weston Jones....61 B7
Weston Longville. 68 C4
Weston
  Lullingfields.. 60 B4
Weston-on-the-
  Green........39 C5
Weston-on-Trent. 63 B8
Weston Patrick.. 26 E4
Weston Rhyn....73 F6
Weston-sub-Edge 51 E6
Weston-super-
  Mare.........22 C5
Weston Turville. 40 C1
Weston under
  Lizard.......62 C2
Weston under
  Penyard.......36 B3
Weston under
  Wetherley.....51 C8
Weston
  Underwood
  Derbys.......76 E2
  M Keynes......53 D6
Westonzoyland.. 23 F5

Westow.........96 C3
West Park......111 F7
West Parley.....13 E8
West Peckham... 29 D7
West Pelton....110 D5
West Pennard... 23 F7
West Pentire.....4 C2
West Perry.....54 C2
Westport Argyll.. 143 F7
  Som..........11 C8
West Putford.....9 C5
West Quantoxhead 22 E3
West Rainton...111 E6
West Rasen.....90 F4
West Raynham...80 E4
West Retford....89 F7
Westrigg......120 C2
West Rounton.. 102 D2
West Row.......55 B7
West Rudham....80 E4
West Runton....81 C7
Westruther.....122 E2
Westry.........66 E3
West Saltoun...121 C7
West Sandwick.. 160 E6
West Scrafton.. 101 F5
West Sleekburn. 117 F8
West Somerton.. 69 C7
West Stafford...12 F5
West Stockwith.. 89 E8
West Stoke.....16 D2
West Stonesdale. 100 D3
West Stoughton. 23 E6
West Stour.....13 B5
West Stourmouth. 31 C6
West Stow.......56 B2
West Stowell....25 C6
West Strathan.. 157 C8
West Stratton.. 26 E3
West Street.....30 D3
West Tanfield... 95 B5
West Taphouse...5 C6
West Tarbert...145 G2
West Thirston.. 117 E7
West Thorney...15 D8
West Thurrock.. 29 B6
West Tilbury....29 B7
West Tisted.....15 B7
West Tofts Norf.. 67 E8
  Perth........133 F8
West Torrington. 90 F5
West Town Hants. 15 E8
  N Som........23 C6
West Tytherley.. 14 B3
West Tytherton.. 24 B4
Westville.......76 E5
West Walton....66 C4
West Walton
  Highway......66 C4
Westward......108 E2
Westward Ho!.....9 B6
Westwell Kent...30 D3
  Oxon.........38 D2
Westwell Leacon. 30 D3
West Wellow....14 C3
West Wemyss...128 E5
Westwick Cambs.. 54 C5
  Durham......101 C5
  Norf..........81 E8
West Wick......23 C5
West Wickham
  Cambs........55 E7
  London.......28 C4
West Williamston 32 D1
West Willoughby. 78 E2
West Winch.....67 C6
West Winterslow. 25 F7
West Wittering.. 15 E8
West Witton....101 F5
Westwood Devon. 10 E5
  Wilts.........24 D3
West Woodburn. 116 F4
West Woodhay...25 C8
West Woodlands.. 24 E2
Westwoodside....89 E8
West Worldham.. 26 F5
West Worlington. 10 C2
West Worthing.. 16 D5
West Wratting... 55 D7
West Wycombe... 39 E8
West Wylam....110 C4
West Yell......160 E6
Wetheral.......108 D4
Wetherby.......95 E7
Wetherden......56 C4
Wetheringsett.. 56 C5
Wethersfield....55 F8
Wethersta.....160 G5
Wetherup Street. 56 C5
Wetley Rocks....75 E6
Wettenhall......74 C3
Wetton.........75 D8
Wetwang........96 D5
Wetwood........74 F4
Wexcombe......25 D7
Wexham Street.. 40 F2
Weybourne......81 C7
Weybread.......69 F5
Weybridge......27 C8
Weycroft.......11 E8
Weydale.......158 D3
Weyhill........25 E8
Weymouth......12 G4
Whaddon Bucks.. 53 F6
  Cambs........54 E4
  Glos.........37 C5
  Wilts.........14 B2
Whale..........99 B7
Whaley.........76 B5
Whaley Bridge... 87 F8
Whaligoe......158 F5
Whalley........93 F7
Whalton........117 F7
Wham..........93 C7
Whaplode......66 B3
Whaplode Drove. 66 C3
Whaplode
  St Catherine.. 66 B3
Wharfe.........93 C7
Wharles.........92 F4
Wharncliffe Side. 88 E3
Wharram le Street. 96 C4
Wharton.........74 C3
Wharton Green... 74 C3
Whashton......101 D6

Whatcombe 13 D6
Whatcote 51 E8
Whatfield 56 E4
Whatley Som 11 D8
 Som 24 E2
Whatlington 18 D4
Whatstandwell 76 D3
Whatton 77 F7
Whauphill 105 E8
Whaw 100 D4
Wheatacre 69 E7
Wheatcroft 76 D3
Wheathampstead 40 C4
Wheathill 61 F6
Wheatley Devon
 Hants 27 E5
 Oxon 39 D5
 S Yorks 89 D6
 W Yorks 87 B8
Wheatley Hill 111 F6
Wheaton Aston 62 C2
Wheddon Cross 21 F8
Wheedlemont 140 B3
Wheelerstreet 27 E7
Wheelock 74 D4
Wheelock Heath 74 D4
Wheelton 86 B4
Wheen 134 B3
Wheldrake 96 E2
Whelford 38 E1
Whelpley Hill 40 D2
Whempstead 41 B6
Whenby 96 C2
Whepstead 56 D2
Wherstead 57 E5
Wherwell 25 E8
Wheston 75 B8
Whetsted 29 E7
Whetstone 64 E2
Whicham 98 F3
Whichford 51 F8
Whickham 110 C5
Whiddon Down 9 E8
Whigstreet 134 E4
Whilton 52 C4
Whimble 9 D5
Whim Farm 120 D5
Whimple 10 E5
Whimpwell Green 69 B6
Whinburgh 68 D3
Whinhall 119 C7
Whinnyfold 153 D10
Whippingham 15 E6
Whipsnade 40 C3
Whipton 10 E4
Whirlow 88 F4
Whisby 78 C2
Whissendine 64 C5
Whissonsett 80 E5
Whistlefield
 Argyll 145 D10
 Argyll 145 D11
Whistley Green 27 B5
Whiston Mers 86 E2
 Staffs 62 C2
 Staffs 75 E7
 S Yorks 88 F5
 W Nhants 53 C6
Whitbeck 98 F3
Whitbourne 50 D2
Whitburn T&W 111 C7
 W Loth 120 C2
Whitburn
 Colliery 111 C7
Whitby Ches W 73 B7
 N Yorks 103 C6
Whitbyheath 73 B7
Whitchurch Bath 23 C8
 Bucks 39 B7
 Cardiff 35 F5
 Devon 6 B2
 Hants 26 E2
 Hereford 36 C2
 Oxon 26 B4
 Pembs 44 C2
 Shrops 74 E2
Whitchurch
 Canonicorum 11 E8
Whitchurch Hill 26 B4
Whitcombe 12 F5
Whitcott Keysett 60 F2
Whiteacen 152 D2
Whiteacre Heath 63 E6
Whitebridge 137 C7
Whitebrook 36 D2
Whiteburn 121 E8
Whitecairn 105 D6
Whitecairns 141 C8
Whitecastle 120 E3
Whitechapel 93 E5
Whitecleat 159 H6
White Coppice 86 C4
Whitecraig 121 B6
Whitecroft 36 D3
Whitecross Corn 4 B4
 Falk 120 B2
 Staffs 62 B2
Whiteface 151 C10
Whitefarland 143 D9
Whitefaulds 112 D2
Whitefield Gtr Man 87 D6
 Perth 134 F1
Whiteford 141 B6
Whitegate 74 C3
Whitehall Blackburn 86 B4
 W Sus 16 B5
Whitehall Village 159 F7
Whitehaven 98 C1
Whitehill 27 F5
Whitehills Aberds 153 B6
 S Lanark 119 D6
Whitehough 87 F8
Whitehouse
 Aberds 140 C5
 Argyll 145 G7
Whiteinch 118 C5
White Kirk 129 F7
White Lackington 12 E5
White Ladies
 Aston 50 D4
Whitelaw 119 E6
Whiteleas 111 C6
Whiteley Bank 15 F6
Whiteley Green 75 B6
Whiteley Village 27 C8
White Lund 92 C4

Whitemans Green 17 B7
White Mill 33 B5
Whitemire 151 F12
Whitemoor 4 D4
Whitemore 75 C5
Whitenap 14 B4
White Ness 160 J5
White Notley 42 C3
Whiteoak Green 38 C3
Whiteparish 14 B3
White Pit 79 B6
White Post 77 D6
Whiterashes 141 B7
White Rocks 35 B8
White Roding 42 C1
Whiterow 158 F5
Whiteshill 37 D5
Whiteside
 Northumb 109 C7
 W Loth 120 C2
Whitesmith 18 D2
Whitestaunton 11 C7
Whitestone Devon 10 E3
 Devon 20 E3
 Warks 63 F7
Whitestones 153 C8
Whitestreet Green 56 F3
Whitewall Corner 96 B3
White Waltham 27 B6
Whiteway Glos 37 C6
 Glos 37 E5
Whitewell Aberds 153 B9
 Lancs 93 E6
Whitewell Bottom 87 B6
Whiteworks 6 B4
Whitfield Kent 31 E7
 Northumb 109 D7
 S Glos 36 E3
 W Nhants 52 F4
Whitford Devon 11 E7
 Flint 72 B5
Whitgift 90 B2
Whitgreave 62 B2
Whitkirk 95 F6
Whitland 32 C2
Whitletts 112 B3
Whitley N Yorks 89 B6
 Reading 26 B5
 Wilts 24 C3
Whitley Bay 111 B6
Whitley Chapel 110 D2
Whitley Lower 88 C3
Whitley Row 29 D5
Whitlock's End 51 B6
Whitminster 36 D4
Whitmore 74 E5
Whitnage 10 C5
Whitnash 51 C8
Whitrigg Cumb 108 D2
 Cumb 108 F2
Whitsbury 14 C2
Whitsome 122 D4
Whitson 35 F7
Whitstable 30 C5
Whitstone 8 E4
Whittingham 117 C6
Whittingslow 60 F4
Whittlebury 52 E4
Whittle-le-Woods 86 B3
Whittlesey 66 E2
Whittlesford 55 E5
Whittlestone Head 86 C5
Whitton Borders 116 B3
 N Lincs 90 B3
 Northumb 117 D6
 Powys 48 C4
 Shrops 49 B7
 Stockton 102 B1
 Suff 56 E5
Whittonditch 25 B7
Whittonstall 110 D3
Whitway 26 D2
Whitwell Derbys 76 B5
 Herts 40 B4
 IoW 15 G6
 N Yorks 101 E7
 Rutland 65 D6
Whitwell-on-the-
 Hill 96 C3
Whitwell Street 81 E7
Whitwick 63 C8
Whitwood 88 B5
Whitworth 87 C6
Whixall 74 F2
Whixley 95 D7
Whoberley 51 B8
Whorlton Durham 101 C6
 N Yorks 102 D2
Whygate 109 B7
Whyle 49 C7
Whyteleafe 28 D4
Wibdon 36 E2
Wibsey 88 A2
Wibtoft 63 F8
Wichenford 50 C2
Wichling 30 D3
Wick BCP 14 E2
 Devon 11 D6
 Highld 158 E5
 S Glos 24 B2
 Shetland 160 K6
 V Glam 21 B8
 Wilts 14 B2
 Worcs 50 E4
 W Sus 16 D4

Wicken Cambs 55 B6
 W Nhants 52 F5
Wicken Bonhunt 55 F5
Wickenby 90 F4
Wicken Green
 Village 80 D4
Wickersley 89 E5
Wickford 42 E3
Wickham Hants 15 C6
 W Berks 25 B8
Wickham Bishops 42 C4
Wickhambreux 31 D6
Wickhambrook 55 D8
Wickhamford 51 E5
Wickham Market 57 D7
Wickhampton 69 D7
Wickham St Paul 56 F2
Wickham Skeith 56 C4
Wickham Street
 Suff 55 D8
 Suff 56 C4
Wick Hill 27 C5
Wicklewood 68 D3
Wickmere 81 D7
Wick St Lawrence 23 C5
Wickwar 36 F4
Widdington 55 F6
Widdrington
 Station 117 E8
Widecombe in the
 Moor 6 B5
Widegates 5 D7
Widemouth Bay 8 D4
Wide Open 110 B5
Widewall 159 J5
Widford Essex 42 D2
 Herts 41 C7
Widham 37 F7
Widmer End 40 E1
Widmerpool 64 B3
Widnes 86 F3
Wigan 86 D3
Wiggaton 11 E6
Wiggenhall St
 Germans 67 C5
Wiggenhall St Mary
 Magdalen 67 C5
Wiggenhall St Mary
 the Virgin 67 C5
Wigginton Herts 40 C2
 Oxon 51 F8
 Staffs 63 D6
 York 95 D8
Wigglesworth 93 D8
Wiggonby 108 D2
Wiggonholt 16 C4
Wighill 95 E7
Wighton 80 D5
Wigley 14 C4
Wigmore Hereford 49 C6
 Medway 30 C2
Wigsley 77 B8
Wigsthorpe 65 F7
Wigston 64 E3
Wigthorpe 89 F6
Wigtoft 79 F5
Wigton 108 E2
Wigtown 105 D8
Wike 95 E6
Wike Well End 89 C7
Wilbarston 64 F5
Wilberfoss 96 D3
Wilberlee 87 C8
Wilburton 55 B5
Wilby N Nhants 53 C6
 Norf 68 F3
 Suff 57 B6
Wilcot 25 C6
Wilcott 60 C3
Wilcrick 35 F8
Wilday Green 76 B3
Wildboarclough 75 C6
Wilden Bedford 53 D8
 Worcs 50 B3
Wildhern 25 D8
Wildhill 41 D5
Wildmoor 50 B4
Wildsworth 90 E2
Wilford 77 F5
Wilkesley 74 E3
Wilkhaven 151 C12
Wilkieston 120 C4
Willand 10 C5
Willaston Ches E 74 D3
 Ches W 73 B7
Willen 53 E6
Willenhall W Mid 51 B8
 W Mid 62 E3
Willerby E Yorks 97 F6
 N Yorks 97 B6
Willersey 51 F6
Willersley 48 E5
Willesborough 30 E4
Willesborough
 Lees 30 E4
Willesden 41 F5
Willett 22 F3
Willey Shrops 61 E6
 Warks 63 F8
Willey Green 27 D7
Williamscott 52 E2
Willian 54 F3
Willingale 42 D1
Willingdon 18 E2
Willingham 54 B5
Willingham by
 Stow 90 F2
Willington Bedford 54 E2
 Derbys 63 B6
 Durham 110 F4
 T&W 111 C6
 Warks 51 F7
Willington Corner 74 C2
Willisham Tye 56 D4
Willitoft 96 F3
Williton 22 E2
Willoughbridge 74 E4
Willoughby Lincs 79 B7
 Warks 52 C3
Willoughby-on-the-
 Wolds 64 B3
Willoughby
 Waterleys 64 E2
Willoughton 90 E3
Willows Green 42 C3
Willsbridge 23 B8
Willsworthy 9 F7
Wilmcote 51 D6
Wilmington Devon 11 E7
 E Sus 18 E2
 Kent 29 B6
Wilminstone 6 B2
Wilmslow 87 F6
Wilnecote 63 D6
Wilpshire 93 F6
Wilsden 94 F3
Wilsford Lincs 78 E3
 Wilts 25 C6
 Wilts 25 D6
Wilsill 94 C4
Wilsley Pound 18 B4

Wilsom 26 F5
Wilson 63 B8
Wilsontown 120 D2
Wilstead 53 E8
Wilsthorpe 65 C7
Wilton Borders 115 C7
 Cumb 98 C2
 N Yorks 103 F6
 Redcar 102 C3
 Wilts 25 C7
 Wilts 25 F5
Wimbish 55 F6
Wimbish Green 55 F7
Wimblebury 62 C4
Wimbledon 28 B3
Wimblington 66 E4
Wimborne Minster 13 E8
Wimborne St Giles 13 C8
Wimbotsham 67 D6
Wimpson 14 C4
Wimpstone 51 E7
Wincanton 12 B5
Wincham 74 B3
Winchburgh 120 B3
Winchcombe 37 B7
Winchelsea 19 D6
Winchelsea Beach 19 D6
Winchester 15 B5
Winchet Hill 29 E8
Winchfield 27 D5
Winchmore Hill
 Bucks 40 E2
 London 41 E6
Wincle 75 C6
Wincobank 88 E4
Windermere 99 E6
Winderton 51 E8
Windhill 151 G8
Windhouse 160 D6
Windlehurst 87 F7
Windlesham 27 C7
Windley 76 E3
Windmill Hill
 E Sus 18 D3
 Som 11 C8
Windrush 38 C1
Windsor N Lincs 89 C8
 Windsor 27 B7
Windsoredge 37 D5
Windygates 128 D5
Windyknowe 120 C2
Windywalls 122 F3
Wineham 17 B6
Winestead 91 B6
Winewall 94 E2
Winfarthing 68 F4
Winford IoW 15 F6
 N Som 23 C7
Winforton 48 E4
Winfrith
 Newburgh 13 F6
Wing Bucks 40 B1
 Rutland 65 D5
Wingate 111 F7
Wingates Gtr Man 86 D4
 Northumb 117 E7
Wingerworth 76 C3
Wingfield C Beds 40 B2
 Suff 57 B6
 Wilts 24 D3
Wingham 31 D6
Wingmore 31 E5
Wingrave 40 C1
Winkburn 77 D7
Winkfield 27 B7
Winkfield Row 27 B6
Winkhill 75 D7
Winklebury 26 D4
Winkleigh 9 D8
Winksley 95 B5
Winkton 14 E2
Winlaton 110 C4
Winless 158 E5
Winmarleigh 92 E4
Winnal 49 F6
Winnall 15 B5
Winnersh 27 B5
Winscales 98 B2
Winscombe 23 D6
Winsford Ches W 74 C3
 Som 21 F8
Winsham 11 D8
Winshill 63 B6
Winskill 109 F5
Winslade 26 E4
Winsley 24 C3
Winslow 39 B7
Winson 37 D7
Winson Green 62 F4
Winsor 14 C4
Winster Derbys 76 C2
 Cumb 99 E6
Winston Durham 101 C6
 Suff 57 C5
Winstone 37 D6
Winston Green 57 C5
Winswell 9 C6
Winterborne
 Clenston 13 D6
Winterborne
 Herringston 12 F4
Winterborne
 Houghton 13 D6
Winterborne
 Kingston 13 E6
Winterborne
 Monkton 12 F4
Winterborne
 Stickland 13 D6
Winterborne
 Whitechurch 13 D6
Winterborne
 Zelston 13 E6
Winterbourne
 S Glos 36 F3
 W Berks 26 B2
Winterbourne
 Abbas 12 E4
Winterbourne
 Bassett 25 B6
Winterbourne
 Dauntsey 25 F6
Winterbourne
 Down 23 B8
Winterbourne
 Earls 25 F6
Winterbourne
 Gunner 25 F6

Winterbourne
 Monkton 25 B6
Winterbourne
 Steepleton 12 F4
Winterbourne
 Stoke 25 E5
Winter Gardens 42 F3
Winteringham 90 B3
Winterley 74 D4
Wintersett 88 C4
Wintershill 15 C6
Winterton 90 C3
Winterton-on-Sea 69 C7
Winthorpe Lincs 79 C8
 Notts 77 D8
Winton BCP 13 E8
 N Yorks 102 D2
 W&F 100 C2
Wintringham 96 B4
Winwick Cambs 65 F8
 Warr 86 E4
 W Nhants 52 B4
Wirksworth 76 D2
Wirksworth Moor 76 D3
Wirswall 74 E2
Wisbech 66 D4
Wisbech St Mary 66 D4
Wisborough Green 16 B4
Wiseton 89 F7
Wishaw N Lanark 119 D7
 Warks 63 E5
Wisley 27 D8
Wispington 78 B5
Wissenden 30 E3
Wissett 57 B7
Wistanstow 60 F4
Wistanswick 61 B6
Wistaston 74 D3
Wistaston Green 74 D3
Wiston Pembs 32 C1
 S Lanark 120 F2
 W Sus 16 C5
Wistow Cambs 66 F2
 N Yorks 95 F8
Wiswell 93 F7
Witcham 66 F4
Witchampton 13 D7
Witchford 55 B6
Witham 42 C4
Witham Friary 24 E2
Witham on the Hill 65 C7
Withcall 78 B5
Withcote 64 D5
Withdean 17 D7
Witherenden Hill 18 C3
Witheridge 10 C3
Witherley 63 E7
Withern 91 F8
Withernsea 91 B7
Withernwick 97 E7
Withersdale Street 69 F5
Withersfield 55 E7
Witherslack 99 F6
Withiel 4 C4
Withiel Florey 21 F8
Withington Glos 37 C7
 Gtr Man 87 E6
 Hereford 49 E7
 Shrops 61 C5
 Staffs 75 F7
Withington Green 74 B5
Withleigh 10 C4
Withnell 86 B4
Withybrook 63 F8
Withycombe 22 E2
Withycombe
 Raleigh 10 F5
Withyham 29 F5
Withypool 21 F7
Witley 27 F7
Witnesham 57 D5
Witney 38 C3
Wittering 65 D7
Wittersham 19 C5
Witton Angus 135 B5
 Worcs 50 C3
Witton Bridge 69 A6
Witton Gilbert 110 E5
Witton-le-Wear 110 F4
Witton Park 110 F4
Wiveliscombe 11 B5
Wivelrod 26 F4
Wivelsfield 17 B7
Wivelsfield Green 17 B7
Wivenhoe 43 B6
Wivenhoe Cross 43 B6
Wiveton 81 C6
Wix 43 B7
Wixford 51 D5
Wixhill 61 B5
Wixoe 55 E8
Woburn 53 F7
Woburn Sands 53 F7
Wokefield Park 26 C4
Woking 27 D8
Wokingham 27 C6
Wolborough 7 B6
Woldingham 28 D4
Wold Newton
 E Yorks 97 B6
 NE Lincs 91 E6
Wolferlow 49 C8
Wolferton 67 B6
Wolfhill 134 F1
Wolf's Castle 44 C4
Wolfsdale 44 C4
Woll 115 B7
Wollaston N Nhants 53 C7
 Shrops 60 C3
Wollaton 76 F5
Wollerton 61 B6
Wollescote 62 F3
Wolsingham 110 F3
Wolstanton 75 E5
Wolston 52 B2
Wolvercote 38 D4
Wolverhampton 62 E3
Wolverley Shrops 73 F8
 Worcs 50 B3
Wolverton Hants 26 D3
 M Keynes 53 E6
 Warks 51 C7
Wolverton
 Common 26 D3
Wolvesnewton 36 E1
Wolvey 63 F8
Wolviston 102 B2
Wombleton 102 F4
Wombourne 62 E2

Wombwell 88 D4
Womenswold 31 D6
Womersley 89 C6
Wonastow 36 C1
Wonersh 27 E8
Wonson 9 E8
Wonston 26 F2
Wooburn 40 F2
Wooburn Green 40 F2
Woodacott 9 D5
Woodale 94 B3
Woodbank 143 D7
Woodbastwick 69 C6
Woodbeck 77 B7
Woodborough
 Notts 77 E6
 Wilts 25 D6
Woodbridge Dorset 12 C5
 Suff 57 E6
Woodbury 10 F5
Woodbury
 Salterton 10 F5
Woodchester 37 D5
Woodchurch Kent 19 B6
 Mers 85 F3
Woodcombe 21 E8
Woodcote 39 F6
Woodcott 26 D2
Woodcroft 36 E2
Woodcutts 13 C7
Wood Dalling 81 E6
Woodditton 55 D7
Woodeaton 39 C5
Woodend Cumb 98 E3
 W Nhants 52 E4
 W Sus 16 D2
Wood End Herts 41 B6
 Warks 51 B6
 Warks 63 E6
Wood Enderby 79 C5
Woodend Green 52 F4
Woodfalls 14 B2
Woodfield Oxon 39 B5
 S Ayrs 112 B3
Wood Field 28 D2
Woodford Corn 8 C4
 Devon 7 D5
 Glos 36 E3
 Gtr Man 87 F6
 London 41 E7
 N Nhants 53 B7
 Soton 14 C5
 Warr 86 E4
Woodford Bridge 41 E7
Woodford Halse 52 D3
Woodgate Devon 11 C6
 Norf 68 C3
 W Mid 62 F3
 W Sus 16 D3
Woodgreen 14 C2
Wood Green 41 E6
Woodhall Herts 41 C5
 Involyd 118 B3
 N Yorks 100 E4
Woodhall Spa 78 C4
Woodham 27 C8
Woodham Ferrers 42 E3
Woodham
 Mortimer 42 D4
Woodham Walter 42 D4
Woodhaven 129 B6
Wood Hayes 62 D3
Woodhead 153 E7
Woodhey 87 C5
Woodhill 61 F7
Woodhorn 117 F8
Woodhouse Leics 64 C2
 N Lincs 89 D8
 S Yorks 88 F5
 W Yorks 88 B4
 W Yorks 95 F5
Woodhouse Eaves 64 C2
Woodhouselee 120 C5
Woodhouselees 108 B3
Woodhouse Park 87 F6
Woodhouses 63 C5
Woodhuish 7 D7
Woodhurst 54 B4
Woodingdean 17 D7
Woodkirk 88 B3
Woodland Devon 7 C5
 Durham 101 B5
Woodlands Aberds 141 E6
 Dorset 13 D8
 Hants 14 C4
 Highld 151 E8
 N Yorks 95 D6
 S Yorks 89 D6
Woodlands Park 27 B6
Woodlands St
 Mary 25 B8
Woodlane 62 B5
Wood Lanes 87 F7
Woodleigh 6 E5
Woodlesford 88 B4
Woodley Gtr Man 87 E7
 Wokingham 27 B5
Woodmancote Glos 36 E4
 Glos 37 B6
 Glos 37 D7
 W Sus 15 D8
 W Sus 17 C6
Woodmancott 26 E3
Woodmansey 97 F6
Woodmansterne 28 D3
Woodminton 13 B8
Woodnesborough 31 D7
Woodnewton 65 E7
Wood Norton 81 E6
Woodplumpton 92 F5
Woodrising 68 D2
Wood's Green 18 B3
Woodside
 Aberdeen 141 D8
 Aberds 153 D10
 Brack 27 B7
 Fife 129 D6
 Hants 14 E4
 Herts 41 D5
 Perth 134 F2
Woodside of
 Arbeadie 141 E6
Woodstock Oxon 38 C4
 Pembs 32 B1
Wood Street Norf 69 B6
Woodthorpe Derbys 76 B4

Woodthorpe continued
 Leics 64 C2
 Lincs 91 F8
 York 95 D8
Woodton 69 E5
Woodtown 9 B6
Woodvale 85 C4
Woodville 63 C7
Wooferton 49 C7
Wookey 23 E7
Wookey Hole 23 E7
Wool 13 F6
Woolacombe 20 E3
Woolage Green 31 E6
Woolaston 36 E2
Woolavington 22 E5
Woolbeding 16 B2
Wooldale 88 D2
Wooler 117 B5
Woolfardisworthy
 Devon 8 B5
 Devon 10 D3
Woolfords
 Cottages 120 D3
Woolhampton 26 C3
Woolhope 49 F8
Woolhope
 Cockshoot 49 F8
Woolland 13 D5
Woollard 23 C8
Woolley Bath 24 C2
 Cambs 54 B2
 Corn 8 C4
 Derbys 76 C3
 W Yorks 88 C4
Woolmer Green 41 C5
Woolmere Green 50 C4
Woolpit 56 C3
Woolscott 52 C2
Woolsington 110 C4
Woolstanwood 74 D3
Woolstaston 60 E4
Woolsthorpe Lincs 65 B6
 Lincs 77 F8
Woolston Devon 6 E5
 Shrops 60 B3
 Shrops 60 F4
 Soton 14 C5
 Warr 86 E4
Woolstone Oxon 38 F2
 M Keynes 53 F6
Woolton 86 F2
Woolton Hill 26 C2
Woolverstone 57 F5
Woolverton 24 D2
Woolwich 28 B5
Woolwich Ferry 28 B5
Woonton 49 D5
Wooperton 117 B6
Woore 74 E4
Wootten Green 57 B6
Wootton Bedford 53 E8
 Hants 14 E3
 Hereford 48 D5
 Kent 31 E6
 N Lincs 90 C4
 Oxon 38 C4
 Oxon 38 D4
 Shrops 49 B6
 Shrops 60 B3
 Staffs 62 B2
 Staffs 75 E8
 W Nhants 53 D5
Wootton Bridge 15 E6
Wootton Common 15 E6
Wootton
 Courtenay 21 E8
Wootton Fitzpaine 11 E8
Wootton Rivers 25 C6
Wootton St
 Lawrence 26 D3
Wootton Wawen 51 C6
Worcester 50 D3
Worcester Park 28 C3
Wordsley 62 F2
Wordwell 56 B2
Worfield 61 E7
Work 159 G5
Workington 98 B1
Worksop 77 B5
Worlaby 90 C4
World's End 26 B2
Worle 23 C5
Worleston 74 D3
Worlingham 69 F7
Worlington 55 B7
Worlingworth 57 C6
Wormald Green 95 C6
Wormbridge 49 F6
Wormegay 67 C6
Wormelow Tump 49 F6
Wormhill 75 B8
Worminghall 39 D6
Wormingford 56 F3
Wormington 50 F5
Worminster 23 E8
Wormit 129 B5
Wormleighton 52 D2
Wormley Herts 41 D6
 Sur 27 F7
Wormley West
 End 41 D6
Wormshill 30 D2
Wormsley 49 E6
Worplesdon 27 D7
Worrall 88 E4
Worsbrough 88 D4
Worsbrough
 Common 88 D4
Worsley 86 D5
Worstead 69 B6
Worsthorne 93 F8
Worston 93 E7
Worswell 6 E3
Worth Kent 31 D7
 W Sus 28 F4
Wortham 56 B4
Worthen 60 D3
Worthenbury 73 E8
Worthing Norf 68 C2
 W Sus 16 D5
Worthington 63 B8
Worth Matravers 13 G7
Worting 26 D4
Wortley S Yorks 88 E4
 W Yorks 95 F5
Worton N Yorks 100 E4

Worton continued
 Wilts 24 D4
Wortwell 69 F5
Wotherton 60 D2
Wotter 6 C3
Wotton 28 E2
Wotton-under-
 Edge 36 E4
Wotton
 Underwood 39 C6
Woughton on the
 Green 53 F6
Wouldham 29 C8
Wrabness 57 F5
Wrafton 20 F3
Wragby Lincs 78 B4
 W Yorks 88 C5
Wragholme 91 E7
Wramplingham 68 D4
Wrangbrook 89 C5
Wrangham 153 E6
Wrangle 79 D7
Wrangle Bank 79 D7
Wrangle Lowgate 79 D7
Wrangway 11 C6
Wrantage 11 B8
Wrawby 90 D4
Wraxall Dorset 12 D3
 N Som 23 B6
 Som 23 F8
Wray 93 C6
Wraysbury 27 B8
Wrayton 93 B6
Wrea Green 92 F3
Wreay Cumb 108 E4
 W&F 99 B6
Wrecclesham 27 E6
Wrecsam
 = Wrexham 73 D7
Wrekenton 111 D5
Wrelton 103 F5
Wrenbury 74 E2
Wrench Green 103 F7
Wreningham 68 E4
Wrentham 69 F7
Wrenthorpe 88 B4
Wrentnall 60 D4
Wressle E Yorks 96 F3
 N Lincs 90 D3
Wrestlingworth 54 E3
Wretham 68 F2
Wretton 67 E6
Wrexham
 = Wrecsam 73 D7
Wrexham Industrial
 Estate 73 E7
Wrightington Bar 86 C3
Wrinehill 74 E4
Wrington 23 C6
Writhlington 24 D2
Writtle 42 D2
Wrockwardine 61 C6
Wroot 89 D8
Wrotham 29 D7
Wrotham Heath 29 D7
Wroughton 37 F8
Wroxall IoW 15 G6
 Warks 51 B7
Wroxeter 61 D5
Wroxham 69 C6
Wroxton 52 E2
Wyaston 75 E8
Wyberton 79 E6
Wyboston 54 D2
Wybunbury 74 E4
Wychbold 50 C4
Wych Cross 28 F5
Wyck 27 F5
Wyck Rissington 38 B1
Wycoller 94 F2
Wycomb 64 B4
Wycombe Marsh 40 E1
Wyddial 54 F4
Wye 30 E4
Wyesham 36 C2
Wyfordby 64 C4
Wyke Dorset 13 B5
 Shrops 61 D6
 Sur 27 D6
 W Yorks 88 B2
Wykeham N Yorks 96 B4
 N Yorks 103 F7
Wyken 63 F7
Wyke Regis 12 G4
Wykey 60 B3
Wylam 110 C4
Wylde Green 62 E5
Wyllie 35 E5
Wylye 24 F5
Wymering 15 D7
Wymeswold 64 B3
Wymington 53 C7
Wymondham Leics 65 C5
 Norf 68 D4
Wyndham 34 E3
Wynford Eagle 12 E3
Wyng 159 J4
Wynyard Village 102 B2
Wyre Piddle 50 E4
Wysall 64 B3
Wythall 51 B5
Wytham 38 D4
Wythburn 99 C5
Wythenshawe 87 F6
Wythop Mill 98 B3
Wyton 54 B3
Wyverstone 56 C4
Wyverstone Street 56 C4
Wyville 65 B5
Wyvis Lodge 150 D7

Yarkhill 49 E8
Yarlet 62 B3
Yarlside 92 C2
Yarm 102 C2
Yarmouth 14 F4
Yarnbrook 24 D3
Yarnfield 75 F5
Yarnscombe 9 B7
Yarnton 38 C4
Yarpole 49 C6
Yarrow 115 B6
Yarrow Feus 115 B6
Yarsop 49 E6
Yarwell 65 E7
Yate 36 F4
Yateley 27 C6
Yatesbury 25 B5
Yattendon 26 B3
Yatton Hereford 49 C6
 N Som 23 C6
Yatton Keynell 24 B3
Yaverland 15 F7
Yaxham 68 C3
Yaxley Cambs 65 E8
 Suff 56 B5
Yazor 49 E6
Y Bala = Bala 72 F3
Y Barri = Barry 22 C3
Y Bont-Faen
 = Cowbridge 21 B8
Y Drenewydd
 = Newtown 59 E8
Yeading 40 F4
Yeadon 94 E5
Yealand Conyers 92 B5
Yealand
 Redmayne 92 B5
Yealmpton 6 D3
Yearby 102 B4
Yearsley 95 B8
Yeaton 60 C4
Yeaveley 75 E8
Yedingham 96 B4
Yeldon 53 C8
Yelford 38 D3
Yelland 20 F3
Yelling 54 C3
Yelvertoft 52 B3
Yelverton Devon 6 C3
 Norf 69 D5
Yenston 12 B5
Yeoford 10 E2
Yeolmbridge 8 F5
Yeo Mill 10 B3
Yeovil 12 C3
Yeovil Marsh 12 C3
Yeovilton 12 B3
Yerbeston 32 D1
Yesnaby 159 G3
Yetlington 117 D6
Yetminster 12 C3
Yettington 11 F5
Yetts o'Muckhart 128 D2
Yieldshields 119 D8
Yiewsley 40 F3
Y Mwmbwls
 = The Mumbles 33 F7
Ynysboeth 34 E4
Ynysddu 35 E5
Ynysgyfflog 58 C3
Ynyshir 34 E4
Ynyslas 58 E3
Ynys-meudwy 33 D8
Ynystawe 33 D7
Ynysybwl 34 E4
Yockenthwaite 94 B2
Yockleton 60 C3
Yokefleet 90 B2
Yoker 118 C5
Yonder Bognie 152 D5
York 95 D8
Yorkletts 30 C4
Yorkley 36 D3
York Town 27 C6
Yorton 60 B5
Youlgreave 76 C2
Youlstone 8 C4
Youlthorpe 96 D3
Youlton 95 C7
Young's End 42 C3
Young Wood 78 B4
Yoxall 62 C5
Yoxford 57 C7
Y Pîl = Pyle 34 F2
Yr Hôb = Hope 73 D7
Y Rhws = Rhoose 22 C2
Y Rhyl = Rhyl 72 A4
Yr Wyddgrug
 = Mold 73 C6
Ysbyty-Cynfyn 47 B6
Ysbyty Ifan 72 E2
Ysbyty Ystwyth 47 B6
Ysceifiog 73 B5
Yspitty 33 E6
Ystalyfera 34 D1
Ystrad 34 E3
Ystrad Aeron 46 D4
Ystradfellte 34 C3
Ystradffin 47 E6
Ystradgynlais 34 C1
Ystradmeurig 47 C6
Ystrad-mynach 35 E5
Ystradowen Carms 33 C8
 V Glam 22 B2
Ystumtuen 47 B6
Ythanbank 153 E9
Ythanwells 153 E6
Ythsie 153 E8

**Y**

Yaddlethorpe 90 D2
Yafford 14 F5
Yafforth 101 E7
Yalding 29 D7
Yanworth 37 C7
Yapham 96 D3
Yapton 16 D3
Yarburgh 91 E7
Yarcombe 11 D7
Yard 22 F2
Yardley 62 F5
Yardley Gobion 53 E5
Yardley Hastings 53 D6

**Z**

Zeal Monachorum 10 D2
Zeals 24 F2
Zelah 4 D3
Zennor 2 C3